Italian Sword
and Sandal Films,
1908–1990

Italian Sword and Sandal Films, 1908–1990

Roy Kinnard *and*
Tony Crnkovich

McFarland & Company, Inc., Publishers
Jefferson, North Carolina

RECENT WORKS ALSO OF INTEREST AND FROM MCFARLAND
The Flash Gordon Serials, 1936–1940: A Heavily Illustrated Guide,
by Roy Kinnard, Tony Crnkovich *and* R.J. Vitone (2008; softcover 2011);
The Films of Fay Wray, by Roy Kinnard *and* Tony Crnkovich (2005;
softcover 2008); *Science Fiction Serials: A Critical Filmography of the 31
Hard SF Cliffhangers; With an Appendix of the 37 Serials with Slight SF
Content,* by Roy Kinnard (1998; softcover 2008); *Horror in Silent Films:
A Filmography, 1896–1929,* by Roy Kinnard (1995; softcover 1999)

Front cover illustration by Tony Crnkovich

Frontispiece: Steve Reeves, *the* sword and sandal superstar.

ISBN (print) 978-1-4766-6291-6
ISBN (ebook) 978-1-4766-2704-5

LIBRARY OF CONGRESS CATALOGUING DATA ARE AVAILABLE

BRITISH LIBRARY CATALOGUING DATA ARE AVAILABLE

© 2017 Roy Kinnard and Tony Crnkovich. All rights reserved

*No part of this book may be reproduced or transmitted in any form
or by any means, electronic or mechanical, including photocopying
or recording, or by any information storage and retrieval system,
without permission in writing from the publisher.*

Printed in the United States of America

*McFarland & Company, Inc., Publishers
Box 611, Jefferson, North Carolina 28640
www.mcfarlandpub.com*

CONTENTS

Acknowledgments
vi

Introduction
1

The Silent Era
7

The Sound Era
15

Appendix: The 1980s Revival
197

Index
209

Acknowledgments

Special thanks for assistance to Carlos Alverio, Al Bielski, Gary Gianni, Jerry Ohlinger, Greg Pierson, Dr. Alice Rader, John Stangeland, Veto Stasiunaitis and Jerry Vermilye.

Introduction

In ancient times, a peaceful village is attacked by marauding warriors, the men brutally slain, the women and children captured. Soon an imposing, heroic figure of superhuman power and endurance arrives on the scene, too late to help the victims. Grimly surveying the horrific tableau of carnage and death, he swears vengeance on the perpetrators and their leader.... So begins many a "sword-and-sandal," or "peplum" movie, a genre of costume adventure film, primarily made in Italy and shown on international screens from 1959 to 1965. The term "peplum" (plural "pepla") refers to the period togas and robes worn by the characters, but the genre is more commonly known (somewhat disdainfully) as "sword-and-sandal." Heavily influenced by earlier spectacles like Cecil B. DeMille's *Samson and Delilah* (1951) and *The Ten Commandments* (1956), the Italian sword-and-sandal films were much more cheaply produced than those big-budget epics, but tried hard to emulate their American models. In their restricted budgets and limited resources, the Italian pepla recalled the American "B" westerns and Saturday matinee serials of earlier decades, and like *those* low-budget, marginalized productions, often had to settle for creating the *impression* of spectacle rather than attaining it. That the pepla (like those westerns and serials) actually *succeeded* in that goal on a regular basis is a tribute to the versatility and ingenuity of their directors, writers and production crews.

The peplum genre had its origins in the silent era, with the release of producer-director Giovanni Pastrone's epic *Cabiria* in 1914. Taking place during the Punic Wars (246 BC to 146 BC), the film startled its contemporary audience with impressive photography and massive sets. Among the characters was Maciste, a loyal, heroic servant possessing superhuman strength, played by Bartolomeo Pagano. Not only was Pagano the first sword-and-sandal strongman, it could be said that he was cinema's first superhero.

Although *Cabiria* was an influential film (among those it influenced was no less a genius than D.W. Griffith, who was inspired to make his own epic, *Intolerance*), and established a market for similar pictures (including two early versions of *Spartacus*), it did not create an enduring genre like the western, and there were few other sword and sandal epics after the beginning of the sound era (one notable exception was *Fabiola*, an Italian gladiator film, released in 1948).

The sword-and-sandal genre as we think of it today did not begin until the arrival of producer Joseph E. Levine. Having entered the movie industry by exploiting double bills of low-budget films, Levine had struck pay dirt in 1956 with the importation of the Japanese horror/sci-fi production *Gojira* which he retitled *Godzilla, King of the Monsters* and released in a re-edited, dubbed version with new scenes of actor Raymond Burr inserted

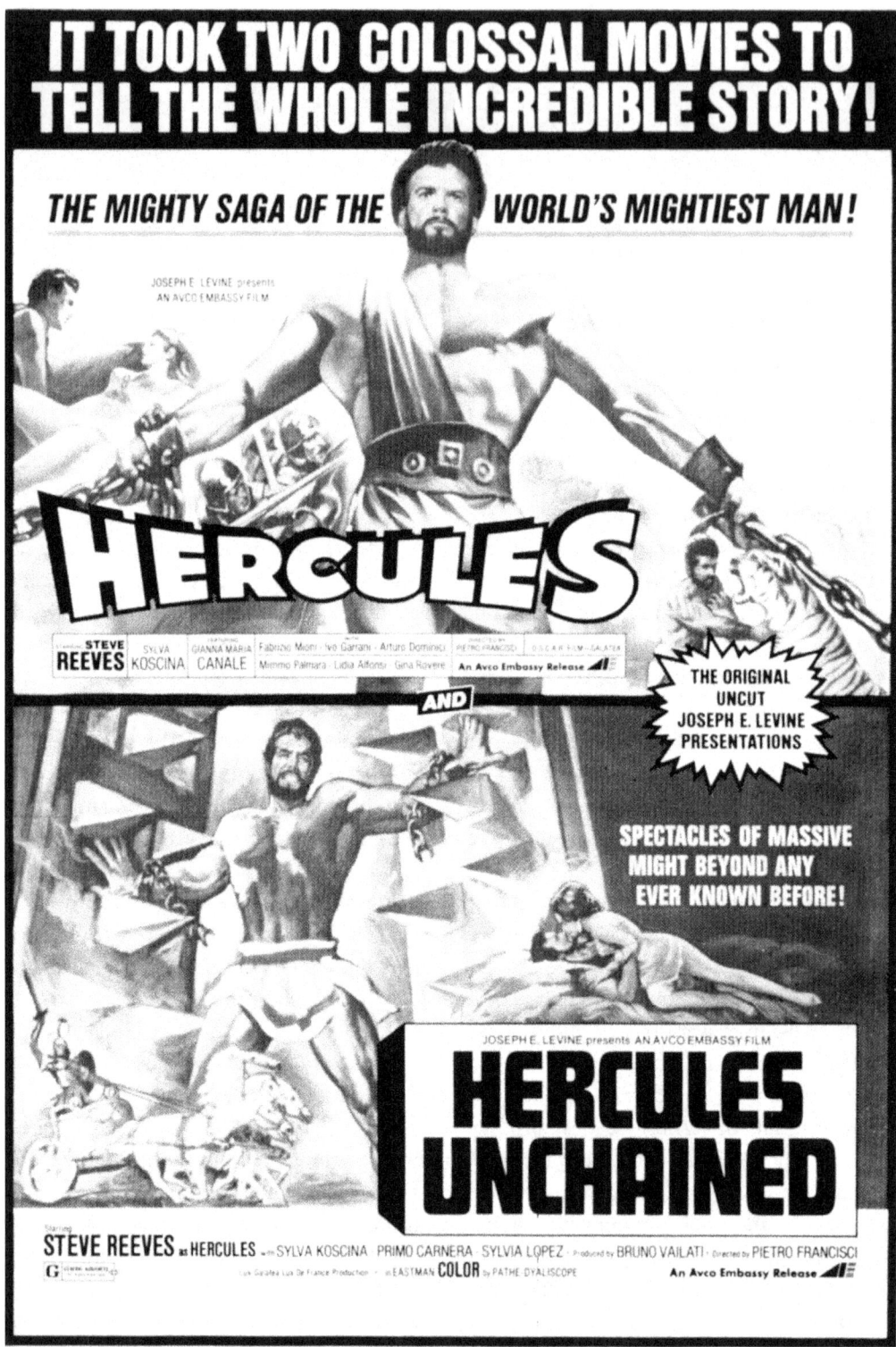

Reissue double-bill ad for two of the greatest sword and sandal films, *Hercules* and *Hercules Unchained*.

for the American release. Levine had made a fortune on *Godzilla*, and repeated the formula three years later when he imported an economically produced Italian spectacle, *Le fatiche di Ercole* (English translation *The Labors of Hercules*), retitled it *Hercules*, and bombarded the American public with a saturation ad campaign that resulted in mammoth box office grosses. Levine had spent $120,000 purchasing the American distribution rights to *Hercules*, another $1,000,000 promoting the film in a multi-media campaign (including chocolate candy bars cast in the image of leading man Steve Reeves), and reaped $5,000,000 in profits. If these figures seem picayune in today's corporate environment, remember that they are in *1959* dollars and at that time placed Levine in the upper tier of film producers and distributors. *Hercules* made an international star of Steve Reeves, professional bodybuilder and holder of the *Mr. Universe* title. Although a successful athlete, Reeves had struggled as an actor. After turning down the lead in DeMille's *Samson and Delilah* because the role demanded a reduction in his weight (and would have disqualified him from athletic competition), his prospects in Hollywood diminished, and he even found himself working for notorious fringe director Ed Wood in the cheapie *Jail Bait*. Reeves' destiny would never take him anywhere near an Academy Award, but he would certainly find his niche with *Hercules*.

Levine had once been quoted as saying, "You can fool all of the people all of the time, if the advertising is right." That sounds like the remark of a tasteless cynic (and may have been said for comic effect as well), but it belies Levine's genuine eye for quality. Both *Godzilla, King of the Monsters* and *Hercules* are good films (in their original foreign as well as imported dubbed versions) on their own modest terms, and it was the innate quality of these movies, abetted by their aggressive marketing campaigns, that the public responded to. Levine's shrewd judgment had single-handedly created a new genre, and the floodgates were opened. Levine soon followed *Hercules* with an immediate sequel, *Hercules Unchained*, and it wasn't long before Steve Reeves had some formidable competition from the likes of Reg Park, Gordon Scott, Mark Forest, Brad Harris, Dan Vadis and Alan Steel. Seemingly, every professional bodybuilder in the world headed for Rome, and some of these newly minted heroes were Italians who had taken anglicized names in order to broaden their commercial appeal. Thus, Lou Degni had rechristened himself "Mark Forest" and Sergio Cianni became "Alan Steel." With the fading Hollywood studio system of the past sputtering and in irreversible decline, film production in America was fading; paradoxically, the film industries in West Germany, Spain and Italy were humming, with plenty of job-seeking American talent heading for Rome. Sword-and-sandal lead Gordon Scott was a Hollywood Tarzan, while such American film industry veterans as Alan Ladd, Anthony Quinn, Jack Palance, Debra Paget, and Broderick Crawford also turn up in pepla, with surprising names like future *Gilligan's Island* star Tina Louise, the spectacular Jayne Mansfield, and even cinematic demigod Orson Welles putting in appearances. Two decades before the Christopher Reeve *Superman* (1978), the movie theatres of the world were flooded with widescreen color superhero and fantasy-adventure movies.

Because of their foreign origin, sometimes tacky production values and obvious vocal dubbing, the sword-and-sandal movies were easy targets for critics, who could lambast the movies without fear of retribution from the major Hollywood studios. Like the "B" westerns and serials, they received little to no respect from the press. To be sure, the pepla had their flaws. The aforementioned dubbing, at times sloppily done, was one. And they certainly *were* cheap, sometimes embarrassingly so. Also like the "B" westerns and serials, they were repetitive in plot and construction, and often seemed to be produced on an assembly-line basis. The same plots (and sometimes even the *same footage*) were used over and over. Many a sword-and-sandal effort proceeded with the muscular hero dispatching 20 or 30 foes (usually highly-trained professional soldiers) at a time without breaking a sweat, while becoming involved, at the film's conclusion, in a tense, prolonged struggle with the movie's antagonist, usually a scrawny, physically unimpressive runt who would be no threat at all under any other circumstances. There *were* absurdities, but even much more respectable films abound in *those*.

Hollywood distributors often believed it necessary to perform surgery on these films before they were shown in America. A good case in point is *Goliath and the Dragon*, released stateside in its dubbed version by American-International in 1960. Entitled *La vendetta di Ercole* (*The Revenge of Hercules*) in its original Italian version, the name of the hero (played by Mark Forest) was changed from Hercules to "Emilius" by AIP, since they believed that the name "Hercules" had been overexposed by that point. The film was also re-edited somewhat, with newly-shot footage of a monstrous dragon (filmed by stop-motion animator Jim Danforth), injected to make the title menace seem more believable and frightening (the human villain, a flabby and debauched Broderick Crawford, certainly didn't seem very imposing on his own). It's debatable whether or not AIP *improved* the film by these efforts, but they certainly increased its commercial viability in America, and it was widely and profitably distributed to drive-ins.

Although most sword-and-sandal epics are set firmly in the Roman era, others embrace different periods and themes, such as biblical stories, pirate adventures, and plots with Vikings or actual historical figures (Caesar or Cleopatra). Fantasy is an essential component in most of these films. With the exception of Hercules, whose status as a demigod is clearly stated in the Steve Reeves films, there is often no explanation of how these super-strong heroes acquired their physical prowess. Like many a comic book hero, they simply are what they are, and in a remote time steeped in mythology, are accepted as such by the normal characters in the films. A few sword-and-sandal epics can be placed in the realm of horror (*Goliath and the Vampires*) or even categorized as science fiction (*Giant of the Metropolis*). While no one is making a claim that these films are or ever were great *art*, they certainly were (and remain) great *entertainment*. Like the Japanese fantasy and horror films, the Italian sword-and-sandal movies have been unfairly criticized and dismissed by many. But, like their Japanese counterparts, the creative personnel and technical craftsmen responsible for these epics-on a budget tried hard to make good films. And they *did*.

To be fair, movies should be judged by the standards of the time that produced them. All that is required to appreciate vintage films is an open mind, a little common sense, and a positive attitude. Special effects, no matter how slick and technologically advanced, do not guarantee quality, nor do enormous budgets. There is much to recommend in the sword-and-sandal films, even on the simplest levels. They are entertaining adventure movies on one hand, and if you like girl watching (and there are plenty of muscular heroes for the ladies in the audience to watch, also), then the pepla have to be one of the sexiest film genres of all time. Again, to draw a parallel between the pepla and the "B" westerns and serials, they were created at a specific point in time for a specific audience; they can and should be enjoyed on that level. Directors like Mario Bava and Riccardo Freda worked long and hard to make these films as entertaining as they are, knowing full well that they would never get the awards and respect they certainly deserved.

Like any craze or fad, the sword-and-sandal movies came to an end. By 1965 they had vanished from the neighborhood theatres and drive-in screens of America, to be replaced almost overnight by the Italian-produced "spaghetti westerns." Hopefully, the sword and sandal films will be preserved for future generations. Most of them were filmed on unstable Eastmancolor film stock, prone to fading and color shifting, and most of the copies accessible on home video are transferred from 16mm Eastmancolor prints which both distort the original color hues *and* crop off the widescreen format, or aspect ratio, the films were shot in. There is some effort underway to rectify this situation, with original 35mm widescreen prints in full, rich color being sought out and transferred to video, but it may be too little, too late. Crazes and fads die, but in the end, only the films themselves remain (that is, *if* they are preserved) and only the films themselves really *matter*.

With this book, the authors have attempted to catalogue the major Italian sword and sandal films of the 1960s, as well as their silent-era predecessors and the brief revival of the genre in the 1980s, in a sort of "introductory overview" of these films. This is a *selective* filmography. While the strict definition of the peplum genre is any period costume film set before 1800, a filmography listing *every* peplum film would have to be a multi-volume set. What we have done here is concentrate on the more heroic "sword-and-sandal" variety, including films that contain elements and/or themes of the fantasy/horror genre.

We have opted to present these films in an alphabetical format, listed by their English titles (since that is how most people know them), with the original Italian title in parentheses. The original year of release (both Italian and American, where known) is given, along with production credits, cast lists, and running times (again, both Italian and American, where known). In the case of silent films, running times are primarily given in terms of length (feet) and/or number of 35mm reels (each reel being equal to 1,000 feet of film — this is done because running times on silent films were variable, dependent on the projection speeds employed by various exhibitors). Each film entry also has a commentary with further information on the movie.

Only *Italian-produced* pepla are examined herein; our focus is on the product of the Italian film industry, since that country was the originator of the peplum genre. Thus, to cite an example, the film *Atlas* (1960), although definitely sword-and-sandal, is not included, since it was an American production (made by Roger Corman), filmed in Greece.

The listings are divided into three sections, the first two covering the silent era and the sound era, with an appendix covering the revival of the genre in the 1980s, with each section listing the films alphabetically.

What we have attempted to do here is compile a straightforward introduction to the Italian sword and-sandal genre, in an accessible format, presented with an unpretentious attitude that is (hopefully) as honest and direct as the films themselves.

One of the pleasures of working on this book has been revisiting movies unseen for years, or discovering others that we had not caught the first time around. Hopefully, the reader will be inspired to seek out many of the films catalogued herein, many of which are available on home video.

THE SILENT ERA

***Cabiria (Cabiria)* (Itala Film, 1914)**

Credits: Producer/Director: Giovanni Pastrone; *Screenplay:* Giovanni Pastrone, Gabriele D'Annunzio (based on a book by Titus Livius and a novel by Emilio Salgari); *Photography:* August Battagliotti, Eugenio Bava, Natale Chiusano, Segundo de Chomón; *Music (live score)*: Manlio Mazza, Ildebrando Pizzetti; *Filmed at Fert Studios, Italy, and on location in Sicily and Tunisia*; running time: 148 minutes; release date (Italy): April 18, 1914.

Cast: Letizia Catena *(Cabiria as a child)*; Lidia Quaranta *(Cabiria)*; Gina Marangoni *(Croessa)*; Dante Testa *(Karthalo, the High Priest)*; Umberto Mozzato *(Fulvio "Fulvius" Axilla)*; Bartolomeo Pagano *(Maciste)*; Raffaele di Napoli *(Bodastoret)*; Emilio Vardannes *(Hannibal)*; Edoardo Davesnes *(Hasdruplal)*; Italia Almirante-Manzini *(Sophonistra)*; Allesandro Bernard *(Syphax)*; Luigi Chellini *(Scipione)*; Vitale di Stefano *(Massinisa)*; Enrico Gemelli *(Archemede)*; Ignazio Lupi *(Arbace)*; with Francesca Bertini; Giuseppe Ferrari; Soava Gallone; Domenico Gambino; Pena Menichelli; Felice Minotti; Amedeo Mustacchi; Fido Schirru.

A poster for the silent classic *Cabiria* (1914).

Comments: One of early cinema's most notable productions, *Cabiria* told the fanciful story of the eponymous heroine, Cabiria (Lidia Quaranta), who is kidnapped by Roman pirates and eventually rescued by nobleman Fulvio Axilla (Umberto Mozzato) and his powerful servant Maciste (Bartolomeo Pagano). Set during the Punic Wars, the film amazed 1914 audiences with its visual extravagance and sumptuous photography. *Cabiria* made an unlikely star of Bartolomeo Pagano (1848–1947), a 6-foot-tall former longshoreman who was cast as Maciste because of his powerful physique. A handsome and charismatic lead, Pagano became so popular that he starred in several later Maciste films *(see separate entries)*. The success of *Cabiria* established the Italian film industry on an international level, and the film was imported to America by distributor George Kleine, and first shown here in June 1914. Upon seeing *Cabiria*, D.W. Griffith, director of *The Birth of a Nation*, was so influenced by the film's design that he resolved to surpass its epic visuals—and *did*—with the Babylonian sequences of his own *Intolerance* (1916). Although *Cabiria* was originally 148 minutes in length, current prints run 123 minutes.

Cabiria star Bartolomeo Pagano.

Cretinetti and the Boots of Brazil (Cretinetti e gli stivali del Brasile) (1916)

Credits: *Director:* André Deed; length: 3,675 feet (4 reels).

Cast: André Deed *(Cretinetti)*; Bartolomeo Pagano *(Maciste)*; Leonie Laporte; Felice Minotti; Gabriel Moreau; Teresa Marangoni.

Comments: Bartolomeo Pagano returned to the role of Maciste in this featurette.

Emperor Maciste (Maciste imperatore) (Fert Film Co., 1924)

Credits: *Director:* Guido Brignone; *Screenplay:* Pier Angelo Mazzolotti; *Photography:* Massimo Terzano; *Distributor:* Società Anonima Stefano Pittaluga; length: 7,001 feet (7 reels); released November 1924.

Cast: Bartolomeo Pagano *(Maciste)*; with Domenico Gambino; Franz Sala; Elena Sangro; Oreste Grandi; Augusto Bandini; Lola Romanos; Gero Zambuto; Felice Minotti; Armand Pouget; Lorenzo Soderini.

Comments: Another appearance by Bartolomeo Pagano as Maciste.

Fabiola (Fabiola) (1913)

Comments: The earliest screen version of the Nicolas Patrick Wiseman novel about Roman gladiators. There is no information available about this first version. The story was filmed again in 1918 and 1948 *(see separate entries)*.

Fabiola (Palatino Film, 1918)

Credits: *Director:* Enrico Guazzoni; *Screenplay:* Fausto Salvatore (based on the novel by Nicholas Patrick Wiseman); *Photography:* Alfredo Lenci; *Sets:* Camillo Innocenti; length: 7,409 feet (8 reels); released March 25, 1918.

Cast: Giulia Cassini-Rizzoto *(Lucina)*; Bruto Castellani *(Quadrato)*; Giorgio Fini, Augusto Mastripietri *(Eurota)*; Amleto Novelli *(Fulvio)*; Livio Pavanelli *(San Sabastiano)*; Signora Poletti *(Sant 'Agnese)*; Valeria Sanfilippo *(Santa Cecilia)*; Maria Antonietta Bartoli-Avveduti [a.k.a. Elena Sangro] *(Fabiola)*; Ljubomir Stanojevic; Singnora Tirelli *(Alfra)*.

Comments: The second film production of

Nicholas Patrick Wiseman's novel about Roman gladiators. The most famous movie version is the sound remake of 1948 *(see separate entry).*

The Fall of Troy *(La caduta di Troia)* (Itala Film, 1911)

Credits: Directors: Luigi Romano Borgnetto, Giovanni Pastrone; *Screenplay:* Giovanni Pastrone; length: 1,969 feet (2 reels); released March 1911.

Cast: Luigi Romano Borgnetto; Giovanni Casaleggio; Madame Davesnes; Emilio Gallo; Olga Giannini Novelli; Giulio Vinà.

Comments: Partially based on the writings of Homer describing the title event, this film was distributed in America by the Motion Picture Distributors and Sales Company. The film was also distributed in England, France, Germany, Ireland, and Spain.

The Giant from the Dolemites *(Il gigante delle Dolomiti)* (Società Anonima Stefano Pittaluga, 1927)

Credits: Director: Guido Brignone; *Photography:* Massimo Terzano; *Production Design:* Domenico Galdo, Giulio Lombardozzi; length: 7,717 feet (8 reels); released January 20, 1927.

Cast: Bartolomeo Pagano *(Maciste, la guida alpina);* Aldo Marus *(il nipotino Hans);* Elena Lunda *(Vanna Dardos);* Dolly Grey *(Maud, la pittrice);* Andrea Habay *(Ing. Ewert);* Luigi Serventi *(Müller, l'avventurieno);* Mario Saio; Augusto Paggioli; Augusto Bandini; Oreste Grandi *(Schulz, il contrabandiere);* Felice Minotti.

Comments: Another Bartolomeo Pagano Maciste film.

Judith and Holophernes *(Giuditta e Oloferne)* (Società Italiana Cines, 1908)

Comments: This film told the story of a vengeful girl who plots to seduce, then assassinate, a tyrant who has conquered her city. Little information is available about this film. Length: 460 feet (short subject); released April 11, 1908.

Judith and Holophernes *(Giuditta e Oloferne)* (Società Anonima Stefano Pittaluga, 1929)

Credits: Director: Baldassarre Negroni; *Photography:* Ubaldo Arata; length: 8,000 feet (8 reels); released January 1929.

Cast: Bartolomeo Pagano; Jia Ruskaja; Franz Sala; Carlo Tedeschi; Giuseppe Brigone; Augusto Bandini; Felice Minotti; Lore Lay; Giorgio Curti; Anna Mari; Andrea Bani; Nino Altieri.

Comments: The second remake of this story *(see entries above for earlier versions)* included Bartolomeo Pagano of *Cabiria* fame in the cast. The plot was reused again in the sound era for the 1959 widescreen color peplum *Head of a Tyrant (see separate entry).*

Judith and Holophernes *(Giuditta e Oloferne)* (Vera Film, 1920)

Credits: Director: Aldo Molinari; *Photography:* Tomasso DeGiorgio; Length: 5,070 feet (6 reels); released September 1920.

Cast: Alfredo Bracci; Guido Guiducci; Ileana Leondoff *(Giuditta).*

Comments: A longer and more elaborate remake of the 1908 version *(see entry above).*

The Last Days of Pompeii *(Gli ultimi giorni di Pompei)* (Ambrosio, 1908)

Credits: Directors: Arturo Ambrosio, Luigi Maggi; *Producer:* Arturo Ambrosio; *Screenplay:* Roberto Omegna (based on the novel by Edward George Bulwer-Lytton); *Photography:* Roberto Omegna, Giovanni Vitrotti; distributor: Società Anonima Ambrosio; length: 1,201 feet (2 reels); released December 1908.

Cast: Luigi Maggi *(Arbace);* Lydia De Roberti *(Nydia);* Umberto Mozzato *(Glauco);* Mirra Principi; Ernesto Vaser *(Nydia's father);* Cesare Gani Carini.

Comments: The Edward George Bulwer-Lytton novel *The Last Days of Pompeii* has been the source for many films, and this short subject was the earliest *(see separate entries for later versions).* Basically, the story equates the factual 79 AD eruption of Vesuvius with divine retribution for the myriad sins of Rome, which, of course (in true DeMille fashion), allows for plenty of onscreen immorality before the eventual catastrophic retribution. The later 1935 Hollywood version took this equation a step further by conflating the volcano eruption with the crucifixion of Jesus, two historical events that were, in fact, separated by 45 years.

The Last Days of Pompeii (Gli ultimi giorni di Pompei) (Ambrosio, 1913)

Credits: Directors: Mario Caserini, Eleuterio Rodolfi; Producer: Arturo Ambrosio; Screenplay: Mario Caserini (based on the novel by Edward George Bulwer-Lytton); Distributor: Giuseppe Barattolo; running time: 88 minutes; released August 24, 1913.

Cast: Fernando Negri Pouget *(Nydia)*; Eugenia Tettoni Fior *(Ione)*; Ubaldo Stefani *(Glaucus)*; Antonio Grisanti *(Arbace)*; Cesare Gani Carini *(Apoecides)*; Vitale Di Stefano *(Claudius)*.

Comments: The second—and more elaborate—Italian film production of George Bulwer-Lytton's moralistic fable involving the eruption of Vesuvius, with two love triangles colliding in ancient Rome. Distributor George Kleine imported this feature-length picture to America and first showed it on August 13, 1913, eleven days before the Italian release.

The Last Days of Pompeii (Gli ultimi giorni di Pompei) (Società Italiana Grandi Films, 1926)

Credits: Directors: Carmine Gallone, Amleto Palmeri; Screenplay: Alfredo Panzini (based on the novel by Edward George Bulwer-Lytton); Photography: Victor Arménise, Alfredo Donelli; Production Design: Vittorio Cafiero; Costumes: Duilio Cambelloti; Running Time: 181 minutes; released March 1926.

Cast: Victor Varconi *(Glauco)*; Rina De Liguoro *(Ione)*; María Corda *(Nydia)*; Bernard Goetzke *(Arbace)*; Emilio Ghione *(Caleno)*; Lia Maris *(Julia)*; Gildo Bacci *(Diomede)*; Enrica Fantis *(Julia's friend)*; Vittorio Evangelisti *(Apecide)*; Ferruccio Biancini *(Olinto)*; Carlo Gualabdri *(Clodio)*; Vasco Creti *(Sallustius)*; Alfredo Martinelli *(Lepidus)*; Giuseppe Pierozzi *(Josio)*; Enrico Monti *(Lidone)*; Enrico Palermi *(Medone)*; Carlo Reiter *(Pansa)*; Carlo Duse *(Burbo)*; Osvaldo Genazzani; Italia Vitalani; Dria Paola; Donatella Neri; Bruto Castellani.

Comments: The last Italian-produced silent version of Edward George Bulwer-Lytton's oft-filmed tale, notable for its sumptuous production values, long running time (over 3 hours), and surprisingly explicit nudity.

The Last Tzar (Gli ultimi zar) (Società Anonima Stefano Pittaluga, 1928)

Credits: Director: Baldassarre Negroni; Photography: Ubaldo Arata; produced and distributed by Società Anonima Stefano Pittaluga; length: 8,380 feet (9 reels).

Cast: Bartolomeo Pagano *(Maciste)*; Elena Lunda; Amilcare Taglienti; Franz Sala; Sandro Ruffini; Elizabeth Grey; Alberto Pasquali; Augusto Bandini; Andrea Miano; Felice Minotti.

Comments: Another Maciste adventure starring Bartolomeo Pagano. Although screened in both Finland and Germany the same year as the Italian release (1928), the film was not distributed in Portugal until 1931.

Maciste Against the Sheikh (Maciste contro lo sceicco) (Fert Film, 1926)

Credits: Director: Mario Camerini; Screenplay: Mario Camerini; distributed by Società Anonima Stefano Pittaluga; running time: 82 minutes; released February 1926.

Cast: Bartolomeo Pagano *(Maciste)*; Cecil Tryan; Rita D'Harcourt; Lido Manetti; Franz Sala; Alex Bernard; Oreste Grandi; Felice Minotti; Armand Pouget; Mario Saio; F.M. Costa; Michele Mikailoff.

Comments: This Bartolomeo Pagano Maciste film is also known under the alternate title *Maciste in Africa*. Actor Lido Manetti was also known as Arnold Kent.

Maciste in Hell (Maciste all inferno) (Fert-Pittaluga, 1926)

Credits: Director: Guido Brignone; Producer: Stefano Pittaluga; Screenplay: Riccardo Artuffo (billed as "Fantaso"); Photography: Ubaldo Arata; Massimo Terzano; Art Direction: Guido Brignone; Set Decoration & Costume Design: Giulio Lombardozzi; Special Effects: Segundo de Chomón; Assistant Director: Sergio Amidei; distributed by Società Anonima Stefano Pittaluga; running time: 95 minutes; released March 31, 1926.

(Pluto, Master of Hell); Mario Saio *(Gerione)*; Pauline Polaire *(Graziella)*; Domenico Serra *(Giorgio)*; Sergio Aidei *(a Devil)*; Andrea Miano, Felice Minotti.

Comments: Perhaps the best and most entertaining of the silent Maciste films, *Maciste in Hell* is borderline horror, with stunning visuals inspired by the work of artist Gustav Doré. The Devil attempts to corrupt Maciste, who literally goes to Hell and does battle with Satan's minions. *Maciste in Hell* was not screened in America until 1931, when it was distributed by Excelsior Pictures Corp. Its grotesque visuals were so extravagant that clips from the movie were later used to illustrate visions of insanity in the 1934 independent film *Maniac*. *Maciste in Hell* survives today, but the version available on home video runs only 66 minutes, almost 30 minutes less than the original Italian release.

Maciste in Love (Maciste innamorato) (Itala Film, 1919)

Credits: Director: Luigi Romano Borgnetto; *Photography:* Alvaro De Simone; distributed by Unione Cinematografica Italiana; length: 6,575 feet (7 reels); released May 1, 1919.

Cast: Bartolomeo Pagano *(Maciste)*; Linda Moglia *(Miss Ada Thompson)*; Ruggero Capodaglio *(Cavicchioni)*; Orlando Ricci *(sig. Thompson)*; Letizia Quaranta.

Comments: A Bartolomeo Pagano Maciste film.

Top: A scene from *Maciste in Hell*. Bartolomeo Pagano threatens Umberto Guarracino. *Above:* Elena Sangro in *Maciste in Hell*.

Cast: Bartolomeo Pagano *(Maciste)*; Elena Sangro *(Porserpina, Pluto's wife)*; Lucia Zanussi *(Luciferina, Pluto's daughter)*; Franz Sala *(Barbariccia/Dottor Nox)*; Umberto Guarracino

Maciste in the Lion's Cage (Maciste nella gabbia dei leoni) (Cinès Pittaluga, 1926)

Credits: Director: Guido Brignone; *Screenplay:* Guido Brignone; *Photography:* Anchise

Brizzi; Massimo Terzano; *Production Design:* Giulio Lombardozzi; length: 7,852 feet (8 reels); released February 10, 1926.

Cast: Bartolomeo Pagano *(Maciste);* Elena Sangro *(Sarah, la cavallerizza);* Luigi Serventi *(Strasser);* Mimi Dovia *(Seida);* Umberto Guarracino *(Sullivan);* Oreste Grandi *(Karl Pommer);* Andrea Habay; Alberto Collo *Giorgio Pommer);* Vittorio Bianchi; Giuseppe Brignone *(Bob, il vecchio clown);* Augusto Bandini; Franz Sala.

Comments: A Bartolomeo Pagano Maciste film, in which the character is hired to capture lions.

Maciste on Vacation *(Maciste in vacanza)* (Itala Film, 1921)

Credits: Director: Luigi Romano Borgnetto; length: 6,257 feet (7 reels); released May 1921.

Cast: Bartolomeo Pagano *(Maciste);* Henriette Bonard; Gemma De Sanctis; Mario Voller-Buzzi; Felice Minotti; Guido De Rege; Emilio Vardannes.

Comments: A Bartolomeo Pagano Maciste film.

Maciste Rescued from the Waters *(Maciste salvato dalle acque)* (Itala Film, 1921)

Credits: Director: Luigi Romano Borgnetto; *Screenplay:* Camillo Bruto Bonzi; length: 5,542 feet (6 reels); released March 1921.

Cast: Bartolomeo Pagano *(Maciste);* Henriette Bonard; Erminia Zago; Guido Clifford; Mario Voller-Buzzi; Emilio Vardannes; Leone Heller; Gino-Lelio Cornelli; Mario Mercati; Felice Minotti.

Comments: A Bartolomeo Pagano Maciste film.

Maciste the Athlete *(Maciste atleta)* (Itala Film, 1918)

Credits: Directors: Vincenzo Denizot, Giovanni Pastrone; length: 7,005 feet (7 reels); released March 1918.

Cast: Bartolomeo Pagano *(Maciste);* Italia Almirante-Manzini; Ruggero Capodaglio; Giulio Andreotti.

Comments: A Bartolomeo Pagano Maciste film, co-directed by Giovanni Pastrone of *Cabiria* fame.

Maciste the Clairvoyant *(Maciste medium)* (Itala Film, 1918)

Credits: Director: Vincenzo Denizot, *Photography:* Giovanni Tomatis; length: 4,774 feet (5 reels); released April 1918.

Cast: Bartolomeo Pagano *(Maciste);* Italia Almirante-Manzini; Ruggero Capodaglio; Elettra Raggio.

Comments: A Bartolomeo Pagano Maciste film.

Maciste the Detective *(Maciste poliziotto)* (Itala Film, 1918)

Credits: Director: Roberto Roberti; *Photography:* Giovanni Tomatis; length: 8,268 feet (9 reels); released March 1918.

Cast: Bartolomeo Pagano *(Maciste);* Italia Almirante-Manzini; Ruggero Capodaglio; Claudia Zambuto; Vittorio Rossi Pianelli; Arnaldo Arnaldi.

Comments: A Bartolomeo Pagano Maciste film.

Maciste the First *(Maciste I)* (Itala Film, 1919)

Credits: Director: Carlo Campogalliani.

Cast: Bartolomeo Pagano *(Maciste);* Letizia Quaranta; Felice Minotti.

Comments: A Bartolomeo Pagano Maciste film.

Maciste the Ranger *(Maciste bersagliere)* (Itala Film, 1916)

Credits: Directors: Luigi Romano Borgnetto, Luigi Maggi.

Cast: Bartolomeo Pagano *(Maciste).*

Comments: A Bartolomeo Pagano Maciste film.

Maciste the Warrior *(Maciste alpino)* (Itala Film, 1916)

Credits: Director: Giovanni Pastrone; *Screenplay:* Giovanni Pastrone; *Photography:* Giovanni Tomatis; *Assistant Directors:* Luigi Romano Borgnetto, Luigi Maggi; *Special Effects:* Segundo de Chomón; length: 6,838 feet (7 reels); released July 16, 1917.

Cast: Bartolomeo Pagano *(Maciste)*; Fido Schirru *(Fritz Pluffer)*; Valentina Frascaroli *(Giulietta)*; Enrico Gernelli *(Conte di Pratolungo)*; Marussia Allesti *(Contessina di Pratolungo)*; Abo Riccioni; Evangelina Vitaliani; Felice Minotti;

Comments: This Bartolomeo Pagano Maciste entry had an off-beat plot. While shooting a Maciste film on location during World War I, Pagano and his crew are captured by the enemy and imprisoned in a concentration camp. Eventually, Pagano/Maciste escapes, fighting off the enemy as he rescues a girl held prisoner in a castle. The Maciste films, for the most part, took place in the present time, possibly as an economic measure to eliminate the need for period sets and costumes; the self-referential story for this one is particularly inventive.

Maciste vs. Maciste (Maciste contro Maciste) (1923)

Cast: Bartolomeo Pagano *(Maciste)*; Helena Makowska.

Comments: Little information is available about this Bartolomeo Pagano Maciste film.

Maciste's American Nephew (Maciste e il nipote d'America) (Fert Film, 1924)

Credits: Director: Eleuterio Rodolfi; *Producer:* Stefano Pittaluga; *Screenplay:* Giovacchino Forzano; *Photography:* Anchise Brizzi, Sergio Goddio; distributed by Società Anonima Stefano Pittaluga; length: 6,365 feet (7 reels); released March 1924.

Cast: Bartolomeo Pagano *(Maciste)*; Diomira Jacobini; Alberto Collo; Pauline Polaire; Augusto Bandini; Oreste Bilancia; Mercedes Brigone.

Comments: A Bartolomeo Pagano Maciste film.

The Marvelous Maciste (Maciste) (Itala Film, 1916)

Credits: Directors: Luigi Romano Borgnetto, Vincenzo Denizot; *Screenplay:* Agnes L. Bain, Giovanni Pastrone; *Production Supervisor:* Giovanni Pastrone; running time: 67 minutes (8,380 feet).

Cast: Bartolomeo Pagano *(Maciste)*; Leone Papa *(Ercole)*; Clementine Gay *(Josefina)*; Amelia Chellini *(Madre di Josefina)*; Didaco Chellini *(il duca Alexis)*; Ada Marangoni.

Comments: This inventive Maciste film tells the story of a young girl, who, pursued by criminals, hides in a movie theatre during a screening of *Cabiria*. Seeing the heroic Maciste in the film, she seeks (and finds) his help in real life. This movie was a co-production of Itala Film and Itala Film of America, and was distributed in the U.S. by Hanover Film Co. For the American version, some cast members had their names anglicized: Clementina Gay was billed as "Arline Costello" in the American prints, Amelia Chellini as "Louise Farnsworth," and Didaco Chellini as "Robert Ormand."

Nero; or the Burning of Rome (Nero; o la caduta di Roma) (Società Anonima Ambrosio, 1909)

Credits: Director: Luigi Maggi; *Producer:* Arturo Ambrosio; *Screenplay:* Decoroso Bonifanti; *Photography:* Giovanni Vitrotti; length: 1,109 feet (2 reels); released October 28, 1909.

Cast: Alberto Capozzi; Lydia De Roberti; Luigi Maggi; Mirra Principi; Ercole Vasser; Ernesto Vasser; Slia Orlandini; Matilde Guerafino Vite; Mario Voller-Buzzi.

Comments: This film, depicting the titular historical event, was originally entitled *Nerone (Nero)*. An alternate title was *Nero; or the Fall of Rome*. It was screened internationally in England, France and Germany, and distributed in America by the Empire Film Co.

Quo Vadis? (Quo Vadis?) (Società Italiana Cines, 1913)

Credits: Director: Enrico Guazzoni; *Screenplay:* Enrico Guazzoni (based on the novel by Henryk Sienkewicz); *Photography:* Eugenio Bava, Alessandro Bona; *Film Editor:* Enrico Guazzoni; *Production Design:* Enrico Guazzoni, Camilo Innocenti; *Art Direction/Costume Design:* Enrico Guazonni; length: 7,382 feet (8 reels); released March 1913.

Cast: Amleto Novelli *(Vinicus)*; Gustavo Serena *(Petronius)*; Amelia Cattaneo *(Eunice)*; Carlo Catnoveltaneo *(Nero)*; Lea Giunchi

(*Lygia*); Augusto Mastripietri (*Chilo*); Cesare Moltini (Tigellinus); Olga Brandini (Poppaea); Ignacio Lupi (Aulus); Giovanni Gizzi (St. Peter); Lia Orlandini; Matilda Guillaume; Ida Carloni Talli; Bruto Castellani (*Ursus*); Giuseppe Gambardella.

Comments: The title, *Quo Vadis?*, a Latin phrase, translates as "Where are you going?," as asked of a Roman soldier by the risen Jesus. This early version of the Henryk Sienkiewiscz novel (which also inspired a 1924 German silent film, as well as the famous 1951 MGM film starring Robert Taylor), was distributed in America by George Kleine.

The Revenge of Maciste (*La rivincita di Maciste*) (Itala Film, 1921)

Credits: Director: Luigi Romano Borgnetto; *Screenplay:* Camillo Bruto Bonzi, Luigi Romano Borgnetto; distributed by Unione Cinematografica Italiana; length: 4,495 feet (5 reels); released August 18, 1921.

Cast: Bartolomeo Pagano (*Maciste*); Henriette Bonard (*Miss Elsa Guappana*); Erminia Zago (*Miss Dorothy Bull-Dog*); Guido Dogliotti; Emilio Vardannes; Leone Heller; Felice Minotti.

Comments: A Bartolomeo Pagano Maciste film.

Spartacus (*Spartaco*) (Latium Film, 1909)

Credits: Director: Oreste Gherardini; length: 1,395 feet; released August 1909.

Cast: Oreste Gherardini (*Spartacus*).

Comments: This earliest screen depiction of the gladiator/slave who led a revolt against Roman tyranny was based on the novel by Raffaello Giovagnoli (the famous 1960 Stanley Kubrick film starring Kirk Douglas was based on a later novel by Howard Fast). Distributed in laboriously hand-colored prints, the film was shown in America by the Empire Film Co.

Spartacus (*Spartaco il gladiatore della Tracia*) (Pasquali e C., 1913)

Credits: Director: Giovanni Enrico Vidali; *Producer:* Ernesto Maria Pasquali; *Music (live score):* Modest Altschuler; running time: 88 minutes; released November 1913.

Cast: Mario Guaita Ausonio [a.k.a. Mario Ausonia] (*Spartacus*); Cristina Ruspoli (*Idamis*); Enrico Bracci (*Marcus Licinius Crassus*); Maria Gandini (*Narona*); Luigi Mele (*Noricus*); Verdi Giovanni (*Artemon*).

Comments: This 1913 version of the Spartacus story was distributed in America by George Kleine.

The Testament of Maciste (*Il testamento di Maciste*) (Itala Film, 1920)

Credits: Director: Carlo Campogalliani; released November 22, 1920; length: 5,657 feet.

Cast: Bartolomeo Pagano (*Maciste*); Letizia Quaranta; Gabriel Moreau; Felice Minotti.

Comments: A Bartolomeo Pagano Maciste Film.

The Trilogy of Maciste (*La trilogia di Maciste*) (Itala Film, 1920)

Credits: Director: Carlo Campogalliani, *Photography:* Fortunato Spinolo; length: 16,638 feet (3 episodes); released May 1920.

Cast: Bartolomeo Pagano (*Maciste*); Letizia Quaranta; Carlo Campogalliani; Vittorio Rossi Pianelli; Pierre Lepetit; Gabriel Moreau; Ria Bruna; Felice Minotti; Oreste Bilancia; Emilio Vardannes.

Comments: This Maciste compilation film consisted of three feature-length installments: (1) *Maciste Faces Death* (*Maciste contro la morte*), (2) *The Voyage of Maciste* (*Il viaggio di Maciste*), and (3) *The Testament of Maciste* (*Il testamento di Maciste*). These episodes were apparently shown separately under the *Trilogy* title. Bartolomeo Pagano became so famous in Italy and was so closely identified with the Maciste role that he was often billed onscreen as "Maciste." The films were immensely popular in Germany and Mexico as well, and Pagano appeared as Maciste in non–Italian films. For instance, *Maciste and the Silver King's Daughter* (*Maciste e la figlia re dell'argento*) [1922], *Maciste and the Chinese Trunk* (*Maciste und die Chinesische Truhe*) [1923], and *Maciste and Prisoner No. 51* (*Maciste und der Sträfling Nr. 51* [1923] were all German productions, as was *Maciste and the Japanese* (*Maciste und die Japanerin*) [1922], while *Maciste the Tourist* (*Maciste Turista*) [1917] was a Mexican production.

THE SOUND ERA

Adventurer of Tortuga (L'avventriero della Tortuga) (Liber Film, 1965)

Credits: Director: Luigi Cauano; *Screenplay:* Luigi Capuano, Fernando Cerchio, Arpad De-Riso, Ottavio Poggi (based on the novel by Emilio Salgari); *Photography:* Guglielmo Mancori (Eastmancolor, ratio 2.35:1); *Film Editor:* Antonietta Zita; *Production Designer:* Giorgio Giovanni; *Costumes:* Giancarlo Bartolini, Salimbeni; *Sound:* Pietro Ortolani; *Fencing Master:* Ferdinando Poggi; running time: 97 minutes; released August 13, 1965.

Cast: Guy Madison (*Alfonso di Montélimar*); Ingeborg Schöner (*Soledad Quintero*); Rik Battaglia (*Pedro Valverde*); Nadia Gray (*Dona Rosita*); Andrea Aureli (*Enrico Vallejo*); Aldo Bufi Landi (*Mendoza*); Mino Doro (*Tarsarios*); Linda Sini (*Paquita*); Giulio Marchetti (*Father of the Bride*); Giulio Battiferi (*Pirate*); Aldo Christiani (*Fernandez*); Bruno Arié (*Pirate*); Riccardo Pizzuti (*Pirate*); Alfredo Danesi; Romano Giomini; Pietro Ceccarelli (*Indian High Priest*); Giulio Maculani (*Spanish Patrol Captain*); Ferdinando Poggi (*Pirate*); Franco Ukmar (*Spanish Soldier*).

Comments: A pirate-adventure film, portions of which were shot on location in Spain, with interiors filmed at Incir De Paolis in Rome. This was a co-production between Italy's Liber Film and Germany's Eichberg-Film. In the English-dubbed version Guy Madison's voice was provided by another actor.

The Adventures of Mandrin (Le avvventure di Mandrin) (Republic Pictures, 1952)

Credits: Director: Mario Soldati; *Producers:* Jacques Bar, Niccolò Theodoli; *Screenplay:* Giorgio Bassani, Augusto Frassinetti, Vittorio Nino Novarese, Mario Soldati (from a story by Giorgio Bassani, Augusto Frassinetti, Vittorio Nino Novarese); *Photography:* Mario Montuori (black-and-white, aspect ratio 1.37:1); *Film Editor:* Roberto Cinquini; *Music:* Mario Nascimbene; *Production Design:* Guido Fiorini; *Costume Design:* Vittorio Nino Novarese; *Makeup:* Amato Garbini; *General Manager:* Elio Scardamaglia; *Production Supervisors:* Fernando Cinquini, Anna Divini; *1st Assistant Director:* Cesare Olivieri; *2nd Assistant Directors:* Renato Cinquini, Agostino Richelmy; *Sound Engineer:* Mario Bartolomei; *Camera Operator:* Amerigo Paolo; *Assistant Camera Operator:* Silvio Fraschetti; *Still Photographer:* Francesco Alessi; *Orchestra Conductor:* Franco Ferrara; running time: 102 minutes; released March 8, 1952 (Italy), May 26, 1955 (U.S.).

Cast: Raf Vallone (*Mandrin*); Jacques Castelot (*Baron de Villemure*); Silvana Pampanini (*Rosetta*); Michèle Philippe (*Marquise de Maubicourt*); Gualtiero Tumiati (*Prince Guido*); Vinicio Sofia (*Stefano Vernet*); Giulio Donnini; Michele Malaspina; Nietta Zocchi; Pietro Capanna (billed as "Piero Capanna"); Richard Armontel; Pina Piovanni; Bruno Smith; Sandro Bianchi; Mariano Di Fulvio; Riccardo Rioli; Alberto Rabagliati (*Behisar*); Dhia Cristiani (*voice dubbing, for Silvana Pampanini*); Lidia Simoneschi (*Voice dubbing, for Michèle Phillippe*); Stefano Sibaldi (*voice dubbing*).

Comments: A costume adventure film with the protagonist based on 18th-century robber-adventurer Louis Mandrin (1725–1755) who is presented here as a Robin-Hood-type figure rebelling against the French tax collection agency. Mandrin's real-life fate (he was eventually captured, tried, and sentenced to a brutal and horrific death by the government) is left unstated in this movie. The film was a co-production of France's Cormoran Films and Italy's Industrie Cinematografiche Sociali (ICS).

The Adventures of Scaramouche (La máscara de Scaramouche) (Embassy, 1963)

Credits: Director: Antonio Isasi-Isamendi; Executive Producer: Juan Campos; Screenplay: Lluís Josep Comerón, Jorge Illa, Antonio Isasi-Isamendi, Jacques Robert, Arturo Rigel; Photography: Alejandro Ulloa (Eastmancolor, Dyaliscope, ratio 2.35:1); Film Editor: Petra di Nieva; Music: Gregorio García Segura; Set Decoration: Enrique Alarcón, Francisco R. Ascencio; Hairdresser: Josefa Rubio; Unit Production Manager: Féliz Moreno; Assistant Director: Ricardo Muñoz Suay; Props: Antonio Luna; Special Effects: Antonio Cortes (models); Stunt Coordinator/Fencing Master: Claude Carliez; Assistant Stunt Coordinator: Antoine Baud; Still Photographer: Simón Lopez; Costumes: Humberto Cornejo; Production Secretary: Carmen Pageo; Music (song, *"Les Comédiens"*): Charles Aznavour (sung by Jacqueline François); running time: 98 minutes; released February 14, 1964 (Italy), November 21, 1964 (U.S.).

Cast: Gérard Barray *(Robert Lafleur, Scaramouche)*; Michèle Girardon *(Diana, Souchil's Ward)*; Gianna Maria Canale *(Suzanne)*; Yvette Lebon *(Alice, Madame de Popignan)*; George Rigaud *(Duc de Lacoste)*; Andrés Mejuto *(Señor de Villancourt)*; Gonzalo Cañas *(Pierot)*; Irán Eory *(Jacqueline, Perot's Girlfriend)*; Rafael Durán *(Señor de Dubalon)*; Jose Brugara *(Marquis de Souchil)*; Antonio Gradoli *(Fernando Montes)*; Xan das Bolas *(Gino)*; Álvaro de Luna; Santiago Ontañón; Gustavo Re; Ángel Álvarez; José Leal; Helga Liné.

Comments: A swashbuckler about the 18th-century French rake constructed along the same lines as the much more famous MGM production of 1952, *Scaramouche*. This inferior but still enjoyable version was a co-production between Italy's Compagnia Cinematografica Mondiale (CCM), Spain's Producciones Benito Perojo, and the French companies Fidès and Capitole Films.

Ali Baba and the Sacred Crown (Le sette fatiche di Alí Babá) (Medallion Pictures, 1962)

Credits: Director: Erminio Salvi; Screenplay: Benito Ilforte, Amrogio Molteni, Erminio Salvi; Photography: Mario Parapetti (Eastmancolor, ratio 2.35:1); Art Director: Giovanni Armadei; running time: 90 minutes; released October 25, 1962 (Italy), 1963 (U.S.); video availability: Something Weird Video.

Cast: Bella Cortez *(Lota)*; Salvatore Furnari; Omero Gargano; Iloosh Koshabe [billed as Rod Flash] *(Ali Baba)*; Aristide Massari; Furio Meniconi *(Mustapha)*; Mario Polletin; Yvonne Sire; Amedeo Trilli *(Hassem Bey)*; Lilliana Zagra.

Comments: An Arabian Nights fantasy-adventure, also known as *The Seven Tasks of Ali Baba*. At a wizard's bidding, Ali Baba delivers a sacred crown to another country, only to find that a tyrant has gained control there, and uses the crown to liberate the people. Iranian-born Iloosh Koshabe (1932–2012) is billed here (and in subsequent films) as "Rod Flash." Stunning Cuban actress Bella Cortez (real name Alicia Paneque; 1944–), is a major asset to this production, as she was in many other genre films. *Ali Baba and the Sacred Crown* was a co-production between two Italian companies, Avis Film and Telexport.

Ali Baba and the Seven Saracens (Simbad contro I sette saraceni) (American-International, 1964)

Credits: Director: Erminio Salvi; Screenplay: Benito Ilforte, Sergio Tocci (based on a story by Erminio Salvi); Photography: Mario Parapetti (Eastmancolor, Totalscope, ratio 2.35:1); Film Editor: Enzo Alfonzi; Production Design/Art Direction: Giuseppe Ranieri; Sound: Bruno Moreal; Costume Design: Giovanna Natili; running time: 94 minutes (Italy), 80 minutes (U.S.); released December 18, 1964 (Italy), 1965 (U.S.), video availability: Something Weird Video.

Bella Cortez in *Ali Baba and the Sacred Crown*.

Cast: Gordon Mitchell *(Omar)*; Bruno Piergentilli [billed as Dan Harrison] *(Sinbad/Ali Baba)*; Bella Cortez *(Fatima, Princess of the Yeridi)*; Carla Calò [billed as Carol Brown] *(Farida, Omar's Lover)*; Armadeo Trilli [billed as Mike Moore] *(Haswan, Fatima's Uncle)*; Luigi Tosi [billed as Nat Coster] *(Meneth, Saracen Leader)*; Tony Di Mitri [billed as Tony Dimitri] *(Sharif)*; Lilli Zander *(Fatima's Friend)*; Attillio Severini *(Gate Guard)*; Tonio Stoppa *(Saracen Leader)*; Franco Doria *(Jukri)*; Maria Pia Conte *(Fatima's Friend)*; Renato Terra [billed as Renato Terra Caizzi] *(Saracen Leader)*; Alberto Conversi *(Momet, a Rebel)*; Artemio Antonini *(Kassim of Zaragan)*; Bruno Caratenuto *(Saracen Leader)*;

Comments: Ali Baba (Sinbad in the original Italian version) battles Omar, an evil king, but falls in love with the despot's beautiful niece. This film was produced by Italy's Avis Film.

Alone Against Rome (Solo contro Rome) (Medallion Pictures, 1962)

Credits: *Director:* Luciano Ricci; *Screenplay:* Gianni Astolfi, Ernesto Gastaldi, Ennio Mancini; *Producer:* Marco Vicaro; *Photography:* Silvano Ippoliti (Technicolor, Totalscope, ratio 2.35:1); *Film Editor:* Roberto Cinquini; *Production Design:* Niko Matul; *Set Decorations:* Piero Poletto; *Costume Design:* Paolo Caraco; *Assistant Director:* Stipe Delic (billed as Stefano Delic); *2nd Unit Director:* Riccardo Freda; *Sound:* Rocco Roy Mangano (billed as Roy Mangano); *Camera Operators:* Raffaele Masciocchi; Riccardo Pallottini; *Horses:* Jadran Film; running time: 95 minutes (Italy), 100 minutes (U.S.); released September 1962 (Italy), December 1963 (U.S.), video availability: Sinister Cinema.

Cast: Lang Jeffries *(Brenno)*; Rossana Posestà

(*Fabiola*); Phillippe Leroy (*Silla*); Gabriele Tinti (*Goruk*); Luciana Angiolillo (*Saron's Servant*); Renato Terra (*Gladiator Trainer*); Goffredo Unger (billed as Frederico Unger); Angelo Bastianoni; Rinaldo Zamperla (*Light Blond Prisoner*); Djorde Nenadovic (*Centurio Caius*); Giancarlo Bastianoni (*Dark Blond Prisoner*); Alfredo Danesi; Franco Nonibasti; Janez Albeht.

Comments: An evil Roman tribune gains control of a town, victimizing the population, until he is opposed and eventually defeated by a warrior. Ten thousand extras were employed in this production. War chariots seen in the Hollywood epic *Ben-Hur* (1959) were borrowed and re-used in this Film. Leading lady Rosanna Podestà was the wife of producer Marco Vicario. *Alone Against Rome* was filmed in Ljubljana, Slovania, Yugoslavia; Pula, Yugoslavia, and Lavrica Skofljica, Slovenia. The film was a co-production between Italy's Atlantica Cinematografica Produzione Films and Yugoslavia's Film Servis.

The Amazons (*Le guerriere dal seno nudo*) (American-International, 1975)

Credits: *Director:* Terence Young; *Producers:* Nino Crisman, André Génovès, Gregorio Sacristán; *Associate Producer:* José Garcia Moreno; *Screenplay:* Massimo De Rita, Arduino Maiuri, Serge de la Roche (based on a story by Richard Aubrey, Robert Graves, Luciano Vincenzoni, Terence Young, Antonio Recoder, Charles Spaak); *Photography:* Aldo Tonti, Alejandro Ulloa (Technicolor, aspect ratio 1.85:1); *Film Editor:* Roger Dwyre; *Music:* Riz Ortolani; *Production Design:* Mario Garbuglia; *Set Decoration:* Julio Molina; *Makeup:* Otello Fava; *Hair Stylist:* Toñy Nieto; *Assistant Director:* John Longmuir; *2nd Unit Director:* Johnny Dwyre; *Special Effects (Matte Painting):* Emilio Ruiz del Rio; *Assistant Film Editor:* John Longmuir; *Choreographer:* Jana Marakova; running time: 105 minutes (Italy), 89 minutes (U.S.); released May 1973 (Italy), March 1975 (U.S.); video availability: Retromedia.

Cast: Alena Johnston (*Antiope*); Sabine Sun (*Oreitheia*); Rosanna Yanni (*Penthesilea*); Helga Liné (*High Priestess*); Rebecca Potok (*Melanippe*); Malissa Longo (*Leuthera*); Lucy Tiller (*Alana*); Almut Berg (*Cynara*); Luciana Paluzzi (*Phaedra*); Angelo Infanti (*Theseus*); Fausto Tozzi (*General*); Ángel del Pozo (*Captain*); Franco Borelli (*Perithous*); Benito Stefanelli (*Commander*); Anna Ardizone (billed as "Anna Maria Ardizzone"); Rita Calderoni (*Amazon*); Francesco D'Adda; Serge de la Roche; Massimo De Rita; Veronique Floret; Arduino Maiuri; Carla Mancini; Ulrike Pesch; Anna Petocchi; Nathalie Plouvie; Virginia Rhodes; Nestore Cavaricci (*Tribesman*); Godela H. Meyer.

Comments: A tribe of Amazons crowns a new queen and battles male enemies in this adventure. Co-produced by Italy's Monteluce Film, France's Les Films de la Boétie, and the Spanish companies Films Montana and Zurbano Films. Some scenes were shot on location in Almeria, Adalucia, Spain.

Amazons of Rome (*La vergini di Roma*) (United Artists, 1961)

Credits: *Directors:* Carlo Ludovico Bragaglia, Vittorio Cottafavi, Peter O'Cord; *Screenplay:* Léo Joannnon, Pierre O'Connell (story by Luigi Emmanuele, Gaetano Loffredo); *Executive Producer:* Arys Nissoti; *Photography:* Marc Fossard (Eastmancolor, ratio 1.75:1); *Film Editor:* Michael Leroy; *Production Design:* Miomir Denic; *Art Direction:* Kosta Krivokapic; *Costume Design:* Piero Sadun; *Makeup:* Hagop Arakelian, Louis Bonnemaison; *Production Manager:* Louis de Masure; *Unit Manager:* Roger Boulais; *Production Supervisor:* Pierre Bochart; *Assistant Directors:* Roger Dallier, Michael Wichard; *Special Effects:* René Le Hénaff, Jean d'Eubonne (models); *Set Design:* Raymond Gabutti; *Sound:* Pierre Goumy (Chief Sound Engineer), Fernand Janisse (Recordist); *Stunts:* Milan Mitic (also Horse Stunts and Stunt Double); *Still Photographer:* Henry Thibalt; running time: 105 minutes (Italy), 93 minutes (U.S.); released March 24, 1961 (Italy), March 1963 (U.S.).

Cast: Louis Jordan (*Drusco*); Sylvia Sims (*Clelia*); Jean Chevrier (*Porcenna, Etruscan Leader*); Nicole Courcel (*Lucilla, Porcenna's Wife*); Ettore Manni (*Horatio/Cocles, Roman Consul*); Paola Falci (*Aurelia*); Renaud Mary (*Stravos*); Michel Piccoli (*Consul Publicola*); Corrado Pani (*Muzio Scevola*); Nicholas Vogel

(Rasmal); Maria Luisa Rolando *(Donna Romana)*; Carlo Giustini *(Bruto)*; Jacques Dufilho; Andrej Gardenin.

Comments: The dashing and sophisticated Louis Jordan *(Gigi)* is miscast as a barbarian leader in this costume adventure yarn, but his charismatic presence is, nonetheless, a welcome addition to the proceedings, and his contribution was apparently considered essential by the producers. During production, animosity between Jordan and assigned director Vittorio Cottafavi resulted in Cottafavi being fired and replaced by Carlo Ludovico Bragaglia

Aphrodite, Goddess of Love (Afrodite, dea dell'amore) (Embassy Pictures, 1966)

Credits: Director: Mario Bonnard; *Producers:* Alberto Manca (billed as "Alberto Manca dell'Assinara"); *Screenplay:* Mario Bonnard, Sergio Leone, Ugo Moretti, Mario di Nardo (based on a story by Mario Bonnard, Alberto Manca); *Photography:* Tino Santoni (Ferraniacolor, Schermiscope, aspect ratio 2.35:1); *Film Editor:* Nella Nannuzzi; *Production Design:* Saverio D'Eugenio; *Set Decoration:* Luigi D'Andria; *Costume Design:* Giancarlo Bartolini Salimbeni *Makeup:* Duilio Giustini, Michele Trimarchi, *Hair Stylists:* Lina Cassini, Gustavo Sisi; *Production Manager:* Adriano Merkel; *Production Supervisors:* Pietro Nofri, Gino Peccerini; *Assistant Director:* Romolo Guerrieri (billed as "Romolo Girolami"); *Assistant Director:* Sergio Leone; *Sound Engineers:* Bruno Francisci, Silvio Santaloce; *Microphone Boom Operator:* Tulio Petricca; *Camera Operators:* Enrico Cignitti, Silvano Mancini; *Special Effects:* Ditta Baciucchi; *Assistant Costume Designer:* Luciana Angelini; *Costumers:* Fausta Scotolani, Irma Tonnini; *Production Secretary:* Diego Alchimede; *Script Supervisor:* Roberto Giandalla; running time: 91 minutes (Italy); released August 29, 1958 (Italy), January 21, 1966 (U.S.).

Cast: Isabelle Corey *(Lerna)*; Anthony Steffen [billed as "Antonio De Teffe"] *(Demetrio)*; Irène Tunc *(Diala)*; Ivo Garrani *(Antigono)*; Giulio Donnini *(Erasto)*; Carlo Tamberlani *(Matteo)*; Gian Paolo Rosmino [billed as "Giampaolo Rosmino"] *(Dineo)*; Andrea Aureli *(Kibur)*; Matteo Spinola *(Glauco)*; Adriano Micantoni *(Ftire)*; Mino Doro *(Crepilo)*; Germano Longo *(Osco)*; Paul Muller *(Asian)*; Livio Lorenzon *(Spy)*; Lilliana Gerace *(Seer)*; Edda Soligo *(Peasant)*; Nada Cortese *(Woman)*; Emma Baron *(Onoria)*; Clara Calamai *(Stenele)*; John Kitzmiller *(Tomoro)*; Massimo Serato *(Quinto Rufo)*; Mimmo Poli *(Trader)*; Renato Montalbano; Ettore Jannetti; Gustavo Serena; Nello Pazzafini, Amerigo Santarelli *(Slave Guard)*.

Comments: Instead of the usual muscular hero, the protagonist in this film is a sensitive artist. At one point, the heroine poses for a sculpture of the goddess Aphrodite, hence the title. This costume adventure was produced by Italy's Schermi Produzione.

The Arena (La rivolta della gladiatrici) (New World Pictures, 1974)

Credits: Director: Steve Carver; *Producer:* Mark Damon; *Executive Producer:* Roger Corman; *Screenplay:* John William Corrington, Joyce Hooper Corrington; *Photography:* Joe D'Amato [billed as "Aristide Massaccesi"] (Technicolor, Techniscope, aspect ratio 2.35:1); *Film Editor:* Piera Bruni; *Music:* Francesco De Masi; *Makeup:* Antonio Mura, Emilio Trani; *Production Manager:* Oscar Santaniello; *2nd Unit Director:* Joe D'Amato (billed as "Michael Wotruba"); *Assistant Director:* Romano Scandariato; *Set Designer:* Mimmo Scavia; *Special Effects:* Sergio Chiusi; *Sound Recordist:* Franco Groppioni; *Sound Effects Editor:* Alvaro Gramigna; *Stunt Co-ordinator:* Franco Pasquetto (billed as "Gianfranco Pasquetto"); *Still Photographer:* Carlo Alberto Cocchi; *Wardrobe:* Renata Morroni; *Orchestra Conductor/Music Arrangements:* Francesco De Masi; *Production Assistants:* Massimo Alberini, Sergio Rosa; *Assistant to the Director:* Jann Carver; *Continuity:* Anita Borgiotti; running time: 90 minutes (Italy), 83 minutes (U.S.); released January 1974 (U.S.), December 27, 1974 (Italy); video availability: Shout! Factory.

Cast: Margaret Markov *(Bodicia)*; Pam Grier *(Mamawi)*; Lucretia Love *(Deidre)*; Paul Muller *(Lucilius)*; Daniele Vargas *(Timarchus)*; Marie Louise Sinclair [billed as "Marie Louise"] *(Livia)*; Maria Pia Conte [billed as "Mary Count"]

(Lucinia); Rosalba Neri [billed as "Sara Bay"] *(Cornelia)*; Vassili Karis [billed as "Vic Karis"] *(Marcus)*; Silvio Lorenzi [billed as "Sid Lawrence"] *(Priscium)*; Mimmo Palmara [billed as "Dick Palmer"] *(Rufinius)*; Antonio Casale [billed as "Anthony Vernon"] *(Lucan)*; Franco Garofalo [billed as "Christopher Oakes"] *(Aemilius)*; Pietro Ceccarelli [billed as "Peter Cester"] *(Septimus)*; Jho Jhenkins *(Quintus)*; Ivan Gasper *(Wulfstan)*; Pietro Torrisi *(Gladiator)*; Salvatore Baccaro *(Winekeeper)*; Anna Melita *(Gladiator Girl)*; Tom Felleghy *(Bidder at Slave Auction)*; Jann Fox *(Centurion)*; Emilio Messina *(Gladiator)*; Roberto Messina *(Gladiator)*; Osiride Pevarello; Mimmo Poli; *(Man at Orgy)*; Claudio Riffini *(Gladiator)*; Sergio Smacchi *(Gladiator)*.

Comments: An all-girl takeoff on *Spartacus* as women gladiators are compelled to fight each other and then rebel against their captors. Produced by Italy's Rover Film, in cooperation with Roger Corman's New World Pictures.

Atlas Against the Cyclops *(Maciste nella terra dei ciclopi)* (Medallion Pictures, 1961)

Credits: *Director:* Antonio Leonviola (billed as Leonviola); *Screenplay:* Oreste Biancoli, Gino Mangini (story by Oreste Biancoli); *Producers:* Luigi Carpentieri, Ermanno Donati; *Photography:* Riccardo Pallotini (Eastmancolor, Dyaliscope, ratio 2.35:1); *Music:* Carlo Innocenzi; *Film Editor:* Mario Serandrei; *Production Designer:* Alberto Boccianti; *Set Decoration:* Ennio Michettoni; *Costume Design:* Giuliano Papi; *Makeup:* Piero Mecacci; *Hair Stylist:* Galileo Mandini; *Production Manager:* Piero Mecacci; *Assistant Directors:* Giovanni Fago; Mariano Laurenti; *Sound:* Gianetto Nardi; *Special Effects:* Giovanni Corridori; *Optical Mattes:* Joseph Nathanson; *Montage Photography:* Galileo Mandini; *Camera Operator:* Stelvio Massi; *Assistant Costume Designer:* Massimo Bolongaro; *Music Director:* Carlo Franci; *Production Assistants:* Giorgio Baldi, Livio Maffei; *Script Girl:* Paola Salva Dori; *English Translator:* Fernando Paolo Girolami; *Secretary to the Producer:* Carlo Zanotti; *Dubbing:* John Davis Hart (English), Maurice LaRoche (French); running time: 94 minutes (Italy), 100 minutes (U.S.); released March 29, 1961 (Italy), April 14, 1963 (U.S.); video availability: Something Weird Video.

Cast: Gordon Mitchell [billed as Mitchell Gordon] *(Maciste)*; Chelo Alonso *(Capys)*; Vira Silenti *(Penope)*; Aldo Bufi Landi *(Sirone)*; Dante DiPaolo *(Iphitos)*; Giotto Tempestini *(Aronio)*; Raffaella Carrá [billed as Raffaella Pelloni] *(Eber)*; Paul Wynter *(Mumba)*; Massimo Righi *(Efros)*; Fabio *(Baby Son of Penope and Agisandro)*; Aldo Pedinotti [billed as Aldo Padinotti] *(Cyclops)*; Tullio Altamura *(Captain of the Guard)*; Antonio Meschini *(Soldier)*; Pietro Ceccarelli *(Prison Guard)*; Moira Orfei *(Peasant Girl)*.

Comments: A 20-foot-tall cyclops terrorizes the land of Sadok until the heroic Maciste arrives to save the day; matters are complicated by the evil queen Capys. This fantasy-adventure was produced by Italy's Panda Film, and shot at Instituto Nazionale Luce in Rome.

Atlas Against the Czar *(Maciste alla corte dello zar)* (Teleworld, 1964)

Credits: *Director:* Tanio Boccia (billed as Amerigo Anton); *Screenplay:* Tanio Boccia (billed as Amerigo Anton), Alberto De Rossi, Mario Moroni (story by Mario Moroni); *Producer:* Luigi Rovere; *Photography:* Aldo Giordani (Technicolor, Techniscope, ratio 2.35:1); *Music:* Carlo Rustichelli; *Set Decoration:* Amedeo Mellone; *Costumes:* Walter Patriarca; *Production Manager:* Renato Panetuzzi; *Art Department:* Italo Tomassi; *Special Effects:* Eugenio Ascani; running time: 91 minutes; released March 4, 1964 (Italy), August 1965 (U.S.); video availability: Something Weird Video.

Cast: Kirk Morris *(Maciste)*; Massimo Serato *(Czar Nicola Nicolajevic)*; Ombretta Colli *(Sonia)*; Gloria Milland *(Nadia)*; Tom Felleghy [billed as Tom Felleghi] *(Akim)*; Giulio Donnini *(Igor)*; Dada Gallotti *(Katia)*; Ugo Sasso; Arnaldo Arnaldi; Howard Ross; Attilio Dottesio; Luigi Scavran; Consalvo Dell'Arti; Spartico Battisti; Giovanni Sabbatini; Franco Pechini; Marco Pasquini; Giorgio Bixio; Nello Pazzafini *(Keeper of the Cave)*.

Comments: Czar Nicholas attempts to recover a lost treasure, with the heroic Maciste inexplicably appearing in medieval Russia to oppose him. As sword and sandal films gradually exhausted their usual plotlines, the stories grew wilder and farther afield in a search for new material. This entry was produced by Italy's Cineluxor at Rome's Cinnecittà Studios.

Attack of the Moors (I Reali di Francia) (American-International Television, 1959)

Credits: Director: Mario Costa; Screenplay: Vittorio Calvino; Nino Stresa (story by Vittorio Calvino); Executive Producer: Adriano Merkel; Producer: Alberto Manca; Photography: Augusto Tiezzi (Color, Dyaliscope, ratio 2.35:1); Film Editor: Otello Colangeli; Music: Carlo Innocenzi; Art Direction: Saverio D'Eugenio; Set Decoration: Emilio D'Andrea; Costume Design: Anna Maria Feo; Makeup: Adriana Cassini; Production Managers: Pietro Nofri, Gino Peccerini; Assistant Director: Mario Tota; Sound: Renato Cadueri; Primiano Muratori, Enzo Silvestri; Special Effects: Angelo Malantrucco (billed as Anglelo Manlandrucco), Maurice Spagnoli; Camera Operator: Mario Sensi; Production Assistant: Tonino Gazarelli; running time: 88 minutes (Italy), 80 minutes (U.S.); released December 11, 1959.

Cast: Chelo Alonso (*Suleima*); Rik Battaglia (*Roland, Count of Besançon*); Gérard Landry (*Gontrano*); Liana Orfei (*Jitana*); Livio Lorenzon (*Basiroco*); Andrea Scotti (*Lanciotto*); Franco Fantasia (*Miguel*); Luisella Boni (*Annette*); Olga Sobelli (*Fazia*); Gino Maturano (*Juanito*); Paola Quattrini (*Princess Maria*); Carlo Tamberlani (*Duke of Chateau Roux*); Cesare Fantoni (*Achirro, Chief of the Moors*); Nerio Bernardi (*King of France*);

Comments: Beautiful Cuban native Chelo Aloso (1933–) [real name Isabella Garcia] was a sultry, charismatic actress who enlivened several pepla. Italian-born leading man Rik Battaglia (1927–2015) appeared in scores of Italian movies, including the Barbara Steele horror entry *Nightmare Castle.* The somewhat convoluted plot here, involving French nobility, Arabian infidels and gypsies, follows the protagonist, Roland, Count of Besançon (Battaglia), as he is dispatched by the King of Spain to defend a castle against invaders. Produced by Italy's Schermi Produzione.

Attack of the Normans (I normanni) (American-International, 1963)

Credits: Director: Giuseppe Vari; Screenplay: Nino Stresa; Photography: Marco Scarpelli, Vittorio Storaro (Eastmancolor, CinemaScope, ratio 2.35:1); Makeup: Alma Santoli, Euclid Santoli; Production Manager: Paolo Mercuri; 2nd Unit Director: Mario Bava; Assistant Directors: Marcello Crescenzi, Tonino Ricci (billed as Teodoro Ricci); Set Design: Giorgio Giovanni; Sound: Kurt Doubrowsky; Music Conductor: Luigi Urbini (billed as Pier Luigi Urbini) Costumes: Casa d'Arte di Firenze; running time: 89 minutes (Italy), 79 minutes (U.S.); released October 19, 1962 (Europe), 1963 (U.S.); video availability: Something Weird Video.

Cast: Cameron Mitchell (*Wilfred, Duke of Saxony*); Geneviève Grad (*Svetania*); Ettore Manni *Oliver D'Anglon*); Philippe Hersent (*James*); Piero Lulli (*Barton*); Paul Muller (*Thomas*); Franca Bettoia (*Queen Patricia*); Raf Baldassarre (*Dag*); Livia Contardi; Tony Di Mitri; Gilberto Galimberti (*Wilfred, Henchman*); Pietro Marascalchi; Gianni Solaro (*King Dagobert*); Rinaldo Zamperla (*William*).

Comments: Court intrigue abounds as the English battle the Normans in this costume-adventure. Mario Bava is credited as 2nd unit director, and battle scenes that he filmed for *Erik the Conqueror* (qv) are used here. *Attack of the Normans* was a co-production between Italy's Galatea Film and France's Lyre Film

Attilla (Atilla il flagello di Dio) (Embassy, 1954)

Credits: Director: Pietro Francisci; Screenplay: Ennio De Concini, Richard C. Sarafian, Primo Zeglio; Executive Producer: Antonio Altoviti; Producers: Dino De Laurentiis, Carlo Ponti; Photography: Aldo Tonti (Technicolor, ratio 1.37:1); Music: Raoul Kraushaar (uncredited); Enzo Masetti; Film Editors: Leo Cattozzo, Helene Turner; Production Design: Flavio Mogherini; Set Decoration: Arrigo Breschi, Riccardo Domenici (billed as Riccardo Dominici); Costume Design: Veniero Colasanti, Esther Scott; Makeup: Jeanne Gallagher, Euclide Santoli; Hair Stylist: Iole Cecchini; Production Director: Georgio

22 Avenger

Adriani; *Production Supervisors:* R.L. Wolf; *Assistant Directors:* Luciano Ercoli, Giorgio Graziosi, Lou Place, Luici Scattini, Aldo Calpini; *Sound Technician:* Biagio Fiorelli; *Sound Recordist:* Robert Post; *Special Effects:* Ivor Beddoes, Stephen B. Grimes; *Camera Operators;* Riccardo Pallotini, Giuseppe Rotunno, Karl Struss, Luciano Trasatti; *Focus Puller:* Dennis Bartlett (uncredited); *Music Director:* Franco Ferrara; *Assistant to Producer:* Joan Altman; *General Organizer:* Antonio Altoviti; *Technicolor Color Consultant:* Joan Bridge; *Choreographer:* Gisa Geert; *Script Girl:* Sherry Proctor; *Sound System:* Western Electric; running time: 77 minutes (Italy), 80 minutes (U.S.); released December 27, 1954 (Italy), May 17, 1958 (U.S.).

Cast: Anthony Quinn *(Attila)*; Sophia Loren *(Honoria)*; Henri Vidal *(Aetius)*; Claude Laydu *(Valentiniano Caesar)*; Irene Papas *(Grune)*; Colette Regis *(Galla Placidia)*; Ettore Manni *(Bleda, Attila's Brother)*; Eduardo Ciannelli [billed as Eduardo Cianelli] *(Onegesius, Counsellor to Attila)*; Georges Bréhat *(Prisco)*; Christian Marquand *(Hun Leader)*; Guido Celano *(Tribal Chieftan)*; Aldo Pini *(Dominicus)*; Marco Guglielmi *(Kadis)*; Antonio Amendola; Richard Bakalyan; Fabio Bellisario; Fernando Birri; Mirella D. Lauri; Cristina Fantoni; Mario Feliciani *(Ippolito)*; Piero Giagnoni; Carlo Hinterman [billed as Carlo Hintermann] *(Tribal Chieftan)*; Dickie Jones; Edilio Kim *(Soldato Unno)*; Rthe enzo Malatesta; Scott Marlowe; Furio Meniconi *(Tribal Leader)*; Aurelio Miserendino; Mimmo Palmara *(Lottatore)*; Piero Pastore *(Tribal Chieftan)*; Aldo Sprovieri; Mario Valente; Henri Vidon; Robert Rietty *(Aetius' Voice)*.

Comments: Iconic star Anthony Quinn portrays 5th-century barbarian leader Attila the Hun as he battles his way across Italy to the gates of Rome. Quinn was acting in the Federico Fellini classic *La Strada* (1954) at the same time he was shooting scenes for *Attila*. Although *Attila* had a much larger budget than *La Strada*, it was not in the same artistic class as Fellini's production. *Attila* was a co-production between Italy's Lux Film and Producciones Ponti–De Laurentiis, in conjunction with France's Compagnie Cinématographique de France.

The Avenger (Le leggenda di Enea) (Medallion Pictures, 1962)

Credits: *Director:* Giorgio Venturini (billed as Giorgio Rivalta); *Screenplay:* Ugo Liberatore, Luigi Mangini, Arrigo Montanari, Nino Stresa, Albert Band, Giuseppe Abbrecia (uncredited), based on the poem *Aeneis* by Publius Vergilius Maro; *Executive Producer:* Piero Ghione, *Producers:* Giorgio Venturini, Albert Band (uncredited); *Music:* Giovanni Fusco; *Photography:* Angelo Lotti (Eastmancolor, Euroscope, ratio 2.35:1); *Film Editor:* Antonietta Zita; *Music Conductor:* Luigi Urbini (billed as Pier Luigi Urbini); *Production Design:* Aleksandar Milovic; *Art Direction/Costume Design:* Arrigo Equini; *Wigs:* Palombi; *Production Manager:* Piero Ghione; *Assistant Directors:* Giuseppe Abbrescia, Stojan Culibrk, Albert Band (uncredited, billed as Alfredo Antonini); *Set Dresser:* Paolo Di Stefano; *Weapons:* E. Rancati (billed as Rancati); *Sound:* Venanzio Biraschi, Pietro Spadoni; *Stunts:* Benito Stefanelli (Fencing Master and Stunt Coordinator); *Assistant Cameramen:* Antonio Orlandini, Mario Pastorini; *Camera Operator:* Elio Polacchi; *Costumes:* Tigano Lofaro; *Footwear:* Pompeii; *Publicist:* Sonia Bencini; *Production Assistants:* Michele Marsala, Arrigo Peri; *Choreographer:* Adriano Vitale; *Titles for U.S. Version:* Associated Advertising and Design; running time: 95 minutes (Italy), 105 minutes (U.S.); released November 28, 1962 (Italy), June 1964 (U.S.); video availability: Retromedia.

Cast: Steve Reeves *(Enea/Aeneas)*; Giacomo Rossi Stuart [billed as Giacomo Rossi-Stuart] *(Euryalus)*; Carla Marlier *(Ravinia, Latino's Daughter)*; Mario Ferrari *(Latino, King of Latium)*; Enzo Fiermonte *(Acate)*; Gianni Garko *(Turno, King of the Rutuli)*; Liana Orfei *(Camilla, Queen of the Volsci)*; Nerio Bernardi *(Drance)*; Robert Bettoni *(Pallante)*; Maurice Poli *(Mezensio, Turno's Henchman)*; Lulla Selli *(Amata, Latino's Wife)*; Pietro Capanna *(Bisia)*; Benito Stefanelli *(Nisius, Euryalus' Friend)*; Adriano Vitale *(Dancer)*: Charles Band [unbilled] *(Ascanio)*; Luciano Benetti [unbilled] *(Sergeste)*; Andrej Gardenin [unbilled] *(Fencer)*; Furio Meniconi [unbilled] *(Turno's Henchman)*; Walter Zappolini [unbilled] *(Dancer)*.

Comments: Hero Aeneas (Steve Reeves) leads refugees from the Trojan war to a new land in Italy. Produced by Italy's Mercury Films, in tandem with France's La Société des Films Sirius and Compagne Industrielle et Commerciale Cinématographique (CICC), and Yugoslavia's Avala Film.

Avenger of the Seven Seas (Il giustiziere dei mari) (American-International Television, 1962)

Credits: Director: Domenico Paolella; *Screenplay:* Ugo Guerra, Luciano Martino, Domenico Paolella, Ernesto Gastaldi (uncredited); *Producer:* Gianni Hecht Lucari; *Photography:* Carlo Bellero (Eastmancolor, Totalscope, aspect ratio 2.35:1); *Film Editor:* Otello Colangeli; *Music:* Egisto Macchi; running time: 90 minutes; released March 22, 1962; video availability: Something Weird Video.

Cast: Richard Harrison *(David Robinson)*; Michèle Mercier *(Jennifer)*; Roldano Lupi *(Redway)*; Marisa Belli *(Nike)*; Walter Barnes *(Van Artz)*; Paul Muller *(Hornblut)*; Carlo Hinterman *(Errol Robinson)*; Lillia Ngyun *(Tahitian Dancer)*; Italo Sain; Romano Giomini.

Comments: A pirate adventure, with hero David Robinson (Richard Harrison), opposing the nefarious Captain Redway (Roldano Lupi). Former male model Richard Harrison (1935–) left an unsuccessful Hollywood acting career for greater success in Italy, appearing in over 100 films. *Avenger of the Seven Seas* was a co-production between Italy's Documento Film and France's Le Louvre Film.

The Avenger of Venice (Il ponte dei sospiri) (Four Star, 1964)

Credits: Directors: Carlo Campogalliani, Pierro Pierotti; *Screenplay:* Oreste Biancoli, Gian Paolo Callegari, Piero Pierotti, Manuel Pilares, Duccio Tessari (from a novel by Michel Zévago; *Photography:* Rafael Pacheco, Luciano Trasatti (Color, ratio 2.35:1); *Music:* Angelo Francesco Lavagnino; *Makeup (Hair):* Iole Cecchini; running time: 91 minutes; released March 16, 1964.

Cast: Brett Halsey *(Rolando Candiano)*; Gianna Maria Canale *(Imperia)*; Burt Nelson *(Scabrino)*; Conrado San Martin *(Capitano Altieri)*; Vira Silenti *(Leonora)*; José Marco Davó *(Bembo Altieri)*; José Nieto *(Dandolo)*; Perla Cristal *(Juana)*; Jean Murat *(Candiano)*; Paolo Gozlino *(Capitano Lorenzo)*; Nino Persello; Andrea Bosic; Lilly Darelli *(Bianca)*; Nello Pazzafini.

Comments: A Count of Monte Cristo–type costume adventure, with a convoluted plot involving a frame-up and false imprisonment, escape, and ultimate revenge. Leading man Brett Halsey (born Charles Oliver Hand in 1933) was another in a long line of frustrated Hollywood actors who immigrated to greater success in Italy (their numbers included Clint Eastwood). At age 34, leading lady Gianna Maria Canale's looks had faded, and this was her last film. *The Avenger of Venice* was produced by Italy's Panda Societa per L'Industria Cinematografica and Spain's Estela Films.

The Avenger, Zorro (El Zorro justicero) (Transeuropa Film/Italian International Film, 1972)

Credits: Director: Rafael Romero Marchent; *Screenplay:* Rafael Romero Marchent, Nino Stresa (based on a story by Rafael Romero Marchent, dialogue by Nino Stresa); *Photography:* Marcello Masciocchi (color, Techniscope, aspect ratio 2.35:1); *Film Editor:* Antonio Gimeno; *Music* Coriolano Gori (billed as "Lallo Gori"); *Art Direction/Set Decoration:* Demofilo Fidani; *Sound:* Paola Esposito; *Script Supervisor:* Alfredo Franchi; running time: 96 minutes (Italy); released February 21, 1972.

Cast: Fabio Testi *(Zorro/Don Diego)*; Simonetta Vitelli [billed as "Simone Blondell"] *(Perla Dominguez)*; Riccardo Garrone; Antonio Gradoli *(Pedro)*; Piero Lulli; Luis Gaspar; Luis Induni *(Sheriff)*; Frank Braña *(Dominguez)*; Eduardo Calvo *(The Judge)*; Andrés Mejuto *(Warner)*; Carlos Romero Marchent *(Fred)*.

Comments: Created by pulp writer Johnston McCulley (1883–1958), the costumed adventurer Zorro first appeared in the 1919 story *The Curse of Capistrano.* Since then, Zorro has appeared in many films, film serials and television shows; the earliest feature-length movie adaptation was the excellent Douglas Fairbanks vehicle *Mark of Zorro* (1920). *The Avenger, Zorro* and the other Italian-produced Zorro films listed herein would perhaps be more accurately defined as spaghetti westerns, but are included here because of their costumed hero. *The Avenger, Zorro* was co-produced by Italy's Transeuropa Film and Italian International Film, in partnership with Spain's Copercines, Cooperativa Cinematográfica. The production was shot at Elios Film in Rome.

The Bacchantes (Le baccanti) (Medallion Pictures, 1961)

Credits: *Director:* Giorgio Ferroni; *Producer:* Giampaolo Bigazzi; *Screenplay:* Giorgio Ferroni, Giorgio Stegani (based on a play by Euripides); *Photography:* Pier Ludovico Pavoni (Technicolor, Techniscope, aspect ratio 2.35:1); *Film Editor:* Giorgio Ferroni; *Music:* Mario Nascimbene; *Orchestra Conductor:* Franco Ferrara; *Production Design:* Antonio Visone; *Set Decorator:* Arrigo Equini; *Costume Design:* Nadia Vitali; *Makeup:* Franco Palombi; *Production Supervisor:* Piero Ghione; *Production Manager:* Giampaolo Bigazzi; *Assistant Director:* Giorgio Stegani; *Sound Engineers:* Oscar De Arcangelis, Raffaele Del Monte; *Camera Operator:* Angelo Lotti; *Assistant Camera Operators:* Giancarlo Granatelli, Dario Regis; *Choreographer:* Herbert Ross; *Script Supervisor:* Cecilia Bigazzi; *Production Secretaries:* Piero Braccialini, Arrigo Peri, Enrico Pili; running time: 100 minutes (Italy), 100 minutes (U.S.); released March 2, 1961 (Italy), 1963 (U.S.).

Cast: Taina Elg *(Dirce)*; Pierre Brice *(Dionysus)*; Alessandra Panaro *(Manto)*; Alberto Lupo *(Pentheus)*; Akim Tamiroff *(Teireslas)*; Raf Mattioli *(Lacdanos)*; Erno Crisa *(Atteon)*; Miranda Campa *(Agave)*; Gérard Landry *(Shepherd)*; Nerio Bernardi *(High Priest)*; Enzo Fiermonte *(Policrates)*.

Comments: In this fantasy, the city of Thebes is visited by the god Dionysus. Based on the ancient Greek play by Euripides. A co-production between the Italian companies Cino del Luca, Vic Film, and the French company Lyre Films. An alternate, and more lurid title, is *Bondage Gladiator Sexy*.

Balboa (Il leggendario conquistadore) (Capitol Film/Cooperativa Cinematográfica Unión, 1963)

Credits: *Director:* José María Elorrieta; *Screenplay:* Federico De Urrutia, José María Elorrieta; *Photography:* Alfonso Nieva (Eastmancolor); *Film Editor:* Antonio Gimeno; *Music:* Federico Contreras; running time: 96 minutes; released October 21, 1963 (Spain).

Cast: Frank Latimore *(Vasco Núñez de Balboa)*; Pilar Cansino *(Anayansi)*; Jesús Puente *(Francisco Pizarro)*; Mario Morales; Alberto Berco; Ángel Ortiz; Juan Barbara; Vincente Ávila; Juan Cortés; Francisco Camoiras; Rufino Inglés; Santiago Rivero; Guillermo Carmona; Antonio Merino; José Villasante; Alfonso de la Vega; Anibal Vela; Manuel Rojas; José Canalejas; Guillermo Méndez; Tito Garcia; Gonzalo Linares; Ángel Menéndez; Rafael Vaquero; Rafaela Aparicio; Teófilo Palou; Juan Cazalilla; Hilda Rodriguez; Belinda Corel; Julian Moreno; Julio Infiesta; Valentin Tornos; Juan Antonio Peral; José Luis Lluch; José Luis Chinchilla; José Maria Ecenarro; Álvaro de Luna; Carlos Casaravilla; Pastor Serrador; Frank Braña; George Martin; Vergilio Teixeira.

Comments: A costume drama involving the real-life Spanish explorer Vasco Núñez de Balboa (circa 1475–1519), who discovered the Pacific Ocean. This film was a co-production between Italy's Capitol Film and Spain's Cooperativa Cinematográfica Unión. Some location scenes were shot in Panama.

Barabbas (Columbia, 1961)

Credits: *Director:* Richard Fleischer; *Producers:* Dino De Laurentiis, Luigi Luraschi; *Screenplay:* Christopher Fry, Nigel Balchin, Diego Fabbri, Ivo Perilli, Salvatore Quasimodo (based on the novel by Pär Lagerkvist), *Photography:* Aldo Tonti; (Technicolor, Super 70 Technirama, aspect ratio 2.35:1); *Film Editors:* Raymond Poulton, Alberto Galitti; *Music:* Mario Nascimbene; *Music Arrangement:* Ennio Morricone; *Orchestra Conductor:* Franco Ferrara; *Art Direction:* Mario Chiari; *Costume Design:* Maria De Matteis; *Assistant Production Manager:* Bud Spencer; *Set Dresser:* Maurizio Chiari; *Stunt Coordinator:*

Nazzareno Zamperla; *Stunts:* Elio Bonadonna, Friedrich von Ledebur; *Production Assistant:* Ralph Serpe; running time: 137 minutes; released December 23, 1961 (Italy), October 10, 1962 (U.S.); video availability: Columbia TriStar Home Video.

Cast: Anthony Quinn *(Barabbas)*; Silvana Mangano *(Rachel)*; Arthur Kennedy *(Pontius Pilate)*; Katy Jurado *(Sara)*; Harry Andrews *(Peter)*; Vittorio Gassman *(Sahak)*; Norman Wooland *(Rufio)*; Valentina Cortese *(Julia)*; Jack Palance *(Torvald)*; Ernest Borgnine *(Lucius)*; Arnoldo Foà *(Joseph of Arimathea)*; Michael Gwynn *(Lazarus)*; Laurence Payne *(Disciple)*; Douglas Fowley *(Vasasio)*; Guido Celano *(Scorpio)*; Enrico Glori; Carlo Giustini *(Officer)*; Giovanni Di Benedetto *(Officer)*; Robert Hall *(Commander of Gladiators)*; Rina Braido *(Tavern Reveler)*; Nando Angelini; Tullio Tomadoni *(Blind Man)*; Joe Robinson *(Gladiator)*; Friederich von Ledebur *(Officer)*; Marcello Di Martire; Spartaco Nale *(Overseer)*; Maria Zanoli *(Beggar Woman)*; Gustavo De Nardo; Vladimiro Picciafuochi; Vanoye Aikens; Anna Alexandrief; Emma Baron *(Maria)*; Roland Bartrop; George Birt; Salvatore Borghese *(Dragged Gladiator)*; William Lyon Brown; Colm Caffrey; Alfio Caltabiano; Miranda Campa *(Maria's Sister)*; E. Cardone; James Frank Clark; Livia Cordaro; Dave Crowley; Dale Cummings; Ralph Dammers; Carolyn De Fonseca *(Woman at Tavern)*; Jim Dolan; Vera Drudi *(Salome)*; Georges Ehling; Jody Excell, Karin Faber; Audrey Fairfax; John Farksen; Charles Fawcett; Rina Franchetti *(Mary Clopas)*; Bente Friedrichsen; Robert Gardett *(Priest)*; Maureen Gavin; Hela Gerber; Eugene Gervasi; Larry Hall; Fernando Hilbeck; John Horne; Rick Howes; William Kiehl *(Soldier)*; Giancarlo Lolli; Marilyn Lombardo; Curt Lowens *(Disciple)*; Natasha Lytess; Rocco Roy Mangano *(Jesus Christ)*; Maria Marchi; Joan Maslow; Walter Maslow; David Maunsell; Ed McReedy; Maria Mizar; Lucia Modugno; David Montressor; Paul Muller *(High Priest)*, Burt Nelson; Remington Olmstead; John Palance; Luciano Palumbo; Piero Pastore *(Nicodemus)*; Joseph Pilcher; Paola Pitagora *(Mary Magdalene)*; Sacha Podgorsky; Massimo Righi; Margherita Sala; Gaetano Scala *(Gladiator)*; Nino Segurini *(John, the Apostle)*; Simone Signoret; Honoré Singer; John Stacy; Malìs Stroyberg; Dan Sturkie; Sharon Tate *(Patrician in Arena)*; Peter Tavis; Jacopo Tecchi; Marilyn Tosatti; Ivan Triesault *(Emperor)*; Wladimiro Tuicovich; A. Valentinsich; Richard Watson; Veronica Wells; Jay Weston; Christa Windish-Graetz.

Comments: A biblical drama based on the tale of a thief, sentenced to death, who is set free in place of the crucified Jesus. This international production was made by Columbia Pictures in cooperation with Italy's Dino De Laurentiis. The movie was shot in Tuscany, among other Italian locations, and director Richard Fleischer made excellent use of a real solar eclipse during filming. One of the better films of its kind thanks to an excellent performance by Anthony Quinn, *Barabbas* was nominated for several international awards.

The Barbarians (Revak, lo schiavo di Cartagine) (Anglo Amalgamated, 1960)

Credits: *Director:* Rudolph Maté; *Producers:* John Lee Mahin, Martin Rackin; *Screenplay:* John Lee Mahin, Martin Rackin (based on the novel by Francis Van Wyck); *Photography:* Carl E. Guthrie (Color, aspect ratio 1:37.1); *Music:* Franco Ferrara; *Film Editor:* Gene Ruggiero; *Sound:* Claude Hitchcock; *Art Director:* Franco Lolli; *Costume Designer:* Mario Giorsi; *Makeup:* Cesare Gambarelli; *Hair Stylist:* Ada Polombi; *Production Manager:* Piero Lazzari;; *Assistant Directors:* Roberto Fizz, Franco Prosperi; *Art Department:* Italo Tomassi; *Production Assistant:* Paolo Gargano; *Master of Arms:* Enzo Musumeci; *Script Supervisor:* Yvonne Axeworthy; running time: 84 minutes (Italy), 90 minutes (U.S.); released October 4, 1960 (U.S.); video availability: Sinister Cinema (as *Revak the Rebel*).

Cast: Jack Palance *(Revak)*; Milly Vitale *(Cherata)*; Guy Rolfe *(Kainus)*; Austin Willis *(Varro)*; Richard Wyler *(Lycursus)*; Deirdre Sullivan *(Valeria)*; John Alderson; Joseph Cuby *(Babu)*; Georges Ehling; Frederic Ross; Melody O'Brian *(Creoda)*; Richard Watson; Pietro Ceccarelli.

Comments: A slave rebels against his Carthaginian masters in this co-production between Italy's Galatea Film, Mahin-Rackin, and the NBC television network.

Battle of the Amazons (Le Amazoni– Donne d'amore e di guerra) (American-International, 1973)

Credits: Director: Alfonso Brescia (billed as "Al Bradley"); *Producer:* Riccardo Brilli; *Executive Producer:* Stenio Fiorentini; *Screenplay:* Mario Amendola, Bruno Corbucci, Fernando Vizcaino (billed as Fernando Izcaino Casas); *Photography:* Fausto Rossi (Technicolor, Techniscope, aspect ratio 2.35:1); *Music:* Franco Micalizzi; *Art Direction:* Mimmo Scavia (billed as "Bartolomeo Scavia"); *Makeup:* Romana González, Raul Ranieri; *Assistant Makeup Artist:* Gino Zamprioli; *Hair Stylist:* Maria Grazia Nardi; *Production Managers:* Pasquale Petricca, Manuel Torres; *Unit Managers:* Vito Di Bari, Julio Himenes; *Assistant Director:* Franco Pasquetto; *2nd Unit Director/Stunts:* Benito Stefanelli; *Props:* Tani; *Sound Technician:* Benedetto Conversi; *Microphone Boom Operator;* Antonio Pantano; *Special Effects:* Sergio Chiusi; *Still Photographer:* Fabio Scatamacchia, *Camera Operator:* Gianfranco Turino; *Assistant Camera Operators:* Giorgio Urbinelli, Domingo Solano; *Gaffer:* Alberto Silvestri; *Chief Grip:* Giancarlo Serravalli; *Wardrobe:* Lucia Costantini; *Continuity:* Giuliana Gherardi; *Soundtrack Album Producer:* Luca di Silverio; running time: 100 minutes (Italy), 91 minutes (U.S.); released August 11, 1973 (Italy), November 21, 1973 (U.S.); video availability: Eurovista.

Cast: Lincoln Tate *(Zeno)*; Lucretia Love *(Eraglia)*; Paolo Todesco *(Valeria)*; Mirta Miller *(Melanippe)*; Benito Stefanelli *(Erno)*; Genie Woods *(Antiope)*; Solvi Stubing *(Sinade)*; Alberto Dell'Acqua *(Lilio)*; Roberto Alessandri; Giancarlo Bastianoni *(Filodos)*; Frank Braña; Luigi Ciavarro *(Turone)*; Pilar Clemens *(Elperia)*; Sonia Ciuffi *(Fara)*; Fernanda Dell'Acqua; Liliana Fioramonti; Leonilde Simoncelli; Luigi Antonio Guerra; Sybilla Barbara Hubner; Patrizia Luparia; Chris McCollins; Riccardo Pizzuti *(Medonte)*; Rosanna Ratcliffe; Nadia Russeau; Edith Shock; Daniela Silvero; Marco Stefanelli *(Medio)*; Franco Ukmar *(Artemio)*.

Comments: The countryside is pillaged and terrorized by a group of ruthless Amazons in this adventure. Co-produced by Italy's Roas Produzioni and Spain's Cinematografica Pelimex.

The Beast of Babylon Against the Son of Hercules (L'eroe di Babilonia) (Embassy, 1963)

Credits: Director: Siro Marcellini; *Producer:* Albino Morandini; *Screenplay:* Gian Paolo Callegari, Siro Marcellini, Albert Valentin; *Photography:* Pier Ludovico Pavoni (Eastmancolor, Euroscope, aspect ratio 2.35:1); *Film Editor:* Nella Nannuzzi; *Production Designer:* Pier Vittorio Marchi; *Costume Designer:* Mario Giorsi; running time: 93 minutes (Italy), 98 minutes (U.S.); released August 23, 1963 (Italy); video availability: Something Weird Video.

Cast: Gordon Scott *(Nippur)*; Geneviève Grad *(Tamira)*; Andrea Scotti *(Namar)*; Célina Cély *(Agar)*; Moira Orfei *(Ura)*; Mario Petri *(Zairo, King of Persia)*; Piero Lulli *(Balthazar)*; Andrea Aureli *(Anarsi)*; Giuseppe Addobbati *(Licardio)*; Paolo Petrini; Harold Bradley *(Mursuk)*; Aldo Pini; Giuseppe Mattei; Oreste Lionello; Consalvo Dell'Arti; Enrico Gozzo; Renato Malavasi.

Comments: The heroic Nippur rescues beautiful slave girl Tamira from evil tyrant Balthazar. The original title was *Hero of Babylon.* Produced by three Italian companies, Compagnia Iternazionale Realizzazioni Artisstiche Cinematografiche (CIRAC), Films Internazionali Artistici (FIA), Gladiator Film, and the French company L.C.J. Editions and Productions.

Behind the Mask of Zorro (Il giuramento di Zorro) (National Telefilm Associates, 1965)

Credits: Director: Ricardo Blasco; *Producers:* Tullio Bruschi, Sergio Newman; *Screenplay:* José Gallardo, Luis Luca Ojeda, Daniel Ribera (based on their story); *Photography:* Vitaliano Natalucci, Mario Vulpiani (Color, aspect ratio 2.35:1); *Music:* Ángel Arteaga; running time: 106 minutes; released September 3, 1965 (West Germany).

Cast: Tony Russel *(Patriciao/Alfonso/Zorro)*; Marí José Alfonso *(Manuela)*; Roberto Paoletti;

Jesús Puente *(General Esteban Garcia)*; Mirella Maravidi *(Alicia)*; Pepe Rubio *(Marcel)*; Ángela Rhu; Agustin González *(Captain)*; Sancho Gracia *(Juan)*; Enrique Navarro; Maria Gónzales; Rafael Corés; Enrico Salvatore; Aldo Cecconi; Joaquin Pamplona; Antonio Moreno; María Luisa Arias; Paquita Cornes; Fernando de Anguita; Rafael Vaquero; Ángel Soler; Ricardo G. Lilló; Jaime Mateos; Luis Durán; Narciso Ojeda; José Torremocha; Inés Rodriguez; Rosita Yarza *(Serafina)*; José María Seoane *(Don Antonio)*.

Comments: Another version of Zorro, produced by Italy's Duca, Duce Compagnia Film, Rodes Cinematografica, and Spain's Hispamer Films. *Oath of Zorro* was an alternate title.

The Bible: In the Beginning (20th Century–Fox, 1966)

Credits: *Director:* John Huston; *Producer:* Dino De Laurentiis; *Associate Producer:* Luigi Luraschi; *Screenplay:* Christopher Fry (with uncredited contributions from Orson Welles, Jonathan Griffin, Mario Soldati); *Music:* Toshirô Mayuzumi, Ennio Morricone; *Music Conductor:* Franco Ferrrara; *Photography:* Giuseppe Rotunno (Deluxe Color, 70mm, aspect ratio 2.35:1); *Film Editors:* Ralph Kemplen, Alberto Gallitti; *Art Director:* Mario Chiari; *Costume Design:* Maria De Matteis; *Makeup:* Alberto De Rossi; *Hairdresser:* Elda Magnanti; *Special Effects:* Linwood G. Dunn, Zeus Ianiro, Augie Lohman, Carlo De Marchis; *Set Dressers:* Bruno Avesani, Enzo Eursepi; *Set Construction:* Aldo Puccini, Mario Scisci; *Assistant Set Decorator:* Luciano Puccini; *Scene Painter:* Italo Tomassi; *Associate Art Director:* Stephen B. Grimes; *Assistant Art Director:* Pasquale Romano; *Property Master:* Tani; *Casting:* Guidarino Guidi; *Production Manager:* Bruno Todini; *2nd Unit Director:* Ernst Haas (Creation sequence); *Assistant Directors:* Vana Caruso, Ottavio Oppo; *Sound:* Fred Hynes; *Sound Recordists:* Murray Spivack, Basil Fenton-Smith; *Sound Editors:* Leslie Hodgson, James D. Young; *Sound Effects Editors:* John Blunk, Wayne Fury, Marvin Walowitz; *Assistant Cameraman:* Giuseppe Di Biase; *Camera Operator:* Giuseppe Maccari; *Assistant Cameraman:* Piero Servo; *Second Unit Photographer:* Donald C. Rogers; *Still Photographer:* Franco Nero; *Assistant Film Editor:* Eunice Mountjoy; *Music Recordist:* Murray Spivack; *Music Editor:* Gilbert D. Marchant; *Music Advisor:* Gofffredo Petrassi; *Production Assistants:* Romano Dandi, Giorgio Morra, Ralph Serpe, Fred Sidewater; *Choreographer:* Katherine Dunham; *Consultants:* Salvatore Garofalo, W.M. Merchant, Angelo Lombardi; *Historical Advisor:* Emilio Villa; *Assistant to John Huston:* Gladys Hill; *Special Contributions:* Mirko Basaldella, Corrado Cagli; running time: 174 minutes; released September 26, 1966 (U.S.); video availability: 20th Century–Fox.

Cast: Michael Parks *(Adam)*; Ulla Bergryd *(Eve)*; Richard Harris *(Cain)*; John Huston *(Noah)*; Stephen Boyd *(Nimrod)*; George C. Scott *(Abraham)*; Ava Gardner *(Sarah)*; Peter O'Toole *(The Three Angels)*; Zoe Sallis *(Hagar)*; Gabriele Ferzetti *(Lot)*; Eleonora Rossi Drago *(Lot's Wife)*; Franco Nero *(Abel)*; Pupella Maggio *(Noah's Wife)*; Robert Rietty *(Abraham's Steward)*; Peter Heinze *(Shem)*; Roger Beaumont; Gianluigi Crescenzi; Maria Grazia Spina *(Daughter of Lot)*; Angelo Boscariol *(Ham)*; Claudie Lange *(Nimrod's Wife)*; Anna Orso *(Shem's Wife)*; Adriana Ambesi *(Daughter of Lot)*; Eric Leutzinger *(Japheth)*; Michael Steinpichler; Gabriella Pallotta *(Ham's Wife)*; Alberto Lucantoni *(Isaac)*; Rosanna Di Rocco *(Japheth's Wife)*; Luciano Conversi *(Ishmael)*; Giovannna Galletti *(Sinful Woman)*; Paola Ambrosi; Flavio Bennati; *(Serpent)*; Salvatore Billa *(Follower of Abraham)*; Giovanni Di Benedetto *(Nimrod's Man)*; Alberico Donadeo *(One of the Sinful Men)*; Aviva Israel; Flavio Nennati; Marie-Christine Pratt; Ivan Rassimov *(Dignitary of Babylon)*; Amru Sani, Elisabetta Velinska.

Comments: This massive picture, based on the opening 22 chapters of the first book of Genesis, was conceived by producer Dino De Laurentiis as the first installment of a planned series of biblical screen adaptations which, due to this film's lukewarm box office performance, never materialized. The movie lost $1,500,000 on release, although it did win several international awards. One of the first major films to allow complete (but tasteful) actor nudity (in the Adam and Eve sequence). Originally, director John Huston had intended to cast Charlie Chaplin as Noah, but when the egotistical Chaplin balked at performing in a film directed by someone other than himself, Huston decided to play the role instead. Scenes of the world's creation were later reused in the campy Raquel Welch prehistoric dinosaur epic *One Million Years B.C.* (1966). Filmed on location in Iceland, Sicily, Egypt, Israel, Morocco, Sardinia, and at studios in Rome.

The Black Archer (*L'arciere nero*) (CTC, 1959)

Credits: Director: Piero Pierotti; *Producer:* Dino Sant'Ambrogio; *Screenplay:* Giorgio Cosantino, Giacomo Gentilomo; Piero Pierotti (based on their story); *Photography:* Aldo Greci (Color, aspect ratio 1.66:1); *Music,* Tarcisio Fusco; *Art Director:* Franco Lolli; running time, 75 minutes; released August 14, 1959 (Italy); video availability: Something Weird Video.

Cast: Gérard Landry (*Corrado*); Federica Ranchi (*Ginevra*); Livio Lorenzon (*Lodrosio*), Carla Strober (*Ubaldina*); Nino Marchesini; Franco Fantasia (*Raniero*); Tom Felleghy; Andrea Fantasia; Renato Navarrini (*Frate Lorenzo*); Fulvia Franco (*La Zingara*); Erno Crisa (*Lodovico*); Jolanda Addolori (*Bianca*); Gianni Baghino; Marisa Cucchi; Stelio Candelli; Terry Mason; Luciana Paoli; Isarco Ravaioli; Piero Pastore; Aldo Moser; Rearmsnato Montalbano; Ignazio Leone; Ivy Holzer; Valeria Vicky; Sandro Baranger.

Comments: In this Robin Hood–type costume drama, an archer opposes his father's murderers, vowing revenge. Produced by Italy's Diamante company.

The Black Corsair (*Il corsaro nero*) (American-International Pictures, 1976)

Credits: Director: Sergio Sollima; *Producer:* Luigi Rovere; *Screenplay:* Emilio Salgari, Alberto Silvestri, Sergio Sollima (based on the books *Il corsaro nero* and *La regina del Craibi*); *Photography:* Alberto Spagnoli (Eastmancolor, Techniscope, aspect ratio 2.35:1); *Film Editor:* Alberto Gallitti; *Music:* Guido De Angelis, Maurizio De Angelis; *Production Design:* Sergio Canivari; *Set Decoration:* Cesare Carmellini; *Costume Design:* Mario Carlini, Dario Cecchi; *Makeup:* Mario Van Riel; *Hair Stylist:* Iolanda Conti; *Production Manager:* Elio De Pietro; *Production Supervisors:* Vasco Mafera, Renato Panetuzzi, Antonio Savini; *2nd Unit Director:* Luciano Sacripanti; *Assistant Directors:* Allan Elledge, Franco Fantasia; *Props:* Giuseppe Ciccocioppo; *Assistant Set Decorator:* Marco Caniveri; *Art Dept. Assistant:* Mario Grilli; *Head Set Construction Grip:* Biagio Nastasi; *Key Grip:* Giacomo Tomaselli; *Gaffer:* Sante Federici; *Sound:* Roberto Petrozzi; *Sound Mixer:* Gianni D'Amico; *Special Effects:* Aldo Gaspari; *Camera Operators:* Sergio Bergamini, Antonio Schiavo Lena; *Assistant Camera Operators:* Giovanni Canfarelli Modica, Fabio Placido; *Still Photographer:* Enzo Falessi; *Chief Seamstress:* Maria Fanetti; *Assistant Film Editor:* Domenico Varone; *Orchestra Conductor:* Gianfranco Plenizio; *Master of Arms:* Franco Fantasia; *Production Secretary:* Vincenzo Cartuccia; *Script Supervisor:* Marion Mertes; *Chief Administrator:* Fernanda Ventimiglia; *Voice Director for English-Dubbed Version:* Peter Fernandez; running time: 126 minutes; released December 22, 1976.

Cast: Kabir Bedi (*The Black Corsair*); Carole André (*Duchessina Van Gould*); Mel Ferrer (*Van Gould*); Angelo Infanti (*Morgan*); Sonja Jeannine (*Yara*); Salvatore Borghese (*Carnaux*); Franco Fantasia (*Van Stiller*); Edoardo Faieta (*L'Olonnais*); Jackie Basehart (*The Red Corsair*); Nicolò Piccolomini (*The Green Corsair*); Guido Alberti (*Governor of Ribeira*); Pietro Torrisi (*Blanchot*); Lionello Pio Di Savoia; Mariano Rigillo; Tony Renis (*José*); Dagmar Lassander (*Marquise of Bermejo*); Pierangeli Llinas (*Indian*).

Comments: India-born Kabir Bedi is the lead in this swashbuckler, as the Black Corsair (aided by the Green Corsair and the Red Corsair) avenges the death of his father, who was murdered by the evil Van Gould.

The Black Devil (*Il diavolo nero*) (Cine Europa-Paradise Film Exchange, 1957)

Credits: Director: Sergio Grieco; *Music:* Roberto Nicolosi; *Photography:* color, aspect ratio 2.35:1); *Master of Arms:* Enzo Musumeci Greco; running time: 80 minutes; released March 29, 1957 (Italy).

Cast: Gérard Landry *(Osvaldo de Marzi)*; Milly Vitale *(Isabella)*; Nadia Gray *(Duchessa Lucrezia)*; Leonora Ruffo *(Stella)*; Maurizio Arena *(Ruggero)*; Andrea Aureli *(Lorenzo di Roccabruna)*; Giulio Battiferri; Nino Crisman *(Don Pedro)*; Ughetto Bertucci; Mariangela Giordano; Enrico Olivieri; Giorgio Ubaldi; Renato Montalbano; Gino Scotti.

Comments: A swashbuckler produced by Italy's Po Film.

The Black Duke *(Il duca nero)* (Hispamer Films/Rodes Cinematografica, 1963)

Credits: Director: Pino Mercanti; *Producer:* Tullio Bruschi; *Screenplay:* Mario Amendola (from a story by Mario Amendola, Tullio Bruschi, Max Di Thiene); *Photography:* Antonio Macasoli (Eastmancolor, aspect ratio 1.66:1); *Music:* Giorgio Fabor; *Film Editor:* Jolanda Benvenuti; *Art Directors:* Paolo D'Andria, Piero Filippone; *Production Design:* Alfredo Montori; *Costume Design:* Maria Luisa Panaro; *Makeup:* Ottorino Censi, Antonio Mura; *Sound:* Goffredo Salvatori; *Production Manager:* Paolo Prestano; *Assistant Directors:* Edmondo Affronti, Gianfranco Baldanello; *Camera Operator:* Claudio Santoni; *Assistant Cameraman:* Maurizio Santoni; *Production Administrator:* Luigi Pinni D'Oliva; *Production Secretaries:* Ferrucio Mosca, Corrado Cespi; *Script Supervisor:* Benilde Vittori; *Master of Arms:* Franco Fantasia; running time: 105 minutes (Italy); released March 11, 1963 (Italy), July 1964 (U.S.).

Cast: Cameron Mitchell *(Cesare Borgia)*; Conrado San Martin *(Riccardo Brancaleone)*; Maria Grazia Spina *(Ginevra)*; Gloria Milland *(Caterina Sforza)*; Franco Fantasia *(Veniero)*; Robert Dean *(Nobleman)*; Silvio Bagolini *(Serafino)*; Antonio Casagrande; Manuel Castiñeiras *(Tancredi)*; Alberto Cevenini; Lilly Darelli; Dina DeSantis *(Lavinia Serpieri)*; Piero Gerlini, *(Gabino)*; Raphael Kores; Giulio Maculani *(Giulio)*; Gilberto Mazzi; Renato Navarrini; Gloria Osuna *(Lucrezia Borgia)*; Nino Persello *(Tito Serpieri)*; Vladimiro Picciafuochi; Walter Pinelli; Gianni Solaro; Giovanni Vari *(Morialdo)*; Lyssa *(Bit)*; Riccardo Pizzuti *(Soldier)*.

Comments: Actor Cameron Mitchell (1919– 1994) more or less abandoned Hollywood in the 1960s for Europe, and here essays the role of Cesare Borgia (1475 [-76?]–1507) who is marked for assassination in this costumer, co-produced by Italy's Rodes Cinematografica and Spain's Hispamer Films.

Brennus, Enemy of Rome *(Brenno il nemico di Roma)* (American International Television, 1963)

Credits: Director: Giacomo Gentilomo; *Producer:* Luigi Mondello; *Screenplay:* Arpad DeRiso, Nino Scolaro, Adriano Bolzoni; *Photography:* Oberdan Troiani (Eastmancolor, Totalscope, aspect ratio 2.35:1); *Film Editor:* Gino Talamo; *Production Design:* Piero Filippone; *Set Decorators:* Camillo Del Signore, Luciano Finocchiaro; *Costume Design:* Giorgio Desideri; *Makeup:* Guglielmo Bonotti; *Hair Stylist:* Maria Arié; *Unit Production Manager:* Augusto Dolfi; *Assistant Director:* Angelo Sangermano; *Sound:* Alessandro Sarandrea; *Camera Operator:* Cesare Allione; *Assistant Camera Operators:* G. Ciulli, Maurizio Santoni, Luigi Troiani; *Still Photographer:* Ermanno Serto; *Assistant Editor:* Beatrice Felici; *Production Secretary:* Marcello Berni; *Script Supervisor:* Paolo Salvadori; running time: 95 minutes (Italy), 90 minutes (U.S.); released December 21, 1963 (Italy).

Cast: Gordon Mitchell *(Brennus)*; Ursula Davis *(Nissia)*; Massimo Serato *(Marco Furio Camillo)*; Tony Kendall *(Quinto Fabio)*; Erno Crisa *(Decio Vatinio)*; Vassili Karis; Margherita Girelli *(Catulla)*; Carla Calò *(Sacerdotessa)*; Nerio Bernardi; Andrea Aureli; Michel Gaida; Anna-Maria Pace; Roland Gray; Carlo Lombardi; Lucio De Santis; Aldo Cecconi; Goffredo Unger; Pietro Tordi *(Vaxo)*; Aldo Pini; Attilio Dottesio; Franco Moruzzi; Claudio Catania *(Bambino)*, Robert Spafford *(Narrator)*.

Comments: A fictional romance is woven into an actual historical event, Gaul's attack on Rome in 390 BC; partially based on a history by Titus Livius. A co-production between Italy's Alta Vista and France's Victory Film.

The Burning of Rome *(Il magnifico avventuriero)* (American International Television, 1963)

Credits: Director: Riccardo Freda; *Producers:* Luigi Carpentieri, Ermanno Donati; *Associate Producer:* Sergio Newman; *Screenplay:* Filippo Sanjust (from his story, adaptation by Antoinette Pellevant from French material); *Photography:* Raffaele Masciocchi, Julio Ortas (Technicolor, aspect ratio 1.85:1); *Film Editor:* Ornella Micheli; *Production Design:* Aurelio Crugnola; *Set Decoration:* Franco Fumagalli; *Costume Design:* Marisa Crimi; *Makeup:* Maurizio Giustini; *Hair Stylist:* Adalgisa Favella; *Production Supervisor:* Alfredo Melidoni; *Production Manager:* Lucio Bompani; *Assistant Directors:* Michel Autin, Goffredo Unger; *Sculptor:* Gianni Gianese; *Special Effects:* Eros Bacciucchi; *Camera Operator:* Antonio Schiavo Lena; *Assistant Camera Operator:* Claudio Ragona; *Editor of Spanish Version:* Rosa G. Salgado; *Script Supervisor:* Silvana Merli; running time: 93 minutes; released August 3, 1963 (Italy); video availability: Something Weird Video.

Cast: Brett Halsey *(Benvenuto Cellini)*; Claudia Mori *(Piera)*; Francoise Fabian *(Lucrezia)*, José Nieto *(Connestabile di Borbone)*; Jacinto San Emeterio *(Francisco I)*, Félix Dafauce *(Frangipani)*; Andrea Bosic *(Michelangelo)*; Rosella Como *(Angela)*; Carla Calò *(Angela's Aunt)*; Bernard Blier *Clemente VII)*; Diego Michelotti *(Carlo V)*; Elio Pandolfi *(Actor)*; Umberto D'Orsi *(Grand Duke di Toscana)*; Giampiero Littera *(Francesco)*; Dany Paris *(Francesco's Mother)*; Bruno Sipioni *(Guard)*; Sandro Dori *(Angela's Uncle)*; Carmelo Artale; Félix Fernández; Rafael Ibáñez; Nazzareno Piana; Mirko Valentin.

Comments: Based on the life of the multi-talented Benvenuto Cellini (1500–1571), who was a draftsman, sculptor, musician, artist, poet and goldsmith, as well as a soldier. Also known under the alternate title *The Magnificent Adventurer*. Director Riccardo Freda (1909–1999) helmed at least a dozen genre productions. Coproduced by Italy's Panda Societa per L'Industria Cinematografica, France's Les Films du Centaure, and Spain's Hispamer Films.

Caesar Against the Pirates (Giulio Cesare contro I pirati) (Capri/Globe Film International, 1962)

Credits: Director: Sergio Grieco; *Producer:* Gastone Gugliemetti; *Screenplay:* Gino Mangini, Fabio De Agostini, Maria Grazia Borgiotti, Sergio Grieco (from a story by Maria Grazia Borgiotti); *Photography:* Vincenzo Seratrice (Eastmancolor, Dyaliscope, aspect ratio 2.35:1); *Music:* Carlo Innocenzi; *Film Editor:* Enzo Alfonzi; *Art Direction:* Alfonso Russo; *Costume Design:* Tigano Lo Faro; *Makeup:* Giuseppe Peruzzi; *Hair Stylist:* Cinzia Bonanni; *Production Supervisor:* Renato De Pasqualis; *General Managers:* Angelo Corso, Lello Luzi; *Assistant Director:* Giulio Pannaccio; *2nd Assistant Director:* Filippo Perrone; *Set Designers:* Alfredo Montori, Alfonso Russo; *Weapons:* Tani; *Sound Engineers:* Eraldo Giordani, Bruno Moreal; *Sound Mixer:* Bruno Mattei; *Camera Operator:* Camillo Bazzoni; *2nd Camera Operator:* Vincenzo Mariani; *Still Photographer:* Enrico Appetito; *Costumer:* Giuliana Ghidini; *Assistant Costumer:* Rosalba Menichelli; *Music Conductor:* Carlo Franci; *Script Supervisor:* Liana Ferri; running time: 93 minutes (Italy); released April 23, 1962 (Italy).

Cast: Gustavo Rojo *(Julius Caesar)*; Abbe Lane *(Plauzia)*; Gordon Mitchell *(Hamar, Cilician Pirate)*; Piero Lulli *(Edom)*; Franca Parisi *(Cornelia, Caesar's Wife)*; Silvana Jachino *(Quintilla, Valerio's Daughter)*; Massimo Carocci *(Publio, Caesar's Friend)*; Ignazio Leone *(Frontone)*; Fedele Gentile *(Valerio Torcuato, Governor of Mileto)*; Pasquale Basile *(Tulio)*; Antonio Basile *(Glauco)*; Aldo Cecconi *(Akim)*; Antonio Gradoli *(Lucio, Roman Consul)*; Nando Angelini *(Roman Officer #1)*; Franco Franchi *(Roman Officer #2)*; Marinella Gennusco *(Handmaiden)*; Erno Crisa *(Silla, Roman Dictator)*; Rosanna Fattori *(Eber, Queen of Famagusta)*; Mario Petri *(Nicomedes, King of Bitinia)*.

Comments: A costume adventure with Julius Caesar battling pirates, this film was produced by Italy's C.A.P.R.I., and shot at INCOM studios in Rome, with the sea battles filmed in Yugoslavia.

Caesar the Conqueror (Giulio Cesare il conquistadore delle Gallie) (Medallion Pictures, 1962)

Credits: Director: Tanio Boccia; *Producers:* Roberto Capitani, Luigi Mondello; *Associate Producer:* René Thévenet; *Screenplay:* Galo Giulio

Cesare, Arpad Deriso, Nino Scolaro (adapted from a book by Galo Giulio Cesare); *Photography:* Romolo Garroni (Eastmancolor, Totalscope, aspect ratio 2.35:1); *Film Editor:* Tanio Boccia; *Art Direction and Set Decoration:* Amedeo Mellone; *Music:* Guido Robuschi, Gian Stellari; *Costume Design:* Maria Luisa Panaro; *Makeup:* Guglielmo Bonotti; *Production Supervisors:* Roberto Capitani, Augusto Dolfi; *Assistant Directors:* Mario Casalini, Angelo Sangermano; *Sound:* Luigi Salvi; *Boom Operator:* Alvaro Orsini; *Dubbing Director:* George Higgins; *Special Effects:* Pasquale Mancino; *Matte Shots:* Joseph Nathanson; *Camera Operator:* Mario Sbrenna; *Assistant Camera Operators:* Mario Cimini, Alfredo Palmieri; *Costumes:* Tigano Lo Faro; *Assistant Costume Designer:* Anna Mallia; *Assistant Film Editor:* Beatrice Felici; *Script Girl:* Maria Luisa Roi; running time: 94 minutes (Italy), 93 minutes (U.S.); released September 27, 1962 (Italy), 1963 (U.S.); video availability: Alpha Video.

Cast: Cameron Mitchell *(Julius Caesar)*; Rik Battaglia *(Vercingetorix)*; Dominique Wilms *(Queen Astrid)*; Ivica Pajer *(Claudius Valerian)*; Raffaella Carrà *(Publia)*; Carlo Tamberlani *(Pompey)*; Cesare Fantoni *(Caius Opio)*; Giulio Donnini *(Eporidorige)*; Nerio Bernardi *(Cicero)*; Carla Calò *(Calpurnia)*; Piero Palermini *(Quintis Sabino)*; Bruno Tocci *(Marc Antony)*; Aldo Pini *(Quintus Cicero)*; Lucia Randi *(Clelia)*; Fedele Gentile *(Centurion)*; Enzo Petracca *(Titus Azius)*; Alberto Manetti.

Comments: In 54 BC, Julius Caesar quells a rebellion to consolidate power. Rik Battaglia plays an actual historical figure (Vercingetorix) in this film. Produced by Italy's Metheus Film and Yugoslavia's Film Servis, the movie was shot at Dino De Laurentiis Cinematografica in Rome, with a few scenes filmed in Yugoslavia.

Captain Blood (Le Capitan) (Da.Ma. Cinematografica/Prisma-Filmverleih, 1960)

Credits: Director: André Hunebelle; *Producers:* René Bezard, Pierre Cabaud; *Screenplay:* Franco Foucard, Jean Halain, André Hunebelle (based on a novel by Michel Zévaco); *Dialogue:* Jean Halain; *Dialogue (Italian Version):* Franco Dalcer; *Photography:* Marcel Grignon (Eastmancolor, Dyaliscope, aspect ratio 2.35:1); *Film Editor:* Jean Feyte; *Production Design:* Georges Lévy; *Set Decorator:* Jean Fontenelle; *Costume Design:* Mirelle Leydet; *Makeup:* Alexandre Marcus; *Makeup Assistants:* Éliane Marcus, Blanche Picot; *Hair Stylists:* Georges Chanteau, Huguette La Laurette; *Music:* Jean Marion; *Production Supervisor:* Paul Cadéac; *Production Manager:* Marcel Lathière; *Unit Manager:* Roger Boulais; *Assistant Unit Managers:* Roger Ferret; Maurice Touati; *Assistant Directors:* Jean-Pierre Guffroy, Jean Tailandier; *Props:* Francois Suné, Michel Suné; *Sound Editor:* René-Christian Forget; *Assistant Sound Editors:* Maurice Dagonneau, Guy Solignac; *Assistant Armorer:* Raoul Birley; *Weapons Master:* Claude Carliez; *Assistant Cameramen:* André Delille, André Marquette, Charles Henri-Montel; *Still Photographer:* Robert Foulon; *Costumer:* Frédéric Junker; *Costume Supervisor:* Marie Gromtseff; *Assistant Film Editor:* Colette Lambert; *Choreography:* Jean Guélis; *Production Secretary:* Charlotte Choquert; *Production Administrator:* Cyril Grize; *Script Supervisor:* Charlotte Lefèvre; *Equestrian Advisor:* Francois Nadal; *Equestrian Assistant:* Rico Lopez; *Voice Dubbing (for Elsa Martinelli):* Claire Guibert; running time: 111 minutes; released October 5, 1960 (France), November 24, 1960 (Italy).

Cast: Jean Marais *(François de Capestan)*; Bourvil *(Cogolin)*; Elsa Martinelli *(Gisèle d'Angoulême)*; Pierrette Bruno *(Giuseppa)*; Lise Delamare *(Marie de Médicis)*; Annie Anderson *(Béatrice de Beaufort)*; Guy Delorme *(Rinaldo)*; Jacqueline Porel *Léonora Galigaï)*; Jean-Paul Coquelin *(Vitry)*; Raphael Patorni *(The Duke d'Angoulême)*; Robert Porte *(Duke de Rohan)*; Jean Berger *(Luynes)*, Piéral *(Lorenzo)*; Jean Blancheur; Alain Janey *(Gisèle's Lackey)*; Michel Thomas, Benoite Labb *(Innkeeper's Wife)*; Marcel Pérès *(Innkeeper of La Pomme d'Or)*; Jean-Michel Rouzière *(A Man from the Province)*; Boby *(The Dog)*; Edmund Beauchamp *(The Governor of The Province)*; Christian Fourcade *(Louis XIII)*; Arnoldo Foà *(Concini)*; Georges Adet *(A Man from the Province)*; Louis Abessier; Michel Arene; Raoul Billery; André Bonnarel; Louis Bugette; Henri Coutet *(Gisèle's Lackey)*;

Fraçoise Deldick *(A Servant at La Pomme d'Or)*; Bernard Dhéran *(Narrator)*; Pierre Durou; Elisabeth Fanty; John-Mary; Georges Montant; Bernard Musson; Dominique Paturel *(A Man from the Province)*; Henri Poirier *(Soldier at Château)*; Jacque Préboist *(Thief)*; Paul Préboist *(Thief)*; René Roussel; Gianni Santuccio; Edmond Tamiz.

Comments: Despite its title, this swashbuckler, set in 17th-century France, is unrelated to the 1935 Errol Flynn movie *Captain Blood*. A co-production between Italy's Da.Ma. Cinematografica and the French companies P.A.C. and Pathé Consortium Cinéma. Filmed on location at various chateaus in France.

Captain Falcon *(Capitan Fuoco)* (Avco Embassy Television, 1958)

Credits: Director: Carlo Campogalliani; *Associate Producer:* Giuliano Simonetti; *Screenplay:* Carlo Campogalliani, Isabella Conino, Gino Mangini, Vittorio Nino Novarese (from a story by Isabella Conino, Gino Mangini, Erminio Salvi); *Photography:* Bitto Albertini (Ferraniacolor); *Film Editor:* Carlo Campogalliani; *Production Design:* Oscar D'Amico, Giuseppe Ranieri; *Set Decoration:* Giorgio Desideri; *Costume Design:* Giovanna Natili; *Makeup:* Romolo de Martino, Marcella Cecchini; *Production Supervisors:* Paolo Mercuri, Decio Salvi; *Production Manager:* Erminio Salvi; *Assistant Directors:* Romolo Guerrieri, Gino Mangini; *Assistant Set Decorator:* Carlo Gentili; *Sound Engineers:* Bruno Moreal, Pietro Ortolani; *Camera Operator:* Carlo Fiore; *Assistant Camera Operator:* Giovanni Bonivento; *Still Photographer:* Cristiano Civirani; *Assistant Film Editor:* Franco Fraticelli; *Orchestra Conductor:* Tito Petralia; *Production Secretary:* Luigi Anastasi; *Script Supervisor:* Roberto Giandalla; running time: 85 minutes, released December 22, 1958 (Italy).

Cast: Lex Barker *(Pietro, Captain Fuoco)*; Rosanna Rory *(Elena di Roccalta)*; Massimo Serato *(Baron Oddo di Serra)*; Anna Maria Ferrero *(Anna)*; Paul Muller *(Rusca)*; Carla Calò Herbert A.E. Böhme *(Count Gualtiero di Roccalta)*; Dante Maggio *(Civetta)*; Piero Lulli *(Lupo)*; Livio Lorenzon *(Captain Manfredo)*; Luigi Cimara *(Eremit)*; Furio Meniconi; Mario Meniconi; Umberto Fiz; Andrea Scotti; Luigi Tosi; Gino Scotti; Luigi Guasco; Lilly Furia; Torino Stoppa.

Comments: The villainous Baron Oddo di Serra persecutes his victims in this costume drama, until his nefarious activities are opposed by Captain Falcon. Like many Hollywood actors whose careers had bottomed out, former Tarzan Lex Barker (1919–1973) was finding steady employment in Italy and Germany at this point.

Captain from Toledo *(L'uomo di Toledo)* (Italcine/Gala Film Distributors, 1965)

Credits: Director: Eugenio Martin; *Producers:* Franco Palombi, Gabriele Silvestri; *Screenplay:* Eugenio Martin, Ugo Moretti (from a story by Ugo Moretti); *Photography:* Franco Villa (color, Techniscope, aspect ratio 2.35:1); *Film Editor:* Maurizio Lucidi; *Costume Designer:* Enrico Fiorentini; *Production Manager:* Orlando Orsini; *Assistant Director:* Roberto Pariante; *Sound:* Oscar De Arcangelis; *Camera Operator:* Aristide Massaccesi; *Electrician:* Francesco Brescini; *Assistant Film Editor:* Anna Amedei; *Script Supervisor:* Bona Magrini; running time: 96 minutes (U.S.); released August 27, 1965 (Italy).

Cast: Stephen Forsyth *(Capt. Miguel)*; Ann Smyrner *(Doña Rosita)*; Norma Bengell *(Myriam)*; Gianni Solaro *(Don Pedro)*; Maria Laura Rocca *(Doña Sol)*; Gabriella Andreini *(Cafat)*; Nerio Bernardi *(Don Alfonso)*; José Calvo *(Don Canio)*; Aldo Cecconi *(Don Raphael)*; Ivan Desny *(Don Felipe)*; Manolo Gómez Bur; Carl Möhner *(Don Ramiro)*; Andrea Sotti *(Carlos)*; Elena Maria Tejeiro *(Juana)*; Rosy Zichel *(Aixa)*; Enrique Ávila *(Pancho)*; Fortunato Arena *(Spanish Grande)*.

Comments: This swashbuckler was produced by Italy's Italcine, the Spanish companies Petruka Films and Procusa, and Germany's TOP-FILM München.

Captain Phantom *(Capitan Fantasma)* (Rank/RCIP, 1953)

Credits: Director: Primo Zeglio; *Producers:* Luigi Carpentieri, Ermanno Donati; *Associate Producer:* Fouad Said; *Screenplay:* Gino De Santis, Agenore Incrocci, Furio Scarpelli, Primo

Zeglio (from a story by Gino De Santis); *Photography:* Carlo Carlini, Marco Scarpelli (Ferraniacolor, aspect ratio 1.37:1); *Music:* Carlo Rustichelli; *Film Editors:* Fouad Said, Mario Serandrei; *Art Direction:* Alberto Boccianti; *Set Decoration:* Gino Brosio; *Costume Design:* Dario Cecchi; *Production Managers:* Antonio Gentile, Silvio Clementelli; *Assistant Production Manager:* Aldo Pomilia; *Assistant Director:* Mariano Savrenti; *2nd Assistant Director:* Luciano Ercoli; *Art Department Manager:* Italo Tomassi; *Assistant Set Decorator:* Giulio Sperabene; *Sound Engineer:* Agostino Moretti; *Camera Operators:* Luigi Filippo Carta, Elio Polacchi, Anthony Steffen; *Assistant Camera Operator:* Ruggero Radicchi; *Stunts:* Nazzareno Zamperla; *Assistant Film Editors:* Ron Honthaner; Ornella Micheli; *Orchestra Conductor:* Ugo Giacomozzi; *Fencing Instructor:* Enzo Musumeci Greco; *Production Assistants:* Aldo Pomilia, Clorindo Zeglio; *Script Supervisor:* Vera Scivicco; running time: 86 minutes; released November 11, 1953 (Italy), 1959 (U.S.).

Cast: Frank Latimore *(Miguel, Duke of Canabil)*; Anna-Maria Sandri *(Consuelo)*; Maxwell Reed *(Don Inigo da Costa)*; Katina Ranieri *(Amparo, the Singer)*; Juan de Landa *(Carlos)*; Paolo Barbara *(Soledad)*; Tino Buazelli *(Damian Pinto)*; Mario Carotenuto *(The Sailor)*; Gianni Cavalieri *(The Doctor)*; Sergio Fantoni *(Officer)*; Fedele Gentile; Carlo Tamberlani; Cesare Fantoni; Mario Feliciani; Aldo Giuffrè; Carlo Lombardi; Franco Marturano; Franco Pastorino; Nico Pepe; Edoardo Toniolo; Anna Maria Ferrero; Ubaldo Lay; Enzo Musumeci Greco; Isarco Ravaioli; Maria Grazia Sandri.

Comments: A seafaring adventure set in the early 1800s. As Spanish legions celebrate their victory over Bonaparte's troops, Miguel, Duke of Canabil, receives word that his father has betrayed Spain by surrendering his fleet to the enemy; knowing that this is untrue, he swears to avenge his father's honor. Produced by Italy's Athena Cinematografica and filmed at Cinecittà Studios, Rome.

Caribbean Hawk *(Lo sparviero dei Carribi)* (Medallion Pictures, 1962)

Credits: *Director:* Piero Regnoli; *Screenplay:* Piero Regnoli; *Photography:* Aldo Greci (Eastmancolor, Totalscope, aspect ratio 2.35:1); *Music:* Aldo Piga; running time: 115 minutes (Italy); released April 5, 1962 (Italy).

Cast: Johnny Desmond *(Juan Rodrigo Olivares)*; Yvonne Monlaur *(Arica Mageiras)*; Armando Francioli *(Esteban)*; Piero Lulli *(Manuel)*; Claudio Undari *(Don Pedro de Alicante)*; Walter Brandi *(Pirate)*; Luigi Batzella *(Pirate)*; Nerio Bernardi; Riccardo De Santis; Carla Foscari *(Corinna)*; Mara Garden; Graziella Granata *(Flora)*; Silvana Jachino; Elvi, Lissiak; Carlo Lombardi; Nino Marchesini *(Vice King of Santa Cruz)*; Vincenzo Musolino *(Pirate)*; Franca Parisi *(Donna Maria de la Rey Sandoval)*; Franco Santi; Amadeo Trilli *(Pao)*.

Comments: A pirate adventure set in the mid–1500s. According to actress Yvonne Monlaur, production difficulties caused a month-long interruption in shooting, with many scripted scenes left unfilmed. Lead Johnny Desmond (1919–1985) had earlier in his career performed with the Bob Crosby and Gene Krupa bands as well as Glenn Miller's military band. Produced by the Italian companies Nord Film Italiana and Remarch Film.

Carthage in Flames *(Cartagine in flamme)* (Columbia Pictures, 1960)

Credits: *Director:* Carmine Gallone; *Screenplay:* Ennio De Concini, Carmine Gallone, Emilio Salgari, Duccio Tessari; *Photography:* Piero Portalupi (Technicolor, Super Technirama 70, aspect ratio 2.20:1); *Music:* Mario Nascimbene; *Film Editor:* Niccolò Lazzari; *Production Design:* Guido Fiorini; *Costume Design:* Veniero Colasanti; *Makeup:* Amato Garbini; *Production Supervisors:* Carmine Gallone, Jr., Renato Jaboni; *Production Managers:* Guido Luzzatto, Marino Vaccà; *Assistant Directors:* Franco Cirino, Andrea Volp; *Scene Painter:* Italo Tomassi; *Sound Engineer:* Bruno Brunacci; *Sound Mixer:* Renato Caduero; *Special Effects:* Giovanni Corridori, Ottavio Mannini; *Stunt Coordinator:* Enzo Musumeci Greco; *Camera Operators:* Enrico Betti Berutto, Idelmo Simonelli; *Assistant Camera Operator:* Neil Binney; *Grip:* Umberto Dessena; *Orchestra Conductor:* Franco Ferrara;

Script Girl: Mimmola Girosi; *Naval Consultant:* Salvatore Prinzi; Running Time: 93 minutes (U.S.); released January 29, 1960 (Italy), January 18, 1961 (U.S.).

Cast: Pierre Brasseur *(Sidone)*; Daniel Gélin *(Phegor)*; Anne Heywood *(Fulvia)*; Aldo Silvani *(Hermon)*; Ilaria Occhini *(Ophir)*; Paolo Stoppa *(Astarito)*; José Suárez *(Hiram)*; Terence Hill *(Tsour)*; Gianrico Tedeschi *(Eleo)*; Edith Peters *(Sarepta)*; Cesare Fantoni *(Assian)*; Erno Crisa *(Asdrubak)*; Fernand Ledoux; Arnoldo Foà; Camillo Piloto; Amedeo Nazzari; Ivo Garrani *(Thala)*; Fortunato Arena *(Soldier on Hiram's Ship)*; Augusto Belardelli; Guido Celano; Clarissa Corner; Lina De Rossi; Piero Giagnoni *(Il bambino)*; Walter Grant; Nadia Lara; Achille Majeroni; Audrey McDonald; Furio Meniconi; Mario Meniconi; Nino Musco; Enzo Musumeci Greco; Mario Passante; Piero Pastore; Andrea Scandurra; Renato Terra; Amedeo Trilli.

Comments: Convoluted soap opera romantics are injected into an account of Carthage's last days. A co-production between the Italian companies Lux Film, Produzione Gallone, and France's Compagnie Cinématografique de France.

Catherine of Russia *(Caterina di Russia)* (National Telefilm Associates, 1963)

Credits: Director: Umberto Lenzi; *Producer:* Fortunato Misiano; *Executive Producer:* Nino Misiano; *Screenplay:* Umberto Lenzi, Guido Maletesta; *Photography:* Augusto Tiezzi (color, Totalscope, aspect ratio 2.35:1); *Music:* Angelo Francesco Lavagnino; *Film Editor:* Jolanda Benvenuti; *Production Design:* Peppino Piccolo; *Set Decoration:* Franco D'Andria; *Costume Design:* Walter Patriarca; *Makeup:* Massimo Giustini; *Hair Stylist:* Violetta Pacelli; *Assistant Directors:* Roberto Giandalla, Ermanno Stel; *Assistant Set Designer:* Giuseppe Ranieri; *Assistant Set Decorator:* Italo Talione; *Sound Engineer:* Franco Groppioni; *Camera Operator:* Luigi Allegretti; *Assistant Film Editor:* Alba Di Salvo; *Production Assistant:* Diego Alchimede; *Continuity:* Maria Luisa Roi; running time: 105 minutes (U.S.); released January 12, 1963 (Italy).

Cast: Hildegard Knef *(Catherine the Great)*; Sergio Fantoni *(Orloff)*; Giacomo Rossi Stuart *(Count Poniatowski)*; Angela Cavo *(Anna, a Chambermaid)*; Ennio Balbo *(Count Panin)*; Leonardo Botta *(Saltikoff)*; Vera Besusso *(Princess Woronzoff)*; Gianni Solaro *(Captain Schverik)*; Enzo Fiermonti *(General Munic)*; Tina Lattanzi *(Czarina Elizabetch)*; Romano Ghini *(Alan)*; Tullio Altamura *(Latouche)*; Janez Vrhovec; Franco Jamonte; G. Voujaklia; Bernard Farber; Luigi D'Acri; Raoul Gassilli *(Czar Peter III)*.

Comments: Catherine the Great discovers that her husband, Count Poniatowski, is plotting her murder. A co-production between Italy's Romano Film, France's Société Nouvelle de Cinématographi (SNC) and Yugoslavia's Zagreb Film.

Cavalier in the Devil's Castle *(Il cavaliere del castello maledetto)* (Walter Manley Enterprises, 1959)

Credits: Director: Mario Costa; *Producer:* Fortunato Misiano; *Screenplay:* Sergio Corbucci, Piero Vivarelli; *Photography:* Augusto Tiezzi (Ferraniacolor, Totalscope, aspect ratio 2.35:1); *Music:* Michele Cozzoli; *Film Editor:* Jolanda Benvenuti; *Production Design:* Alfredo Montori; *Costume Design:* Giancarlo Bartolini Salimbeni; running time: 80 minutes (Italy); released March 21, 1959 (Italy); video availability: Something Weird Video.

Cast: Massimo Serato *(Capt. Ugone di Collefeltro)*; Irène Tunc *(Marquise Fiamma)*; Luisella Boni *(Countess Isabella)*; Pierre Cressoy *(Astolfo)*; Livio Lorenzon *(Guidobaldo Fortebraccio)*; Maria Sima *(Violante)*; Carlo Tamberlani *(Count Oliviero)*; Aldo Bufi Landi *(Duccio)*; Luciano Marin *(Gianetto)*; Ignazio Balsamo; Miranda Campa; Andrea Fantasia; Franco Fantasia; Gina Mascetti; Ugo Sasso; Amedeo Trilli.

Comments: The evil Captain Ugone di Collefeltro imprisons a benign ruler and attempts to marry his daughter, but his schemes are opposed by a masked crusader. Produced by Italy's Romana Film, this color film is only available in America in the form of a black-and-white print.

The Centurion *(Il conquistatore de Corinto)* (Producers International, 1961)

Credits: Director: Mario Costa; *Producer:* Manlio Morelli; *Screenplay:* Nino Stresa; *Photography:* Pier Ludovico Pavoni (Eastmancolor, aspect ratio 2.35:1); *Music:* Carlo Innocenzi; *Film Editor:* Antonietta Zita; *Costume Design:* Mario Giorsi; *Art Department:* Italo Tomassi; *Special Effects:* Antonio Visone; running time: 105 minutes (Italy), 77 minutes (U.S.); released October 21, 1961 (Italy), August 1962 (U.S.); video availability: Sinister Cinema.

Cast: Jacques Sernas *(Caius Vinicius)*; John Drew Barrymore *(Diaeus)*; Geneviève Grad *(Hebe)*; Gianna Maria Canale *(Artemide)*; Gordon Mitchell *(General Metellus)*; Gianni Santuccio *(Critolaus)*; Nando Tamberlani *(Callicrates)*; Ivano Staccioli *(Hippolytus)*; Andrea Fantasia *(Lucius Mummius)*; Gianni Solaro *(Caesar)*; José Jaspe *(Traitor)*; Vassili Karis *(Egeo)*; Dina De Santis *(Chimene)*; Milena Vukotic *(Ancella)*; Adriana Vianello *(Cleo)*; Miranda Campa; Franco Fantasia *(Corinthian Aristocrat)*; Luciano Pigozzi *(Corinthian Messenger)*.

Comments: Set in 146 BC, this film deals with the battle of Corinth, in which the city is destroyed and its treasures plundered. Originally running 105 minutes, *The Centurion* was recut to 77 minutes by its American distributor, losing nearly 30 minutes of footage, which resulted in continuity gaps. Produced by Italy's Europa Cinematografica, in association with France's C.F.P.C.

Challenge of the Gladiator (Il gladiatore che sfidò l'impero) (American International Television, 1965)

Credits: Director: Domenico Paolella; *Screenplay:* Alessandro Ferraù, Domenico Paolella; *Photography:* Raffaele Masciocchi (color, Totalscope, aspect ratio 2.35:1); *Music:* Giuseppe Piccillo; *Film Editor:* Antonietta Zita; *Makeup:* Duilio Scarozza; *Hair Stylist:* Adriana Cassini; *Set Designer:* Camillo Del Signore; *Unit Manager:* Ferdinand Felicioni; *Assistant Director:* Tersicore Kolosoff; *Sound:* Franco Groppioni; running time: 103 minutes (Italy), 90 minutes (U.S.); released April 4, 1965 (Italy).

Cast: Peter Lupus [billed as "Rock Stevens"] *(Spartacus)*; Massimo Serato *(Senator Lucio Quintillus)*; Livio Lorenzon *(Commodio)*; Gloria Milland *(Livia)*; Piero Lulli *(Consul Metello)*; Walter Barnes *(Terenzo)*; Andrea Checchi; Dario Michaelis; Franco Ressel; Bruno Scipioni; Giulio Tomei; Giovanni Petrucci; John Bartha *(Roman Messenger)*; Salvatore Borghese *(Gladiator)*; Jeff Cameron *(Gladiator)*; Mimmo Poli *(Roman at Orgy)*; Alfonso Giganti *(Spectator at Tent Match)*.

Comments: Accompanied by his beautiful daughter Livia, Roman senator Lucius Quintillus searches for treasure in Thrace, but is opposed by rebel gladiator Spartacus. Produced by Italy's Jonia Film.

Charge of the Black Lancers (I lanceri neri) (Paramount Television, 1962)

Credits: Director: Giacomo Gentilomo; *Producer:* Jone Tuzi; *Screenplay:* Ottavio Alessi, Ernesto Gastaldi, Ugo Guerra, Luciano Martino; *Photography:* Raffaele Masciocchi (Eastmancolor, CinemaScope, aspect ratio 2.35:1); *Music:* Mario Nascimbene; *Production Design:* Kosta Krivokapic; running time: 97 minutes (Italy); released August 31, 1962 (Italy); video availability: Something Weird Video.

Cast: Mel Ferrer *(Andrea)*; Yvonne Furneaux *(Jassa)*; Letícia Román *(Mascia)*; Lorella De Luca *(Samal)*; Jean Claudio *(Sergio Di Tula)*; Annibale Ninchi *(Prince Nikiev)*; Franco Silva *(Gamul)*; Nando Tamberlani *(King Stefano III)*; Giulio Battiferri *(Mascia's Jailer)*; Claudio Biava *(Alfiere Di Sergio)*; Remo De Angelis *(Officiale)*; Renato De Carmine *(Prince Polacco)*; Arturo Dominici *(Chief of Krevires)*; Mirko Ellis *(Member of the Counsel)*; Andrej Gardenin *(Fencer)*; Piero Lulli, Piero Palermini; Umberto Raho *(Another Member of the Council)*.

Comments: It's the Poles vs. the Tartars in this action drama, co-produced by Italy's Royal Film, France's France-Cinéma Productions, and Yugoslavia's C.F.S. Košutnjak.

Cleopatra's Daughter (Il sepolcro dei re) (Medallion Pictures, 1960)

Credits: Director: Fernando Cerchio; *Screenplay:* Damiano Damiani, Fernando Cerchio; *Photography:* Anchise Brizzi (Technicolor, Ultrascope, aspect ratio: 2.35:1); *Music:* Giovanni Fusco; *Film Editor:* Antonietta Zita; *Art Direction:*

Arrigo Equini; *Art Department Manager:* Italo Tomassi; *Costume Design:* Giancarlo Bartolini Salimbeni, *Assistant Director:* Giuliano Betti; *Sound (English Dubbing):* Richard Mcnamara; running time: 109 minutes; released December 7, 1960 (Italy), February 1963 (U.S.); video availability: Sinister Cinema.

Cast: Debra Paget *(Shila, Cleopatra's Daughter)*; Ettore Manni *(Resi, Pharoah's Physician)*; Erno Crisa *(Kefren, Tegi's Councellor)*; Corrado Pani *(Pharoah Nemorat/Keops)*; Yvette Lebon *(Queen Mother Tegi)*; Andreina Rossi *(Kefren's Mistress)*; Ivano Staccioli; Angelo Dessy; Renato Mambor; Nando Tamberlani; Stefania Ré; Rosalba Neri; Betsy Bell; Amerigo Santarelli; Pietro Ceccarelli *(Sutek)*; Vittorio Ripamonti; Pino Sciacqua; Vando Tress; Robert Alda *(Inuni, Pharoah's Architect)*; Veriano Ginesi.

Comments: The lovely Debra Paget *(The Ten Commandments)* plays Cleopatra's (fictional) daughter, with Cleopatra entrusting her offspring to the Assyrians after the death of the pharaoh Nemorat. Produced by Italy's Explorer Film '58 and France's Comptoir Français du Productions.

Colossus and the Amazon Queen *(La regina delle amazzoni)* (American International, 1960)

Credits: *Director:* Vittorio Sala; *Producer:* Enzo Merolle; *Screenplay:* Ennio De Concini, Fulvio Fo, Augusto Frassinetti, Giorgio Mordini, Vittorio Nino, Novarese, Vittorio Sala, Duccio Tessari; *Photography:* Bitto Albertini (Eastmancolor, Dyaliscope, aspect ratio: 2.35:1); *Film Editor:* Mario Serandrei; *Music:* Roberto Nicolosi; *Art Direction:* Ottavio Scotti; *Costume Design:* Gaia Romanini; *Makeup:* Anacieto Giustini; *Hair Stylist:* Mirella Ginnoto; *Production Manager:* Armando Grottini; *Production Organization:* Sergio Merolle; *Assistant Directors:* Daniele G. Luisi, Duccio Tessari; *Art Department Manager:* Italo Tomassi; *Sound:* Amelio Verona; *Special Effects:* Joseph Nathanson; *Camera Operator:* Carlo Fiore; *Assistant Camera Operator:* Franco Di Giacomo; *Assistant Film Editor:* Lina Caterini; *Orchestra Conductor:* Luigi Urbini; *Choreography:* Tito LeDuc; *Production Secretaries:* Tonino Garzarelli, Ardulino Mercuri; *Script Supervisor:* Mimmola Girosi; running time: 98 minutes (Italy), 84 minutes (U.S.); released September 8, 1960 (Italy), 1964 (U.S.); video availability: Retromedia Entertainment.

Cast: Rod Taylor *(Pirro)*; Ed Fury *(Glauco)*; Dorian Gray *(Antiope)*; Daniela Rocca *(Melitta)*; Gianna Maria Canale *(La Regina)*; Alberto Farnese *(Losco, a Pirate)*; Giorgia Moll *(Amazon)*; Folco Lulli; Ignazio Leone *(Sopho)*; Adriana Facchetti *(Sacerdota)*; Paola Falchi *(Amazon)*; Enzo Cerusico *(Menandro)*; Marco Tulli *(Eumio-Oste)*; Marilù Tolo *(Amazon)*; Nadia Bianchi *(Amazon)*; Maria Luisa Rispoli *(Amazon)*; Carla Dody *(Amazon)*; Germana Francioli *(Amazon)*; Alfredo Varelli *(Merchant #1)*; Gino Buzzanca *(Merchant #2)*; Lily Mantovani *(Amazon)*; Tilde Damiani *(Amazon)*; Renato Tagliani *(Nando)*; Francesca Dean *(Amazon)*; Dori Hassan *(Amazon)*; Marina Lucatelli *(Amazon)*; Loredana Nusciak *(Amazon)*; Tiberio Murgia, Luciana Angiolillo *(Amazon)*; Mariangela Giordano *(Amazon)*; Maria Pia Cohen *(Amazon)*; Marietta Gennusco *(Amazon)*; Lia Lena *(Amazon)*.

Comments: In this comedic adventure, a swindler looking for treasure (Rod Taylor) travels to an island with his companion (Ed Fury) and discovers a society of Amazons. This very campy film was disliked intensely by Taylor, but is nevertheless one of his most enjoyable movies. Co-produced by the Italian companies Galatea Film, Glomer Film and Alta Vista.

Colossus and the Headhunters *(Maciste contro I cacciatori di teste)* (American International, 1963)

Credits: *Director:* Guido Malatesta; *Producer:* Giorgio Marzelli; *Screenplay:* Guido Malatesta (from his story); *Photography:* Domenico Scala (Eastmancolor, CinemaScope, aspect ratio 2.35:1); *Music:* Guido Robuschi, Gian Stellari; *Film Editor:* Enzo Alfonzi; *Art Direction:* Giuseppe Ranieri; *Costume Design:* Nadia Vitale; *Sound:* Bruno Moreal; running time: 81 minutes (Italy), 79 minutes (U.S.); released January 10, 1963 (Italy); video availability: Alpha Video.

Cast: Kirk Morris *(Maciste)*; Laura Brown *(Queen Amoha)*; Demeter Bitenc *(Ariel)*; Frank Leroy *(Kermes)*; Alfredo Zammi *(Tyran)*; Corinne Capri *(Dancer)*; Luigi Esposito *(Aris)*; Nello Pazzafini *(Gunk)*; Alessio Pregara *(King Olibana)*; Ines Holder *(Asmyn)*; Letizia Stephan *(Moana, the Islander)*.

Comments: The beautiful Queen Amoha seeks the help of Maciste as she struggles against the oppressors of her people. Produced by the Italian companies RCM Produzione Cinematografica and Alta Vista, portions of this film were shot in Ljubljana, Slovenia, in Yugoslavia.

The Colossus of Rhodes (Il colosso di Rodi) (MGM, 1961)

Credits: Director: Sergio Leone; *Executive Producer:* Michele Scaglione; *Screenplay:* Ennio De Concini, Sergio Leone, Cesare Seccia, Luciano Martino, Ageo Savioli, Luciano Chtarrini, Carlo Gualtieri (from their story); *Photography:* Antonio L. Ballesteros (Eastmancolor, Supertotalscope, aspect ratio 2.35:1); *Film Editor:* Eraldo Da Roma; *Music:* Angelo Francesco Lavagnino; *Production Design:* Ramiro Gómez; *Costume Design:* Vittorio Rossi; *Makeup:* Angela Malandrucco, Carlos Nin; *Production Managers:* Eduardo de la Fuente, Cesare Seccia; *Assistant Director:* Jorge Grau; *2nd Assistant Directors:* Luis Lasala, Mahnahén Velasco, Yves Boisset; *Collaborating Director:* Michael Lupo; *Trainee Assistant Director:* Roberto Bordegas; *Set Designer:* Jesús Mateos; *Construction:* Francisco Rodriguez Asensio; *Assistant Art Director:* Giuseppe Raineri; *Sound:* Mario Amari, Giuseppe Turco; *Special Effects:* Erasmo Bacciucchi, Vittorio Galiano; *Sound Effects:* Tonino Cacciottolo; *Special Makeup*

Original Italian poster for *Colossus and the Headhunters* (*Maciste contro I caccitori di teste*).

Poster for *The Colossus of Rhodes*.

Rory Calhoun in *The Colossus of Rhodes*.

Effects: Francisco Rodriguez Asensio; *2nd Unit Directors of Photography:* Emilio Foriscot, Mariano Ruiz; *Camera Operator:* Eduardo Noé; *Assistant Camera Operators:* Franco Frazzi, Gianni Maddaleni; *Key Grip:* Aldo Colanzi; *Stunts:* Alfio Contalbiano; *Costumes:* Irma Tonnini, Maria Pia Mancini; *Assistant Costume Designer:* Antonio Cortés; *Assistant Film Editors:* Marisa Mengoli, Maria Luisa Pino; *Production Secretaries:* José Castanyer, Maria Isabel, Capillas Ruiz; *Choreography:* Carla Leone; *Voice Dubbing (for Lea Massari):* Lidia Simoneschi. running time: 139 minutes (Italy), 127 minutes (U.S.); released August 25, 1961 (Italy), December 13, 1961 (U.S.); video availability: Warner Home Video.

Cast: Rory Calhoun *(Darios)*; Lea Massari *(Diala)*; Georges Marchal *(Peliocles)*; Conrado San Martin *(Thar)*; Ángel Aranda *(Koros)*; Mabel Karr *(Mirte)*; Mimmo Palmara *(Ares)*; Roberto Camardiel *(Serse)*; Alfio Caltabiano *(Creonte)*; George Rigaud *(Lissipu)*; Yann Larvor *(Mahor)*; Carlo Tamberlani *(Xenon)*; Félix Fernández *(Carete)*; Ignazio Dolce; Antonio Casas *(Phoenician Ambassador)*; Fernando Calzado *(Sirone)*; Álvaro de Luna; Arturo Cabré; Rafael Menéndez; Nello Pazzafini; Gustavo Re *(Mercader)*; Norman Rose *(Voice)*; José María Vilches *(Eros)*.

Comments: Set in 280 BC, this adventure follows a Greek military hero as he rebels against the evil King Serse and is sentenced to combat in the arena after he is captured. Moral retribution arrives in the form of a concluding earthquake. Rory Calhoun (star of the American television show *The Texan*) was cast in this film on only one day's notice. *The Colossus of Rhodes* was Sergio Leone's first credited directorial effort, although he had directed (unbilled) earlier movies. The historical Colossus of Rhodes stood 32 meters high and was erected on a hill, while the structure depicted in the film is supposed to be 110 meters tall and stands astride a harbor. Leone was dissuaded from giving the figure the face of Benito Mussolini, as he had planned. Leone married choreographer Carla Ranalli during production. Some portions of the film were shot on location in Spain. Produced by the Italian companies Produzioni Atlas Consorziate (P.A.C.) and Cine Produzioni Associate, Spain's Procusa, and the French companies Comptoir Français du Productions Cinématographiques (CFPC) and Cinema Television International (CTI).

The Conqueror of Atlantis
(Il conquistatore di atlantide)
(ABC Films, 1965)

Credits: *Director:* Alfonso Brescia; *Producers:* Giorgio Agliani; Alberto Chimenz, Pier Ludovico Pavoni; *Screenplay:* Alfonso Brescia, Franco Cobianchi; *Photography:* Fausto Rossi (Technicolor, Techniscope, aspect ratio 2.35:1); *Film Editor:* Nella Nannuzzi; *Music:* Ugo Filippini; *Production Design and Costume Design:* Mario Giorsi; *Assistant Director:* Filiberto Fiaschi; *Fencing Master:* Giorgio Ubaldi; *English Dubbing Director:* Richard McNamara; running time: 93 minutes (U.S.); released April 1, 1965 (Italy); video availability: Something Weird Video.

Cast: Kirk Morris *(Heracles)*; Luciana Gilli *(Vima)*; Piero Lulli *(Ramir)*; Andrea Scotti *(Karr)*; Mahmoud El-Sabbaa *(Assur)*; Caterina Trentini; Livia Rossetti; Rinaldo Zamperla; Hélène Chanel *(Queen Ming)*; Mohammed Tawfik; Fortunato Arena *(Golden Ghost Man)*.

Comments: A rare excursion into the realm of sci-fi for the peplum genre, dealing with the lost city of Atlantis and featuring androids and futuristic machinery. Somewhat reminiscent of a low-budget serial, and just as enjoyable. Produced by Doina Cine, Copro Film and PCA.

Conqueror of Maracaibo
(Il conquitatore di Maracaibo)
(Medallion Pictures, 1961)

Credits: *Director:* Eugenio Marti; *Producer:* Leonardo Martin; *Screenplay:* Gianfranco Parolini, Giovanni Simonelli (from their story); *Photography:* Francesco Izzarelli (color, Totalscope, aspect ratio 2.35:1); *Film Editor:* Antonio Gimeno; *Music:* Miguel Asins Arbó; *Production Design:* Francisco Canet; *Art Direction:* Gianfranco Parolini; *Costume Design:* Vittorio Rossi; *Hair Stylist:* E. Ibañez; *Production Managers:* Manolo Torrs, Attilio Tosato; *General Manager:* Michele Scaglione; *Assistant Directors:* Francisco Pérez-Dolz, Giovanni Simonelli; *Assistant Production Designer:* Giuseppe Ranieri; *Sound:* Giuseppe Turco; *Special Effects:* Ramón Leros; *Camera Operator:* Miguel Agudo; *Costume Seamstress:* Valeria Sponsali; *Master at Arms:* Joe Baldi; running time: 101 minutes (Italy); released April 29, 1961 (Italy).

Cast: Hans Von Borsody *(Alan Drake)*; Luisella Boni *(Altagracia)*; Helga Liné *(Moira/El Valiente)*; Luis Induni *(Blaine)*; Xan das Bolas *(Slave Auctioneer)*; Carlos Casaravilla *(Brasseur)*; Salvatore Furnari *(Veleno)*; José Marco *(Costello)*; José Maria Caffarel *(Pirate)*; Conrad Anderson *(Puritano)*; Carlo Tamberlani *(Governor)*; Jany Clair *(Doña Isabella Valdez)*; Barta Barri *(Wilde)*; Frank Braña; Livia Contardi *(Rosario)*; José Manuel Martin; Luis Sánchez Polack *(Don Miguel Ortega)*.

Comments: The beautiful Helga Liné is featured as a girl pirate in this seafaring costumer, produced by Italy's Produzion Associate, in conjunction with the Spanish companies Procusa and Época Films S.A. Partially filmed on location in Spain.

The Conqueror of the Orient
(Il conquistatore dell'Oriente)
(Avco Embassy, 1960)

Credits: *Director:* Tanio Boccia; *Producer:* Giuliano Simonetti; *Executive Producer:* Nino Misiano; *Screenplay:* Tanio Boccia, Gianni Mauro, Mario Moroni (from a story by Tanio Boccia); *Photography:* Vincenzo Seratrice (locations), Luciano Trasatti (interiors), Ferraniacolor, Dyaliscope, aspect ratio 2.35:1); *Film Editor:* Mario Sansoni; *Music:* Giovanni Fassino; *Set Decoration:* Ennio Michettoni; *Costume Design:* Adriana Berselli; *Makeup:* Duilio Giustini; *Production Manager:* Michelangelo Ciafré; *Production Secretary:* Claudio Agostinelli; *Assistant*

Director: Mario Moroni; *Set Designer:* Piero Filippone; *Sound:* Biagio Fiorelli; *Camera Operators:* Camillo Bazzoni, Franco Villa; *Still Photographers:* Bruno Bruni, Luigi Quattrini; *Orchestra Conductor:* Giovanni Fassino; *Continuity:* Carla Fierro, Maria Luisa Roi; *Production Secretary:* Claudio Agostinelli; *Assistant to the Director:* Mario Casalini; *Laboratory Owner:* Ettore Catalucci; *Fencing Master:* Enzo Musumeci Greco; *Dialogue for English Language Version:* John Davis Hart; *Production Inspectors:* Diego Alchimede, Giuliano Simonetti; running time: 102 minutes (Italy), 86 minutes (U.S.); released October 12, 1960 (Italy); video availability: Mill Creek.

Cast: Gianna Maria Canale *(Dinazar/Zobeida)*; Rik Battaglia *(Nadir)*; Irène Tunc *(Fatima)*; Edda Ferronao *(Fatima Maid #1)*; Attilio Torelli *(Leader of the Red Robes Tribe)*; Riccardo Ferri *(Leader of the White Robes Tribe)*; Myriam Cordella *(Fatima Maid #2)*; Aldo Pini *(Chief of Prison Guards)*; Renato Montalbano, Paul Muller *(Sultan Dakar)*; Tatiana Farnese *(Katiscia)*; Franco Balducci *(Nureddin, Nadir's Companion)*; Giulio Donnini *(Rato, the Chancellor)*; Fosco Giachetti *(Omar, Nadir's Father)*.

Comments: Set in the Orient, hero Nadir (Rik Battaglia) rebels against the evil Sultan Dakar (Paul Muller) in this costume adventure. Produced by Italy's Produzioni Europee Associati (PEA) in tandem with Germany's Tabos Film, and shot at Dino De Laurentiis Cinematografica Studios in Rome.

Constantine and the Cross *(Costanto il grande)* (Embassy, 1961)

Credits: *Director:* Lionello De Felice; *Producers:* Joseph E. Levine, Ferdinand Felicioni; *Screenplay:* Ennio De Concini, Lionello De Felice, Diego Fabbri, Ernesto Guida, Franco Rossetti, Guglielmo Santangelo (from a story by Fulvio Palmieri); *Dialogue:* Michael Audley; *Photography:* Massimo Dallamano (Eastmancolor, Totalscope, aspect ratio 2.35:1); *Music:* Mario Nascimbene; *Film Editors:* Mario Serandrei, Gabriele Varriale; *Art Direction:* Franco Lolli; *Costume Design:* Giancarlo Bartolini Salimbeni; *Master of Arms:* Franco Fantasia; running time: 120 minutes (U.S.); released January 1961 (Italy) December 1962 (U.S.); video availability: Alpha Video.

Cast: Cornel Wilde *(Constantine)*; Belinda Lee *(Fausta)*; Massimo Serato *(Maxentius)*; Christine Kaufmann *(Livia)*; Fausto Tozzi *(Hadrian)*; Tino Carraro *(Emperor Maximanus)*; Carlo Ninchi *(Constantius Chlorus)*; Vittorio Sanipoli *(Apuleius)*; Elisa Cegani *(Elena)*; Lia Angeleri *Clavia, a Christian)*; Franco Fantasia *(Roman Soldier)*; Lauro Gazzolo *(Amodius)*; Nando Gazzolo *(Licinius)*; Veriano Ginesi *(Torturer)*; Loris Gizzi *(Roman Prosecutor)*; Enrico Glori *(Livia's Father)*; Jole Mauro *(Celi, Fausto's Maid)*; Annibale Ninchi *(Galarius)*; Carlo Tamberlani *(Diocletian)*; Renato Terra *(Jailer)*.

Comments: Constantine (280–337 AD) converts Rome to Christianity in this historical epic. Produced by Italy's Jonia Film, Yugoslavia's Jadran Film and Beaver-Champion Attractions, this film was shot at Incir De Paolis Studios in Rome.

The Cossacks *(I cosacchi)* (Universal, 1960)

Credits: *Directors:* Viktor Tourjansky, Giorgio Venturini; *Producer:* Giampaolo Bigazzi; *Screenplay:* Damiano Damiani, Ugo Liberatore, Viktor Tourjansky, Federico Zardi (from a story by Damiano Damiani); *Photography:* Massimo Dallamano (Eastmancolor, Totalscope, aspect ratio 2.35:1); *Film Editor:* Antonietta Zita; *Music:* Giovanni Fusco; *Production Design:* Miodrag Nikolic; *Art Direction:* Jovan Radic; *Head Scenic Painter:* Italo Tomassi; *Costume Design:* Giancarlo Bartolini Salimbeni; running time: 100 minutes (Italy), 114 minutes (U.S.); released February 4, 1960 (Italy), May 1960 (U.S.).

Cast: Edmund Purdom *(Shamil)*; John Drew Barrymore *(Giamal)*; Giorgia Moll *(Tatiana)*; Pierre Brice *(Boris)*; Elena Zareschi *(Patimat)*; Erno Crisa *(Casi)*; Massimo Girotti *(Alexander II)*; Maria Grazia Spina *(Alina)*; Mario Pisu *(Voronzov)*; Laura Carli *(Ferguson)*; Louis Seigner, Maria Badmajew; Nerio Bernardi; Mara Berni; Liana Del Balzo; Andrea Fantasia; Franco Fantasia; Maria Letizia Gazzoni; Giuliano Gemma; Marcello Giorda; Toma Jovanovic; Rita Rubirosa; Marilù Sangiorgi; Luigi Tosi, Janez Vrhovec.

Comments: Russia expands southeast to

invade the Chechen people in this historical drama, set in the mid–1800s. Avoiding the usual stereotypes and one-dimensional characterizations, the treatment here is unusually sensitive and fair-minded to both sides of the conflict. Produced by the Italian companies Explorer Film '58, Faro Film and Wanguard Film, in association with France's Comptoir Français du Productions Cinématographiques (CFPC) and Yugoslavia's C.F.S. Košutnjak.

The Count of Monte Cristo *(Le Comte de Monte-Cristo)* (Cineroma/La Société des Films Sirius, 1954)

Credits: Director: Robert Vernay; *Producers:* Lucien Masson, Jacques Roitfeld; *Screenplay:* Daniel Ivernel (based on the novel by Alexandre Dumas, adapted by Robert Vernay and Georges Neveux, dialogue by Georges Neveux); *Photography:* Robert Juillard (Gevacolor, aspect ratio 1.37:1); *Film Editor:* Monique Kirsanoff; *Music:* Jean Wiener; *Production Design:* Robert Clavel; *Costume Design:* Georges K. Benda; *Makeup:* Alexandre Marcus; *Assistant Makeup Artist:* Yvonne Barrie; *Hair Stylist:* Jules Chanteau; *Production Manager:* Wladimir Roitfeld; *Unit Production Manager:* Jean Mottet; *Assistant Unit Manager:* Roger Drescoffre; *Assistant Director:* Paul Feyder; *Assistant Director (part 2 only):* Roberto Savarese; *2nd Assistant Director:* Édouard Molinaro; *Assistant Production Designers:* Marc Desages, Jacques Douy; *Set Dresser:* Charles Merangel; *Sound:* Jean Rieul; *Boom Operator:* Marcel Corvaisier; *Camera Operator:* Jacques Robin; *Assistant Cameraman:* Bob Pater; *2nd Assistant Cameraman:* Daniel Diot; *Still Photographer:* Roger Corbeau; *Costumes:* Raymonde Catherine; *Costumer:* Victor Noeppel; *Costumer (for Jean Marais):* André Bardot; *Assistant Film Editors:* Raymonde Delor; Anne-Marie Forrer; *Orchestra Conductor:* Ernest Guillon; *Script Girl:* Nicole Bénard; *Press Representative:* Pierre Hani; running time: 183 minutes (released in 2 parts); released January 14, 1954 (France), August 20, 1954 (Italy).

Cast: Jean Marais *(Edmond Dantès/The Count of Monte Cristo)*; Lia Amanda *(Mercédès Herrera)*; Daniel Ivernel *(Gaspard Caderousse)*; Folco Lulli *(Jacopo)*; Louis Seigner *(Joannès, the Jeweler)*; Claude Génia *(La Carconte)*; Jean Témerson *(Kingi Louis XVIII)*; France Asselin *(Renée de Villefort)*; Julian Bertheau *(Emperor Napoléon)*; Lucien Blondeau *(Dantès' Father)*; André Brunot *(Morel)*; Gualtiero Tumiati *(Abbot Faria)*; Jacques Castelot *(Gérard de Villefort)*; Noël Roquevert *(Col. Noirtier de Villefort)*; Roger Pigaut *(Fernand de Morcerf)*; Paolo Stoppa *(Bertuccio)*; Simone Paris *(Émilienne de Beaugency)*; Genica Athanasiou *(Fatima)*; Daniel Cauchy *(Bruno)*; Jean-Pierre Mocky *(Albert de Morcerf)*; Marcel Journet *(President of the Chamber of Chamber of Peers)*; Pierre Flourens; Cristina Grado *(Haydée)*; Frédéric Valmain; André Var; Paul Azais *(Jailer)*; Paul Barge *(Policeman)*; Charles Bayard *(Assessor in the Chamber of Peers)*; Léon Berton *(The Inspector's Secretary)*; José Casa *(Innkeeper)*; Jacques Couturier; Marcel Delaître *(Jailer)*; Édouard Francomme; Fernand Gilbert *(The "Professor")*; Raymonf Girard; Marcel Loche *(Bailiff)*; Julien Maffre; Franck Maurice; Pierre Morin *(Grand Marshall)*; Bernard Musson *(Lawyer)*; Nathalie Nerval; Maryse Pallet *(Valentine)*; Philippe Richard *(Inspector)*; Made Siamé; Paul Villé *(The Governor)*; Roger Vincent; Léon Walther *(Courier)*; Janine Zorelli *(La Picard)*.

Comments: Filmed in two parts, this was the first color screen adaptation of the Alexandre Dumas novel. Produced by Italy's Cineroma, Fono Roma and Lux Film companies, in association with the French companies La Société des Films Sirius and Les Productions Jaques Roitfeld.

Cyrano and D'Artagnan *(Cyrano et d'Artagnan)* (Circe Production/Compagnia Cinematografica Champion, 1964)

Credits: Director: Abel Gance; *Associate Producer:* Nino Constantini; *Screenplay:* Abel Gance, Rafael Garcia Serrano (Spanish Version), José Luis Dibildos (Spanish Version), based on a story by Abel Gance; *Photography:* Otello Martelli (Eastmancolor); *Film Editors:* Eraldo Da Roma, Pedro del Rey; *Costume Design:* Dario Cecchi; *2nd Unit Director:* Nathan Juran; *2nd Unit Camera Operators:* Nelly Kaplan, Juan Mariné; *Master of Arms:* Enzo Musumeci Greco;

running time: 145 minutes; released September 25, 1964 (U.S.).

Cast: José Ferrer *(Cyrano de Bergerac)*; Jean-Pierre Cassel *(D'Artagnan)*; Sylva Koscina *(Ninon de l'Eclos)*; Daliah Lavi *(Marion de l'Orme)*; Rafael Rivelles *(Cardinal Duc de Richelieu)*; Laura Valenzuela *(Queen Anne of Austria)*; Julián Mateos *(Marquis de Cinq-Mars)*; Michel Simon *(Le Grognard)*; Phillippe Noiret *(King Louis XIII)*; Gabrielle Dorziat [billed as "Gabrielle D'Orziat"] *(Mme. De Mauvières)*; Enrique Ávila; Jacinto San Emeterio; Jesús Puente; Barta Barri; Fernando Cebrián; Alfredo Mayo; José Jaspe; Ivo Garrani; Franco Bevardi *(Aramis)*; Henri Crémieux *(Messire Jean)*; Carlo Dori *(Linières)*; Guy Henry *(Athos)*; Josette La Roche *(Duchess de Chevreuse)*; Andre Lauriault *(La Colombe)*; Diego Michelotti *(Scarron)*; Bob Morel *(Porthos)*; Massimo Pietrobon *(Saint-Simon)*; Ferdinand Guillaume.

Comments: José Ferrer reprises his role of Cyrano de Bergerac (from the 1950 United Artists film produced by Stanley Kramer) in this Italian-French-Spanish co-production. Produced by the Italian companies Compagnia Cinematografica Champion and Constantini Film, with France's Circe Production and Spain's Ágata Films S.A.

Damon and Pythias *(Il tiranno di Siracusa)* (MGM, 1962)

Credits: *Director:* Curtis Bernhardt; *Producer:* Franco Riganti; *Associate Producers:* Sam Jaffe, Samuel Marx; *Screenplay:* Samuel Marx, Franco Riganti, Paolo Ojetti, Bridget Bolnand, Barry Oringer (from a story by Samuel Marx, Paola Ojetti, Franco Riganti); *Photography:* Aldo Tonti (Metrocolor); *Film Editor:* Niccolò Lazzari; *Music:* Angelo Francesco Lavagnino; *Production Design:* Alberto Boccianti; *Set Decoration:* Ennio Michettoni; *Costume Design:* Adriana Berselli; *Makeup:* Nilo Jacopini; *Hair Stylist:*

Don Burnett (left) and Guy Williams in *Damon and Pythias*.

Rosa Luciani; *Production Manager:* Giorgio Riganti; *Assistant Director:* Alberto Cardone; *Manager of Art Department:* Italo Tomassi; *Camera Operator:* Luigi Kuveiller; *Matte Shots:* Joseph Nathanson; *Orchestra Conductor:* Franco Ferrara (Orchestra Filarmonica Romana); *Fencing Master:* Franco Fantasia; running time: 101 minutes (Italy), 99 minutes (U.S.); released August 30, 1962 (Italy), June 1962 (U.S.).

Cast: Guy Williams *(Damon)*; Don Burnett *(Pythias)*; Ilaria Occhini *(Nerissa)*; Liana Orfei *(Adriana)*; Marina Berti *(Merika, Nerissa's Friend)*; Arnoldo Foà *(Dionysius, the Tyrant)*; Carlo Gustini *(Cariso)*; Aldo Silvani *(Patriarch)*; Andrea Bosic *(Arcanos)*; Maurizio Baldoni *(Dionysius the Younger)*; Franco Fantasia *(Rumius, the Fencing Master)*; Osvaldo Ruggieri *(Demetrius, Nerissa's Brother)*; Lawrence Montaigne *(Flute Player)*; Enrico Glori *(Nikos)*; Gianni Bonagura *(Phylemon)*; Vittorio Bonos *(Digenis)*; Carlo Rizzo *(Lìbìa)*; Giovanna Maculani *(Hermione)*; Enzo Fiermonte; Tiberio Mitri; Franco Ressel; Tiberio Murgia; Luigi Bonos; Maurizio Bedoni; Carolyn De Fonseca *(Chloe)*; Carla Bonavera; Enrico Salvatore.

Comments: When he is sentenced to death by the cruel tyrant Dionysius, Pythias' brother Damon offers to sacrifice himself instead. Based on accounts by the 4th century BC philosopher Aristoxenus. Dionysius I of Syracuse (405 BC–367 BC) was an actual historical figure, a military commander who seized power in a coup. Filmed on location at the baths of Caracalla, Rome, and at Rome's Cinecittà Studios. An International Motion Picture Enterprises production.

Liana Orfei and Guy Williams in *Damon and Pythias*.

David and Goliath (David e Golia) (Allied Artists, 1960)

Credits: Directors: Ferdinando Baldi, Richard Pottier, Orson Welles (uncredited); *Producer:* Erminio Salvi; *Screenplay:* Umberto Scarpelli, Gino Mangini, Ambrogio Molteni, Erminio Salvi; *Photography:* Carlo Fiore, Bitto Albertini (Eastmancolor, Totalscope, aspect ratio 2.35:1); *Film Editor:* Franco Fraticelli; *Music:* Carlo Innocenzi; *Art Direction:* Oscar D'Amico; *Costume Design:* Giovanna Natili; *Makeup:* Guglielmo Bonotti; *Hair Stylist:* Giovanni Palombi; *Assistant Director:* Gianfranco Baldenello; *Sound:* Bruno Moreal, Pietro Ortolani; *Scenic Photographer:* Cristiano Civirani; *Orchestra Conductor:* Giuseppe Savagnone; *Choreographer:* Carla Leone; *Administrative Director:* Decio Salvi; *Voice Dubbing:* Gino Cervi (for Orson Welles); Lidia Simoneschi (for Eleonora Rossi Drago); running time: 113 minutes (Italy), 95 minutes (U.S.); released January

Left to right: Massimo Serato, Pierre Cressoy and Orson Welles in *David and Goliath*.

22, 1960 (Italy), May 28, 1961 (U.S.); video availability: Alpha Video.

Cast: Orson Welles *(King Saul)*; Ivica Pajer *(David)*; Eleonora Rossi Drago *(Merab)*; Massimo Serato *(Abner)*; Giulia Rubini *(Micol)*; Pierre Cressoy *(Gionata)*; Hilton Edwards *(Prophet Samuel)*; Furio Meniconi *(Asrod, King of the Philistines)*; Aldo Pedinotti *(Goliath)*; Dante Maggio *(Cret)*; Luigi Tosi *(Benjamin Di Gaba)*; Umberto Fiz *(Lazar)*; Ugo Sasso *(Huro)*; Ileana Danelli *(Sarah)*; Emma Baron *(Anna, Mother of David)*; Olimpo Gargano; Simonetta Simeoni *(Egla)*; Marina Riccardi *(Girl)*; Carla Foscari; Stefano Valle; Arpad Kertes *(Father Isaiah)*; Renato Terra; Fabrizio Capucci; Gabriele Tinti; Carlo D'Angelo; Roberto Miali; Nadia Lara *(Girl)*; Armando Annuale.

Comments: Cinematic icon Orson Welles appeared—and also directed his own scenes—in this Italian-Yugoslavian co-production, based on the biblical tale. Filmed at Incir De Paolis Studios, Rome, Amato Studios in Rome, and on location in Yugoslavia and Jerusalem. Produced by Italy's Ansa company in association with Yugoslavia's Dubrava Film.

The Defeat of Hannibal (Scipione l'africano) (Esperia Film Distributing, 1937)

Credits: *Director:* Carmine Gallone; *Producer:* Frederic Curiosi; *Executive Producer:* Vittorio Mussolini; *Screenplay:* Carmine Gallone, Camillo Mariani Dell'Aguillara, Sebastiano A. Luciani, Silvio Maurano (based on a story by Carmine Gallone, Camilo Mariana Dell'Aguillara, Sebastiano A Luciani); *Photography:* Ubaldo Arata, Anchise Brizzi (black & white); *Film Editor:* Oswald Hafenrichter; *Music:* Ildebrando Pizzetti; *Production Design and Costume Design::* Pietro Aschieri; *Set Decoration:* Carmine Gallone; *Makeup:* Mario Giuseppe Paoletti; *Production Manager:* Federico Curioni; *Assistant Directors:* Giorgio Ferroni, Giorgio Mannini, Romolo Marcellini; *2nd Assistant Directors:* Francesco di

Sirignano, Paolo Moffa, Domenico Paolella, Ferdinando Maria Poggioli; *Set Designer:* Ettore Corso; *Scenic Painter:* Italo Tomassi; *Sound:* Vittorio Trentino; *Camera Operators:* Ugo Lombardi, Giorgio Orsini; *Assistant Costume Designer:* Maria De Matteis; *Military Advisors:* Francesco Poggi, Alberto Riggi; *Voice Dubbing:* Giovanna Scotto (for Francesca Braggiotti); running time: 117 minutes (Italy), 83 minutes (U.S.); released August 4, 1937 (Italy), September 21, 1939 (U.S.).

Cast: Annibale Ninchi *(Publius Cornelius Scipio)*; Camillo Pilotto *(Hannibal)*; Fosco Giachetti *(Captain Massinissa)*; Francesca Braggiotti *(Queen Sophonisba)*; Marcello Giorda *(King Syphace)*; Guglielmo Barnabò *(Furius, the Fat Roman)*; Isa Miranda *(Velia, a Roman Woman)*; Memo Benassi *(Cato)*; Franco Coop *(Mezio, a Roman Soldier)*; Ciro Galvani *(Quinto Fabio Massimo)*; Carlo Lombardi *(Lucio)*; Marcello Spada *(Arunte)*; Piero Carnabucci *(Battle Veteran)*; Carlo Ninchi *(Lelius)*; Lamberto Picasso *(Hasdrubal, Advisor to Hannibal)*; Diana Lante *(Scipione's Mother)*; Raimondo Van Riel *(Maharbale)*; Achille Majeroni; Carlo Tamberlani *(Ambassador Romano)*; Gino Viotti *(Merchant Fenicio)*; Clara Padoa *(Sofonisba's Slave)*; Ugo Sasso *(Official)*; Mario Gallina *(Carthaginian Ambassador)*; Olinto Cristina *(Carthaginian Ambassador #2)*; Carlo Duse *(Messo di Magone)*; Franco Brambilla *Romano)*; Antonella Steni *(Little Girl)*; Enzo Biliotti; Bruno Calabretta; Alberto Campi; Gustavo Conforti; Giorgio Covi; Federico De Martino; Cesare Gambarelli; Walter Lazzaro; Guglielmo Longo; Giorgio Marcello; Otello Polini; Albino Principe; Gennaro Sabatino; Carlo Simoneschi; Ernesto Torrini; Vittorio Vaser; Amedeo Vecci; Franca Vella; Carla Zaccaria; Armando Zuccarelli; Rosina Adrario; Nino Altieri; Ruggero Angeletti; Sandro Bianchi; Vittorio Capanni; Antimo Reyner; Alberto Sordi; Alfredo De Antoni; Fernando Solieri; Mario Carotenuto *(Extra)*; Alberto De Martino *(Son of Scipio)*.

Comments: Italian dictator Benito Mussolini was one of the main forces behind this historical account of Hannibal's defeat as he crossed the Alps during the Second Punic Wars (218–201 BC), a major conflict between Carthage and Rome. This production employed 6,000 extras, with directors of photography Ubaldo Arata and Anchise Brizzi using one of the earliest zoom lenses. Co-produced by Italy's Consorzione *Scipio l'Africano*, Ente Nazionale Industrie Cinematografiche (ENIC), and France's L.C.J. Editions and Productions.

The Defeat of the Barbarians *(Re Manfredi)* (Retix Cinematografica, 1962)

Credits: Directors: Paolo Lombardo, Piero Regnoli; *Photography:* color, Supercinescope, aspect ratio 2.35:1; running time: 92 minutes, released 1962.

Cast: Ken Clark *(Astolfo)*; Gérard Landry *(Riccardo)*; Moira Orfei *(Grenda)*; Piero Lulli *(Manfredi)*; Renata Monteduro *(Orabile)*; Vittorio André; Anita Berti; Marcello Bonini Olas; Carla Calò *(Bibiana)*; Beryl Cunningham *(Grenda's Black Maid Servant)*; Joe Kamel; Piero Leri *(Giordano)*; Gianni Loti; Nino Musco *(Orabile's Father)*; Renato Navarrini; Aldo Peri *(Baron Berthold)*; Daniela Regnoli *(Grenda's Maid Servant)*.

Comments: This action-adventure was produced by Italy's Retix Cinematografica. Leading man Ken Clark also starred in Roger Corman's cult horror opus *Attack of the Giant Leeches*.

Desert Desperadoes *(La peccatrice del deserto)* (Principal Distributing, 1959)

Credits: Directors: Steve Sekely, Gianni Vernuccio; *Producer:* John G. Nasht; *Screenplay:* Victor Stoloff (from his story); *Photography:* Massimo Dellamano (black & white, aspect ratio 1.37:1); *Music:* Mario Nascimbene; *Costume Design:* Giancarlo Bartolini Salimbeni; running time: 81 minutes; released July 1959 (U.S.).

Cast: Ruth Roman *(The Woman)*; Akim Tamiroff *(The Merchant)*; Otello Toso *(Verrus)*; Gianni Musy *(Fabius)*; Arnoldo Foà *(The Chaldean)*; Alan Furlan *(Rais)*; Nino Marchetti *(Metullius)*.

Comments: A quasi-biblical tale dealing with King Herod's edict condemning all male children to death. Produced by Italy's Venturini-Express-Nasht, and filmed in Egypt and Turin, Italy.

Desert Warrior (Los amantes del desierto) (Medallion Pictures, 1957)

Credits: Directors: Goffredo Alessandrini, Fernando Cerchio, León Klimovsky, Gianni Vernuccio; *Producers:* Carlo Infascelli, Benito Perojo; *Line Producer:* Miguel Tudela; *Screenplay:* Edoardo Anton, Oreste Biancoli, Leo Bomba, Giuseppe Mangione (from a story by Manuel Villegas López, adaptation by Alfonso Paso, Mariano Ozares); *Photography:* Antonio L. Ballesteros, Mario Damicelli (Eastmancolor, CinemaScope, aspect ratio 2.35:1); *Film Editor:* Antonio Ramírez de Loaysa; *Music:* Michel Michelet; *Production Design and Set Decoration:* Sigfrido Burmann, Mario Garbuglia; *Costume Design:* Beni Montresor; *Makeup:* Carmen Martín; *Hair Stylist:* Josefa Rubio; *Production Managers:* Manuel Castedo, Enrique F. Sagaseta; *Assistant Director:* Ricardo Muñoz Suay; *Props:* Manuel Martínez, Miguel Pérez Marián; *Construction Coordinator:* Francisco Rodríguez Asensio; *Camera Operators:* Allejandro Ulloa, Ricardo Navarrete; *Assistant Cameramen:* Fernando Guillot, José Marina, Luis Peña; *Still Photographers:* Luis Beringola, Miguel Ángel García Basabé, Miguel Guzmán, Nicholás Javier, Antonio Lara, Simón López, Antonio Ortas; *Assistant Film Editors:* Teresa Bort, Maria Teresa Ortiz; *Orchestrators:* José Garcia Bernalt, Alberto Moya; *Production Assistant:* Ricardo Diaz; *Script Supervisor:* Carmen Pageo; running time: 87 minutes (Italy); released December 22, 1958 (Italy), November 1961 (U.S.).

Cast: Carmen Sevilla *(Princess Amina)*; Ricardo Montalban *(Prince Said)*; Gino Cervi *(Ibrahim)*; José Guardiola *(Kamal)*; Franca Bettoia *(Suleika)*; Manuel Guitián; Domingo Rivas; Manuel Alcón; Mariangela Giordano; Joaquín Bergía; Félix Briones; Pilar Gómez Ferrer; Anna Maria Ferrero; Arnoldo Foà; Samia Gamal.

Comments: Prince Said vows revenge on the evil Ibrahim, who has murdered his father. Produced by Italy's Films Benito Perojo and Roma Film, in association with France's Parc Film and Germany's Rialto Film.

Devil of the Desert Against the Son of Hercules (Anthar l'invincibile) (Avco Embassy, 1964)

Credits: Director: Antonio Margheriti; *Producer:* Luigi Nannerini; *Screenplay:* Guido Malatesta, Arturo Rigel, André Tabet (from their story); *Photography:* Alejandro Ulloa (Technicolor, Techniscope, aspect ratio: 2.35:1); *Film Editors:* Otello Colangeli, Antonio Ramírez Loaysa; *Music:* Georges Garvarentz; *Set Decoration:* Ottavio Scotti; *Costume Design:* Vittorio Rossi; *Special Effects:* Dino Galiano; *Production Manager:* Nino Masini; *Assistant Director:* Ruggero Deodato; running time: 114 minutes (Italy), 93 minutes (U.S.); released June 27, 1964 (Italy); video availability: Something Weird Video.

Cast: Kirk Morris *(Anthar)*; Michèle Girardon *(Princess Soraya)*; Renato Baldini *(Kamal)*; Mario Feliciani *(Ganor)*; José Jaspe *(Akrim)*; Manuel Gallardo *(Prince Daikor)*; Nadine Verdier *(Slave Girl)*; Roberto Dell'Acqua *(Aimu, the Mute)*; Howard Ross *(Hasien)*; Pietro Tordi *(Slave Market Bidder)*; Ugo Sasso *(Murad)*; Giacomo Furia *(Salene)*; Laura Nucci *(Adonna)*; Tanya Lopert *(Slave Girl)*; Fedele Gentile *(Slave Market Bidder)*; Serena Michelotti *(Slave Girl)*; Beryl Cunningham *(Black Slave Girl)*; Goffredo Unger *(Rabek)*.

Comments: Heroic rebel Anthar falls in love with the beautiful Princess Soraya, and aids her in regaining the throne usurped by evil tyrant Ganor, who murdered her father. Originally titled *Anthar the Invincible (Anthar l'Invincibile)*, this film was retitled *The Devil of the Desert Against the Son of Hercules* for inclusion in Avco Embassy's *The Sons of Hercules* syndicated television series. This series involved a group of 14 peplum (all *qv*), retitled and re-edited, distributed under the title *The Sons of Hercules*. Only two of the series titles *(Ulysses Against the Son of Hercules,* originally *Ulysses Against Hercules)* and *The Son of Hercules in the Land of Darkness,* originally *Hercules the Invincible)* actually featured the Hercules character; four of the other titles had originally been Maciste films, two were Ursus movies, and the other six were random gladiator titles, all unified under *The Sons of Hercules* umbrella. The 14 titles were: *Ursus, Son of Hercules* (originally *The Mighty Ursus*), *Mole Men vs. the Son of Hercules* (originally *Maciste, the Strongest Man in the World*), *Triumph of the Son of Hercules* (originally *The Triumph of Maciste*), *Fire Monsters Against the Son of Hercules* (originally *Maciste vs. the Monsters*), *Venus Against the Son of Hercules* (originally *Mars, God of War*), *Ulysses Against the Son of Hercules* (originally *Ulysses Against Hercules*), *Medusa Against the Son of Hercules* (originally *Perseus the Invincible*), *The Son of Hercules in the Land of Fire* (originally *Ursus in the Land of Fire*), *The Tyrant of Lydia Against the Son of Hercules* (originally *Goliath and the Rebel Slave*), *Messalina Against the Son of Hercules* (originally *The Last Gladiator*), *The Beast of Babylon Against the Son of Hercules* (originally *Hero of Babylon*), *The Terror of Rome Against the Son of Hercules* (originally *Maciste, Gladiator of Sparta*), *The Son of Hercules in the Land of Darkness* (originally *Hercules the Invincible*), and the title under discussion here, *The Devil of the Desert against the Son of Hercules*, which, in addition to its original title of *Anthar the Invincible*, was also known as *The Slave Merchants* and *Soraya, Queen of the Desert*. A further illusion of series continuity was provided by a catchy introductory theme song belted out by a male chorus.

The Devil's Cavaliers (I cavalieri del diablo) (Galassia Cinematografica, 1959)

Credits: *Director:* Siro Marcellini; *Producers:* Argy Robelli, Edoardo Robelli; *Executive Producer:* Giulio Fiasch; *Screenplay:* Carlo Alberto Chiesa, Siro Marcellini (from a story by Jean Blondel and Siro Marcellini); *Dialogue:* Ugo Moretti; *Photography:* Luciano Trasatti (Eastmancolor); *Film Editor:* Edmond Lozzi; *Music:* Carmine Rizzo; *Art Direction:* Oscar D'Amico; *Set Decoration:* Bruno Avesani; *Costume Design:* Manta Louisa Danari; *Makeup:* Guglielmo Bonotti; Andrea Riva; *Hair Stylist:* Rocchetti; *Production Managers:* Antonio Dalumb, Aio Robelli; *Assistant Director:* Franco Balbintlio; *Sound:* Adriano Taloni; *Camera Operator:* Franco Villa; *Assistant Camera Operator:* Saverio Diamante; *Music Director:* Pietro Argento; *Fencing Masters:* Franco Fantasia, Andrea Fantasia; *Assistant to the Director:* Filiberto Fiaschi; *Continuity:* Lucia Yagunta; *Production Secretary:* Luigi Ebstanian; running time: 92 minutes (U.S.); released June 26, 1959 (Italy); video availability: Something Weird Video.

Cast: Frank Latimore *(Capt. Richard Stiller)*; Emma Danieli *(Countess Louise Valance)*; Gianna Maria Canale *(Baroness Elaine of Faldone)*; Gabriella Palotta *(Giuselle, Louise's Maid)*; Anthony Steffen *(Richmond)*; Andrea Aureli *(Duke of Vas)*; Federica Ranchi *(Derolia, the Barmaid)*; Franco Fantasia *(Duneil, the Swordsman)*; Mirko Ellis *(Paul, Stiller's Henchman)*; José Jaspe *(Jermaine, Stiller's Henchman)*; Oreste Lionello; Andrea Fantasia; Carlo Bressan; Pasquale De Filippo; Franco Diana; Fedele Gentile; Loris Gizzi; Lea Monaco; Nino Musco; Bruno Parisio; Andrea Scotti; Nunzio Gallo; Regina Dainelli.

Comments: A costume drama set in the Late French Renaissance period, featuring a rebellion against the nobility. Produced by Italy's Galassia Cinematografica, and filmed at Castello di Ostia, Ostia Antica, Rome, and Monte Gelato Falls on the Treja River, Lazio, Italy.

Diary of a Roman Virgin (Diario di una vergine Romana) (1973)

Credits: *Director:* Joe D'Amato; *Screenplay:* Joe D'Amato (billed as "Michael Wotruba"); *Music:* Berto Pisano; *Photography:* Joe D'Amato [billed as "Aristide Massaccesi"] (color); *Film Editor:* Piera Bruni; running time: 75 minutes, released 1973 (Italy).

Cast: Lucretia Love; Linda Sini; Atilo Dottesio; Edmondo Tieghi; Stefano Spitoni; Danilo Mezzetti; Antonio Casale; Emanuele Seguino; Luigi Antonio Guerra; Domenico Maggio.

Comments: This low-budget film was padded with footage lifted from *The Last Days of Pompeii* (1960), *Triumph of the Ten Gladiators* (1964), and *The Arena* (1974). Co-produced by Italy's 1 Aprile Cinematografica and Galassia Cinematografica.

Don Cesare di Bazan (Don Cesare di Bazan) (Artisti Associati, 1942)

Credits: *Director/Producer:* Riccardo Freda; *Screenplay:* Sergio Amidei, Vitaliano Brancati, Giacomo De Benedetti, Philippe Dumanoir, Cesare Zavattini, Riccardo Freda (based on a play by Adolphe d'Ennery); *Photography:* Mario Craveri (black-and-white, aspect ratio 1.37:1);

Film Editor: Rolando Benedetti; *Music:* Franco d'Achiardi; *Production Design:* Gastone Medin; *Set Decoration:* Guglielmo G. Borzone; *Costume Design:* Gino Sensani, Maria De Matteis; *Production Supervisor:* Paolo Frasca; *Production Manager:* Piero Cocco; *1st Assistant Director:* Fede Arnaud, *2nd Assistant Director:* Mario Tarchetti; *Construction Coordinator:* Savino Fino; *Sound Engineer:* Tommaso Barberini; *Camera Operators:* Amieto Daissé, Ubaldo Marelli; *Assistant Camera Operator:* Marcello Gatti; running time: 78 minutes; released October 4, 1942.

Cast: Gino Cervi *(Don Cesare Di Bazan)*; Annelise Uhlig *(Renée Dumas)*; Paolo Stoppa *(Sancho)*; Enrico Glori *(Viscount di Beaumont)*; Enzo Biliotti *(Filippo IV)*; Giovanni Grasso *(Don José of Nogueira)*; Carlo Duse *("The Crow," The Viscount's Messenger)*; Antonio Marietti *(Young Count)*; Alfredo Robert *(Pasquale Cornalis)*; Sandrino Morino *(Child)*; Anna Maria Dionisi *(Renée's Maid)*; Ermanno Donati *(Velasquez)*; Antonio Acqua *(Capt. Ribera)*; Armando Francioli *(Knight)*; Alfredo Martinelli *(Conspirator)*; Angelo Dessy *(Conspirator)*; Pietro Tordi *(Actor)*; Cellio Bucchi *(Duke of Orovesa)*; Umberto Scianizza *(Innkeeper)*; Evaristo Signorini *(Conspirator)*, Mario Besesti *(Voice Dubbing for Giovanni Grasso)*; Tina Lattanzi *(Voice Dubbing for Annelise Uhlig)*; Stefano Sibaldi *(Voice Dubbing for Enzo Biliotti)*.

Comments: Catalonia attempts to secede from the Spanish Empire in this costume drama, filmed during Mussolini's reign. Produced by Italy's Artisti Associati and Elica Film. Remade (by the same director) as *The Seventh Sword* (1962) *(qv)*.

Dragon's Blood (Sigfrido) (Fortunia Film, 1957)

Credits: Director: Giacomo Gentilomo; *Producer:* Antonio Ferrigno; *Screenplay:* Giorgio Costantini, Antonio Ferrigno, Giacomo Gentilomo, Cesare Vico Ludovico; *Photography:* Carlo Nebiolo (Eastmancolor, Supercinescope, aspect ratio 2.35:1); *Film Editor:* Rodolfo Novelli; *Music:* Franco Langella; *Production Design:* Beni Montresor; *Makeup:* Antonio Marini, Oscar Pacelli; *Hair Stylist:* Anna Fabrizi; *Production Managers:* Alberto Cinquini, Gennaro Masullo, Fernando Rossi; *Assistant Directors:* Franco Cirino, Ettore Maria Fizzarotti; *Sound:* Kurt Doubrowsky, Emilio Rosa; (Westrex Sound System); *Assistant Art Directors:* Giuseppe Ranieri, Mario Sertoli; *Special Effects (Dragon):* Carlo Rambaldi; *Matte Shots:* Joseph Nathanson; *Laboratory:* Sviluppo Pelicole e Stampa (SPEC), Rome, Italy; *Camera Operator:* Stelvio Massi; *Assistant Cameraman:* Antonio Belviso; *2nd Assistant Cameramen:* Luigi Bernardini, Mario Mancini; *2nd Unit Camera Operator:* Enrico Cignitti; *2nd Unit Assistant Cameraman:* Enrico Priori; *Still Photographer:* Tito Consolazione; *Wardrobe:* Elena Nicolai; *Assistant Costume Designers:* Luciana Angelini, Adriana Berselli; *Color Timer:* Giovanni Taccari; *Script Supervisors:* Gennaro Ballistrieri, Lina D'Amico; running time: 93 minutes (Italy), 97 minutes (U.S.); released 1957.

Cast: Sebastian Fischer *(Siegfried)*; Ilaria Occhini *(Kriemhild)*; Rolf Tasna *(Hagen)*; Katharina Mayberg *(Brunhild)*; Giorgio Costantini *(Gunther)*; Franca Mazzoni *(Ute)*; Giulio Donnini *(Alberico)*; Alberto Cinquini *(Mime)*; Enrico Olivieri *(Gisselher)*; Germano Longo *(Gerenot)*; Tina Gloriani *(Siglinde)*; Philippe Hersent *(Danwarth)*; Livio Lorenzon; Pietro Tordi; Bianca Doria; Stelio Candelli; Gregor Bals; John Gambino; Brunetta Ameliese; Joky Gambino; Cristina De Angelis.

Comments: A medieval fantasy based on Germany's 13th century Nibelungenlied Saga. The giant dragon in this film is one of the earliest creations of special effects technician Carlo Rambaldi, who was later responsible for *King Kong* (1976) and *E.T.* (1982).

The Dream of Zorro (Il sogno di Zorro) (Industrie Cinematografiche Sociali/Titanus, 1952)

Credits: Director: Mario Soldati; *Producer:* Niccolò Theodoli; *Screenplay:* Mario Amendola, Marcello Marchesi (based on a story by Mario Amendola, Sandro Continenza, Ruggero Maccari, Marcello Marchesi, Vittorio Metz); *Photography:* Carlo Montuori, Mario Montuori (black-and-white, aspect ratio 1.37:1); *Film Editor:* Renato Cinquini; *Music:* Mario Nascimbene; *Costume Design:* Vittorio Nino Novarese; *Master of Arms:* Enzo Musumeci Greco; running time: 93 minutes; released March 26, 1952.

Cast: Walter Chiari *(Don Reimundo Esteban);* Delia Scala *(Gloria/Estrella/Dolores);* Vittorio Gassman *(Don Antonio/Juan);* Umberto Aquillino *(José);* Anna Arena *(Innkeeper);* Sandro Bianchi *(Pablo/Ramon);* Pietro Capanna *(Manuel);* Giorgio Costantini *(Captain);* Juan de Landa *(César/Pedro);* Augusto Di Giovanni *(Don Formoso);* Giovanni Dolfini *(Don Alonzo);* Claudio Ermelli *(Maestro);* Giacomo Furia *(Panchito);* Sophia Loren [billed as "Sofia Scicolone"] *(Conchita);* Michele Malaspina *(Perez);* Gisella Monaldi *(Luisa/Consuelo);* Guido Morisi *(Ignazio);* Luigi Pavese *(Don Garcia Fernandez);* Michèle Philippe *(Maria/Marta);* Riccardo Rioli *(Notaio);* Gualtiero Tumiati *(Don Cesar Alcazan);* Nietta Zocchi *(Dona Hermosa Alcazan).*

Comments: Another Italian film adaptation of Zorro, produced by Industrie Cinematografiche Sociali in association with Titanus.

Duel of Champions (Orazi e Curiazi) (Medallion Pictures, 1961)

Credits: Director: Ferdinando Baldi; *Producer:* Angelo Ferrara; *Screenplay:* Ennio De Concini, Carlo Lizzani, Giuliano Montaldo (from a story by Luciano Vincenzoni); *Photography:* Amerigo Gengarelli (Eastmancolor, Totalscope, aspect ratio 2.35:1); *Film Editor:* Renzo Lucidi; *Music;* Angelo Francesco Lavagnino; *Production Designers:* Dragoljub Ivkov, Massimo Palmiri; *Art Direction:* Giulio Bongini, Vlado Brankovic; *Costume Design:* Mario Giorsi; *Makeup:* Michele Trimarchi; *Hair Stylist:* Lina Cassini; *Production Manager:* Luigi Bigerna; *Assistant Director:* Andrea Volpe; *Art Dept. Manager:* Italo Tomassi; *Assistant Set Decorator:* Giorgina Baldoni; *Camera Operator:* Cesare Allione; *Orchestra Conductor:* Luigi Urbini; *Production Assistants:* Angelo Binarelli, Angelo Cittadini, Mauro Sacripanti; running time: 90 minutes (Italy), 105 minutes (U.S.); released October 19, 1961 (Italy) August 1964 (U.S.); video availability: VCI.

Cast: Alan Ladd *(Horatio);* Franca Bettoia *(Marcia);* Franco Fabrizi *(Curazio);* Robert Keith *(Tullio Hostillo, King of Rome);* Jacqueline Derval *(Horatia);* Luciano Marin *(Eli);* Andrea Aureli *(King of Alba);* Mino Doro *(Caius);* Osvaldo Ruggieri *(Warrior of Alba);* Piero Palermini *(Nevio);* Violette Marceau *(Slave);* Umberto Raho *(Grand Priest);* Alfredo Varelli *(Sabinus);* Evi Marandi *(Slave);* Alana Ladd *(Scilla);* Nando Angelini *(Official);* Franca Pasut *(Slave);* Jacques Sernas *(Marcus);* William Conroy *(Roman Soldier);* Andrej Gardenin *(Fencer).*

Comments: A tired Alan Ladd, his Hollywood film career over, stars in this epic, co-produced by Italy's Lux Film and Tiberia Film, in association with Yugoslavia's Lovcen Film. Shot at Centralni Filmski Studio in Belgrade, Serbia.

Duel of the Titans (Romolo e Remo) (Paramount, 1961)

Credits: Director: Sergio Corbucci; *Supervising Producers:* Sergio Borelli, Roberto Moretti; *General Producer:* Mario Musy Glori; *Producers:* Tonino Cervi, Alessandro Jacovini; *Screenplay:* Luciano Martino, Sergio Carbucci, Ennio De Concini, Luciano Martino, Franco Rossetti, Duccio Tessari, Sergio Leone (from a story by Luciano Martino, Sergio Corbucci, Sergio Leone); *Dialogue:* Adriano Bolzoni, Sergio Leone; *Photography:* Enzo Barboni (Eastmancolor, CinemaScope, aspect ratio 2.35:1); *Film Editor:* Gabriele Varriale; *Music:* Piero Piccioni; *Production Design:* Saverio D'Eugenio; *Set Decoration:* Carlo Simi; *Costume Design:* Cesare Rovatti; *Makeup:* Thea Boggiatto, Mario Van Riel; *Hair Stylist:* Anna Cristofani; *Production Manager:* Franco Palaggi; *2nd Unit Production Manager:* Vittorio Musy Glori; *Assistant Directors:* Roberto Fizz, Mimmola Girosi, Guido Zurli; *2nd Unit Director:* Franco Giraldi; *Assistant Set Decorators:* Giovanni Axeri, Gianfranco Lowle; *Tapestries:* Alfredo D'Angelo; *Special Effects:* Lamberto Verde; *Weapons Supervisor:* Domenico Damiani; *Fencing Master:* Benito Stefanelli; *Stunts:* Nicola Di Gioia; *Camera Operators:* Emilio Giannini, Stelvio Massi; *2nd Unit Director of Photography:* Dario Di Palma; *Key Grip:* Romolo Romangoli; *Gaffer:* Remo Dolci; *Still Photographer:* G.B. Poletto; *Costume Seamstress:* Adriana Masseroni; *Orchestra Conductor:* Piero Piccioni; *Production Assistants:* Gianni di

Stolfo; Alberto Giomareli, Francesco Merli; *Script Supervisors:* Renata Melingò, Eschilo Tarquini; *Laboratory:* Technostampa (Rome, Italy); running time: 108 minutes (Italy), 89 minutes (U.S.); released December 6, 1961 (Italy), June 1963 (U.S.); video availability: Sinister Cinema.

Cast: Steve Reeves *(Romulus)*; Gordon Scott *(Remus)*; Virna Lisi *(Julia)*; Franco Volpi *(Amulio)*; Laura Solari *(Rea Silvia)*; Piero Lulli *(Sulpicius)*; José Greci *(Estia)*; Gianni Musy *(Romulus' Companion)*; Inger Milton *(Sira)*; Enzo Cerusico *(Numa Pompillo)*; Andrea Bosic *(Faustolo)*; Enrico Glori *(Citizen of Alba)*; Franco Balducci *(Acilio)*; Germano Longo *(Scebro)*; Bruno Tocci *(Pristino)*; Giuliano Dell'Ovo *(Publio)*; Nando Angelini *(Roman Soldier)*; Massimo Girotti *(King Tazio)*; Ornella Vanoni *(Tarpeia)*; Jacques Sernas *(Curzio)*; Giovanni Di Benedetto *(Official)*; Mimmo Poli *(Pastore)*; Consalvo Dell'Arti *(Spectator at Games)*; Benito Stefanelli *(Soldier)*; Giovanni Cianfriglia *(Man with Whip)*.

Comments: The producers originally planned to cast Steve Reeves as *both* Romulus and Remus (the legendary founders of Rome) in this epic, but when Reeves balked at playing a dual role, he recommended Gordon Scott for the part of Remus. This film was a co-production between Italy's Titanus and Ajace Produzioni Cinematografiche and France's Société Nouvelle Pathé Cinéma (S.N.L.P.) and Société Générale de Cinématographie. The production was shot at Titanus Studios, Rome and at Teatri della Farnesina, Rome.

El Cid (Il Cid) (Allied Artists, 1961)

Credits: Director: Anthony Mann; *Producer:* Samuel Bronston; *Associate Producers:* Jaime Prades, Michal Waszynski; *Screenplay:* Philip Yordan, Fredric M. Frank, Ben Barzman (from a story by Fredric M. Frank); *Photography:* Robert Krasker (Technicolor, Technirama, aspect ratio 2.35:1); *Film Editor:* Robert Lawrence; *Music:* Miklós Rózsa; *Production Design, Set Decoration and Costume Design:* Veniero Colasanti, John Moore; *Makeup:* Mario Van Riel; *Hair Stylist:* Grazia De Rossi; *Production Managers:* Leon Chooluck, Guy Luongo; *Unit Manager;* Tadeo Villalba; *2nd Unit Director:* Yakima Canutt; *Assistant Directors:* José López Rodero, José María Ochoa; *First Assistant Director:* Luciano Sacripanti; *Assistant Set Decorators:* José María Alarcón, Vicente Sempere; *Paintings and Drawings:* Marciak Piotrowski; *Painter:* Julián Martín; *Props:* Stanley Detlie; *Sound:* Jack Solomon; *Sound Editor:* Verna Fields; *Sound Mixing:* Gordon K. McCallum; *Special Effects:* Jack Erikson, Alex Weldon; *Special Effects Assistants:* Antonio Baquero, Antonio Bueno; *Stunts:* Buff Brady, Jerry Brown, Joe Canutt, Tap Canutt, Enzo Musumeci Greco, Miguel Pedregosa, Jack Williams; *2nd Unit Director of Photography:* Manuel Berenguer; *Camera Operator:* John Harris; *Head Grip:* Carl Gibson; *Supervising Electrician:* Norton Kurland; *Wardrobe Director:* Gloria Musetta; *Assistant to the Editor:* Magdalena Paradell; *Music Editor:* Edna Bullock; *Orchestrator:* Eugene Zador; *Orchestra Leader:* Lucie Svehlova; *Writer of Italian Version:* Diego Fabbri; *2nd Assistant to the Director:* Julio Sempere; *Design Consultant:* Armondo Linus Acosta; *Fencing Instructor:* Enzo Musumeci Greco; *Script Supervisor:* Pat Miller; running time: 182 minutes; released October 24, 1961 (Italy), December 14, 1961 (U.S.); video availability: Genius Products.

Cast: Charlton Heston *(El Cid Rodrigo de Vivar)*; Sophia Loren *(Jimena)*; Raf Vallone *(Count Ordóñez)*; Geneviève Page *(Princess Urraca)*; John Fraser *(Prince Alfonso)*; Gary Raymond *(Prince Sancho)*; Hurd Hatfield *(Arias)*; Massimo Serato *(Fanez)*; Frank Thring *(Al Kadir)*; Michael Hordern *(Don Diego)*; Andrew Cruickshank *(Count Gormaz)*; Douglas Wilmer *(Moutamin)*; Tullio Carminati *(Priest)*; Ralph Truman *(King Ferdinand)*; Christopher Rhodes *(Don Martin)*; Carlo Giustini *(Bermúdez)*; Gérard Tichy *(King Ramirez)*; Fausto Tozzi *(Dolfos)*; Barbara Everest *(Mother Superior)*; Katina Noble *(Nun)*; Nerio Bernardi *(Soldier)*; Franco Fantasia *(Soldier)*; Herbert Lom *(Ben Yussuf)*; Antonio Mayans; Paul Muller *(Arabian Assistant Doctor)*; Paul Naschy; Rosalba Neri *(Harem Girl)*; Robert Rietty *(Voice of Fanez)*; Vergilio Teixeira.

Comments: An action-filled profile of the Castillian nobleman and military leader Rodrigo de Vivar (circa 1043–1099) and his adventures in medieval Spain. An impressive production that grossed in excess of $26,000,000 and was nominated for three Academy Awards—for Art Direction, Best Music Score, and Original Song, although it did not win in any of these categories. There was some degree of animosity between Charlton Heston and Sophia Loren during production, resulting in difficulties, particularly in their more intimate scenes together. Loren was one of the first actresses to receive a $1,000,000 fee for her services, which was more than Heston's salary. A 1993 restoration added 16 minutes of previously cut footage to the movie. Produced by Samuel Bronston in association with Italy's Dear Film Produzione. Filmed at Rome's Titanus Studios and various locations in Spain.

Erik the Conqueror (Gli invasori) (American International, 1961)

Credits: *Director:* Mario Bava; *Producer:* Ferruccio De Martino; *Screenplay:* Mario Bava, Oreste Biancoli, Piero Pierotti (based on their story); *Photography:* Mario Bava (Technicolor, Dyaliscope, aspect ratio 2.35:1); *Film Editor:* Mario Serandrei; *Music:* Les Baxter (U.S. Release), Roberto Nicolosi; *Makeup:* Euclide Santoli; *Hair Stylist:* Mara Rocchetti; *Production Manager:* Massimo De Rita; *Unit Managers:* Armando Govoni, Paolo Mercuri; *Assistant Directors:* Franco Prosperi, Tonino Ricci; *Set Designer:* Giorgio Giovannini; *Set Dresser:* Massimo Tavazzi; *Sound:* Roberto Mattioli; *Supervising Sound Editor:* Pierta Vesperini; *Boom Operator:* Aldo Zanni; *Stunts:* Nicola Di Gioia; *Camera Operators:* Giovanni Narzisi, Ubaldo Terzano; *1st Assistant Cameraman:* Enrico Fontana; *2nd Assistant Cameraman:* Giuseppe Berta; *Wardrobe:* Tina Grani; *Assistant Film Editor:* Lina Caterini; *Orchestra Conductor:* Luigi Urbini; *Soundtrack Album Producer:* Luca di Silvetro; *Choreography:* Leopoldo Sonova; *Voice Dubbing:* Fiorella Betti (for Ellen Kessler); Maria Pia Di Meo (for Alice Kessler); *Production Secretary:* Arturo Padovani; running time: 98 minutes (Italy), 81 minutes (U.S.); released December 7, 1961 (Italy), June 12, 1963 (U.S.); video availability: Anchor Bay.

Cast: Cameron Mitchell *(Eron)*; Alice Kessler *(Rama)*; Ellen Kessler *(Daya)*; George Ardisson *(Erik, Duke of Helford)*; Andrea Checchi *(Sir Rutford)*; Jean-Jacques Delbo *(Olaf)*; Franco Giacobini *(Rustchello)*; Raf Baldassarre *(Blak)*; Enzo Doria *(Bennet)*; Gianni Solaro *(Ranco)*; Franco Ressel *(King Lotar)*; Livia Contardi *(Hadda)*; Folco Lulli *(Harad, re dei Vichinghi)*; Françoise Christophe *(Regina Alice)*; Joe Robinson *(Garlan)*.

Comments: An excellent Viking adventure (taking place in 786 AD), well-made by director Mario Bava (1914–1980), who always knew how to get the most out of his production money and resources. Co-produced by Italy's Galatea Film, with France's Lyre Film and Critérion Film. Shot at Rome's Titanus Studios.

Esther and the King (Ester e il re) (20th Century–Fox, 1960)

Credits: *Directors:* Raoul Walsh, Mario Bava (Italian Version); *Producer:* Raoul Walsh; *Associate Producer:* John Twist; *Screenplay:* Raoul Walsh, Michael Elkins, Ennio De Concini; *Photography:* Mario Bava (Technicolor, CinemaScope, aspect ratio 2.35:1); *Film Editor:* Jerry Webb; *Music:* Angelo Francesco Lavagnino, Roberto Nicolosi; *Art Direction:* Giorgio Giovannini; *Makeup:* Euclide Santoli; *Hair Stylist:* Manilo Rocchetti; *Production Supervisor:* Ferruccio De Martino; *Production Manager:* Mike Holden; *Unit Manager:* Massimo De Rita; *Assistant Director:* Ottavio Oppo; *Camera Operator:* Ubaldo Terzano; *Costume Supervisor:* Anna Maria Feo; *Producer of Soundtrack Album:* Luca di Silverio; *Dialogue Coach:* Harriet Medin; running time: 109 minutes; released February 17, 1961 (Italy), November 18, 1960 (U.S.); video availability: St. Clair Vision.

Cast: Joan Collins *(Esther)*; Richard Egan *(King Ahasuerus)*; Denis O'Dea *(Mordecai)*; Sergio Fantoni *(Haman)*; Rik Battaglia *(Simon)*; Renato Baldini *(Klydrathes)*; Gabriele Tinti *(Samual)*; Rosalba Neri *(Keresh)*; Robert Buchanan *(Hegai)*; Daniela Rocca *(Queen Vashti)*; Folco Lulli *(Tobiah)*; Pietro Ceccarelli *(Bald Gladiator)*; Ombretta Ostenda; Aldo Pini *(Captain of the Guards)*; Howard Ross *(Gladiator)*; Claudio Ruffini *(Persian Guard)*; Attilo Severini *(Persian Soldier Giving a Cup to Ahasuerus)*; Italo Tancredi *(Gisco)*.

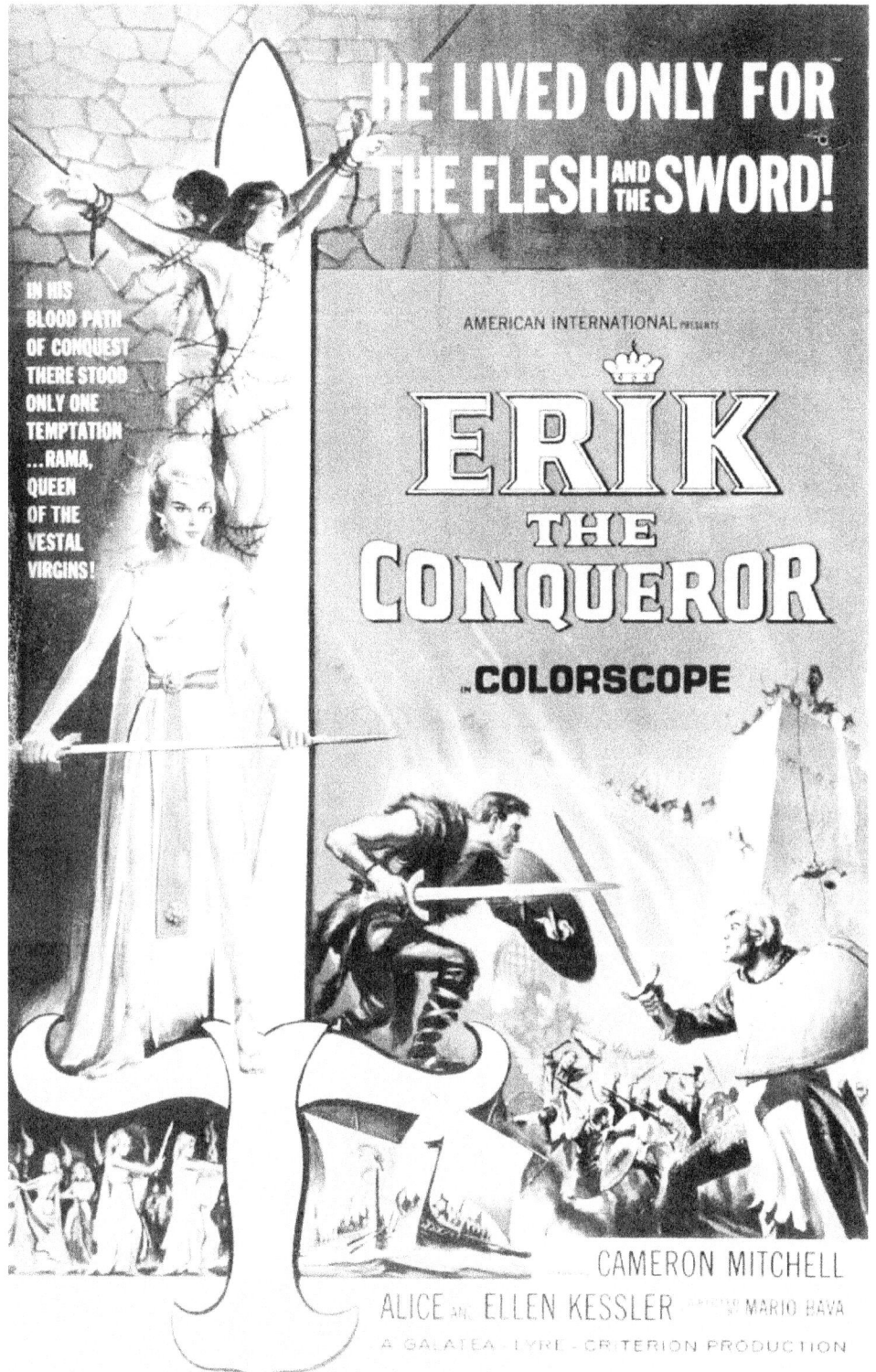

Poster for *Erik the Conqueror*.

Comments: An Old Testament story of court intrigue, which had originally been intended (just after her appearance in DeMille's *Samson and Delilah*) as a vehicle for Hedy Lamarr. Produced by Italy's Galatea Film and Titanus in association with Twentieth Century–Fox.

The Executioner of Venice (Il boia di Venezia) (Liber Film, 1963)

Credits: Director: Luigi Capuano; *Producer:* Ottavio Poggi; *Executive Producer:* Nino Battiferri; *Screenplay:* Luigi Capuano, Arpad DeRiso, Milton Krims (from a story by Ottavio Poggi); *Photography:* Alvaro Mancori (Eastmancolor, Totalscope, aspect ratio 2.35:1); *Film Editor:* Antonietta Zita, *Music:* Carlo Rustichelli; *Set Decoration:* Ernest Kromberg; *Costume Design and Set Design:* Giancarlo Bartolini Salimbeni; *Makeup:* Eligio Trani; *Hair Stylist:* Marisa Fraticelli; *Assistant Director:* John Alarimo; *Sound:* Magia Fiorenzo; *Camera Operator:* Sandro Mancori; *Assistant Cameraman:* Grillo Spadini; *Still Photographer:* Rinascimento Laselli; *Assistant Costume Designer:* Elio Micheli; *Production Assistants:* Diego Alchimede, Arrigo Peri; *Continuity:* Anna Maria Padoan, Maria Luisa Rosen; *Director of English Language Version:* Richard McNamara; running time: 90 minutes; released September 20, 1963 (Italy); video availability: Sinister Cinema.

Cast: Lex Barker *(Sandrigo Bembo)*; Guy Madison *(Rodrigo Zeno)*; Alessandra Panaro *(Leonora Danin)*; Mario Petri *(Boia Guamieri)*; Alberto Farnese *(Michele Arcà)*; Giulio Marchetti *(Bartolo)*; Feodor Chaliapin, Jr. *(Doge Giovanni Bembo)*; Franco Fantasia *(Pietro)*; Raf Baldassarre *(Messere Grimani)*; Mirella Roxy *(Smeralda)*; Marija Tocinoski; John Bartha *(Messere Leonardo)*; Attilio Severini; Giulio Maculani; Giuliana Farnese; Romano Giomini.

Comments: This swashbuckler, set in the 17th century, was produced by Italy's Liber Film, with scenes shot on location in Venice.

Fabiola (United Artists, 1949)

Credits: Director: Alessandro Blasetti; *Producer:* Salvo D'Angelo; *Screenplay:* Alessandro Blasetti, Jean-Georges Auriol, Antonio Pietrangeli, Diego Fabbri, Cesare Zavattini, Emilio Cecchi, Vitaliano Brancati, Corrado Pavolini, Umberto Barbaro, Renato Castellani, Suso Cecchi D'Amico, Mario Chiari, Lionello De Felice, Alberto Vecchietti (from a story by Alessandro Blasetti, Mario Chiari, Diego Fabbri, based on the novel by Nicholas Patrick Wiseman); *Photography:* Mario Craveri, Ubaldo Marelli (black & white, aspect ratio 1.37:1); *Film Editor:* Mario Serandrei; *Music:* Enzo Masetti; *Production Design:* Arnaldo Foschini; *Set Decoration and Costume Design:* Veniero Colasanti; *Makeup:* Guglielmo Bonotti, Camillo De Rossi; *Production Supervisor:* Orlando Orsini; *Production Managers:* Attilo Fattori, Renato Silvestri; *Assistant Directors:* Lionello De Felice, Sergio Leone; *2nd Assistant Directors:* Marcello Baldi, Isa Bartalini; *Second 2nd Assistant Director:* Carlo Romano; *Collaborating Director:* Mario Chiari; *Set Designers:* Franco Lolli, Aldo Tommasini; *Assistant Production Designer:* Demofilo Fidani; *Construction:* Italo Tomassi; *Sound:* Ovidio Del Grande, Giovanni Paris; *Camera Operators:* Amleto Dessie, Ubaldo Marelli; *Assistant Cameraman:* Mario Sensi; *Still Photographer:* Osvaldo Civirani; *Orchestra Conductor:* Willy Ferrero;

Michèle Morgan in *Fabiola*.

Production Assistants: Giacomo Aragno, Gualtero Bagnoli, Claude Heymann; *Literary Advisor:* Giuseppe Della Torre; *Voice Dubbing:* Mario Besesti (for Michel Simon); Gualtiero De Angelis (for Massimo Girotti); Laura Gazzolo (for Sergio Tofano); Giuseppe Rinaldi (for Henri Vidal); Carlo Romano (for Guglielmo Barnabò); Sandro Ruffini (for Louis Salou); Lidia Simoneschi (for Michèle Morgan); released March 3, 1949 (Italy), May 29, 1951 (U.S.); running time: 183 minutes (Italy), 96 minutes (U.S.).

Cast: Michèle Morgan *(Fabiola)*; Henri Vidal *(Rhual)*; Michel Simon *(Senator Fabius Severus)*; Louis Salou *(Fulvius Petronius)*; Elisa Cegani *(Sira)*; Massimo Girotti *(Sebastian)*; Gino Cervi *(Quadratus)*; Sergio Tofano *(Luciano)*; Rina Morelli *(Faustina)*; Paolo Stoppa *(Proconsul Manlius Valerian)*; Carlo Ninchi *(Galba)*; Franco Interlenghi *(Corvino)*; Guglielmo Barnabò *(Antoniano Leto)*; Aldo Silvani *(Cassiano)*;, Silvana Jachino *(Lucilla)*; Umberto Sacripante *(Official)*; Gollarda Sapienza *(Cecilla)*; Virgilio Riento *(Pietro)*; Ludmilla Dudarova *(Giulia)*; Nerio Bernardi *(Imperial Messenger)*; Bella Starace Sainati *(Guardian of the Catacombs)*; Ugo Sasso, Amedeo Trilli; Hans Hinrich *(Judge/Inquisitor)*; Maurizio Di Nardo *(Tarcisio)*; Annibale Beltrone; Giovanni Caporilli; Lorena Berg *(1stt Young Patrician Woman)*; Lucciana Danieli *(2nd Young Patrician Woman)*; Flavia Grande *(3rd Young Patrician Woman)*; Olga Vittoria Gentilli; Victor Ledda; Vinicio Sofia; Paolo Ferrari; Luca Cortese *(Corbulo)*; Guido Celano *(Pompey)*; Erminio Spalla; Egisto Olivieri; Carlo Jachino; Laura Gore; Helena Makowska; Gabriele Ferzetti *(Claudius)*; Walter Lazzaro *(Armondian)*; Amalia Pellegrini; Michele Sakara; Armando Annuale; Rinaldo Smordoni; Gino Leurini; Beppe Tosi; Nino Javert; Riccardo Mangano; Paul Muller; Umberto Silvestri; Federico Collino; Gino Saltamerenda; Anna De Angelis; Darix Togni; Carla Rovere.

Comments: This drama about the virtuous daughter of a Roman senator who falls in love with a gladiator had been filmed before in the silent era *(qv)*. Today, *Fabiola*, with its blend of period romance and spectacle, looks almost like a prescient template for the scores of peplum that would appear in the 1960s. Produced by Italy's Universalia Film.

Falcon of the Desert (*La magnifica sfida*) (Wonder Films, 1965)

Credits: Director: Miguel Lluch; *Producers:* Osvaldo Civirani, María Ángel Coma Borrás; *Screenplay:* Osvaldo Civirani, Roberto Gianviti, María del Carmen, Martinez Román (from their story); *Photography:* Osvaldo Civirani (Technicolor, Techniscope, aspect ratio 2.35:1); *Music:* Ugo Filippini; *Art Direction:* Teddy Villalba; *Costume Design:* Antonio Randaccio; *Sound:* Pietro Spadoni; running time: 98 minutes (Italy); released September 10, 1965 (Italy).

Cast: Kirk Morris *(Kadir)*; Dina Loy *(Princess Amar)*; Aldo Sambrell *(Kames)*; Tomás Picó *(Hussein)*; Erika Jones *(Semira, the Dancer)*; Franco Fantasia *(Atatur)*; José Riesgo *(Omar)*; Howard Ross *(Jafar)*; Ignazio Dolce *(Sirup)*; Claudio Scarchilli *(Ali, the Innkeeper)*; Roberto Messina; Juan Cortés.

Comments: The heroic Kadir opposes the tyrant Atatur, who has conquered the city of Semares in the Arabian desert. A co-production between Italy's Wonder Films and Spain's Hispamer Films.

The Fall of Rome (*Il crollo di Roma*) (Medallion Pictures, 1963)

Credits: Director: Antonio Margheriti; *Producer:* Marco Vicario; *Screenplay:* Gianni Astolfi, Mauro Mancini, Antonio Margheriti; *Photography:* Ricardo Pallottini (Eastmancolor, Totalscope, aspect ratio 2.35:1); *Film Editor:* Renato Cinquini; *Music:* Riz Ortolani; *Makeup:* Sergio Angeloni, Franco Di Girolamo, Giuseppe Ferranti; *Hair Stylists:* Rosa Luciani, Silvana Senzacqua; *Wigs:* Silvana Senzacqua; *Production Supervisor:* Gianni di Stolfo; *Production Directors:* Nino Masini, Natalino Vicario; *Assistant Director:* Ettore Maria Fizzarotti; *Scenic Artist/Set Dresser:* Riccardo Domenici; *Sound:* Giorgio Messina, Carlo Minotrio; *Special Effects:* Dino Galiano; *Camera Operators:* Danilo Desideri, Enrico Fontana; *2nd Unit Photographer:* Nino Cristiani; *Assistant Cameramen:* Aldo Bernardini, Luigi Bernardini, Giuseppe Silva; *Wardrobe Mistresses:* Maria Pia Mancini, Maria Tonnini;

Weapons Consultant: Goffredo Unger; *Script Girl:* Tersicore Kolosoff; running time: 89 minutes; released February 28, 1963 (Italy).

Cast: Carl Möhner *(Marcus)*; Loredana Nusciak *(Svetla)*; Ida Galli *(Licia)*; Andrea Aureli *(Rako)*; Piero Palermini *(Valerio)*; Giancarlo Sbragia *(Giunio)*; Nando Tamberlani *(Matteo)*; Maria Grazia Buccella *(Xenia)*; Jim Dolen *(Caius)*; Richard Ricci *(Tulio)*; Mimmo Maggio; Robert Bettoni; Ferdinando Poggi; Claudio Scarchilli; Renato Terra; Joe Pollini.

Comments: The titular event is detailed in this epic, produced by Italy's Atlantica Cinematografica Produzione Films.

The Fighting Musketeers (Les Trois Mousquetaires: Premiere Époque— Les Ferrets de la reine) (Prodis, 1961)

Credits: Director: Bernard Borderie; *Producer:* Raymond Borderie; *Screenplay:* Jean Bernard-Luc, Bernard Borderie (adapted from the novel *The Three Musketeers* by Alexandre Dumas); *Photography:* Armand Thirard (Eastmancolor, Franscope, aspect ratio 2.35:1); *Film Editor:* Christian Gaudin; *Music:* Paul Misraki; *Set Decoration:* René Moulaert; *Costume Design:* Rosine Delamare; *Makeup:* Jean Paul Ulysse, Micheline Chaperon, Denise Lemoigne; *Hair Stylists:* Micheline Chaperon, Denise Lemoigne; *Production Manager:* Henri Jaquillard, Paul Lemaire; *Assistant Directors:* Claude Clément, Paul Nuyttens; *Assistant Set Decorators:* Sydney Bettex, Henri Sonois; *Set Dressers:* Roger Ronsin, Daniel Villeroy; *Props:* Albert Volper; *Props (Exteriors):* Pierre Roudeix, Roger Volper; *Sound:* René Sarazin (Westrex Recording System); *Assistant Sound Technicians:* Paul Pauwels, Jean Zann; *Sound Mixer:* Jean Neny; *Cameramen:* Gilles Bonneau, Louis Née; *Camera Operator:* Henri Persin; *Assistant Camera Operators:* Robert Florent, André Tixador; *Still Photographer:* Raoul Foulon; *Wardrobe:* Simone Henry, Ginette Manzon; *Costumer:* Georgette Fillon; *Assistant Film Editors:* Jacqueline Givord, Suzanne Rondeau; *Orchestra Conductor:* Jacques Métehen; *Administrator:* Roger Morand; *Stunt Advisor:* Henri Cogan; *Fencing Advisor:* Claude Carliez; *Equine Advisor:* François Nadal; *Accountant:* Robert Chevereau; *Production Secretary:* Simone Clément; *Script Supervisor:* Lily Hargous; *Laboratory:* Laboratoires Franay L.T.C. Saint-Cloud; running time: 102 minutes; released October 4, 1961 (France); video availability: Studio Canal.

Cast: Gérard Barray *(D'Artagnan)*; Georges Desecrières *(Athos)*; Bernard Woringer *(Porthos)*; Jacques Toja *(Aramis)*; Mylène Demongeot *(Milady)*; Jean Carmet *(Planchet)*; Guy Delorme *(Rochefort)*; Robert Berri *(Bonacieux)*; Anne Tonietti *(Ketty)*; Guy Tréjan *(Louis XIII)*; Henri Nassiet *(M. de Tréville)*; Jacques Berthier *(Buckingham)*; Françoise Christophe *(Ann d'Autriche)*; Daniel Sorano *(Richelieu)*; Perrette Pradier *(Constance Bonacieux)*; Jacques Seiler *(Grimaud)*; André Weber *(Bazin)*; Henri Cogan *(Mousqueton)*; Léna Skerla *(Madame de Chevreuse)*; Philippe March *(De Wardes)*; Malka Ribowska *(Madame de Lannoy)*; Hubert de Lapparent *(Seguier)*; Espanita Cortez *(Doña Estafania)*; Pierre Mirat *(Innkeeper of Amiens)*; Dominique Zardi *(Innkeeper Meuny)*; Jean Degrave *(M. de la Porte)*; Jacques Hilling *(La Chesnaye)*; Jean Ozenne *(Chambellan de Buckingham)*; Claude Salez *(The Cardinal's Henchman)*; Jean Gras.

Comments: This version of Dumas' *The Three Musketeers* was co-produced by Italy's Fono Roma and the French companies Films Borderie, Les Films Moderenes and Le Film d'Art. The production was filmed at various locations in France. Dumas' material had previously been adapted onscreen as early as 1903.

Fire Monsters Against the Son of Hercules (Maciste contro I mostri) (Avco Embassy, 1962)

Credits: Director: Guido Maletesta; *Producers:* Giorgio Marzelli, Alfio Quattrini; *Screenplay:* Arpad DeRiso, Guido Maletesta; *Photography:* Giuseppe La Torre (Eastmancolor, Totalscope, aspect ratio 2.35:1); *Film Editor:*

Opposite, top: Margaret Lee in *Fire Monsters Against the Son of Hercules. Opposite, bottom:* A monster attacks in *Fire Monsters Against the Son of Hercules.*

Enzo Alfonzi; *Music:* Guido Robuschi, Gian Stellari; *Production Design:* Umberta Cesarano; *Costume Design:* Mario Giorsi; *Makeup:* Giovanni Ranieri; *Special Makeup Effects:* Carlo Rambaldi; *Hair Stylist/Wigs:* Rocchetti; *Production Supervisor:* Attilio Tosato; *Assistant Director:* G. Cesare Marmol; *2nd Unit Director:* Gianfranco Baldanello; *Sound:* Bruno Moreal, B. Spadini; *Sound Editor:* Bruno Mattei; *Camera Operator:* Mario Mancini; *Assistant Cameraman:* Mario Pastorini; *Costumes:* Tigano Lo Faro; *Footwear:* E. Pompei; running time: 82 minutes (Italy); released April 25, 1962 (Italy); video availability: Something Weird Video.

Cast: Reg Lewis *(Maciste/Maxus/Germanicus)*; Margaret Lee *(Moah)*; Luciano Marin *(Aydar of the Sun People)*; Andrea Aureli *(Rhia)*; Birgit Bergen *(Agmir, Nude Blonde)*; Nello Pazzafini *(Chief of the Cave People)*; Maria Kent *(Agmin, Nab's Girlfriend)*; Fulvia Gasser *(Girl of the Sun People)*; Rocco Spataro *(Dorak)*; Mimmo Maggio *(Man of the Sun People)*; Nando Angelini *(Man of the Cave People)*; Ivan Pengow *(Agur)*; Tanja Snidersic *(Girl of the Sun People)*; Demeter Bitenc *(Dorak, Father of Aydar)*; Laura Brown *(Sacrificed Girl of the Sun People)*; Alfredo Zammi *(Fire Keeper of the Sun People)*.

Comments: The powerful warrior Maxxus (called Maciste in this version) is embroiled in a conflict between warring tribes, the Sun Worshippers and the Moon Worshippers. This film was also known as both *Maciste vs. the Monsters (Maciste contro I mostri)* and *Colossus of the Stone Age*. A co-production of Italy's Euro International Film (EIA) and Yugoslavia's Caserbib. Filmed at Incir De Paolis Studios, Rome, and on location in the caves of Ljubljana, in Slovenia, Yugoslavia.

Fire Over Rome (Il incendio di Roma) (American International, 1965)

Credits: *Director:* Guido Maletesta; *Producer:* Giorgio Marzelli; *Screenplay:* Guido Maletesta, Giorgio Marzelli; *Photography:* Aldo Greci (Color, Techniscope, aspect ratio 2.35:1); *Film Editor:* Enzo Alfonzi; *Music:* Guido Robuschi, Gian Stellari; *Production Design:* Oscar D'Amico; *Costume Design:* Mario Giorsi, Rosalba Menichelli; *Makeup:* Giovanni Amadei; *Hair Stylist:* Eda Delich; *Production Manager:* Michelangelo Ciafré; *Unit Production Managers:* Luigi Esposito, Valerio Marzelli; *Assistant Director:* Gianfranco Baldanello; *Sound:* Mario Sisti; *Special Effects:* Pasquale Mancino; *Production Secretary:* Claudio Sinibaldi; *Script Supervisors:* Grazia Baldanello, Mirella Maletesta; running time: 80 minutes (Italy); released March 20, 1965 (Italy).

Cast: Lang Jeffries *(Marcus Valerius)*; Cristina Galoni *(Giulia)*; Moira Orfei *(Poppaea)*; Mario Felliciani *(Seneca)*; Luciano Marin *(Fulvius)*; Evi Maltagliati *(Livia Augusta, Mother of Marcus)*; Franco Fantasia *(Clodius)*; Massimo Carocci *(Young Christian)*; Vladimir Medar *(Nero)*; Vladimir Bacic; Anita Todesco; Mimmo Maggio; Franco Daddi; Riccardo Pizzuti; Demeter Bitenc *(Menecrate)*; Petar Dobric.

Comments: When he falls in love with a Christian girl, Roman consul Marcus Valerius is sentenced to fight in the arena as a gladiator. Produced by Italy's GMC and Jadran Film.

The Four Musketeers (I quattro moschettieri) (Société Générale de Cinématographie [S.G.C.]/ Titanus, 1963)

Credits: *Director:* Carlo Ludovico Bragaglia; *Producer:* Gianni Buffardi; *Screenplay:* Bruno Corbucci, Giovanni Grimaldi (from their story); *Photography:* Tino Santoni (Eastmancolor); *Film Editor:* Giulianna Attenni; *Music:* Gianni Ferrio; *Production Design:* Giorgio Giovannini; *Costume Design:* Giuliano Papi; *Assistant Director:* Elsa Carnavali; *Sound:* Giulio Tagliacozzo; *Microphone Boom Operator:* Primiano Muratori; running time: 105 minutes; released 1963.

Cast: Aldo Fabrizi *(Bouboule)*; Nino Taranto; Erminio Macario; Carlo Croccolo; Lisa Gastoni *(Milady de Winter)*; Carla Malier *(Constance Bonacieux)*; Béatrice Altariba *(Annd d'Autriche)*; Peppino De Filippo *(Cardinal Richelieu)*; Francesco Mulé *(King Louis XIII)*; George Rivière *(D'Artagnan)*; Betto Di Paolo *(Aramis)*; Ferdinando Poggi *(Athos)*; Andrea Aureli *(Porthos)*; Francis Lane *(Bonacieux)*; Franco Ressel *(Lord Buckingham)*; Alberto Bonucci *(Cyrano de Bergerac)*; Nino Terzo *(Captain of the Guard)*; Anna Campori.

Comments: A comedic take on *The Three*

Musketeers, although no relation to the 1974 Richard Lester film of the same title. In this story, four men impersonate the Musketeers and attempt to steal the Queen's necklace. Co-produced by Italy's Titanus and France's Société Générale de Cinematographie (S.G.C.)

Fury of Achilles (L'ira di Achille) (American International, 1963)

Credits: Director: Marino Girolami; *Producers:* Samuel Z. Arkoff, James H. Nicholson; *Screenplay:* Gino De Santis; *Photography:* Mario Fioretti (color, Ultrascope, aspect ratio 2.35:1); *Film Editor:* Mirella Casini; *Music:* Carlo Savina; *Production Design:* Saverio D'Eugenio; running time: 118 minutes (Italy), 95 minutes (U.S.); released September 23, 1963 (Italy); video availability: Alpha Video.

Cast: Gordon Mitchell *(Achilles)*; Jacques Bergerac *(Hector)*; Cristina Gaioni *(Xenia)*; Gloria Milland *(Brisels)*; Piero Lulli *(Odysseus)*; Roberto Risso *(Paris)*; Mario Petri *(Agamemnon)*; Eleonora Bianchi *(Criséide)*; Erminio Spalla *(Nestor)*; Fosco Giachetti *(Priamos)*; Nando Tamerlani *(Cressus)*; Ennio Girolami *(Patrocius)*; Tina Gloriani *(Andromace)*; Remo De Angelis; Manfred Freyberger; Dada Gallotti; Romano Ghini; Gina Mascetti; Edith Peters *(Nubian Slave)*; Maria Laura Rocca; Gian Paolo Rosmino; Anita Todesco; Nestore Cavaricci *(Soldier)*.

Comments: A sword-and-sandal opus with supernatural overtones as Achilles (Gordon Mitchell) exhibits god-like powers of invincibility in this Trojan War story. At 6'3", Gordon Mitchell (1923–2003) was a genre regular who, when the peplum craze faded, segued easily into spaghetti westerns. *Fury of Achilles* was produced by Italy's Uneurop Film.

The Fury of Hercules (La furia di Ercole) (Medallion Pictures, 1962)

Credits: Director: Gianfranco Parolini; *Producer:* Mario Maggi; *Screenplay:* M. D'Amiens, Angelo DeRiso, Gianfranco Parolini, Giovanni Simonelli, Sergio Sollima (from a story by Larry Madison, Gianfranco Parolini, Giovanni Simonelli); *Dialogue:* John Davis Hart (for English version); *Photography:* Francesco Izzarelli (Eastmancolor, Totalscope, aspect ratio: 2.35:1); *Film Editor:* Mario Sansoni; *Music:* Carlo Innocenzi; *Production Design and Art Direction:* Oscar D'Amico; *Set Decoration:* Giuseppe Ranieri; *Costume Design:* Vittorio Rossi; *Makeup:* Antonio Marini, Pierantonio Mecacci; *Hair Stylist:* Galileo Mandini; *Production Manager:* Ernesto Gentili; *Production Supervisor:* Toscano Giuntini; *1st Assistant Directors:* V.S. Scega, Giovanni Simonelli, Niksa Stefanini; *2nd Assistant Director:* Ante Jukas; *3rd Assistant Director:* Ignazio Dolce; *Construction Coordinator:* Fernando Filoni; *Sound:* Gianetto Nardi; *Boom Operator:* Michele Cossu; *Sound Effects:* Renato Marinelli; *Dubbing Director:* Richard McNamara (for English version); *Special Effects:* F. Cardinali, Rolando Morelli; *Camera Operators:* M. Baric, Emilio Giannini, Matija Ergles, Valentin Serak; *Assistant Camera Operators:* Josip Akcic, A. Manganiello; *Chief Electrician:* Gustavo Bonfigli; *Wardrobe:* Irma Tonnini; *Wardrobe Assistant:* M.P. Mancini; *Footwear:* Ditta Pompei; *Wigs:* Palombi; *Assistant Editors:* Nadia Bonifazi, A. Gianini; *Orchestra Conductor:* Carlo Franci; *Production Assistant:* Luciano Giustini; *Chief Crewman:* Alberto Manni; *Fencing Master:* Giuseppe Mattei; *Continuity:* J. Cindri; *Optical Effects Laboratory:* Sviluppo Pellicole e Stampa (SPES), Rome, Italy; running time: 97 minutes (Italy); released March 21, 1962 (Italy), 1963 (U.S.); video availability: Something Weird Video.

Cast: Brad Harris *(Hercules)*; Luisella Boni *(Daria)*; Mara Berni *(Cnidia)*; Elke Arendt; Carlo Tamberlani *(Eridione)*; Serge Gainsbourg *(Menistus)*; Alan Steel *(Kaldos)*; Franco Gasparri; Irena Prosen; Romano Ghini; Ivan Dobric; Niksa Stefanini *(Robur)*; Natascia Polavshenko; Manja Golec.

Comments: Hercules falls in love with an evil queen's handmaiden, while the ruthless monarch has her own plans for the mighty hero. Muscular lead Brad Harris (1933–) was a prolific sword-and-sandal regular who later starred in spaghetti westerns. *Fury of Hercules* was produced by Italy's Cinematografica Associati (C.I.A.S.), and France's Comptoir Français du Film Production (CFFP). Shot at Dubrava Film, Zagreb, Croatia, and at locations in Zagreb.

Fury of the Pagans (La furia dei barbari) (Columbia Pictures, 1960)

Credits: *Director:* Guido Maletesta; *Producers:* Mario Bartoloni, Giuliano Simonetti; *Executive Producer:* Paolo Ricci; *Screenplay:* Gino Mangini, Umberto Scarpelli (based on a novel by Gino Mangini); *Photography:* Vincenzo Seratrice (Eastmancolor, Dyaliscope, aspect ratio 2.35:1); *Film Editors:* Roberto Giandalla, Mario Sansoni; *Music:* Guido Robuschi, Gian Stellari; *Production Design:* Pier Vittorio Marchi, Alfonso Russo; *Art Direction:* Gino Mangini; *Costume Design:* Giorgio Desideri; *Sound:* Mario Bartolomei; *Production Manager:* Michelangelo Ciafré; *Camera Operator:* Camillo Bazzoni; *Assistant Camera Operators:* Luigi Allegretti, Vitaliano Natalucci; running time: 95 minutes (Italy), 86 minutes (U.S.); released October 27, 1960 (Italy), May 1963 (U.S.).

Cast: Edmund Purdom *(Toryok)*; Rossana Podestà *(Leonora)*; Livio Lorenzon *(Kovo)*; Carla Calò; Daniele Vargas *(Napur)*; Andrea Fantasia *(Nogaric)*; Vittoria Febbi *(Daritza)*; Ljubica Jovic *(Kathrina)*; Luciano Marin *(Donar)*; Raffaella Carrà *(Maritza)*; Giulio Massimini *(Laszlo)*; Simonetta Simeoni; Niksa Stefanini *(Schonak)*; Amedeo Trilli *(Ragon)*.

Comments: In this sword-and-sandal epic (set in 568 AD), warrior Toryok seeks revenge on the cruel Barbarian leader Kovo, who has raped and murdered Toryok's wife. Produced by Italy's Arion company. Director Guido Maletesta was sometimes billed as "James Read."

The Giant of Marathon (La battaglia di Maratona) (MGM, 1959)

Credits: *Directors:* Jacques Tourneur, Mario Bava; *Producer:* Bruno Vailati; *Supervising Producer:* Renato Angiolini; *Secretary of Production:* Paolo Mercuri; *Screenplay:* Ennio De Concini, Augusto Frassinetti, Bruno Vailati (from their story, based on an idea by Alberto Barsanti and Raffaello Pacini); *Photography:* Mario Bava (Eastmancolor, Dyaliscope, and, for underwater scenes, Totalscope, aspect ratio 2.35:1); *Film Editor:* Mario Serandrei; *Music:* Roberto Nicolosi; *Production Design:* Aleksandar Milovic; *Art Direction:* Marcello del Prato; *Set Decoration:* Massimo Tavazzi; *Costume Design:* Pier Luigi Pizzi; *Makeup:* Otello Fava; *Hair Stylist:* Mara Rocchetti; *Production Manager:* Ferrucio De Martino; *Assistant Production Manager:* Massimo De Rita; *Assistant Directors:* Odoardo Fiory, Ottavio Oppo; *Assistant Art Director:* Gianni D'Aloisio; *Storyboard Artist:* Mario Chiari; *Sound:* Massimo Tagliaferri; *Sound Engineers:* Giulio Tagliacozzo, Louis Kieffer; *Special Effects:* Mario Bava; *Fencing Master:* Enzo Musumeci Greco; *Camera Operators:* Massimo Terzano, Ubaldo Terzano; *Underwater Cameraman:* Masino Manunza; *Wardrobe:* Armando Govoni; *Costumer:* Marisa Crimi; *Orchestra Conductor:* Luigi Urbini; *Secretary to the Director:* Barbara Fusch; *Continuity:* Armando Govoni; *Weapons:* Rancati; running time: 90 minutes (Italy), 92 minutes (director's cut); released December 3, 1959 (Italy), May 25, 1960 (U.S.); video availability: Retromedia.

Cast: Steve Reeves *(Phillipides)*; Mylène Demongeot *(Andromeda)*; Sergio Fantoni *(Teocrito)*; Alberto Lupo *(Milziade)*; Daniele Vargas *(Darius, King of Persia)*; Gianni Loti *(Teucro)*; Miranda Campa *(Andromeda's Friend)*; Ivo Garrani *(Creuso)*; Daniela Rocca *(Karis)*; Sergio Ciani [Alan Steel] *(Euros)*; Franco Fantasia *(The Senator)*; Carlo Lombardi, Ignazio Balsamo *(Ship's Captain)*; Gian Paolo Rosmino; Walter Grant; Maria Grazia Sandri *(Andromeda's Handmaiden)*; Paule Emanuele *(Dubbed Voice of Karis)*; Richard Francoeur *(Dubbed Voice of The Senator)*; Jean-Claude Michel *(Dubbed Voice of Phillipides)*; Roger Tréville *(Dubbed Voice of Darius, King of Persia)*; Gérard Herter *(Hippia)*; Rinaldo Zamperla *(Gladiator)*.

Comments: In 490 BC Greek warrior Phillipides (Steve Reeves) rises up in opposition to the Persian armies sweeping the world. Director Jacques Tourneur had been hired on a 10-month contract, and when Tourneur was unable to finish on time and refused to sign a contract extension, the production was entrusted to Mario Bava, whose efficiency on this film earned him permission to film his great horror classic *Black Sunday*. A co-production between Italy's Titanus and Galatea Film, and France's Lux Compagnie Cinématographique de France and Societé Cinématographique Lyre. Filmed at Titanus

Poster for *The Giant of Marathon*.

Studios in Rome and Centralni Filmski Studio Košutnjak in Belgrade, Serbia.

The Giant of Metropolis (Il gigante di Metropolis) (Goldstone Film Enterprises, 1961)

Credits: Director: Umberto Scarpelli; *Producers:* Decio Salvi, Erminio Salvi; *Screenplay:* Sabatino Ciuffini, Ambrogio Molteni, Oreste Palella, Erminio Salvi, Gino Stafford (from a story by Gino Stafford); *Photography:* Oberdan Troiani (Eastmancolor, aspect ratio 2.35:1); *Film Editor:* Franco Fraticelli; *Production Design:* Giorgio Giovannini; *Set Decoration:* Giuseppe Ranieri; *Costume Design:* Giovanna Natili; *Makeup:* Romolo de Martino; *Hair Stylists:* Adalgisa Favella; *Wigs:* Rocchetti; *Production Supervisor/Unit Manager:* Franco di Mauro; *General Manager:* Decio Salvi; *Production Manager:* Elios Vercelloni; *Assistant Director:* Mario Tota; *Set Construction:* Sergio Scalia; *Sound Engineer:* Alessandro Sarandrea; *Special Effects:* Joseph Nathanson; *Camera Operator:* Mario Sensi; *Assistant Camera Operator:* Silvano Mancini; *Still Photographer:* Cristiano Civirani; *Wardrobe Assistant:* Maria Teresa Morelli; *Assistant Film Editor:* Sergio Fraticelli; *Dubbing Director (English Version):* Richard McNamara; *Colorist:* Andrea Gargano; *Orchestra Conductor:* Armando Trovajoli; *Fencing Master:* Bruno Ukmar; *Choreographer:* Leopoldo Savona; *Footwear:* Pompei; *Script Supervisors:* Adriana Bellanti; Leo Scuccuglia; *Production Secretary:* Luigi Guasco; *Script (English Dubbed Version):* John Davis Hart; running time: 98 minutes (Italy); released October 26, 1961 (Italy), November 20, 1963 (U.S.); video availability: Retromedia.

Cast: Gordon Mitchell *(Obro)*; Bella Cortez *(Princess Mecede)*; Roldano Lupi *(King Yotar)*; Marietto *(Elmos)*; Omero Gargano *(Wise Man)*; Mario Meniconi *(Obro's Friend)*; Carlo Tamberlani; Luigi Moneta *(The Prime Minister)*; Ugo Sasso *(Captain of the Guard)*; Renato Terra *(Young Scientist)*; Carlo Enrici; Leopoldo Sa-

Gordon Mitchell and Bella Cortez star in *The Giant of Metropolis*.

Original Italian poster for *The Giant of Metropolis*.

vona *(Danzatori)*; Furio Meniconi *(Egon, Yota's Father)*; Liana Orfei *(Queen Texen)*; Alberto Farnese; Aldo Pedinotti.

Comments: The heroic Obro vs. the evil king Yotar, ruler of the scientifically-advanced city of Metropolis. A rare peplum in its strong sci-fi overtones, almost reminiscent of Universal's 1930s *Flash Gordon* serials in its mixture of the primitive and the futuristic. Leading lady Bella Cortez, as always, helps to engage (male) viewer interest. Filmed at Incir De Paolis Studios, Rome.

Giant of the Evil Island (Il mistero dell'isola maledetta) (American International, 1965)

Credits: Director: Piero Pierotti; *Producer:* Fortunato Misiano; *Screenplay:* Arpad DeRiso, Piero Pierotti; *Photography:* Augusto Tiezzi (Eastmancolor, Totalscope, aspect ratio 2.35:1); *Film Editor:* Jolanda Benvenuti; *Music:* Angelo Francesco Lavagnino; *Set Decoration:* Franco Anoria; *Sound:* Bernardino Fronzetti; *Assistant Director:* Giancarlo Romitelli; running time: 80 minutes; released 1965; video availability: Something Weird Video.

Cast: Peter Lupus [billed as "Rock Stevens"] *(Pedro Valverde)*; Halina Zalewska *(Doña Alma Morales)*; Arturo Dominici *(Don Alvarado)*; Monique Renaud *(Consuelo)*; Nello Pazzafini *(Malik)*; Dina De Santis *(Bianca)*; Amedeo Trilli *(Captain Jose Rivera)*; Loris Gizzi *(The Doctor)*; Nando Angelini *(Ramon)*; Nino Vingelli *(Tortilla)*; Attilio Dottesio *(Lt. Esteban)*; Rosy De Leo *(Girl)*; Salvatore Borghese *(Crow, a Pirate)*; Ignazio Balsamo *(Navarro)*; Franco Jamonte *(Sanch)*; Gianni Baghino *(Pirate)*; Aldo Cristiani; Gaetano Scala; Emilio Messina *(Man at the Market)*; Gino Soldi; Ricardo Castelli; Luigi D'Acri; Gilberto Galimberti.

Comments: A pirate adventure with hero Pedro Valverde (Peter Lupus) arriving on Evil Island to combat a band of pirates. A relative latecomer to the peplum genre, Peter Lupus was billed as "Rock Stevens" in these films at the suggestion of American-International's Sam Arkoff, who commented that he thought Lupus' real name "sounded like a disease." Lupus would later become better known as the musclebound member of a government secret agent team in the network television series *Mission Impossible*.

Giants of Rome (I giganti di Roma) (Walter Manley Enterprises, 1964)

Credits: Director: Antonio Margheriti; *Producers:* Mino Loy, Luciano Martino; *Screenplay:*

Ernesto Gastaldi, Luciano Martino; *Dialogue:* Arlette Combret; *Photography:* Fausto Zuccoli (Eastmancolor, Totalscope, aspect ratio 2.35:1); *Film Editor:* Romana Fortini; *Music:* Carlo Rustchelli; *Production Design:* Jean-Paul Coutan-Laboureur; *Costume Design:* Riccardo Domenici; *Makeup:* Franco Freda; *Assistant Directors:* Nino Fruscella, Roberto Pariante; running time: 95 minutes (Italy); released September 10, 1964 (Italy); video availability: Alpha Video.

Cast: Richard Harrison *(Claudius Marcellus)*; Wandisa Guida *(Livilla)*; Ettore Manni *(Castor)*; Philippe Hersent *(Drusus)*; Ralph Hudson *(Germanicus)*; Nicole Tessier *(Edua)*; Goffredo Unger *(Varo)*; Renato Baldini *(Drood)*; Piero Lulli *(Pompeus)*; Alessandro Sperli *(Julius Caesar)*; Aldo Cecconi; Maurizio Conti; Alberto Dell'Acqua *(Valerius)*; Jean Claude Madal; Renato Montalbano; Claudio Scarchilli; Gianni Solaro.

Comments: Julius Caesar sends a group of warriors to destroy the Druids' secret weapon, which is revealed to be a giant catapult. A coproduction of the Italian companies Devon Film and N.C., in tandem with the French company Radius Productions.

The Giants of Thessaly (I giganti della Tessaglia) (Medallion Pictures, 1960)

Credits: *Director:* Riccardo Freda; *Producers:* Virgilio De Blasi, Giuliano Sambati; *Screenplay:* Giuseppe Masini, Mario Rossetti, Riccardo Freda, Ennio De Concini; *Photography:* Raffaele Masciocchi, Václav Vich (Eastmancolor, Totalscope, aspect ratio 2.35:1); *Film Editor:* Otello Colangeli; *Music:* Carlo Rustichelli; *Set Decoration:* Antonio Visone; *Costume Design:* Mario Giorsi; *Makeup:* Giuseppe Peruzzi; *Hair Stylist:* Anna Graziosi; *Assistant Director:* Odoardo Fiory; *Set Designer:* Franco Lolli; *Props:* E. Rancati; *Sound:* Luigi Puri; *Assistant Sound Technician:* Renato Cadueri; *Camera Operators:* Enrico Cortese, Antonio Schiavo Lena; *Assistant Camera Operator:* Enrico Cortese; *Still Photographer:* Alfio Quattrini; *Special Effects:* Carlo Rambaldi; *Costumes:* Tigano Lo Faro; *Assistant Costumer:* Antonio Randaccio; *Footwear:* Pompei; *Wigs:* Rocchetti; *Music Director:* Franco Ferrara; *Production Assistant:* Enrique Bologna; *Continuity:* Vittoria Vigorelli; running time: 98 minutes (Italy), 86 minutes (U.S.); released December 4, 1960 (Italy), July 7, 1963 (U.S.); video availability: Alpha Video.

Cast: Roland Carey *(Jason)*; Ziva Rodann *(Creusa)*; Alberto Farnese *(Adrasto)*; Massimo Girotti *(Orfeo)*; Nadia Sanders *(Queen Gaia)*; Luciano Marin *(Euristio)*; Cathia Caro *(Aglaia)*; Alfredo Varelli *(Argo)*; Gil Delamare *(Alceo)*; Maria Teresa Vianello *(Olivia-Sorella di Gaia)*; Nando Tamberlani *(Aglaia's Father)*; Alberto Sorrentino *(Licaone)*; Massimo Pianforini *(Argo's Father)*; Paolo Gozlino *(Laerte)*; Raf Baldassarre *(Antinoo)*; Nando Angelini *(Jason's Friend)*; Takis Kavouras; Franco Gentili; Jacques Stany *(Jason's Friend)*; Gualberto Titta *(Council Member)*; Salvatore Furnari *(Nano)*; Pietro Tordi *(Telamone)*; Raimondo Magni *(Peleo)*; Giovanni Sabbatini; Tino Vetrani; Pietro Capanna; Alice Clements *(Prima Ballerina)*; Piero Pastore *(Citizen of Jolco)*; Franco Sertili *(Council Member)*; Gabriele Ferrari; Fortunato Arena *(Argonaut)*; Moira Orfei *(Atalanta)*.

Comments: A version of Jason and the Argonauts, and their search for the magical Golden Fleece. Co-produced by Italy's Alexandra Produzioni and by France's Société Cinématographique Lyre. Filmed at Cinecittà Studios and LUCE Studios in Rome. The material used here would be more fully exploited by stop-motion animator Ray Harryhausen in the Columbia Pictures production *Jason and the Argonauts*, released the same year in America (1963).

Gideon and Samson (I grandi condottieri) (San Pablo Films, 1965)

Credits: *Directors:* Marcello Baldi, Francisco Pérez-Dolz; *Producer:* Toni Di Carlo; *Screenplay:* Ottavio Jemma, Flavio Niccolini, Marcello Baldi, Tonino Guerra; *Photography:* Marcello Masciocchi (Eastmancolor, aspect ratio 2.35:1); *Film Editor:* Giulianna Atteni; *Production Design:* Sigfrido Burmann, Ottavio Scotti; *Set Decoration:* Arrigo Breschi, Adolfo Cofiño; *Costume Design:* Giorgio Desideri; *Makeup:* José Maria Alonso Pesquera, Miguel Fernández de Prada, Vittorio Galiano, Diego Gómez Sempere; *Assistant Directors:* José López Rodero, Flavio Niccolini, Renato

Rizzuto; *Sound:* Giorgio Pallotta; *Special Effects:* Dino Galiano, Vitantonio Ricci; *Optical Effects:* Luciano Vittori; *Camera Operators:* Salvador Gil, Ubaldo Terzano; *Assistant Camera Operators:* José Antonio Hoya, Otello Spila; *Assistant Film Editor:* Lucia Coos; *Orchestra Conductor:* Alberto Zedda; *Titles:* Luciano Vittory; *Script Supervisors:* Rometta Pietrostefani, Ricardo Huertas; *Laboratory:* Tecnostampa, Rome, Italy; running time: 101 minutes; released October 5, 1965 (Italy); video availability: VCI.

Cast: Anton Geesink *(Samson)*; Ivo Garrani *(Gideon)*; Rosalba Neri *(Delilah)*; Fernando Rey *(The Stranger, The Angel of the Lord)*; Paolo Gozlino *(Prince of Gaza)*; Ana Maria Noé *(Samson's Mother)*; Maruchi Fresno *(Gideon's Wife)*; Giorgio Cerioni *(Jeter, Gideon's Son)*; Piero Gerlini *(Ferim)*; Lucio De Santis *(Nabur)*; Sergio Ammirata *(Philistine General)*; Barta Barri *(Fara)*; José Jaspe *(Zeba)*; Consalvo Dell'Arti; Beni Deus *(Salmunna)*; Mirko Ellis; Pepe Martin.

Comments: Samson here is the biblical figure, not the mythical strongman of peplum lore. This story is adapted from chapters 6 through 8 and chapters 13 through 16 of the Book of Judges. Produced by Italy's San Paolo Films. Shot at Cinecittà Studios in Rome, with some location work in Almeria, Spain.

Gladiator of Rome *(Il gladiatore di Roma)* (Medallion Pictures, 1962)

Credits: *Director:* Mario Costa; *Producer:* Giorgio Agliani; *Screenplay:* Gian Paolo Callegari, Giuseppe Mariani (from their story); *Photography:* Pier Ludovico Pavoni (Eastmancolor, Euroscope, aspect ratio 2.35:1); *Film Editor:* Antonietta Zita; *Music:* Carlo Franci; *Art Direction:* Piero Poletto; *Set Decoration:* Francesco D'Andria; *Costume Design:* Giorgio Desideri; *Production Manager:* Adriano Merkel; *Assistant Director:* Mario Tota; *Sound:* Giovanni Bianchi; Raffaele Del Monte; *Sound System:* Westrex; *Camera Operator:* Fausto Rossi; *Continuity:* Alberto Salvatori; running time: 100 minutes (Italy), 80 minutes (U.S.); released September 13, 1962 (Italy), 1963 (U.S.); video availability: Something Weird Video.

Cast: Gordon Scott *(Marcus Lucilius)*; Wandisa Guida *(Nisa)*; Roberto Risso *(Valerio, Jr.)*; Ombretta Colli *(Aglae)*; Alberto Farnese *(Magistrate Vezio Rufo)*; Gianni Solaro *(Senator Macrino)*; Charles Borromel *(Anio)*; Piero Lulli *(General Astarte)*; Mirko Ellis *(Frasto)*; Pietro De Vico *(Pompilio)*; Nando Tamberlani *(Valerio's Father)*; Andrea Aureli *(Settimio)*; Eleonora Vargas *(Prisca)*; Pietro Ceccarelli *(Bald Gladiator)*; Pietro Tordi *(Slave Guard)*; Nello Pazzafini *(Gladiator)*; Giulio Cali *(Old Christian)*; Raf Baldassarre *(Gladiator)*; Giulio Battiferri *(Slave Spy)*; Miranda Campa *(Porzia, Valerio's Mother)*; Gualtiero Isnenghi *(Senator)*; Amedeo Trilli *(Innkeeper)*; Célina Cély; Leo Garavaglia; Germana Francioli; Artemio Antonini *(Gladiator)*; Harold Bradley *(Gladiator)*; Veriano Ginesi.

Comments: A gladiator protects a slave girl who is, in reality, a princess. Gordon Scott (1926–2007), real name Gordon Acton Werschkul, was a 6'3" body builder who starred in six Hollywood Tarzan movies before he segued into the Italian sword-and-sandal scene. He was briefly married to actress Vera Miles. This movie was produced by Italy's Compagnie Internazionale Realizzazioni Artistiche Cinematografiche (CIRAC) and Giorgio Agliani Cinematografica companies. Shot at Titanus Studios in Rome.

Gladiators 7 *(I sette gladiatori)* (MGM, 1962)

Credits: *Director:* Pedro Lazaga; *Producers:* Anacleto Fontini, Italo Zingarelli; *Screenplay:* Sandro Continenza, Bruno Corbucci, Alberto De Martino, Giovanni Grimaldi (from a story by Alberto De Martino and Italo Zingarelli); *Photography:* Bitto Albertini, Eloy Mella (Eastmancolor, Tehniscope, aspect ratio 2.35:1); *Film Editor:* Otello Cólangeli; *Production Design:* Piero Poletto, Antonio Simont; *Costume Design:* Franco Antonelli, Mario Giorsi; *Production Managers:* Ángel Monís, Roberto Pailaggi; *Makeup:* Franco Corridoni; *Hair Stylist:* Esther Nin; *Assistant Director:* Alfonso Brescia; *Sound Engineers:* Mario Morigi, Alessandro Sarandrea; *Sound Mixer:* Guido Felicioni; *Sound System:* Westrex; *Special Effects:* Emilio Ruiz del Rio; *Camera Operator:* Cesare Allione; *Assistant Camera Operator:* José María Moreno; *Script Supervisor:* Adriana Ballanti; *Master of Arms:*

Original Italian poster for *Gladiator of Rome*.

Giorgio Ubaldi; running time: 105 minutes (Italy), 92 minutes (U.S.); released October 11, 1962 (Italy), May 6, 1964 (U.S.); video availability: Something Weird Video.

Cast: Richard Harrison *(Darius)*; Loredana Nusciak *(Aglala)*; Livio Lorenzon *(Panurgus)*; Gérard Tichy *(Hiarba)*; Edoardo Toniolo *(Milan)*; José Marco *(Xeno)*; Barta Barri *(Flaccus)*; Nazzareno Zamperla *(Vargas)*; Franca Badeschi *(Licia)*; Enrique Ávila *(Livius)*; Antonio Molino Rojo *(Macrobius)*; Antonio Rubio *(Mados)*; Emilia Wolkowicz *(Ismere)*.

Comments: This film contains plot elements lifted from Kurosawa's *The Seven Samurai* as a freed gladiator seeks revenge for the murder of his father, and finds his lover in the clutches of an evil tyrant. This production was filmed in some of the same locations as *El Cid*.

Goddess of Love (La Venere di Cheronea) (20th Century–Fox, 1957)

Credits: Directors: Fernando Cerchio, Viktor Tourjansky; *Producer:* Giampaolo Bigazzi; *Screenplay:* Damiano Damiani, Federico Zardi; *Photography:* Arturo Gallea (Ferraniacolor, Totalscope, aspect ratio 2.35:1); *Music:* Michel Michelet; *Art Director:* Italo Tomassi; *Assistant Director:* Sergio Bergonzelli; running time: 90 minutes (Italy), 68 minutes (U.S.); released December 5, 1957 (Italy), November 1960 (U.S.).

Cast: Belinda Lee *(Aphrodite)*; Jacques Sernas *(Laertes)*; Massimo Girotti *(Prassitele)*; Maria Frau; Luigi Tosi; Claudio Gora *(Armodio)*; Elli Parvo *(Elena)*; Camillo Pilotto *(Polibio)*; Enzo Fiermonte.

Comments: This film was produced by the Italian companies Faro Film and Prora Industrie Cinematografiche e Dello Spettacolo, and Germany's Rialto Film.

Gold for the Caesars (Oro per i Cesari) (MGM, 1963)

Credits: Directors: André De Toth, Sabatino Ciuffini, Riccardo Freda; *Producer:* Joseph Fryd; *Photography:* Raffaele Masciocchi (Technicolor, aspect ratio 1.66:1); *Film Editor:* Franco Fraticelli; *Music:* Franco Mannino; *Art Direction:* Ottavio Scotti; *Costume Design:* Mario Giorsi; *Makeup:* Maurizio Giustini; *Hair Stylist:* Giancarlo Marin; *Production Manager:* Luciano Cattania; *Assistant Production Manager:* Paolo Gorgano; *Assistant Director:* Jerzy Maco; *2nd Unit Director:* Riccardo Freda; *Set Dresser:* Arrigo Breschi; *Sound:* Giovanni Rossi; *Special Effects:* Eros Bacciucchi; *Camera Operator:* Antonio Schiavo Lena; *Assistant Camera Operator:* Remo Grisanti; *Still Photographer:* Angelo Pennoni; *Orchestra Conductor:* Franco Mannino; *Fencing Master:* Bruno Ukmar; *Script Girl:* Anna Gruber; running time: 98 minutes (Italy), 86 minutes (U.S.); released March 3, 1963 (Italy), June 1964 (U.S.); video availability: Warner Home Video.

Cast: Jeffrey Hunter *(Lacer)*; Mylène Demongeot *(Penelope)*; Ron Randell *(Centurion Rufus)*; Massimo Girotti *(Pro-Consul Caius Cornelius Maximus)*; Giulio Bosetti *(Scipio)*; Ettore Manni *(Luna, the Celt)*; Georges Lycan *(Malendi, the Celt)*; Furio Meniconi *(Dax, the Gaul)*; Tonino Cervi; Laura Nucci; Jacques Stany.

Comments: Attacked by Celtic warriors, an enslaved architect leads an expedition to the Valley of the Sil in search of gold. Produced by Italy's Adelphia Compagnia Cinematographica and SFA, with the French companies Compagnie Industrielle et Commerciale Cinématographique (CICC) and Films Borderie.

The Golden Arrow (L'arciere delle mille e una notte) (MGM, 1962)

Credits: Director: Antonio Margheriti; *Producer:* Goffredo Lombardo; *Screenplay:* Giorgio Arlorio, Augusto Frassinetti, Giorgio Prosperi, Filippo Sanjust, Bruno Vailati; *Photography:* Gábor Pogány (Technicolor, Technirama, aspect ratio 2.35:1); *Film Editor:* Mario Serandrei; *Art Direction:* Flavio Mogherini; *Set Decoration:* Massimo Tavazzi; *Costume Design:* Giorgio Desideri; *Makeup:* Franco Di Girolamo; *Hair Stylist:* Anna Cristofani; *Production Supervisor:* Folco Laudati; *Assistant Director:* Giovanni Fago; *2nd Unit Director:* Ettore Maria Fizzarotti; *Sound:* Mario Messina; *Sound System:* Westrex; *Special Effects:* Fernando Mazza; *Special Effects Laboratory:* Technicolor Italiana; *2nd Unit Cameraman:* Giovanni Raffaldi; *Still Photographer:* G.B. Poletto; *Orchestra Conductor:* Franco Ferrara; *Production Assistant:* Mario Dalla Pria;

Script Girl: Franca Franco; *Dialogue Director (U.S. Dubbed Version):* George Higgins; running time: 91 minutes (U.S.); released September 7, 1962 (Italy), May 1964 (U.S.).

Cast: Tab Hunter *(Hassan)*; Rossana Podestà *(Jamila)*; Umberto Melnati *(Thin Genie)*; Mario Feliciani *(Baktiar)*; Dominique Boschero *(Queen of Rocky Valley)*; Renato Baldini *(Prince of Bassora)*; Giustino Durano *(Absent-Minded Genie)*; Franco Scandurra; Gloria Milland; Renato Montalbano; Rosario Borelli *(Prince of Aleppo)*; Calisto Calisti *(Prince of Bassora's General)*; Abdel Moneim Ibrahim *(Captain Hamit)*; José Jaspe *(Sabrath)*; Gian Paolo Rosmino *(Mokbar)*; Claudio Scarchilli *(Bandit)*; Ceco Zamurovich *(Prince of Samarkand)*; Omar Zolficar *(Magician)*.

Comments: A comedic fantasy involving a magical golden arrow. Filmed at Rome's Titanus studios.

Goliath Against the Giants (Goliath contro I giganti) (Medallion Pictures, 1961)

Credits: *Director:* Guido Maletesta; *Screenplay:* Arpad DeRiso, Gianfranco Parolini, Cesare Seccia (from a story by Cesare Seccia, Giovanni Simonelli, Sergio Sollima); *Photography:* Alejandro Ulloa (Eastmancolor, SuperTotalscope, aspect ratio 2.35:1); *Film Editors:* Edmond Lozzi, Mario Sansoni; *Music:* Carlo Innocenzi; *Production Design:* Gianfranco Parolini; *Costume Design:* Vittorio Rossi; *Makeup:* Angelo Malantrucco, Carmen Martin; *Production Managers:* Manuel Pérez, Cesare Seccia; *Assistant Directors:* Juan Athena, Romolo Guerrieri, Mahnahén Velasco; *2nd Unit Director:* Jorge Grau; *Set Designers:* Ramiro Gómez, Carlos Santonocito; *Special*

Poster for *Goliath Against the Giants.*

Effects: Erasmo Bacciucchi, Beppe Domenici, Vittorio Galiano; *Fencing Master:* Nello Pazzafini; *Director of English- Dubbed Version:* Richard McNamara; *Script for English-Dubbed Version:* John Davis Hart; running time: 98 minutes (Italy), 90 minutes (U.S.); released May 14, 1961 (Italy), April 14, 1963 (U.S.); video availability: Something Weird Video.

Cast: Brad Harris *(Goliath)*; Gloria Milland *(Princess Elea)*; Fernando Rey *(Bokan, the Usurper)*; Barbara Carroll *(Daina)*; Carmen de Lirio *(Diamira)*; Pepe Rubio *(Briseo)*; Fernando Sancho *(Namathos)*; Lina Rosales; Arnaldo Martelli; Ignazio Dolce; Luigi Marturano; Franco Gasparri; Nello Pazzafini *(Jagoran)*;

Francisco Bernal; Manuel Arbó; Ángel Ortiz; Rufino Inglés; Lluis Marco; Angel Aranda; Bruno Arié *(Sailor with Goliath)*.

Comments: The heroic Goliath has his work cut out for him as he battles sea monsters, giants, Amazonian warriors, gorillas and lions in this sword-and-sandal epic. Produced by Italy's Cinematographica Associati (CI.AS.) and Spain's Procusa.

Goliath and the Barbarians (Il terrore dei barbari) (American International, 1959)

Credits: Director: Carlo Campogalliani; *Producer:* Erminio Salvi; *Screenplay:* Gino Mangini, Erminio Salvi, Nino Stresa, Giuseppe Taffarel; *Photography:* Bitto Albertini (Ferraniacolor, Totalscope, aspect ratio 2.35:1); *Film Editor:* Franco Fraticelli; *Music:* Carlo Innocenzi (rescored by Les Baxter for U.S. release); *Production Design:* Oscar D'Amico; *Costume Design:* Giorgio Desideri; Giovanna Natili; *Assistant Directors:* Sergio Bergonzelli, Romolo Guerrieri; *Director for English-Dubbed Version:* George Gonneau; running time: 85 minutes (Italy), 86 minutes (U.S.); released June 30, 1959 (Italy), November 1959 (U.S.).

Cast: Steve Reeves *(Emiliano, known as "Goliath")*; Chelo Alonso *(Landa)*; Bruce Cabot *(Alboino)*; Giulia Rubini *(Lidia)*; Arturo Dominici *(Svevo)*; Gino Scotti *(Count Daniele)*; Livio Lorenzon *(Igor)*; Luciano Marin *(Marco)*; Andrea Checci *(Delfo, Londo's Father)*; Carla Calò *(Bruno's Mother)*; Fabrizio Capucci *(Bruno)*; Clara Coppola; Cesare Fantoni; Carla Foscari; Veriano Ginesi *(Barbarian Fighter)*; Furio Meniconi *(Hulderich)*; Chery Million; Ugo Sasso; Renato Terra; Gabriele Tinti; Luigi Tosi; Amedeo Trilli; Eleonora Vargas; Ivanhoe Vela.

Comments: Goliath wages a one-man war against invading barbarians, and still finds time to romance the beautiful Landa. Produced by Italy's Standard Produzione and Alta Vista companies, this sword-and-sandal epic was completed on production money from American-International Pictures, which had the film in theatres only five months after Reeves' *Hercules*. Third-billed in the cast is

Left: Steve Reeves and Chelo Alonso in *Goliath and the Barbarians*. *Right:* Chelo Alonso in *Goliath and the Barbarians*.

Chelo Alonso and Livio Lorenzon in *Goliath and the Barbarians*.

Bruce Cabot, who, a quarter of a century earlier, had starred in the original *King Kong*.

Goliath and the Dragon (*La vendetta di Ercole*) (American International, 1960)

Credits: Director: Vittorio Cottafavi; *Producers:* Gianni Fuchs, Achille Piazzi; *Supervising Producer:* Armando Mirandi; *Executive Producer:* Alessandro Tasca; *Screenplay:* Marcello Baldi, Duccio Tessari, Mario Ferrari, Nicolò Ferrari, Fabio Carpi, Ennio De Concini, Franco Rossetti (from a story by Marcello Baldi, Nicolò Ferrari); *Dialogue for French Version:* Pierre Cholot, Bruno Guillaume; *Photography:* Mario Montuori (Technicolor, Totalscope, aspect ratio 2.35:1); *Film Editors (English-Dubbed Version):* Salvatore Billitteri, Maurizio Lucidi; *Music:* Alexandre Derevitsky; *Music for English-Dubbed Version:* Les Baxter; *Production Design:* Franco Lolli; *Costume Design:* Giulia Mafai; *Makeup:* Romolo de Martino; *Special Makeup Effects:* Carlo Rambaldi; *Hair Stylist:* Adriana Cassini; *Production Manager:* Danilo Marciani; *2nd Unit Director:* Giorgio Cristallini; *Assistant Director:* Emilio Miraglia; *Props:* E. Rancati; *Sound:* Franco Groppioni; *Special Effects:* Costel Grozea; *Special Effects for U.S. Version:* Jim Danforth; *Camera Operators:* Giuseppe Bernardini, Alfio Contini; *Costumes:* Ruggero Peruzzi; *Gowns:* Pompei; *Orchestra Conductor:* Al Simms; *Production Assistants:* Giorgio Baldi, Sergio Borelli; *Master of Arms:* Enzo Musumeci Greco; *Director of English-Dubbed Version:* Lee Kresel; running time:

Opposite, top: **Wandisa Guida and Broderick Crawford in *Goliath and the Dragon*. *Opposite, bottom:* Mark Forest and Sandro Moretti (lying on ground) in *Goliath and the Dragon*.**

Poster for *Goliath and the Dragon*.

87 minutes (U.S.); released August 12, 1960 (Italy), November 1960 (U.S.); video availability: Something Weird Video.

Cast: Mark Forest *(Emilius, Known as "Goliath")*; Broderick Crawford *(King Eurystheus)*; Gaby André *(Ismene)*, Renato Terra; Federica Ranchi *(Thea)*; Ugo Sasso *(Timocleo of Medar)*; Sandro Moretti *(Illo)*; Salvatore Furnari *(Little Peasant)*; Giancarlo Sbragia *(Tindaro)*; Michele Gentilini; Wandisa Guida *(Alcinoe)*; Nino Milano

(Lica); Leonora Ruffo (Dejanira); Spartaco Nale; Carla Calò (La Sibilla); Franco Loffredi; Piero Pastore (Prison Guard); Fedele Gentile (Peasant); Corrado Sonni; Graziella Cori; Claudio Undari (Polimorfeo); Roberto Ceccacci; Grazia Collodi, (Iride, Thea's Slave); Stefano Valle; Philippe Hersent (Androcio).

Comments: Originally a Hercules film, American-International changed the hero's name to "Emilius" (also known as "Goliath," as a helpful introductory title informs us), and added a stop-motion animation sequence involving a monstrous dragon. A tired Broderick Crawford (barely a decade after his Academy Award–winning performance in *All the King's Men*), provides the villainous opposition to Goliath here, although Crawford's voice is dubbed by another actor *impersonating* Crawford. Gaby André and Wandisa Guida provide the feminine interest, with Guida especially good in a treacherous but ultimately sympathetic role. Beautifully photographed with lush colors by Mario Montuori. Star Mark Forest (1933–), born Lorenzo Luis Degni, was an imposing 6-footer who anglicized his name for the sword-and-sandal films. Forest used the money he earned from his peplum films to fund a second career in opera, and he teaches music today in California. *Goliath and the Dragon* was co-produced by the Italian companies Achille Piazzi Produzioni Cinematografica and Produzione Gianni Fuchs, in cooperation with the French company Comptoir Français du Film Production (CFFP).

Goliath and the Sins of Babylon (Maciste l'eroe più grande del mondo) (American International, 1963)

Credits: Director: Michele Lupo; *Producer:* Elio Scardamaglia; *Associate Producer:* Salvatore Billitteri; *Screenplay:* Roberto Gianviti, Francesco Scardamaglia, Lionello De Felice (from a story by Roberto Gianviti, Francesco Scardamaglia); *Photography:* Guglielmo Mancori (Technicolor, Techniscope, aspect ratio 2.35:1); *Film Editor:* Alberto Gallitti; *Film Editor of U.S. Version:* Christopher Holmes; *Music:* Francesco De Masi; *Art Direction:* Pier Vittorio Marchi; *Costume Design:* Mario Giorsi; *Makeup:* Amato Garbini; *Hair Stylist:* Amalia Paoletti; *Production Manager:* Paolo Gargano; *Sound:* Alessandro Sarandrea; *Camera Operator:* Mario Sbrenna; *Music for U.S. Version:* Les Baxter; running time: 92 minutes (Italy), 80 minutes (U.S.); released: August 22, 1963 (Italy), December 25, 1963 (U.S.); video availability: Retromedia.

Cast: Mark Forest (*Maciste/Goliath/Marcellus*); José Greci (*Regia/Chelima*); Giuliano Gemma (*Xandros*); Erno Crisa (*Morakeb*); Mimmo Palmara (*Alceas*); Livio Lorenzon (*Evandro*); Piero Lulli (*Pergasos*); Paul Muller (*King Rukus*); Eleonora Bianchi (*Sacrificial Victim*); Jacques Herlin (*Phoenician Merchant*); Alfio Caltabiano (*Meneos*); Arnaldo Fabrizio (*Goliath, the Dwarf*); Ugo Sasso (*Sacrificial Victim's Father*); Harold Bradley (*Regia's Servant*); Calisto Caisti (*Delos, the King's Advisor*); Nello Pazzafini (*Gladiator*); Loris Loddi (*Sacrificial Victim's Young Brother*); Giancarlo Bastianoni; Joe Kamel (*Gladiator*); Piero Pastore (*Farmer Witness*); Jeff Cameron (*Gladiator*); Pietro Ceccarelli (*Gong-Ringing Soldier*); Veriano Ginesi (*Soldier*); Emilio Messina (*Guard*); Gaetano Quartararo (*Shipwreck Survivor*).

Comments: Goliath (Maciste in the original Italian version) fights to free Babylon from a tyrannical ruler. Produced by Italy's Leone Film with portions shot at Monte Gelato Waterfall, Mazzano Romano, Italy.

Goliath and the Vampires (Maciste contro il vampiro) (American International, 1961)

Credits: Directors: Sergio Corbucci, Giacomo Gentilomo; *Producer:* Paolo Moffa; *Executive Producer:* Dino De Laurentiis; *Producer of U.S. Version:* Salvatore Billitteri; *Production Supervisor:* Sergio Borelli; *Screenplay:* Sergio Corbucci, Duccio Tessari; *Photography:* Alvaro Mancori (Technicolor, Totalscope, aspect ratio 2.35:1); *Film Editor:* Eraldo Da Roma; *Music:* Angelo Francesco Lavagnino; *Music for U.S. Version:* Les Baxter; *Production Design:* Kosta Krivokapic, Gianni Polidori; *Art Direction:* Slobodan Mijacevic, Aleksandar Milovic; *Makeup:* Antonio Marini; *Hair Stylist:* Galileo Mandini; *Production Manager:* Franco Palaggi; *Assistant Director:* Guido Zurli; *Sound Supervisor:* Sergio Borelli;

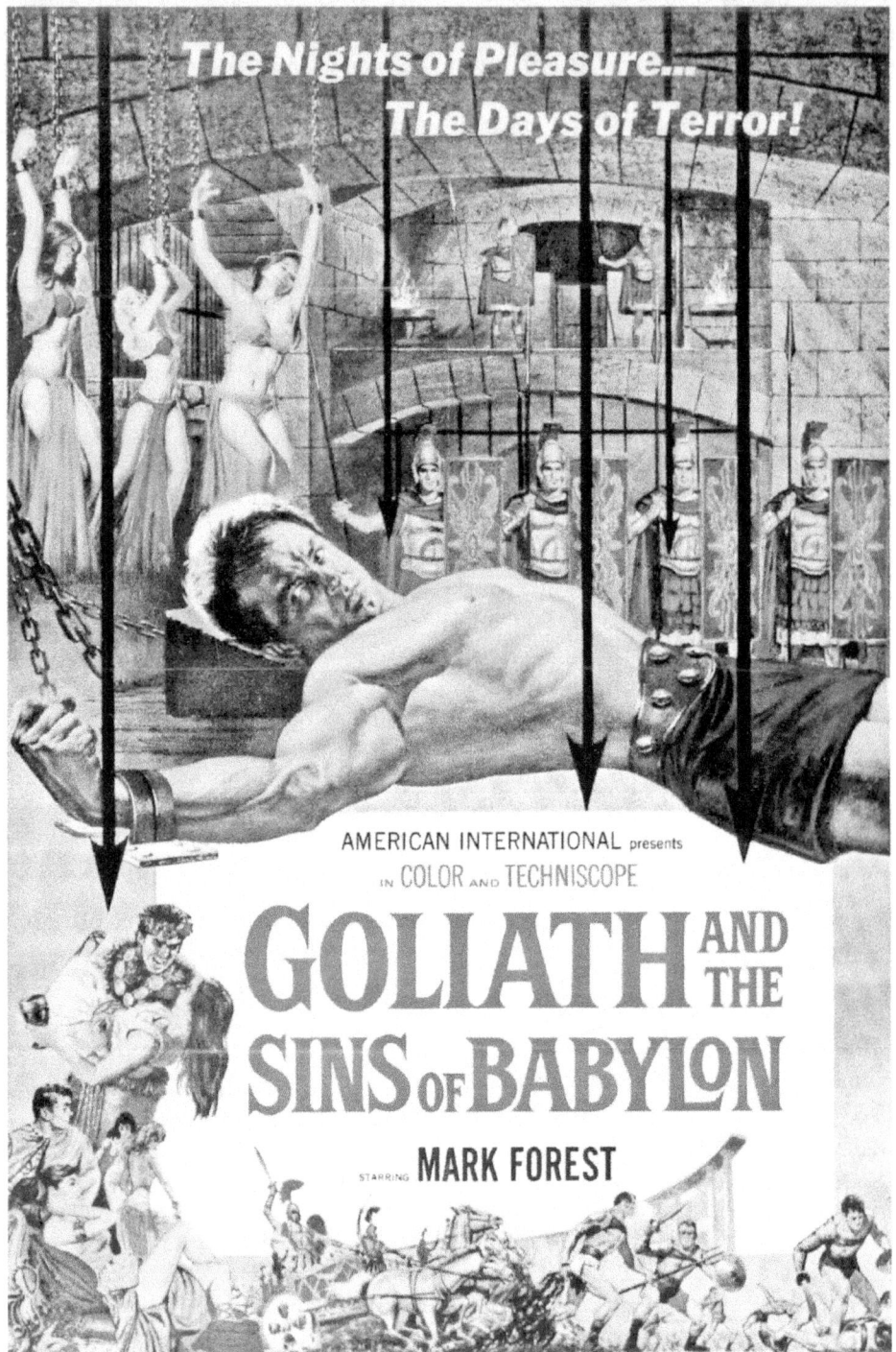

Poster for *Goliath and the Sins of Babylon*.

Top: Gordon Scott in *Goliath and the Vampires*. *Bottom:* The faceless vampires attack in *Goliath and the Vampires*.

Guido Solano in *Goliath and the Vampires*.

Sound Technicians: Mario Amari, Fiorenzo Magli; *Stunts:* Giovanni Cianfriglia; *Camera Operator:* Sandro Mancori; *Wardrobe Mistress:* Irma Tonnini; *Costumer:* Vittorio Rossi; *Music Director:* Carlo Savina; *Weapons Consultant:* Benito Stefanelli; running time: 92 minutes (Italy), 91 minutes (U.S.); released August 21, 1961 (Italy), April 1964 (U.S.); video availability: Something Weird Video.

Cast: Gordon Scott *(Maciste/Goliath)*; Leonora Ruffo *(Guja)*; Jacques Sernas *(Kurtik)*, Gianna Maria Canale *(Astra)*; Rocco Vitolazzi *(Ciro)*; Mario Feliciani *(Sultan Abdul/Omar)*; Vanoye Aikens *(Annahil)*; Annabella Incontrera *(Magda)*; Guido Celano *(Kobrak, the Vampire)*; Emma Baron *(Maciste's Mother)*; Renato Terra.

Comments: Gordon Scott's first peplum finds Goliath up against the vampiric fiend Kobrak and his hellish minions. The production design of Kosta Krivokapic and Gianni Polidori, aided by Alvaro Mancori's cinematography, is striking in this memorable entry, and it is unfortunate that most of the available prints have faded color. Produced by Italy's Ambrosiana Cinematografica.

Goliath at the Conquest of Damascus (Golia alla conquista di Bagdad) (American International, 1965)

Credits: Director: Domenico Paolella; *Producer:* Fortunato Misiano; *Screenplay:* Luciano Martino, Domenico Paolella, Ernesto Gastaldi; *Photography:* Augusto Tiezzi (Eastmancolor, aspect ratio 2.35:1); *Music:* Angelo Francesco Lavagnino; *Production Design:* Pier Vittorio Marchi; *Costume Design:* Walter Patriarca; running time: 95 minutes (Italy), 85 minutes (U.S.); released March 3, 1965; video availability: Something Weird Video.

Cast: Peter Lupus [billed as "Rock Stevens"] *(Goliath)*; Mario Petri *(Yssour)*; Helga Liné *(Fatma)*; Arturo Domenici *(Kalchev)*; Piero

Lulli *(Thor)*; Anna Maria Polani *(Myriam)*; Marino Masé *(Phir)*; Daniele Vargas *(Saud)*; Mino Doro *(King Selim)*; Andrea Aureli *(Bhalek)*; Nello Pazzafini *(Horval)*; Dario Michaelis *(Safawidi)*; Fedele Gentile *(King Selim's Officer)*; Ignazio Balsamo *(Messenger)*; Bernardina Sarrocco; Mirko Valentin.

Comments: Goliath rescues a princess and helps an exiled king regain his throne in this adventure, produced by Italy's Titanus and Romana Film.

Guns of the Black Witch *(Il terrore dei mari)* (American International, 1961)

Credits: Director and Producer: Domenico Paolella; *Screenplay:* Ugo Guerra, Luciano Martino, Ernesto Gastaldi; *Photography:* Carlo Bellero (Eastmancolor, Totalscope, aspect ratio 2.35:1); *Film Editor:* Jolanda Benvenuti; *Music:* Michele Cozzoli; *Music for U.S. Version:* Les Baxter, Ronald Stein; *Art Direction:* Giancarlo Bartolini Salimbeni; *Set Decoration:* Alfredo Montori; *Costume Design:* Italia Scandariato; *Makeup:* Massimo Giustini; *Production Supervisors:* Diego Alchimede, Pasquale Misiano; *Executive Production Manager:* Nino Misiano; *Production Manager:* Fortunato Misiano; *Assistant Director:* Umberto Lenzi; *Sound:* Mario Del Pezzo; *Camera Operator:* Gaetano Valle; *Assistant Camera Operators:* Saverio Diamante, Guglielmo Vincioni; *Action Scenes Coordinator/Nautical Advisor:* Walter Bertolazzi; *Script Girl:* Lina D'Amico; running time; 98 minutes (Italy), 81 minutes (U.S.); released February 24, 1961 (Italy), December 1961 (U.S.); video availability: Sinister Cinema.

Cast: Don Megowan *(Jean)*; Silvana Pampanini *(Delores)*; Emma Danieli *(Elisa)*; Livio Lorenzon *(Guzman)*; Germano Longo *(Michel)*; Loris Gizzi *(Governor)*; Philippe Hersent *(Jean's Stepfather)*; Anna Lina Alberti *(Elisa's Maid)*; Annie Alberti *(Conchita)*; Tullio Altamura; Nando Angelini; Corrado Annicelli; Gianni Baghino; Teodoro Corrà; Nada Cortese; Pasquale De Filippo; Francesco De Leone; Franco Jamonte *(Captain Teach)*; Cesare Lancia; Sina Relli.

Comments: In this 17th-century pirate adventure, two children who escape death at the hands of the Spanish vow revenge when they grow to manhood. Co-produced by Italy's Romana Film and France's Societe Nouvelle de Cinematographie (SNC). Filmed at Lake Garda in Italy. Lead Don Megowan was a Hollywood veteran whose most famous movie is probably Universal-International's *The Creature Walks Among Us* (1956), the second sequel to *The Creature from the Black Lagoon* (1954).

Hannibal *(Annibale)* (Warner Bros., 1959)

Credits: Directors: Carlo Ludovico Bragaglia, Edgar G. Ulmer; *Producers:* Ottavio Poggi, Jack Dietz; *Screenplay:* Mortimer Braus, Sandro Continenza, Edgar G. Ulmer (from a story by Ottavio Poggi); *Photography:* Raffaele Masciocchi (Eastmancolor, Supercinescope, aspect ratio 2.35:1); *Film Editor:* Renato Cinquini; *Music:* Carlo Rustchelli; *Art Direction:* Ernest Kromberg; *Set Decoration:* Carlo Gentili; *Costume Design:* Giancarlo Bartolini Salimbeni; *Makeup:* Mirella Ginnoto; *Production Managers:* Nino Battiferri, Lucio Bompani; *Assistant Director:* Nino Zanchin; *Set Designer:* Amedeo Mellone; *Sound:* Raffaele Del Monte, Franco Groppioni; *Sound System:* Westrex; *Special Effects:* Anacieto Giustini; *Camera Operator:* Marcello Masciocchi; *Orchestra Conductor:* Franco Ferrara; *Script Supervisor:* Shirley Ulmer; running time: 95 minutes (Italy), 103 minutes (U.S.); released December 21, 1959 (Italy), June 18, 1960 (U.S.).

Cast: Victor Mature *(Hannibal)*; Gabriele Ferzetti *(Fabius Maximus)*; Rita Gam *(Sylvia)*; Milly Vitale *(Danila)*; Rik Battaglia *(Hasdrubal)*; Franco Silva *(Maharbal)*; Terence Hill [billed as "Mario Girotti"] *(Quintillus)*; Mirko Ellis *(Mago)*; Andrea Aureli *(Gajus Terentius Varro)*; Andrea Fantasia *(Konsul Paulus Emilius)*; Renzo Cesana; Bud Spencer *(Rutario)*; Pina Bottin; Remo De Angelis; Piero Mitri; Mario Pisu; Franco Dominici *(Minitius)*; Enzo Fiermonte, *(Announcer in Senate)*; Andrea Esterhazy *(Slave)*; Piero Tiberi *(Hannibal's Son)*; Bruno Arié *(Wrestler)*; Nello Pazzafini *(Wrestler—Last Winner)*.

Comments: Another historical drama based on the story of Carthaginian general Hannibal (circa 247 BC–circa 181 BC) crossing the Alps in his military campaign against Rome during the Second Punic War in 218 BC Hollywood producer Jack Dietz went uncredited on this production; it was his last film. Low-budget auteur Edgar G. Ulmer *(Detour)* co-directed this production. Produced by Italy's Liber Films, with portions shot at Avala Studios in Belgrade, Serbia.

Head of a Tyrant *(Giuditta e Oloferne)* (Universal, 1959)

Credits: Director: Fernando Cerchio; *Producer:* Piero Ghione; *Screenplay:* Gian Paolo Callegari, Fernando Cerchio, Damiano Damiani, Guido Maletesta (based on a play by Friedrich Hebbel); *Photography:* Pier Ludovico Pavoni (Ferraniacolor, [U.S. prints Technicolor], Totalscope, aspect ratio 2.35:1); *Film Editor:* Gianmaria Messeri; *Music:* Carlo Savina; *Set Decoration:* Giorgio Scalco; *Costume Design:* Vittorio Nino Novarese; *Production Manager:* Giampaolo Bigazzi; *Assistant Director:* Vincenzo Gamna; *Art Department Manager:* Italo Tomassi; *Sound:* Oscar De Arcangelis, Raffaele Del Monte; *Camera Operator:* Angelo Lotti; *Supervising Film Editor:* Antonietta Zita; *Assistant Film Editor:* Nino Fedeluca; running time: 94 minutes (Italy); released February 26, 1959 (Italy), April 1960 (U.S.); video availability: Sinister Cinema.

Cast: Massimo Girotti *(Holophernes)*; Isabelle Corey *(Judith)*; Renato Baldini *(Arbar)*; Yvette Masson *(Rispa)*; Gianni Rizzo *(Ozia)*; Camillo Pilotto *(Belial)*; Lucia Banti *(Servant Girl)*; Ricardo Valle *(Isaac)*; Leonardo Botta *(Gabriele)*; Franco Balducci *(Galaad)*; Luigi Tosi *(Iras)*; Gabriele Antonini *(Brother)*; Daniela Rocca *(Naomi)*; Enzo Doria *(Daniel)*; Alberto Archetti; Luciano Ciccarone; Enzo Fiermonte; Fedele Gentile; Chery Million; Diego Pozzetto.

Comments: A virtuous girl seduces a tyrant who has conquered her people, planning to assassinate him. Previously filmed several times in the silent era under the original title of this production, *Judith and Holophernes* *(qv)*. Co-produced by the Italian companies Explorer Film '58, Faro Film and Vic Film, in cooperation with the French company C.F.P.C.

Hercules *(Le fatiche di Ercole)* (Warner Bros., 1958)

Credits: Director: Pietro Francisci; *Producers:* Federico Teti, Joseph E. Levine; *Screenplay:* Ennio De Concini, Pietro Francisci, Gaio Frattini, Agenore Incrocci, Furio Scarpelli (adaptation by Pietro Francisci from the poem *The Argonautica* by Apollonios Rhodios); *Photography:* Mario Bava (Eastmancolor, Dyaliscope, aspect ratio 2.35:1); *Film Editor:* Mario Serandrei; *Music:* Enzo Masetti; *Art Direction and Set Decoration:* Flavio Mogherini; *Costume Design:* Giulio Coltellacci; *Makeup:* Euclide Santoni; *Hair Stylist:* Mara Rochetti; *Production Manager:*

Steve Reeves and Sylva Koscina in *Hercules*.

Top and bottom: **Steve Reeves as *Hercules*.**

Mario Pisani; *Assistant Director:* Pietro Nuccorini; *Assistant Set Designer:* Gianni D'Aloisio; *Sound:* Renato Cadueri; Guido Tagliacozzo; *Special Effects:* Mario Bava; *Stunts:* Giovanni Cianfriglia, Nazzareno Zamperla; *Camera Operator:* Corrado Bartoloni; *Assistant Camera Operator:* Silvio Frashetti; *Lighting Technician:* Mario Bava; *Costumes:* Assunto Lazzazzera; *Assistant Costume Designer:* Paolo Tommasi; *Editing Secretary:* Gigliola Rosmino; *Music Director:* Carlo Savina; *Choreography:* Gisa Geert; *Production Secretary:* Spartaco Conversi; *Executive Director:* Ferruccio De Martino; *Executive Director's Assistant:* Massimo De Rita;, *Director's Assistant:* Ettore Mattia; *Assistant Film Editor:* Titta Perozzi; *Laboratory:* Stacofilm S. p. a., Rome, Italy; *Master of Arms:* Enzo Musumeci Greco; running time: 104 minutes (Italy), 107 minutes (U.S.); released February 20, 1958 (Italy), July 22, 1959 (U.S.); video availability: Sinister Cinema.

Cast: Steve Reeves *(Hercules)*; Sylva Koscina *(Iole, Daughter of Pelias)*; Fabrizio Mioni *(Jason)*; Ivo Garrani *(Pelias, King of Iolcus)*; Gianna Maria Canale *(Antea, Queen of the Amazons)*; Arturo Dominici *(Eurysteus)*; Mimmo Palmara *(Iphitus, Son of Pelias)*; Lidia Alfonsi *(The Sybil)*; Gabriele Antonini *(Ulysses)*; Aldo Fiorelli *(Argos)*; Andrea Fantasia *(Laertes)*; Luciana Paluzzi *(Iole's Maid)*; Afro Poli *(Chironi)*; Gian Paolo Rosmino *(Aesculapius)*; Willi Colombini *(Pollux)*; Fulvio Carrara *(Castor)*; Gino Mattera *(Orpheus)*; Gina Rovere *(Amazon #1)*; Lily Granado *(Amazon #2)*; Aldo Pini *(Tifi)*; Guido Martufi *(Iphitus as a Child)*; Paola Quattrini *(Iole as a Child)*; Romano Barbieri; Augusto Belardelli; Spartaco Nale.

Comments: *The* peplum, and *the* sword-and-sandal epic that started the 1960s craze. Producer Joseph E. Levine spent more money promoting *Hercules* than the film had originally cost. Levine bought the American film rights for $120,000 and grossed $1,000,000 in the first ten days of the film's release. Levine had 600 prints of the film struck, and used nationwide saturation booking to maximize his profits; this was an uncommon practice at the time. Among the many promotional gambits was a comic book printed by Dell Publishing, which sold 500,000 copies. *Hercules* and its immediate sequel *Hercules Unchained (qv)* were also the two highest-grossing films in Italian film history. Producer Edward Small had announced a Hercules film project in 1953, with Lex Barker in the lead, but the movie was never produced. Steve Reeves *was* Hercules; he made the role his own, despite the fact that audiences never heard his real voice; he was dubbed by Richard McNamara (a former American GI who stayed in Italy after World War II to work in the film industry) and, in some foreign versions, by Norman Rose. According to the great director Mario Bava, who worked on *Hercules* as a lighting technician, he was the one who suggested that Reeves grow a beard for the role. With *Hercules,* Steve Reeves joined an elite group of actors (Bela Lugosi as Dracula, Buster Crabbe as Flash Gordon, George Reeves as Superman, and Clayton Moore as the Lone Ranger) who define, perpetuate, and *own* their iconic roles, no matter who else plays the characters. With *Hercules* and its sequel *Hercules Unchained,* director Pietro Francisci (1906–1977) laid down the blueprint for what was to become an extensive and very successful film genre, and the quality of Francisci's work has yet to be fully acknowledged. *Hercules* was originally produced by the Italian companies Galatea Film and O.S.C.A.R., in cooperation with Spain's Urania Film. There are four different cuts of *Hercules,* running 98, 103 and 104 minutes, with the longest version—the Italian original—at 107 minutes containing more semi-nudity than the others.

Hercules Against Rome *(Ercole contro Roma)* (American International, 1964)

Credits: *Director:* Piero Pierotti; *Producer:* Fortunato Misiano; *Screenplay:* Arpad DeRiso, Piero Pierotti (from a story by Arpad DeRiso and Nino Scolaro); *Photography:* Augusto Tiezzi (color, Totalscope, aspect ratio 2.35:1); *Film Editor:* Jolanda Benvenuti; *Music:* Angelo Francisco Lavagnino; *Art Direction:* Salvatore Giancotti; *Assistant Director:* Sergio Martino; running time: 94 minutes (Italy); 87 minutes (U.S.); released May 15, 1964 (Italy).

Cast: Alan Steel *(Hercules)*; Wandisa Guida *(Ulpia)*; Livio Lorenzon *(Mansurio)*; Daniele Vargas *(Filippo Afro)*; Andrea Aureli *(Rosio)*;

Dina De Santis *(Arminia)*; Carlo Tamberlani *(Emperor Gordiano)*; Tulio Altamura *(Lucilio)*; Simonetta Simeoni *(Erika)*; Walter Licastro *(Rezio)*; Renato Navarrini *(Argeso)*; Alberto Cevenini *(Dario)*; Amedeo Trilli *(Miro)*; Calisto Calisti *(Mercante)*; Nello Pazzafini *(Segesto)*; Ignazio Balsamo *(Taurus)*; Gaetano Scala *(Indovino Sirio)*; Emma Valloni *(Girl in Tavern)*; Armando Guarnieri *(Giano)*; Anna Arena *(Fenicia)*; Atilo Dottesio *(Satiro)*; Salvatore Borghese *(Mirko)*; Mimmo Palmara *(Lucio Traiano)*.

Comments: A Roman emperor, the victim of a plot by his Pretorinan guards, is recued by Hercules. Produced by the Italian company Romana Film, France's Regina Films and SFF Alfred Rose.

Hercules Against the Barbarians (Maciste nell'inferno di Gengis Khan) (American International, 1964)

Credits: Director: Domenico Paolella; *Producers:* Jacopo Comin, Felice Felicioni; *Supervising Producer:* Giulio Pappagallo; *Screenplay:* Domenico Paolella, Alessandro Ferraù, Luciano Martino (from a story by Domenico Paolella and Alessandro Ferraù); *Photography:* Raffaele Masciocchi (color, Totalscope, aspect ratio 2.35:1); *Film Editor:* Otello Colangeli; *Music:* Giuseppe Piccillo; *Art Direction:* Alfredo Montori; *Set Decoration:* Camillo Del Signore; *Costume Design:* Vera Marzot; *Assistant Director:* Tersicore Kolosoff; *Sound:* Mario Morigi' Pietro Ortolani; *Camera Operator:* Antonio Schiavo Lena; *Orchestra Conductor:* Carlo Savina; *Continuity:* Alberto Salvatore; *Producers of English-Dubbed Version:* Samuel Z. Arkoff, James H. Nicholson; *Director of English-Dubbed Version:* Robert Spafford; running time: 96 minutes (Italy); released April 16, 1964 (Italy); video availability: Something Weird Video.

Cast: Mark Forest *(Hercules)*; José Greci *(Armina)*; Ken Clark *(Kubilai)*; Gloria Milland *(Arias)*; Howard Ross *(Gason)*; Tullio Altamura *(Christian Priest)*; Roldano Lupi *(Genghis Khan)*; Mirko Ellis *(King Vladimir)*; Renato Terra; Bruno Scipioni; Harold Bradley; Mirko Valentin; Elisabetta Wu *(Genghis Khan's Lover)*; Daniela Igliozzi; Renato Navarrini; Ugo Sasso.

Comments: Improbably appearing in the 12th century, Hercules rescues a princess from Genghis Khan. Produced by Italy's Jonia Film.

Hercules Against the Mongols (Maciste contro i Mongoli) (American-International, 1963)

Credits: Director: Domenico Paolella; *Pro-*

Poster for *Hercules Against the Mongols*.

ducer: Jacopo Comin; *Screenplay:* Alessandro Ferraù, Luciano Martino, Domenico Paolella; *Photography:* Raffaele Masciocchi (Eastmancolor, Totalscope, aspect ratio 2.35:1); *Film Editor:* Otello Colangeli; *Music:* Carlo Savina; *Art Direction:* Alfredo Montori; *Costume Design:* Vera; *Makeup:* Otello Sisi; *Hair Dresser:* Adriana Cassini; *Production Supervisor:* Giulio Pappagallo; *Production Manager:* Ferdinand Felicioni; *Assistant Director:* Tersicore Kolosoff; *Set Dresser:* Camillo Del Signore; *Sound:* Mario Morigi, Pietro Ortolani; *Camera Operator:* Antonio Schiavo Lena; *Script Girl:* Nellita Zampieri; running time: 90 minutes (Italy), 90 minutes (U.S.); released November 29, 1963 (Italy); video availability: Something Weird Video.

Cast: Mark Forest *(Maciste)*; José Greci *(Bianca de Tuleda)*; Maria Grazia Spina *(Ljuba)*; Ken Clark *(Sayan)*; Howard Ross [billed as "Renato Rossini"] *(Susadl)*; Nadir Moretti [billed as "Nadir Baltimore"] *(Kin Khan)*; Tullio Altamura *(Osvaldo)*; Bianca Doria *(Raja)*; Fedele Gentile *(Bernard)*; Loris Loddi *(Alessio)*; Giuseppe Addobbati [billed as "John Douglas"] *(The King)*; Bruno Scipioni; Renato Terra *(Karikan)*.

Comments: After the death of Genghis Khan in 1227 AD, Hercules rescues the beautiful princess Bianca from the dead warlord's three ruthless sons. Produced by the Italian companies Alta Vista and Jonia Film, and shot at Incir De Paolis Studios in Rome.

Hercules Against the Moon Men *(Maciste e la regina di Samar)* (Governor Films, 1964)

Credits: *Director:* Giacomo Gentilomo; *Producers:* Luigi Mondello, Robert de Nesle; *Assis-

Poster for *Hercules Against the Moon Men.*

Jany Clair and Alan Steel in *Hercules Against the Moon Men.*

tant *Producer:* Renato Rizzuto; *Supervising Producer:* Augusto Dolfi; *Photography:* Oberdan Troiani (Eastmancolor, Cromoscope, aspect ratio 2.35:1); *Film Editor:* Beatrice Felici; *Music:* Carlo Franci; *Art Direction:* Amedeo Mellone; *Set Decoration:* Giorgio Hermann; *Costume Design:* Maria Luisa Panaro; *Makeup:* Antonio Marini; *Hair Stylist:* Italia Marini; *Assistant Director:* Angelo Sangermano; *Sound:* Luigi Puri; *Special Effects:* Ugo Amadoro; *Laboratory:* Tecnostampa, Rome, Italy; *Camera Operator:* Antonio Modica; *Assistant Camera Operators:* Pier Luigi Santi, Luigi Troiani; *Production Secretary:* Marcello Berni; *Footwear:* E. Pompei; *Wigs:* G. Rochetti; running time: 90 minutes (Italy), 88 minutes (U.S.); released June 27, 1964 (Italy), May 1965 (U.S.); video availability: Something Weird Video.

Cast: Alan Steel *(Hercules)*; Jany Clair *(Queen Samara)*; Anna Maria Polani *(Agar, Gladius' Daughter)*; Nando Tamberlani *(Gladius, the Chancellor)*; Della D'Alberti *(Princess Billis/Selene)*; Goffredo Unger *(Remar)*; Anna Maria Dionisio *(Taris, Tirteo's Wife)*; Paola Pitti *(Tirteo's Daughter)*; Giuliano Raffaelli *(Tirteo, the Innkeeper)*; Stefano Carletti *(Mogol)*; Roberto Ceccacci *(Rudolphis)*; Atilo Dottesio *(Xelon)*; Franco Moruzzi *(Timor)*; Jean-Pierre Honoré *(Darix, Samara's Cousin)*; Salvatore Borghese *(Leader of Ambush Against Hercules)*; Antonio Corevi *(Rubio)*; Angelo Sangermano *(Man at Inn)*.

Comments: In this entry, which veers into the sci-fi realm, evil aliens from the moon land on Earth and conquer the city of Samar. The city's beautiful, wicked queen, Samara, makes a pact with the Moon Men and agrees to provide them with human sacrifices in exchange for their help in conquering the world; Hercules arrives to thwart her plans. Lead Alan Steel (1935–2015), born Sergio Ciani, was an excellent Hercules, and as fellow peplum stars Gordon Mitchell and Brad Harris also did, he went on to appear in spaghetti westerns after the sword-and-sandal craze had faded. *Hercules Against the Moon Men* was co-produced by Italy's Nike Cinematografica and France's Comptoir Français du Cinématographiques (CFPC) and filmed at Cinecittà Studios in Rome.

Hercules Against the Sons of the Sun (Ercole contro I figli del sole) (Walter Manley Enterprises, 1964)

Credits: Director and Producer: Osvaldo Civirani; *Screenplay:* Osvaldo Civirani, Franco Tannuzzini (from their story, adapted by María del Carmen, Martinez Román); *Photography:* Julio Ortas, Osvaldo Civirani (Eastmancolor, Techniscope, aspect ratio 2.35:1); *Film Editors:* Rosa G. Salgado, Nella Nannuzzi; *Music:* Coriolano Gori; *Costume Design:* Mario Giorsi; *Makeup:* Gianni Baneri, Anacieto Giustini; *Hairstylists:* Liliana Celi, Otello Santangeli; *Production Managers:* Paolo Mercuri, Ángel Rosson y Rubio; *Assistant Directors:* Emilio Miraglia, José Montes; *Set Designer:* Pier Vittorio Marchi; *Sound:* Luigi Puri; *Microphone Technician:* Alvaro Orsini; *Stunts:* Nicola Di Gioia; *Camera Operators:* Mario Cimini, Fausto Rossi, Maurizio Scanzani; *Assistant Camera Operators:* Roberto Brega, Walter Civirani, Enrico Cortese, Maurizio Lucchini, Claudio Morabito, Mario Pastorini; *Choreography:* Gino Landi; Archie Savage; *Production Assistant:* Romolo Germano; *Continuity:* Liana Ferri; *Supervisor, English-Dubbed Version:* Richard McNamara; running time: 88 minutes (Italy); released August 8, 1964 (Italy); video availability: Trimark Home Video.

Cast: Mark Forest *(Hercules)*; Anna-Maria Pace *(Princess Hamara)*; Giuliano Gemma *(Princess Maytha)*; Ángela Rhu *(Queen)*; Giulio Donnini *(High Priest)*; German Grech *(Captain of the Guards)*; Andrea Scotti *(Hino)*; Franco Fantasia *(King Ata Hualpa)*; Carlo Latimer *(Chako, the Village Leader)*; Romano Ghini *(Cleor)*; José Riesgo *(King Huasca)*; Antonio Acqua *(Maytha's Priest)*; Stefano Conti *(Adro)*; Gilberto Galvani *(Prisoner)*; Assia Zezon *(Handmaiden)*; Audrey Anderson *(Dancing Girl)*; Ricardo Valle *(Aflos)*; José Carlos Arévalo; Juan Antonio Arévalo; Jose Fresco *(King Juasca)*; Rafael Ibáñez; Javier de Rivera; Andrea Scoppi; Rosalba Neri *(Queen)*.

Comments: After he is shipwrecked in South America, Hercules battles the Incas and rescues a deposed king. As the sword-and-sandal producers grew more and more desperate for story material they went farther and farther afield in the geographical settings and timeframes of their scripts. This particularly anachronistic entry was co-produced by Italy's Wonder films and Spain's Hispamer Films; it was shot at Elios Studios and Vides Cinematografica in Rome.

Hercules and the Black Pirates (Sansone contro il corsaro nero) (American International, 1964)

Credits: Director: Luigi Capuano; *Producer:* Fortunato Misiano; *Screenplay:* Arpad DeRiso, Piero Pierotti; *Photography:* Augusto Tiezzi (Eastmancolor, Totalscope, aspect ratio 2.35:1); *Film Editor:* Jolanda Benvenuti; *Music:* Angelo Francisco Lavagnino; *Production Design:* Pier Vittorio Marchi; *Costume Design:* Walter Patriarca; *Sound:* Leopoldo Rosi; running time: 93 minutes (Italy); released January 25, 1964 (Italy), 1964 (U.S.); video availability: Image Entertainment.

Cast: Alan Steel *(Hercules/Samson)*; Rosalba Neri *(Rosita)*; Piero Lulli *(Rodrigo Sanchez)*; Andrea Aureli *(The Black Corsair)*; Enzo Maggio; Elisa Mainardi *(Carmelita)*; Simonetta Simeoni; Nello Pazzafini *(The Black Corsair's Assistant)*; Margherita Bosi; Cinzia Bruno *(Alma)*; Nerio Bernardi *(Governor of Hermosa)*; Anna Arena; Ignazio Balsamo; Giulio Battiferri; Gilberto Galimberti *(Pirate)*.

Comments: Called Samson in the original Italian version, Hercules joins the Royal Army and battles pirates for the hand of the beautiful Rosita, daughter of the governor. Produced by Italy's Romana Film.

Hercules and the Captive Women (Ercole alla coquista di Atlantide) (Woolner Bros., 1961)

Top and bottom: Alan Steel in *Hercules and the Black Pirates.*

Credits: Director: Vittorio Cottafavi; *Producer:* Achille Piazzi; *Screenplay:* Vittorio Cottafavi, Sandro Continenza, Duccio Tessari, Pierre Benoit, Nicolò Ferrari (from a story by Nicolò Ferrari); *Photography:* Carlo Carlini (Technicolor, Super Tecnirama 70, aspect ratio 2.20:1); *Film Editor:* Maurizio Lucidi; *Music:* Gino Marinuzzi, Jr., Armando Trovajoli; *Production Design:* Franco Lolli; *Costume Design:* Vittorio Rossi; *Production Manager:* Danilo Marciani; *2nd Unit Director:* Giorgio Cristallini; *Art Department Manager:* Italo Tomassi; *Sound:* Umberto Picistrelli; *Special Effects:* Mario Bava; *Orchestra Conductor:* Gino Marinuzzi, Jr.; *Choreography:* Peter Vander Sloot; *Volcano Shots:* Haroun Tazieff; *Soundtrack Album Producer:* Luca di Silverlo; *Producer/Editor of U.S. Dubbed Version:* Hugo Grimaldi; *Voice Actors in U.S.—Dubbed Version:* Georges Aminel; Louis Albressier; Lucien Bryonne; Gabriel Cattand; Jany Clair; Jacques Deschamps; Michel Gatineau; Michel Gudin; Claire Guibert; Jean-Louis Jemma; Hubert Noël; Serge Sauvion; Maria Tamar; Paul Villé; Jean Violette; *Narrator of U.S.-Dubbed Version:* Leon Selznick; running time: 101 minutes (Italy), 94 minutes (U.S.); released August 19, 1961 (Italy), April 15, 1963 (U.S.); video availability: Mill Creek Entertainment.

Cast: Reg Park *(Hercules)*; Fay Spain *(Queen Antinea of Atlantis)*; Ettore Manni *(Androclo, King of Thebes)*; Luciano Marin *(Illo)*; Laura Efrikian *(Ismene, Antinea's Daughter)*; Enrico Maria Salerno *(King of Megara)*; Ivo Garrani *(King of di Megalia)*; Gian Maria Volonté *(King of Sparta)*; Mimmo Palmara *(Astor, The Grand Vizier)*; Mario Petri *(Zenith, Priest of Uranus)*; Mino Doro *(Oraclo)*; Salvatore Furnari *(Timoteo, the Dwarf)*; Alessandro Sperli *(King with Mother)*; Mario Valdemarin *(Gabor)*; Luciana Angiolillo *(Delanira, Hercules' Wife)*; Maurizio Coffarelli *(Proteus, the Monster)*; Tulio Altamura; Raf Baldassarre *(Captain of the Guard)*; Ignazio Dolce; Nando Tamberlani *(Tiresia)*; Nazzareno Zamperla *(Man in Tavern Fight)*; Jimmy il Fenomeno *(Man in Tavern Fight #2)*.

Comments: Hercules rescues a girl who accompanies him to the lost kingdom of Atlantis, where he learns that the queen is planning to conquer the world. Produced by Italy's SpA Cinematografica in cooperation with France's Comptoir Français du Film Production (CFFP). This is the only Italian Hercules film shot in the 70mm format. The American soundtrack features music borrowed from *The Creature from the Black Lagoon* (1954).

Hercules and the Masked Rider (*Golia e il cavaliere mascherato*) (American International, 1963)

Credits: Director: Piero Pierotti; *Producer:* Fortunato Misiano; *Producers of U.S.-Dubbed Version:* Samuel Z. Arkoff, James H. Nicholson; *Screenplay:* Luciano Martino, Piero Perotti, Ernesto Gastaldi, Arpad DeRiso (from a story by Luciano Martino, Piero Perotti); *Photography:* Augusto Tiezzi (Eastmancolor, Totalscope, aspect ratio 2.35:1); *Film Editor:* Jolanda Benvenuti; *Art Direction:* Salvatore Giancotti; *Costume Design:* Walter Patriarca; *Assistant Director:* Giancarlo Romitelli; *Sound:* Franco Groppioni, Bruno Moreal; *Camera Operator:* Luigi Allegretti; *Assistant Camera Operator:* Renato Mascagno; *Assistant Film Editor:* Alba Di Salvo; running time: 85 minutes (Italy); 86 minutes (U.S.), released November 17, 1963 (Italy), 1964 (U.S.); video availability: Mill Creek Entertainment.

Cast: Alan Steel *(Hercules)*; Mimmo Palmara *(Don Juan)*; José Greci *(Doña Blanca, Francisco's Daughter)*; Pilar Cansino *(Estella, the Gypsy Queen)*; Arturo Dominici *(Don Ramiro Suarez)*; Dina De Santis *(Dolores, Blanca's Handmaid)*; Piero Leri *(Felipe)*; Renato Navarrini *(Don Francisco)*; Loris Gizzi *(Pedro, the King's Envoy)*; Ettore Manni *(Captain Blasco)*; Tulio Altamura *(Ruiz)*; Ugo Sasso *(Hermann)*; Armando Guarnieri *(Don Alvarez)*; Gianni Baghino *(Goha, the Treasurer)*; Nando Angelini; Piero Pastore *(Head Guard at Prison)*; Antonio Corevi; Ignazio Balsamo; Gaetano Scala *(Esteban)*; Mauro Mannatrizio; Fidel Gonzáles *(Palomito)*; Nello Pazzafini *(Gypsy)*; Salvatore Borghese *(Gypsy)*.

Opposite, top: Reg Park battles a monster in *Hercules and the Captive Women*. *Opposite, bottom:* The monster poses smugly for the camera in *Hercules and the Captive Women*.

88 *Hercules*

Comments: Called Goliath in the original Italian version, Hercules is reduced to guest star status in this swashbuckling tale (which is apparently set in the 15th or 16th century) pitting a masked, Zorro-type hero against Spanish Conquistadors. Produced by Italy's Romana Film.

Hercules and the Treasure of the Incas (Sansone e il tesoro degli Incas) (American-International Television, 1964)

Credits: Director: Piero Pierotti; *Producer:* Fortunato Misiano; *Screenplay:* Arpad DeRiso, Piero Pierotti; *Photography:* Augusto Tiezzi (color, Totalscope, 2.35:1); *Music:* Angelo Francesco Lavagnino; *Production Design:* Pier Vittorio Marchi; *Costume Design:* Walter Patriarca; *Makeup:* Anacieto Giustini; *Hair Stylist:* Violetta Pacelli; *Production Manager:* Pasquale Misiano; *Camera Operator:* Luigi Allegretti; *Assistant Camera Operator:* Renato Mascagno; *Production Secretary:* Elio Saroli; running time: 105 minutes (Italy), 90 minutes (U.S.); released October 15, 1964; video availability: Sinister Cinema.

Cast: Alan Steel *(William Smith/Samson)*; Tony Sailer *(Alan Fox)*; Wolfgang Lukschy *(El Puma)*; Brigitte Heiberg *(Jenny Nixon)*; Mario Petri *(Jerry Darmon)*; Anna Maria Polani *(Queen Mysia)*; Pierre Cressoy *(Vince)*; Federico Boido *(Tex)*; Rosy De Leo; Elisabetta Fanti *(Urpia)*; Gilberto Galimberti *(Aztec)*; Dada Gallotti *(Ilona)*; Omero Gargano *(Bartender)*; Antonio Gradoli *(Castoro)*; Franco Jamonte *(Darmon's Accomplice)*; Gino Marturano *(Barracuda)*; Harry Riebauer *(Sheriff)*; Bruno Scipioni *Darmon's Henchman)*; Andrea Scotti *(Stagecoach Passenger)*; Attilio Severini *(Grizzly)*; Umberto Spadoro *(Darmon's Henchman)*; Carlo Tamberlani *(Burt Nixon)*; Giulio Tomei; Amedeo Trilli *(Barber)*; Nino Vingelli *(Indian)*.

Comments: In this convoluted, anachronistic tale, Hercules winds up on the Yucatan peninsula, dealing with the Incas. Hercules was called Samson in the original Italian version. Co-produced by Italy's Romana Film and France's Ulysse Productions.

Hercules and the Tyrants of Babylon (Ercole contro I tiranni di Babilonia) (American International, 1964)

Poster for *Hercules and the Tyrants of Babylon.*

Credits: Director: Domenico Paolella; *Producer:* Fortunato Misiano; *Screenplay:* Luciano Martino, Domenico Paolella); *Photography:* Augusto Tiezzi (color, Totalscope, aspect ratio 2.35:1); *Film Editor:* Jolanda Benvenuti; *Music:* Angelo Francisco Lavagnino; *Art Direction:* Pier Vittorio Marchi; *Makeup:* Massimo Giustini; *Hair Stylist:* Violetta Pacelli; *Production Manager:* Nino Misiano; *Wardrobe Supervisor:* Walter Patriarca; *Producers of U.S.-Dubbed Version:* Samuel Z. Arkoff, James H. Nicholson; running time: 96 minutes (Italy), 86 minutes (U.S.); released December 25, 1964 (Italy), 1965 (U.S.); video availability: Mill Creek Entertainment.

Cast: Peter Lupus [billed as "Rock Stevens"] *(Hercules)*; Helga Liné *(Taneal/Tanit)*; Mario Petri *(King Phaleg)*; Livio Lorenzon *(Salman Osar)*; Anna Maria Polani *(Asparta/Esperia))*; Tullio Altamura *(Azur)*; Franco Balducci *(Bahar)*; Diego Pozetto *(Bomar)*; Mirko Valentin *(Glaucone)*; Diego Michelotti *(Chritophisis)*; Rosy De Leo *(Lady in Waiting)*; Eugenio Bottari *(Azur's Major Domo)*; Andrea Scotti *(Young Shepherd)*; Salvatore Borghese; Jeff Cameron *(Soldier)*; Pietro Ceccarelli *(Fighter)*; Arturo Dominici; Gilberto Galimberti; Piero Lulli; Emilio Messina; Amerigo Santarelli *(Wrestler)*; Pietro Torrisi *(Wrestler)*; Daniele Vargas.

Comments: Hercules frees the people of Babylon from an evil sorceress. Produced by Italy's Romana Film.

Hercules in the Haunted World *(Ercole al centro della Terra)* (Woolner Bros., 1961)

Credits: Directors: Mario Bava, Franco Prosperi; *Producer:* Achille Piazzi; *Screenplay:* Mario Bava, Sandro Continenza, Franco Prosperi, Duccio Tessari (from a story by Mario Bava); *Photography:* Mario Bava (Technicolor, Totalscope Super 100, aspect ratio 2.35:1); *Film Editor:* Mario Serandrei; *Music:* Armando Trovajoli; *Production Design and Art Direction:* Franco Lolli; *Costume Design:* Mario Giorsi;

Reg Park in *Hercules in the Haunted World*.

Makeup: Renzo Francioni, Franco Palombi; *Hair Stylist:* Nicla Palombi; *Production Manager:* Danilo Marciani; *Art Department Manager:* Italo Tomassi; *Assistant Set Designer:* Antonio Sarzi-Braga; *Sound:* Luigi Puri; *Special Visual Effects/Sound Effects:* Tonino Cacciottolo; *Assistant Camera Operator:* Joe D'Amato; *Wardrobe:* Maria Luisa Onorati, Valeria Sponsali; *Soundtrack Album Producer:* Luca di Silverio; *Voice Dubbing for Italian Version:* Emilio Cigoli (for Reg Park); Lauro Gazzolo (for Christopher Lee); running time: 93 minutes (Italy); released November 16, 1961 (Italy), April 1964 (U.S.); video availability: Fantoma.

Cast: Reg Park *(Hercules)*; Christopher Lee *(King Lico)*; Leonora Ruffo *(Princess Deianira)*; George Ardisson *(Thesus)*; Marisa Beli *(Aretusa)*; Ida Galli *(Persephone)*; Franco Giacobini *(Telemachus)*; Mino Doro *(Keros)*, Rosalba Neri *(Helena)*; Ely Drago *(Jocasta)*; Gaia Germani *(Medea)*; Raf Baldassarre *(Mercenary)*; Elisabetta Paven *(Tamar)*; Aldo Pedinotti *(Sunis)*; Claudio Marzulli; Garzia Collodi *(Elettra)*.

Comments: Hercules, accompanied by his friends Theseus and Telemachus, journeys to Hades in search of a cure for his mesmerized lover Deianara, who is being held captive by the evil King Lico. One of the greatest of all Hercules films. Extremely well-directed and designed by the great Mario Bava, who gets the most out of extremely limited resources. Reg Park is excellent as Hercules, exhibiting a wider emotional range than expected, and Hammer Films' Dracula Christopher Lee (although voice-dubbed by another actor) is a major asset to this production. Produced by Italy's SpA Cinematografica. A beautifully-restored, high quality DVD of this film was released by Fantoma.

Hercules in the Valley of Woe (Maciste contro Ercole nella valle dei guri) (Embassy, 1961)

Credits: Director: Mario Mattoli; *Producer:* Italo Martinenghi; *Screenplay:* Marcello Marchesi, Vittorio Metz; *Photography:* Enzo Oddone (color, Totalscope, aspect ratio 2.35:1); *Film Editor:* Roberto Cinquini; *Music:* Gianni Ferrio; *Makeup:* Michele Trimarchi; *Hair Stylist:* Marcella De Marzi; *Production Supervisor:* Renato De Pasqualis; *Production Manager:* Ignazio Luceri; *Assistant Director:* Gabriele Palmieri; *Sound:* Pietro Ortolani; *Script Supervisor:* Mirella Gamacchio; running time: 90 minutes (Italy); released December 19, 1961 (Italy); video availability: Alpha Video.

Cast: Kirk Morris *(Maciste)*;

French poster for *Hercules in the Haunted World*.

Frank Gordon (*Hercules*); Bice Valori; Raimondo Vianello (*Rusteghin*); Mario Carotenuto (*Comendatore*); Liana Orfei (*Dejanira*); Carlo Croccolo (*Fetonte*); Franco Franchi (*Francheo*); Gino Bramieri; Ciccio Ingrassia; Ave Ninchi; Sondra Mondaini; Gino Buzzanca; Gianni Cajafa; Gianna Cobelli; Fanfulla; Renato Maddalena; Francesco Mulé; Ombretta Ostenda; Riccardo Paladini; Rita Salvati; Renato Terra; Santo Versace.

Comments: In this decidedly comedic entry, two fast-talking boxing promoters travel back in time and meet Hercules, who rescues them from Genghis Khan.

Hercules of the Desert (*La valle dell'eco tonante*) (American International, 1964)

Credits: Director: Tanio Boccia (billed as "Amerigo Anton"); *Producer:* Luigi Rovere; *Screenplay:* Mario Moroni, Alberto De Rossi, Tanio Boccia (from a story by Mario Moroni, Alberto De Rossi); *Photography:* Aldo Giordani (Technicolor, Techniscope, aspect ratio 2.35:1); *Film Editor:* Tanio Boccia; *Music:* Carlo Rustichelli; *Production Design:* Amedeo Mellone; *Costume Design:* Walter Patriarca; *Makeup:* Duilio Giustini; *Hair Stylist:* Gustavo Sisi; *Production Manager:* Renato Panetuzzi; *Assistant Director:* Mario Casalini; *Assistant Production Designer:* Oreste Sabatini; *Set Construction:* Carlo Agate, Angelo Zambo; *Sound:* Oscar Di Santo, Umberto Picistrelli; *Sound Recordist:* Eugenio Fiori; *Microphone Boom Operator:* Guido Ortenzi; *Special Effects:* Pasquale Mancino; *Camera Operator:* Sergio Bergamini; *Assistant Camera Operator:* Nello Renzi; *Still Photographer:* Mario Mazzoni; *Assistant Costume Designers:* Domenico Casu, Angiolina Menichelli; *Assistant Film Editor:* Alba Di Salvo; *Administrative Director:* Fernanda Ventimiglia; *Production Secretary:* Maurizio Rotundi; *Script Supervisor:* Grazia Baldanello; running time: 95 minutes (Italy); released October 9, 1964 (Italy), 1965 (U.S.); video availability: Something Weird Video.

Cast: Kirk Morris (*Maciste*); Hélène Chanel (*Farida*); Alberto Farnese (*Masura*); Spela Rozin (*Selina*); Furio Meniconi (*Manatha*); Rosalba Neri (*Ramhis*); Geneviève Audry; Nando Tamberlani (*Manata, the Sage*); Dante Posani; Mara Carisi; Nadir Moretti; Aldo Cecconi; Marco Pasquini; Luigi Scavran; Franco Pechini; Wladimiro Tuicovich.

Comments: Heroic Maciste comes to the rescue when evil Queen Farida attempts to conquer the peaceful Gameli tribe and their beautiful leader Selina. Produced by Italy's Cineluxor.

Hercules, Prisoner of Evil (*Ursus, il terrore dei kinorghisi*) (American-International, 1964)

Credits: Directors: Antonio Margheriti (billed as "Anthony Dawson"), Ruggero Deodato; *Producer:* Adelpho Ambrosiano; *Screenplay:* Marcello Sartarelli; *Photography:* Gábor Pogány (Eastmancolor, Totalscope, aspect ratio 2.35:1); *Film Editor:* Otello Colangeli; *Music:* Franco Mannino (billed as "Franco Trinacria"); *Production Supervisor:* Natalino Vicario; *Production Manager:* Luciano Cattania; *Production Design:* Riccardo Domenici; *Makeup:* Maurizio Giustini; *Hair Stylist:* Iolanda Conti; *Assistant Director:* Ruggero Deodato; *Sound:* Mario Morigi, Giulio Tagliacozzo; *Camera Operators:* Mario Capriotti; Claudio Ragona; *Assistant Film Editor:* Maria Napoleoni; running time: 100 minutes (Italy), 90 minutes (U.S.); released July 31, 1964 (Italy); video availability: Retromedia.

Cast: Reg Park (*Ursus*); Mireille Granelli (*Amiko*); Ettore Manni (*Ilo*); Furio Meniconi (*Zereteli*); María Teresa Orsini (*Kato*); Lilli Mantovani (*Slave*); Nino Fuscagni (*Miko*); Giulio Maculani (*Varos*); Ugo Carboni; Claudio Scarchilli (*Lava*); Piero Pastore (*Amko*); Gaetano Quartararo; Claudio Ruffini (*Frido*).

Comments: Hercules defends villagers from the cruel Prince Zereteli and the evil sorceress Amiko, who has the ability to transform men into bestial monsters. Produced by Italy's Ambrosiana Cinematografica and Adelphia Productions.

Hercules, Samson and Ulysses (*Ercole sfida Sansone*) (MGM, 1963)

Credits: Director: Pietro Francisci; *Producer:* Joseph Fryd; *Screenplay:* Pietro Francisci; *Photography:* Silvano Ippoliti (Metrocolor, aspect ratio 1.85:1); *Music:* Angelo Francesco Lavagnino;

Art Direction: Giorgio Giovannini; *Costume Design:* Gaia Romanini; *Makeup:* Euclide Santoli; *Hair Stylist:* Amalia Paoletti; *Sound:* Antonio Bramonti; *Sound System:* Westrex; *Camera Operator:* Franco Di Giacomo; *Orchestra Conductor:* Carlo Savina; *Choreographer:* Wilbert Bradley; running time: 93 minutes (Italy), 86 minutes (U.S.); released December 20, 1963 (Italy); May 1965 (U.S.); video availability: Warner Home Video.

Cast: Kirk Morris *(Hercules)*; Iloosh Khoshabe [billed as "Richard Lloyd"] *(Samson)*; Liana Orfei *(Delilah, Philistine Queen)*; Diletta D'Andrea *(Leria, Hercules' Wife)*; Enzo Cerusico *(Ulysses)*; Fulvia Franco *(Queen of Ithaca)*; Aldo Giuffrè *(Seren, Philistine King)*; Andrea Fantasia *(Laertes, King of Ithaca)*; Nando Angelini *(Rower)*; Marco Mariani; Jole Mauro; Pietro Tordi *(Azer)*; Mario De Simone *(Daros)*; Aldo Pini; Ettore Zamperini; Ugo Sasso; Mario Wassilli; Fortunato Arena; Giovanni Di Benedetto; Willi Colombini; Cinzia Bruno; Fulvio Carrara; Loris Lodi *(Iro)*; Stefania Sabatini; Walter Grant; Rina Mascetti; Antonio Corevi; Halina Zalewska; Wladimiro Tuicovich; Cyrus Elias; Franco Fantasia.

Comments: The three heroic title characters form an alliance to defeat a sea monster and the evil ruler of the Philistines. Produced by I.C.D.

Hercules the Avenger *(La sfida dei giganti)* (American International, 1965)

Credits: Director: Maurizio Lucidi (Billed as "Maurice A. Bright"); *Screenplay:* Lorenzo Gicca Palli (billed as "Enzo Gicca"); *Photography:* Alvaro Mancori (color, Techniscope, aspect ratio 2.35:1); *Film Editor:* Maurizio Lucidi; *Art Direction:* Giorgio Giovannini; *Costume Design:* Tina Grani; *Special Effects:* Emilio Trani; running time: 96 minutes (Italy), 90 minutes (U.S.); released August 13, 1965 (Italy); video availability: Retromedia.

Cast: Reg Park *(Hercules)*; Gia Sandri *(Queen Leda)*; Giovanni Cianfriglia *(Anteo)*; Adriana Ambesi *(Deyanira)*; Gianni Solaro *(Teseo)*; Luigi Barbini *(Xantos)*; Franco Ressel *(Eteocles)*; Luigi Donato *(Timoniere)*; Marisa Belli *(Queen of the Children of the Sun)*; Corrado Sonni; Mimmo Poli *(Gerone)*; Giulio Maculani.

Comments: Hercules battles zombies and monsters in this weak but interesting production, which consists almost entirely of re-edited footage culled from *Hercules in the Haunted World (qv)* and *Hercules and the Captive Women (qv)*. Produced by Italy's Plaza Film and Schermi Riuniti.

Hercules Unchained *(Ercole e la regina di Lidia)* (Warner Bros., 1959)

Credits: Director: Pietro Francisci; *Producers:* Bruno Vailati, Joseph E. Levine; *Executive Producer:* Ferruccio De Martino; *Screenplay:* Ennio De Concini, Pietro Francisci (from a story by Pietro Francisci, based on plays by Sophocles and Aeschylus); *Photography:* Mario Bava (Eastmancolor, Dyaliscope, aspect ratio 2.35:1); *Film Editor:* Mario Serandrei; *Music:* Enzo Masetti; *Set Decoration:* Massimo Tavazzi; *Costume Design:* Maria Baroni; *Makeup:* Otello Fava; *Hair Stylist:* Maria Miccinilli; *Wigs:* Rocchetti; *Assistant Directors:* Pietro Nuccorini, Mario Bava; *Architect:* Flavio Mogherini; *Assistant Architects:* Gianni D'Aloisio, Giorgio Giovannini; *Weapons/Props:* E. Rancati; *Set Dresser:* Tani; *Sound:* Renato Cadueri, Paolo Ketoff; *Sound Technician:* Giulio Tagliacozzo; *Microphone Operator:* Bruno Zanoli; *Special Effects:* Mario Bava; *Stunts:* Nazzareno Zamperla; *Camera Operator:* Ubaldo Terzano; *Assistant Camera Operators:* Danilo Desideri, Mario Mancini; *Lighting Director:* Mario Bava; *Still Photographer:* Aldo Galfano; *Dressmakers:* Assunto Lazzazzera, Mimma Olivieri; *Footwear:* Pompei; *Assistant Film Editor:* Misa Gabrini; *Orchestra Conductor:* Carlo Savina; *Soundtrack Album Producer:* Luca di Silverio; *Choreographer:* Johnny Blysdeal; *Production Secretaries:* Dante Brini, Spartaco Conversi; *Production Assistant:* Massimo De Rita; *Locations:* Salvatore Siciliano; *Fencing Master:* Enzo Musumeci Greco; *Continuity:* Barbara Fusch; running time: 98 minutes (Italy), 105 minutes (U.S.); released February 14, 1959 (Italy), July 13, 1960 (U.S.); video availability: Alpha Video.

Cast: Steve Reeves *(Hercules)*; Sylva Koscina *(Iole, Hercules' Wife)*; Sylvia Lopez *(Queen Ofale, of Lydia)*; Patrizia Della Rovere *(Penelope)*; Primo Carnera *(Antaeus, the Giant)*; Carlo D'Angelo *(Creonte, High Priest of Thebes)*; Gabriele

Top: **Steve Reeves grapples with Primo Carnera in** *Hercules Unchained.* *Bottom:* **Steve Reeves and Sylvia Lopez in** *Hercules Unchained.*

Antonini *(Ulysses, Son of Laertes)*; Cesare Fantoni *(Edipus, King of Thebes)*; Mimmo Palmara *(Polinices)*; Andrea Fantasia *(laertes, King of Ithaca)*; Aldo Fiorelli *(Argos, the Shipbuilder)*; Gino Mattera *(Orpheo)*; Aldo Pini *(Tifi, Pilot of the Argo)*; Nino Marchetti *(Fossore)*; Daniele Vargas *(Anfiarao)*; Sergio Fantoni *(Eteocles)*; Elda Tattoli *(Altmea, Mother of Ulysses' Girlfriend)*; Ugo Sasso *(Polinice's Officer)*; Fulvio Carrara *(Pollux)*; Willi Combini *(Castor, Laertes' Assistant)*; Fulvia Franco *(Anticlea, Ulysses' Mother)*; Angelo Zanolli *(Admeo)*; Walter Grant *(Aesculapio)*; Marisa Valenti *(Ulysses' Bride)*; Gianni Loti *(Sandone, Captain of the Lydian Guard)*; Nando Cicero *(Lastene)*; Colleen Bennet *(Ballerina at Palace)*; Sergio Ciani (a. k. a. Alan Steel); Fabrizio Mioni *(Jason)*.

Comments: Although *Hercules* certainly established a global demand for sword-and-sandal epics, it was this immediate sequel that really propelled the genre forward into the craze that it became. In this continuation of the Steve Reeves original, the heroic young Ulysses attempts to rescue Hercules, who has lost his memory under the influence of the beautiful Queen Ofale of Lydia, with whom he has fallen in love while his wife Iole awaits his return. In many ways a more visually exciting production than the first movie (thanks to the special effects and design influence of Mario Bava), *Hercules Unchained* also benefits from the copious feminine pulchritude on display, especially the French-born Sylvia Lopez as Queen Ofale. Tragically, Lopez (a stunning beauty at age 26) was afflicted with leukemia, and died shortly after completing this film. Croatian-born Sylva Koscina (1933–1994) had a long career in Italian and European films, and, with her bright, wholesome sex appeal, contributes a great deal to this film as well as the original. Former heavyweight boxing champion Primo Carnera (in his last film role) appears here as Antaeus the Earth God, who draws his enormous strength from contact with the soil. He proves a tough opponent for Hercules until the secret of his power is revealed, prompting Hercules to simply throw him in the water (curiously, the German release of *Hercules Unchained* omits any mention of Antaeus' godhood, rendering Hercules' difficulty in defeating him somewhat puzzling). *Hercules Unchained* was co-produced by Italy's Galatea Film and Lux Film, in cooperation with France's Lux Compagnie Cinématographique de France and Spain's Urania Film; and was shot at Rome's Titanus Studios. A later double-bill reissue paired it up with the original film.

Steve Reeves in *Hercules Unchained.*

Hercules vs. the Hydra (Gli amori di Ercole) (Walter Manley Enterprises, 1966)

Credits: Director: Carlo Ludovico Bragaglia; *Producer:* Alberto Manca; *Associate Producer:* Alberto Salvatori; *Screenplay:* Sandro Continenza, Luciano Doria (from a story by Alberto Manca); *Photography:* Enzo Serafin (Eastmancolor, CinemaScope, aspect ratio 2.35:1); *Film Editor:* Renato Cinquini; *Music:* Carlo Innocenzi; *Production Design:* Alberto Boccianti; *Set Decoration:* Fortunato Frasca; *Costume Design:* Maria Baroni, Dario Cecchi; *Makeup Director:* Amato Garbini; *Makeup Artist:* Duilio Scarozza; *Assistant Makeup Artist:* Angelo Grisoni; *Hair Stylists:* Gabriella Borzelli, Rosa Luciani; *Production Manager:* Gianni Solitro; *Assistant Directors:* John Hanau, Nino Zanchin; *2nd Assistant Directors:* Giovanni Fago, Jean Josipovici; *Art Department Manager:* Italo Tomassi; *Sound:* Oscar Di Santo; *Sound Engineer:* Luigi Puri; *Sound Recordist:* Pietro Spadoni; *Microphone Boom Operator:* Mario Ligobbi; *Special Effects:* Nino Battistelli, Augusto Vivani; *Camera Operator:* Claudio Ragona; *2nd Unit Camera Operators:* Luigi Allegretti, Vittorio Bernini, Vincenzo Seratrice; *Assistant Camera Operators:* Nello Renzi, Sergio Salvati; *Assistant Film Editor:* Cleofe Conversi; *Orchestra Conductor:* Carlo Franci; *Fencing Master:* Enzo Musumeci Greco; *Equine Supervisor:* Luigi Padovani; *Script Supervisor:* Nelly Cavallo; running time: 97 minutes (Italy), 98 minutes (U.S.); released August 19, 1960 (Italy), 1966 (U.S.); video availability: Something Weird Video.

Cast: Jayne Mansfield *(Queen Delanira/Hippolyta)*; Mickey Hargitay *(Hercules)*; Massimo Serato *(Licos)*; René Dary *(The General)*; Moira Orfei *(Némée)*; Gil Vidal *(Achilles)*; Sandrine; Rossella Como; Andrea Scotti; Arturo Bragaglia; Andrea Aureli; Olga Solbelli; Giulio

Husband and wife stars Mickey Hargitay and Jayne Mansfield in *Hercules vs. the Hydra.*

Mickey Hargitay and Jayne Mansfield in *Hercules vs. the Hydra*.

Donnini; Lidia Alfonsi; Barbara Florian; Aldo Pedinotti; Tina Gloriani; Antonio Gradoli; Cesare Fantoni; Giovanni Galletti; Gianni Loti; Sergio Calò; *Voice Dubbing Actors:* Nadine Alari; Pierre Asso; René Bériard; Jean-Henri Chambois; Jacqueline Ferrière; Lucienne Givry; Claire Guibert; Camile Guérini; Michel Le Royer; Héléna Manson; Roland Ménard; Hubert Noël.

Comments: Hollywood icon Jayne Mansfield and her husband Mickey Hargitay star in this very atypical entry, in which Hercules battles the mythical Hydra and rescues his lover Delanira from the traitorous King Licos. Mickey Hargitay (an underrated performer) is very good as Hercules, and blonde bombshell Jayne Mansfield (her physical assets on full display here in a dual role) is a stunning lead. An alternate title is *The Loves of Hercules*. Produced by the Italian company Grandi Schermi Italiani in cooperation with the French companies Contact Organization and Paris Productions (PIP).

Hercules vs. the Moloch (*Ercole contro Moloch*) (Embassy, 1963)

Credits: *Director:* Giorgio Ferroni; *Producers:* Diego Alchimede, Robert de Nesle; *Screenplay:* Remigio Del Grosso, Arrigo Equini, Giorgio Ferroni; *Photography:* Augusto Tiezzi (Eastmancolor, Euroscope, aspect ratio 2.35:1); *Film Editor:* Antonietta Zita; *Production Design:* Arrigo Equini; *Costume Design:* Elio Micheli; *Makeup:* Massimo Giustini; *Hair Stylist:* Violetta Pacelli; *Production Supervisor:* Diego Alchimede; *Assistant Director:* Giancarlo Romitelli; *Sound Engineers:* Armando Bondani, Franco Groppioni; *Director of U.S.-Dubbed Version:* Richard McNamara; *Script for U.S.-Dubbed Version:* John Davis Hart; running time: 102 minutes (Italy); released December 21, 1963 (Italy), December 15, 1965 (U.S.); video availability: Trimark Home Video.

Cast: Gordon Scott *(Hercules)*; Alessandra Panaro *(Medea, Queen of Tyro)*; Rosalba Neri

Original Italian poster for *Hercules vs. the Hydra*.

(Demeter, Queen of Micenas); Arturo Dominici (Penthius, General of Micenas); Michel Lemoine (Euneos); Jany Clair (Deianira); Nerio Bernardi (Asterion, High Priest); Nello Pazzafini (Archepolos); Gaetano Scala; Geneviève Grad (Pasifae); Pietro Marascalchi; Mario Lodolini; Fortunato Arena (Gladiator Instructor); Jeff Cameron (Gladiator); Veriano Ginesi (Gladiator).

Comments: Hercules defeats a pagan cult that worships a hideous monster as their god in this entry, which has a somewhat more horrific slant than most. Produced by Italy's Explorer Film '58 and France's Comptoir Français du Film Production (CFFP).

Hero of Rome (Il colosso di Roma) (Embassy Pictures, 1964)

Credits: *Director:* Giorgio Ferroni; *Screenplay:* Remigio Del Grosso, Antonio Visone (from a story by Alberta Montanti); *Photography:* Augusto Tiezzi (Eastmancolor, Spesvision, aspect ratio 2.35:1); *Film Editor:* Antonietta Zita; *Music:* Angelo Francesco Lavagnino; *Production Design:* Antonio Visone; *Art Direction:* Gérard Cohen, Joëlle Janin; *Set Decoration:* Carlo Gentili; *Costume Design:* Elio Micheli; *Makeup:* Massimo Giustini; *Hair Stylists:* Salvatore Cotroneo, Violetta Pacelli; *Sound:* Guido Felicioni, Pietro Ortolani; *Production Supervisor:* Italo Tallone; *Production Manager:* Diego Alchimede; *Assistant Director:* Giorgio Stegani; *Camera Operator:* Luigi Allegretti; *Assistant Camera Operators:* Giovanni Bonivento, Renato Mascagno; *Assistant Film Editor:* Graziella Zita; *Script Supervisor:* Giovanni Siracusa; running time: 90 minutes (Italy), 90 minutes (U.S.); released June 25, 1964 (Italy); video availability: Synergy Entertainment.

Cast: Gordon Scott (Mucius); Gabriella Pallotta (Cielia); Massimo Serato (Tarquinius); Gabriele Antonini (Arunte); Maria Pia Conte (Valeria); Roldano Lupi (Porsenna); Philippe Hersent (Publicola); Franco Fantasia (Claudius); Bernard Farber (Milone); Nando Angelini (Etruscan Soldier); Fortunato Arena (Etruscan Soldier); Tullio Altamura (Senator); Valerio Tordi (Servius); Attilio Dottesio (Senator); Gaetano Quartararo (Senator); Antonio Corevi (Etruscan Physician); Gianni Baghino (Etruscan Soldier).

Comments: After Tarquinius, the vile ruler of Rome, is dethroned in an uprising, he plots to regain power, but is opposed by the heroic warrior Muscius. Produced by Italy's Dorica Film and Produzi Associati (PEA), in cooperation with France's Unicité and Les Films Jacques Lettienne.

Herod the Great (Erode il grande) (Allied Artists, 1960)

Credits: *Director:* Viktor Tourjansky (billed

Edmund Purdom and Sylvia Lopez in *Herod the Great*.

as "Arnaldo Genoino"); *Producer:* Viktor Tourjansky; *Executive Producer:* Giampaolo Bigazzi; *Supervising Producers:* Umberto Falciani, Piero Ghione; *Screenplay:* Damiano Damiani, Federico Zardi, Fernando Cerchio, Viktor Tourjansky (from a story by Damiano Damiani and Tullio Pinelli); *Photography:* Massimo Dallamano (Eastmancolor, Totalscope, aspect ratio 2.35:1); *Film Editor:* Antonietta Zita; *Music:* Carlo Savina; *Set Decoration:* Nedo Azzini, Riccardo Domenici, Giorgio Scala; *Costume Design:* Vittorio Nino Novarese; *Makeup:* Franco Palombi, Attilio Camarda; *Hair Stylist:* Nicla Palombi; *Production Managers:* Umberto Falciani, Piero Ghione; *Assistant Directors:* Sergio Bergonzelli, Fernando Cerchio; *Art Department Manager:* Italo Tomassi; *Set Designer:* Giorgio Scalo; *Sound:* Franco Bassi, Raffaele Del Monte; *Special Effects:* Joseph Nathanson; *Camera Operator:* Cesare Allione; *Assistant Camera Operators:* Sergio D'Offizi, Dario Regis; *Still Photographer:* Paul Ronald; *Assistant Costume Designer:* Marisa Crimi; *Assistant Film Editor:* Nina Jadelica; *Production Secretary:* Cecilia Bigazzi; *Continuity:* Vyera Golconich; *Producer of English-Dubbed Version:* Sam Schneider; running time: 93 minutes (Italy); released January 1, 1959 (Italy), December 5, 1960 (U.S.); video availability: Alpha Video.

Cast: Edmund Purdom *(Herod)*; Sandra Milo *(Sarah)*; Elena Zareschi *(Alexandra)*; Alberto Lupo *(Aaron)*; Sylvia Lopez *(Miriam)*; Andrea Giordana *(Daniel)*; Corrado Pani *(Herod Antipas)*; Renato Baldini *(Claudio)*; Camillo Pilotto *(High Priest)*; Carlo D'Angelo *(Man Who Saw Jesus' Birth)*; Enrico Glori *(Taret)*; Adolfo Geri; Fedele Gentile *(Oreb)*; Enzo Fiermonte; Renato Montalbano; Nino Marchetti; Diego Pozzetto; Jean Mollier; Tonino Cervasato *(Baby)*; Feodor Chaliapin, Jr.; Valeria Gramignani; Massimo Girotti *(Ottaviano/Augustus)*; Arnoldo Foà.

Comments: After Herod, King of Judea, is captured by the Romans, his faithful lieutenant Aaron attempts to free him. Produced by the Italian companies Vic Film, Faro Film and Explorer Film,'58 in tandem with the French company Comptoir Français du Productions Cinématographiques (CFPC).

The Huns *(La regina dei tartari)* (Producers International, 1960)

Credits: *Director:* Sergio Grieco; *Producer:* Carlo Lombardi; *Screenplay:* Marcello Ciorciolini, Rate Furlan (from a story by Eric Klaus); *Photography:* Alfio Contini (Eastmancolor, Totalscope, aspect ratio 2.35:1); *Film Editor:* Enzo Alfonzi; *Music:* Bruno Canfora; *Art Direction:* Alberto Bocciantini; *Costume Design:* Mario Giorsi; running time: 102 minutes (Italy); released October 5, 1960 (Italy), November 14, 1962 (U.S.).

Cast: Chelo Alonso *(Tanya, Queen of the Tartars)*; Jacques Sernas *(Malok)*; Folco Lulli *(Igor)*; Philippe Hersent *(Katermal)*; Andrea Scotti *(Chagatai)*; Ciquita Coffelli *(Oruska)*; Raf Baldassarre *(Prisoner of the Tartars)*; Pietro Tordi *(Morobas)*; Mario Petri *(Timur)*; Piero Lulli *(Seikor)*.

Comments: A costume adventure with nonstop action, with the beautiful Chelo Alonso in the lead. A co-production of Italy's Columbus Films and France's Comptoir Français du Film Production (CFFP).

Invasion 1700 *(Col ferro e col fuoco)* (Medallion Pictures, 1962)

Credits: *Director:* Fernando Cerchio; *Screenplay:* Ugo Liberatore, Remigio Del Grosso, Enrico Ribulsi, George St. George (based on the novel *With Fire and Sword* by Henryk Sienkiewicz); *Photography:* Pier Ludovico Pavoni (Eastmancolor, Euroscope, aspect ratio 2.35:1); *Film Editor:* Antonietta Zita; *Music:* Francesco De Masi, Giovanni Fusco; *Production Design:* Arrigo Equini, Jovan Radic; *Art Direction:* Lazar Stefanovic, Milan Todorovic; *Set Decoration:* Paolo Janni; *Costume Design:* Giancarlo Bartolini Salimbeni; *Makeup Artist:* Raul Ranieri; *Hair Stylist:* Giovanni Palombi; *Production Managers:* Piero Ghione, Aleksander Krstic; *General Manager:* Giampaolo Bigazzi; *2nd Unit Director:* Sergio Berganzelli; *Assistant Director:* Pasquale De Florio; *Sound:* Raffaele Del Monte, Ferdinando Pescetelli; *Camera Operator:* Fausto Rossi; *2nd Unit Camera Operator:* Angelo Lotti; *Assistant Costume Designer:* Nadia Vitali; *Master of Arms:* Milutin Dimitrijevic; *Production Secretary:* Michele Marsala; *Script Supervisor:* Lula Milano; running time: 112 minutes (Italy); released July 1962 (Italy), January 1965 (U.S.).

Cast: Jeanne Crain *(Helen)*; Pierre Brice *(Jan Ketusky)*; Elena Zareschi *(Princess Kurzevich)*; Akim Tamiroff *(Mielski Zasloba)*; Raoul Grassilli *(Basillio)*; Bruno Nessi *(Longin)*; Eleonora Vargas *(Horpina)*; Gabriella Andreini *(Anussia)*; Nerio Bernardi *(Geremia)*; Nando Angelini; Nico Stefanini; Marcello Selmi; Alberto Mareschalchi; Alberto Archetti; Milena Vukotic; John Drew Barrymore *(Bohun)*; Gordon Mitchell *(Ulrich)*; Giacomo Rossi Stuart; Ornella Vanoni.

Comments: A Tartar invasion occurs in this costume adventure, produced by Italy's Avala Film and Film Europa in cooperation with France's Comptoir Français du Film Production (CFFP) and Yugoslavia's Košutnjak.

The Invincible Brothers Maciste *(Gli invincibli fratelli Maciste)* (ABS Films, 1964)

Credits: Director: Roberto Mauri; *Producer:* Domenico Seymandi; *Screenplay:* Roberto Mauri, Edoardo Mulargia; *Photography:* Romolo Garroni (Eastmancolor, aspect ratio 2.35:1); *Film Editor:* Enzo Alabiso; *Production Design:* Giuseppe Ranieri; *Costume Design:* Sergio Selli; *Special Effects:* Augusto Possanza; running time: 90 minutes (Italy), 92 minutes (U.S.); released December 18, 1964 (Italy).

Cast: Iloosh Koshabe [billed as "Richard Lloyd"] *(Maciste the Elder)*; Mario Novelli [billed as "Tony Freeman"] *(Maciste the Younger)*; Claudie Lange *(Queen Thaliade)*; Anthony Steffen [billed as "Antonio De Teffè"] *(Prince Akim)*; Ursula Davis *(Jana)*; Gia Sandri *(Nice)*; Stevenson Lang; Franco Visconti; Ruth von Hagen; Noelle Dumas; Ferruccio Viotti.

Comments: An evil queen rules a hidden land in this atypical entry, which is distinguished by a partially jazz-influenced music score. Produced by Italy's IFESA.

The Invincible Gladiator *(Il gladiatore invincibile)* (Goldstone/Seven Arts, 1961)

Credits: Directors and Producers: Alberto De Martino, Antonio Momplet; *Producers of U.S.-Dubbed Version:* Anacleto Fontini, Italo Zingarelli; *Screenplay:* Francesco De Feo, Alberto De Martino, Anacleto Fontini, Antonio Momplet, Francesco Thellung, Natividad Zaro (from a story by Francesco De Feo, Anacleto Fontini, Francesco Thellung and Natividad Zaro); *Dialogue for Spanish-Dubbed Version:* Rafael Garcia Serrano; *Photography:* Eloy Mella (Technicolor, Techniscope, aspect ratio 2.35:1); *Film Editor:* Otello Colangeli; *Sound:* Westrex Sound System; *Production Design:* Santiago Ontañón; *Production Management:* Roberto Palaggi; running time: 105 minutes (Italy), 96 minutes (U.S.);

Richard Harrison in *The Invincible Gladiator*.

Top: Richard Harrison (right) squares off against an opponent in *The Invincible Gladiator. Left:* Richard Harrison and Isabelle Corey in *The Invincible Gladiator.*

released October 13, 1961 (Italy), September 1963 (U.S.); video availability: Image Entertainment.

Cast: Richard Harrison *(Rezius)*; Isabelle Corey *(Sira)*; Livio Lorenzon *(Itus)*; Leo Anchóriz *(Prime Minister Rabirius)*; Edoardo Nevola *(Prince Darius)*; José Marco *(Livius)*; Jole Mauro *(Xenia)*; Ricardo Canales *(Samanthius, Former Royal Councillor)*; Antonio Molino Rojo *(Euclante)*; Giorgio Ubaldi *(Gladiator)*; Tomás Blanco *(Senior Conspirator)*; George Martin *(Gladiator)*; Barta Barri *(Gladiator)*.

Comments: Rezius, a Roman warrior, rebels against the evil Prime Minister Rabirius. Produced by Italy's Films Columbus and Variety Film Production in association with Spain's Athenea Films and shot at Incir De Paolis Studios in Rome.

The Invincible Masked Rider (L'invincibile cavaliere mascherato) (Embassy Pictures, 1963)

Credits: Director: Umberto Lenzi; *Producer:* Fortunato Misiano; *Screenplay:* Gino De Santis, Umberto Lenzi, Guido Maletesta, Luciano Martino (based on a novel by Johnston McCulley); *Photography:* Bitto Albertini, Augusto Tiezzi (Eastmancolor, Totalscope, aspect ratio 2.35:1); *Film Editor:* Jolanda Benvenuti; *Music:* Angelino Francesco Lavagnino; *Set Decoration:* Peppino Piccolo; *Costume Design:* Walter Patriarca; *Production Manager:* Nino Misiano; running time: 96 minutes (Italy & U.S.); released March 29, 1963 (Italy), July 1967 (U.S.).

Cast: Pierre Brice *(Don Diego)*; Daniele Vargas *(Don Luis)*; Hélène Chanel *(Carmencita)*; Massimo Serato *(Don Rodrigo)*; Gisella Arden *(Maria)*; Aldo Bufi Landi *(Francisco)*; Carlo Latimer *(Tabuca)*; Nerio Bernardi *(Don Gomez)*; Romano Ghini *(Maurillo)*; Tullio Altamura *(Dr. Bernarinus)*; Ignazio Balsamo; Clara Bindi; Salvatore Campochiaro *(Alvarez)*; Guido Celano *(Dr. Aguilera)*; Gino Marturano *(Ortega)*; Eleonora Morana *(Rosario)*; Piero Pastore; Nello Pazzafini *(Alonzo)*; Sina Relli *(Kidnapped Girl)*; Gino Soldi *(Miguel)*; Attilio Torelli *(The Innkeeper)*; Amedeo Trilli *(merchant)*.

Comments: A Zorro-type masked hero adventure, set in 17th-century Spain. Produced by Italy's Romana Film and France's Socété Nouvelle de Cinematographié (SNC).

Ivanhoe, the Norman Swordsman (La spada Normanna) (Les Films Corona/Oceania Produzioni Internazionali Cinematografiche/Talia Films, 1971)

Credits: Director: Roberto Mauri; *Screenplay:* Piero Regnoli, Manuel Torres, André Tranché (based on their story); *Photography:* Sandro Mancori (Eastmancolor, Totalscope, aspect ratio 2.35:1); *Film Editor:* Adriano Tagliavia; *Music:* Roberto Pregadio (billed as "H. Pregadio"); running time: 99 minutes; released April 29, 1971.

Cast: Mark Damon *(Ivanhoe)*; Luis Dávila *(Stephen of Cunningham)*; Krista Nell *(Brenda)*; Aveline Frederica *(Kitty)*; Aldo Berti *(Art)*; Spartaco Conversi *(Kitts)*; Luis de Tejada (billed as "Luis Tejada"); Arnaldo Dell'Acqua *(Scottish Tribal Leader)*; Vittorio Fanfoni *(Announcer)*; Vassili Karis *(Trigul)*; Nello Pazzafini *(Ghippo)*; Maurizio Mannola *(Ghippo's Man)*; Luciano Pigozzi [billed as "Alan Collin"] *(Mortimer, the Principal)*; Linda Sini *(Mortimer's Wife)*; Rinaldo Zamperla; Manuel Zarzo *(Oliver)*; Renzo Pevarello *(Ghippo, a Gang Member)*.

Comments: Returning from the Crusades in the 12th century, heroic Ivanhoe saves the throne of England from an evil usurper. Co-produced by Italy's Oceania Produzioni Cinematografiche, France's Les Films Corona and Spain's Talia Films. Partially shot on location at Cardona's Castle in Barcelona, Spain, and Cardona's Collegiate Church in Barcelona.

Jacob, the Man Who Fought with God (Giacobbe, l'uomo lottò con Dio) (San Paolo Films, 1963)

Credits: Director: Marcello Baldi; *Screenplay:* Ottavio Jemma, Giuseppe Mangione; *Photography:* Marcello Masciocchi (color, aspect ratio 1.85:1); *Film Editors:* Giulianna Attenni, Lina Caterini; *Production Design:* Piero Poletto; running time: 84 minutes; released 1963; video availability: VCI.

Cast: Giorgio Cerioni *(Jacob)*; Jean Morcier; Judy Parker *(Rachel)*; Alfredo Rizzo; Giuseppe Addobbati [billed as "John Douglas"] *(Adam)*; Sergio Ammarata; Nando Angelini; Letitia Bollante; Piero Bugli; Consalvo Dell'Arti; Luisa Della Noce *(Leah)*; Elena Demerik; Dario Dolci; Bernard Farber Fosco Giachetti *(Abraham)*; Massimo Giuliani; Rosalia Maggio; Roberto Mannoni; Lily Mantovani; Jole Mauro; Roberto Miali; Glauco Onorato; Anna Orso; Roberto Paoletti; Claudio Perone; Paolo Pieri; Massimo Pietrobon; Pino Sciaqua; Vinicio Sofia; Moa Tahi; Ruth von Hagen.

Comments: Old Testament tales of Abraham are featured in this biblical drama, produced by Italy's San Paolo Films.

Journey Beneath the Desert (Antinea, l'amante della cità sepolta) (Embassy Pictures, 1961)

Credits: Directors: Giuseppe Masini, Edgar G. Ulmer, Frank Borzage (uncredited); *Producer:* Luigi Nannerini; *Screenplay:* Remigio Del Grosso, Ugo Liberatore, André Tabet (based on *L'Atlantide* by Pierre Benôit); *Photography:* Enzo Serafin (Technicolor, Technirama, aspect ratio 2.20:1 [35mm prints], 2.35:1 [70mm prints]); *Film Editor:* Renato Cinquini; *Music:* Carlo Rustichelli; *Production Design:* Edgar G. Ulmer; *Art Direction:* Piero Filippone; *Costume Design:* Vittorio Rossi; *2nd Unit Director:* Mario Caiano; *Assistant Art Director:* Manfredo Manfredi; *Special Effects:* Giovanni Ventimiglia; *Music Direction:* Franco Ferrara; *Dialogue Coach:* Arianne Ulmer; *Script Supervisor:* Shirley Ulmer; running time: 105 minutes; released May 5, 1961 (Italy), July 1967 (U.S.); video availability: Something Weird Video.

Cast: Jean-Louid Trintignant *(Pierre)*; Haya Harareet *(Queen Antinea)*; Georges Revière *(John)*; James Westmoreland [billed as "Rad Fulton"] *(Robert)*; Amadeo Nazzari *(Tamal)*; Giulia Rubini *(Zinah)*; Gabriele Tinti *(Max)*; Ignazio Dulce; Gian Maria Volonté *(Tarath)*.

Comments: After their helicopter crashes in the desert, the stranded crew discovers the legendary city of Atlantis hidden beneath the sands. Veteran director Frank Borzage was slated to helm this adventure-fantasy, and began the production, but due to illness was replaced by legendary Poverty Row stylist Edgar G. Ulmer. Exhibited in both 35mm and 70mm.

Kerim, Son of the Sheik (Il figlio dello sceicco) (CFFF/Mercury Films, 1962)

Credits: Director: Mario Costa; *Producer:* Jean-Philippe Mérand; *Screenplay:* Nino Stresa (based on his story); *Photography:* Angelo Lotti (color, Euroscope, aspect ratio 2.35:1); *Film Editor:* Antonietta Zita; *Music:* Francesco Di Masi; *Production Design:* Giancarlo Bartolini; *Set Decoration:* Antonio Visone; *Costume Design:* Giancarlo Bartolini Salimbeni; *Makeup:* Raul Ranieri; *Hair Stylist:* Giovanni Palombi; *Production Manager:* Piero Ghione; *Assistant Directors:* Jean-Philippe Mérand, Mario Tota; *Sound:* Pietro Spadoni; *Camera Operator:* Silvano Mancini; *Assistant Camera Operators:* Giancarlo Granatelli, Mario Pastorini; *Orchestra Conductor:* Francesco Di Masi; *Production Secretary:* Michele Marsala; *Master of Arms:* Luciano Benetti; *Script Supervisor:* Sonia Bencini; running time: 85 minutes; released June 29, 1962 (Italy).

Cast: Gordon Scott *(Kerim)*; Cristina Gaioni *(Fawzia)*; Moira Orfei *(Zahira)*; Alberto Farnese *(Omar)*; Jany Clair *(Imprisoned Woman)*; Maria Grazia Spina *(Laila)*; Nando Tamberlani *(Mansur)*; Luciano Benetti *(Prince Ahmed)*; Gordon Mitchell *(Yussuf)*; Nando Angelini *(Akim)*; Lulla Selli *(Selima)*.

Comments: Set in the Middle East of the 1860s, this costume adventure follows the heroic Kerim as he avenges the death of his sister Laila, who has been killed by the evil usurper Omar. Produced by Italy's Mercury Films and France's CFFF.

Kindar the Invulnerable (Kindar l'invulnerabile) (Wonder Films/ ABC Films, 1965)

Credits: Director/Producer: Osvaldo Civirani; *Screenplay:* Alessandro Ferraù, Roberto Gianviti (from their story); *Photography:* Osvaldo Civirani (Technicolor, Techniscope, aspect ratio 2.35:1); *Film Editor:* Nella Nannuzzi; *Art Direction:* Pier Vittorio Marchi; *Set Decoration:* Franco D'Andria; *Costume Design:* Mario Giorsi; *Makeup:* Duilio Giustini; *Makeup Assistant:* Cinzia Landi; *Hair Stylist:* Valeria Ferri; *Production Manager:* Umberto Chinigo; *Director of U.S.-Dubbed Version:* Richard McNamara; *Production Manager for U.S.-Dubbed Version:* Adriano Merkel; *Dialogue for U.S.-Dubbed Version:* Luciano Trasatti (billed as "John Collins"); *Assistant Director:* Bona Magrini; *Set Designer:* Pier Vittorio Marchi; *Weapons:* E. Rancati; *Sound:* Vittorio Massi; *Microphone Technician:* Armando Loffredi; *Camera Operators:* Franco Frazzi; Gianni Savelli; *Assistant Camera Operators:* Gianni Antinori, Walter Civirani; *Key Grip:* Franco Tocci; *Chief Electrician:* Emanuele Di Cola; *Costumes:* Maria Antonelli; *Assistant Costume Designer:* Antonio Randaccio; *Wardrobe:* Anna Onori; *Wigs:* Palombi; *Footwear:* Pompei; *Jeweler:* Donatella; *Production Assistant:* Mario Campollunghi; *Continuity:* Maurizio Tanfani;

running time: 96 minutes (Italy); Released March 5, 1965 (Italy); video availability: Alpha Video.

Cast: Mark Forest *(Kindar)*; Mimmo Palmara *(Seymuth)*; Rosalba Neri *(Kira)*; Dea Flowers *(Nefer)*; Howard Ross [billed as "Red Ross"] *(Siro)*; Giulio Tomasini *(Eman, King of Utor)*; Hussein Kandil *(Humi)*; Omar Zolficar; Sherifa Maher.

Comments: The son of a sultan is kidnapped by a desert bandit, but discovers his true identity after he grows to manhood. Produced by Italy's Wonder Films and Copro Films, this film was shot on location near the Great Pyramids in the Nile River area of Egypt, with further location work in Tunisia. Interiors were shot at Incir De Paolis Studios in Rome.

Knight Without a Country (Il cavaliere senza terra) (Diamante, 1959)

Credits: Director: Giacomo Gentilomo; *Photography:* Anchise Brizzi (Ferraniacolor, Panoramica, aspect ratio 2.35:1); *Music:* Ezio Carabella; *Art Direction:* Franco Lolli; running time: 111 minutes (Italy); released February 14, 1959 (Italy).

Cast: Gérard Landry *(Rolando)*; Constance Smith *(Laura)*; Wandisa Guida; Alberto Farnese *(Rizzerio, Duke of Villalta)*; Giacomo Rossi Stuart *(Ruggero)*; Valeria Fabrizi *(Countess of Holten)*; Franco Fantasia; Ivano Staccioli; Nino Musco; Andrea Fantasia; José Jaspe; Gino Buzzanca; Ettore Bevilacqua; Nino Marchesini; Pietro Tordi; Diego Pozzetto; Alfredo Bianchini; Mario Passante; Renato Montalbano; Cristina De Angelis; Luciano Manara; Michele Zentillini.

Comments: A costume adventure produced by Italy's Diamante.

Knights of Terror (Il terrore dei mantelli rossi) (Cine Europa-Paradise Film Exchange, 1963)

Credits: Director: Mario Costa; *Producer:* Georges Combret; *Screenplay:* Eduardo Falletti, Nino Lillo (from their story); *Photography:* Julio Ortas (Eastmancolor, Isco-Scope, aspect ratio 2.35:1); *Film Editor:* Jolanda Benvenuti; *Music:* Carlo Rusticelli; *Dialogue for French Version:* Pierre Maudru; running time: 86 minutes; released August 12, 1963 (Italy), 1963 (U.S.).

Cast: Tony Russel *(Paolo)*; Scilla Gabel *(Cristina)*; Yves Vincent *(Captain Mirko)*; Jacques Dacqmine *(Vladimir)*; Nerio Bernardi; Carla Calò; Pilar Clemens; Tony Soler; Pierre Torodi; Claude Brasseur; Beni Deus; Alfonso Rojas; Alf Marholm.

Comments: Heroic Captain Mirko defends a village terrorized by a group of horsemen known only as The Knights of Terror. This costume adventure was produced by Italy's Pamec Cinematografica in cooperation with France's Radius Productions and Spain's Hispamer Films.

Knives of the Avenger (I coltelli del vendicatore) (World Entertainment Corp., 1966)

Credits: Director: Mario Bava; *Screenplay:* Mario Bava (billed as "John Hold"), Alberto Liberati, Giorgio Simonelli; *Photography:* Antonio Rinaldi, Mario Bava (Technicolor, Techniscope, aspect ratio 2.35:1); *Film Editor:* Otello Colangeli; *Music:* Marcello Giombini; *Production Design/Set Decoration:* Alberto Tavazzi; *Art Direction:* Piero Filippone (billed as "Peter Felt"); *Costume Design:* Giorgio Desideri; *Assistant Director:* Roberto Giandalla; *Camera Operator:* Saverio Diamante; *Assistant Camera Operator:* Giorgio Aureli; running time: 85 minutes (Italy); released May 30, 1966 (Italy), January 1968 (U.S.); video availability: Anchor Bay Entertainment.

Cast: Cameron Mitchell *(Rurik/Helmut)*; Fausto Tozzi [billed as "Frank Ross"] *(Hagen)*; Giacomo Rossi Stuart [billed as "Jack Stuart"] *(King Arald)*; Luciano Pollentin [billed as "Louis Pollentin] *(Moki)*; Amedeo Trilli [billed as "Michael Moore"] *(Viking King)*; Renato Terra *(Hagen's Henchman)*; Sergio Cortona *(Hagen's Henchman)*; Elissa Pichelli [billed as "Lisa Wagner"] *(Karin)*; Bruno Arté *(Hut Intruder)*; Osiride Pevarello *(Hagen's Henchman)*; Goffredo Unger *(Hagen's Henchman)*.

Comments: Karin, the wife of King Arald, whom she believes dead, flees with her son as her husband's enemy Hagen is in pursuit; they are protected by Rurik, a virtuous warrior who eventually defeats Hagen. This was a troubled production salvaged by the talented Mario Bava, who rewrote and reshot the movie, finishing the production in just 6 days. Produced by Italy's Sider Film and shot at Titanus Studios in Rome.

The Last Days of Pompeii (Gli ultimi giomi di Pompei) (United Artists, 1959)

Credits: Directors: Mario Bonnard, Sergio Leone; *Producer:* Paolo Moffa; *Associate Producer:* Lucio Fulci; *Screenplay:* Sergio Corbucci, Ennio De Concini, Luigi Emmanuele, Sergio Leone, Duccio Tessari (based on the novel by Edward George Bulwer-Lytton); *Photography:* Antonio L. Ballesteros (Eastmancolor, Supertotalscope, aspect ratio 2.35:1); *Film Editors:* Eraldo Da Roma, Julio Peña; *Music:* Angelo Francesco Lavagnino; *Production Design:* Ramiro Gómez, Aldo Tommasini; *Set Decoration:* Ramiro Gómez; *Costume Design:* Duilio Cambellotti, Vittorio Rossi; *Makeup:* Angelo Malantrucco; *Production Managers:* Paolo Moffa, Renato Silvestri; *Assistant Director:* Duccio Tessari; *2nd Unit Assistant Directors:* Sergio Corbucci, Sergio Leone; *Sound:* Mario Amari, Giovanni Percelli; *Microphone Boom Operator:* Primiano Muratori; *Special Effects:* Dino Galiano (billed as "Cataldo Galiano"); *Matte Shots:* Emilio Ruiz del Rio; *2nd Unit Photography:* Enzo Barboni; *Assistant Costume Designer:* Luciana Bagni; *Color Consultant:* Jorge Grau; *2nd Assistant Film Editor:* Maria Luisa Pino; *Production Secretary:* Alfonso Fabrizio; running time: 100 minutes (Italy), 103 minutes (U.S.); released November 12, 1959 (Italy), July 17, 1960 (U.S.); video availability: Something Weird Video.

Cast: Steve Reeves *(Glaucus)*; Christine Kaufmann *(Ione)*; Fernando Rey *(Arbacès, High Priest)*; Barbara Carroll *(Nydia)*; Anne-Marie Baumann *(Julia)*; Mimmo Palmara *(Gallinus)*;

An arena scene from *The Last Days of Pompeii*.

Guillermo Marin *(Ascanius)*; Carlo Tamberlani *(Leader of the Christians)*; Mino Doro *(Consul)*; Mario Berriatúa *(Praetorian Guard)*; Mario Morales *(Praetorian Guard)*; Ángel Ortiz *(Praetorian Guard)*; Ignazio Dolce; Ángel Aranda *(Antonius)*; Tony Richards; Antonio Casas; Lola Torres; Vicky Lagos; Ignaz Cole; Jesús Puente; Maria Silva; Pedro Fenollar *(Pregonaro)*.

Comments: A widescreen color version of the dependable Edward George Bulwer-Lytton novel, filmed many times before as a silent and in Hollywood in 1935. Credited director Mario Bonnard fell ill during production and most of the production was actually shot by an uncredited Sergio Leone, who also contributed to the screenplay. Leone used much of the same production crew when he directed *The Colossus of Rhodes (qv)*. Produced by Italy's Cinematografica Associati (CI.AS.) and Domiciana, in cooperation with Spain's Procusa and the Danish company Transocean-Film. Shot on location in Pompeii, Naples.

The Last of the Vikings *(L'ultimo dei Vikinghi)* (Medallion Pictures, 1961)

Credits: *Director:* Giacomo Gentilomo; *Producers:* Roberto Capitani, Luigi Mondello; *Producer of U.S.-Dubbed Version:* Sam Schneider; *Screenplay:* Arpad DeRiso, Guido Zurli, Giacomo Gentilomo (from a story by Arpad DeRiso, Luigi Mondello, Guido Zurli); *Photography:* Enzo Serafin (Eastmancolor, Dyaliscope, aspect ratio 2.35:1); *Film Editor:* Gino Talamo; *Music:* Roberto Nicolosi; *Art Direction:* Italo Tomassi; *Costume Design:* Maria Luisa Panaro; *Production Supervisors:* Augusto Dolfi, Tonino Garzarelli; *Production Manager:* Roberto Capitani; *General Manager:* Luigi Mondello; *Assistant Director:* G. Cesare Marmol; *2nd Unit Directors:* Pino Mercanti, Guido Zurli; *Set Designer:* Saverio D'Eugenio; *2nd Unit Photography:* Alvaro Mancori; *Lighting Director:* Enzo Serafin; *Costumes:* Tigano Lofaro; *Seamstress:* Assunto Lazzazzera; *Orchestra Conductor:* Luigi Urbini; *Script Supervisor:* Maria Luisa Roi; *2nd Unit Script Supervisor:* Anita Borgiotti; running time: 103 minutes (U.S.); released February 8, 1961 (Italy), May 1962 (U.S.); video availability: Mill Creek Entertainment.

Cast: Cameron Mitchell *(Harald)*; Edmund Purdom *(King Sveno)*; Isabelle Corey *(Hilde)*; Hélène Rémy *(Edith/Elga)*; Andrea Aureli *(Haakon)*; Mario Feleciani; Aldo Bufi Landi *(Londborg)*; Carla Calò *(Herta)*; Corrado Annacelli *(Godrun)*; Nando Tamberlani *(Gultred)*; Nando Angelini *(Simon, King Sveno's Man)*; Piero Berlini; George Ardisson *(Guntar)*; Piero Lulli *(Hardak King Sveno's Man)*; Benito Steffanelli *(Lorig, Guntar's Friend)*.

Comments: Viking brothers Harald and Guntar avenge their murdered father. Produced by Italy's Tiberius Film and Galatea Film in cooperation with France's Critérion Film and Les Films du Cyclope.

Legions of the Nile *(Le legioni di Cleopatra)* (20th Century–Fox, 1959)

Credits: *Director:* Vittorio Cottafavi; *Producers:* Virgilio De Blasi, Robert de Nesle, Natividad Zaro, Italo Zingarelli; *Screenplay:* Vittorio Cottafavi, Giorgio Cristallini, Ennio De Concini (from a story by Ennio De Concini, Arnaldo Marrosu); *Dialogue for Spanish-Dubbed Version:* Natividad Zaro; *Photography:* Mario Pacheco (Eastmancolor, Supercinescope, aspect ratio 2.35:1); *Film Editors:* Luciano Cavalieri, Julio Peña; *Music:* Renzo Rossellini; *Art Direction:* Antonio Simont; *Costume Design:* Vittorio Rossi; *Makeup:* José María Sánchez, Franco Titi; *Hair Stylist:* Carmen Sánchez; *Assistant Directors:* Antoni Ribas, Ceco Zamurovich; *2nd Unit Director:* Giorgio Cristallini; *Art Department Manager:* Italo Tomassi; *Props:* Luis Buchs, Juan Garcia; *Sound:* Oscar De Arcangelis; *Camera Operators:* Luigi Allegretti, Rafael Pacheco; *Assistant Camera Operators:* Sante Achilli, Ramón Fernández; *Assistant Film Editor:* Sergio Montanari; *Music Director:* Alberto Paoletti; *Choreography:* Peter Vander Sloot; *Production Assistants:* Carlo Audisio, Mario Giovannini, José Herrera; *Master of Arms:* Giorgio Ubaldi; *Script Supervisor:* Manuel de la Cueva; running time: 100 minutes (Italy), 91 minutes (U.S.); released November 27, 1959 (Italy), December 1960 (U.S.).

Cast: Linda Cristal *(Cleopatra/ Berenice)*; Ettore Manni *(Curridio)*; Georges Marchal *(Mark*

Antony); Conrado San Martin (Gotarzo); Maria Mahor (Marianna); Alfredo Mayo (Ottaviano); Daniela Rocca (Teyrè); Mino Doro (Domiziano); Andrea Aureli (Imotio); Stefano Terra; Stefano Oppedisano; Salvatore Furnari (Dwarf); Rafael Durán (Egyptian Priest); Juan Maján (Vezio); Tomás Blanco (Ovidio); Jany Clair; Mary Carrillo (Iras); Guillermo Amengual; Vicente Bañó; Juan Casalilla; F. Gomez Vazquez; Joaquin Guillén; Abraham Ventero; Ángel Álvarez (Slave Trader); Rafael Luis Carlo.

Comments: Cleopatra and lover Marc Antony vs. Roman Emperor Octavian. Twentieth Century–Fox bought and shelved this film to prevent competition with their currently-filming Elizabeth Taylor spectacle *Cleopatra* (released in 1963). *Legions of the Nile* was produced by Italy's Alexandra Produzioni Cinematografiche (Alexandra P.C.), France's Lyre Films and Comptoir Français du Productions Cinématographiques (CFPC), in cooperation with Spain's Atenea Films and Estela Films. The production was shot at C.E.A. Studios in Madrid, Spain and at Cinecittà Studios in Rome.

The Lion of St. Mark (Il leone di San Marco) (Embassy Pictures, 1963)

Credits: Director: Luigi Capuano; *Producer:* Ottavio Poggi; *Executive Producer:* Nino Battiferri; *Screenplay:* Luigi Capuano, Arpad DeRiso, Ottavio Poggi; *Photography:* Alvaro Mancori (Eastmancolor, Totalscope, aspect ratio 2.35:1); *Film Editor:* Antonietta Zita; *Music:* Carlo Rustichelli; *Production Design/Costume Design:* Giancarlo Bartolini Salimbeni; *Art Direction:* Ernest Kromberg; *Makeup:* Eligio Trani; *Production Manager:* Diego Alchimede; *Assistant Director:* Gianfranco Baldanello; *Construction Manager:* Salvatore Siciliano; *Sound:* Fiorenzo Magli; *Camera Operator:* Sandro Mancori; *Assistant Camera Operator:* Giulio Spadoni; *Assistant Costumer:* Elio Micheli; *Production Secretary:* Arrigo Peri; *Script Supervisor:* Maria Luisa Rosen; running time: 106 minutes; released November 21, 1963 (Italy), July 1967 (U.S.); video availability: Something Weird Video.

Cast: Gordon Scott (Manrico Venier); Gianna Maria Canale (Rosanna Melzi); Alberto Farnese (Titta); Giulio Marchetti (Gualtiero); Rik Battaglia (Giandolo); Franca Bettoia (Isabella Fieschi); Feodor Chaliapin, Jr., (The Doge); John Bartha (Count Fieschi); Mirko Ellis (Civetta); Franco Fantasia (Vipera); Giulio Maculani (Capt. Ostenburg); Anna Maria Padoan (Mrs. Fieschi); Attillio Severini (Pirate).

Comments: This tale of Pirates on the Adriatic coast takes place in 1620. Produced by Italy's Liber.

The Lion of Thebes (Leone di Tebe) (Embassy Pictures, 1964)

Credits: Director: Giorgio Ferroni; *Producer:* Diego Alchimede; *Executive Producer:* Giorgio Ferroni; *Screenplay:* Remigio Del Grosso, Georgio Feroni, Andrey De Coligny, Jean Velter (from a story by Andrey De Coligny); *Photography:* Angelo Lotti (Eastmancolor, Euroscope, aspect ratio: 2.35:1); *Film Editor:* Antonietta Zita; *Music:* Francesco De Masi; *Production Design:* Arrigo Equini; *Set Decoration:* Carlo Gentili; *Costume Design:* Elio Micheli; *Makeup:* Giovanni Ranieri; *Hair Stylist:* Violetta Pacelli; *Assistant Directors:* Giancarlo Romitelli, Giorgio Stegani; *Sound:* Raffaele Del Monte, Alessandro Sarandrea; *Fencing Master:* Franco Fantasia; *Director of U.S.-Dubbed Version:* Richard McNamara; running time: 88 minutes (Italy), 89 minutes (U.S.); released June 28, 1964 (Italy), 1965 (U.S.); video availability: Something Weird Video.

Cast: Mark Forest (Arian); Yvonne Furneaux (Helen of Troy); Massimo Serato (Tutmes); Pierre Cressoy ((Ramses); Nerio Bernardi (Xesostus); Rosalba Neri (Nais); Carlo Tamberlani (Menophis); Nello Pazzafini (Wrestler); Pietro Capanna; Roberto Messina (Wrestler); Tullio Altamura (Jewel Merchant); Enzo Fiermonte (Official for Tutmes); Valerio Tordi; Diego Michelotti; Alberto Lupo (Menelao); Franco Ukmar (Soldier).

Comments: The heroic Arian guards Helen of Troy when she is shipwrecked and stranded in Egypt. Produced by Italy's Filmes and the French company La Société des Films Sirius.

Long Live Robin Hood (L'arciere di fuoco) (Universal Cinema, 1976)

Credits: Director: Giorgio Ferroni; *Producer:*

Top: **Mark Forest in** *The Lion of Thebes.* *Bottom:* **Yvonne Furneaux and Rosalba Neri in** *The Lion of Thebes.*

A desert action scene from *The Lion of Thebes*.

Ernest Boetan; *Screenplay:* Ennio De Concini, Mauel Torres Larreda, Giorgio Stegani, André Tranché (based on a story by Ennio De Concini); *Photography:* Giuseppe Pinori (Eastmancolor, Techniscope, aspect ratio 2.35:1); *Film Editor:* Antonietta Zita; *Music:* Gianni Ferrio; *Set Decoration:* Enrique Alarcón, Arrigo Equini; *Camera Operator:* Sebastiano Celeste; *Stunts:* Nazzareno Zamperla; running time: 103 minutes; released March 12, 1971 (Italy), 1976 (U.S.).

Cast: Giuliano Gemma *(Robin Hood)*; Mark Damon *(Allen)*; Silvia Dionisio *(Lady Marianne di Manson)*; Mario Adorf *(Brother Tuck)*; Daniele Dublino *(Prince John)*; Valerie Forques; Nello Pazzafini *(Little John)*; Manuel Zarzo *(Will Scarlet)*; Lars Bloch *(King Richard Lionheart)*; Giovanni Cianfriglia *(Archer at Tournament)*; Valerio Colombaioni *(Muck Scape)*; Pierre Cressoy *(Sir Guy)*; Pupo De Luca [billed as "Gianni De Luca"] *(Wrong Priest)*; Giulio Donnini *(Priest at Wedding Ceremony)*; Luis Dávila *(Sir Robert)*; Vittorio Fanfoni; Gaetano Imbró; Helga Liné *(Matilde)*; Furio Meniconi *(Innkeeper)*; Riccardo Petrazzi *(Sheriff's Guard)*; Osiride Pevarello *(Man at Wedding Ceremony)*; Antonio Pica; Nazzareno Zamperla; Ettore Arena *(Man at Gallows)*; Bruno Arié *(One of Sir Robert's Men)*; Sisto Brunetti *(One of Robin's Men)*; Franco Daddi *(One of Robin's Men)*; Wladimir Daddi *(Man Bringing Horse)*; Roberto Dell'Acqua *(Gary)*; Oscar Giustini *(Soldier)*; Franco Maruzzi *(Archer at Tournament)*; Filippo Perego *(One of Sir Robert's Men)*; Renzo Pevarello *(Roland Watson)*; Ottorino Polentini *(One of Robin's Men)*; Claudio Ruffini *(One of Robin's Men)*; Sergio Smacchi *(Archer at Tournament)*; Bruno Ukmar *(Soldier)*; Clemente Ukmar *(Hangman)*; Franco Ukmar *(One of Sir Robert's Men)*; Rinaldo Zamperla *(One of Robin's Men)*.

Comments: Another interpretation of the Robin Hood legend, Produced by Italy's Oceana Produzioni Internazionali Cinematografiche, France's Les Films Corona, and Spain's Talia Films. Partially shot at Colegiata y Castillo de Cardona in Barcelona, Spain.

The Loves and Times of Scaramouche (La avventure e gli amori di Scaramouche) (Avco Embassy Pictures, 1976)

Credits: Director: Enzo G. Castellari; *Producer:* Federico Alcardi; *Screenplay:* Enzo G. Castellari, Tito Carpi (from a story by Tito Carpi); *Photography:* Giovanni Bergamini (Telecolor); *Film Editor:* Gianfranco Amicucci; *Music:* Franco Bixio, Fabio Frizzi, Vince Tempera; *Art Direction:* Enzo Bulgarelli; *Costume Design:* Luciano Sagoni; *Sound:* Pietro Spadoni; *Stunt Coordinator:* Rocco Lerro; *Horse Stunts:* Milan Mitic; *Still Photographer:* Ermanno Serto; *Casting:* Damir Mejovsek; *Dialogue Coach:* Ian Danby; released March 17, 1976.

Cast: Michael Sarrazin *(Scaramouche)*; Ursula Andress *(Joséphine De Beauharnais)*; Aldo Maccione *(Napoléon Bonaparte)*; Giancarlo Prete *(Whistle, the Barber)*; Michael Forest *(Danglar)*; Salvatore Borghese *(Chagrin, the Bomber)*; Nico il Grande *(Scribe)*; Gisela Hahn *(Babette)*; Karen Fiedler; Vera De Oliveira *(Josephine's Maid)*; Romano Puppo; Massimo Vanni; Alex Togni; Adolfo Belletti *(Old Husband)*; Dante Cleri *(Voyeur)*; Riccardo Garrone *Captain)*; Renzo Marignano *(Barber's Client)*; Damir Mejovsek *(General)*; Nerina Montagnani *(Old Wife)*; Luciano Pigozzi *(Babbette's Husband)*; Peter Berling; Rocco Lerro *(French Lieutenant)*.

Comments: This costume adventure was produced by Embassy Pictures, Italy's Epee Cinematographica, Yugoslavia's Jadran Film and Denmark's Lisa Film. Shot at Monte Gelato Falls on the Treja River in Lazio, Italy, and in Zagreb, Croatia.

The Loves of Salammbo (Salambò) (20th Century–Fox, 1960)

Credits: Director: Sergio Grieco; *Producer:* Luigi Nannerini; *Screenplay:* Mario Caiano, Sergio Grieco, Giuseppe Mangione, André Tabet, Georges Tabet (based on the novel *Salammbo* by Gustave Flaubert); *Photography:* Piero Portalupi (Eastmancolor, Totalscope, aspect ratio 2.35:1); *Laboratory:* L.T.C. Saint Cloud, France; *Production Design:* Franco Lolli; *Art Direction:* Antonio Visone; *Assistant Directors:* Mario Caiano, Benchekroun Larbi; *Assistant Film Editor:* Bruno Mattei; *Master of Arms:* Enzo Musumeci Greco; *Production Assistant:* Abdou Chraibi; running time: 110 minutes (Italy), 72 minutes (U.S.); released September 16, 1960 (Italy), October 1962 (U.S.); video availability: Sinister Cinema.

Cast: Jeanne Valérie *(Salambò)*; Jacques Sernas *(Mathos)*; Edmund Purdom *(Narr Havas)*; Arnoldo Foà *(Spendius)*; Riccardo Garrone *(Hamilcar)*; Kamala Devi *(Maiden)*; Charles Fawcett *(Annone)*; Brunella Bovo *(Neshma)*; Andrea Aureli *(Kohamir)*; Raf Baldassarre *(Chief Mercenary)*; Nando Tamberlani *(High Priest)*; Ivano Staccioli *(Gell)*; Antonio Basile; Pasquale Basile; Vittorio Duse; Franco Franchi; Ferdinando Poggi; Faustone Signoretti; Rinaldo Zamperla.

Comments: The Carthaginians employ an army of Barbarians to fight the Romans in this costume adventure, set in the 3rd century BC Co-produced by Italy's Stella Film and France's Fides Films.

Maciste Against the Sheik (Maciste contro lo scecio) (Medallion Pictures, 1962)

Credits: Director: Domenico Paolella; *Producer:* Alberto Manca; *Screenplay:* Gian Paolo Callegari, Alessandro Ferraù, Alberto Manca, Domenico Paolella, Sergio Sollima; *Photography:* Carlo Bellero (Eastmancolor, Totalscope, aspect ratio 2.35:1); *Film Editor:* Giacinto Solito; *Music:* Carlo Savina; *Production Design and Art Direction:* Alfredo Montori; *Costume Design:* Giorgio Desideri; *Makeup:* Romolo de Martino; *Hair Stylist:* Lina Cassini; *Assistant Director:* Tersicore Kolosoff; *Camera Operator:* Gaetano Valle; *Sound:* Giulio Tagliacozzo; *Microphone Boom Operator:* Giorgio Minoprio; running time: 95 minutes (Italy); released April 21, 1962 (Italy), 1963 (U.S.); video availability: Sinister Cinema.

Cast: Ed Fury *(Maciste)*; Erno Crisa *(The

Sheik); Gisella Arden *(Isabella);* Piero Lulli *(Ramiro);* Mara Berni *(Zuleima);* Anna Ranalli *(Consuelo);* Massimo Carocci *(Antonio);* Giuseppe Addobbati [billed as "John MacDouglas"] *(Duke of Malaga);* Carlo Pisacane *(Ali);* Adriano Micantoni *(Don Alfredo Alvarez);* Carlo Latimer *(Selim);* Edy Nogara *(Mother Superior);* Mimmo Poli *(Chamberlain);* Bruno Scipioni *(Luis);* Gino Soli *(Benda Nera);* Amedeo Trilli *(Captain);* Ettore Manni; Fortunato Arena *(Fighter);* Pasquale Fasciano *(Fighter);* Claudio Ruffini *(Fighter);* Amerigo Santarelli *(Torturer);* Nazzareno Zamperla *(Fighter).*

Comments: The heroic Maciste and his friend Antonio rescue the beautiful Isabella, daughter of the Duke of Malaga. Produced by Italy's Compagnia Italiani Grandi Film.

Maciste, the Avenger of the Mayans (Maciste il vendicatore dei Maya) (Urias Films, 1965)

Credits: *Director/Screenplay:* Guido Malatesta; *Photography:* Romolo Garroni (color, Totalscope, aspect ratio 2.35:1); *Film Editor:* Enzo Alfonzi; *Music:* Ugo Filippini; *Special Effects:* Eugenio Ascani; *Assistant Director* Giancarlo Romitelli; running time: 85 minutes (Italy); released May 26, 1965.

Cast: Kirk Morris *(Hercules/Maciste);* Barbara Loy *(Aloha);* Andrea Aureli *(Manur);* Demeter Bitenc *(Gruno);* Lucia Bomez; Mimmo Maggio; Rita Klein; Luciana Paoli; Luciano Marin *(Donar);* Antonio Casale *(Berak);* Koloss *(Goliath);* Nando Angelini; Artemio Antonini *(Manur Warrior);* Fortunato Arena *(Manur Warrior);* Bruno Arié *(Madir);* Federico Boido *(Ulmar Guard);* Jeff Cameron *(Manur Warrior);* Gilberto Galimberti *(Manur Warrior);* Nello Pazzafini *(Ulmar Leader);* Attilio Severini *(Manur Warrior).*

Comments: This "cut and paste" effort combines footage from two previous films *The Fire Monsters vs. The Son of Hercules* and *Colossus Against the Headhunters* (both qv). Interesting as an exercise in editorial desperation, if nothing else. Produced by Italy's Urias Films.

The Magnificent Gladiator (Il magnifico gladiatore) (Seven Film, 1964)

Credits: *Director/Screenplay:* Alfonso Brescia; *Producer:* Anacleto Fontini; *Photography:* Pier Ludovico Pavoni (Technicolor, Techniscope, aspect ratio 2.35:1); *Film Editor:* Nella Nannuzzi; *Music:* Marcello Giombini; *Production Design:* Pier Vittorio Marchi; *Costume Design:* Mario Giorsi; *Makeup:* Andrea Riva; *Hair Stylist:* Lina Cassini; *Production Supervisor:* Albino Morandini; *Production Manager:* Carlo Vassalle; *Assistant Director:* Filiberto Fiaschi; *Sound:* Franco Groppioni, Mario Morigi, Sandro Occhetti; *Microphone Boom Operator:* Raul Montesanti; *Camera Operator:* Fausto Rossi; *Assistant Camera Operator:* Mario Pastorini; *Costume Assistant:* Silvano Giusti; *Script Editor:* Filippo Perrone; running time: 95 minutes (Italy); released December 31, 1964 (Italy); video availability: Retromedia.

Cast: Mark Forest *(Hercules/Attalus);* Marilù Tolo *(Velida);* Paolo Gozlino *(Zulio);* Jolanda Modio *(Clea);* Franco Cobianchi *(Emperor Caesar Galienus);* Oreste Lionello *(Drusius);* Nazzareno Zamperla *(Horatius);* Fedele Gentile *(Arminius);* Giulio Tomei; Renato Montalbano; Fortunato Arena; Giuseppe Mattei; Emilio Messina; Nello Pazzafini; Franco Ukmar *(Gladiator);* Ferruccio Viotti *(Quintilius).*

Comments: Hercules is captured by Roman soldiers and forced to perform as a gladiator in the Colosseum. Produced by Italy's Seven Film.

The Magnificent Robin Hood (Il magnifico Robin Hood) (Marco Claudia Cinematografica/ RM Films/Cire Films, 1970)

Credits: *Director:* Roberto Bianchi Montero; *Producers:* Marco Claudio, Angelo Santaniello, Oscar Santaniello; *Screenplay:* Juan Benito Alarcón, Arpad DeRiso, Angelo Sangermano (from a story by Angelo Sangermano); *Dialogue for Spanish Version:* Manuel Iglesias; *Photography:* Jaime Deu Casas (Technicolor, Techniscope, aspect ratio 2.35:1); *Film Editor:* Cesare Bianchi; *Music:* Augusto Martelli; *Production Design:* Ivo Battelli; *Costume Design:* Oscar Capponi; *Assistant Costume Designer:* Giuliana Serano; *Makeup:* Angelo Ron Caioli; *Assistant Makeup Artist:* Massimo Civiletti; *Hair Stylist:* Nerea Rosmanit; *Production Manager:* Oscar Santaniello; *General*

Manager: Marcello Berni; *Assistant Director:* Mario Bianchi; *Sound Engineer:* Ivo Benedetti; *Camera Operators:* Sebastiano Celeste, Claudio Morabito; *Assistant Camera Operator:* Enrico Priori; *Orchestra Conductor:* Augusto Martelli; *Script Supervisor:* Luigina Lovan; running time: 91 minutes (Italy); released September 18, 1970 (Italy).

Cast: George Martin *(Robin Hood)*; Spela Rozin [billed as "Sheila Rossin"] *(Rowina)*; Frank Braña *(Prince John)*; Massimo Righi [billed as "Max Dean"] *(Sir Jack Beacham)*; Aldo Cecconi [billed as "Jim Clay"] *(Friar Tuck)*; Cris Huerta [billed as "Chris Huerta"] *(Little John)*; Antonella Murgia *(Marian)*; Benito Pacifico [billed as "Dennis Colt"] *(Mellin)*; Luciano Conti *(Will)*; Clemente Ukmar; Michele Branca *(Lowell)*; Silvano Zignani; Carla Mancini; Ivana Novak *(Alice)*; Francesco Vietri; Gippo Leone; Gualtiero Isnenghi; Pietro Ceccarelli *(Attacker)*; Atilo Dottesio *(Sir William Prescott)*; Mara Krupp *(Cook)*.

Comments: A 1970s version of the Robin Hood legend, produced by Italy's Marco Claudia Cinematografica and Spain's RM Films.

Marco Polo *(L'avventura di un italiano in Cina)* (American International, 1962)

Credits: Directors: Piero Pierotti and (U.S.-Dubbed Version) Hugo Fregonese; *Producers:* Luigi Carpentieri, Ermanno Donati; *Screenplay:* Oreste Biancoli, Ennio De Concini, Eliana De Sabata, Antoinette Pellevant, Piero Pierotti, Duccio Tessari; *Photography:* Ricardo Pallottini (Technicolor, CinemaScope, aspect ratio 2.35:1); *Laboratory:* Technicolor; *Film Editor:* Ornella Micheli; *Music:* Angelo Francisco Lavagnino; *Production Design:* Zoran Zorcic; *Art Direction:* Aurelio Crugnola, Franco Fumagalli, Miodrag Miric, Jovan Radic; *Costume Design:* Mario Giorsi; *Makeup:* Euclide Santoli; *Production Supervisor:* Livio Maffei; *Production Managers:* Gianni Minervini, Lucio Orlandini; *Assistant Director:* Michelangelo Panaro; *Assistant Set Designer:* Aldo Fumagalli; *Assistant Costume Designer:* Silvano Giusti; *Choreography:* Franca Bartolomei; *Music for U.S.-Dubbed Version:* Les Baxter; *Musicians:* Dale L. Anderson (percussion), Larry Bunker (percussion), Clare Fischer (piano); running time: 95 minutes (U.S.); released June 21, 1962 (Italy), August 1962 (U.S.); video availability: Prism Entertainment Corp.

Cast: Rory Calhoun *(Marco Polo)*; Yòko Tani *(Princess Amurroy)*; Camillo Pilotto *(Grand Khan)*; Pierre Cressoy *(Cuday)*; Michael Chow *(Ciu-Lin)*; Tiny Young [billed as "Thien-Huong"] *(Tai-Au)*; Franco Ammirata; Tonino Cianci; Paolo Falchi; Angelo Galassi; Anna Maestri; Spartaco Nale; Ching Jen Pai; Roberto Paoletti; Ada Passeri; Bianca Pividori; Franco Ressel; Poing Ping Sam; Giacomo Tchang *(Old Chinese Man)*; Janine Tramony; Claudio Undari *(Mongka)*.

Comments: The Italian explorer Marco Polo (1254–1324) rescues the daughter of Kublai Khan in this fabricated adventure, produced by Italy's Alta Vista Filmorsa and Panda Film. Many of this production's sets (as well as actress Yòko Tani) were reused for *Samson and the 7 Miracles of the World* (qv).

Marco the Magnificent *(Le fabuleuse aventure de Marco Polo)* (MGM, 1966)

Credits: Directors: Denys de La Patellière, Raoul Lévy; *Co-Director:* Noël Howard; *Producer:* Raoul Lévy; *Screenplay:* Noël Howard, Raoul Lévy, Jean-Paul Rappeneau, Jacques Rémy, Denys de La Patellière; *Photography:* Wladimir Ivanov, Claude Renoir, Armand Thiraud (Eastmancolor, Franscope, aspect ratio 2.35:1); *Film Editors:* Noëlle Balenci, Jacqueline Thiédot, Albert Jurgenson; *Music:* Mario Bua, M.J. Coignard-Helison, Georges Garvarentz; *Production Design:* Jacques Saulnier; *Art Direction:* Veljko Despotovic, Slobodan Mijacevic, Miodrag Miric, Miodrag Nikolic; *Costume Design:* Jacques Fonteray; *Makeup:* Radmila Todorovic; *Production Manager:* Alfredo Nicolai; *Assistant Director:* Cliff Lyons; *Sound:* Pierre-Henri Goumy, Jacques Labussière; *Sound Recordist:* Vladimir Stankovic; *Special Effects:* Roscoe Cline; *Stunts:* Milan Mitic; Slavoljub Plavsic-Zvonce, Dragomir Stanojevic; *Theme Song Vocals:* Jerry Vale; released December 14, 1966.

Cast: Horst Buchholz *(Marco Polo)*; Anthony Quinn *(Kublai Khan, Mongol Emperor of China)*; Akim Tamiroff *(The Old Man of the Mountain)*;

Elsa Martinelli *(The Woman with the Whip)*; Robert Hossein *(Prince Nayam, Mongol Rebel Leader)*; Grégore Aslan *(Achmed Abdullah)*; Omar Sharif *(Sheik Alla Hou)*; Orson Welles *(Akerman)*; Massimo Girotti *(Nicolo, Marco's Father)*; Folco Lulli *(Spinello)*; Guido Alberti *(Pope Gregory X)*; Lynne Sue Moon *(Princess Gogatine)*; Bruno Cremer *(Guillaume de Tripoli, a Knight Templar)*; Jacques Monod *(Nicolo de Vicenza, a Knight Templar)*; Mica Orlovic *(Matteo, Marco's Uncle)*; Maria Virginia Onorato; Mansoureh Rihai *(Taha)*; Dragomir Felba; Myriam Michelson *(Chinese Princess)*; Mansuareh Risai; Ljubo Skiljevic; Aleksandar Stojkovic; Janez Vrhovec; Andrej Gardenin *(Fencer)*; Noël Howard; Cliff Lyons; Lucille Soong *(Princess Bride)*.

Comments: Another fictionalized account of the Italian explorer Marco Polo. This film was produced by Italy's Prodi Cinematografica, in association with France's Société Nouvelle de Cinématographie (SNC), with further production assistance from ITTAC, Italaf Kaboul, Mounir Rafla, and Yugoslavia's Avala Film. Orson Welles wrote his own (as well as Omar Sharif's) dialogue.

Mark of Zorro *(E io lo dico a Zzzzorro!)* (Iniziative Cinematografiche Internazional [ICI]/Estela Films, 1975)

Credits: *Director:* Franco Lo Cascio; *Co-Producer:* José María Cunillés; *Screenplay:* Augusto Finocchi, Francisco Lara Polop [billed as "Francisco Lara"] (from a story by Augusto Finocchi); *Photography:* Juan Gelpi (billed as "Juan Gelpi Puig"), Franco Villa (Eastmancolor); *Music/Orchestra Conductor:* Gianfranco Plenizio; *Script Supervisor:* Silvia Petroni; running time: 97 minutes; released July 3, 1975.

Cast: George Hilton *(Philip Mackintosh/Don Alba de Mendoza)*; Lionel Stander *(Padre Donato)*; Charo López *(Rosita Florenda)*; Rodolfo Licari [billed as "Rod Licari"] *(Count Manuel de Pas)*; Antonio Pica *(Major de Colignac)*; Gino Pagnani *(Drunk)*; Tito García; Flora Corasello *(Donna Florinda)*; Biel Moll; Giulio Baraghini; Dante Cleri; Rinaldo Zamperla; Franco Virgilio; Franco Daddi; Maria Tedeschi; Mario Proietti; Ettore Arena *(French Soldier)*; Bruno Bertocci; Giuseppe Talarico; Filippo Perego; Wilma Palmieri; Amerigo Castrighella *(Executioner)*; Bruno Alias *(Townsman)*; Rossana Canghiari *(Wedding Guest)*; Aristide Caporale *(Restaurant Guest)*; Enrico Cesaretti *(Colignac Soldier)*; Franz Colangeli *(Townsman)*; Wladimir Daddi *(Brawler)*; Ottaviano Dell'Acqua *(Brawler)*; Roberto Dell'Acqua *(Brawler)*; Raniero Dorascenzi *(Wedding Guest)*; Iolanda Fortini *(Townswoman)*; Lina Franchi *(Townswoman)*; Ferruchio Fregonese *(Wedding Guest)*; Oscar Giustini *(Brawler)*; Margherita Horowitz *(Wedding Guest)*; Giuseppe Marrocco *(Wedding Guest)*; Fulvio Pellegrino *(Townsman)*; Renzo Pevarello *(Brawler)*; Domenico Ravenna *(Politician)*; Nando Sarlo *(Townsman)*; Franca Scagnetti *(Townswoman)*; Pupita Lea Scuderoni *(Wedding Guest)*; Pietro Torrisi *(Brawler)*; Lidia Zanussi *(Woman in Church)*; Luciano Zanussi *(Politician)*.

Comments: Another cinematic incarnation of Zorro, produced by Italy's Iniziative Cinematografiche Internazionali (ICI) and Spain's Estela Films.

Mars, God of War *(Marte, dio della guerra)* (Embassy Pictures, 1962)

Credits: *Director:* Marcello Baldi; *Screenplay:* Marcello Baldi, Sandro Continenza (from a story by Ernesto Gastaldi and Ugo Guerra); *Photography:* Marcello Masciocchi (Eastmancolor, Totalscope, aspect ratio 2.35:1); *Film Editor:* Maurizio Lucidi; *Production Design:* Piero Poletto; *Costume Design:* Mario Giorsi; *Sound:* Pietro Ortolani; running time: 98 minutes; released June 24, 1962 (Italy); video availability: Something Weird Video.

Cast: Roger Browne *(Mars)*; Jocelyn Lane *(Daphne)*; Linda Sini *(Ecuba)*; Dante DiPaolo *(Frixos)*; Renato Speziali; Michèle Bailly *(Venere)*; John Kitzmiller *(Afros)*; Giuseppe Addobbati; Renato Navarrini; Corrado Annicelli; Claudio Perone; Massimo Serato *(Antarus)*; Aldo Bufi Landi; Giulio Donnini; Livio Lorenzon; Folco Lulli; Gianni Solaro.

Comments: This fanciful tale of the ancient gods on Mt. Olympus is also known as *The Son of Hercules vs. Venus*. Produced by the Italian companies Galatea Film, Incei Film, and SpA Cinematografica.

Mask of the Musketeers (Zorro e i tre moschettieri) (American International, 1963)

Credits: *Director:* Luigi Capuano; *Producer:* Marino Vacca; *Executive Producer:* Ferdinand Felicioni; *Screenplay:* Roberto Gianviti, Italo De Tuddo (from a story by Fernando Felicioni); *Photography:* Carlo Bellero (Pathé Color, Totalscope, aspect ratio 2.35:1); *Film Editor:* Antonietta Zita; *Music:* Carlo Savina; *Art Direction:* Alfredo Montori; *Set Decoration:* Antonio Fratalocchi; *Costume Design:* Elio Micheli; *Makeup:* Duilio Scarozza; *Hair Stylist:* Marcella Favella; *Production Supervisor:* Giulio Pappagallo; *Assistant Director:* Gianfranco Baldanello; *Assistant Art Director:* Giuseppe Ranieri; *Sound:* Raffaele Del Monte, Mario Del Pezzo; *Camera Operator:* Mario Sensi; *Master of Arms:* Franco Fantasia; *Script Supervisor:* Nellita Zampieri; running time: 100 minutes (Italy), 101 minutes (U.S.); released February 14, 1963 (Italy); video availability: Something Weird Video.

Cast: Gordon Scott *(Zorro)*; José Greci *(Isabella)*; Giacomo Rossi Stuart *(Athos)*; Livio Lorenzon *(Porthos)*; Franco Fantasia *(Count of Savilla)*; Nazzareno Zamperla [billed as "Tony Zamperla"] *(D'Artagnan)*; Nerio Bernardi *(Cardinal Richelieu)*; Ignazio Leone; Mario Pisu *(Count of Tequel)*; Giuseppe Addobbati; Giulio Maculani; Ignazio Balsamo; Enzo Maggio; Luciano Bonnani; Renato Malavasi; Pasquale De Filippo; Amina Pirani Maggi; Jan De Vecchi; Ugo Sasso; Andrea Fantasia; Bruno Scipioni; Charles Fawcett; Benito Stefanelli; Nando Tamberlani; Gianni Rizzo *(King Philip)*; Maria Grazia Spina *(Manuela)*; Roberto Risso *(Aramis)*.

Comments: Another Zorro adventure, starring Gordon Scott as the masked hero. Produced by Italy's Alta Vista and Jonia Film.

The Masked Conqueror (Zorro alla corte di Spagna) (American International, 1962)

Credits: *Director:* Luigi Capuano; *Producer:* Ferdinand Felicioni; *Screenplay:* Arpad DeRiso, Nino Scolaro (from their story); *Photography:* Oberdan Troiani (Eastmancolor, Dyaliscope, aspect ratio 2.35:1); *Film Editor:* Antonietta Zita; *Music:* Carlo Savina; *Production Design:* Alfredo Montori; *Costume Design:* Camillo Del Signore; *Sound:* Pietro Ortolani; *Assistant Director:* Gianfranco Baldanello; running time: 92 minutes (Italy), 94 minutes (U.S.); released June 29, 1962 (Italy).

Cast: George Ardisson *(Riccardo Di Villa Verde/Zorro)*; Alberto Lupo *(Miguel)*; Nadia Marlowa *(Bianca Rodriguez)*; Maria Letizia Gazzoni *(Infanta Isabella)*; Franco Fantasia *(Manuel Garcia)*; Antonio Gradoli *(L'Oste)*; Carlo Tamberlani *(Marquis Pedro Di Villa Verde)*; Amedeo Trilli *(Friar)*; Maria Grazia Spina *(Consuelo)*; Nazzareno Zamperla *(Paquito)*; Carla Calò *(Francisca Di Villa Verde)*; Nerio Bernardini *(Col. Vargas)*; Tullio Altamura *(Count of Toledo)*; Andreina Paul *(Queen Maria Cristina)*; Gloria Parri *(Rosita)*; Pasquale Di Filippo *(Valet)*; Ugo Sasso *(Dignitary)*; Gianni Rizzo *(Don Carlos)*; Livio Lorenzon *(Capt. Morales)*.

Comments: A Zorro adventure, produced by Italy's Jonia Film.

The Masked Man Against the Pirates (L'uomo mascherato contro i piratti) (ABC Films, 1964)

Credits: *Director:* Vertunnio De Angelis; *Producer:* Pino Addario; *Screenplay:* Aldo Barni, Giorgio Costantini, Vertunnio De Angelis, Dino Sant'Ambrogio; *Photography:* Antonio Belviso, Gino Santini (Eastmancolor, aspect ratio 2.35:1); *Film Editor:* Mariano Arditi; *Music:* Alessandro Nadin; *Set Decoration:* Demofilo Fidani; *Costume Design:* Mila Vitelli Valenza; *Production Manager:* Gianni Solitro; *Assistant Directors:* Gennaro Ballistrieri, Tony Pretetto; *Sound:* Alfredo Neri; *Special Effects:* Agostino Possanza; *Production Assistant:* Rosetta Sestili; running time: 105 minutes (U.S.); released July 12, 1964 (Italy); video availability: Something Weird Video.

Cast: George Hilton *(Suarez)*; Claude Dantes *(Princess Anne)*; Giovanni Vari *(Capt. Pedro Ramon Garcia)*; José Torres *(Josh, the Raven)*; Pietro De Vico; Tony Kendall *(Capt. Ruiz)*; Gina Rovere; Luciano Benetti; Lucio De Santis; Mario Zicavo; Giorgio Costantini; Laura Forest; Adriana Tucci; Christa Windish-Graetz.

Comments: A pirate adventure with a Zorro-type masked avenger thrown into the proceedings. Produced by the Italian companies Rio Film, Seven Film and Titanus.

Massacre in the Black Forest (Il massacro della foresta nera) (Majestic Pictures, 1967)

Credits: Directors: Ferdinando Baldi (billed as "Ferdy Baldwin"), Rudolf Nussgruber; *Screenplay:* Ferdinando Baldi, Adriano Bolzoni, Alessandro Ferraù; *Photography:* Lucky Satson (color, aspect ratio 1.85:1); *Film Editor:* Otello Colangeli (billed as "Othello"); *Music:* Carlo Savina (billed as "Charles Hanger"); *Production Design:* Miodrag Nikolic; *Art Direction:* Jovan Radic, Louis Shake, Milan Todorovic; *Costume Design:* Donald Dawn; *Makeup:* Donald Coach; *Production Manager:* Bob Ensascaller, Jr.; *Assistant Director:* Norman Wood; *Stunts:* Slavoljub Plavsic-Zvonce; *Producer of Soundtrack Album:* Luca di Silverio; running time: 82 minutes; released 1967.

Cast: Cameron Mitchell *(Consul Aulus Sessnia)*; Antonella Lualdi *(Tusnelda)*; Hans Von Borsody *(Arminius)*; Beba Loncar *(Livia)*; Dieter Eppler; Remo De Angelis; Peter Carsten; Aleksandar Gavric; Paul Windsor; Beli Bolin; Vladimir Medar; Andrej Gardenin.

Comments: Led by a former member of the Roman Army, Teutonic warriors rise up against Rome in the 1st century AD Produced by Italy's Debora Film, Yugoslavia's Avala Film and Germany's Peter Carsten Productions.

Medusa Against the Son of Hercules (Perseo l'invincibile) (Embassy, 1963)

Credits: Director: Alberto De Martino; *Producer:* Erno Bistolfi; *Screenplay:* Ernesto Gastaldi, Mario Caiano, Alberto De Martino, Luciano

Soldiers encounter the horrendous Medusa in *Medusa Against the Son of Hercules.*

Martino, Mario Guerra, José Mallorqui, Tonino Guerra (from a story by Mario Guerra, Alberto De Martino, based on an idea by Edoardo G. Conti); *Photography:* Eloy Mella, Dario Di Palma (Eastmancolor, Totalscope, aspect ratio 2.35:1); *Film Editors:* Mercedes Alonso, Otello Colangeli; *Music:* Carlo Franci, Manuel Parada; *Production Design:* Franco Lolli; *Set Decoration:* Enzo Constantini, José Luis Garcia, Jaime Pérez Cubero; *Costume Design:* Angiolina Menichelli; *Makeup:* Romolo De Martino; *Hair Stylist:* Italia Marini; *Production Managers:* Gervasio Banciella, José Luis Jerez Aloza; *Assistant Directors:* Luciano Palmera, Vittorio Vighi; *Art Department Manager:* Italo Tomassi; *Sound:* Luigi Puri; *Special Effects:* Carlo Rambaldi, Amando de Orsario; *Matte Shots:* Emilio Ruiz del Rio; *Stunts:* Valentino Pelizzi; *2nd Assistant Cameraman:* Ricardo Poblete; *Fencing Master:* Giorgio Ubaldi; *Director of U.S.-Dubbed Version:* Richard Mcnamara; *Script for U.S.-Dubbed Version:* John Davis Hart; running time: 90 minutes (Italy); released February 7, 1963 (Italy); video availability: Sinister Cinema.

Cast: Richard Harrison *(Perseus)*; Anna Ranalli *(Andromeda)*; Arturo Dominici *(Acrisio)*; Elisa Cegani *(Danae)*; Leo Anchóriz *(Galenore)*; Antonio Molino Rojo *(Tarpete)*; Roberto Camardiel *(Cefeo)*; Ángel Jordán *(Medusa)*; Fernando Liger; Bruno Scipioni; Frank Braña *(Prince)*; Miguel de la Riva *(Prince)*; José Luis Ferreiro; Miguel González; Rufino Inglés; Enrique Novarro *(Stheno)*; Ángela Pia *(Euryale)*; Lorenzo Robledo *(Prince)*; José Sepúlveda.

Comments: Originally called *Perseus Against the Monsters*, this entry deals with the legendary Medusa, whose supernatural gaze can petrify men and turn them into stone. There are equal parts of sword-and-sandal and horror-fantasy in this above-average production. Co-produced by Italy's Cineproduzione Emo Bistolfi and Spain's Copercines Cooperativa Cinematografica.

Anna Ranalli in *Medusa Against the Son of Hercules.*

Messalina (*Messalina Venere imperatrice*) (American-International, 1960)

Credits: *Director:* Vittorio Cottafavi; *Producer:* Erno Bistolfi; *Screenplay:* Ennio De Concini, Mario Guerra, Carlo Romano, Duccio Tessari (from their story); *Photography:* Marco Scarpelli (Technicolor, Technirama, aspect ratio 2.35:1); *Music:* Angelo Francesco Lavagnino; *Art Direction:* Franco Lolli; *Art Direction:* Italo Tomassi; *Camera Operator:* Pasqualino De Santis; *Assistant Director:* Duccio Tessari; *Orchestra Conductor:* Carlo Savina; running time: 96 minutes (Italy), 84 minutes (U.S.); released March 12, 1960 (Italy), 1962 (U.S.).

Cast: Belinda Lee *(Messalina/Valeris)*; Spiros Focás *(Lucio Massimo)*; Carlo Giustini *(Lusio Geta)*; Giancarlo Sbraglia *(Aulo Celso)*; Giulio Donnini *(Narciso)*; Arturo Dominici *(Caio Sillio)*; Ida Galli *(Silvia)*; Marcello Giorda *(Claudio)*; Mino Doro *(Suplicio)*; Annie Gorassini *(Aulo Ceso's Courtesan)*; Arnoldo Tieri *(Pirgo Pollinice)*; Giuliano Gemma *(Marcello)*; Lia Angeleri *(Vipidia)*; Vittorio Congia *(Ortotrago)*; Paola Pitagora; Spartaco Nale *(Tibuleno)*; Vladimiro Picciafuochi; Nando Angelini *(Glauco, Armenian Campaign Veteran)*; Giorgio Zuccaro; Mimmo Poli *(Drunk Disguised as Bacchus)*; Bruno Pagilari; Pietro Di Giulio; Nino Orsini;

Original Italian poster for *Medusa Against the Son of Hercules*.

Bruno Scipioni; Benito Stefanelli; Calisto Calisti; Bruna Cealti; Paolo Di Mario; Alberto Plebani; Gilberto Mazzi *(Consul)*; Roberto Caporali; Antonio Correri; Alfio Caltabiano; Paolo Gargaloni; Janine Hendy *(Dancer)*; Pix Mullet, Ennio Sammartino *(Dancer)*.

Comments: The cruel and wanton Messalina (circa 17 or 20 AD–48 AD) was the third wife of the Roman Emperor Claudius, and she is played to the hilt in this production by Belinda Lee. Produced by Italy's Cineproduzione Emo Bistolfi and filmed at Cinecittà Studios in Rome.

Messalina vs. The Son of Hercules (L'ultimo gladiatore) (Avco Embassy, 1964)

Credits: Director: Umberto Lenzi; *Producer:* Alfonso Sansone; *Screenplay:* Gian Paolo Callegari, Albert Valentin (from their story); *Photography:* Pier Ludovico Pavoni (Eastmancolor, Techniscope, aspect ratio 2.35:1); *Film Editor:* Nella Nannuzzi; *Music:* Carlo Franci; *Production Design:* Pier Vittorio Marchi; *Set Decoration:* Franco D'Andria; *Costume Design:* Mario Giorsi; *Makeup:* Otello Fava; *Hair Stylist:* Renata Magnanti; *Production Manager:* Carlo Vassalle; *Assistant Directors:* Filiberto Fiaschi, Viktor Tourjansky, Larby Towns; *Sound Engineer:* Franco Groppioni; *Camera Operator:* Fausto Rossi; *Assistant Camera Operator:* Mario Pastorini; *Costumer:* Tigano Lo Faro; *Assistant Costume Designer:* Antonio Randaccio; *Production Secretary:* Albino Morandini; *Script Supervisor:* Liana Ferri; *Master of Arms:* Bruno Ukmar; running time: 98 minutes (Italy), 98 minutes (U.S.); released June 27, 1964; video availability: Something Weird Video.

Cast: Richard Harrison *(Glaucus)*; Lisa Gastoni *(Messalina)*; Marilù Tolo *(Ena)*; Philippe Hersent *(Claudio)*; Livio Lorenzon *(Prefect of the Court)*; Jean Claudio *(Gaio Silio)*; Lidia Alfonsi; Gianni Solari *(Cassius Chaerea)*; Enzo Fiermonte; Giuseppe Addobbati *(Lucilius)*; Maria Laura Rocca *(Procusa)*; Charles Borromel *(Caligola)*; Lucia Bomez; Ettore Arena *(Roman Soldier)*; Fortunato Arena *(Bearded Soldier/Attacker)*; Aldo Canti *(Fighter with Glaucus)*; Arnaldo Fabrizio *(Caligola's Dwarf)*; Jimmy il Fenomeno *(a Briton)*; Gilberto Galimberti *(Soldier Holding Glaucus)*; Emilio Messina *(Gladiator)*; Paul Naschy *(Extra)*; Piero Pastore *(Ambassador to Britain)*; Nello Pazzafini *(Member of Lucilius' Escort)*; Bruno Ukmar *(Hitman/Soldier)*; Franco Ukmar *(Hitman/Soldier)*.

Comments: The evil Empress Messalina threatens the virginal Ena with death in order to force Ena's lover Glaucus to assassinate the Emperor Claudius. Lisa Gastoni, cast here as Messalina, had a wider dramatic range than most of the peplum actresses, and was adept at either virtuous or sinister roles. Produced by Italy's Promoteo Film S.R.L. and Sancro Film, in association with the French companies Unicité and Les Films Jacques Leitienne.

Michael Strogoff (Michel Strogoff) (Continental Distributing, 1956)

Credits: Director: Carmine Gallone; *Producer:* Emile Natan; *Screenplay:* Marc-Gilbert Sauvajon (based on the novel by Jules Verne); *Photography:* Robert Lefebvre (Eastmancolor, CinemaScope, aspect ratio 2.35:1); *Film Editors:* Niccolò Lazzari, Armand Ridel; *Production Design:* Léon Barsacq, Kosta Krivokapic; *Art Direction:* Vlastimir Gavrik, Aleksandar Milovic; *Set Decoration:* Robert Christidès; *Costume Design:* Marcel Escoffier, Jean Zay; *Makeup:* Alberto De Rossi, Lina Gallet; *Production Manager:* Louis Wipf; *Unit Managers:* Lucien Lippens, Radomir Popovic, Milenko Stakovic; *1st Assistant Director:* Georges Friedman; *Assistant Directors:* Stojan Culibrk, Dejan Kosanovic, Nikola Rajic; *Set Designers:* Vlastimir Gavrik, Kosta Krivokapic; *Assistant Set Decorators:* Jacques Chalvet, André Dakst; *Scenic Artists:* Lj. Borisavljevic, P. Novakovic, M. Sreckovic; *Sound:* Vorke Scarlett; *Sound Engineer:* Louis Hochet; *Sound System:* Western Electric; *Camera Operators:* Roger Delpuech, Albert Militon; *Assistant Camera Operators:* Luc Mirot, Gaston Muller, Gilbert Sarthre; *Still Photographer:* Walter Limot; *Wardrobe:* Jean Zay; *Orchestra Conductor:* Serge Baudo; *Production Supervisors:* Joseph Spigler, George Vallon; *Production Assistant/Script Supervisor:* Dagmar Bolin; *Military Advisor:* Zivojin Gugic; running time: 111 minutes; released December 14, 1956 (France), May 20, 1960 (U.S.).

Cast: Curt Jurgens *(Michael Strogoff)*; Geneviève Page *(Nadia Fédor)*; Jacques Dacqmine *(The Grand Duke)*; Sylva Koscina *(Sangarre)*; Gérard Buhr *(Henry Blount)*; Louis Arbressier *(Tsar Alexandre II)*; Fernand Fabre; Michel Etcheverry *(General Krisloff)*; Paul Demange *(Telegraph Employee)*; Valéry Inkijinoff *(Féofor Khan)*; Francoise Fabian *(Natko)*; Henri Nassiet *(Ivan Ogareff)*; Sylvie *(Marfa, Strogoff's Mother)*; Jean Parédès *(Alcide Jolivet)*; Dusan Janicijevic; Milivoje Popovic-Mavid; Léonce Corne; Vladimir Medar; Pavle Mincic.

Comments: During a Tartar rebellion in 19th century Russia, the Tsar entrusts Capt. Michael Strogoff with the task of delivering a vital message to the Tsar's brother, fighting in Serbia. Based on the 1876 novel by Jules Verne. Produced by Italy's Illiria Film and Produzione Gallone, in association with France's Les Films Modernes and Yugoslavia's Udruzenje Filmskih Umetnika Srbije (UFUS).

The Mighty Crusaders (La Gerusalemme liberata) (Falcon, 1961)

Credits: *Director:* Carlo Ludovico Bragaglia; *Producer:* Ottavio Poggi; *Screenplay:* Sandro Continenza (based on material by Torquato Tasso; script for English version by Annalena Limentani, Frederica Nutter); *Photography:* Rodolfo Lombardi (Ferraniacolor, Supercinescope, aspect ratio 2.35:1); *Film Editor:* Renato Cinquini; *Music:* Roberto Nicolosi; *Art Direction:* Ernest Kromberg; *Costume Design:* Giancarlo Bartolini Salimbeni; *Makeup:* Goffredo Rochetti; *Production Manager:* Lucio Bompani; *Sound:* Bruno Francisci; *Assistant Film Editor:* Bruno Mattei; *Production Supervisor:* Cesare Torri; running time: 97 minutes (Italy), 87 minutes (U.S.); released January 1961 (U.S.).

Cast: Francisco Rabal *(Tancredi d'Altavilla)*; Sylva Koscina *(Clorinda)*; Gianna Maria Canale *(Armida)*; Rik Battaglia *(Rinaldo d'Este)*; Philippe Hersent *(Goffredo di Buglione)*; Andrea Aureli *(Argante)*; Alba Arnova *(Harem Dancer)*; Nando Tamberlani *(Pietro the Hermit)*; Cesare Fantoni *(Aladino)*; Edoardo Toniolo *Raimondo da Tolosa)*; Carlo Hinterman *(Dilone)*; Ugo Sasso *(Gernando di Norvegia)*; Leonardo Bragaglia *(Achille Sforza)*; Fedele Gentile *(Presidio Commander)*; Giulio Battiferri *(Muslim Ambassador)*; Fernando Ghia *(Squire of Rinaldo)*; Teresa Ferrone *(Angelica)*; Joe Kamel; Tomás Torres; Giovanni Panzetti *(Beggar)*; Lino Basile *(Squire of Tancredi)*; Livia Contardi *(Erminia)*.

Comments: An account of the Crusades, produced by Italy's MAX Film.

The Mighty Ursus (Ursus) (United Artists, 1962)

Credits: *Director:* Carlo Campogalliani; *Producer/Executive Producer:* Italo Zingarelli; *Screenplay:* Giuliano Carnimeo, Giuseppe Mangione, Sergio Sollima (from a story by Giuseppe Mangione); *Photography:* Eloy Mella (Eastmancolor, Totalscope, aspect ratio 2.35:1); *Film Editors:* Franco Fraticelli, Julio Peña; *Music:* Roman Vlad; *Art Direction:* Piero Poletto, Antonio Simont; *Set Decoration:* Giulio Cabras, Julio Molina; *Costume Design:* Antonio Cortés, Piero Sadun; *Makeup:* Michele Trimarchi; *Unit Managers:* Giorgio Migliarini, Ángel Monis; *Assistant Directors:* Romolo Guerrieri, Pepe Herrera; *Special Effects:* Raffaele Del Monte, Mario Del Pezzo, Rolando Morelli; *Camera Operators:* Stelvio Massi, Ricardo Poblete (billed as "Ricardo Poblette"); *Production Assistant:* Roberto Palaggi; *Script Supervisors:* Roberto Giandalla, Maria Teresa Ramos; *Choreographer:* Gino Landi; running time: 90 minutes; released February 1, 1961 (Italy), April 11, 1962 (U.S.).

Cast: Ed Fury *(Ursus)*; Cristina Gaioni [billed as "Cristina Gajoni"] *(Magali)*; Moira Orfei *(Attea)*; Mario Scaccia *(Kymos)*; Maria Luisa Merlo [billed as "Mary Marion"] *(Doreide)*; Luis Prendes *(Setas)*; Rafael Luis Calvo [billed as "Raphael Luis Calvo"] *(Mok)*; Mariangela Giordano *(Miriam)*; Nino Fuscagni *(Kymos' Guest)*; Soledad Miranda *(Iside)*; Eliana Grimaldi *(Fillis)*; Antonio Gil *(Adelfo)*; Ángela Pla; Cris Huerta *(Challenging Wrestler)*; Roberto Camardiel [billed as "Roberto Gamardiel"] *(Cleonte)*; Manuel Arbó; José Balbuena *(Bullfighter)*; Vicente Bañó; Tomás Blanco; José de la Cal *(Bullfighter)*; Ángel Calero; Rafael Calvo Revilla; Adelino Carvalho *(Bullfighter)*; Óscar Cortina; Alfredo David *(Bullfighter)*; Carmelo Garcia; Manuel Gil; Teresa Gisbert; José Gosálvez; Julio Infiesta; Rufino Inglés; Isleño *(Bullfighter)*; José

Ed Fury in *The Mighty Ursus*.

Timoteo López *(Bullfighter)*; Ángel Menéndez; Ray Palolo *(Fighter)*; Luis Roses; Ventura Ruiz *(Fighter)*.

Comments: Also known as *Ursus*. In this sword-and-sandal adventure, strongman Ursus searches for his fiancée Attea, who has been kidnapped by a religious sect that sacrifices virgins to pagan gods. A scene in which Ed Fury grapples with a bull in the arena is particularly impressive. Many sets from director Nicholas Ray's *King of Kings* (1961) were reused for this movie. Produced by Italy's Cine-Italia Films, Spain's Atenea Films and Yugoslavia's Film Servis. Shot at Cinecittà in Rome, with some location work in Algetete, Madrid, Spain.

Minotaur, the Wild Beast of Crete (*Teseo contro il minotauro*) (United Artists, 1960)

Credits: *Director:* Silvio Amadio; *Producers:* Giorgio Agliani, Gino Mordini, Rudolphe Solmesne; *Screenplay:* Gian Paolo Callegari, Sandro Continenza; *Photography:* Aldo Giordani (Technicolor, Totalscope, aspect ratio 2.35:1); *Film Editor:* Nella Nannuzzi; *Music:* Carlo Rustichelli; *Production Designer:* Piero Poletto; *Makeup:* Duilio Giustini, Manrico Spagnoli; *Hair Stylist:* Marisa Fraticelli; *Production Manager:* Adriano Merkel; *Assistant Director:* Alberto De Martino; *Props:* E. Rancati, C. Sormani; *Sound:* Mario Del Pezzo; *Special Effects (Matte Shots):* Joseph Nathanson; *Horse Stunts/Stunt Double:* Milan Mitic; *Unit Photographer:* Renato Del Frate; *Wardrobe:* Enzo Bulgarelli; *Music Director:* Franco Ferrara; *Unit Director:* Giorgio Capitani; *Master of Arms:* Enzo Musumeci Greco; *Choreography:* Adriano Vitale; *English-Language Script:* Daniel Mainwaring; running time: 105 minutes (Italy); released November 25, 1960 (Italy), April 1961 (U.S.); video availability: Something Weird Video.

Cast: Bob Mathias *(Prince Teseo)*; Rosanna Schiaffino *(Princess Fedra/Arianna)*; Alberto Lupo *(Chirone)*; Rik Battaglia *(Demetrio)*; Carlo

Poster for *The Mighty Ursus.*

Tamberlani *(Minos, King of Crete)*; Nico Pepe *(Gerione)*; Susanne Loret *(Anfitrite)*; Nerio Bernardi *(King of Athens)*; Paul Muller *(Court Physician)*; Tiziana Casetti *(Illia, Xanto's Daughter)*; Alberto Plebani *(Xanto)*; Tina Lattanzi *(Queen Pasiphae)*; Milo Malagoli *(Minotaur)*; Alberto Barberito; Emma Baron *(Arianna's Foster Mother)*; Maria Maleff; Vanni Materassi; Adriano Micantoni *(Sunis, the High Priest)*; Vladimiro Picciafuochi *(Jailer)*; Andrea Scotti *(Alcmene)*; Erminio Spalla *(Arianna's Foster Father)*; Amedeo Trilli *(Ctesiphorus)*; Vittorio Vaser *(Timon)*; Elena Zareschi.

Comments: In 1600 BC, the heroic Prince Teseo saves Princess Arianna from the legendary Minotaur. Lead Bob Mathias (1930–2006) was a two-time Olympic gold medalist (in the 1948 and 1952 Games), served as a United States Marine Corps officer, and was a Republican Congressman representing California from 1967 to 1975. This film was produced by the Italian companies Gino Mordini, Giorgio Agliani Cinematografica, and Illiria Film.

Mole Men Against the Son of Hercules (Maciste l'uomo più forte del mondo) (Embassy, 1961)

Credits: *Director:* Antonio Leonviola; *Executive Producer:* Elio Scardamaglia; *Screenplay:* Marcello Baldi, Giuseppe Mangione (from a story by Antonio Leonviola and Giuseppe Mangione; dialogue for English-dubbed version by Stephen Garrett, Frank Gregory); *Photography:* Alvaro Mancori (color, Totalscope, aspect ratio 2.35:1); *Film Editor:* Otello Colangeli; *Music:* Armando Trovajoli; *Production Design/Set Decoration:* Franco Lolli; *Art Direction:* Italo Tomassi; *Costume Design:* Gaia Romanini; *Makeup:* Amato Garbini; *Hair Stylist:* Mirella Ginnoto; *Production Manager:* Piero Lazzari; *Unit Manager:* Paolo Gargano; *Assistant Director:* Sergio Donà; *Set Design:* Aristide Spila; *Assistant Set Designers:* Francesco Cuppini, Gianfranco Fini; *Sound Engineers:* Ovidio Del Grande, S. Occhetti; *Camera Operator:* Sandro Mancori; *Chief Electricians:* Marcello Zucchè, M. Fino; *Assistant Costumers:* Lolly Fugagnolli, A. Quilici; *Assistant Film Editor:* Paolo Lucignani; *Continuity:* Nellita Zampieri; running time: 90 minutes; released October 10, 1961; video availability: Something Weird Video.

Cast: Mark Forest *(Maciste, Son of Hercules)*; Moira Orfei *(Queen Halis Mojab)*; Paul Wynter *(Bango)*; Gianni Garko *(Kathar, Kahab's Son)*; Enrico Glori *(Kahab, the High Priest)*; Raffaella Carrà *(Princess Salirah)*; Roberto Miali *(Loth)*; Nando Tamberlani *(Khur, King of Aran)*; Carla Foscari; Rosalia Gavo; Graziella Granata *(Queen's Handmaid)*; Janine Hendy *(Queen's Handmaid Playing Harp)*; Grazia Campori *(Queen's Handmaid)*; Mara Lombardo *(Queen's Handmaid)*; Luciana Vivaldi *(Queen's Handmaid)*; Franca Polesello *(Queen's Handmaid)*; Cinzia Cam *(Queen's Handmaid)*; Bruna Mori *(Queen's Handmaid)*; Anna De Martino *(Queen's Handmaid)*; Gloria Hendy *(Tulac, Bango's Friend)*.

Comments: Maciste battles monsters and an evil queen in an underground city to rescue Princess Salirah. Produced by Italy's Leone Film and shot at Cinecittà in Rome.

The Mongols (I mongoli) (Colorama Features, 1961)

Credits: *Directors:* André De Toth, Leopoldo Savona, Riccardo Freda; *Producer:* Guido Giambartolomei; *Screenplay:* Ottavio Alessi, Alessandro Ferraù, Ernesto Gastaldi, Ugo Guerra, Luciano Martino; *Photography:* Aldo Giordani (Eastmancolor, CinemaScope, aspect ratio 2.35:1); *Film Editor:* Otello Colangeli; *Music:* Mario Nascimbene; *Production Design:* Aleksandar Milovic Angelo Zambo; *Art Direction:* Milan Todorovic; *Set Decoration:* Arrigo Breschi; *Costume Design:* Enzo Bulgarelli; *Production Manager:* Carlo Bessi; *Assistant Director:* Alberto Cardone; *2nd Unit Director (action scenes):* Riccardo Freda; *Stunts:* Milan Mitic; *2nd Unit Director of Photography:* Renato Del Frate; *Camera Operators:* Sergio Bergamini, Giovanni Bergamini; *Still Photographers:* Guglielmo Coluzzi, Aldo Galfano; *Music Director:* Franco Ferrara; *Scenery:* Ottavio Scotti; *Choreography:* Dino Solari; running time: 115 minutes (Italy), 105 minutes (U.S.); released August 31, 1961 (Italy), September 26, 1966 (U.S.); video availability: Something Weird Video.

Cast: Jack Palance *(Ogatai)*; Anita Ekberg *(Hulina)*; Antonella Lualdi *(Amina)*; Franco

Top: Anita Ekberg in *The Mongols*. *Bottom:* Anita Ekberg confronts a torture victim in *The Mongols*.

Silva *(Stepen of Crakow)*; Gianni Garko *(Henry de Valois)*; Roldano Lupi *(Genghis Khan)*; Gabriele Antonini *(Temugin)*; Pierre Cressoy *(Igor)*; Mario Colli *(Boris)*; Lawrence Montaigne *(Prince Stefan's Ally)*; George Wang *(Subodai)*; Andrej Gardenin *(Fencer)*; Vittorio Sanipoli; Janine Hendy *(Harem Dancer)*.

Comments: Genghis Khan and his Mongols invade Poland and conquer the city of Krakow. After the invasion, they are ready to make peace with the King, but Genghis Khan's brutal son Ogatai wants to crush the city. Genghis Khan here is portrayed as considerably more reasonable than the actual historical warlord, who by most accounts was responsible for 20 million deaths (10 percent of the known world population at that time!). Produced by Italy's Royal Film and France's France Cinéma Productions. Filmed at Centralni Filmski Studio, Košutnjak, Belgrade, Serbia.

Morgan, the Pirate *(Morgan il pirata)* (MGM, 1960)

Credits: *Directors:* André De Toth, Primo Zeglio; *Producer:* Joseph E. Levine; *Screenplay:* Filippo Sanjust, André De Toth, Primo Zeglio; *Photography:* Tonino Delli Colli (Technicolor, CinemaScope, aspect ratio 2.35:1); *Film Editor:* Maurizio Lucidi; *Music:* Franco Mannino; *Production Design:* Gianni Polidori; *Art Direction:* Josette France; *Costume Design:* Filippo Sanjust; *Makeup:* Angelo Giustini; *Hair Stylists:* Lina Cassini, Mirella Ginnoto; *Production Supervisors:* Roberto Onori, Nicolò Pomilia; *Assistant Director:* Alberto Cardone; *Sound:* Fausto Ancillai, Enzo Silvestri; *Sound Engineer:* Georges Leblond; *Microphone Boom Operator:* Primiano Muratori; *Special Effects:* Eros Bacciucchi; *Camera Operator:* Franco Delli Colli; *Assistant Camera Operators:* Pino Santini, Gioacchino Sofia; *Still Photographer:* Angelo Pennoni; *Assistant Film Editors:* Alberto Cardone, Andrea Volpe; *Orchestra Conductor:* Franco Mannino; *Technical Director:* Simone Dauvillier; *Fencing Master:* Enzo Musumeci Greco; running time: 95 minutes (Italy), 93 minutes (U.S.); released November 17, 1960 (Italy), July 6, 1961 (U.S.).

Cast: Steve Reeves *(Henry Morgan)*; Valérie Lagrange *(Doña Inez)*; Ivo Garrani *(Governor Don José Guzman)*; Lidia Alfonsi *(Doña Maria)*; Giulio Bosetti *(Sir Thomas Modyford)*; Angelo Zanolli *(David)*; George Ardisson *(Walter)*; Dino Malacrida *(Duke)*; Anita Todesco; Armand Mestral *(Francois L'Olonnais)*; Chelo Alonso *(Consuela)*; Angelo Boscariol *(Pirate)*; Giovanni Cianfriglia *(Slave Trader's Assistant)*; Veriano Ginesi *(Pirate)*; Aldo Pini *(Pirate)*; Mimmo Poli *(Pirate)*.

Comments: Welsh pirate Sir Henry Morgan (circa 1635–1688) sets out to conquer Panama, where he was once enslaved. Produced by the Italian companies Adelphia Compagnia Cinematografica and Lux Film, in association with the French companie Compagnie Cinématographique de France.

Musketeers of the Sea *(Il moschettieri del mare)* (American-International, 1962)

Credits: *Director:* Massimo Patrizi Steno; *Producers:* Roberto Chabert, Alfredo Mirabile, Orlando Orsini; *Screenplay:* Marcello Fondato, Roberto Gianviti, Vittorio Metz Steno; *Photography:* Carlo Carlini (color, aspect ratio 2.35:1); *Music:* Carlo Rustichelli; *Production Design:* Gianni Polidori; *Assistant Director:* Nando Cicero; *2nd Unit 1st Assistant Director:* Mariano Laurenti; *Master of Arms:* Goffredo Unger; running time: 116 minutes; released November 28, 1962 (Italy), 1964 (U.S.).

Cast: Pier Angeli *(Consuelo/Gracia)*; Channing Pollock *(Pierre de Savigny)*; Aldo Ray *(Moreau)*; Philippe Clay *(Gosselin)*; Robert Alda *(Vice-Governor Gomez)*; Raymond Bussières *(Colonel Ortona)*; Carlo Ninchi *(Count di Lorna)*; Mario Scaccia *(King of France)*; Carla Calò *(Zalamea)*; Mario Siletti *(The Treasurer)*; Cesare Fantoni *(Father Milita)*; Gino Buzzanca *(Crew Leader)*; Pietro Tordi *(Bosun)*; Furio Meniconi *(Pirate Captain)*; Lamberto Antinori; Erika Jorgen; Rinaldo Zamperla *(Soldier)*.

Comments: A tongue-in-cheek swashbuckler, produced by Italy's Morino Film and France's France Cinéma Productions.

The Mysterious Swordsman *(Lo spadaccino misterioso)* (Po Film, 1956)

Credits: Director: Sergio Grieco; *Producer:* Ottavio Poggi; *Screenplay:* Sergio Grieco, Carlo Veo (from a story by Ottavio Poggi, Aldo Segri); *Photography:* Ferraniacolor, CinemaScope, aspect ratio 2.35:1); *Music:* Ezio Carabella; *Production Design:* Ernest Kromberg; *Master of Arms:* Enzo Musumeci Greco; running time: 90 minutes; released May 25, 1956 (Italy).

Cast: Frank Latimore *(Riccardo Degli Argentari)*; Fiorella Mari *(Laura)*; Gérard Landry *(Duke Ubaldo)*; Tamara Lees; Andrea Aureli; Giulio Battiferri; Antonio Corevi; Remo De Angelis; Lidia Del Faro; Enrico Glori; Gianni Luda; Nino Milano; Susan Terry.

Comments: A low-budget swashbuckler, produced by Italy's Po Film.

Nero and the Burning of Rome *(Nerone e Messalina)* (Cinefilms/ Four Star Television, 1953)

Credits: Director: Primo Zeglio; *Screenplay:* Paolo Levi, Riccardo Testa, Primo Zeglio (adaptation by Fulvio Palmieri, from a novel by David Bluhmen); *Photography:* Mario Albertelli, Tonino Delli Colli (black-and-white, aspect ratio 1.37:1); *Film Editor:* Giancarlo Cappelli; *Production Design:* Italo Cremona; *Art Direction:* Giulio Bongini; *Set Decoration:* Ugo Pericoli; *Costume Design:* Giulio Bongini, Italo Cremona; *General Production Manager:* Luciano Doria; *Production Manager:* Gualtero Bagnoli; *Assistant Production Managers:* Angelo Battiferri, Armando Morandi; *Sound:* Leopoldo Rosi; running time: 106 minutes (Italy), 97 minutes (U.S.); released August 28, 1953.

Cast: Gino Cervi *(Nero)*; Paolo Barbara *(Agrippina)*; Yvonne Sanson *(Stabillia Messalina)*; Milly Vitale *(Atte)*; Jole Fierro *(Poppea)*; Steve Barclay *(Chariot Commander)*; Bella Starace Sainati *(Locusta)*; Ludmilla Dudarova *(Valeria Messalina)*; Carlo Giustini *(Brittanico)*; Memmo Carotenuto; Lamberto Picasso *(Seneca)*; Silvana Jachino *(Eunike)*; Mario Molfesi; Renzo Ricci *(Petronio)*; Carlo Tamberlani *(Tigellino)*; Elisa Vazzoler; Aldo Alimonti; Corrado Annicelli; Armando Annuale; Cesare Bettarini; Jenny Folchi *(Nero's Concubine)*; Loris Gizzi; *(Decius Metellus)*; Gianni Musy; Enrico Poli.

Comments: The titular event is depicted in this early peplum, filmed in black-and-white and produced by Italy's Spettacolo Film.

The New Adventures of Zorro *(Zorro il dominatore)* (Duca Internazionale/ Producciones Cinematográficas/ Hispamer Films/Rosa Films, S.A., 1969)

Credits: Director: José Luis Merino; *Producer:* Ángel Rosson y Rubio; *Photography:* Emanuele Di Cola (Eastmancolor); *Film Editor:* Giuseppe Giacobino; *Music:* Coriolano Gori; running time: 89 minutes; released 1969.

Cast: Carlos Quiney *(Antonio Sandoval/ Zorro)*; Maria Pia Conte *(Isabel)*; Aldo Bufi Landi *(Colonel Mauricio de Córdoba)*; José Jaspe *(Governor)*; Juan Cortés *(Capitán Álvaro Mendoza)*.

Comments: Another quickly-made Zorro adventure, Produced by Italy's Duca Internazionale with Spain's Producciones Cinematograficas and Hispamer Films.

The Night of the Great Attack *(La notte del grande assalto)* (Four Star Television, 1959)

Credits: Director: Giuseppe Maria Scotese; *Producers:* Angelo Faccenna, Giuseppe Maria Scotese; *Co-Producer:* René Thévenet; *Screenplay:* Arnaldo Marrosu, Giuseppe Maria Scotese; *Photography:* Pier Ludovico Pavoni (color, Totalscope, aspect ratio 2.35:1); *Film Editor:* Otello Colangeli; *Music:* Carlo Rustichelli; *Production Design:* Carlo Vignati; *Set Decoration:* Franco Fontana; *Costume Design:* Maria Luisa Panaro; *Makeup:* Guglielmo Bonotti; *Production Manager:* Giancarlo Ferrando; *Assistant Cameramen:* Luigi Conversi, Angelo Lotti; *Sound:* Renato Cadueri, Mario Del Pezzo; *Production Assistant:* Louis Duchesne; running time: 95 minutes; released October 29, 1959 (Italy).

Cast: Agnès Laurent *(Isabella)*; Fausto Tozzi *(Zanco)*; Kerima *(Maya)*; Sergio Fantoni *(Marco)*; Gianni Rizzo; Alfredo Varelli; Giacomo Rossi Stuart; Luisa Mattioli; Sandrine; Olga Solbelli; José Jaspe; Bruno Corelli *(Giuliare Di Borgia)*; Ignazio Leone; Aldo Pini; Remo De Angelis; Raf Baldassarre; Ezio Vergari; Arrigo Peri; Mario Bordi; Alberto Farnese; René Dary.

Comments: A costume adventure produced by Italy's Italcaribe and France's Contact Organisation and Paris Interproductions (PIP).

The Night They Killed Rasputin
(Les Nuits de Raspoutine)
(Brigadier Films, 1960)

Credits: Director: Pierre Chenal; *Producers:* Giampaolo Bigazzi, Robert de Nesle, Vincent Fotre; *Screenplay:* Pierre Chenal, Ugo Liberatore, André Tabet; *Photography:* Bitto Albertini (Eastmancolor); *Film Editors:* Eraldo Da Roma, Antonietta Zita; *Music:* Angelo Francesco Lavagnino; *Art Direction:* Arrigo Equini; *Art Direction:* Italo Tomassi; *Assistant Director:* Giuliano Betti; *Orchestra Conductor:* Alessandro Nadin; running time: 87 minutes (U.S.); released May 12, 1960 (Italy), October 1962 (U.S.).

Cast: Edmund Purdom *(Rasputin);* Gianna Maria Canale *(Czarina Alexandra);* John Drew Barrymore *(Prince Felix Yousoupoff);* Jany Clair *(Irina Yousoupoff);* Ugo Sasso *(Czar);* Nerio Bernardi; Livio Lorenzon; Yvette Lebon; Marco Guglielmi; Enrico Glori; Piero Palermini; Jole Fierro; Miranda Campa; Rita Rubirosa; Anita Todesco; Silla Bettini; Maria Grazia Buccella; Feodor Chaliapin, Jr.; Liana Del Balzo; Élida Dey; Ivo Garrani; Michele Malaspina; Giulia Rubini.

Comments: An account of the life of Gregori Rasputin (1869–1916), the Russian peasant and mystic who exerted great influence over Nicholas II, the last Tsar of Russia. This film was produced by the Italian companies Explorer Film '58, Faro Film and Wanguard Film, in association with France's Comptoir Français du Productions Cinématographiques (CFPC), and the German company Rialto Film. This subject was exploited more fully in the Christopher Lee film *Rasputin, the Mad Monk.*

Nights and Loves of Don Juan
(Le calde notti di Don Giovanni)
(Fénix Cooperativa Cinematográfica/Italo Spagnola/Luis Film, 1971)

Credits: Director: Alfonso Brescia; *Producers:* Arturo Marcus, Luigi Mondello; *Screenplay:* Arturo Marcus, Arpad DeRiso, Aldo Crudo (from a story by Keith Lugar, Arturo Marcos, character of "Don Juan Tenorio" created by José Zorrilla); *Photography:* Julio Ortas (billed as "Julio Ortas Plaza"), Godofredo Pachecho (Eastmancolor, Techniscope, aspect ratio 2.35:1); *Film Editor:* Rolando Salvatori; *Music:* Carlo Savina; *Production Design:* José Luis Galicia; *Costume Design:* Camillo Del Signore, Jaime Pérez Cubero; *Assistant Costume Designer:* Maria Luisa Panaro; *Wigs:* S. Rocchetti; *Production Managers:* Augusto Dolfi, Piero Ghione; *Unit Production Manager:* Miguel Ángel Bermejo; *1st Assistant Director:* Filippo Perrone; *2nd Assistant Director:* Paulino González; *Camera Operators:* Cesare Allione, Claudio Morabito; *Assistant Camera Operator:* Carlo Di Biase; *Still Photographer:* Ermanno Serto; *Orchestra Conductor:* Carlo Savina; *Master of Arms:* Franco Fantasia; *Footwear:* E. Pompei; *Set Furnishings:* E. Rancati; *Production Secretary:* Rinaldo Scorcelletti; *Script Supervisor:* Giuliana Gherardi; running time: 110 minutes (Italy); released March 10, 1971.

Cast: Robert Hoffman *(Don Juan Tenorio);* Barbara Bouchet *(Esmeralda);* Ira von Fürstenberg [billed as "Ira Furstenberg"] *(Isabella Gonzales);* Annabella Incontrera *(Maddalena);* Lucretia Love *(Queen of Cipro);* Edwige Fenech *(Aiscia);* Pasquale Nigro (billed as "Pat Nigro"); María Montez; José Calvo [billed as "Pepe Calvo"] *(Sultan Selim);* Adriano Micantoni *(Emir Omar);* Franco Fantasia *(Mahid);* Pietro Torrisi [billed as "Peter Thorys"] *(Alìl);* Cris Huerta; Franco Marletta; Francisco Amords; Fortunato Arena *(Warden);* Emma Baron *(Mother Superior);* José Maria Caffarel; Antonio Cintado; Gabriel Llopart; Osiride Pevarello *(Warden);* Santiago Rivero.

Comments: A retelling of Don Juan's misadventures, produced by Italy's Italo Spagnola and Luis Film, and Spain's Fénix Cooperativa Cinematográfica.

The Nights of Lucretia Borgia
(La notte di Lucrezia Borgia)
(Columbia, 1960)

Credits: Director: Sergio Grieco; *Screenplay:* Carlo Caiano, Sergio Grieco; *Photography:* Massimo Dallamano (Eastmancolor, Totalscope, aspect ratio: 2.35:1); *Music:* Alexandre Derevitsky,

Angelo Francesco Lavagnino; *Costume Design:* Vittorio Rossi; *Assistant Film Editor:* Bruno Mattei; running time: 108 minutes (U.S.); released October 5, 1960 (U.S.).

Cast: Belinda Lee *(Lucretia Borgia)*; Jacques Sernas *(Frederico)*; Arnoldo Foà *(Astorre)*; Michèle Mercier *(Dana d'Alva)*; Franco Fabrizi *(Cesare Borgia)*; Marco Tulli; Lilli Scaringi; Germano Longo; Nando Tamberlani; Raf Baldassarre; Gianni Loti; Stelio Candelli; Ricardo Valle; Chery Million.

Comments: Aristocrat Cesare Borgia brings an impoverished nobleman, Federico, into his service, only to find that his evil sister Lucretia expresses a carnal interest in him. Produced by Italy's Musa and France's Fidès companies.

The Old Testament *(Il vecchio testamento)* (Four Star Television, 1963)

Credits: *Director:* Gianfranco Parolini; *Screenplay:* Gianfranco Parolini, Giovanni Simonelli (based on a story by Ghigo De Chiara, Luciano Martino, Giorgio Prosperi); *Photography:* Francesco Izzarelli (Eastmancolor, Supertotalscope, aspect ratio 2.35:1); *Film Editor:* Edmond Lozzi; *Music:* Angelo Francesco Lavagnino; *Production Design:* Niko Matul, Giuseppe Ranieri; *Costume Design:* Vittorio Rossi; *Makeup:* Piero Mecacci; *Assistant Makeup Artist:* Pierantonio Mecacci; *Hair Stylist:* Galileo Mandini; *Production Supervisor:* Luciano Volpato; *Production Manager:* Mario Damiani; *General Manager:* Mario Maggi; *Assistant Directors:* Ignazio Dulce, Giovanni Simonelli; *Special Effects:* Roberto Morelli; *Camera Operator:* T. Zaro; *Assistant Camera Operator:* A. Mananiello; *Assistant Film Editor:* Amedeo Giomini; *Orchestra Conductor:* Carlo Franci; *Production Secretary:* Enzo Doria; *Script Supervisor:* S. Gardner; *Stunts:* Brad Harris; *Master of Arms:* Giuseppe Mattei; running time: 115 minutes (Italy), 88 minutes (U.S.); released April 10, 1963 (Italy); video availability: Goodtimes Video.

Cast: Brad Harris *(Simone)*; Ivano Staccioli [billed as "John Heston"]; Franca Parisi [billed as "Margaret Taylor"]; *(Miza)*; Mara Lane *(Diotima)*; Philippe Hersent *(Namele)*; Carlo Tamberlani *(Mattaia)*; Jacques Berthier *(Appolonio)*; Djordje Nenadovic *(Judas)*; Ivy Stewart; Enzo Doria *(Gionata)*; Ignazio Dolce; Isarco Ravaioli *(Giovanni)*; Vladimir Lieb *(Antenone)*; Niksa Stefanini; Giuseppe Mattei; Arnaldo Martelli; Vladimir Bacic; Sava Severova; Irena Prosen; Susan Paget; Alan Steel; Fulvia Gasser; Luisella Boni; Maks Furijan.

Comments: Old Testament Bible stories are featured in this movie, produced by Italy's Cinematografica Associati (CI. AS.), France's Comptoir Français du Film Production (CFFP), and Yugoslavia's Filmservis.

100 Horsemen *(I cento cavalieri)* (Embassy Pictures, 1964)

Credits: *Director:* Vittorio Cottafavi; *Screenplay:* Vittorio Cottafavi, Giorgio Prosperi, Enrico Ribulsi, José Maria Otero, Antonio Ecelza, José Luis Guarner (based on a story by Vittorio Cottafavi, Giorgio Prosperi); *Photography:* Francisco Marin (Technicolor, Techniscope, aspect ratio 2.35:1); *Film Editor:* Maurizio Lucidi; *Music:* Antonio Pérez Olea; *Production Design:* Ramiro Gómez; *Costume Design:* Vittorio Rossi; *Assistant Makeup Artist:* José Luis Pérez; *Production Manager:* Eduardo de la Fuente; *General Manager:* Gabriele Silvestri; *Sound Engineer:* Domenico Curia; *Assistant Film Editor:* Anna Amedei; *2nd Unit Director:* Odoardo Fiory; *Master of Arms:* Giorgio Ubaldi; running time: 115 minutes (Italy), 85 minutes (U.S.); released December 30, 1964 (Italy), 1965 (U.S.).

Cast: Mark Damon *(Don Fernando Herrera y Menendez)*; Antonella Lualdi *(Sancha Ordoñez)*; Gastone Moschin *(Friar Carmelo)*; Wolfgang Preiss *(Sheik Albengalbon)*; Barbara Frey *(Laurencia)*; Rafael Alonso *(Don Jaime Badaloz)*; Hans Nielsen *(Alfonso Ordoñez, Mayor)*; Manuel Gallardo *(Halaf)*; Salvatore Furnari *(Head of the Thieves)*; Giorgio Ubaldi; Enrico Ribulsi *(Count of Castille)*; Mario Feliciani *(Ambassador of the Sheik)*; Arnoldo Foà *(Don Gonzalo Herrera y Menendez)*; Rafael Albaicin *(Mohammed)*; Manuel Arbó; Omán de Bengala; Fernando Bilbao; Francisco Camoiras; José Canalejas *(Moorish Warrior)*; Juan Cazalilla; Hans Clarin; Alfonso de la Vega; Mirko Ellis *(One-Eyed Nobleman)*; Orlando Galas; Marcelo Gonzalez; Rafael Hernández; José Luis Lluch; Venancio Muro; Juan

Olaguibel; Antonio Orengo; Ángel Ortiz; Antonio Padilla; Antonio Perea; Héctor Quiroga; Mariano Rabanal; Ricardo Rubinstein; Aldo Sambrell *(Alfaqui)*; Pedro Solis; Ángel Ter; Charo Tijero Pernana; Rafael Vaquero; María Vico; Mariano Vidal Molina; José Villasante.

Comments: In Medieval Spain, Don Fernando, son of El Cid, struggles to overthrow the Moors. Produced by Italy's Domiziana Internazionale Cinematografica, Spain's Procusa, and Germany's International Germania Film.

The Pharaoh's Woman *(La donna dei faraoni)* (Universal, 1960)

Credits: Director: Viktor Tourjansky; *Producer:* Giorgio Venturini; *Executive Producer:* Piero Ghione; *Executive Producer (International Version):* Giampaolo Bigazzi; *Screenplay:* Remigio Del Grosso, Ugo Liberatore (based on a story by Virgilio Tosi, Massimo Vitalo); *Photography:* Pier Ludovico Pavoni (Technicolor, Techniscope, aspect ratio 2.35:1); *Film Editor:* Antonietta Zita; *Music:* Giovanni Fusco; *Art Direction:* Arrigo Equini; *Costume Design:* Giancarlo Bartolini Salimbeni; *Makeup:* Franco Palombi; *Hair Stylist:* Nicla Palombi; *Production Manager:* Charles Lifshitz; *Production Manager (Location Scenes):* Thomas Sagone; *Assistant Directors:* Sergio Bergonzelli, Giuliano Betti *(International Version)*; *2nd Unit Directors:* Giorgio Venturini, G. Adami Romani *(International Version)*; *Set Dresser:* Carlo Gentili; *Props and Weapons:* E. Rancati; *Art Direction:* Italo Tomassi; *Sound:* Raffaele Del Monte, Umberto Picistrelli; *Special Effects:* Joseph Nathanson; *Camera Operator:* Angelo Lotti; *Assistant Cameramen:* Gianni Antinori, Emidio Cirillo; *Still Photographer:* Vasilis Fotopoulos; *Wigs:* Palombi; *Costumes:* Ruggero Peruzzi; *Wardrobe:* Nadia Vitali; *Footwear:* Pompei; *Laboratory:* Sviluppo Pellicole a Stampa (SPES), Rome, Italy; *Laboratory Director:* Ettore Catalucci; *Choreography:* Adriano Vitale; *Continuity:* Cecilia Bigazzi, Franca Carotenuto; running time: 87 minutes (Italy), 106 minutes (U.S.); released December 10, 1960 (Italy), May 1961 (U.S.).

Cast: Linda Cristal *(Akis)*; Pierre Brice *(Amosis, the Physician)*; Armando Francioli *(Ramses, Prince of Thebes)*; John Drew Barrymore *(Sabaku, Prince of Bubastis)*; Lilli Lembo *(Mareth)*; Nerio Bernardi; Guido Celano; Andreina Rossi *(High Priestess)*; Ugo Sasso; Nando Angelini; Nadia Brivio; Enzo Fiermonte; Luciano Francioli; Fedele Gentile; Nino Marchetti; Anna Placido; Wilma Sempetery; Anita Todesco.

Comments: A power struggle erupts between the rival princes of Upper and Lower Egypt, with two young lovers caught up in the conflict. Produced by the Italian companies Vic Film and Faro Film and shot at Cinecittà Studios in Rome with some location work in Egypt.

Pia of Ptolemy *(Pia de' Tolomei)* (Film Do. Re. Mi., 1958)

Credits: Director: Sergio Grieco; *Producer:* Carlo Infascelli; *Screenplay:* Edoardo Anton; *Photography:* Tino Santoni (color, Supercinescope, aspect ratio 2.35:1); *Film Editor:* Giacinto Solito; *Music:* Carlo Rustichelli; *Set Decoration:* Beni Montresor; *Makeup:* Rino Carboni; *Hair Stylist:* Iole Cecchini; *Production Supervisors:* Paolo Giovanardi, Enzo Provenzale; *Unit Production Managers:* Eliseo Boschi, Sergio Iacobis; *Assistant Directors:* Luigi Bazzoni, Mario Caiano; *Camera Operator:* Enrico Cignitti; *Art Department:* Italo Tomassi; *Set Designer:* Peppino Piccolo; *Props:* Giorgio Hermann; *Script Supervisor:* Anna Veo; running time: 102 minutes (Italy); released December 29, 1958 (Italy); video availability: Sinister Cinema.

Cast: Jacques Sernas *(Ghino Perticari)*; Ilaria Occhini *(Pia of Ptolomey)*; Arnoldo Foà *(Nello Della Piettra)*; Bella Darvi *(Bice)*; Franca Mazzoni; Conrad Andersen; Raf Baldassarre; Giulio Cali; Renato Chiantoni; Tom Felleghy; Fausto Guerzoni; Herbert Knippenberg; Adriano Micantoni; Marco Paoletti; Marcella Rovena; Umberto Sacripante; Ivano Staccioli; Renato Terra; Edoardo Toniolo.

Comments: Star-crossed lovers are separated by warring clans in this costume drama, produced by Italy's Film Do. Re. Mi. and France's Procinex.

The Pirate and the Slave Girl *(La scimitarra del saraceno)* (Crest Film Distributors, 1959)

Credits: Director: Piero Perotti; *Executive*

Producers: Fortunato Misiano, René Pignières; *Screenplay:* Luciano Martino, Piero Pierotti, Bruno Rasia; *Photography:* Augusto Tiezzi (Ferraniacolor, Totalscope, aspect ratio 2.35:1); *Film Editor:* Jolanda Benvenuti; *Music:* Michele Cozzoli; *Art Direction:* Bruno Rasia; *Set Decoration:* Alfredo Montori, Camillo Del Signore; *Costume Design:* Giancarlo Bartolini Salimbeni; *Production Manager:* Fortunato Misiano; *Assistant Director:* Gianfranco Baldanello; *Sound:* Bruno Moreal, Pietro Ortolani; *Director of Action Scenes:* Walter Bertolazzi; *Production Assistant:* Diego Alchimede; running time: 99 minutes (Italy); released October 22, 1959 (Italy), September 1961 (U.S.).

Cast: Lex Barker *(Dragon Drakut)*; Chelo Alonso *(Princess Miriam)*; Massimo Serato *(Roberto Diego)*; Graziella Granata *(Bianca)*; Daniele Vargas *(Gamal)*; Gianni Rizzo *(Nikopoulos)*; Luigi Tosi *(Francisco, the Castillian Painter)*; Michele Malaspina *(Governor of Rhodes)*; Enzo Maggio *(Candela)*; Anna Arena *(Zaira)*; Bruno Corelli *(Selim, the Sultan)*; Franco Fantasia *(Captain Volan)*; Giulio Battiferri *(Drunk at Tavern)*; Clara Bindi *(Prostitute at Tavern)*; Ignazio Balsamo; Fernando Cerulli; Alberto Cinquini; Ugo Sasso; Gino Scotti *(Chief of the Oarsmen)*; Franco Jamonte *(Gambler at Tavern)*; Erminio Spalla *(Malik)*; Amedeo Trilli *(Chu-Lin)*; Geneviève Audry; Valeria Gramignani; Nadia Brivio; Ubaldo Lay *(Tripolino)*; Nino Musco; Takis Kavouras; Renato Navarrini *(Omar)*; Evelina Laudani; Rina Mascetti; Elena May; Teresa Volpe; Corinne Capri; Stefania Ré; Paolo Prestano; Paolo Fiorino; Fedele Gentile; Giovanni Vari; Andrea Fantasia *(Captain Furlan)*.

Comments: A pirate adventure, portions of which were filmed at Lake Garda in Italy. Produced by Italy's Romana Film and France's Société Nouvelle de Cinématographie (SNC).

The Pirate of the Black Hawk (Il pirata dello sparviero nero) (Filmgroup, 1958)

Credits: *Director:* Sergio Grieco; *Producers:* Carlo Prescino, Giorgio Prescino; *Executive Producer:* Guido Paolucci; *Screenplay:* Engo Alfonsi, Mario Caiano, Sergio Greco, Guido Zurli; *Photography:* Vincenzo Seratrice (Ferraniacolor, Supercinescope, aspect ratio 2.35:1); *Film Editor:* Enzo Alfonzi; *Music:* Roberto Nicolosi; *Production Design:* Saverio D'Eugenio; *Set Decoration:* Luigi D'Andria; *Costume Design:* Giulia Mafai; *Makeup:* Manrico Spagnoli; *Production Manager:* Dino Sant'Ambrogio; *Assistant Director:* Mario Caiano; *Sound:* Franco Groppioni; *Assistant Film Editor:* Bruno Mattei; *Fencing Master:* Enzo Musumeci Greco; running time: 72 minutes; released November 13, 1958 (Italy), December 1961 (U.S.); video availability: St. Clair Vision.

Cast: Gérard Landry *(Capt. Riccardo)*; Pina Bottin *(Eva)*; Andrea Aureli *(Manfredo do Monteforte)*; Mijanou Bardot *(Elena di Monteforte)*; Ettore Manni *(Giovanni)*; Eloisa Cianni *(Stella, Riccardo's Sister)*; Germano Longo *(Marco)*; Raf Baldassarre *(Pirate)*; Giulio Battiferri *(Nerone)*; Andria Miano *(Pirate with Barbo)*; Lea Migliorini; Maurizio Placenti *(Pirate)*; Piero Giagnoni *(Hector)*; Giovanni Cianfriglia *(Soldier on Ship)*; Franco Cobianchi *(Elena's Father)*; Veriano Ginesi *(Torturer)*; Ferdinando Poggi *(Soldier)*; Nazzareno Zamperla *(Pirate with Ambassador Francesca)*.

Comments: In this pirate story, it's Capt. Riccardo, commander of the pirate ship *Black Hawk* versus Saracen brigand Manfredo do Monteforte. Produced by Italy's Emmepi Cinematografica and France's Comptoir Français du Productions Cinématographiques (CFPC). Filmed at Incir De Paolis Studios in Rome. Although lensed in Ferraniacolor, *The Pirate of the Black Hawk* was exhibited in black-and-white for its American theatrical distribution.

Pirate of the Half Moon (Il corsaro della mezzaluna) (Glomer Film, 1959)

Credits: *Director:* Giuseppe Maria Scotese; *Producer:* Enzo Merolle; *Screenplay:* Mario Amendola, Riccardo Pazzaglia, Giuseppe Maria Scotese (with additional dialogue by Alma Neille, Kay Ouseby); *Photography:* Bitto Albertini (Eastmancolor, CinemaScope, aspect ratio 2.35:1); *Music:* Renzo Rossellini; *Production Design:* Saverio D'Eugenio; running time: 95 minutes; released January 2, 1959.

Cast: John Derek *(Nadir El Krim/Paul de Vellenera)*; Ingeborg Schöner *(Angela)*; Gianna Maria Canale *(Infanta Caterina)*; Alberto Farnese *(Alonzo de Carmona/Ugo van Berg)*; Camillo Pilotto *(Baron Alfonso di Carmerlata)*; Raf Mattioli *(Vasco)*; Gianni Rizzo *(Visconte di Grand)*; Paul Muller *(Carlo)*; Yvette Masson *(Rosa)*; Raf Baldassarre *(Pirate)*; Furio Meniconi; Carol Carter *(Dancer)*; Fausto Guerzoni *(Maestro Anselmo)*; Ignazio Leone *(Nicola)*; Amina Pirani Maggi *(Nurse)*; Carlo Hinterman; Fanny Landini *(Marquuise di Gredon)*; Alberto Varelli *(Tatun)*; Piero Giagnoni *(Antonio)*; Mimmo Poli *(Fat Pirate)*; Silvio Lillo *(Vasquez)*; Gabriella De Victor; Annamaria Mustari.

Comments: A pirate adventure, produced by Italy's Glomer Film.

Pirates of the Coast *(I pirati della costa)* (Warner Bros. Television, 1960)

Credits: *Director:* Domenico Paolella; *Producer:* Fortunato Misiano; *Screenplay:* Ugo Guerra, Luciano Martino, Bruno Rasia, Ernesto Gastaldi; *Photography:* Augusto Tiezzi (color, Totalscope, aspect ratio 2.35:1); *Film Editor:* Jolanda Benvenuti; *Music:* Michele Cozzoli; *Production Design:* Giancarlo Bartolini Salimbeni; Alfredo Montori; *Art Direction:* Bruno Rasia; *Costume Design:* Giancarlo Bartolini Salimbeni, Italia Scandariato; *Sound:* Giovanni Bianchi; running time: 102 minutes (U.S.); released December 1, 1960 (Italy).

Cast: Lex Barker *(Luis Monterrey)*; Estella Blain *(Isabela Linares)*; Livio Lorenzon *(Olonese)*; Liana Orfei *(Ana del Perú)*; Loris Gizzi *(Don Fernando Linares)*; John Kitzmiller *(Rock)*; Nino Vingelli *(Porro)*; Ignazio Balsamo *(Brook)*; Nando Angelini *(Manolito)*; Gianni Solaro *(LaMotte)*; Enzo Fiermonte *(Mascella)*; Corrado Annicelli *(Pedro Salvador)*; Tullio Altamura *(Governor of Santa Cruz)*; Giovanni Vari *(Pirate)*; Nada Cortese *(Lady in Court #1)*; Eleonora Morana *(Lady in Court #2)*; Franco Jamonte *(Pirate)*; Gianni Baghino *(Sailor)*; Pasquale De Filippo *(Chief Gunner)*; Emilio Nazzaro *(Prisoner)*; Giulio Battiferri *(Doctor)*; Pina Cornel *(Prostitute)*; Sina Relli *(Prostitute)*; Giulio Amauli *(Judge)*; Giuseppe Chinnici *(Court Clerk)*; Gérard Landry *(Prosecutor)*; Veriano Ginesi *(Soldier)*.

Comments: A colorful pirate tale, with both Lex Barker and Estella Blain *(The Diabolical Doctor Z)* well-cast. Co-produced by Italy's Romana Film and France's Société Nouvelle de Cinematographie (SNC).

Pontius Pilate *(Ponzio Pilato)* (U.S. Films, 1962)

Credits: *Directors:* Gian Paolo Callegari, Irving Rapper; *Producer:* Enzo Merolle; *Screenplay:* Oreste Biancoli, Gian Paolo Callegari, Gino De Santis, Guy Elmes, Ivo Perilli, Guglielmo Santangelo (based on a story by Gino De Santis); *Photography:* Massimo Dallamano (color, Supertechnirama 70, negative ratio 2.20:1, 35mm print ratio 2.35:1); *Film Editors:* Renzo Lucidi, Frederick Muller; *Music:* Angelo Francesco Lavagnino; *Production Design:* Ugo Pericoli; *Set Decoration:* Ottavio Scotti; *Costume Design:* Ugo Pericoli; *Makeup:* Anacieto Giustini; *Hair Stylist:* Italia Cambi; *Production Manager:* Armando Grottini; *Unit Production Manager:* Sergio Merolle; *Art Dept. Manager:* Italo Tomassi; *Assistant Directors:* Colette Lariviere, Luciano Ricci, Giancarlo Romani; *Camera Operators:* Carlo Fiore, Fausto Zuccoli; *Assistant Camera Operators:* Pasquale Fanetti, Otello Spila; *Sound:* Mario Amari, Oscar De Arcangelis; *Sound (French Version):* Louis Kieffer; *Orchestra Conductor:* Luigi Urbini; *Choreography:* Claude Marchand; *Script Girl:* Paolo Salvadori; *Technical Director (French Version):* Simone Dauvillie; running time: 100 minutes (Italy); released February 15, 1962 (Italy), 1967 (U.S.); video availability: Synergy Entertainment.

Cast: Jean Marais *(Pontius Pilate)*; Jeanne Crain *(Claudia Procula)*; Basil Rathbone *(Caiaphus)*; Leticia Román *(Sarah)*; Massimo Serato *(Nicodemus)*; Riccardo Garrone *(Galba)*; Livio Lorenzon *(Barabbas)*; Gianni Garko *(Jonathan)*; John Drew Barrymore *(Jesus/Judas)*; Roger Tréville *(Aaron El Mesin)*; Carlo Giustini *(Decio)*; Dante DiPaolo *(Simone)*; Paul Muller *(Mehlik)*; Alfredo Varelli *(Giuseppe d'Arimatea)*; Manuela Ballard *(Ester)*; Emma Baron *(Dirce)*; Raffaella Carrà *(Jessica)*; Aldo Pini *(Isaac)*; Claudio Scarchilli *(Disma)*; Charles Borromel

(Caesar); Roger Browne; Nicola Di Gioia *(Council Official)*; John Karlsen *(Roman Senator)*; John Stacy *(Roman Senator)*.

Comments: The Passion of Christ, as seen through the eyes of Pontius Pilate (Jean Marais). Basil Rathbone, who plays Caiaphus here, had played Pilate himself in the 1935 R.K.O. film *The Last Days of Pompeii*. This film is unique in that the same actor, John Drew Barrymore, plays both Judas and Jesus, although his interpretation of Jesus is seen only from behind, from the side, or is depicted through closeups of the eyes. Produced by Italy's Glomer Film in association with France's Wx Compagnie Cinématographique de France. Filmed in 70mm, but also exhibited in 35mm.

The Prisoner of the Iron Mask *(La vendetta della maschera di ferro)* (American-International, 1961)

Credits: Director: Francesco De Feo; *Producers:* Robert de Nesle, Francesco Thellung; *Producer (English Version):* Salvatore Billitteri; *Screenplay:* Silvio Amadio, Francesco De Feo, Ruggero Jacobbi; *Photography:* Antonio Schiavo Lena (Eastmancolor, Techniscope, aspect ratio 2.35:1); *Film Editor:* Luciano Cavalieri; *Production Design:* Piero Poletto; *Set Decoration:* Ennio Michettoni; *Costume Design:* Adriana Berselli; *Makeup:* Oscar Pacelli; *Hair Stylist:* Violetta Pacelli; *Dubbing Director (U.S. Version):* Lee Kresel; running time: 80 minutes (U.S.); released August 24, 1961 (Italy), June 1962 (U.S.).

Cast: Pietro Albani; Silvio Bagolini; Emma Baron; Andrea Bosic; Tiziana Casetti; Jany Clair; Francesco De Leone; Andrea Fantasia; Wandisa Guida *(Christina)*; Joe Kamel; Michel Lemoine *(Marco)*; Vanni Materassi; Piero Pastore; Mimmo Poli; Erminio Spalla; Nando Tamberlani; Marco Tulli.

Comments: A retelling of *The Man in the Iron Mask*, produced by Italy's Cinematografica Associati (CI. AS.) and France's Comptoir Français du Film Production (CFFP).

Punches, Pirates and Karate *(Pugni, pirati e karatè)* (1973)

Credits: Director: Joe D'Amato (billed as "Michael Wotruba"); *Photography:* color; running time: 84 minutes; released December 9, 1973 (Italy).

Cast: Richard Harrison *(Gargantua/"Garga")*; Roberto Dell'Acqua *(Mano di Velluto)*; Giorgio Dolfin; Atilo Dottesio *(Governor)*; Olga Janowski; Nello Pazzafini *(Head of Chinese Karate School)*; Mario Pedone *(Man at Tavern)*.

Comments: Two pirates are stranded on a remote island in this comic adventure. Produced by Italy's 1 Aprile Cinematografica. This low-budget film reuses footage of combat scenes from *Conqueror of Maracaibo* (1961) *(qv)*.

A Queen for Caesar *(Una regina per Cesare)* (Commonwealth United, 1962)

Credits: Director: Piero Pierotti, Viktor Tourjansky; *Producers:* Alberto Chimenz, Vico Pavoni, Giorgio Venturini; *Screenplay:* Fulvio Gicca Palli, Arrigo Montanari (based on a story by Fulvio Gicca Palli); *Photography:* Angelo Lotti, Pier Ludovico Pavoni (color, Euroscope, aspect ratio 2.35:1); *Film Editor:* Luciano Cavalieri; *Music:* Michel Michelet; *Costume Design:* Nadia Vitali; *Makeup:* Raul Ranieri; *Hair Stylist:* Giovanni Palombi; *Set Designer:* Paolo Janni; *Sound:* Mario Del Pezzo; *Camera Operator:* Fausto Rossi; *Music Director:* Francesco De Masi; *Production Assistant:* Cecilia Bigazzi; *Continuity:* Bixie Banfi; *Fencing Master:* Benito Stefanelli; *Supervisor of English-Dubbed Version:* Richard McNamara; running time: 90 minutes (U.S.); released December 22, 1962 (Italy).

Cast: Pascale Petit *(Cleopatra)*; George Ardisson *(Achilles)*; Rik Battaglia *(Lucio Settimio)*; Corrado Pani *(Ptolomaio)*; Franco Volpi *(Apollodoro)*; Ennio Balbo *(Theodoto)*; Nerio Bernardi *(Scauro)*; Aurora de Alba *(Rabis)*; Nando Angelini *(Sexto Pompeio)*; Barbara Loy; Nino Marchetti *(Messenger)*; Barbara Nardi *(Ancella)*; Piero Palermini *(Afranio)*; Akim Tamiroff *(Gnaeo Pompeio)*; Gordon Scott *(Julies Caesar)*; Giovanni Cianfriglia *(Dealer #1)*; Benito Stefanelli *(Dealer #2)*.

Comments: A power struggle erupts between Queen Cleopatra of Egypt and her brother Ptolemy. The name "Cleopatra" was kept out of the film's title, most likely in deference to the impending release of 20th Century–Fox's mammoth production *Cleopatra*, starring Elizabeth Taylor. Produced by Italy's Filmes Cinematografica and France's C.F.P.C.

The Queen of Sheba (La regina di saba) (Lippert Pictures, 1952)

Credits: Director: Pietro Francisci; *Producer:* Mario Francisci; *Screenplay:* Raul De Sarro, Pietro Francisci, Giorgio Graziosi, Vittorio Nino Novarese (based on a story by Raul De Sarro, Pietro Francisci, Giorgio Graziosi); *Photography:* Mario Montuori (black-and-white, aspect ratio 1.37:1); *Music:* Nino Rota; *Art Direction:* Giulio Bongini, William Cameron Menzies; *Costume Design:* Vittorio Nino Novarese; *Hair Stylist:* Iole Cecchini; *Production Manager:* Carlo Bessi; *Orchestra Conductor:* Franco Ferrara; *Master of Arms:* Enzo Musumeci Greco; *Supervisor of U.S.-Dubbed Version:* Richard Heinz; *Voice Dubbing (for Marina Berti):* Tina Lattanzi; running time: 110 minutes (Italy), 99 minutes (U.S.); released November 6, 1952 (Italy), November 3, 1953 (U.S.).

Cast: Leonora Ruffo *(Balkis, Queen of Sheba)*; Gino Cervi *(King Solomon of Jerusalem)*; Gino Leurini *(Prince Rehoboam of Jerusalem)*; Marina Berti *(Zamira, Rehoboam's Betrothed)*; Franco Silva *(Kabaal, Commander of the Serbian Army)*; Mario Ferrari *(Chaldis, High Priest of Sheba)*; Isa Pola *(Tabula, Leader of the Handmaidens)*; Nyta Dover *(Kinor, a Handmaiden)*; Umberto Silvestri *(Isachar, Companion of Rehoboam)*; Dorian Gray *(Ati)*; Franca Tamantini *(The False Mother)*; Fulvia Mammi *(The True Mother)*; Ugo Sasso; Edda Albertini; Maria Bernardini; Rossana Galli; Leda Rivarolo; Pietro Tordi *(Onabar)*.

Comments: King Solomon dispatches his son on a spy mission to Sheba, but he falls in love with the queen, and tries to prevent a war. Produced by Italy's Oro Film, this low-budget black-and-white film was distributed in America by Lippert Pictures. The film's major asset is its leading lady, Leonora Ruffo.

Queen of the Nile (Nefertite, regina del Nilo) (Colorama Features, 1961)

Credits: Director: Fernando Cerchio; *Producer:* Ottavio Poggi; *Screenplay:* John Byrne, Fernando Cerchio, Emerico Papp, Ottavio Poggi; *Photography:* Massimo Dallamano (Eastmancolor, Superscinescope, aspect ratio 2.35:1); *Film Editor:* Renato Cinquini; *Music:* Carlo Rustichelli; *Production Design:* Ernest Kromberg, Amedeo Mellone; *Set Decoration:* Gianfranco Lowle; *Costume Design:* Giancarlo Bartolini Salimbeni; *Makeup:* Eligio Trani; *Hair Stylist:* Mara Rochetti; *Wigs:* S. Rocchetti; *Executive in Charge of Production:* Roberto Capitani; *Production Manager:* Nino Battiferri; *Assistant Directors:* John Alarimo, Mauro Severino; *Set Construction:* Salvatore Siciliano; *Sound:* Mario Amari, Mario Del Pezzo; *Optical Effects:* Enrico Catalucci; *Camera Operator:* Carlo Fiore; *Electrician:*

Left and right: Jeanne Crain in *Queen of the Nile*.

Francesco Brescini; *Assistant Costume Designer:* Elio Micheli; *Orchestra Conductor:* Luigi Urbini; *Production Assistants:* Giovanni Albanese, Diego Alchimede; *Choreography:* Wilbert Bradley; *Script Supervisors:* Anna Maria Padoan, Juli Poggi; *Fencing Master:* Luigi Marturano; *Footwear:* Luigi Pompei; *Weapons:* Rancati; running time: 106 minutes (Italy), 97 minutes (U.S.); released September 20, 1961 (Italy), January 15, 1964 (U.S.); video availability: Something Weird Video.

Cast: Jeanne Crain *(Nefertiti)*; Vincent Price *(Benakon)*; Edmund Purdom *(Tumos, the Sculptor)*; Amedeo Nazzari *(Amenophis IV)*; Liana Orfei *(Merith)*; Carlo D'Angelo *(Seper)*; Alberto Farnese *(Dakim)*; Clelia Matania *(Penaba)*; Giulio Marchetti *(Meck)*; Piero Palermini *(Nagor)*; Umberto Raho; Luigi Marturano; Romano Giomini; Raf Baldassarre; Adriano Vitale; Gino Talamo.

Comments: In 1300 BC the pharaoh Amenhotep IV marries Nefertiti, but she really loves the sculptor Tumos, who carves the world-famous bust of her. This fabricated period soap opera was produced by Italy's MAX Film and shot at Incir De Paolis Studios in Rome.

The Queen of the Pirates (*La Venere dei pirati*) (Columbia, 1960)

Credits: *Director:* Mario Costa; *Producer:* Ottavio Poggi; *Screenplay:* John Byrne, Nino Stresa (from a story by Kurt Nachmann, Rolf Olsen); *Photography:* Raffaele Masciocchi (Eastmancolor, Supercinescope, aspect ratio 2.35:1); *Film Editor:* Renato Cinquini; *Music:* Carlo Rustichelli; *Art Direction:* Ernest Kromberg; *Set Decoration:* Amedeo Mellone; *Sound System:* Westrex; *Costume Design:* Giancarlo Bartolini Salimbeni; *Makeup:* Maurizio Giustini; running time: 80 minutes; released August 26, 1960 (Italy), July 26, 1961 (U.S.).

Cast: Gianna Maria Canale *(Sandra)*; Massimo Serato *(Cesare, Count of Santa Croce)*; Scilla Gabel *(Isabella)*; Livio Lorenzon *(Pirate Chief)*; Paul Muller *(Duke Zulian)*; Moira Orfei *(Jana)*; José Jaspe *(Capt. Mirko)*; Giustino Durano *(Battista)*; Andrea Aureli; Franco Fantasia; Nando Tamberlani; Giulio Battiferri; Luigi Marturano; Gianni Solaro; Annamaria Mustari; Raf Baldassarre.

Comments: A pirate adventure with a female lead, produced by Italy's MAX Film, with some location work at Monte Argentario Grosseto in Tuscany, Italy.

Queen of the Seas (*La avventure di Mary Read*) (American-International Television, 1961)

Credits: *Director:* Umberto Lenzi; *Producer:* Fortunato Misiano; *Screenplay:* Ugo Guerra, Luciano Martino, Ernesto Gastaldi; *Photography:* Augusto Tiezzi (Eastmancolor, Totalscope, aspect ratio 2.35:1); *Film Editor:* Jolanda Benvenuti; *Music:* Gino Filippini; *Set Decoration:* Alfredo Montori; *Production Supervisor:* Pasquale Misiano; *Production Manager:* Nino Misiano; *Assistant Director:* Tersicore Kolosoff; *Supervisor of Action Scenes:* Walter Bertolazzi; running time: 87 minutes; released December 1, 1961 (Italy), 1964 (U.S.); video availability: Something Weird Video.

Cast: Lisa Gastoni *(Mary Read)*; Jerome Courtland *(Peter Goodwin)*; Walter Barnes *(Capt. Poof)*; Agostino Salvietti *(Mangiatrippa, a Pirate)*; Germano Longo *(Ivan, a Pirate)*; Gianni Solaro *(Governor of Florida)*; Gisella Arden *(French Dancer)*; Dina De Santis *(Lady Flirting with Peter)*; Tullio Altamura *(Don Pedro Alvarez)*; Ignazio Balsamo *(Captain of the Guard)*; Anna Arena *(Signora Sulla Diligenza)*; Giulio Battiferri *(Prison Guard)*; Franco Jamonte *(Horse-Riding Instructor)*; Edoardo Toniolo *(Lord Goodwin)*; Piero Pastore *(Protocol Instructor)*; Loris Gizzi *(Prison Director)*; Gualtiero Isnenghi *(Captain of English Ship)*; Eleonora Morana *(Miss Elizabeth)*; Maria Teresa Angele; Nada Cortese; Luigi D'Acri; Walter Licastro; Bruno Scipioni; Mimmo Poli *(Falling Fat Man)*.

Comments: A lady jewel thief becomes a pirate in this costume adventure, produced by Italy's Romana Film and France's Société Nouvelle de Cinématographie (SNC).

Rage of the Buccaneers (*Gordon il pirata nero*) (Colorama Features, 1961)

Credits: *Director:* Mario Costa; *Producer:* Ottavio Poggi; *Screenplay:* John Byrne, Ottavio Poggi; *Photography:* Carlo Bellero (Eastmancolor, Totalscope, aspect ratio 2.35:1); *Film Editor:* Renato Cinquini; *Music:* Carlo Rustichelli; *Art Direction:* Ernest Kromberg, Amedeo Mellone; *Costume Design:* Giancarlo Bartolini Salimbeni; running time: 88 minutes; released December 15, 1961 (Italy), August 1963 (U.S.).

Cast: Ricardo Montalban *(Capt. Gordon, the Black Pirate)*; Vincent Price *(Romero)*; Giulia Rubini *(Manuela, the Governor's Daughter)*; Liana Orfei *(Luana)*; Mario Feliciani *(The Governor)*; Giustino Durano *(Juan)*; Gisella Sofio *(Rosita, Manuela's Maid)*, José Jaspe *(Capt. Tortuga)*; Edoardo Toniolo *(Felipe Cortez)*; Gino Marturano *(Tarto)*; Andrea Fantasia *(Bonifacio)*; Franco Fantasia *(Officer on Slave Ship)*; Giulio Battiferri; Romano Giomini; Paolo Pieri; Adriano Vitale; Vanoye Aikens; Wilbert Bradley; Mario Rezzera; Bruno Arté *(Pirate)*; Walter Barnes; Frank Wolff *(Bonifatius)*.

Comments: A pirate adventure, produced by Italy's Max Production, With some location work at Monte Argentario Grosseto and Porto Ercole in Tuscany, Italy.

Rampage of Evil *(Capitani di ventura)* (Artix, 1961)

Credits: *Director:* Angelo Dorigo; *Music:* Aldo Piga; *Photography:* color, Totalscope, aspect ratio 2.35:1; running time: 90 minutes; released August 12, 1961 (Italy).

Cast: Raf Baldassarre; Luigi Batzella *(Prince Giuliani)*; Andrea Fantasia; Wandisa Guida *(Duchess Belinda)*; José Jaspe; Gérard Landry *(Brunello Montenotte)*; Gianni Loti; Paul Muller *(Count Falcino)*; Nino Musco; Renato Navarrini; Franco Odoardi; Franca Parisi *(Rosalba)*; Mario Petri *(Capt. Hans)*; Lido Pini; Benito Stefanelli; Cesira Vianello.

Comments: The heroic Brunello Montenotte attempts to rescue Prince Giuliani, who is being held prisoner. Produced by Italy's Artix.

The Rebel Gladiators *(Ursus, il gladiatore ribelle)* (Medallion Pictures, 1962)

Credits: *Director:* Domenico Paolella; *Producer:* Ignazio Luceri; *Screenplay:* Alessandro Ferraù, Domenico Paolella, Sergio Sollima; *Photography:* Carlo Bellero (Eastmancolor, Techniscope, aspect ratio 2.35:1); *Music:* Carlo Savina; *Art Direction:* Alfredo Montori; running time: 95 minutes; released November 15, 1962 (Italy), 1963 (U.S.); video availability: Something Weird Video.

Cast: Dan Vadis *(Ursus)*; Gloria Milland *(Marzia)*; José Greci *(Arminia)*; Sergio Ciani *(Commodus)*; Andrea Aureli *(Gladiatorial Instructor)*; Tullio Altamura *(Antoninus)*; Nando Tamberlani *(Marcus Aurelius)*; Salvatore Borghese *(Gladiator)*; Gianni Santuccio *(Senator Emilius Letus)*; Consalvo Dell'Arti *(Senator Lucius)*; Carlo Delmi *(Settimus Letus)*; Marco Mariani; Pietro Ceccarelli; Bruno Scipioni; Claudio Marzulli; Artemio Antonini *(Gladiator)*; Bruno Arié *(Gladiator)*; Valéry Inkijinoff *(Torturer)*; Roberto Messina *(Gladiator)*; Mario Novelli *(Gladiator)*; Nello Pazzafini *(Gladiator)*.

Comments: The heroic Ursus is forced to battle gladiator Marcus Aurelius in the arena to save his village. Produced by Italy's Splendor Film.

The Red Cloak *(Il mantello rosso)* (Sefo Films International, 1955)

Credits: *Director:* Giuseppe Maria Scotese; *Producer:* Elios Vercelloni; *Executive Producer:* Albino Principe; *Screenplay:* Guglielmo Santangelo, Albino Principe (story adaptation: Jacopo Corsi, Pierre Kast, Riccardo Pazzaglia, France Roche, Giuseppe Maria Scotese); *Photography:* Bitto Albertini (Ferraniacolor, Stereocinescope, aspect ratio 2.35:1); *Film Editor:* Renzo Lucidi; *Music:* Gino Marinuzzi, Jr.; *Art Direction and Set Decoration:* Lamberto Giovagnoli; *Production Manager:* Elios Varcelloni; *Costumes:* Ugo Pericoli; *Master of Arms:* Enzo Musumeci Greco; running time: 102 minutes; released September 15, 1955 (Italy), 1961 (U.S.).

Cast: Patricia Medina *(Laura Lanfranch)*; Fausto Tozzi *(Luca deBardi)*; Jean Murat *(Cosimo)*; Bruce Cabot *(Capt. Raniero d'Anversa)*; Colette Deréal; Guy Mairesse; Lyla Rocco *(Stella)*; Domenico Modugno; *(Saro)*; Nyta Dover; Jean-François Calvé; Aldo Pensa; Erminio Spalla; Franco Caruso; Eduardo de Santis; Jeanne Fusier-Gir; Giorgio Gandos; giacomo Rossi Stuart; Franco Fantasia; Andrea Fantasia; Giulio Battiferri; Carlo Marrazzini, Edoardo Davila.

Comments: A costume drama co-produced by three Italian companies: Centro Cinema, Franca Film, and Trio Film.

The Red Falcon (Il falco rosso) (Forum Film/Briguglio Films, 1949)

Credits: Director: Carlo Ludovico Bragaglia; *Producers:* Raffaele Colamonici, Umberto Montesi; *Screenplay:* Vittorio Nino Novarese, Fulvio Palmieri, Bruno Valeri; *Photography:* Carlo Montuori (black-and-white, aspect ratio 1.37:1); *Film Editor:* Mario Sansoni; *Music:* Franco Casavola; *Production Design:* Raffaele Colamonici; *Production Manager:* Raffaele Colamonici; *Sound:* Kurt Doubrowsky; *Camera Operator:* Mario Montuori; running time: 87 minutes; released December 5, 1949.

Cast: Jacques Sernas *(Raniero d'Atri)*; Tamara Lees *(Clotilde di Tuscolo)*; Paul Muller *(Baron Goffredo)*; Victor Ledda *(Count Tuscolo)*; Pietro Tordi *(Demetrio)*; Ugo Sasso *(Pietro)*; Piero Palermini *(Gilberto)*; Carla Calò *(Marfa)*; Gemma Bolognesi *(Berta)*; Arturo Bragaglia; Anna Di Lorenzo *(Rosalinda)*; Nino Javert; Renato Valente.

Comments: When a young man returns home to find an evil baron terrorizing his people, he opposes him as the heroic masked "Red Falcon." Produced by Italy's Forum Film.

The Red Sheik (Lo sceicco rosso) (Medallion Pictures, 1962)

Credits: Director: Fernando Cerchio; *Producer:* Bruno Turchetto; *Screenplay:* Luigi Capuano, Remigio Del Grosso, Arrigo Montanari, Vittoriano Petrilli (story by Gino De Santis); *Photography:* Angelo Lotti, Elio Polacchi (Eastmancolor, Euroscope, aspect ratio 2.35:1); *Film Editor:* Gino Talamo; *Music:* Francesco De Masi, Giovanni Fusco; *Production Designer:* Antonio Visone; *Costume Design:* Giancarlo Bartolini Salimbeni; *Sound:* Raffaele Del Monte; running time: 90 minutes; released October 1, 1962 (Italy), December 1963 (U.S.).

Cast: Channing Pollock *(Ruiz da Silva)*; Luciana Gilli *(Amina)*; Mel Welles *(Hassan)*; Rosalba Neri *(Hammel)*; Ettore Manni *(Mohammad)*; Pietro De Vico *(Ignacio)*; Glauco Onorato *(Yussuf)*; Ahmed Amer *(Ajabar)*; Mary Welles *(Izmir)*; Alberto Archetti; Giulio Battiferri *(Canceriere)*; Marcello Selmi.

Comments: The mysterious "Red Sheik" defends oppressed peasants. Produced by Italy's Explorer Film '58.

Return of Sandokan (Sandokan contro il leopardo di Sarawak) (Screen Gems Television, 1964)

Credits: Director: Luigi Capuano; *Producer:* Ottavio Poggi; *Screenplay:* Luigi Capuano, Arpad DeRiso (based on the novel by Emilio Salgari); *Photography:* Bitto Albertini (Eastmancolor, Totalscope, aspect ratio 2.35:1); *Film Editor:* Antonietta Zita; *Music:* Carlo Rustichelli; *Art Direction:* Giancarlo Bartolini Salimbeni; *Costume Design:* Elio Micheli; *Sound:* Vittorio Trentino; *Weapons:* Ferdinando Poggi; running time: 88 minutes; released October 18, 1964 (Italy).

Cast: Ray Danton *(Sandokan)*; Franca Bettoia *(Samoa)*; Guy Madison *(Yanez)*; Mario Petri *(Sir Charles Brooks)*; Alberto Farnese *(Tremal Naik)*; Mino Doro *(Lumbo)*; Aldo Bufi Landi *(Rajani)*; Giulio Marchetti *(Sagapar)*; Romano Giomini; Adriano Vitale; Giuliana Farnese; Ferdinando Poggi *(Assumbata)*; Franco Fantasia *(Kuron)*; Hal Frederick *(Kalam)*.

Comments: Sandokan, heroic Prince of Malaysia, rescues the beautiful Samoa, who has been hypnotized by an evil magician. Third in the Sandokan series, based on the character created by novelist Emilio Salgari. Co-produced by Italy's Liber Film and Germany's Eichberg-Film.

Return of the Black Eagle (Acquila nera) (Lux Film, 1946)

Credits: Director: Riccardo Freda; *Producer:* Dino De Laurentiis; *Screenplay:* Baccio Agnoletti, Mario Monicelli, Steno; Federico Fellini, Riccardo Freda (based on a story by Alexander Pushkin); *Photography:* Guglielmo Lombardi, Rodolfo Lombardi (black-and-white, aspect ratio 1.37:1); *Film Editor:* Otello Colangeli; *Music:* Franco Casavola; *Production Design:* Arrigo Equinni; *Production Managers:* Romolo Laurenti, Franco Palaggi; *Costume Design:* Vasco Glori; *Assistant Director:* Giorgio Lastricati;

Camera Operator: Ugo Lombardi; running time: 97 minutes; released September 21, 1946.

Cast: Rossano Brazzi (*Vladimir Dubrovski*); Irasima Dilián (*Mascia Petrovic*); Gino Cervi (*Kirila Petrovic*); Rina Morelli (*Irina*); Harry Feist (*Sergej Ivanovic*); Paolo Stoppa (*Bandit*); Inga Gort (*Maria*); Pietro Sharoff (*Count Andrea Dubrovski*); Luigi Pavese (*Servant*); Angelo Calabrese; Cesare Polacco; Angelo Bassanelli; Gianna Maria Canale; Dante Nello Carapelli; Pietro Ciriaci; Magda Forlenza; Armando Francioli; Loris Gizzi; Gina Lollobrigida; Piero Pastore; Felice Romano; Yvonne Sanson; Ugo Sasso; Mario Siletti.

Comments: This costume drama featured the earliest film appearance of Gina Lollobrigida, in a small role; future director Federico Fellini contributed to the script. Produced by Italy's Lux Film. A sequel, *Revenge of the Black Eagle* (qv), followed.

Revenge of Black Eagle (*La vendetta di Aquila Nera*) (Walter Manley/ Screen Gems, 1951)

Cast: *Director:* Riccardo Freda; *Producers:* Carlo Calano, Umberto Momi; *Screenplay:* Carlo Calano, Sandro Continenza, Ennio De Concini, Riccardo Freda; *Photography:* Toni Frenguelli (black-and-white, aspect ratio 1.37:1); *Film Editor:* Otello Coangeli; *Music:* Renzo Rossellini; *Art Direction:* Piero Filippone; running time: 97 minutes; released October 31, 1951 (Italy).

Cast: Rossano Brazzi (*Vladimir Dubrovski*); Gianna Maria Canale (*Tatiana Cernicevski*); Peter Trent (*Igor Cernicevski*); Vittorio Sanipoli (*Prince Boris Yuravleff*); Franca Marzi (*Katia*); Nerio Bernardi (*Czar Paolo III*); Giovanni Del Panta (*Ivan*); Ughetto Bertucci (*Kurin*); Guido Sissia (*Andrej Dubrovskij*); Atilo Dottesio (*Prince Boris' Guard*); Fausto Gerzoni (*Pastor*); Ileana Simova (*Maruska*); Dante Nello Carapelli (*Selim*); Franco Jamonte (*Ilya*); Arnaldo Mochetti; Raffaele Tana; Pasquale Fasciano; Guido Moroni Celsi.

Comments: A sequel to *Return of the Black Eagle* (qv). Produced by Italy's Associati Produttori Independenti Film (API).

The Revenge of Ivanhoe (*La rivincita de Ivanhoe*) (Trans-American Films, 1965)

Credits: *Director:* Tanio Boccia; *Producers:* Roberto Capitani, Néstor Gaffet, *Screenplay:* Arpad DeRiso, Nino Scolaro, Flomenica Sánchez; *Photography:* Romolo Garroni (Eastmancolor, Totalscope, aspect ratio 2.35:1); *Music:* Giuseppe Piccillo; *Costume Design:* Walter Patriarca; *Production Manager:* Roberto Capitani; *Assistant Production Manager:* Virgilio Muzio; *Set Designer:* Armedeo Mellone; *Sound:* Pietro Vesperini; *Assistant Director:* Mario Casalini; *Camera Operators:* Emilio Giannini, Aldo Ricci; *Assistant Camera Operators:* Gino Giorgi, Claudio Morabito; *Costumes:* Tigano Lo Faro; *Assistant Film Editor:* Valentina Guerra; *Orchestra Conductor:* Carlo Franci; *Continuity:* Priscilla Contardi; *Production Secretary:* Vincenzo Tocci; *Master of Arms:* Franco Pasquetto; running time: 100 minutes; released January 22, 1965 (Italy); video availability: Sinister Cinema.

Cast: Rik Van Nutter [billed as "Clyde Rogers"] (*Ivanhoe*); Gilda Lousek (*Rowena of Stratford*); Andrea Aureli (*Bertrand of Hastings*); Duilio Marzio (*Cedric of Hastings*); Glauco Onorato (*Lockheel*); Furio Meniconi (*Etimbaldo*); Nando Tamberlani (*Prior of Wessex*); Ariana Gorini (*Isabella*); Tullio Altamura (*Wilfred Cox*); Wladimiro Tuicovich (*Redbourne*); Nerio Bernardi (*Donald, the Dungeon Master*); Marco Pasquini (*Arthur of Stratford*); Vladimiro Picciafuochi (*Chester*); Renato Terra (*Tuck*); Giovanni Cianfriglia (*One of Lockey's Men*); Rainer Brandt (*Dubbed Voice of Ivanhoe*); Franco Pasquetto.

Comments: In 12th-century England, Ivanhoe returns from the Crusades and frees the Saxons from bondage. Produced by Italy's Tevere Film. Shot at Rome's Cinecittà Studios.

Revenge of the Barbarians (*La vendetta dei barbari*) (American-International Television, 1960)

Credits: *Director:* Giuseppe Vari; *Producer:* Alessandro Santini; *Screenplay:* Gastone Ramazzotti (from a story by Enrico Formai); *Photography:* Sergio Pesce (Eastmancolor, Dyaliscope, aspect ratio 2.35:1); *Film Editor:* Giuseppe Vari;

Music: Roberto Nicolosi; *Production Design:* Ivo Battelli; *Set Decoration:* Fulvio Barsotti; *Costume Design:* Giorgio Desideri; *Production Supervisor:* Enrico Formai; *Sound:* Mario Faraoni, Bruno Moreal; *Microphone Boom Operator:* Primiano Muratori; *Orchestra Conductor:* Luigi Urbini; running time: 105 minutes (Italy), 104 minutes (U.S.); released December 23, 1960 (Italy), 1964 (U.S.).

Cast: Daniela Rocca *(Galla Placidia, Onorius' Sister)*; Anthony Steel *(Olympius, Consul of Rome)*; Robert Alda *(Ataulf)*; José Greci *(Sabina)*; Mario Scaccia *(Onorius, Emperor of the West)*; Evi Marandi *(Ameria, Slave Girl)*; Arturo Dominici *(Antemius)*; Cesare Fantoni *(Alaric, King of the Visigoths)*; Gilberto Mazzi; Dario Dolci; Anita Todesco; Amedeo Trilli; Giulio Maculani; Paolo Reale; Andrea Petricca; Joe Kamel; Sergio Calò; Tom Felleghy *(Roman Officer)*; Giovanni Vari; Juan Valejo; Antonio Gradoli; Artemio Antonini *(Soldier)*; Salvatore Borghese *(Gothic Warrior)*; Nello Pazzafini *(Visigoth Warrior)*.

Comments: In 408 AD, Alaric, King of the Visigoths, leads his warriors in an invasion of Italy and the sacking of Rome. Produced by Italy's Oriental Film.

Revenge of the Conquered (Drakut il vendicatore) (American-International Television, 1963)

Credits: Director: Luigi Capuano; *Producer:* Felice Felicioni; *Screenplay:* Italo De Tuddo, Roberto Gianviti, Nino Stresa (based on a story by Nino Stresa); *Photography:* Sergio Pesce (Pathécolor [U.S.] Eastmancolor [Italy], Colorscope [U.S.] Totalscope [Italy], aspect ratio 2.35:1); *Film Editor:* Antonietta Zita; *Music:* Franco Ferrara, Carlo Innocenzi; *Production Design:* Alfredo Montori; *Costume Design:* Marilù Alianello; *Assistant Director:* Gianfranco Baldanello; *Sound:* R. Del Monte, Bruno Francisci; *Orchestra Conductor:* Franco Ferrara; running time: 93 minutes (Italy), 84 minutes (U.S.); released 1963 (Italy), 1964 (U.S.), video availability: Something Weird Video.

Cast: Burt Nelson *(Drakut)*; Wandisa Guida *(Princess Irina)*; Mario Petri *(Grand Duke Atanas)*; Moira Orfei *(Edmea)*; Maria Grazia Spina; Franco Fantasia; Ugo Sasso; Rosalia Maggio; Nando Tamberlani; Carla Calò; Albedrakutrto Lupo; Gianni Baghino; Walter Barnes; Massimo Carocci; Elio Crovetto.

Comments: After the gypsy Drakut rescues Princess Irina from bandits and saves her from a forced marriage, she falls in love with him and makes him a prince in gratitude. Produced by Italy's Jonia Film.

Revenge of the Gladiators (La vendetta dei gladiatori) (American-International, Television, 1964)

Credits: Director: Luigi Capuano; *Screenplay:* Arpad DeRiso, Roberto Gianviti (from a story by Arpad DeRiso, Luigi Capuano); *Photography:* Raffaele Masciocchi (Pathécolor [U.S.] Eastmancolor [Italy], Colorscope [U.S.] Euroscope [Italy], aspect ratio 2.35:1), *Film Editor:* Antonietta Zita; *Music:* Giuseppe Piccillo; *Production Design:* Giuseppe Ranieri; *Costume Design:* Elio Micheli; *Sound:* Franco Borni, Raffaele Del Monte, Franco Groppioni; running time: 98 minutes (Italy), 90 minutes (U.S.); released December 31, 1964 (Italy), 1965 (U.S.).

Cast: Mickey Hargitay *(Fabio)*; José Greci *(Priscilla)*; Livio Lorenzon *(Genserico, a Vandal)*; Renato Baldini *(General Ezio)*; Roldano Lupi *(Valentiniano III)*; Andrea Checchi *(Gavinio)*; Nerio Bernardi *(Tidone)*; Andreina Paul *(Calpurnia)*; Bruno Scipioni; Mirko Ellis *(Vilfredo, Genserico's Son)*, Giulio Tomei *(Christian Official)*; Dante Maggio *(Drunk in Tavern)*; Aldo Canti *(Lucio, a Gladiator)*; Luigi Casellato; Giovanni Cianfriglia *(Fulvio, a Gladiator)*; Antonio Corevi *(Callisto)*; Andrea Costa; Aldo Cristiani *(Gladiator)*; Franco Daddi *(Gladiator)*; Pasquale De Filippo *(Crasso, a Senator)*; Consalvo Dell'Arti *(Roman Officer in Tavern)*; Emilia Della Rocca *(Handmaid)*; Giulio Maculani *(Gladiator)*; Gino Marturano *(Vilfredo's Friend)*; Benito Stefanelli *(Ardenzio, a Gladiator)*; Amedeo Trilli *(Head Guard at Fortress)*.

Comments: Vandals, led by Genserico, attack Rome in 454 AD They are opposed by the heroic Fabio. Produced by Italy's Splendor Film. This film is not related to *Revenge of the Gladiators* (also 1964) *(qv)*, which was alternately titled *The Revenge of Spartacus.*

Revenge of the Gladiators
(La vendetta di Spartacus) (Paramount, 1964)

Credits: Director: Michele Lupo; *Producer:* Elio Scardamaglia; *Screenplay:* Lionello De Felice, Ernesto Guida, Ernesto Gastaldi; *Photography:* Guglielmo Mancori (Technicolor, Techniscope, aspect ratio 2.35:1); *Film Editor:* Alberto Gallitti; *Music:* Francesco De Masi; *Costume Design:* Walter Patriarca; *Set Design:* Pier Vittorio Marchi; *Special Effects:* Armando Grilli; running time: 105 minutes; released September 24, 1964 (Italy), September 1965 (U.S.).

Cast: Roger Browne *(Valerio)*; Scilla Gabel *(Cinzia)*; Giacomo Rossi Stuart *(Fulvius)*; Daniele Vargas *(Lucius Transone)*; Germano Longo *(Marcellus)*; Gianni Solaro; Franco Di Tocchio; Gian Paolo Rosmino, Alfo Contabiano; Pietro Ceccarelli; Petro Marascalchi; Mario Novelli; Nello Pazzafini; Calisto Calisti; Antonio Corevi; Eugenio Galadini; Leonilde Montesi; Aldo Pini *(Cayo Rutilo)*; Adriano Vitale; Gordon Mitchell *(Arminio)*; Mary Arden; Fortunato Arena *(Roman Mercenary)*; John Bartha *(Roman Soldier)*.

Comments: In this contrived, unofficial sequel (no relation to the 1960 Stanley Kubrick film *Spartacus*), the survivors of Spartacus' slave revolt make an attempt to rescue their crucified leader. Produced by Italy's Leone Film. An alternate title was *The Revenge of Spartacus*.

Revenge of the Mercenaries
(Il capitano di ferro) (Taurisano Film/Dubrava Film, 1962)

Credits: Director: Sergio Grieco; *Producer:* Lello Luzi; *Screenplay:* Fabio De Agostini, Stipe Delic, Aldo Segri (based on their story), *Photography:* Guglielmo Mancori (color, CinemaScope, aspect ratio 2.35:1), *Film Editor:* Enzo Alfonzi; *Music:* Carlo Savina; *Production Design:* Oscar D'Amico; *Costume Design:* Mario Giorsi; *Makeup:* Antonio Marini; *Hair Stylists:* Galileo Mandini, Manlio Rocchetti; *Production Managers:* Renato De Pasqualis; *Assistant Directors:* Stipe Delic, Giulio Pannaccio, Filippo Ferrone; *Props:* Ditta Tani; *Sound:* Bruno Moreal, Luigi Puri; *Stunts:* Valentino Pelizzi; *Camera Operator:* Sandro Mancori; *Assistant Camera Operator:* Giancarlo Martella; *Still Photographer:* Enrico Appetito; *Costumes:* Virgilio Ciarlo; *Costume Assistant:* Silvano Giusti; *Footwear:* Pompei; *Assistant Film Editor:* Laura Caccianti; *Master of Arms:* Aldo Cecconi; *Script Supervisor:* Liana Ferri; released October 26, 1962 (Italy).

Cast: Gustavo Rojo; Barbara Steele; Mario Petri; Fred Williams; Nando Angelini; Andrea Aureli; Relja Basic; Antonio Basile; Aldo Cecconi; Lilly Darelli; Fedele Gentile; Jose Gregorin; Joza Gregorin; Silvana Jachino; Vladimir Krstulovic; Drago Mitrovic; Liliana Palazio; Milan Ruikavine; Andrea Scotti; Niksa Stefanini, Leopoldo Valentini.

Comments: Hero Furio returns to his village only to find that it has been ravaged by German invaders. Italian horror icon Barbara Steele receives second billing in this film, even though her screen time is minimal. Co-produced by Italy's Taurisano Film and Yugoslavia's Dubrava Film.

Revenge of the Musketeers
(D'Artagnan contro i 3 moschettieri) (American-International Television, 1963)

Credits: Director: Fulvio Tului; *Producers:* Felice Felicioni, Jacobo Savini; *Screenplay:* Tito Carpi, Roberto Gianviti (from their story); *Photography:* Oberdan Troiani Dyaliscope, aspect ratio 2.35:1); *Film Editor:* Antonietta Zita; *Music:* Carlo Savina; *Production Design:* Alfredo Montori; *Set Decoration:* Camillo Del Signore; *Costume Design:* Vera Marzot; *Makeup:* Duilio Scarozza; *Hair Stylist:* Adrianna Cassini; *Camera Operator:* Mario Sensi; *Production Manager:* Ferdinand Felicioni; *General Production Manager:* Jacopo Comin; *Assistant Director:* Alberto Cardone; *Master of Arms:* Franco Fantasia; *Script Supervisor:* Nellita Zampieri; running time: 90 minutes (Italy), 97 minutes (U.S.); released 1963 (Italy), 1965 (U.S.).

Cast: Fernando Lamas *(D'Atagnan)*; Gloria Milland *(Olimpia Mancini)*; Roberto Risso *(Aramis)*; Walter Barnes *(Porthos)*; Franco Fantasia *(Athos)*; Folco Lulli *(Cardinal Mazarini)*; Andreina Paul *(Queen Anne)*; Gabriele Antonini *(King Charles II)*; Renzo Palmer; Piero Lulli;

Ugo Sasso; Carla Calò; Ignazio Leone; Romano Ghini; Carlo Lombardi; Fedele Gentile; Franco Ressel; Andrea Fantasia; Enzo Maggio; Benito Stefanelli; Leopoldo Valentini; Anita Todesco.

Comments: In this swashbuckler, the Three Musketeers save a young king from an evil cardinal. Produced by Italy's Jonia Film.

Revolt of the Barbarians *(La rivolta dei barbari)* (Protor Film S. r. L., 1964)

Credits: Director: Guido Maletesta; *Producer:* Pier Luigi Torri; *Photography:* Luciano Trasatti (Eastmancolor, aspect ratio 2.35:1); *Film Editor:* Enzo Alfonsi; *Music:* Carlo Franci; *Costumes:* Gaia Romanini; *Set Design:* Oscar D'Amico; *Production Supervisors:* Michelangelo Ciafre, Salvatore Vizzinibisaccia; *Camera Operator:* Vitaliano Natalucci; *Assistant Director:* Franco Longo; *Special Effects:* Agostino Possanza; *Still Photographer:* Bruno Ceria; *Wigs:* Lina Rinaldi; *Footwear:* Pompei; *Master of Arms:* Gaetano Scala; running time: 80 minutes (Italy), 99 minutes (U.S.); released December 18, 1964 (Italy); video availability: Retromedia.

Cast: Roland Carey *(Darius)*; Maria Grazia Spina *(Lydia)*; Mario Feliciani; Gabriele Antonini; Andrea Aureli; Susan Sullivan; Gaetano Scala; Franco Beltramme; Gilberto Galimberti.

Comments: A Roman Consul investigates gold theft in Gaul, only to discover that the gold is being stolen by a tribe in league with the local governor. Produced by Italy's Protor Film S.r.L.

Revolt of the Mercenaries *(La rivolta dei mercenari)* (Warner Bros. Television, 1961)

Credits: Director: Piero Costa; *Producer:* Antonio Canelli; *Screenplay:* Antonio Boccaci, Piero Costa, Eduardo Falletti, Carlo Musso, Luciano Vincenzoni (from a story by Luciano Vincenzoni); *Photography:* Julio Ortas, Godofredo Pacheco (Eastmancolor, Totalscope, aspect ratio 2.35:1); *Film Editors:* Pablo G. del Amo, Julio Peña, Mario Serandrei; *Music:* Carlo Innocenzi; *Production Design:* Saverio D'Eugenio, Augusto Lega; *Costume Design:* Franco Nardelli; *Makeup:* Cesare Gambarelli, Maria Teresa; *Hair Stylist:* Gamborino Rocchetti; *Orchestra Conductor:* Carlo Franci; *Production Assistant:* Julio Parra; running time: 89 minutes (U.S.); released July 27, 1961 (Italy), January 1964 (U.S.).

Cast: Virginia Mayo *(Lady Patrizia, Duchess of Rivalta)*; Conrado San Martin *(Capt. Lucio Di Rialto)*; Susana Canales *(Katia)*; Livio Lorenzon *(Count Keller Paroll)*; Carla Calò *(Miriam du Marchant)*; Franco Fantasia *(Ilario)*; Alfredo Mayo *(Marco)*; John Kitzmiller *(Tago)*; Tomás Blanco *(Capt. Brann)*; Anita Todesco *(Prisca)*; Pilar Cansino, *(Simonetta)*; Marco Tulli *(Stefano, Prince of Siena)*; Luciano Benetti *(One of Lucio's Men)*; Enzo Fiermonte *(Cizzania)*; Ugo Sasso; Amedeo Trilli *(Pintar, Katia's Father)*; Marilù Sangiorgi *(Gypsy Girl)*; Xan das Bolas *(Katia's Companion)*; Ángel del Pozo *(Arrigo)*; Diana Lorys *(Nora)*; Franco Pesce *(Old Man)*; Giovanni Petrucci; Alberto Cevenini *(Alessandro)*.

Comments: In Friuli, Italy, during the Renaissance, Duchess Patrizia tries to prevent the acquisition of her lands by Count Keller through marriage to the influential Prince Stefano, even though she does not love him; she is ultimately saved from this fate by the mercenary leader Lucio Di Rialto. This costume drama was co-produced by Italy's Prodas and Spain's Chapalo Films S.A.

Revolt of the Praetorians *(La rivolta dei pretoriani)* (ABC Films, 1964)

Credits: Director: Alfonso Brescia; *Producer:* Carlo Vassalle; *Screenplay:* Gian Paolo Callegari; *Photography:* Pier Ludovico Pavoni (Technicolor, Techniscope, aspect ratio 2.35:1); *Film Editor:* Nella Nannuzzi; *Music:* Carlo Franci; *Production Design:* Pier Vittorio Marchi; *Costume Design:* Mario Giorsi; *Master of Arms:* Bruno Ukmar; running time: 100 minutes (Italy), 95 minutes (U.S.); released September 4, 1964 (Italy).

Cast: Richard Harrison *(Valerio Ruffo)*; Moira Orfei *(Artamne)*; Piero Lulli *(Domitian)*; Giuliano Gemma *(Cocceio Nerva)*; Paola Pitti *(Lucilla)*; Ivy Holzer *(Zusa)*; Fedele Gentile *(Fabio Lucilio)*; Amedeo Trilli *(Guardian of the Quarry)*; Mirko Ellis *(Seiano)*; Renato Montalbano *(Sotero)*; Salvatore Furnari *(Elpidion)*; Massimo Carocci; Aldo Cecconi *(Soterus)*; Andrea Fantasia *(Usurper)*; Osiride Pevarello *(Fireflasher)*; Bruno Ukmar *(Roman Soldier)*.

Comments: Rome trembles under the tyrannical rule of Emperor Domitian and his Egyptian consort Artamme, until a masked hero known only as "The Red Wolf" appears to oppose them. Produced by Italy's Prometeo Film S.r.L.

The Revolt of the Seven (La rivolta dei sette) (Sanson Film, 1964)

Credits: Director: Alberto De Martino; *Producer:* Joseph Fryd; *Screenplay:* Sandro Continenza, Alberto De Martino, Vincenzo Mannino; *Photography:* Pier Ludovico Pavoni (Eastmancolor, Techniscope, aspect ratio 2.35:1); *Film Editor:* Otello Colangeli; *Music:* Franco Mannino, Angelo Francesco Lavagnino; *Art Direction:* Piero Poletto; *Costume Design:* Mario Giorsi; *Makeup:* Romolo de Martino; *Sound Engineer:* Alessandro Sarandrea; *Sound Post-Synchronization:* Gene Luotto; *Camera Operator:* Fausto Rossi; *Orchestra Conductor:* Franco Mannino; running time: 90 minutes (Italy), 85 minutes (U.S.); released December 28, 1964 (Italy).

Cast: Tony Russel *(Keros)*; Massimo Serato *(Baxo)*; Nando Gazzolo *(Sar/Milo)*; Livio Lorenzon *(Nemete)*; Piero Lulli *(Silone)*; Helga Liné *(Aspasia)*; Paola Pitti *(Helea)*; Howard Ross *(Croto)*; Pietro Capanna *(Mardok)*; Walter Maestosi *(Critone)*; Gaetano Quartararo *(Acrone)*; Nando Angelini *(Spying Gladiator)*; Fortunato Arena *(Gladiator)*; Jeff Cameron *(Gladiator)*; Angelo Casadei *(Soldier)*; Dakar *(Jagull)*; Alfonso Giganti *(Spectator)*; Osiride Pevarello *(Gladiator)*; Renzo Pevarello *(Gladiator)*; Bruno Ukmar *(Soldier)*; Franco Ukmar *(Soldier)*.

Comments: A group of seven warriors from Sparta oppose a villainous traitor. Produced by Italy's Sanson Film.

Revolt of the Slaves (La rivolta degli schiavi) (United Artists, 1960)

Credits: Director: Nunzio Malasomma; *Producer:* Paolo Moffa; *Screenplay:* Stefano Srucchi, Duccio Tessari (based on the novel *Fabiola* by Nicholas Patrick Wiseman); *English-Language Dialogue:* Daniel Mainwaring; *Photography:* Cecilio Paniagua (Technicolor, Techniscope, aspect ratio 2.35:1); *Film Editor:* Eraldo Da Roma; *Music:* Angelo Francesco Lavagnino; *Art Direction/Set Decoration:* Ramiro Gómez; *Costume Design:* Vittorio Rossi; *Makeup:* Carmen Martin; running time: 100 minutes (Italy); 102 minutes (U.S.); released December 20, 1960 (Italy); June 1961 (U.S.).

Cast: Rhonda Fleming *(Fabiola)*; Lang Jeffries *(Vibio)*; Darío Moreno *(Massimiano)*; Ettore Manni *(San Sabastiano)*; Wandisa Guida *(Agnese)*; Gino Cervi *(Fabio)*; Fernando Rey *(Valerio)*; Serge Gainsbourg *(Corvino)*; José Nieto *(Sesto)*; Benno Hoffman *(Pretoriano)*; Rainer Penkert *(Massimo)*; Antonio Casas *(Tertulio)*; Vanoye Aikens *(Iface)*; Dolores Francine *(Liubaia)*; Burt Nelson *(Catulo)*; Julio Peña *(Torquato)*; Rafael Rivelles *(Rutilio)*.

Comments: A Christian slave falls in love with a Patrician woman during the last years of the Roman Empire. Another version of *Fabiola (qv)*, filmed previously in 1949 and also in the silent era. Co-produced by Italy's Ambrosiana Cinematografica, Spain's C.B. Films S.A., and Germany's Ultra Film.

Robin Hood and the Pirates (Robin Hood e i pirati) (Embassy Pictures, 1960)

Credits: Director: Giorgio Simonelli; *Producers:* Leo Bomba, Carlo Infascelli; *Screenplay:* Edoardo Anton, Leo Bomba, Marcello Ciorciolini, Carlo Infascelli, Enrico Spadorcia (from a story by Carlo Infascelli); *Photography:* Raffaele Masciocchi ((Eastmancolor, Totalscope, aspect ratio 2.35:1); *Film Editor:* Dolores Tamburini; *Music:* Guido Robuschi, Gian Stellari; *Production Design:* Lamberto Giovagnoli; *Costume Design:* Dina Di Bari; *Sound:* Remo Palmieri; running time: 88 minutes (U.S.); released December 24, 1960 (Italy), 1964 (U.S.).

Cast: Lex Barker *(Robin Hood)*; Jocelyn Lane *(Karin Blain)*; Rosanna Rory *(Lizbeth Brooks)*; Mario Scaccia *(Jonathan Brooks)*; Walter Barnes *(Guercio/Orbo)*; Edith Peters *(Palla di Grasso/Bambola)*; Giulio Donnini *(Golia/Hunchback Clown)*; Renato Chiantoni *(Gladiacove)*; Mario Passante *(Brooks' Friend)*; Marco Tulli *(Friar Lorenzo)*; Gino Buzzanca *(Capt. Uncino)*; Renato Maddalena *(Trinca)*; Renato Terra *(Bambanera)*; Umberto Sacripante *(Philips, Karin's*

Uncle); Edda Soligo *(Olga, Karin's Nurse)*; Enrico Salvatore *(John)*; Mario Ambrosino *(Sacristan/Philosopher Pirate)*; Giovanni Vari *(Sospiri)*; Amalia Bracale *(Saracen Woman)*; Lilian Nguyen *(Saracen Woman)*; Ignazio Balsamo; Antonio Corevi; Italo Gasperini; Janine Hendy *(Saracen Woman)*; Gloria Hendy *(Saracen Woman)*; Anna Malasardi *(Saracen Woman)*; Sergio Mioni; Subkmanati Rukmini; Alberto Togliani; Corrado Zingaro; Bruno Tocci.

Comments: A loose interpretation of the Robin Hood legend. The hero of Sherwood Forest winds up in the Mediterranean, where he is shipwrecked and rescued by pirates. Produced by Italy's Finanziaria Cinematografica Italiana (FICIT).

Robin Hood, the Invincible Archer (Robin Hood, l'invincibile arciere) (Cinematografica Lomberda/ Hispamer Films, 1970)

Credits: Director: José Luis Merino; *Screenplay:* José Luis Merino, Piero Pierotti (from a story by Piero Pierotti); *Photography:* Umberto Lanzano (Eastmancolor); *Music:* Bruno Nicolai; running time: 84 minutes; released March 27, 1970.

Cast: Carlos Quine [billed as "Charles Quiney"] *(Robin Hood)*; Luis Barboo; Pasquale Basile; Alfredo Calles; Antonio Mayans *(John)*; Carina Monti; Franca Polesello; Paolo Senatore; Claudio Trionfi; Dan van Husen; Mariano Vidal Molina.

Comments: A continuation of the Robin Hood legend, co-produced by Italy's Cinematografica Lombarda and Neptunia Films, in tandem with Spain's Hispamer Films and Tyrys Films.

Roland the Mighty (Orlando e i Paladini di Francia) (ABC Films, 1956)

Credits: Director: Pietro Francisci; *Screenplay:* Ennio De Concini; *Photography:* Mario Bava (Eastmancolor, Gammascope, aspect ratio 2.35:1); *Music:* Angelo Francesco Lavagnino; *Art Direction:* Giulio Bongini; *Master of Arms:* Enzo Musumeci Greco; running time: 110 minutes (Italy), 99 minutes (U.S.); released December 6, 1956, video availability: Retromedia.

Cast: Rik Battaglia *(Orlando/Roland)*; Rosanna Schiaffino *(Angelica/Angélique)*; Lorella De Luca *(Alda/Aude)*; Fabrizio Mioni *(Rinaldo)*; Vittorio Sanipoli *(Gano di Maganza)*; Clelia Matania *(Nurse)*; Ivo Garrani *(Carlo Magno)*; Ugo Sasso *(Agramante)*; Franco Cobianchi; Cesare Fantoni; Gian Paolo Rosmino; Mimmo Palmara *(Argalia)*; Antonio Amendola; Lamberto Antinori *(Guglielmo)*; Alberto Archetti; Gino Buzzanca; Nando Cicero; Rosella Como *(Dolores)*; Anna Di Lorenzo *(Lena)*; Germano Longo *(Gualtiero)*; Gianni Luda; Nino Marchetti; Furio Meniconi; Gina Rovere *(Fiamma)*; Attilio Severini; Pietro Tordi *Ubaldo)*; Claudio Undari; Marisa Valenti.

Comments: The Saracens vs. Charlemagne's army in the Pyrenean foothills; a beautiful seductress is employed by the Saracen Agramante to aid in subverting Charlemagne's troops. Produced by Italy's Italgamma.

Rome 1585 (I masnadieri) (American-International Television, 1961)

Credits: Director: Mario Bonnard; *Producer:* Mario Pellegrino; *Screenplay:* Mario Bonnard, Nino Minuto (from a story by Nino Minuto); *Photography:* Marco Scarpelli (Eastmancolor, Dyaliscope, aspect ratio 2.35:1); *Film Editor:* Nella Nannuzzi; *Music:* Giulio Bonnard; *Production Design:* Amedeo Mellone; *Set Decoration:* Massimo Tavazzi; *Makeup:* Anacieto Giustini; *Hair Stylist:* Anna Fabrizzi; *Production Manager:* Mario Pellegrino; *Assistant Production Managers:* Gennaro Masullo, Bice Paoletti; *Assistant Directors:* Ettore Maria Fizzarotti, Milo Panaro; *2nd Assistant Directors:* Tonino Ricci; Vittorio Salerno; *Sound:* Guido Barboni; *Camera Operator:* Mario Mancini; *Assistant Camera Operators:* Giovanni Ciarlo, Federico Del Zoppo; *Assistant Film Editor:* Andreina Giglietti; *Orchestra Conductor:* Carlo Franci; *Production Secretaries:* Maria Celli, Arturo Padovani, *Script Supervisor:* Maria Bonnard; *Masters of Arms:* Colombini, Negroni, Pleboni; running time: 110 minutes (Italy), 85 minutes (U.S.); released August 9, 1961; video availability: Sinister Cinema.

Cast: Daniela Rocca *(Alba)*; Antonio Cifariello *(Leonetto)*; Yvonne Sanson; Livio Lorenzon;

Giulio Donnini; Gianni Solaro; Nerio Bernardi; José Torres; Leopoldo Valentini; Mino Doro; Roberto Paoletti; Ettore Ribotta; Consalvo Dell'Arti; Franco Ressel; Tony Di Mitri; Fernando Baltoni; Bruno Tocci; Gaita Di Seta; Salvo Randone *(Sisto V)*; Folco Lulli *(Fra Silenzio)*; Debra Paget *(Esmeralda, the Gypsy)*; Andrea Petricca; Renzo Bagagli *(Swordsman)*; Liana Del Belzo.

Comments: A mercenary leader falls in love with a princess. Produced by Italy's Leda Film.

The Rover *(L'avventuriero)* (Cinerama Releasing Corporation, 1971)

Credits: Director: Terence Young; *Producers:* Alfredo Bini, Selig J. Seligman; *Screenplay:* Jo Eisinger, Luciano Vincenzoni (from their story, based on the novel *The Rover,* by Joseph Conrad); *Photography:* Leonida Barboni (color); *Film Editor:* Peter Thornton; *Music:* Ennio Morricone; *Art Direction:* Gianni Polidori, Alberto Cardone; *Costume Design:* Veniero Colasanti; *Production Manager:* Fernando Franchi; *Assistant Director:* Giancarlo Zagni; *Orchestra Conductor:* Bruno Nicolai; *Soloist:* Angelo Stefanato; *Production Associate:* Mike Stern; *Naval Advisor:* Marc-Antonio Bragadin; running time: 103 minutes (U.S.); released September 8, 1967 (Italy), 1971 (U.S.).

Cast: Anthony Quinn *(Peyrol)*; Rosanna Schiaffino *(Arlette)*; Rita Hayworth *(Aunt Caterina)*; Richard Johnson *(Real)*; Ivo Garrani *(Scevola)*; Mino Doro *(Dussard)*; Luciano Rossi *(Michel)*; Mirko Valentin *(Jacot)*; Giovanni Di Benedetto *(Lt. Bolt)*; Anthony Dawson *(Capt. Vincent)*; Franco Giornelli *(Simmons)*; Franco Fantasia *(French Admiral)*; Fabrizio Jovine *(Archives Officer)*; John Lane *(Captain of the Port)*; Vittorio Venturoli *(French Officer)*; Gustavo Gionni *(Sans-Culotte)*; Lucio De Santis *(Fisherman)*; Raffaella Miciella *(Arlette as a Child)*; Paola Bossalino *(Girl)*; Rita Klein *(Girl)*; Catherine Alexander *(Girl)*; Ruggero Salvadori *(Hood)*; Andrea Fantasia; Giulio Marchetti; Giovanni Ivan Scratuglia *(Young Sailor)*.

Comments: During the Napoleonic Era, a former pirate befriends a mentally ill girl who then becomes romantically involved with a French Navy officer. Although reinforced by the presence of two major stars (Anthony Quinn and Rita Hayworth), this interesting film (which contains some worthwhile action and sea battles alongside the human drama) was barely released in America. Shot in 1966, it was minimally distributed by Cinerama in the U.S., in 1971. Co-produced by Italy's Arco Film, and the American Broadcasting Company (ABC), with Selmur Productions.

Samson *(Sansone)* (Medallion Pictures, 1961)

Credits: Director: Gianfranco Parolini; *Screenplay:* Oscar D'Amico, Gianfranco Parolini, Giovanni Simonelli (from a story by G. Madison, Gianfranco Parolini, Giovanni Simonelli); *Photography:* Francesco Izzarelli (Eastmancolor, Totalscope, aspect ratio 2.35:1); *Film Editor:* Mario Sansoni; *Music:* Carlo Innocenzi; *Production Design:* Oscar D'Amico; *Costume Design:* Vittorio Rossi; *Makeup Artist:* Antonio Marini, Pierantonio Mecacci; *Production Manager:* Ernesto Gentili; *General Production Manager:* Mario Maggi; *Assistant Director:* Giovanni Simonelli; *Assistant Production Designer:* Giuseppe Ranieri; *Sound Engineer:* Gianetto Nardi; *Special Effects:* F. Cardinelli, Roberto Morelli; *Camera Operator:* Emilio Giannini; *Assistant Camera Operator:* A. Mangianello; *Assistant Film Editor:* Amedeo Giomini; *Stunts:* Brad Harris; *Orchestra Conductor:* Carlo Franci; running time: 100 minutes (Italy), 99 minutes (U.S.); released December 23, 1961 (Italy); 1963 (U.S.); video availability: Sinister Cinema.

Cast: Brad Harris *(Samson)*; Alan Steel *(Macigno/Hercules)*; Mara Berni *(Romilda)*; Serge Gainsbourg *(Warkalla)*; Luisella Boni [billed as "Brigitte Corey"] *(Janine)*; Carlo Tamberlani *(Botan)*; Irena Prosen *(Mila)*; Franco Gasparri *(Mila's Son)*; Manja Golec; Romano Ghini; Niksa Stefanini [billed as Nicola Stefanini].

Comments: Samson discovers that the Kingdom of Sulom has been conquered by a tyrant who has murdered the queen. Produced by Italy's Cinematografica Associati (CI. AS.). The Samson character of the sword-and-sandal films is a heroic, Hercules-type fictional strongman, and has no relation to the biblical figure bearing the same name.

Samson Against the Pirates (Sansone contro i pirati) (American-International Television, 1963)

Credits: Director: Tanio Boccia [billed as "Amerigo Anton"]; *Producer:* Fortunato Misiano; *Screenplay:* Guido Maletesta; *Cinematography:* Augusto Tiezzi (Eastmancolor, Totalscope, aspect ratio 2.35:1); *Film Editor:* Jolanda Benvenuti; *Production Design:* Salvatore Giancotti; *Set Decoration:* Franco D'Andra; *Music:* Angelo Francesco Lavagnino; *Costume Design:* Walter Patriarca; *Makeup:* Massimo Giustini; *Hair Stylists:* Salvatore Controneo Violetta Pacelli; *Production Manager:* Nino Misiano; *Assistant Directors:* Mario Moroni, Giancarlo Romitelli; *Sound:* Mario Faraoni, Bruno Moreal; *Sound Effects:* Italo Cameracanna; *Camera Operator:* Luigi Allegretti; *Assistant Camera Operator:* Renato Mascagno [billed as "Renato Mascagni"]; *Production Coordinator:* Pasquale Misiano; *Script Girl:* Mirella Malatesta; *Nautical Advisor:* Walter Bertolazzi; running time: 89 minutes (Italy); released July 29, 1963 (Italy); video availability: Sinister Cinema.

Cast: Kirk Morris *(Samson);* Margaret Lee *(Amanda);* Daniele Vargas *(Murad);* Aldo Bufi Landi *(Manuel);* Tullio Altamura *(Mobed);* Adriana Ambesi *(Sarah);* Franco Peruzzi [billed as "Frank Leroy"] *(Ramon);* Gianna Serra; Attilio Dottesio *(Alvarez);* Calisto Calisti *(Ibrahim);* Gino Soldi; Nello Pazzafini *(Sandor);* Sina Scarfone; Teresa De Leo; Antonio Vezza; Pasquale De Filippo; John Bartha; Adalberto Roni; Andrea Scotti *(Daikon).*

Comments: In this adventure, set in 1630, Samson is involved with pirates on Devil's Island. An alternate title was *Samson and the Sea Beasts.* Produced by Italy's Romana Film.

Samson and the Mighty Challenge (Ercole, Sansone, Maciste e Ursus gli invincibli) (Rank, 1964)

Credits: Director: Giorgio Capitani; *Producer:* Giorgio Cristallini; *Screenplay:* Sandro Continenza, Roberto Gianviti (from their story, Spanish adaptation by Sebastián Luca de Tana); *Photography:* Carlo Bellero (Eastmancolor, aspect ratio 1.85:1); *Film Editor:* Roberto Cinquini; *Music:* Piero Umilani; *Set Decoration:* Gianfranco Ramacci; *Production Manager:* Attilio Tosato; *2nd Unit Director:* Giorgio Cristallini; *2nd Assistant Cameramen:* Luis Cuadrado, Gaetano Valle; *2nd Assistant Cameraman/Underwater Cameraman:* M. Mamura; running time: 100 minutes (Italy); released November 12, 1964 (Italy).

Cast: Alan Steel *(Hercules);* Howard Ross *(Maciste);* Nadir Moretti [billed as "Nadir Baltimore"] *(Samson);* Yann Larvor [billed as "Yann L'Arvor"] *(Ursus);* Luciano Marin *(Inor);* Hélène Chanel; Lia Zoppelli *(Nemea);* Moira Orfei *(Dalila);* Arnaldo Fabrizio *(Goliath, the Dwarf);* Livio Lorenzon; Nino Dal Fabbro; Elisa Montés *(Omphale);* María Luisa Ponte *(Ursus' Woman);* Conrado San Martin *(Marinaro);* Valentino Macchi; Nino Marchetti; Carlo Tamberlani; Gaetano Moretti; Attilio Tosato.

Comments: The world's four mightiest heroes—Hercules, Maciste, Samson and Ursus—battle one another, then team up to fight an evil tyrant. Produced by Italy's Senior Cinematografica, France's Films Régent, and Spain's PE Films (Productores Exibidores Films S.A.).

Samson and the 7 Miracles of the World (Maciste alla corte del Gran Khan) (American-International, 1961)

Credits: Director: Riccardo Freda; *Producers:* Salvatore Billitteri [U.S. version], Luigi Carpentieri, Ermanno Donati; *Screenplay:* Oreste Biancoli, Duccio Tessari (from a story by Oresti Biancoli) [script for U.S. version by George Gonneau, Lee Kresel]; *Photography:* Riccardo Pallotini (Eastmancolor, Superinescope [Colorscope in U.S.], aspect ratio 2.35:1); *Film Editor:* Ornella Micheli; *Music:* Les Baxter (U.S. version), Carlo Innocenzi; *Art Direction:* Piero Filippone; *Set Decoration:* Ennio Michettoni, Athos Danilo Zanetti; *Costume Design:* Massimo Bolongaro; *Production Supervisors:* Mario Damiani, Livio Maffei; *Assistant Director:* Giuliano Betti; *Sound:* Raffaele Del Monte, Mario Del Pezzo; *Special Effects:* Piero Mecacci; *Camera Operator:* Stelvio Massi; *Assistant Cameraman:* Giulio Spadoni; *Orchestra Conductor:* Carlo Savina; *Music Coordinator:* Al Sims; *Choreography:*

Poster for *Samson Against the Pirates*.

Wilbert Bradley; *Dubbing (U.S. version)*: George Gonneau, Lee Kresel; running time: 95 minutes (Italy), 80 minutes (U.S.); released October 31, 1961 (Italy), December 1962 (U.S.); video availability: Retromedia.

Cast: Gordon Scott *(Maciste/Samson)*; Yôko Tani *(Princess Lei-ling)*; Dante DiPaolo *(Bayan)*; Gabriele Antonini *(Cho)*; Leonardo Severini *(Garak, the Great Khan)*; Valéry Inkijinoff *(Taoist High Priest)*; Franco Ressel *(Captain of the Khan's Guards)*; Ely Yeh *(Emperor Wung)*; Ham-Chau Luong [billed as "Luong-Ham Chan"] *(Buddhist High Priest)*; Chu Lai Chit *(Prince Tai Sung)*; Sergio Ukmar; Tonnino Cianci (billed as "Antonio Cianci"); Giacomo Tchang *(Old Chinese Priest)*; Georges Aminel; René Arrieu; Henry Djanik; Jean-Pierre Ducos; Raymond Loyer; Roger Rudel; Martine Sarcey; Jacques Thébault; Pietro Torrisi *(Comparsa)*; George Gonneau *(Narrator [U.S. version]/Garak, The Great Khan [voice])*.

Comments: In the Orient, a beautiful Asian princess is rescued by Samson. The sets (as well as actress Yôko Tani) were leftovers from *Marco Polo* (1962) *(qv)*. This film also re-uses Les Baxter's score from *Goliath and the Barbarians (qv)*. The original title was *Maciste alla corte del Gran Khan (Maciste at the Court of the Great Khan)*, and an alternate title was *Goliath and the Golden City*. Co-produced by Italy's Panda Film and France's Gallus Films.

Samson and the Slave Queen *(Zorro contro Maciste)* (American-International, 1963)

Credits: *Director:* Umberto Lenzi; *Producer:* Fortunato Misiano; *Screenplay:* Umberto Lenzi, Guido Maletesta; *Photography:* Augusto Tiezzi (Eastmancolor, Totalscope, aspect ratio 2.35:1); *Film Editor:* Jolanda Benvenuti; *Music:* Les Baxter (U.S. version), Angelo Francesco Lavagnino; *Set Decoration:* Salvatore Giancotti; *Costume Design:* Walter Patriarca; *Assistant Director:* Giancarlo Romitelli; running time: 90 minutes (Italy), 86 minutes (U.S.); released August 23, 1963 (Italy), December 13, 1963 (U.S.).

Cast: Pierre Brice *(Zorro/Ramon)*; Alan Steel *(Maciste/Samson)*; Moira Orfei *(Malva)*; Maria Grazia Spina *(Isabella de Alazon)*; Andrea Aureli *(Rabek)*; Massimo Serato *(Garcia de Higuera)*;

Left: Pierre Brice leaps above Alan Steel in *Samson and the Slave Queen*. *Right:* Alan Steel in *Samson and the Slave Queen*.

Andrea Scotti *(Pedro)*; Aldo Bufi Landi *(Deikor)*; Gianni Baghino *(Paco)*; Ignazio Balsamo *(Joaquim)*; Antonio Corevi *(Don Manuel)*; Rosy De Leo *(Carmencita)*; Franco De Simone; Attilo Dettesio *(Gen. Saveria)*; Loris Gizzi *(Don Alvarez)*; Renato Malevasi *(Alonzo)*; Nello Pazzafini *(Rabek's Henchman)*; Sina Relli; Gaetano Scala; Attilio Torelli; Amedeo Trilli *(L'Oste)*; Nazzareno Zamperla *(Sadoch)*.

Comments: One of two women, the blonde and virtuous Isabella, and the evil, dark-haired Malva, is heir to the throne, and search for a will that determines their fate; Samson and Zorro aid them in their quest. Produced by Italy's Romana Film.

Samson in King Solomon's Mines (Maciste nelle miniere de re Salomone) (Embassy, 1964)

Credits: *Director:* Piero Regnoli (billed as "Martin Andrews"); *Producers:* Luigi Carpentieri, Ermanno Donati; *Supervising Producer:* Ennio Di Meo; *Screenplay:* Piero Regnoli; *Photography:* Mario Capriotti, Luciano Trasatti (Technicolor, Techniscope, aspect ratio 2.35:1), *Film Editor:* Ornella Michelli; *Production Secretary:* Ennio De Meo; *Art Direction:* Aurelio Crugnola; *Costume Design:* Franco Loquenzi; *Makeup:* Maurizio Giustini; *Hair Stylist:* Iolanda Conti; *Assistant Director:* Vittorio Sindoni; *Assistant Art Director:* Aldo Capuano; *Sound:* Alessandro Sarandrea; *Camera Operator:* Gino Santini; *Assistant Film Editor:* Rossana Landi; *Music Arrangements/Orchestra Conductor:* Francesco De Masi; *Continuity:* Bruna Malaguti; *Production Assistant:* Franco Cuccu; *Master of Arms:* Bruna Malaguti; running time: 92 minutes (Italy), 92 minutes (U.S.); released June 25, 1964 (Italy); video availability: Alpha Video.

Cast: Reg Park *(Samson/Maciste)*; Wandisa Guida *(Fazira)*; Bruno Piergentili [billed as "Dan Harrison"] *(Abucar)*; Eleonora Bianchi *(Samara)*; Elio Jotta [billed as "Leonard G. Elliot"] *(Riad)*; Carlo Tamberlani *(Zelea)*; Giuseppe Addobbati *(Namar)*; Nino Persello *(Belal)*; Bruno Scipioni *(Kadar)*; Loris Loddi *(Vazma, Heir to the Throne)*.

Comments: The heroic Maciste is captured

Reg Park in *Samson in King Solomon's Mines.*

and forced to work as a slave in an African mine. Produced by Italy's Panda Societa per L'Industria Cinematografica. Filmed at Incir De Paolis Studios in Rome, with some location shooting done in South Africa for the wildlife scenes.

Sandokan Fights Back (Sandokan alla riscossa) (Screen Gems Television, 1964)

Credits: Director: Luigi Capuano; *Producer:* Ottavio Poggi; *Screenplay:* Luigi Capuano, Arpad DeRiso (based on a novel by Emilio Salgari); *Photography:* Bitto Albertini (Eastmancolor, Totalscope, aspect ratio 2.35:1); *Film Editor:* Antonietta Zita; *Art Direction:* Giancarlo Bartolini Salimbeni, Ernest Kromberg; *Set Decoration:* Massimo Tavazzi; *Costume Design:* Giancarlo Batolini Salimbeni; *Production Managers:* Nino Battiferri, Romano Cardarelli, Günther Kulakowski; *Sound:* Vittorio Trentino; *Fencing Master:* Ferdinando Poggi; running time: 91 minutes (Italy); released August 13, 1964 (Italy); video availability: Sinister Cinema.

Cast: Ray Danton *(Sandokan)*; Guy Madison *(Yanez)*; Franca Bettoia *(Samoa)*; Mario Petri *(Sir Charles Brooks)*; Alberto Farnese *(Tremal Naik)*; Mino Doro *(Lumbo)*; Giulio Marchetti *(Sagapar)*; Sandro Moretti *(Kammamuri)*; Ferdinando Poggi *(Teotrokis' Accomplice)*; Raf Baldassarre *(Tetrokis the Greek)*; Isarco Ravaioli *(Sitar)*; Veriano Ginesi *(Executor)*.

Comments: Sandokan claims his rightful destiny as ruler of Malaysia. An alternate title was *The Conqueror and the Empress*. Produced by Italy's Liber Film and Germany's Eichberg-Film. Followed by *Return of Sandokan* (1964) *(qv)*.

Sandokan, Pirate of Malaysia (I pirati della Malesia) (Arce Films, 1964)

Credits: Director: Umberto Lenzi; *Producer:* Solly V. Bianco; *Screenplay:* Victor Andrés Catena, Jaime Comas Gil, Ugo Liberatore (from a story adaptation by Ugo Liberatore, based on a novel by Emilio Salgari); *Photography:* Federico G. Larraya, Angelo Lotti (color, Techniscope, aspect ratio 2.35:1); *Film Editor:* Jolanda Benvenuti; *Music:* Giovanni Fusco; *Production Design:* Arrigo Equini; *Costume Design:* Giancarlo Bartolini Salimbeni; *Makeup:* Raul Ranieri; *Production Manager:* Tomasso Sagone; *Set Dresser:* Carlo Gentili; *Camera Operators:* Luigi Allegretti, Elio Polacchi; *Assistant Camera Operators:* Giorgio Garibaldi Schwarze, Giancarlo Granatelli; *Director of English-Dubbed Version:* Richard McNamara; running time: 110 minutes (Italy), 106 minutes (U.S.); released October 16, 1964 (Italy).

Cast: Steve Reeves *(Sandokan)*; Jacqueline Sassard *(Princess Hada)*; Mimmo Palmara *(Tremal-Naik)*; Andrea Bosic *(Yanez)*; Nando Gazzolo *(Lt. Clintock)*; Leo Anchóriz); *(Lord Brook)*; Franco Balducci *(Sambigliong)*; Pierre Cressoy *(Captain of The Young India)*; Giuseppe Addobbati *(Muda Hassin)*; Nando Angelini; Dakar [billed as "Alejandro Barrera Dakar"] *(Kammamuuri)*; George Wang *(Sho Pa)*; Sujata Rubener *(Dancer)*; Asoka Rubener *(Dancer)*; Fortunato Arena *(English Officer)*; Domenico Cianfriglia; José Torres *(Homat)*; Nazzareno Zamperla *(Durango)*.

Comments: Malaysian rebel Sandokan opposes a corrupt British general in Singapore. The sequel to *Sandokan the Great* (1963) *(qv)*. Alternate titles were *The Pirates of Malaysia* and *The Pirates of the Seven Seas*. Co-Produced by Italy's Euro International Film (EIA), France's La Société des Films Sirius, and Spain's Lacy International Films.

Sandokan the Great (Sandokan la tigre di Mompracem) (MGM, 1963)

Credits: Director: Umberto Lenzi; *Producer:* Giovanni Fusco; *Screenplay:* Victor Andrés Catena, Fulvio Gicca Palli, Umberto Lenzi (based on the novel *Le tigri di Mompracem* by Emilio Salgari); *Photography:* Aurelio G. Larraya, Angelo Lotti, Giovanni Scarpellini (Technicolor, Techniscope, aspect ratio 2,35:1); *Film Editors:* Jolanda Benvenuti, Antonietta Zita; *Music:* Giovanni Fusco; *Production Design:* Arrigo Equini; *Set Decoration:* Arrigo Equini, Juan Alberto Soler; *Costume Design:* Giancarlo Bartolini Salimbeni; *Makeup:* Raul Ranieri; *Hair Stylist:* Giovanni Palombi; *Production Supervisors:* Cecilia Bigazzi, Averroè Stefani; *Production Manager:* Tommaso Sagone; *General Manager (Sri Lanka Locations)*; Sardha Rathnarive; *1st Assistant Directors:* Jean Maury, Viktor Tourjansky;

Geneviève Grad and Steve Reeves in *Sandokan the Great*.

2nd Assistant Director: Giancarlo Romitelli; *Camera Operators:* Fausto Rossi, Antonio Schiavo Lena; *Assistant Camera Operator:* Giorgio Garibaldi Schwarze; *Assistant Costume Designer:* Nadia Vitali; *Assistant to the Director:* Jean Maumy; *Script Supervisor:* Laura Vignola; running time: 95 minutes (Italy), 105 minutes (U.S.); released December 19, 1963 (Italy), May 1965 (U.S.); video availability: Warner Home Video.

Cast: Steve Reeves *(Sandokan)*; Geneviève Grad *(Mary Ann)*; Andrea Bosic *(Yanez)*; Rik Battaglia *(Sambigliong)*; Mario Valdemarin *(Lt. Ross)*; Enzo Fiermonte *(Sgt. Mitchell)*; Wilbert Bradley *(Pataan)*; Maurice Poli *(Girobatol)*; Gino Marturano *(Kanandurian)*; Nazzareno Zamperla *(Hirangù)*; Giovanni Cianfriglia; Pietro Capanna; Ananda Kumar *(Twang Long)*; Adolfo Celi; Mimmo Palmara; Jacqueline Sassard; Emilio Cigoli *(Steve Reeves' Dubbed Voice)*.

Comments: Malaysian rebel Sandokan opposes British colonial domination in this action yarn, based on the character created by novelist Emilio Salgari. Followed by *Sandokan, Pirate of Malaysia*. Produced by Italy's Films S.A., France's Comptoir Français du Film Production (CFFP), and Spain's Ocean Films.

The Saracens (*Il pirati del diavolo*) (American-International Television, 1963)

Credits: *Director:* Roberto Mauri; *Screenplay:*

Opposite, top: Steve Reeves protects Geneviève Grad from attack in *Sandokan the Great*. *Opposite, bottom:* Steve Reeves and Geneviève Grad in *Sandokan the Great*.

Mario Calucci, Roberto Mauri; *Photography:* Angelo Baistrocchi (color, Totalscope, aspect ratio 2.35:1); *Film Editor:* Mariano Arditi; *Music:* Aldo Piga; running time: 89 minutes (U.S.); released June 21, 1963 (Italy).

Cast: Richard Harrison *(Marco Trevisan)*; Walter Brandi *(Ranieri)*; Annamaria Ubaldi *(Alina)*; Gino Turini [billed as "John Turner"] *(Count Trevisan)*; Maretta Procaccini *(The Child)*; Lorenzo Artale *(Giovanni)*; Anita Todesco *(Zoraide)*; Liana Dori *(Velia)*; Lilly Landers *(Caterina)*; Demeter Bitenc *(Rabaneck)*; Luigi Batzella [billed as "Paolo Solvay"] *(Mahmud)*.

Comments: Hero Marco Trevisan vs. Turkish pirates on the Dalmatian coast in Croatia. Produced by Italy's Walmar Cinematografica and Yugoslavia's Triglav Film.

Saul and David *(Saul e David)* (Screen Gems Television, 1964)

Credits: Director: Marcello Baldi; *Producers:* Emilio Cordero, Toni Di Carlo; *Screenplay:* Marcello Baldi, Emilio Cordero, Tonino Guerra, Ottavio Jemma, Flavio Niccolini, A. Rubio Fuentes; *Photography:* Marcello Masciocchi, Juan Ruiz Romero (Eastmancolor, Techniscope, aspect ratio 2.35:1); *Film Editor:* Giulianna Attenni; *Music:* Teo Usuelli; *Art Direction:* Sigfrido Burmann; *Costume Design:* Giorgio Desideri; *Production Manager:* José María Alonso Pesquera; *Stunts:* Miguel Pedregosa; *Orchestra Conductor:* Alberto Zedda; *Dialogue Director:* Clement Lister; running time: 105 minutes (U.S.); released December 31, 1964 (Italy), June 1968 (U.S.); video availability: VCI.

Cast: Norman Wooland *(King Saul)*; Gianni Garko *(David)*; Elisa Cegani *(Akhinoam)*; Luz Márquez *(Abigail)*; Pilar Clemens *(Michal)*; Virgilio Teixeira *(Abner)*; Antonio Mayans *(Jonathan)*; Carlos Casaravilla *(Samuel)*; Stefy Lang *(Goliath)*; Marco Paoletti *(David, as a Boy)*; Paolo Gozlino *(Joab)*; Andrea Sciré; Raffaele Romano; Dante Maggio *(Abdon)*; Giorgio Cerioni; Antonio Molino Rojo; Aldo Sambrell; Barta Barri; Ricardo G. Lilló; Antonio Vela *(David's Child Friend)*; José Jaspe; Nino Persello.

Comments: David of Bethlehem slays Goliath in this biblical drama, produced by Italy's San Paolo Films and shot at Rome's Cinecittà Studios. An alternate U.S. television title was the nondescript *Sibling Rivalry.*

Scheherazade *(Shéhérazade)* (Shawn International, 1963)

Credits: Director: Pierre Gaspard-Huit; *Producers:* Michael Safra, Serge Silberman; *Screenplay:* Pierre Gaspard-Huit, José Gutiérrez Maesso, Marc Gilbert Sauvajon (from their story); *Photography:* André Domage, Christian Mattras (Eastmancolor, Superpanorama 70, aspect ratio 2.20:1 [65mm]); *Film Editor:* Louisette Hautecoeur; *Music:* André Hossein; *Set Decoration:* Francisco Canet, Georges Wakhévitch; *Costume Design:* Georges Wakhévitch; *Production Manager:* Henri Baum; *2nd Unit Director:* Jacques Bourdon; *Sound:* Antoine Petitjean (Westrex sound system, 70mm 6-track); *Choreography:* Jeanine Charrat; *Fencing Master:* Claude Carliez; running time: 124 minutes; released September 5, 1963 (Italy), May 12, 1965 (U.S.).

Cast: Anna Karina *(Shéhérazade)*; Gérard Barray *(Renaud de Villecroix)*; Antonio Vilar *(Haroun-al-Raschid)*; Giuliano Gemma *(Didier)*; Marilluc ù Tolo *(Shirin)*; Fausto Tozzi *(Barmak)*; Gil Vidal *(Thierry)*; Jorge Mistral *(Grand Vizir Zajean-ccar)*; Fernando Rey; Joëlle LaTour *(Anira)*; Rafael Albaicín; Karamoko Cisse; María Calvi; José Calvo; Félix Fernández; María Granada; José Manuel Martin; Lorella De Luca; Jean-Luc Goddard.

Comments: Three knights offer the beautiful Shéhérazade to a sultan as a gift. Actress Anna Karina was married to French "New Wave" director Jean-Luc Goddard and appeared in his films (most notably *Alphaville*); Goddard himself appears in a cameo here.

The Sea Pirate *(Surcouf, l'eroe dei sette mari)* (Paramount, 1967)

Credits: Director: Sergio Bergonzelli; *Director of International Version:* Roy Rowland; *Producers:* Roy Rowland, Nat Wachsberger; *Screenplay:* Georges de La Grandière, Gerald Savery, Giovanni Simonelli, José Antonio de la Loma (from a story by Georges de La Grandière, Jacques Séverac; dialogue by Guy Farrell); *Photography:* Juan Gelpi (Technicolor, Techniscope, aspect ratio 2.35:1); *Film Editor:* Jean-Michel Gautier;

Music: Georges Garvarentz; *Production Design:* Juan Alberto Soler; *Costume Design:* Román Calatayud; *Makeup:* Vittorio Biseo; *Production Managers:* Luigi Nannerini, Valentin Salient; *Production Supervisor:* Franco Sormani; *Assistant Directors:* Antonio Di Paolo, Tony Puente; *Sound:* Pietro Spadoni; *Special Effects:* John P. Fulton; *Assistant Film Editor:* Juan Luis Oliver; *Script Supervisor:* Isabel Mulá; *Production Secretary:* Filippo Nannerini; running time: 85 minutes (U.S.); released March 24, 1967 (Italy), June 28, 1967 (U.S.).

Cast: Gérard Barray *(Capt. Robert Surcouf)*; Antonella Lualdi *(Margaret Carruthers/Lady Blackwood)*; Terrence Morgan *(Lord Blackwood)*; Geneviève Casile *(Marie-Catherine Blaise)*; Armand Mestral *(Capt. Hans Fell)*; Gérard Tichy *(Kernan)*; Alberto Cevenini *(Garneray)*; Giani Esposito *(Napoléon)*; Antonio Molino Rojo *(Andre Chambles)*; Gonzalo de Esquiroz *(Captain Toward)*; George Rigaud *(Admiral Decrès)*; Rosella Bergamonti *(Louise)*; Mónica Randall *(Joséphine de Beauharnais)*; Anne Vernon; Virgilio Teixeira; Ivano Staccioli; Tomás Blanco *(Gov. Malartic)*; Frank Oliveras *(Nicolas Surcouf)*; Mariano Vidal Molina *(André Chamblais)*; Aldo Sambrell *(Sailor on La Bombarde)*; Luis Barboo; José Maria Caffarel *(Blaise, Marie-Catherine's Father)*; Victor Israel; Francisco Tuset.

Comments: A pirate yarn set during the Napoleonic Era. Co-produced by Italy's Arco Film, the French companies Edition et Diffusion Cinématographique (E.D.I.C.), Rialto Film, and the Spanish company Balcázar Producciones Cinematograficas. According to lead Gérard Barray, Roy Rowland actually directed the entire film and Sergio Bergonzelli was credited only for contractual reasons.

The Secret Mark of D'Artagnan (Il colpo segreto di d'Artagnan) (Medallion Pictures, 1962)

Credits: Director: Siro Marcellini; *Producer:* Ottavio Poggi; *Screenplay:* Milton Krims, Siro Marcellini, Ottavio Poggi; *Photography:* Alvaro Mancori (Technicolor, Totalscope, aspect ratio 2.35:1); *Film Editor:* Renato Cinquini; *Music:* Carlo Rustichelli; *Art Direction:* Amedeo Mellone; *Construction Manager:* Salvatore Siciliano; running time: 91 minutes (U.S.); released August 12, 1962 (Italy), 1963 (U.S.); video availability: Something Weird Video.

Cast: George Nader *(D'artagnan)*; Magali Nöel *(Carlotta)*; Georges Marchal *(Duke of Montserrat)*; Massimo Serato *(Cardinal Richelieu)*; Alessandra Panaro *(Diana)*; Mario Petri *(Porthos)*; Franco Fantasia; Raf Baldassarre; Giulio Marchetti; Andrea Fantasia; Romano Giomini; Piero Pastore.

Comments: Two of the Three Musketeers, D'Artagnan and Porthos, attempt to thwart an assassination plot against King Louis XIII. Produced by Italy's Liber Film and France's Les Films Agiman.

The Secret Seven (Gli invincibli sette) (MGM, 1963)

Credits: Director: Alberto De Martino; *Producers:* Anacleto Fontini, Italo Zingarelli; *Screenplay:* Alberto De Martino (from a story by Alberto De Martino, Sandro Continenza); *Photography:* Eloy Mella (Eastmancolor, Techniscope, aspect ratio 2.35:1); *Film Editors:* Otello Colangeli, José Luis Matesanz; *Music:* Carlo Franci; *Art Direction:* José Antonio de la Guerra, Piero Poletto; *Costume Design:* Mario Giorsi; *Makeup:* Romolo de Martino; *Hair Stylist:* Manolita Castro; *Production Managers:* Ángel Monís, Roberto Palaggi; *Assistant Director:* Jaime Bayarri; *Sound:* Julio Carvajal, Mario Morigi, Mario Sensi, Gene Luotto; *Camera Operator:* Giovanni Bergamini; *Costume Assistant:* Silvano Giusti; *Assistant Film Editor:* Aurelio Pennacchia; *Script Supervisor:* Maria Pia Rocco; *Master of Arms:* Giorgio Ubaldi; running time: 92 minutes (Italy); released October 31, 1963 (Italy), April 1966 (U.S.).

Cast: Tony Russel *(Leslio)*; Helga Liné *(Lydia)*; Massimo Serato *(Axel)*; Gérard Tichy *(Rabirio)*; Renato Baldini *(Kadem)*; Livio Lorenzon *(Rubio)*; Barta Barri *(Baxo)*; José Marco *(Luzar)*; Cris Huerta *(Gular)*; Gianni Solaro *(Nakassar)*; Francesco Sormano *(Aristocrat)*; Emma Baron *(Mother)*; Pedro Mari Sánchez *(Ario)*; Tomás Blanco *(Panuzio)*; Renato Montalbano *(Aristocrat)*.

Comments: In Lebanon during the 4th Century AD, the tyrannical King Rabirio sentences heroic Axel to death, but Axel's brother Leslio and five rebel slaves rescue him; the seven of them form a team and ultimately defeat Rabirio. Co-produced by Italy's Film Columbus and Spain's Atenea Films. In Britain, *The Secret Seven* was released on a double-bill with the Christopher Lee movie *The Devil-Ship Pirates* (1964).

Seven from Thebes (Sette a Tebe) (Avala Film/P.A.C./Zebra, 1964)

Credits: Director: Luigi Vanzi (billed as "Roy Ferguson"); *Music:* Carlo Savina; *Photography:* Technicolor, Techniscope, aspect ratio 2.35:1; *Production Design:* Aleksandar Milovic; *Art Direction:* Jovan Radic, Milan Todorovic; *Costume Design:* Mira Gilsic; running time: 105 minutes (Italy), 88 minutes (U.S.); released December 31, 1964 (Italy).

Cast: André Lawrence *(Diomedes)*; Lena von Martens *(Doride)*; Burt Plesher *(Hipolito)*; Loredana Nusciak *(Cirene)*; Raf Baldassarre *(Leonidas)*; Paul Windsor; Mariangela Giordano (billed as "Mary Jordan"); Bert Silver; Stole Arandjelovic, Andrej Gardenin *(Fencer)*; Dusan Janicijevic; Dragan Ocokoljic; Branko Plesa; Milivoje Popovic-Mavid; Bert Sotlar; Pavle Vuisic (billed as "Pavle Vujisic").

Comments: The heroic Diomedes and his warriors embark on the overthrow of Sparta, which dominates the city of Thebes. Produced by Italy's Zebra Films, the French companies P.A.C. and Société Nouvelle des Établissements Gaumont (SNEG), and Yugoslavia's Avala Film. Shot in Rome, with some location work in Yugoslavia.

Seven Rebel Gladiators (Sette contro tutti) (Leone Film, 1965)

Credits: Director: Michele Lupo; *Producer:* Elio Scardamaglia; *Screenplay:* Lionello De Felice, Francesco Scardamaglia (from a story by Ernesto Gastaldi); *Photography:* Sandro Mancori (Technicolor, Techniscope, aspect ratio 2.35:1); *Film Editor:* Alberto Gallitti; *Music:* Francesco De Masi; *Production Manager:* Piero Lazzari; running time: 90 minutes (Italy); released August 26, 1965 (Italy).

Cast: Roger Browne [billed as "Roger Browne"] *(Marcus Aulus)*; José Greci [billed as "Liz Havilland"] *(Assuer)*; Alfio Caltabiano [billed as "Al Northton"] *(Vladius)*; Harold Bradley *(Tucos)*; Mario Novelli [billed as "Anthony Freeman"] *(Physios)*; Erno Crisa *(Morakeb)*; Carlo Tamberlani [billed as "Bud Stevenson"] *(King Krontal)*; Arnaldo Fabrizio [billed as "Little Goliath"] *(Goliath)*; Pietro Tordi (billed as "Peter Barclay"); Jeff Cameron; Pietro Ceccarelli; Dakar; Sam Hamilton; Bill Miller; Ugo Sasso (billed as "Gordon Stevens"); Nazzareno Zamperla (billed as "Nick Anderson").

Comments: Marcus Aulus, a Roman centurion, joins forces with six gladiators to defeat Vadius, an evil Roman tribune. Produced by Italy's Leone Film. This movie reuses some footage from *The Mole Men Against the Son of Hercules* (qv).

The Seven Revenges (Le sette sfide) (Embassy Pictures, 1961)

Credits: Director: Primo Zeglio; *Producer:* Erminio Salvi; *Screenplay:* Sabatino Ciuffini, Roberto Natale, Erminio Salvi, Giuseppe Taffarel, Primo Zeglio, Sergio Leone (from a story by Erminio Salvi); *Photography:* Bitto Albertini (Eastmancolor, Totalscope, aspect ratio 2.35:1); *Film Editor:* Franco Fraticelli; *Music:* Carlo Innocenzi; *Art Direction:* Oscar D'Amico; *Costume Design:* Giovanna Natili; *Sound:* Bruno Moreal; running time: 92 minutes (Italy); released April 1, 1961 (Italy); July 9, 1967 (U.S.).

Cast: Ed Fury *(Ivan)*; Elaine Stewart *(Tamara)*; Bella Cortez *(Suani)*; Roldano Lupi *(The Great Khan)*; Paolo Barbara *(Deniza)*; Furio Meniconi *(Amok)*; Gabriele Antonini *Kir, Ivan's Brother)*; Sergio Ukmar *(Yakub, Amok's Brother)*; Franco Ukmar *(Ostop, Amok's Brother)*; Bruno Ukmar *(Amok's Brother)*; Relja Basic; Omero Gargano *(The Great Khan's Advisor)*; Renato Terrs (billed as "Renato Terra Caizzi").

Comments: Rival Mongol chiefs battle to the death in this action-adventure, co-produced by Italy's Adelphia Compagnia Cinematografica and Yugoslavia's Dubrava Film.

Seven Seas to Calais (Il dominatore dei 7 mari) (MGM, 1963)

Credits: Director: Rudolph Maté, Primo Zeglio; *Producer:* Paolo Moffa; *Screenplay:* Filippo Sanjust; *Photography:* Giulio Gianini; (Eastmancolor, CinemaScope, aspect ratio 2.35:1); *Film Editor:* Franco Fraticelli; *Music:* Franco Mannino; *Art Direction:* Nicola Cantatore; *Costume Design:* Filippo Sanjust; *Makeup:* Maurizio Giustini; *Sound:* Primiano Muritori (Westrex sound system); *Special Effects:* Eros Bacciucchi; *Script Girl:* Anna Gruber; running time: 102 minutes (Italy); released March 1963 (U.S.).

Cast: Rod Taylor *(Sir Francis Drake)*; Keith Michell *(Malcolm Marsh)*; Edy Vessel *(Arabella Ducleau)*; Terence Hill [billed as Mario Girotti] *(Babington)*; Basil Dignam *(Sir Francis Walsingham)*; Anthony Dawson *(Lord Burleigh)*; Gianni Cajafa *(Tom Moon)*; Irene Worth *(Queen Elizabeth I)*; Arturo Dominici *(Don Bernardino de Mendoza, the Spanish Ambassador)*; Marco Guglielmi *(Fletcher)*; Esmeralda Ruspoli *(Mary of Scotland)*; Rosella D'Aquino *(Potato)*; Umberto Raho *(King Philip of Spain)*; Aldo Bufi Landi *(Vigeois)*; Giuseppe Abbrescia *(Chester)*; Luciana Gilli *(Indian Wife)*; Massimo Righi *(Lord of the Royal Court)*; Anna Santarsiero *(Indian Wife)*; Gianni Solaro *(Admiral Maria Sedonia)*; Jacopo Tecchi *(Garcia)*; Bruno Ukmar *(Emmanuel)*; Franco Ukmar *(Francisco)*; Adriano Vitale *(Recalde)*.

Comments: Sir Francis Drake steals gold from the Spaniards on an expedition to the New World, and then returns to England to thwart spies plotting against Queen Elizabeth I. Produced by Italy's Adelphi Compagnia Cinematografica. Shot in Rome, with the ocean scenes filmed at the Bay of Naples and Salerno, Campania. Co-director Rudolph Maté's last movie.

Seven Slaves Against the World (Gli schiavi più forti del mondo) (Paramount, 1964)

Credits: *Director:* Michele Lupo; *Producer:* Elio Scardamaglia; *Screenplay:* Roberto Gianviti, Michele Lupo; *Photography:* Guglielmo Mancori (Technicolor, Techniscope, aspect ratio 2.35:1); *Film Editor:* Alberto Gallitti; *Music:* Francesco De Masi; *Art Direction:* Pier Vittorio Marchi; *Costume Design:* Walter Patriarca; *Special Effects:* Armando Grilli; *Choreography:* Alfio Caltabiano; running time: 96 minutes (U.S.), released August 28, 1964 (Italy); November 1965 (U.S.).

Cast: Roger Browne *(Marcus)*; Gordon Mitchell *(Balisten)*; Arnaldo Fabrizio *(Goliath)*; Scilla Gabel *(Claudia)*; Aldo Pini *(Traidor)*; Alfredo Rizzo *(Efrem)*; Giacomo Rossi Stuart *(Gaius)*; Carlo Tamberlani *(Lucius Terentius)*; Germano Longo *(Lucius Emilius)*; Luciana Vincenzi; Alfio Caltabiano *(Gladiator)*; Calisto Calisti *(Selim)*; Pietro Ceccarelli; Mario Novelli; Nello Pazzafini; Aldo Pedinotti; Adriano Vitale.

Comments: On the desert fringes of the Roman Empire, a group of slaves escape during a revolt at a construction site. Produced by Italy's Leone Film.

The Seventh Sword (Le sette spade del vendicatore) (Medallion Pictures, 1962)

Credits: *Director:* Riccardo Freda; *Producer:* Cino Del Duca; *Screenplay:* Filippo Sanjust, Adolphe d'Ennery; *Photography:* Raffaele Masciocchi (Technicolor, aspect ratio 2.35:1); *Music:* Franco Mannino; *Production Design/Set Decoration:* Antonio Martini; *Special Effects:* Eros Bacciucchi; running time: 94 minutes (Italy); 84 minutes (U.S.); released October 30, 1962 (Italy), 1963 (U.S.).

Cast: Brett Halsey *(Don Carlos de Bazan)*; Béatrice Altariba *(Isabella)*; Giulio Bosetti *(Duke of Saavedra)*; Gabriele Antonini *(Phillip II)*; Gabriele Tinti *(Corvo)*; Mario Scaccia *(The Cardinal)*; Alberto Sorrentino *(Sancho)*; Jacopo Tecchi *(Mayor)*; Anita Todesco *(Caterina)*; Gary Conklin; Antonio Corevi *(Conspirator)*; John Karlsen *(Old Actor)*; Jacques Stany *(Officer at Don Carlos' Execution)*.

Comments: The basic material for this swashbuckler was filmed previously (by the same director, Riccardo Freda) as *Don Cesare di Bazan* in 1942 *(qv)*. This remake was co-produced by Italy's Adelphia, and the French companies Comptoir Français du Film Production (CFFP) and Francisco Film.

79 A.D. (Anno 79: La distruzione di Ercolano) (American-International Television, 1962)

Credits: *Director:* Gianfranco Parolini; *Producer:* Robert de Nesle; *Screenplay:* Gianfranco Parolini, Giovanni Simonelli (from their story, dialogue by Helmut Haran); *Photography:* Francesco Izzarelli (color, Totalscope, aspect ratio 2.35:1); *Film Editor:* Edmond Lozzi; *Music:* Carlo Franci; *Production Design:* Niko Matul, Giuseppe Ranieri; *Costume Design:* Vittorio Rossi; *Makeup:* Galileo Mandini; *Assistant Makeup Artist:* Pierantonio Mecacci; *Production Managers:* Mario Damiani, Mario Maggi; *General Production Manager:* Luciano Volpato; *Assistant Directors:* Sergio Bazzini, Ignazio Dolce; *Sound Engineer:* Gianetto Nardi; *Sound Mixer:* M. Cossu; *Special Effects:* Roberto Morelli; *Camera Operators:* Bruno Mattei, T. Zarkov; *Assistant Camera Operator:* A. Mangianello; *Key Grip:* Alfonso Merola; *Assistant Costume Designer:* R. Amorotti; *Master of Arms:* Giuseppe Mattei; *Script Supervisor:* Slava Gartner; running time: 88 minutes (Italy), 113 minutes (U.S.); released December 23, 1962 (Italy).

Cast: Susan Paget *(Livia)*; Brad Harris *(Marcus Tiberius)*; Mara Lane *(Diomira)*; Jacques Berthier *(Tercius)*; Jany Clair *(Myrta)*; Carlo Tamberlani *(Furius)*; Philippe Hersent *(Titus Flavius)*; Ivy Holzer [billed as "Ivy Stewart"] *(Claudia)*; Isarco Ravaioli *(Licinius)*; Djordje Nenadovic [billed as "George Nenadovic"] *(Samson)*; Vladimir Leib [billed as "Vladimiro Leib"] *(Lepidus)*; Niksa Stefanini [billed as "Nicola Stefanini"] *(Valerius)*; Giuseppe Mattei [billed as "Pino Mattei] *(Drago)*; Arnaldo Martelli [billed as "Ray Martino"] *(Saurus)*; Milo Kaciceva [billed as "Mila Kacic"] *(Armodia)*; Vladimir Bacic [billed as "Vladimiro Bacic"] *(Migiurtis)*; Giuseppe Marotti; Maks Furijan [billed as "Max Furjan"] *(Menezio)*; Ignazio Dolce; Mila Kacic *(Armodia)*; Mario Matiradonna; Janez Vrhovec *(Ciparisso)*.

Comments: In 79 AD, the city of Herculaneum is destroyed by the eruption of Mt. Vesuvius. Produced by Italy's Cinematografica Associati (CI. AS.) and France's Comptoir Français du Film Production (CFFP).

The Shadow of Zorro (L'ombra di Zorro) (Allied Artists Television, 1962)

Credits: *Director:* Joaquin Luis Romero Marchent; *Producer:* Alberto Grimaldi; *Executive Producer:* Attilio Tosato; *Screenplay:* José Mallorqui, Joaquin Romero Hernández (from their story); *Photography:* Enrico Betti Berutto [Italian version], Rafael Pacheco (Eastmancolor, Dyaliscope, aspect ratio 2.35:1); *Film Editor:* Mercedes Alonso; *Music:* Francesco De Masi (Italian version), Manuel Parada; *Production Design:* Luciano Vincenti; *Set Decoration:* José Luis Galicia. Jaime Pérez Cubero; *Makeup:* Antonio Florido, Cesare Pacelli; *Assistant Makeup Artist:* Isabel; *Hair Stylist:* Antonia López, *Production Supervisor:* Pietro Nofri; *Production Managers:* Norberto Soliño, Attilio Tosato; *Unit Production Managers:* Manuel Castedo, Carlo Caiano; *1st Assistant Director:* Serafin Garcia; *Assistant Directors:* Giuseppe Passalacqua (Italian version), Rafael Romero Marchent; *Sound:* Pietro Ortolani; *Microphone Boom Operator:* Raul Montesanti; *Camera Operators:* Mario Sensi (Italian version), Jorge Herrero; *Assistant Camera Operators:* Mario Caiano (Italian version); Diego Úbeda; *Still Photographer:* Miguel Guzmán; *Wardrobe:* Paquita Pons; *Assistant Film Editor:* María Dolores Laguna; *Final Colorist:* Andrea Gargano; *Production Assistants:* Juan Campos, Jesús Rancaño; *Secretary to the Producer:* Franco Sernia; *Script Girl:* Lucía Martin; running time: 87 minutes (Italy); released December 22, 1962 (Italy).

Cast: Frank Latimore *(Don José de la Torre/Zorro)*; María Luz Gallicia *(María)*; Paul Piaget *(Dan)*; Claudio Undari [billed as "Robert Hundar"] *(Billy)*; José Marco Davó *(Governor)*; Jesús Tordesillas *(Don Cesar dela Torre)*; Mario Feliciani [billed as "Marco Feliciani"] *(McDonald)*; María Silva *(Irene)*; José Marco *(Olo)*; Diana Lorys *(Mestiza)*; Raf Baldassarre *(Chinto)*; Marco Tulli *(Tom Gray)*; Juan Antonio Arévalo *(Fernando)*; Carlos Romero Marchent *(Chema)*; Sira Origo *(Governor's Wife)*; Xan das Bolas *(Banker)*; Raffaella Carrà *(Camela)*; Miguel Merino *(Raimundo)*; Simón Arriaga; Elena Montoya *(Child)*; Gonzalo de Esquiroz; Alberto Cubi; Pedro Rodriguez de Quevedo *(Banker)*; Rufino Inglés *(Coachman)*; Francisco Coamoiras *(Sordomudo)*; Gianni Santuccio *(Minister)*; Guillermo Méndez *(Fencing Master)*; Lorenzo Robledo *(Captain)*; Howard Vernon *(General)*.

Comments: Another version of Zorro. Coproduced by Italy's Explorer Film '58 and Produzioni Europee Associati (PEA), and France's

Lesoeur, and Spain's Copercines Cooperativa Cinemátográfica.

Siege of Syracuse (L'assedio di Siracusa) (Paramount, 1960)

Credits: Director: Pietro Francisci; *Producer:* Enzo Merolle; *Screenplay:* Pietro Francisci, Giorgio Graziosi, Ennio De Concini (from a story by Pietro Francisci, Giorgio Graziosi); *Photography:* Carlo Carlini (Eastmancolor, Dyaliscope, aspect ratio 2.35:1); *Film Editor:* Nino Baragli; *Music:* Angelo Francesco Lavagnino; *Production Design:* Ottavio Scotti; *Set Decoration:* Ugo Pericoli; *Costume Design:* Gaia Romanini; *Makeup:* Anacieto Giustini; *Hair Stylist:* Mirella Ginnoto; *Production Supervisor:* Sergio Merolle; *General Production Manager:* Rino Merolle; *Production Managers:* Armando Grottini, Giovanni Laterza; *Assistant Director:* Pietro Nuccorini; *Art Dept. Manager:* Italo Tomassi; *Assistant Set Decorator:* Franco Loquenzi; *Sound:* Bruno Moreal, Amelio Verona (Western Electric sound system); *Special Effects:* Joseph Nathanson; *Camera Operator:* Luigi Filippo Carta; *Assistant Camera Operators:* Franco Di Giacomo, Ruggero Radicchi; *Laboratory:* Stacofilm S. p. a., Rome, Italy; *Assistant Film Editor:* A. Maria Girosi; *Production Secretaries:* Spartaco Conversi, Remo De Angelis; running time: 118 minutes (Italy), 97 minutes (U.S.); released March 17, 1960 (Italy), January 31, 1962 (U.S.); video availability: Sinister Cinema.

Cast: Rossano Brazzi *(Archimedes);* Tina Louise *(Diana/Artemide/Lucrezia);* Sylva Koscina *(Clio);* Enrico Maria Salerno *(Gorgia);* Gino Cervi *(Gerone);* Alberto Farnese *(Marcello);* Luciano Marin *(Marco);* Alfredo Varelli *(Kriton);* Walter Grant *(Tiresias);* Mara Lombardo *(Dancer);* Corinne Capri *(Girl in Troupe);* Enzo Cerusico *(Young Student);* Cesare Fantoni *(Archimede's Father);* Veriano Ginesi *(Man at Tavern);* Enrico Olivieri *(Young Apprentice);* Erminio Spalla *(Innkeeper).*

Comments: At the Siege of Syracuse during the Second Punic Wars (214 BC–212 BC), elements of sci-fi enter the plot as the brilliant Archimedes invents a reflective sun disk to defeat the Romans. Produced by Italy's Glomer Film and Galatea Film with France's Societé Cinématografica Lyre.

Sign of the Gladiator (Nel segno di Roma) (American-International, 1959)

Credits: Director: Guido Brignone; *Producer:* Enzo Merolle; *Screenplay:* Francesco Tellung, Francesco De Feo, Sergio Leone, Giuseppe Mangione, Guido Brignone; *Photography:* Luciano Trasatti (Eastmancolor, Dyaliscope, aspect ratio 2.35:1); *Film Editor:* Nino Baragli; *Music:* Angelo Francesco Lavagninio; *Art Direction:* Ottavio Scotti; *Set Decoration:* Ugo Pericoli; *Costume Design:* Vittorio Nino Novarese; *Makeup:* Giuliano Laurenti; *Hair Stylist:* Ada Palombi; *Production Supervisors:* Fernando Cinquini, Sergio Merolle; *Production Manager:* Rino Merolle; *Assistant Directors:* Michele Lupo, Sergio Leone; *2nd Unit Directors:* Riccardo Freda, Michelangelo Antonioni, Vittorio Musy Glori; *Sound:* Mario Amari, Adriano Taloni (Westrex sound system); *Special Effects:* Joseph Nathanson; *Camera Operator:* Franco Villa; *Costumes:* Enzo Bulgarelli; *Editorial Secretary:* Gigliola Rosmino; *General Supervisor:* Guido Brignone; *Choreographer:* Claude Marchand; *Production Assistants:* Sante Chimirri, Tonino Garzarelli; running time: 98 minutes (Italy); released March 5, 1959 (Italy), September 23, 1959 (U.S.).

Cast: Anita Ekberg *(Zenobia, Queen of Palmira);* Georges Marchal *(Marcus Valerius, Roman Consul);* Folco Lulli *(Zemanzius, Zenobia's Prime Minister);* Chelo Alonso *(Erica, Zemanzius' Favorite Dancer);* Gino Cervi *(Aurelianus, Emperor of Rome);* Jacques Sernas *(Julianus, Roman Centurion);* Lorella De Luca *(Bathsheba, the Vestal Virgin);* Alberto Farnese *(Marcello);* Paul Muller *(Slavemaster);* Mimmo Palmara *(Lator);* Alfredo Varelli *(Vithos);* Sergio Sauro *(Flavio);* Arturo Bragaglia, Remo De Angelis; *Voice Dubbing Actors:* Gianfranco Bellini *(for Sergio Sauro);* Giorgio Capecchi *(for Folco Lulli);* Emilio Cigoli *(for Georges Marchal);* Dhia Cristiani *(for Chelo Alonso);* Maria Pia Di Meo *(for Lorella De Luca);* Nando Gazzolo *(for Alberto Farnese);* Pino Locchi *(for Jacques Sernas);* Glauco Onorato *(for Mimmo Palmara);* Giuseppe Rinaldi *(for Alfredo Varelli);* Lidia Simoneschi *(for Anita Ekberg);* Renato Turi *(for Arturo Dominici).*

Comments: Roman troops under the command of Marcus Valerius are defeated by Zenobia, Queen of Palmira. This film was produced by Italy's Glomer Film and Lux Film, with France's Societé Cinématographique, Germany's Tele Film GmbH, and Yugoslavia's Dubrava Film. Shot at Globus-Dubrava Film Studio in Croatia.

Sinbad and the Caliph of Baghdad (Simbad e il califfo di Bagdad) (Buton Film Roas Produzioni, 1973)

Credits: Director/Screenplay/Film Editor: Pietro Francisci; *Producer:* Angelo Faccenna; *Executive Producer:* Vittorio Russo; *Photography:* Gino Santini (color); *Supervising Film Editor:* Otello Colangeli; *Music:* Carlo Jachino; *Costume Design:* Maria Luisa Panaro; *Production Manager:* Mario Pellegrino; running time: 101 minutes (Italy); released June 23, 1973.

Cast: Robert Malcolm *(Sinbad)*; Sonia Wilson *(Sherazade)*; Luigi Bonos *(Finùz)*; Leo Valeriano *(Bamàn)*; Spartaco Conversi; Arturo Dominici *(Visir)*; Franco Fantasia; Eugene Walter *(Zenebi)*; Paul Oxon; Maria Luigia Biscardi; Gianfranco Clerici billed as "Mac Davis"); Eva Maria Gabriel (billed as "Eva Maria Grubmiller"); Carla Mancini; Alessandro Perrella.

Comments: Seafaring adventurer Sinbad versus a power-mad Caliph. Produced by the Italian companies Buton Film and Roas Produzioni. Filmed at Elios Film Studios in Rome with some location work in Cairo, Egypt.

Sins of Rome (Spartaco) (RKO, 1953)

Credits: Director: Riccardo Freda (billed as "Robert Hampton"); *Producer:* Carlo Caiano; *Screenplay:* Maria Bory, Jean Ferry, Gino Visentini (from a story by Maria Bory); *Photography:* Gábor Pogány (black & white, aspect ratio 1.37:1); *Film Editor:* Mario Serandrei; *Music:* Renzo Rosselini; *Art Direction:* Franco Lolli; *Costume Design:* Dina Di Bari; *Production Manager:* Roberto Fabbri; *Camera Operator:* Guglielmo Garroni; running time: 94 minutes (Italy), 75 minutes (U.S.); released January 28, 1953 (Italy), June 1954 (U.S.); video availability: Something Weird Video.

Cast: Massimo Girotti *(Spartacus)*; Ludmilla Tchérina *(Amitys)*; Yves Vincent *(Ocnormas, Spartacus' Lieutenant)*; Gianna Maria Canale *(Sabina Crassus)*; Carlo Ninchi *(Marcus Licinius Crassus)*; Vittorio Sanipoli *(Marcus Virilius Rufus)*; Carlo Giustini *(Artorige)*; Umberto Silvestri *(Lentulus)*; Teresa Franchini *(Spartacus' Mother)*; Renato Baldini *(Gladiator)*; Nerio Bernardi; Cesare Bettarini; Darix Togni *(Gladiator)*.

Comments: In this version of the slave revolt led by Spartacus (which precedes the Stanley Kubrick *Spartacus* by seven years), Spartacus is a young Roman officer who is condemned to slavery because he strikes a superior. Co-produced by the Italian copanies Associati Produttori Indepenti Film (API) and Consorzio Spartacus, with the French company Rialto Film, an Es Establissments Sinag

The Slave (Il figlio di Spartacus) (MGM, 1962)

Credits: Director: Sergio Corbucci; *Producer:* Franco Palaggi; *Screenplay:* Adriano Bolzoni, Giovanni Grimaldi, Bruno Corbucci (from a story by Adriano Bolzoni); *Photography:* Enzo Barboni (Metrocolor, CinemaScope, aspect ratio 2.35:1); *Film Editor:* Ruggero Mastroianni; *Music:* Piero Piccioni; *Production Design:* Ottavio Scotti; *Set Decoration:* Riccardo Domenici; *Costume Design:* Mario Giorsi; *Makeup:* Franco Di Girolamo, Pierantonio Mecacci; *Hair Stylist:* Mara Rochetti; *Sound: Westrex sound system*; *Production Supervisor:* Sergio Borelli; *Production Manager:* Franco Palaggi; *Assistant Directors:* Mimmola Girosi, Franco Rossellini; *2nd Unit Director:* Franco Giraldi; *Camera Operator:* Stelvio Massi; *Orchestra Conductor:* Luigi Urbini; *Fencing Master:* Benito Stefanelli; *Laboratory:* Technostampa, Rome, Italy; running time: 100 minutes (Italy); released August 24, 1962 (Italy), May 29, 1963 (U.S.).

Cast: Steve Reeves *(Randus, Spartacus' Son)*; Jacques Sernas *(Vetius, Spartacus' Friend)*; Gianna Maria Canale *(Claudia, Crassus' Wife)*; Claudio Gora *(Crassus, Governor of Egypt)*; Ombretta Colli *(Saide, Egyptian Slavegirl)*; Roland Bartrop *(Lumonius, Randus' Friend)*; Franco Balducci *(Verus, Ship's Commander)*; Enzo Fiermonte

Steve Reeves in *The Slave*.

(*Gulbar, Slave Wrestling Randus*); Renato Baldini (*Verulus, Caesar's Adjutant*); Gloria Parri (*Egyptian Slave Woman*); Giovanni Cianfriglia (*Soldier Whipping Saide*); Benito Stefanelli (*Blonde Slave*); Attillio Severini (*Nubian*); Ahmed Ramzy (*Murdok, Lybian Chief*); Hassan Ahmed (*Lybian Prince*); Ivo Garrani (*Julius Caesar*).

Comments: Randus discovers that he is the son of Spartacus. The original Italian title translates to *The Son of Spartacus*, but this was changed to the more generic *The Slave* by MGM to avoid conflict with Stanley Kubrick's 1960 *Spartacus*. This was the final sword-and-sandal effort for Steve Reeves; after this he made two Sandokan films, a spaghetti western, and then retired from the screen. Produced by Italy's Titanus in association with Arta Cinematografica S.P.A. and Les Film Jacques Willemetz. Portions were filmed at the Great Pyramids and the Sphinx on the Gaza Plateau in Egypt.

Slave Girls of Sheba (*Le verdi bandiere di Allah*) (American-International Television, 1963)

Credits: *Directors:* Giacomo Gentilomo, Guido Zurli; *Screenplay:* Adriano Bolzoni, Umberto Lenzi, Sergio Leone, Amedeo Marrosu, Guido Zurli (from a story by Umberto Lenzi); *Photography:* Luciano Trasatti, Franco Villa (Eastmancolor [Italian prints], Pathecolor [U.S. prints], Totalscope [Italian prints], Colorscope [U.S. prints], aspect ratio 2.35:1); *Film Editor:* Otello Colangeli; *Production Design:* Oscar D'Amico; running time: 100 minutes (Italy); released May 24, 1963 (Italy); video availability: Something Weird Video.

Cast: José Suárez (*Omar*); Linda Cristal (*Olivia*); Cristina Gaioni (*Ursula*); Mimmo Palmara (*Hibrahim*); Walter Barnes; Hélène Chanel (*Harem Girl*); Vittorio Sanipoli (*Sheik Selim*); José Jaspe (*Friar*); Renato Montalbano.

Comments: A costume adventure co-produced by Italy's Italia Produzione and Yugoslavia's Dubrava Film.

Slave of Rome (*La schiava di Roma*) (Medallion Pictures, 1961)

Credits: *Directors:* Sergio Grieco, Franco Prosperi; *Producer:* Marci Vicario; *Screenplay:* Franco Prosperi, Silvano Reina, Marco Vicario; *Photography:* Vincenzo Seratrice (Eastmancolor, Totalscope, aspect ratio 2.35:1); *Film Editor:* Enzo Alfonzi; *Music:* Armando Trovajoli; *Production Design:* Franco Lolli; *Costume Design:* Mario Giorsi; *Art Dept. Manager:* Italo Tomassi; *1st Assistant Director:* Mario Caiano; *2nd Assistant Director:* Stipe Delic; *3rd Assistant Director:* Franco Prosperi; running time: 98 minutes (Italy), 85 minutes (U.S.); released February 3, 1961 (Italy); video availability: Something Weird Video.

Cast: Rossana Podestà (*Antea*); Guy Madison (*Marcus Valerius*); Mario Petri (*Lysircos*); Giacomo Rossi Stuart (*Claudius*); Raf Baldassarre (*Lucio*); Ignazio Leone; Ferdinando Poggi (billed as "Nando Poggi"); Mirko Boman (billed as "Mirko Roman"); Goffredo Unger (billed as "Fredy Hunger); Niksa Stefanini (billed as "Nicola Stefanini"); Nazzareno Zamperla; Pasquale Basile; Antonio Basile; Angelo Bastianoni; Giancarlo Bastianoni; Stipe Delic (billed as "Stefano Delic"); Giuseppe Batisti; Rinaldo Zamperla; Milo Rucavina; Simone Ilic; Djordje Nenadovic (billed as "Giorgio Nenadovic").

Comments: Marcus Valerius is sent by Rome

to punish the Gauls, who have violated their treaty with the empire. Produced by Italy's Atlantica Cinematografica Produzione Films.

Slave Queen of Babylon (lo Semiramide) (American-International Television, 1963)

Credits: Director: Primo Zeglio; *Producer:* Aldo Pomilia; *Screenplay:* Fede Arnaud, Alberto Liberati, Primo Zeglio (from a story by Luigi De Santis, Sergio Spina); *Photography:* Alvaro Mancori (Eastmancolor, CinemaScope, aspect ratio 2.35:1); *Film Editor:* Alberto Gallitti; *Music:* Carlo Savina; *Production Design:* Maria Baroni; *Makeup:* Eligio Trani; *Hair Stylist:* Marisa Fraticelli; *Production Supervisor:* Alessandro Tasca; *Production Manager:* Piero Lazzari; *Assistant Director:* Giorgio Gentili; *Sound:* Umberto Picistrelli; *Special Effects:* Giancarlo Urbisaglia; *Master of Arms:* Alfio Caltabiano; *Camera Operator:* Sandro Mancori; *Still Photographer:* Angelo Pennoni; *Costumes:* Antonella Cappuccio; *Orchestra Conductor:* Carlo Savina; *Production Secretary:* Enrico Albani; *Script Supervisor:* Bona Magrini; running time: 101 minutes (U.S.); released March 22, 1963 (Italy).

Cast: Yvonne Furneaux *(Semiramide)*; John Ericson *(Kir)*; Renzo Ricci *(Minurte)*; Gianni Rizzo *(Ghelas)*; Germano Longo *(Omnos)*; John Bartha [billed as "Gian Barta"] *(Althar)*; Nino Di Napoli *(Adath, the King's Son)*; Valérie Camille *(Ballerina)*; Mario Laurentino *(Oerte)*; Piero Pastore *(Shabli)*; Mario Passante *(Naval Constructor)*; Ugo Sasso *(Omnos' Officer)*; Annamaria Ubaldi *(Maid)*; Harold Bradley *(Semiramide's Black Slave)*; Antonio Corevi *(Zagros)*; Lucio De Santis *(Marduk)*; Charles Fawcett *(High Priest)*; Massimo Giuliani *(Adarte)*; Umberto Silvestri *(Wrestler)*; José Torres *(Pharaoh's Messenger)*; Aldo Vasco *(Wrestler)*; Fortunato Arena *(Captain of the Guard)*; Calisto Calisti *(Slave Attendant)*; Alfio Caltabiano *(Zagos)*; Jeff Cameron *(Desenio Darak)*; Amerigo Santarelli *(Slave)*.

Comments: In 810 BC the beautiful Semiramide overthrows the King produced by the Minurte in the Assyrian capital of Ninevah, and eventually builds the city known as Babylon. Produced by the Italian companies Apo Film and Globe Film International.

Sodom and Gomorrah (Sodoma e Gomora) (Twentieth Century–Fox, 1962)

Credits: Director: Robert Aldrich; *Producers:* Joseph E. Levine, Goffredo Lombardo; *Executive Producer:* Maurizio Lodi-Fè; *Screenplay:* Hugo Butler, Giorgio Prosperi, Ernesto Gastaldi (based on a novel by Richard Wormser); *Photography:* Silvano Ippoliti, Cyril J. Knowles, Mario Montuori, Alfio Contini (Technicolor, aspect ratio 1.85:1); *Film Editors:* Peter Tanner, Mario Serandrei; *Music:* Miklós Rózsa; *Production Design:* Ken Adam; *Set Decoration:* Gino Brosio, Emilio D'Andria; *Costume Design:* Giancarlo Bartolini Salimbeni; *Makeup:* Euclide Santoli, *Hair Stylist:* Amalia Paoletti; *Production Managers:* Giorgio Adriani, Mario Del Papa, Giorgio Zambon; *1st Assistant Director:* Gus Agosti; *2nd Unit Directors:* Oscar Rudolph, Sergio Leone; *2nd Unit Assistant Director:* Giorgio Gentili; *Assistant Directors:* Franco Cirino, Benchekroun Larbi; *Assistant Production Designer:* Giorgio Giovannini; *Scene Painter:* Italo Tomassi; *Sound:* Kurt Doubrowsky (Westrex sound system); *Sound Effects Editor:* Leslie Hodgson; *Microphone Boom Operator:* Primiano Muratori; *Special Effects:* Serse Urbisaglia, Wally Veevers, Lee Zavitz, Leonardo Bianchi, Aldo De Robertis, Cyril J. Knowles; *Stunts:* Nazzareno Zamperla; *Camera Operators:* Leonardo Bedini, Aldo De Robertis; *Still Photographers:* Lorenzo Papi, G.B. Poletto; *Assistant Costume Designer:* Giuliana Ghidini; *Music Orchestrator:* Eugene Zador; *Orchestra Conductor:* Carlo Savina; *Dialogue Director:* Michael Audley; *Choreography:* Archie Savage; *Prologue and Main Title Design:* Maurice Binder; running time: 154 minutes; released October 4, 1962 (Italy), January 23, 1963 (U.S.); video availability: Twentieth Century–Fox Home Video.

Cast: Stewart Granger *(Lot)*; Pier Angeli *(Ildith)*; Stanley Baker *(Astaroth)*; Rossana Podestà *(Shuah)*; Rik Battaglia *(Melchior)*; Giacomo Rossi Stuart *(Ishmael)*; Scilla Gabel *(Tamar)*; Anthony Steffen [billed as "Antonio De Teffe"] *(The Captain)*; Enzo Fiermonte *(Eber)*; Gabriele Tinti *(Lieutenant)*; Daniele Vargas *(Segur)*; Claudia Mori *(Maleb)*; Feodor

Chaliapin, Jr. *(Alabias)*; Mitsuko Takara *(Orphea)*; Massimo Pietrobon *(Isaac)*; Mimmo Palmara *(Arno)*; Liana Del Balzo *(Rich Hebrew Woman)*; Francesco Tensi *(1st Old Man)*; Andrea Tagliabue *(Eber's Son)*; Alice Kessler *(Dancer)*; Ellen Kessler *(Dancer)*; Emillio Messina; Roberto Messina; Aldo Silvani *(Nakur)*; Anouk Aimée *(The Queen)*; Vittorio Artesi *(Eber's Other Son)*; Salvatore Borghese; Pietro Ceccarelli *(Officer in Sodom)*; Calogero Chiarenza; Tom Felleghy; Giovanni Galletti *(Malik)*; Renato Giuia; Valentino Macchi; Primo Moroni *(2nd Old Man)*; Mimmo Poli *Queen's Cupbearer)*; Renato Terra; Maria Pia Di Meo *(Dubbed Voice for Pier Angeli)*; Rosetta Calavetta *(Dubbed Voice for Anouk Aimée)*.

Comments: The biblical story of Lot, as told by director Robert Aldrich, the auteur of *Kiss Me Deadly*, and a surprising choice to helm a religious epic. Filmed on an 11-month schedule, the original budget for this production was $2,000,000, but the final cost was $5,000,000. According to Aldrich, he fired 2nd unit director Sergio Leone during production because Leone was giving preferential treatment to the Italian cast and crew members. Co-produced by Italy's Titanus Studios and the French companies Pathé Consortium Cinéma and Société Générale de Cinématographie (S.G.C.), and filmed on location in the twin cities of Aït Benhaddou in Morocco, and, for the flood and battle scenes, in Marrakech, Morocco.

The Son of Captain Blood *(El hijo del capitán Blood)* (Paramount, 1964)

Credits: Director: Tulio Demicheli; *Producers:* Harry Joe Brown, Benito Perojo; *Screenplay:* Casey Robinson, Arturo Rigel, [and, for Italian version] Mario Caiano (based on a story by Casey Robinson and characters from the novel by Rafael Sabatini); *Photography:* Antonio L. Bellesteros, Alejandro Ulloa (Eastmancolor, Dyaliscope, aspect ratio 2.35:1); *Film Editors:* Renato Cinquini, Antonio Ramírez de Loaysa; *Music:* Gregorio Garcia Segura; *Production Design:* Piero Filippone; *Art Direction:* Enrique Alarcón; *Set Decoration:* Enrique Alarcón, Luis Pérez Espinosa; *Costume Design:* Humberto Cornejo; *Production Manager:* Miguel Tudela; *Assistant Production Manager:* Tadeo Villalba; *2nd Unit Director:* Yakima Canutt; *Assistant Directors:* Mara Di Paolo, Augusto Fenollar; *Camera Operator:* Clemente Manzano; *Composers (for song "Quindici uomini"):* Angelo Francesco Lavagnino, Simoni; *Orchestra/Choir Conductor:* Riccardo Vantellini; *Laboratory:* Technicolor; running time: 88 minutes (U.S.); released March 1964 (U.S.).

Cast: Sean Flynn *(Robert Blood)*; Alessandra Panaro *(Abigail "Abby" McBride)*; Ann Todd *(Arabella Blood)*; José Nieto *(Capt. De Malagon)*; Roberto Camardiel *(Oliver Orguelthorpe)*; Fernando Sancho *(Timothy Thomas)*; Luisa de Córdoba *(Mme. Prue)*; Carlos Casaravilla *(Capt. Murdock)*; John Kitzmiller *(Moses)*; Ángeles Macua *(Prostitute)*; José María Caffarel *(Gov. Dawson)*; Carmen Esbri; Barta Barri *(Kirby)*; Xan das Bolas *(Matt)*; Raf Baldassarre *(Bruno)*; Simonetta Simeoni; Luz Romero; Rafael Bardem; Ettore Ribotta; Mario Matiradonna; Ángel Ortiz; Julio Infiesta; Francisco Bernal; Antonio Casas *(Capt. of the Negrier)*; Mery Leyva; María Sánchez Aroca; Carmen Lozano; Juan Cortés; Angel Menéndez; José González Talavera; Dolores Tórres; Harold de Weeks; Enrique Macedo; Antonio Braña; Sixto Lecón; Álvaro de Luna *(Pirate)*; Arnaldo Martelli.

Comments: The son of Captain Blood, played by, literally, the son of "Captain Blood." Errol Flynn had filmed *Captain Blood* for Warner Bros. in 1935 under the direction of Michael Curtiz, and Flynn's son Sean is cast here as the pirate's offspring. Although physically fit for the role, Sean Flynn exhibits considerably less charisma than his father, and *The Son of Captain Blood* is certainly less of a film than *Captain Blood*, although it is still an entertaining pirate adventure. Produced by Italy's Compagnia Cinematografica Mondiale (CCM) and Spain's Producciones Benito Perojo, in association with Harry Joe Brown Productions. Shot on location in Spain. In the United States, Paramount Pictures, incredibly, distributed *The Son of Captain Blood* on a double bill with the Jerry Lewis comedy *The Patsy*!

Son of Cleopatra *(Il figlio di Cleopatra)* (United Artists, 1964)

Credits: *Director:* Ferdinando Baldi; *Producers:* Anacieto Fontini, Francesco Tellung; *Executive Producer:* Nino Milano; *Screenplay:* Ferdinando Baldi, Franco Airaldi, Anacleto Fontini (from a story by Anacleto Fontini); *Photography:* Bitto Albertini (Technicolor, Techniscope, aspect ratio 2.35:1); *Film Editor:* Otello Colangeli; *Music:* Carlo Rustichelli; *Production Design:* Oscar D'Amico; *Costume Design:* Adriana Spadaro; *(Makeup:* Duilio Scarozza; *Hair Stylist:* Adriana Cassini; *Production Manager:* Nino Milano; *Assistant Director:* Mauro Scaripanti; *Sound:* Mario Del Pezzo; *Sound Mixers:* Sandro Occhetti, Fausto Achilli; *Camera Operator:* Carlo Fiore; *Assistant Camera Operators:* Maurizio Salvatori, Sergio Martinelli; *Still Photographer:* Mario Sabatelli; *Assistant Film Editor:* Aurelio Pennacchia; *Orchestra Conductor:* Franco Ferrara; running time: 128 minutes (Italy); released December 31, 1964 (Italy); video availability: Retromedia.

Cast: Mark Damon *(El Kebir)*; Scilla Gabel *(Livia)*; Arnoldo Foà *(Varrone)*; Livio Lorenzon *(Petronio)*; Samira Ahmed *(Meroe)*; Alberto Lupo *(Octavian)*; Shukry Sarhan *(Akro)*; Leila Fawzi *(Hermia)*; Paolo Gozlino *(Furio)*; Yehia Chahine *(Safar)*; Hassan Yousef *(Uro)*; Corrado Annicelli *(Longino)*; Franco Fantasia *(Vetero)*; Alberto Cevenini; Mahmoud Farag *(Tarok)*; Abdel Khalek Saleh *(Priest)*; Ivan Basta; William Conroy *(Roman Soldier)*; Attilio Severini *(Messenger)*.

Comments: The heroic El Kebir learns that he is the son of Cleopatra and rebels against the evil governor Petronius. Co-produced by the Italian companies Seven Film, Tiki Film, and the Egyptian companies Egyptian General Company for International Film Production (PARC) and Copro Film.

The Son of D'Artagnan *(Il figlio d'Artagnan)* (Augustus Film/Cocinor, 1950)

Credits: *Director:* Riccardo Freda; *Producers:* Raffaele Colamonici, Umberto Montesi; *Screenplay:* Riccardo Freda [billed as "Dick Jordan"] (based on his story); *Photography:* Sergio Pesce (black-and-white, aspect ratio 1.37:1); *Film Editor:* Renato Cinquini; *Music:* Carlo Jachino; *Production Design/Set Decoration:* Alberto Boccianti; *Costume Design:* Maria De Matteis; *Production Manager:* Raffaele Colamonici; *Sound Engineer:* Umberto Picistrelli; *Assistant Director:* Valentino Trevisaneto (billed as "Valentino Trevisanato"); running time: 86 minutes (Italy); released March 8, 1950 (Italy).

Cast: Carlo Ninchi *(Maresciallo D'Artagnan)*; Gianna Maria Canale *(Linda)*; Franca Marzi *(The Countess)*; Peter Trent *(Duke de Malvoisin)*; Paolo Stoppa *(Paolo)*; Piero Palermini *Raoul d'Artagnan)*; Enzo Fiermonte *(Visconte di Langlass)*; Nerio Bernardi; Ugo Sasso; Pietro Tordi; Luigi Garrone (billed as "Luigi A. Garrone"); Miranda Campa; Furio Meniconi; Mario Meniconi; Nello Meniconi.

Comments: Living a peaceful life as a novice in a monastery, the son of D'Artagnan decides to follow his father's heroic example. Produced by Italy's Augustus Film.

The Son of Hercules in the Land of Darkness *(Ercole l'invincibile)* (Embassy Pictures, 1964)

Credits: *Director/Producer:* Alvaro Mancori; *Screenplay:* Kirk Mayer, Pat Kein, Alvaro Mancori (from a story by Pat Kein, Kirk Mayer); *Photography:* Claude Haroy (Technicolor, Techniscope, aspect ratio 2.35:1); *Film Editor:* Frank Robertson; *Music:* Francesco De Masi; *Art Direction:* Huld Wreim; *Costume Design:* Anna Maria Chretien; *Makeup:* Jean-Pierre Harvey, Antony Chanel; *Wigs:* Gabriel Gotan; *Production Manager:* Lewis Mann; *Assistant Director:* Pat Klein; *Sound:* Floni Garden; *Special Effects:* Rasmo Bradley; *Still Photographer:* Angel Pat; *Laboratory:* Technicolor. *Master of Arms:* Enzo Musumeci Greco; *Weapons Consultant:* Franco Fantasia; running time: 85 minutes (Italy), 81 minutes (U.S.); released March 19, 1964; video availability: Mill Creek Entertainment.

Cast: Dan Vadis *(Hercules)*; Spela Rozin *(Telca)*; Carla Calò [billed as "Carol Brown"] *(Queen Ella)*; Ken Clark *(Kabol)*; Maria Fiore [billed as "Joan Simons"] *(Melissa)*; Jannette Barton *(Etel)*; Ugo Sasso [billed as "Hugo Arden"] *(King Tedaeo, Telca's Father)*; Howard Ross [billed as "Red Ross"] *(Captain of the Guard)*; Olga Solbelli [billed as "Sand Beauty"]

(The Prophetess); Alberto Cevenini [billed as "Kirk Bent"] *(Telca's Brother)*; Paul Mac Lee *(Guard)*; Kriss Moss *(Guard)*; Rosemarie Lindt *(Slave Girl)*; Michaela Ariston *(Slave Girl)*; Christine Mathius *(Slave Girl)*; Jannette Le Roy *(Slave Girl)*; Sara Laurier *(Slave Girl)*.

Comments: Hercules battles a dragon, a lion and a bear to rescue Princess Telca. Produced by the Italian companies Metheus Films and Alvaro Mancori Produzioni Cinematografica. For the version of the film distributed in America, the dragon footage was cut and replaced by the dragon scene from Steve Reeves' *Hercules*.

Son of Samson *(Maciste nella valle dei Re)* (Medallion Pictures, 1960)

Credits: *Director:* Carlo Campogalliani; *Producers:* Luigi Carpentieri, Ermanno Donati; *Executive Producer:* Piero Donati; *Producer of English-Dubbed Version:* Sam Schneider; *Screenplay:* Oreste Biancoli, Ennio De Concini (from their story); *Photography:* Riccardo Pallottini (Technicolor, Techniscope, aspect ratio 2.35:1); *Film Editor:* Roberto Cinquini; *Music:* Carlo Innocenzi; *Art Direction:* Oscar D'Amico; *Costume Design:* Maria De Matteis; *Assistant Makeup Artist:* Halid Redzebasic; *Hair Stylist:* Galileo Mandini; *Production Supervisors:* Giorgio Baldi, Livio Maffei; *Assistant Director:* Romolo Guerrieri; *2nd Unit Directors:* Mario Bava, Mate Relja; *Props:* Ennio Michettoni; *Sound:* Leopoldo Rosi; *Special Effects:* Piero Mecacci; *Camera Operator:* Stelvio Massi; *Costumes:* Tigano Lo Faro; *Assistant Costume Designer:* Marisa Crimi; *Assistant Editor:* Ornella Micheli; *Orchestra Conductor:* Carlo Franci; *Choreographer:* Tito LeDuc; *Stunts/Master of Arms:* Andrea Fantasia; *Continuity:* Benilde Vittori; *Laboratory:* S.P.E.S., Rome,

Chelo Alonso and Mark Forest in *Son of Samson*.

Chelo Alonso in *Son of Samson*.

Italy; running time: 94 minutes (Italy), 89 minutes (U.S.); released November 24, 1960 (Italy), June 2, 1962 (U.S.); video availability: Retromedia Entertainment.

Cast: Mark Forest *(Maciste)*; Chelo Alonso *(Queen Smedes)*; Vira Silenti *(Tekaet)*; Angelo Zanolli *(Pharaoh Kenamun)*; Federica Ranchi *(Nofret)*; Carlo Tamberlani *(Pharaoh Armiteo I)*; Nino Musco *(Senneka the Camel Driver)*; Zvonimir Rogoz *(Grand Visir)*; Ignazio Dolce *(Tradesman)*; Andrea Fantasia *(Blacksmith)*; Petar Dobric *(High Priest)*; Ada Ruggeri.

Comments: In Egypt, Maciste leads a revolt against the evil Queen Smedes. Produced by Italy's Panda Societa L'Industria Cinematografica, the French companies Films Borderie and Gallus Films and Yugoslavia's Dubrava Film. Shot at Interstudio in Rome and on location in the Valley of the Kings in Egypt.

Son of the Red Corsair *(Il figlio del corsaro rosso)* (Medallion Pictures, 1959)

Credits: *Director:* Primo Zeglio; *Producers:* Luigi Carpentieri, Ermanno Donati; *Screenplay:* Fede Arnaud, Alberto Liberati, Primo Zeglio (based on a novel by Emilio Salgari, English dialogue by Polly Stevens); *Photography:* Carlo Carlini (Eastmancolor, Totalscope, aspect ratio 2.35:1); *Film Editor:* Roberto Cinquini; *Music:* Roman Vlad; *Production Design:* Mario Chiari; *Set Decoration:* Alfredo Montori; *Costume Design:* Maria De Matteis; *Makeup:* Franco Freda; *Hair Stylist:* Anna Fabrizzi; *Production Supervisor:* Pasquale Misiano; *Production Manager:* Fede Arnaud; *Assistant Production Manager:* Giorgio Baldi; *Assistant Director:* Sergio Leone; *Props:* Pasquale Roscedo; *Sound Technicians:* Mario Amari, Leopoldo Rosi; *English Dialogue Recordist:* Don Brown; *Camera Operator:* Luigi

Filippo Carta; *Choreography:* Archie Savage; *Production Secretary:* Paolo Gargano; *Script Supervisor:* Elvira D'Amico; *Master of Arms:* Franco Fantasia; running time: 96 minutes (Italy); released June 25, 1959 (Italy), December 1963 (U.S.); video availability: Something Weird Video.

Cast: Lex Barker *(Enrico di Ventimiglia)*; Sylvia Lopez *(Carmen di Montélimar)*; Vira Silenti *(Neala di Ventimiglia)*; Luciano Marin *(Miguel di Montélimar)*; Antonio Crast *(Don Juan de Sasebo)*; Fanfulla [billed as "Luigi Visconti"] *(Marquese di Montélimar)*; Vicky Lagos *(Paquita)*; Roberto Paoletti *(Barrejo)*; Nietta Zocchi *(Isabella)*; Saro Urzi *(Mendoza)*; Elio Pandolfi *(Sergeant)*; Livio Lorenzon *(José, a Pirate)*; Diego Michelotti *(Juan Herrero)*; Franco Fantasia *(Dorado)*; Giorgio Costantini *(Van Hais)*; Annamaria Mustari; Tiziano Cortini *(Alfonso)*; Gianni Solaro *(Spanish Ship Captain)*; Luigi Bracale *(Martin)*; Arone De Carlo; Veriano Ginesi *(Pirate)*; Nello Pazzafini *(Spanish Soldier)*; Mimmo Poli *(Tavern Patron)*.

Comments: A Spanish Count, the son of the legendary pirate the Red Corsair, avenges his father's death. Produced by Italy's Athena Cinematografica and Panda Film, in association with the companies Carpentieri and Donati.

Sons of Thunder *(Arrivano i titani)* (United Artists, 1962)

Credits: Director: Duccio Tessari; *Producers:* Franco Cristaldi, Alexandre Minouchkine; *Screenplay:* Ennio De Concini, Duccio Tessari; *Photography:* Alfio Contini (Technicolor, aspect ratio 1.85:1); *Film Editor:* Maurizio Lucidi; *Music:* Carlo Rustichelli; *Production Design:* Ottavio Scotti; *Set Decoration:* Carlo Gentili; *Costume Design:* Vittorio Rossi; *Production Supervisor:* Rodolfo Martello; *Production Manager:* Giorgio Cristallini; *Assistant Directors:* Odoardo Fiory, Ariane Minouchkine, Fabio Rinaudo, Nino Zanchin; *Assistant Set Decorator:* Fabio Vergoz; *Sound:* Adriano Taloni; *Special Effects:* Joseph Nathanson; *Master of Arms:* Giorgio Ubaldi; *Camera Operator:* Maurizio Scanzani; *2nd Unit Camera Operator:* Renato Del Frate; *Assistant Camera Operator:* José María Moreno; *Orchestra Conductor:* Franco Ferrara; *Production Secretaries:* Nino Fruscella, Albino Morandini, Andrea Petricca; *Production Administrator:* Riccardo Caneva; *Laboratory:* Technicolor; *Script Supervisor:* Lucia Avanzi; *Producer of Soundtrack Album:* Luca di Silverio; running time: 120 minutes (Italy), 111 minutes (U.S.); released May 4, 1962 (Italy), September 18, 1963 (U.S.).

Cast: Pedro Armendáriz *(Cadmo)*; Giuliano Gemma *(Krios)*; Antonella Lualdi *(Ermione)*; Serge Nubret *(Rator)*; Jacqueline Sassard *(Antiope)*; Gérard Séty *(Aquiles)*; Tanya Lopert *(Licina)*; Ingrid Schoeller *(Emerate)*; Franco Lantieri *(Tarete)*; Monica Berger; Maria Luisa Rispoli *(Marzia)*; Isarco Ravaioli *(Centinela)*; Fernando Rey *(High Priest)*; Aldo Pedinotti *(A Titan)*; Fernando Sancho; Erika Spaggiari; Angelo Casadei *(Townsman)*.

Comments: Krios, one of the mythical Titans of Greek legend, arrives on Earth to overthrow the evil King Cadmo. Produced by Italy's Vides Cinematografica in association with the French companies Filmsonor and Les Films Arlane.

Spartacus and the Ten Gladiators *(Gli invincibli dieci gladiatori)* (Four Star Television, 1964)

Credits: Director: Nick Nostro; *Producer:* Armando Morandi; *Screenplay:* Sergio Sollima (billed as "Simon Sterling"), Nick Nostro, Alfonso Balcázar (from their story); *Photography:* Tino Santoni (Technicolor, Techniscope, aspect ratio 2.35:1); *Film Editor:* Bruno Mattei; *Music:* Carlo Savina; *Art Direction:* Giorgio Postiglione; *Set Decoration:* Carlo Gervasi; *Costume Design:* Massimo Bolongaro; *Makeup:* Piero Mecacci; *Hair Stylist:* Galileo Mandini; *Production Manager:* Rodolfo Frattaioli; *Assistant Director:* Stefano Rollo; *Sound Technician:* Fausto Ancillai; *Camera Operators:* Giovanni Bergamini, Alfredo Marganiello; *Assistant Camera Operators:* Riccardo Damiani, Gianni Maddaleni; *Chief Grip:* Domenico Mattei; *Gaffer:* Gino Vinciguerra; *Wardrobe Mistress:* Elisabetta Costantini; *Costumes:* Tigano Lo Faro; *Fencing Master:* Emilio Messina; *Orchestra Conductor:* Carlo Savina; *Final Colorist:* Andrea Gargano; *Production Assistant:* Leo Daviddi; *Script Supervisor:* Olga Pehar; running time: 88 minutes (Italy), 99 minutes (U.S.); released December 24, 1964 (Italy); video availability: Mill Creek Entertainment.

Cast: Dan Vadis *(Roccia, a Gladiator);* Helga Liné *(Daliah);* Ivano Staccioli (billed as "John Heston"); Alfredo Varelli [billed as "John Warren"] *(Spartacus);* Ursula Davis *(Lydia);* Giuliano Dell'Ovo [billed as "Julian Dower"] *(Bearded Gladiator);* Enzo Fiermonte [billed as "William Bird"] *(Rizio, a Gladiator);* Frank Oliveras; Vassili Karis (billed as "Marco Vassilli"); Salvatore Borghese *(Mute Gladiator);* Emilio Messina *(Lepto, a Gladiator);* Ugo Sasso [billed as "Gordon Steve"] *(Gladiator);* Jeff Cameron *(Gladiator);* Aldo Canti [billed as "Alan Lancaster"] *(Gladiator);* Gianni Rizzo *(Senator Sesto Vetulio);* Pietro Torrisi [billed as "Fred Hudson"] *(Gladiator);* Artemio Antonini *(Julius Varros);* Pietro Ceccarelli *(Matateo);* Roberto Messina *(Old Gladiator);* Riccardo Pizzuti *(Roman Senator);* Milton Reid *(Chimbro);* Fortunato Arena *(Prison Warden);* Bruno Arié *(Gladiator);* Armando Bottin *(Gladiator);* Vincenzo Maggio *Gladiator);* Cesare Martignon *(Senator);* Nello Pazzafini *(Soldier);* Aldo Pedinotti *(Senator);* Nando Sarlo *(Senator).*

Comments: Spartacus and ten loyal gladiators rebel against Rome. Produced by Italy's Cine Produzioni Associate, France's Les Films Copernic, and Spain's Balcázar Producciones Cinematograficas. Shot in Rome and on location in Barcelona, Spain.

The Story of Joseph and His Brethren (Giuseppe venduto dai fratelli) (Colorama Features, 1961)

Credits: Directors: Irving Rapper (English version), Luciano Ricci (Italian version); *Producers:* Luigi Carpentieri, Ermanno Donati; *Screenplay:* Guglielmo Santangelo, Oreste Biancoli, Ennio De Concini (from a story by Guglielmo Santangelo) [Italian version], Guy Elmes (English version); *Photography:* Riccardo Pallottini (Eastmancolor, Totalscope, aspect ratio 2.35:1); *Film Editor:* Mario Serandrei; *Music:* Mario Nascimbene; *Art Direction:* Oscar D'Amico; *Set Decoration:* Ennio Michettoni; *Costume Design:* Maria De Matteis; *Makeup:* Sergio Angeloni, Piero Mecacci; *Hair Stylist:* Galileo Mandini; *Production Manager:* Piero Donati; *Assistant Director:* Giovanni Fago; *Sculptor:* Gianni Gianese; *Sound:* Raffaele Del Monte, Mario Messina; *Microphone Boom Operator:* Primiano Muratori; *Matte Shots:* Joseph Nathanson; *Camera Operators:* Sandro Mancori, Stelvio Massi; *Electrician:* Stjepan Milic; *Wardrobe:* Marisa Crimi; Giuliano Papi; *Assistant Film Editor:* Ornella Micheli; *Orchestra Conductor:* Franco Ferrara; *Production Supervisor:* Luciano Ricci; *Production Assistants:* Giorgio Baldi, Livio Maffei; *Continuity:* Paola Salvadori, Pina Zani; *Historical Consultants:* Jacob W. Nathan, Guido Pala; *Dialogue Director (for English-Dubbed Version):* Richard Mcnamara; running time: 103 minutes (U.S.); released August 24, 1961 (Italy), November 30, 1962 (U.S.); video availability: VCI Home Video.

Cast: Geoffrey Horne *(Joseph);* Robert Morley *(Potiphar);* Belinda Lee *(Henet);* Vira Silenti *(Asenath);* Terence Hill [billed as "Mario Girotti"] *(Benjamin);* Carlo Giustini *(Reuben);* Finlay Currie *(Jacob);* Arturo Dominici *(Rekmira);* Robert Rietty *(Pharaoh);* Julian Brooks *(Chief Baker);* Mimo Billi *(Chief Butler);* Marietto *(Benjamin, as a Child);* Marco Guglielmi *(Judah);* Dante DiPaolo *(Simeon);* Charles Borromel *(Dan);* Helmuth Schneider *(Zebulon);* Loris Bazzocchi *(Issachar);* Marin Marija *(Asher);* Nino Segurini *(Gad);* Tonko Sacevic *(Levi);* Bruno Arié *(Debating Man);* Enrico Chiappafredo *(Debating Man);* Victor Rietti *(Baker);* Pietro Tordi *(Enemy).*

Comments: The Old Testament story of Joseph, produced on a modest scale. Produced by the Italian companies Jolly Film and Cosmopolis, in association with Yugoslavia's Dubrava Film. This was originally a Columbia Pictures project conceived by studio head Harry Cohn as a vehicle for Rita Hayworth, but the production was cancelled.

Strogoff (Michel Strogoff, corriere dello zar) (Cineriz Distributori Associati, 1970)

Credits: Director: Eriprando Visconti; *Producers:* Artur Brauner, Nicola Domilia, Alfonso Sansone; *Screenplay:* Giampiero Bona, Ladislas Fodor, Albert Kantof, Georges Lautner, Stefano Strucchi, Eriprando Visconti (based on the novel *Michael Strogoff* by Jules Verne); *Photography:* Luigi Kuveiller (Technicolor, SuperTotalscope, aspect ratio 2.35:1); *Film Editor:* Franco Arcalli; *Music:* Teo Usuelli; *Costume Design:* Maria Sotirova; *Sound:* Primiano Muratori; *Assistant Sound Technician:* Luciano Muratori; *Electrician:* Vasil Kamenov; *Orchestra Conductor:* Alberto Zedda.

Cast: John Phillip Law *(Michael Strogoff)*; Mimsy Farmer *(Nadia)*; Hiram Keller *(Ivan Ogareff)*; Delia Boccardo *(Sangarre)*; Kurt Meisel *(Feofar Khan)*; Elisabeth Bergner *(Marfa Strogoff)*; Claudio Gora [billed as "Claudio Cora"] *(General Dubelt)*; Donato Castellaneta *(Alcide Jolivet)*; Jacques Maury *(Capt. Alexandre Chélépine)*; Christian Marin *(Harry Blount)*; Jean-Pierre Dorat *(Vassili Feodor)*; Bianca Doria; Jean Dudan; Enzo Fiermonte *(Colonel With Gen. Debelt)*; Quinto Parmeggiani; Herbert Fux *(Pope)*.

Comments: Another version of the Jules Verne novel *Michael Strogoff.* Produced by Italy's Sancrosiap S.p.A., France's Les Films Corona, Germany's CCC Filmkunst & Co. KG Artur Brauner, and Studiya za igralni filmi "Boyana."

Suleiman the Conqueror (Solimano il conquistatore) (Medallion Pictures, 1961)

Credits: *Directors:* Vatroslav Mimica, Mario Tota; *Producer:* Vatroslav Mimica; *Screenplay:* Mario Caiano, Stipe Delic, Michelangelo Frieri, Vatroslav Mimica; *Photography:* Giuseppe La Torre (Eastmancolor, Totalscope, aspect ratio 2.35:1); *Music:* Francesco De Masi; *Production Design:* Kosta Krivokapic, Alfredo Montori; *Costume Design:* Giorgio Desideri; *Special Effects:* Celeste Franzi, Walfrido Traversari; *Assistant Film Editor:* Bruno Mattei; running time: 99 minutes (Italy); released December 7, 1961 (Italy), 1963 (U.S.); video availability: Something Weird Video.

Cast: Edmund Purdom *(Ibrahim Pascià)*; Giorgia Moll *(Vesna Orlovich)*; Alberto Farnese *(Gaspard)*; Luciano Marin *(Ivan)*; Loris Gizzi *(Suleiman II)*; Stane Potokar *(Capt. Nicholas Orlovich)*; Evi Maltagliati *(Anna, the Housekeeper)*; Raf Baldassarre *(Lieutenant)*; Nando Tamberlani *(Chancellor of Vienna)*; Giuseppe Addobbati [billed as "John Douglas"]; Andrea Aureli *(Yurik)*; Silvio Bagolini *(Drunk in Tavern)*; Enzo Doria *(Suleiman's Confidante)*; Andrej Gardenin *(Fencer)*; Dusan Janicijevic; Nada Kasapic; Vladimir Medar *(Blacksmith)*; Mira Tapavica *(Aicha)*; Amedeo Trilli; Janez Vrhovec.

Comments: The Turkish Sultan Suleiman tries to conquer Vienna in this costume adventure. Produced by Italy's Cine Produzione Astoria and Yugoslavia's C.F.S. Košutnjak.

The Sword and the Cross (Le Schiave di Cartagine) (Valiant Films, 1956)

Credits: *Director:* Guido Brignone; *Producer:* Gregorio Walerstein; *Screenplay:* Francesco De Feo, Mario Guerra, Nicola Manzari, Francesco Thellung (from a story by G. Maggi, Francesco Thellung, Italo Zingarelli); *Photography:* Bitto Albertini (Ferraniacolor, Cinetotalscope, aspect ratio 2.35:1); *Film Editor:* Jolanda Benvenuti; *Music:* Enzo Masetti; *Costume Design:* Enzo Bulgarelli; *Production Manager:* Italo Zingarelli; *Art Dept. Manager:* Italo Tomassi; *Orchestra Conductor:* Ugo Giacomozzi; *Master of Arms:* Enzo Musumeci Greco; running time: 87 minutes (U.S.); released December 14, 1956 (Italy), April 1960 (U.S.).

Cast: Gianna Maria Canale *(Julia Martia)*; Jorge Mistral *(Marcus Valerius)*; Marisa Allasio *(Lea)*; Ana Luisa Peluffo *(Esther)*; Rubén Rojo *(Flavius Metellus)*; Luigi Pavese *(Publius Cornelius)*; Germán Cobos *(Tullius)*; Ricardo Valle *(Stephen)*; Nando Tamberlani *(Proconsul)*; Albert Hehn [billed as "Alberto Helm"] *(Livius)*; Marcello Giorda; Carlo Lombardi; Nicola Manzari; Renato Navarrini; Emilio Petacci; Ugo Sasso; Vinicio Sofia; Edoardo Toniolo; Nietta Zocchi; Lilla Brignone *(Dubbed Voice for Gianna Maria Canale)*.

Comments: This gladiator adventure is a loose remake of *Fabiola.* Co-produced by Italy's Società Italiana Cines, Spain's Yago Films, and Cinematográfica Filmex S.A.

Sword of Damascus (Il ladro di Damasco) (American-International Television, 1964)

Credits: *Director:* Mario Amendola (billed as "Irving Jacobs"); *Producer:* Tulio Bruschi; *Screenplay:* Mario Amendola; *Photography:* Luciano Trasatti (Eastmancolor, aspect ratio 1.85:1); *Film Editor:* Nella Nannuzzi; *Production Design:*

Alfredo Montori; *Assistant Director:* Alfonso Brescia; running time: 103 minutes (Italy), 93 minutes (U.S.); released February 19, 1964 (Italy); video availability: Something Weird Video.

Cast: Tony Russel *(Jesen)*; Luciana Gilli [billed as "Luciana Gillj"] *(Miriam)*; Gianni Solaro *(Tibullo)*; Ferruccio Amendola *(Tisba)*; Enrico Salvatore; Bruno Ukmar; Adriana Limiti; Pietro Tordi (billed as "Peter White"); Irena Prosen; Renato Baldini *(Uria)*; Giuseppe Fortis *(Mannae)*; Rate Furlan.

Comments: The Romans and the Syrians clash in this epic. Produced by Italy's Rodes Cinematografica. Fourth-billed Ferruccio Amendola was the nephew of director Mario Amendola.

The Sword of El Cid *(La spada del Cid)* (PRO International Pictures, 1962)

Credits: Director: Miguel Iglesias; *Screenplay:* Luis G. de Blain, Miguel Iglesias, Antonio Navarro Linares, Victor M. Tarruella (from a story by Ferdinando Baldi, Alfredo Giannetti, additional dialogue by Noel Clarasó); *Photography:* Francisco Marin (Eastmancolor, Supercinescope, aspect ratio 2.35:1); *Film Editor:* Otello Colangeli; *Production Design:* Juan Alberto Soler; *Assistant Camera Operator:* Juan Prous; running time: 86 minutes (U.S.); released December 24, 1962 (Italy); February 1964 (U.S.).

Cast: Roland Carey *(Bernardo)*; Sandro Moretti *(Ramon)*; Chantal Deberg *(Maria Sol)*; Eliana Grimaldi *(Bianca)*; José Luis Pellicena *(Felix Muñoz)*; Daniela Bianchi *(Elvira)*; Fernando Cebrián; Ramón Centenero; Félix de Pomés; Andrea Fantasia; Joaquín Ferré; Pedro Gil; Luis Induni; Daniel Martín; Andrés Mejuto; Nino Milano; Juan Monfort; Frank Oliveras; Josefina Tapias; Francisco Tuset; Ramón Vaccaro.

Comments: This unofficial and contrived "sequel" to *El Cid (qv)* relates the adventures of El Cid's two daughters. Co-produced by Italy's Alexandra Produzioni Cinematografiche, in association with Spain's Cintera and Victor M. Tarruela, P.C. Supporting actress Daniela Bianchi was also seen in the Sean Connery James Bond film *From Russia with Love.*

Sword of Rebellion *(Il ribelle di Castlemonte)* (Industrie Cinetelevisive, 1964)

Credits: Director: Vertunnio De Angelis; *Screenplay:* Aldo Berni (from a story by Luigi Bonelli); *Music:* Aldo Piga; running time: 82 minutes (U.S.); released September 16, 1964 (Italy); video availability: Something Weird Video.

Cast: Gérard Landry *(Marco Degli Ammannati)*; Annie Alberti *(Bianca)*; Luciano Benetti *(Captain of the Guards)*; Aldo Bufi Landi *(Rizzio)*; Ivano Staccioli *(Duke Albere Di Castlemonte)*; Liana Trouche *(Amanda)*; John Kitzmiller *(Ali)*; Anna Maria Aveta *(Farmer's Wife)*; Giulio Cali; Felice Minotti; Franco Pizarro *(Don Ruiz)*; Gino Turini [billed as "John Turner"] *(Count Kurt Von Utreht)*.

Comments: Count Marco opposes the evil Duke Albere for the hand of Duchess Bianca. This action-adventure was produced by Italy's Industrie Cinetelevisive.

Sword of the Conqueror *(Rosmunda e Alboino)* (United Artists, 1961)

Credits: Director: Carlo Campogalliani; *Producer:* Gilberto Carbone; *Screenplay:* Paolo Barbara, Carlo Campogalliani, Alessandro Ferraù, Roberto Gianviti, Primo Zeglio; *Photography:* Angelo Baistrocchi, Raffaele Masiocchi (Eastmancolor, Colorscope, aspect ratio 2.35:1); *Film Editor:* Mario Serandrei; *Music:* Carlo Rustichelli; *Production Design:* Massimo Tavazzi; *Costume Design:* Giuliana Ghidini; *Makeup:* Mario Van Riel; *Hair Stylist:* Grazia De Rossi; *Production Managers:* Renato Parravicini, Aristodemo Petri, Gastone Tomassoni; *Unit Manager:* Aristodeus Petri; *2nd Unit Director:* Romolo Guerrieri; *Assistant Directors:* Ettore Maria Fizzarotti, Luigi Petrini, Tonino Ricci; *Sound:* Giulio Tagliacozzo (Westrex sound system); *Camera Operator:* Antonio Schiavo Lena; *2nd Camera Operator:* Elio Polacchi; *Still Photographer:* G.B. Poletto; *Orchestra Conductor:* Carlo Savina; *Fencing Master:* Ferdinando Poggi; *Script Supervisors:* Adolfo Dragone, Maria Luisa Roi; *Dialogue Coach:* Harriet Medin; running time: 96 minutes (Italy); released August 24, 1961 (Italy), September 1962 (U.S.).

Cast: Jack Palance *(Alboino)*; Eleonora Rossi Drago *(Rosmunda)*; Guy Madison *(Amalchi)*; Carlo D'Angelo *(Falisque)*; Edy Vessel *(Matilda)*; Andrea Bosic *(King Cunimond)*; Ivan Palance *(Ulderico)*; Vittorio Sanipoli *(Wolfango)*; Raf Baldassarre; Guido Celano; Guido Mafrino; Lamberto Antinori; Roberto Altamura; Calisto Calisti; Edda Ferronao; Elio Folgaresi; Franco Jamonte; Renato Mori; Amina Pirani Maggi; Robert Hall; Barbara Nardi; Walter Grant; Alfredo Marchetti; Vittorio Vaser; Spartaco Nale; Aldo Pini; Vladimiro Tuicovich; Olga Romanelli; John Camel; Giovanni Vari; Elio Bonadonna; Angelo Boscariol; Mario De Persio; Vittorio Cuocolo.

Comments: In 566 AD, the heroic Amalchi battles the evil Alboino for the hand of Rosmunda. Produced by Titanus.

Sword of the Empire *(Una spada per l'impero)* (American-International Television, 1964)

Credits: Director: Sergio Grieco; *Producer:* Giorgio Marzelli; *Screenplay:* Fulvio Tului; *Photography:* Romolo Garroni (Eastmancolor, CinemaScope, aspect ratio 2.35:1); *Film Editor:* Enzo Alfonzi; *Music:* Guido Robuschi, Gian Stellari; *Production Design:* Athos Danilo Zanetti; *Costume Design:* Angiolina Menichelli; *Electrician:* Francesco Brescini; running time: 81 minutes (Italy); released October 21, 1964 (Italy).

Cast: Lang Jeffries *(Quintus Marcus, Roman Consul)*; José Greci *(Nissia, Blonde Slave)*; Enzo Terascio *(Emperor Commodus)*; Howard Ross [billed as "Renato Rossini"] *(Leto)*; Mila Stanic *(Marcia, a Christian)*; Angela Angelucci *(Omah, Brunette Slave)*; Giuseppe Addobbati *(Pertinacius)*; Ignazio Leone *(Tigerio)*; Adriano Micantoni *(Artale)*; Edgardo Siroli *(Sisto)*; Antonio Devi *(Fabio)*; Mario Ghignone *(Roman Christian)*; Fedele Gentile *(Valerio)*; Paolo Di Mario *(Lucilla)*; Pasquale Basile *(Orazio)*; Piero Pastore *(Ottavio)*; Mimmo Maggio; Giulio Tomei *(Cleandro)*; Ennio Antonelli *(Roman Christian)*; Nando Gazzolo *(Quintus Marcus, Roman Consul)* [dubbed voice]; Pietro Torrisi *(Wrestler)*.

Comments: A low-budget take-off on *The Fall of the Roman Empire,* released the same year. Produced by Italy's Assia International Film.

Sword of Zorro *(Le tre spade di Zorro)* (National Telefilm Associates, 1963)

Credits: Director: Ricardo Blasco; *Producers:* Tullio Bruschi, Sergio Newman; *Screenplay:* Mario Amendola, José Gallardo, Luis Lucas Ojeda, Daniel Ribera (from a story by Mario Amendola); *Photography:* Julio Ortas (color, aspect ratio 2.35:1); *Film Editor:* Jolanda Benvenuti; *Music:* Antonio Ramirez Ángel; *Art Direction:* Teddy Villalba; *Assistant Director:* José Luis Monter; running time: 88 minutes (U.S.); released October 23, 1963 (Portugal); video availability: Sinister Cinema.

Cast: Guy Stockwell *(Zorro)*; Gloria Milland *(Virginia)*; Mikaela [billed as "Mikaela Wood"] *(Maria)*; Antonio Prieto *(Don Manuel Paredes)*; Giuseppe Addobbati [billed as "John Douglas"] *(Marques de Santa Ana)*; Franco Fantasia *(Col. Martinez)*; Julio Cesar Sempere [billed as "Julio Cesar"] *(Little Diego)*; Juan Luis Gallardo [billed as "Robert Dean"] *(Felipe)*; Guillermo Vera *(Mexican)*; Alfonso Rojas *(Capt. Gonzalez)*; Manrico Melchiorre *(Lieutenant)*; Santiago Rivero *(The New Governor)*; Anna Petocchi *(Ana)*; Luis Marin *(Soldier)*; Pilar Gómez Ferrer *(Nodriza)*; Manuel Arbó *(Tavern Customer)*; Vicente Bañó; Dolores Bermudez; Ana Carvajal *(Maid)*; Milagros Guijarro *(Flamenco Dancer)*; Antonio Jiménez Escribano *(Peasant)*; José Luis Lizalde *(Soldier)*; José Luis Lluch *(Soldier)*; Conchita Rodriguez del Valle *(Maria, the Girl)*; Jacinto San Emeterio *(Don Garcia Pulido)*.

Comments: Zorro opposes corrupt government officials in this adventure set in 1830 Mexico. Co-produced by Italy's Rodes Cinematografica and Spain's Hispamer Films. Some scenes were filmed on location at Colmenar de Oreja, Madrid, Spain.

Sword Without a Country *(Spada senza bandiera)* (Embassy Pictures, 1961)

Credits: Director: Carlo Veo; *Producer:* Lello Luzi; *Screenplay:* Andrea Gava, Carlo Veo; *Photography:* Aldo Greci (Eastmancolor, aspect ratio 2.35:1); *Music:* Carlo Innocenzi; *Production Design:* Giorgio Gionannini; released February

25, 1961 (Italy); video availability: Something Weird Video.

Cast: Folco Lulli *(Diego Benvenuti di Pianora)*; Leonora Ruffo *(Gigliola)*; Claudio Gora *(Duke of Belvarco)*; Renato Speziali *(Cino)*; Mara Berni *(Isabella)*; Piero Lulli *(Benedetto)*; Gérard Landry *(Costanzo)*; José Jaspe; Ivano Staccioli *(Amico di Cino)*; Enzo Doria; Dina De Santis; Gianni Perelli; Nadia Lara; Fedele Gentile; Franco Pizarro; Piergiorgio Gragnani; Flora Carosello; Nino Fuscagni; Tony Di Mitri; Mauro Del Vecchio; Roberto Ceccacci; Enzo Staiola; Ruth von Hagen; Bruno Tocci; Carla Calò; Rina Brado.

Comments: When a humble troubadour kills the unwanted fiancée the lovely Gigliola, his friends help him to escape with her, and they join a group of rebels trying to overthrow the corrupt government. Produced by Italy's A.D. Cinematografica.

Swordsman of Siena *(La congiura dei dieci)* (MGM, 1962)

Credits: *Directors:* Baccio Bandini (Italian version), Etienne Périer (English and French versions); *Producer:* Jacques Bar; *Screenplay:* Michael Kanin, Fay Kanin, Alec Coppel (English version), Sandro Continenza, Dominique Fabre (Italian version), based on the novel *The Swordsman of Terror* by Anthony Marshall; *Photography:* Tonino Delli Colli (Metrocolor, CinemaScope, aspect ratio 2.35:1); *Film Editors:* Monique Isnardon, Robert Isnardon (English version), Renzo Lucidi (Italian version); *Music:* Mario Nascimbene; *Costume Design:* Dario Cecchi; *Production Manager (Italian version)*: Bianca Lattuada; *1st Assistant Director (Italian version)*: Franco Cirino; *2nd Assistant Director:* Gus Agosti; *Production Designers (Italian version)*: Alberto Boccianti, Franco Lolli; *Set Decorator (Italian version)*: Giorgio Mecchia Madalena; *Sound Recording Supervisor:* Kurt Doubrowsky; *Camera Operator:* Franco Delli Colli; *Music Director (Italian version)*: Carlo Rustichelli; *Orchestra Conductor:* Franco Ferrara; *Stunt Double:* Buddy Van Horn; running time: 97 minutes (U.S.); released December 5, 1962 (U.S.); video availability: Warner Home Video.

Cast: Stewart Granger *(Thomas Stanswood)*; Sylva Koscina *(Orietta Arconti)*; Christine Kaufmann *(Serenella Arconti)*; Riccardo Garrone *(Don Carlos)*; Alberto Lupo *(Andrea Paresi)*; Marina Berti *(Countess of Osta)*; Tullio Carminati *(Father Giacomo)*; Claudio Gora *(Leoni)*; Fanfulla; Giulio Marchetti *(Carlos' Servant)*; Carlo Rizzo *(Gino)*; Ignazio Dolce; Fausto Tozzi *(Hugo)*; Tom Felleghy *(Spanish Captain)*; Antonio Ricci *(Child)*; Mario Passante; Loris Gizzi *(Councillor)*.

Comments: In this swashbuckler influenced by *Scaramouche* (which also starred Stewart Granger) the bodyguard of a Spanish overlord falls in love with the overlord's betrothed, and then joins a group of rebels opposing the corrupt government. Co-produced by Italy's Monica Film and France's Compagnie Internationale de Productions Cinématographique (CIPRA).

Taras Bulba, the Cossack *(Taras Bulba, il cosacco)* (Universal Television, 1970)

Credits: *Director:* Ferdinando Baldi; *Screenplay:* Ennio De Concini (based on a novel by Nicolai Gogol); *Photography:* Amerigo Gingarelli (color, aspect ratio 2.35:1); *Film Editor:* Renzo Lucidi; *Music:* Guido Robuschi, Gian Stellari; *Costume Design:* Mario Giorsi; *Assistant Makeup Artist:* Halid Redzebasic; released May 7, 1970.

Cast: Vladimir Medar *(Taras Bulba)*; Jean François Poron *(Andrei Bulba)*; George Reich *(Ostapi)*; Hugo Santana *(Gurko)*; Lorella De Luca *(Natalia)*; Fosco-Giachetti *(Voivode)*; Sylvia Sorrente; Erno Crisa; Mirko Ellis; Andrea Scotti; Dada Gallotti.

Comments: Cossack chief Taras Bulba goes to war against Poland and the Tartars. Based on the novel by Nikolai Gogol. The character of Taras Bulba was based on several historical personalities, and was personified to greater effect onscreen by Yul Brynner in 1962. This lesser adaptation was produced by Italy's I.A.C.EI.D.C. This 1963 film was not distributed in America until 1970.

Tartar Invasion *(Ursus e la regazza tartara)* (Medallion Pictures, 1963)

Credits: Director/Screenplay: Remigio Del Grosso; *Producer:* Nino Battiferri; *Photography:* Anchise Brizzi (Eastmancolor, Techniscope, aspect ratio 2.35:1); *Film Editor:* Antonietta Zita; *Music:* Angelo Francesco Lavagnino; *Art Direction:* Antonio Visone; *Costume Design:* Giancarlo Bartolini Salimbeni; *Makeup:* Anacieto Giustini; *Production Manager:* Nino Battiferri; *Assistant Director:* Gianfranco Baldinello; *2nd Unit Directors:* Sergio Bergonzelli, Giorgio Capitani; *Sound Technicians:* Raffaele Del Monte, Mario Del Pezzo; *Camera Operator:* Antonio Modica; *Assistant Camera Operator:* Pier Luigi Santi (billed as "Pierluigi Santi"); *1st Production Assistant:* Diego Alchimede; *Production Assistants:* Angelo Iocono (billed as "Angelo Jacono"), Arrigo Peri; *Fencing Master:* Bruno Arié (billed as "Bruno Arrie"); *Stunts:* Valentino Pelizzi; *Continuity:* Liliana Gatti (billed as "Lilla Gatti"); *Director of English-Dubbed Version:* Richard McNamara; running time: 100 minutes (Italy), 85 minutes (U.S.); released December 13, 1961 (Italy), 1963 (U.S.); video availability: Something Weird Video.

Cast: Yôko Tani *(Princess Ila)*; Ettore Manni *(Prince Stefan)*; Roland Lesaffre *(Ivan)*; Maria Grazia Spina *(Amia)*; Tom Felleghy [billed as "Tom Felleghi"] *(Suleiman)*; Andrea Aureli *(Ibrahim)*; Ivano Staccioli *(Prince Ahmed)*; Joe Robinson *(Ursus)*; Antonio Piretti *(Ursus' Son)*; Mario Landolini; Pino Sciacqua; Jacopo Tecchi; Anita Todesco; Adriano Vitale; Akim Tamiroff *(Khan of the Tartars)*; Bruno Arié *(Polish Soldier)*; Giancarlo Bastianoni *(Polish Soldier)*; Angelo Casadei *(Tartar)*; Veriano Ginesi *(Leader of Horses)*; Oscar Giustini *(Soldier)*; Emilio Messina *(Battle Victim)*; Nello Pazzafini *(Tartar)*; Gianni Solaro *(Polish War Leader)*; Sergio Ukmar *(Tartar)*.

Comments: Eastern hordes threaten Europe in this action yarn, co-produced by Italy's Explorer '58 and France's Comptoir Français du Film Production (CFFP).

The Tartars (I tartari) (MGM, 1962)

Credits: Directors: Richard Thorpe, Ferdinando Baldi; *Producer:* Riccardo Gualino; *Screenplay:* Domenico Salvati, Sabatino Ciuffini, Oreste Palella, Gaio Frattini, Ambroglio Moltini, Julian De Kassel (from their story); *Photography:* Amerigo Gengarelli (Technicolor, Techniscope, aspect ratio 2.35:1); *Film Editor:* Maurizio Lucidi; *Music:* Renzo Rossellini; *Production Design:* Oscar D'Amico, Pasquale Dal Pino; *Set Decoration:* Antonio Fratalocchi; *Costume Design:* Giovanna Natili; *Makeup:* Renato Bornarzi; *Hair Stylist:* Giovanni Palombi; *Production Supervisor:* Roberto Onori; *General Production Manager:* Alessandro Tasca; *Production Managers:* Renato Jaboni, Elios Vercelloni; *Assistant Directors:* Giorgio Gentili, Ambrogio Molteni; *Sound:* Kurt Doubrowsky; *Special Effects:* Costel Grozea; *Camera Operator:* Carlo Fiore; *Assistant Camera Operators:* Mario Cimini, Silvano Mancini; *Orchestra Conductor:* Luigi Urbini; *Production Secretaries:* Carlo Bartolini, Luigi Guasco; *Script Supervisor:* Anna Tasca; *Master of Arms:* Franco Fantasia; running time: 83 minutes (U.S.); released June 20, 1962 (U.S.).

Cast: Victor Mature *(Oleg)*; Orson Welles

Liana Orfei and Victor Mature in *The Tartars*.

Above: Orson Welles (right) in *The Tartars*. *Left:* Liana Orfei in *The Tartars*.

(Burundai); Liana Orfei (Helga); Arnoldo Foà (Ciu Lang); Luciano Marin (Eric); Bella Cortez (Samia); Furio Meniconi (Sigrun); Pietro Ceccarelli; Renato Terra; Folco Lulli (Togrul); Spartaco Nale.

Comments: It's Tartar leader Burundai versus Viking chief Oleg in this epic. Lead Victor Mature was in the waning years of a mediocre career at this point and was insecure about his role, especially since he was playing opposite a genuine talent like Orson Welles, and there was some tension between Mature and Welles on the set, which led Mature to wear lifts in his shoes at one point so that he would appear taller than Welles. This film was co-produced by Italy's Lux Film and Yugoslavia's Dubrava Film. Shot at Titanus studios in Rome, with some location work in Yugoslavia.

Taur, the Mighty (Taur, il re della forza bruta) (American-International Television, 1963)

Credits: *Director:* Antonio Leonviola; *Producer:*

Alfredo Guarini; *Screenplay:* Antonio Leonviola, Fabio Piccioni, Sofia Scandurra (from a story by Fabio Piccioni); *Photography:* Guglielmo Mancori (Eastmancolor, Totalscope, aspect ratio 2.35:1); *Film Editor:* Renato Cinquini; *Music:* Roberto Nicolosi; *Orchestra Conductor:* Luigi Urbini; *Laboratory:* Technostampa, Rome, Italy; running time: 95 minutes (Italy), 89 minutes (U.S.); released June 30, 1963 (Italy); video availability: Sinister Cinema.

Cast: Joe Robinson *(Taur)*; Harry Baird *(Ubaratautu)*; Bella Cortez *(Queen Akiba)*; Antonio Leonviola *(El Kab)*; Alberto Cevenini *(Syros)*; Thea Fleming *(Illa)*; Carla Foscari *(Ararut)*; Claudia Capone *(Tuja)*; Erminio Spalla *(King Surupak)*; Miranda Crovato *(The Queen)*; José Torres *(El Khad)*; Janine Hendy *(Afer)*.

Comments: King Surupak is murdered by warriors from Kixos, who kidnap his daughters; the girls are rescued by the heroic Taurus. The character of Taurus had originally been called "Tarzan" until a lawsuit by the Edgar Rice Burroughs estate forced a name change. Co-produced by the Italian companies Coronet, S.R.L., Cosmopolis, Galatea Film and Italia Film, with Yugoslavia's Dubrava Film. Filmed in Italy and on location at Postojna Cave in Yugoslavia.

Temple of the White Elephant (Sandok, il Maciste della giungla) (American-International Television, 1964)

Credits: Director: Umberto Lenzi; *Producer:* Solly V. Bianco; *Screenplay:* Fulvio Gicca Palli, Umberto Lenzi; *Photography:* Angelo Lotti (color, Techniscope, aspect ratio 2.35:1); *Film Editor:* Jolanda Benvenuti; *Music:* Georges Garvarentz; *Set Decoration:* Arrigo Equini; running time: 85 minutes (U.S.); released March 24, 1964 (Italy).

Cast: Sean Flynn *(Lt. Dick Ramsey)*; Alessandra Panaro *(Cynthia Montague)*; Marie Versini *(Princess Dhara)*; Mimmo Palmara *(Parvati Sandok)*; Arturo Dominici *(Maharajah)*; Giacomo Rossi Stuart *(Reginal Milliner)*; Fortunato Arena *(Sect Member)*; Salvatore Borghese *(Sect Member)*; Andrea Bosic *(Colonel)*; Giorgio Cerioni *(John Willoughby)*; Giovanni Cianfriglia *(Krishna)*; Dakar *(Sect Member)*; Enzo Fiermonte *(Sgt. Major)*; Jacques Herlin *(English Officer)*; Nello Pazzafini *(Sect Member)*; Redilly B. Rajapa *(Prince Baram)*; Seyna Seyn (Sara).

Comments: In India, a British lieutenant and the viceroy's daughter are captured by members of a fanatical religious sect known as "The White Elephant"; they are eventually rescued by Lt. Dick Ramsey of the Lancers. Co-produced by Italy's Filmes and France's Capitole Films.

The Ten Gladiators (I dieci gladiatori) (American-International Television, 1963)

Credits: Director: Gianfranco Parolini; *Screenplay:* Giovanni Simonelli; Sergio Sollima, Gianfranco Parolini (from their story); *Photography:* Francesco Izzarelli (color, Supertotalscope, aspect ratio 2.35:1); *Film Editor:* Edmond Lozzi; *Music:* Angelo Francesco Lavagnino; *Production Design:* Giorgio Postiglione, Giuseppe Ranieri; *Costume Design:* Vittorio Rossi; *Sound:* Gianetto Nardi; *Special Effects:* Renato Marinelli; running time: 110 minutes (Italy), 104 minutes (U.S.); released December 14, 1963 (Italy); video availability: Sinister Cinema.

Cast: Roger Browne *(Glaucus Valerius)*; José Greci [billed as "Susan Paget"] *(Livia)*; Dan Vadis *(Roccia/The Rock)*; Franca Parisi [as "Margaret Taylor"] *(Poppea)*; Gianni Rizzo *(Claudius Nero)*; Mimmo Palmara [billed as "Dick Palmer"] *(Tigelinus)*; Ugo Sasso *(Resius)*; Mirko Ellis *(Servius Galba)*; Giuseppe Mattei (billed as "Pino Mattei"); Gianfranco Parolini *(Livius Verus)*; Vassili Karis *(Epaphrodito)*; Emilio Messina *(Gladiator Leptus)*; Aldo Canti *(Gladiator)*; Salvatore Borghese *(Milo/Minius, the Mute)*; Giancarlo Bastianoni; Giuliano Dell'Ovo *(Gladiator)*; Gino Turini (billed as "John Turner"); Pietro Torrisi *(Gladiator)*; Arnaldo Fabrizio *(Glaucus' Servant)*; Romano Giomini; Milton Reid *(Bald Wrestler)*; Ivano Staccioli *(Gladiator)*; Veriano Ginesi *(Geriel, the Ship's Drummer)*; Roberto Messina *(Methodius)*.

Comments: Roman patrician Glaucus Valerius enlists the aid of Roccia ("The Rock"), a heroic gladiator, in his quest to overthrow the tyrannical Nero. Produced by Italy's Cine-Produzioni Associate.

The Terror of Rome Against the Son of Hercules (Maciste, gladiatore di sparta) (Embassy Pictures, 1964)

Credits: *Director:* Mario Caiano; *Screenplay:* Mario Amendola, Alfonso Brecia, Albert Valentin (based on their story); *Photography:* Pier Ludovico Pavoni (Technicolor, Techniscope, aspect ratio 2.35:1); *Film Editor:* Nella Nannuzzi; *Music:* Carlo Franci; *Production Design:* Pier Vittorio Marchi; *Set Decoration:* Franco D'Andria; *Costume Design:* Mario Giorsi; *Makeup:* Otello Fava; *Hair Stylist:* Renata Magnanti; *Production Supervisor:* Albino Morandini; *1st Assistant Director:* Antonio Brescia; *Assistant Director:* Bertrand Tavernier; *Sound:* Franco Groppioni; *Camera Operator:* Fausto Rossi; *Assistant Camera Operator:* Mario Pastorini; *Assistant Costume Designer:* Antonio Randaccio; *Fencing Director:* Alfio Caltabiano; *Master of Arms:* Bruno Ukmar; *Production Secretary:* Carlo Vassalle; *Script Supervisor:* Filiberto Fiaschi; *Script for English-Dubbed Version:* Tamara Lees; *Director of English-Dubbed Version:* Richard McNamara; *Laboratory:* Technicolor; running time: 103 minutes (Italy); released March 26, 1964 (Italy), video availability: Something Weird Video.

Cast: Mark Forest *(Maciste)*; Marilù Tolo *(Olympia)*; Elisabetta Fanti *(Livia)*; Claudio Undari *(Zefatius)*; Franco Cobianchi *(Vittelius)*; Ferruccio Amendola *(Dammatius)*; Lea Monaco; Renato Navarrini; Ugo Attanasio; Giuseppe Addobbati *(Marcellus)*; Bruno Ukmar *(Tirfeo)*; Jacques Stany *(Epialte)*; Enrico Salvatore; Fortunato Arena *(Gladiator)*; Mario Caiano; Giuliano Giulian; Emilio Messina *(Gladiator)*; Roberto Messina *(Gladiator)*; Nello Pazzafini *(Gladiator)*; Franco Ukmar *(Gladiator)*.

Mark Forest in *The Terror of Rome Against the Son of Hercules.*

Mark Forest in *The Terror of Rome Against the Son of Hercules.*

Comments: In 69 BC, heroic strongman Macist opposes the evil ruler Vittelius. Co-produced by Italy's Prometeo Film S.r.L, France's Les Films Jacques Leitienne and Samcro Film SpA.

Terror of the Red Mask (*Il terrore della maschera rossa*) (Four Star Television, 1960)

Credits: Director: Luigi Capuano; *Producer:* Jacopo Comin; *Screenplay:* Vittorio Metz, Marcello Ciorciolini, Luigi Capuano, Roberto Gianviti; *Photography:* Carlo Montuori (Eastmancolor, Totalscope, aspect ratio 2.35:1); *Film Editor:* Antonietta Zita; *Art Direction/Costume Design:* Giancarlo Bartolini Salimbeni; *Production Manager:* Ferdinand Felicioni; *Sound:* Raffaele Del Monte, Franco Groppioni; *Assistant Directors:* Federico Chentrens, Daniele G. Luisi; running time: 92 minutes (Italy), 88 minutes (U.S.); released January 23, 1960 (Italy); video availability: Something Weird Video.

Cast: Lex Barker *(Marco)*; Chelo Alonso *(Karima)*; Livio Lorenzon *(Astolfo)*; Liana Orfei *(Jolanda)*; Franco Fantasia *(Egidio)*; Elio Crovetto *(Uguccione)*; Enrico Glori; Ugo Sasso; *(Rebel Leader)*; Bruno Scipioni *(Rebel)*; Luigi Tosi *(Martino)*; Oscar Andriani; Arturo Bragaglia; Mario Meniconi; Benito Stefanelli; Marco Guglielmi *(Ivano)*; Riccardo Billi *(Fanello)*; Nello Pazzafini; Amerigo Santarelli *(Torturer)*; Eugenia Tavani; Franco Ukmar *(Soldier)*; Sergio Ukmar *(Soldier)*;

Comments: A mysterious hero known as "The Red Mask" opposes the tyranny of Astolfo, a cruel overlord. Produced by Italy's De Paolis Studios in Rome.

Terror of the Steppes (*I predoni della steppa*) (Embassy Pictures, 1964)

Credits: Director: Tanio Boccia; *Producer:* Luigi Rovere; *Screenplay:* Tanio Boccia (billed as "Amerigo Anton"), Mario Moroni; *Photography:* Aldo Giordani (Technicolor, Techniscope, aspect ratio 2.35:1); *Music:* Carlo Rustichelli; *Set Decoration:* Amedeo Mellone; *Costume Design:* Walter Patriarca; *Art Dept. Manager:* Italo Tomassi; *Production Manager:* Renato Panetuzzi; running time: 97 minutes (Italy); released January 30, 1964 (Italy); video availability: Something Weird Video.

Cast: Kirk Morris *(Sandar Khan)*; Moira Orfei *(Malina)*; Daniele Vargas *(Altan Khan)*; Ombretta Colli *(Samira)*; Franco Cobianchi [billed as "Peter White"] *(Yesen Khan)*; Giulio Donnini *(The Khan's Advisor)*; Ugo Sasso *(Ciukhai)*; Furio Meniconi *(Kublai)*; Sina Scarfone; Marco Pasquini; Luigi Scavran; Attilio Dottesio; Anna Mazzelli; Gabriella Schettini; Franco Pechini; Claudio Marzulli; Fortunato Arena *(Sandar Khan's Soldier)*; Tony Casale *(Man)*; Amerigo Santarelli *(Guard)*.

Comments: The heroic Sandar Khan versus the Tartars. Produced by Italy's Cineluxor.

Tharus, Son of Attila (Tharus figlio di Attila) (American International, 1962)

Credits: Director: Roberto Bianchi Montero; Screenplay: Roberto Bianchi Montero, Leo Bomba (from a story by Leo Bomba); Photography: Giuseppe La Torre (color, aspect ratio 2.35:1); Production Design: Oscar D'Amico; Music: Alexandre Derevitsky, Mario Miglardi; Assistant Film Editor: Bruno Mattei; running time: 89 minutes (Italy), 90 minutes (U.S.); released March 30, 1962 (Italy); video availability: Something Weird Video.

Cast: Jerome Courtland (Tharus); Lisa Gastoni (Princess Tamall); Mimmo Palmara (Kudrum); Rik Van Nutter (Otto); Livio Lorenzon (King Haadem); Giuseppe Addobbati; Liana Dori; Daniele Igor; Christiane Martel; Lorenzo Artale; Riccardo Montalbano.

Comments: Attila the Hun's brother, King Bohlem, dispatches his son Otto and nephew Tharus to form an alliance with King Haadem. Haadem, though, has joined forces with-and betrothed his daughter to-Kudrum, who is opposed to King Bohlem's interests. Kudrum turns against Otto and Tharus, murdering King Haadem, but he is eventually defeated by Tharus. Co-produced by Italy's P.T. Cinematografica and Spain's IFI Producción S.A.

Theodora, Slave Empress (Teodora, imperatrice di Bizano) (I.F.E. Releasing Corp., 1954)

Credits: Director: Riccardo Freda; Screenplay: René Wheeler, Claude Accursi, Ranieri Cochetti, Riccardo Freda (from a story by André-Paul Antoine, Riccardo Freda); Photography: Rodolfo Lombardi (Ferraniacolor, aspect ratio 1.37:1); Film Editor: Mario Serandrei; Music: Renzo Rossellini; Production Design: Filiberto Sbardella, Antonio Valente; Art Direction: Riccardo Freda, Franco Lolli; Set Decoration: Flora Capponi; Costume Design: Veniero Colasanti; Makeup: Giuseppe Annunziata, Giuseppe Peruzzi; Hair Stylists: Lina Cassini, Renata Longari; Production Supervisor: Gino Fanano; Production Manager: Giuseppe Fatigati; Unit Manager: Riccardo Freda; Assistant Directors: Ranieri Cochetti, Giuseppe Divita, Mario Mambretti, Rolando Stragliati; Sound: Aldo Calpini, Giovanni Nesci (Western Electric sound system); Camera Operators: Mario Alberti, Giorgio Attili, Guglielmo Lombardi; Still Photographer: Foto Civirani; Orchestra Conductor: Franco Ferrara; Production Secretary: Franco Adorno; Script Supervisor: Augusto Zanelli; running time: 124 minutes (Italy), 88 minutes (U.S.); released September 29, 1954 (Italy), December 20, 1954 (U.S.).

Cast: Georges Marchal (Giustiniano); Gianna Maria Canale (Theodora); Renato Baldini (Arcas); Irene Papas (Faidia); Carlo Sposito (Scarpios); Nerio Bernardi (Belisario); Olga Solbelli (Egina); Alessandro Fersen (Metropolita); Loris Gizzi (Smimos); Umberto Silvestri (Blind Athlete); Mario Siletti (Magistrate); Oscar Andriani (Scarpios' Defender); Giovanni Fagioli (Court Clerk); Henri Guisol (John of Cappadocia); Roger Pigaut (Andres); Armando Annuale (Sandal Merchant); Fortunato Arena (Guard); Pietro Capanna; Libero Intorre; Giorgio Murri; Michele Riccardini (Jailer); Dubbing Actors: Denise Bosc (for Irene Papas in French version); Giorgio Capecchi (for Alessandro Fersen); Emilio Cigoli (for Georges Marchal); Dhia Cristiani (for Irene Papas); Gualtiero De Angelis (for Roger Rigaut); Camille Fournier (for Gianna Maria Canale in French version); Richard Francoeur (for Mario Siletti in French version); Lauro Gazzolo (for Mario Siletti); Pino Locchi (for Renato Baldini); Pierre Morin (for Nerio Beernardi in French version); Lita Recio (for Olga Solbelli in French version); Carlo Romano (for Carletto Sposito); Stefano Sibaldi (for Henri Guisol); Lidia Simoneschi (for Gianna Maria Canale); Jacques Thébault (for Giovanni Fagioli in French version); Paul Villé (for Armando Annuale in French version).

Comments: Theodora, a Roman courtesan, marries the emperor Justinian, but turns against him when she seeks justice for her people. Co-produced by Italy's Lux Film-Roma and France's Lux Compagnie Cinématographique de France. Shot at S.S.F.A. Studios in Rome. Some of the sets were constructed on fairgrounds that had been abandoned during World War II.

The Thief of Baghdad (Il ladro di Bagdad) (MGM, 1961)

Credits: Directors: Arthur Lubin, Bruno Vailati; *Producer:* Bruno Vailati (presented by Joseph E. Levine); *Screenplay:* Augusto Frassinetti, Filippo Sanjust, Bruno Vailati (from their story); *Photography:* Tonino Delli Colli (Eastmancolor, CinemaScope, aspect ratio 2.35:1); *Film Editor:* Gene Ruggiero; *Music:* Carlo Rustichelli; *Art Direction:* Flavio Mogherini; *Costume Design:* Georges K. Benda; *Makeup:* Romolo De Martino; *Hair Stylist:* Adalgisa Favella; *Production Manager:* Nello Meniconi; *Assistant Director:* Roberto Fizz; *Set Dresser:* Massimo Tavazzi; *Special Effects:* Tom Howard; *Camera Operator:* Franco Delli Colli; *Production Assistants:* Mario Basili, Mario Di Biase; *Location Manager (Tunisia Scenes):* André Bessis; *Choreography:* Paul Steffen; *Script Supervisor:* Barbara Fusch; running time: 100 minutes (Italy); released March 23, 1961 (Italy), August 10, 1961 (U.S.); video availability: Embassy Home Entertainment.

Cast: Steve Reeves *(Karim)*; Giorgia Moll *(Amina)*; Edy Vessel *(Kadeejah)*; Arturo Dominici *(Prince Osman)*; Daniele Vargas *(Gamal)*; Antonio Battistella *(Sultan of Baghdad)*; Fanfulla [billed as "Luigi Visconti'] *(Abdul)*; Giancarlo Zarfati *(Farid)*; Gina Mascetti *(Governess)*; Antonio Rosmino; Ignazio Dolce; Mohammed Agrebi; Joudi Mohammed Jamil; Georges Chamarat *(Magician)*; Eduardo Bergamo; Rosario Borelli; Chignone; Franco Cobianchi; Walter Grant; Mario Passante; Gail Pearl *(Dancer)*; Archie Savage; Anita Todesco *(Ancella)*; Fortunato Arena *(Prison Guard Captain)*.

Comments: In this tongue-in-cheek fantasy/adventure, Prince Karim is subjected to seven tests in his quest to recover a magical blue rose that will save the life of his love, a comatose princess. The same basic material was filmed previously in 1924, with Douglas Fairbanks, Sr., and in 1940 with Sabu. This Steve Reeves version was co-produced by Italy's Titanus Studios and France's Lux Compagne Cinématographique de France. Filmed at Monte Gelato Falls on the Treja River in Italy, and on location in Tunisia.

Thor and the Amazon Women (Le gladiatrici) (American-International Television, 1963)

Credits: Director: Antonio Leonviola; *Producers:* Ennio De Concini, Alfredo Guarini; *Executive Producer:* Livio Maffei; *Screenplay:* Antonio Leonviola, Fabio Piccioni, Sofia Scandurra (from a story by Antonio Leonviola, Fabio Piccioni); *Photography:* Guglielmo Mancori (Eastmancolor, Totalscope [Colorscope in U.S. prints], aspect ratio 2.35:1); *Film Editor:* Renato Cinquini; *Music:* Roberto Nicolosi; *Production Design:* Oscar D'Amico; *Costume Design:* Serenilla Staccioli; *Makeup:* Marcello Di Paolo; *Hair Stylist:* Lilla Polyák; *Production Manager:* Giorgio Baldi; *Assistant Directors:* Tonino Ricci, Sofia Scandurra; *Set Dresser:* Camillo Del Signore; *Special Effects:* Dino Galiano; *Orchestra Conductor:* Luigi Urbini; *Production Assistant:* Carlo Zanotti; *Script Supervisor:* Nuri Zschokke; *Laboratory:* Technostampa, Rome, Italy; running time: 95 minutes (Italy), 84 minutes (U.S.); released August 9, 1963 (Italy); video availability: Sinister Cinema.

Cast: Susy Andersen *(Tamar)*; Joe Robinson *(Thor)*; Harry Baird *(Ubarautu)*; Janine Hendy *(The Black Queen)*; Maria Fiore *(Yamad)*; Alberto Cevenini *(Siros)*; Tony Ante; Robert Baca; Anna Majurec; Claudia Capone *(Agarit)*; Carla Foscari *(Ghebel Gor)*.

Comments: The heroic Thor (no relation to the Norse God of Thunder) rescues men enslaved by a race of Amazons. Co-produced by Italy's Italia Film, Greece's Coronet Film and Yugoslavia's Dubrava Film. Produced at the same time as *Taur the Mighty (qv)*. Shot on location in Serbia, and at Postojna Cave in Yugoslavia, Otosko Cave in Postajna, Slovenia, and in Italy.

3 Avengers (Gli invincibili tre) (ABC Films, 1964)

Credits: Director: Gianfranco Parolini; *Screenplay:* Lionello De Felice, Arnaldo Marrosu, Gianfranco Parolini; *Photography:* Francesco Izzarelli (Eastmancolor, Totalscope, aspect ratio 2.35:1); *Film Editor:* Edmond Lozzi; running time: 101 minutes (Italy), 97 minutes (U.S.); released November 26, 1964 (Italy).

Cast: Alan Steel *(Ursus)*; Mimmo Palmara *(False Ursus)*; Lisa Gastoni *(Alina)*; Rosalba Neri *(Demora)*; Carlo Tamberlani *(King Igos)*; Orchidea De Santis *(Blonde Girl)*; Thomas King; Gianni Rizzo *(Teomoco)*; Enzo Maggio *(Manina)*; Nello Pazzafini *(Samur)*; Enzo Doria; Arnaldo Dell'Acqua; Giuseppe Mattei (billed as "Pino Mattei"); Vassili Karis *(Prince Dario)*; Tony Maggio; Franco Ukmar *(Dario's Henchman)*.

Comments: The mighty Ursus opposes a cruel tyrant in this epic. Co-produced by Italy's Cine-Italia Film and France's International Production Cinématographique.

The Three Pirates *(I tre corsari)* (L.C.J. Editions and Productions/Ponti-De Laurentiis Cinematografica, 1952)

Credits: *Director:* Mario Soldati; *Producers:* Dino De Laurentiis, Carlo Ponti; *Screenplay:* Emilio Salgari, Ennio De Concini, Agenore Incrocci, Furio Scarpelli; *Photography:* Tonino Delli Colli (black-and-white, aspect ratio 1.37:1); *Film Editor:* Leo Cattozzo; *Music:* Nino Rota; *Art Direction:* Flavio Mogherini; *Set Decoration:* Piero Gherardi; *Costume Design:* Dario Checci; *General Manager:* Bruno Todini; *Production Supervisor:* Fernando Cinquini; *Assistant Directors:* Sergio Leone, Cesare Olivieri; *Sound:* Biagio Fiorelli; *Camera Operator:* Sergio Bergamini; *Assistant Camera Operator:* Bianco Bernardini; *Production Secretary:* Angelo Binarelli; *Script Supervisors:* Pio Angeletti, Sergio Leone, Rometta Pietrostefani; *Master of Arms:* Enzo Musumeci Greco; running time: 88 minutes (Italy); released October 16, 1952 (Italy).

Cast: Ettore Manni *(The Black Corsair, Enrico di Ventimiglia)*; Marc Lawrence *(Van Gould)*; Barbara Florian *(Isabella)*; Renato Salvatori *(The Red Corair, Rolando di Ventimiglia)*; Cesare Danova *(The Green Corsair, Carlo di Ventimiglia)*; Alberto Sorrentino *(Agonia)*; Gualtiero Tumiati *(Count do Ventimiglia)*; Ignazio Balsamo *(Van Stiller)*; Joop Van Hulzen *(Viceroy de S.M.)*; Ubaldo Lay *(Alvaro, the Jailer)*; Amedeo Dejana *(Enfer)*; Tiberio Mitri *(Jordan Graumont)*; Fernando Iannilli *(Sharp)*; Gianni Luda *(Gillent)*; Giorgio Costantini *(Capt. Esöpagnol)*; Mario Glori *(Diego)*; Ettore Jannetti *(Ruben)*; Piero Pastore *(Capt. Du Galion)*; Lili Cerasoli [billed as "Liliana Cerasoli"] *(Margherita)*; Marga Cella *(Manoela)*; Mimo Billi *(Innkeeper)*; Felice Minotti; Silvana Maldi.

Comments: A pirate adventure, co-produced by Italy's Ponti-De Laurentiis Cinematografica and France's L.C.J. Editions & Productions.

Three Swords for Rome *(I tre centurioni)* (Ca.Pi Film S.r.l./Radius Productions, 1964)

Credits: *Director:* Roberto Mauri; *Screenplay:* Roberto Mauri, Edoardo Mulargia; *Photography:* Vitaliano Natalucci (color, Totalscope, aspect ratio 2.35:1); *Music:* Aldo Piga; running time: 95 minutes (Italy), 85 minutes (U.S.); released December 31, 1964 (Italy).

Cast: Roger Browne *(Fabio)*; Mimmo Palmara *(Maximo)*; Mario Novelli [billed as "Tony Freeman"] *(Julio)*; Lisa Gastoni *(Elena)*; Mario Feliciani; Philippe Hersent; Walter Brandi; Nerio Bernardi; Véra Valmont.

Comments: This sword-and-sandal action yarn was co-produced by Italy's Ca. Pi Film S.r.L. and France's Radius Productions.

Thunder of Battle *(Coriolano, eroe senza patria)* (Comptoir Français du Film Production/CFFP/Doria Film, 1964)

Credits: *Director:* Giorgio Ferroni; *Producer:* Diego Alchimede; *Screenplay:* Remigio Del Grosso; *Photography:* Augusto Tiezzi (Eastmancolor, Euroscope, aspect ratio 2.35:1); *Film Editor:* Antonietta Zita; *Music:* Carlo Rustichelli; running time: 96 minutes (Italy); released March 5, 1964 (Italy).

Cast: Gordon Scott *(Coriolanus)*; Alberto Lupo *(Escinio)*; Lilla Brignone *(Volumnia)*; Philippe Hersent *(Consul Cominio)*; Rosalba Neri *(Virginia)*; Aldo Bufi Landi *(Marco)*; Angela Minervini *(Livia)*; Pierre Cressoy *(King Aufidio)*; Gaetano Quartararo *(Junio Bruto)*; Nerio Bernardi *(Menenio Agripa)*; Valerio Tordi; Piero Pastore; Tullio Altamura *(Advisor)*; Nello Pazzafini *(Prisoner)*; Fortunato Arena *(Servant)*; Salvatore Borghese *(Addetto)*.

Comments: It's Coriolanus versus the Roman

Empire in this epic, which re-uses footage from *The Trojan Horse* and *Hannibal* (both *qv*). Co-produced by Italy's Doria Film, Explorer '58 and France's Comptoir Français du Film Production (CFFP).

Tiger of the Seven Seas (La tigre dei sette mari) (Embassy Pictures, 1962)

Credits: Director: Luigi Capuano; *Producer:* Ottavio Poggi; *Executive Producer:* Nino Battiferri; *Screenplay:* Luigi Capuano, Arpad DeRiso, Ottavio Poggi (from a story by Nino Battiferri); *Photography:* Alvaro Mancori (Eastmancolor, Totalscope, aspect ratio 2.35:1); *Film Editor:* Renato Cinquini; *Music:* Carlo Rustichelli; *Art Direction:* Ernest Kromberg, Amedeo Mellone; *Costume Design:* Giancarlo Bartolini Salimbeni; *Makeup:* Eligio Trani; *Hair Stylist:* Marisa Fraticelli; *Production Manager:* Antonio Sarno; *Assistant Director:* Gianfranco Baldanello; *Construction Manager:* Salvatore Siciliano; *Sound:* Fiorenzo Magli; *Camera Operator:* Sandro Mancori; *Production Secretary:* Arrigo Perri; *Script Supervisor:* Maria Luisa Rosen; *Master of Arms:* Bruno Arié; running time: 90 minutes (Italy); released December 23, 1962 (Italy), October 1964 (U.S.).

Cast: Gianna Maria Canale *(Consuelo)*; Anthony Steel *(William Scott)*; Maria Grazia Spina *(Anna de Cordoba)*; Ernesto Callindri *(Inigio de Cordoba)*; Andrea Aureli *(Robert, Consuelo's Father)*; Carlo Ninchi *(Tiger)*; John Kitzmiller *(Serpente)*; Carlo Pisacane *(Pirate)*; Nazzareno Zamperla *(Rick)*; Pasquale De Filippo; Giulio Battiferri *(Innkeeper)*; Renato Giomini; Renato Izzo; Salvatore Borghese.

Comments: Consuelo, the daughter of a pirate captain, joins forces with the heroic William Scott to recover a hidden treasure. Co-produced by Italy's Euro International Film (EIA) and Liber Film. Some scenes were filmed on Lake Garda in Italy. Footage from *The Lion of St. Mark* (*qv*) was reused in this film.

Treasure of the Petrified Forest (Il tesoro della Foresta Pietrificata) (Asteria Film/Avis Film, 1965)

Credits: Director: Erminio Salvi; *Producer:* Olga Chart; *Executive Producers:* Dante Chiappini, Pietro Fea; *Screenplay:* Luigi Tosi, Adriano Antonelli, Benito Ilforte, Erminio Salvi (from a story by Erminio Salvi); *Photography:* Mario Parapetti (Eastmancolor, Asterscope, aspect ratio 2.35:1); *Film Editor:* Enzo Alfonzi; *Music:* Rolf Ferraro; *Casting:* Pietro Nuccorini, Erminio Salvi; *Art Direction:* Peppino Ranceri; *Set Decoration:* Antonio Fratalocchi; *Makeup:* Guglielmo Bonotti; *Hair Stylist:* Constantino Teodori; *Production Supervisor:* Spartaco Conversi; *Production Manager:* Antonio Raffa; *Assistant Directors:* Graziella Marsetti, Pietro Nuccorini; *Sound:* Pietro Ortolani (Westrex sound system); *Sound Editor:* Cesare Bianchini; *Camera Operator:* Emilio Varriano; *Still Photographer:* Mario Sabatelli; *Fencing Master:* Pietro Ceccarelli; *Production Supervisor:* Spartaco Conversi; *Production Assistant:* Giosue Gardani; *Production Secretary:* Luigi Anastasi; running time: 111 minutes; released June 13, 1965 (Italy).

Cast: Gordon Mitchell *(Hunding)*; Ivica Pajer [billed as "Ivo Payer"] *(Sigmund)*; Eleonora Bianchi *(Siglinde)*; Pamela Tudor; Amedeo Trilli (billed as "Mike Moore"); Nat Coster (billed as "Nat Koster"); Pietro Ceccarelli (billed as "Puccio Ceccarelli"); Franco Doria; Attililo Severini; Franco Beltramme; Lella Cattaneo *(Witch)*; Lia Giordano; Giorgio Tesei; Giovanni Ivan Scratuglia (billed as "Ivan Scratuglia"); Luisa Rivelli *(Erika)*.

Comments: A loose re-interpretation of Germany's Nibelungenlied Saga, produced by the Italian companies Asteria Film, Avis Film and Olga Chart. Shot at Incir De Paolis Studios, Rome.

The Triumph of Michael Strogoff (Le triomphe de Michel Strogoff) (Fono Roma/Screen Gems Television, 1961)

Credits: Director: Victor Tourjansky (billed as "W. Tourjansky"); *Producer:* Emile Natan; *Screenplay:* Marc-Gilbert Sauvajon (based on the novel *Michael Strogoff* by Jules Verne); *Photography:* Edmond Séchan (Eastmancolor, Dyaliscope, aspect ratio 2.35:1); *Film Editors:* Armand Ridel, Henri Traverna; *Music:* Christian Chevallier, Hubert Giraud; *Production Design:*

René Renoux; *Assistant Production Designers:* André Bakst, Pierre Tyberghein; *Makeup:* Boris de Fast, Georges Klein, Maguy Vernadet; *Production Manager:* Ludmilla Goulian; *Unit Production Managers:* Pierre Cottance, Paul Laffargue, Suzanne Wiesenfeld; *Assistant Director:* Guy Lacourt; *Set Dresser:* Robert Turlure; *Sound Engineer:* Jean Monchablon; *Matte Shots:* Joseph Nathanson; *Camera Operator:* Pierre Goupil; *1st Assistant Camera Operator:* André Villard; *Assistant Camera Operators:* Guy Delattre, Arlette Massay; *Still Photographer:* Walter Limot; *Costume Supervisor:* Gladys de Segonzac; *Costumer:* Luce Scatena; *Assistant Film Editor:* Arlette Lalande; *General Administration:* Joseph Spigler; *Choreography:* Irina Grjebina; *Script Girl:* Claude Vériat; running time: 118 minutes; released December 15, 1961.

Cast: Curt Jurgens *(Michael Strogoff)*; Jacques Bézard; Capucine *(Tatoa, a Volskaya)*; Daniel Emilfork *(Ben Routh)*; Raymond Gérôme; Valéry Inkijinoff *(Amektal)*; Georges Lycan *(The Khan)*; Pierre Massimi [billed as "Pierre Massini"] *(Serge de Bachenberg)*; Pierre Mirat; Henri Massiet; Albert Pierjac *(Ivan)*; Claude Titre *(Igor Vassiliev)*; Simone Valère *(The Empress)*.

Comments: A sequel to *Michael Strogoff (qv)*. Co-produced by Italy's Fono Roma and France's Les Films Modernes.

The Triumph of Robin Hood (*Il trionfo di Robin Hood*) (Embassy Pictures, 1962)

Credits: Director: Umberto Lenzi; *Producer:* Tiziano Longo; *Screenplay:* Giancarlo Romitelli; *Photography:* Angelo Filippini (color, Totalscope, aspect ratio 2.35:1); *Music:* Aldo Piga; *Set Decoration:* Giuseppe Ranieri; *Production Manager:* Aurelio Serafinelli; *Assistant Director:* Giancarlo Romitelli; released September 15, 1962 (Italy).

Cast: Don Burnett *(Robin Hood)*; Gia Scala *(Anna)*; Samson Burke; Philippe Noël; Vincenzo Musolino; Gaia Germani; Germano Longo; Arturo Dominici; Enrico Luzi; Daniela Igliozzi; Vinicio Sofia; Gianni Solaro; Maks Furijan; Nello Pazzafini; Jurica Djakovic; Mauro Mannatrizio; Edda Ferronao; Janez Vrhovec *(John Lackland)*.

Comments: Basically an unofficial remake of Errol Flynn's classic *The Adventures of Robin Hood* (1938), with virtually the same plot. Produced by Italy's Buona Vista and Yugoslavia's Triglav Film. The scenes featuring the Sheriff of Nottingham's castle were filmed at Otocec, Slovenia, and the scene of King Richard's return from the Crusades were filmed at Bistra, Vrhnika, Slovenia.

The Triumph of the Son of Hercules (*Il trionfo di Maciste*) (Embassy Pictures, 1961)

Credits: Director: Tanio Boccia (billed as "Amerigo Anton"); *Producer:* Roberto Capitani; *Screenplay:* Arpad DeRiso, Giovanni Scolaro [billed as "Nino Scolaro'] (based on their story); *Cinematography:* Oberdan Troiani (Eastmancolor, Totalscope, aspect ratio 2.35:1); *Film Editor:* Gino Talamo; *Music:* Carlo Innocenzi, Guido Robuschi, Gian Stellari; *Production Design:* Amedeo Mellone; *Costume Design:* Walter Patriarca; *Makeup:* Romeo Fraticelli; *Hair Stylist:* Maria-Luisa Fraticelli; *Production Manager:* Roberto Capitani; *Assistant Director:* Mario Moroni; *Sound:* Alessandro Sarandrea; *Sound Recordist:* Giulio Fellicioni; *Sound Effects:* Raul Montesanti; *Special Effects:* Dino Galiano (billed as "Cataldo Galliano"), Vitantonio Ricci; *Camera Operator:* Mario Sensi; *Assistant Camera Operator:* Luigi Troiani; *Colorist:* Joseph Nathanson; *Still Photographer:* Alfio Quattrini; *Wardrobe:* Assunto Lazzazzera; *Production Assistant:* Augusto Dolfi; *Production Secretary:* Giulio Biagetti; *Continuity:* Silvana Vincenti; *Choreography:* Wilbert Bradley; running time: 88 minutes (Italy), 87 minutes (U.S.); released October 2, 1961 (Italy).

Cast: Kirk Morris *(Maciste)*; Cathia Caro *(Antea)*; Liuba Bodina *(Queen Tenefi)*; Cesare Fantoni *(Agadon)*; Giulio Donnini *(Omnes, the Merchant)*; Attilio Dottesio *(Arsinoe)*; Bruno Tocci *(Santos, Iram's Bodyguard)*; Salvatore Lago; Piero Leri *(Prince Iram)*; Lucia Randi [billed as "Lucy Randi"] *(Rais)*; Alfredo Salvatori [billed as "Alfredo Salvadori"] *(Tabor)*; Calisto Calisti *(Rais' and Tabor's Father)*; Cesare Lancia; Romano Ghini; Wilbert Bradley *(Dancer with Firebrands)*; Aldo Bufi Landi *(Themail)*; Carla Calò *(Yalis, the Oracle)*.

Comments: Maciste versus Tenefi, the evil Queen of Memphis, who sacrifices young women to the God of Fire. Produced by Italy's Jork Produzione Cinematografica. This film was the debut of Kirk Morris (1938–), real name Adriano Bellini. After his sword-and-sandal tenure had ended, Morris began a second career in advertising, then later returned to the film industry as a producer.

Triumph of the Ten Gladiators (Il trionfo dei dieci gladiatori) (Four Star Television, 1964)

Credits: Director: Nick Nostro; *Producer:* Armando Morandi; *Screenplay:* Nick Nostro, Sergio Sollima (from a story by Nick Nostro); *Photography:* Tino Santoni, Francisco Marin (Technicolor, Techniscope, aspect ratio 2.35:1); *Film Editor:* Enzo Alfonzi; *Music:* Carlo Savina; *Art Direction:* Giorgio Postiglione; *Set Decoration:* Carlo Gervasi; *Costume Design:* Massimo Bolongaro; *Makeup:* Piero Mecacci; *Hair Stylist:* Guido Mandini; *Production Manager:* Rodolfo Frattaioli; *Assistant Director:* Stefano Rollo; *Sound Engineer:* Fausto Ancillai; *Sound Effects:* Italo Cameracanna; *Camera Operators:* Giovanni Bergamini, Alfredo Marganiello; *Assistant Camera Operators:* Riccardo Damiani, Gianni Maddaleni; *Chief Grip:* Domenico Mattei; *Gaffer:* Gino Vinciguerra; *Wardrobe Mistress:* Elisabetta Costantini; *Assistant Film Editor:* Bruno Mattei; *Production Assistant:* Leo Daviddi; *Fencing Master:* Emilio Messina; *Script Supervisor:* Olga Pehar; running time: 106 minutes (Italy); released November 26, 1964 (Italy); video availability: Sinister Cinema.

Cast: Dan Vadis *(Roccia);* Helga Liné *(Queen Moluya);* Stelio Candelli [billed as "Stanley Kent"] *(Glauco Marcio);* Gianni Rizzo *(Sesto Vitullio);* Halina Zalewska *(Myrta);* Enzo Fiermonte [billed as "William Bird"] *(Rizio);* Leontine May *(Selima);* Carlo Tamberlani *(Publio Rufo);* Ivano Staccioli [billed as "John Heston"] *(Arimandro);* Emilio Messina [billed as "Don Emil Messina"] *(Lepto);* Ugo Sasso (billed as "Gordon Steve"); Salvatore Borghese (billed as "Sal Borgese"); Frank Oliveras (billed as "Frank Oliveiras"); Aldo Canti (billed as "Alan Lancaster"); Giuliano Dell'Ovo [billed as "Julian Dower"] *(Livurno);* Jeff Cameron; Pietro Torrisi; (billed as "Fred Hudson"); Dean Daves; Pietro Ceccarelli *(Matateo);* Franco Pesce; Mimmo Poli *(Tavern Owner).*

Comments: The heroic Roccia and his gladiators, sent on a mission by the consul of Syria, join forces with Glauco and kidnap Queen Moluya to prevent a war with Rome.

The Trojan Horse (La guerra di troia) (Colorama Features, 1961)

Credits: Director: Giorgio Ferroni; *Producer:* Giampaolo Bigazzi; *Screenplay:* Giorgio Ferroni, Ugo Liberatore, Giorgio Stegani, Federico Zardi; *Photography:* Reno Filippini (Technicolor, Techniscope, aspect ratio 2.35:1); *Film Editor:* Antonietta Zita; *Music:* Mario Ammonini, Giovanni Fusco; *Production Design:* Pier Vittorio Marchi, Zoran Zorcic; *Art Direction:* Dragoljub Ivkov, Jovan Radic, Milan Todorovic; *Optical Effects:* Enrico Catalucci; *Wardrobe:* Milanka Sultanovic; *Weapons Consultant:* Benito Stefanelli; *Soundtrack Album Producer:* Luca di Silverio; running time: 115 minutes (Italy), 105 minutes (U.S.); released October 26, 1961 (Italy), July 1962 (U.S.); video availability: Trimark Home Video.

Cast: Steve Reeves *(Aeneas);* Juliette Mayniel *(Creusa);* John Drew Barrymore *(Ulysses);* Edy Vessel *(Helen);* Lidia Alfonsi *(Cassandra);* Warner Bentivegna *(Paris);* Luciana Angiolillo *(Andromache);* Arturo Dominici *(Achilles);* Mimmo Palmara *(Ajax);* Nerio Bernardi *(Agamemnon);* Nando Tamberlani *(Menelaus);* Carlo Tamberlani *(Priam);* Giancarlo Bastianoni; Giovanni Cianfriglia; Luigi Ciavarro; Giulio Maculani; Nello Pazzafini; Andrej Gardenin.

Comments: The familiar story of the Trojan Horse, which was used to smuggle concealed warriors into the walled city of Troy. Co-produced by Italy's Europa Cinematografica, the French companies Compagnie Industrielle et Commerciale Cinématographique (CICC), Les Films Modernes, and Yugoslavia's Lovcen Film. Shot at Centralni Filmski Studio, Kosutnak, Belgrade, Serbia.

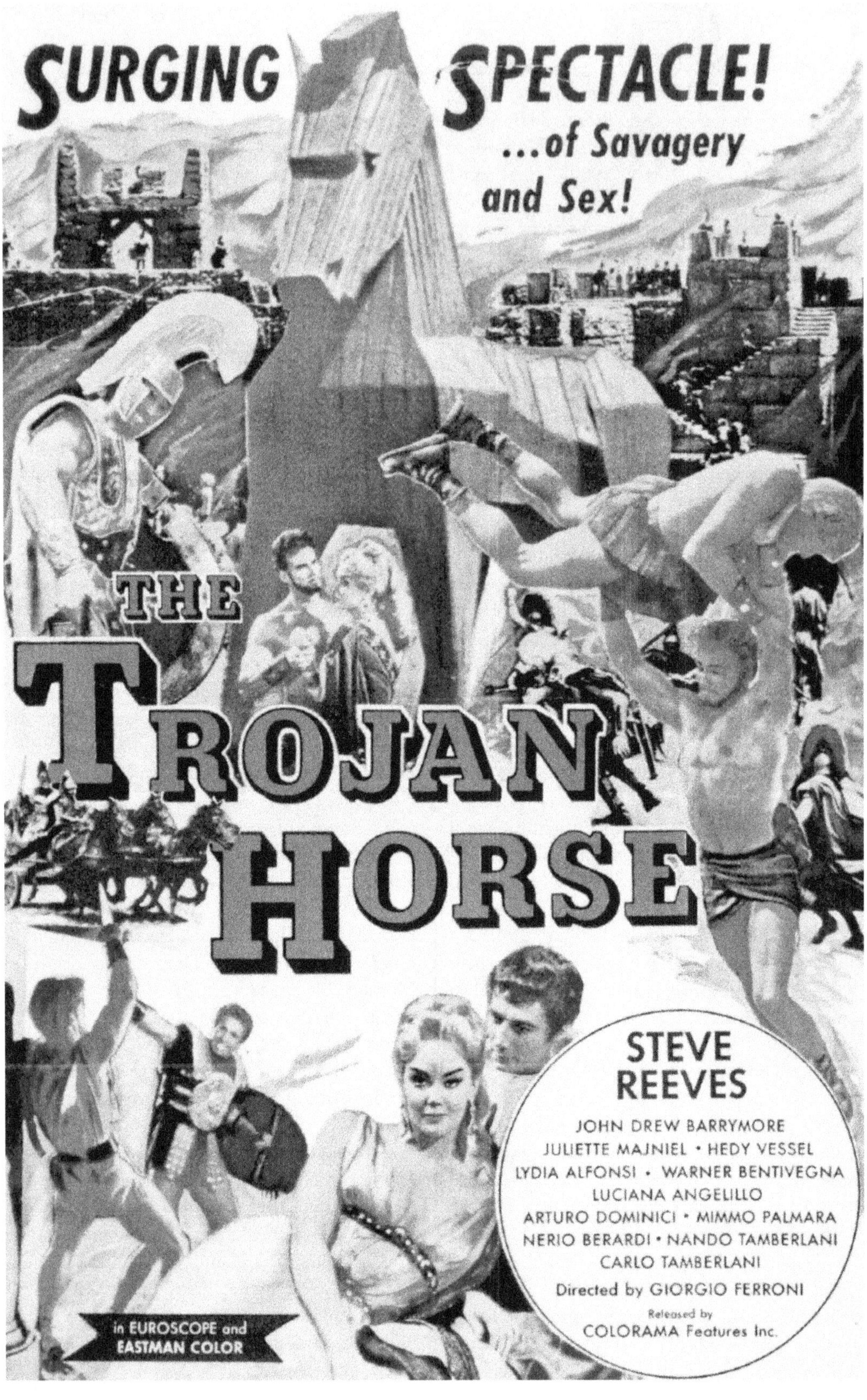
SURGING SPECTACLE!
...of Savagery and Sex!
THE TROJAN HORSE
STEVE REEVES
JOHN DREW BARRYMORE
JULIETTE MAJNIEL • HEDY VESSEL
LYDIA ALFONSI • WARNER BENTIVEGNA
LUCIANA ANGELILLO
ARTURO DOMINICI • MIMMO PALMARA
NERIO BERARDI • NANDO TAMBERLANI
CARLO TAMBERLANI
Directed by GIORGIO FERRONI
Released by
COLORAMA Features Inc.
in EUROSCOPE and EASTMAN COLOR

The Two Gladiators (I due gladiatori) (ABC Films, 1964)

Credits: Director: Mario Caiano; *Screenplay:* Mario Amendola, Alfonso Brescia (from their story), dialogue for English-dubbed version: Tamara Lees; *Photography:* Pier Ludovico Pavoni (Eastmancolor [some prints Technicolor], Techniscope, aspect ratio 2.25:1); *Film Editor:* Nella Mannuzzi; *Music:* Carlo Franci; *Production Design:* Pier Vittorio Marchi; *Set Decoration:* Franco D'Andria; *Costume Design:* Mario Giorsi; *Makeup:* Otello Fava; *Hair Stylist:* Elda Magnanti; *Wig Maker:* Rocchetti; *Production Supervisor:* Albino Morandini; *Production Manager:* Carlo Vassalle; *Assistant Directors:* Filiberto Fiaschi, Filippo Perrone; *2nd Unit Director:* Alfonso Brescia; *Set Designer:* Pier Vittorio Marchi; *Sound:* Franco Groppioni; *Weapons and Props:* E. Rancati; *Footwear:* Pompei; *Fencing Master:* Bruno Ukmar; *Camera Operator:* Fausto Rossi; *Assistant Camera Operator:* Mario Pastorini; *Costumes:* Tigano Lo Faro; *Assistant Costume Designer:* Antonio Randaccio; *Script Supervisor:* Liana Ferri; running time: 100 minutes (Italy), released July 10, 1964 (Italy); video availability: Mill Creek Entertainment.

Cast: Richard Harrison *(Lucius Crassus)*; Moira Orfei *(Marzia)*; Alberto Farnese *(Leto)*; Mimmo Palmara *(Commodus)*; Mirko Ellis *(Pertinance)*; Piero Lulli *(Cleandro)*; Enzo Fiermonte *(Gen. Ottavio Cratico)*; Ivy Holzer *(Emilia)*; Giuliano Gemma *(Orazio)*; Álvaro de Luna *(Pannunzio)*; Adriano Micantoni [billed as "Peter White"] *(Pompeo)*; Gianni Solaro *(Tarrunio)*; Renato Montalbano *(Centurion Prison Guard)*; Nello Pazzafini *(Settler Leader)*; Fortunato Arena; Franco Pasquetto; Osiride Pevarello; Renzo Pevarello; Bruno Ukmar; Franco Ukmar.

Comments: The insane Emperor Commodus leads Rome on a downward path toward self-destruction. Produced by Italy's Prometeo Film S.r.L. Filmed at De Paolis Studios, Rome.

Two Nights with Cleopatra (Due notti con Cleopatra) (Ultra Pictures Corp., 1954)

Top and above: **Sophia Loren in** *Two Nights with Cleopatra.*

Opposite: **Poster for** *The Trojan Horse.*

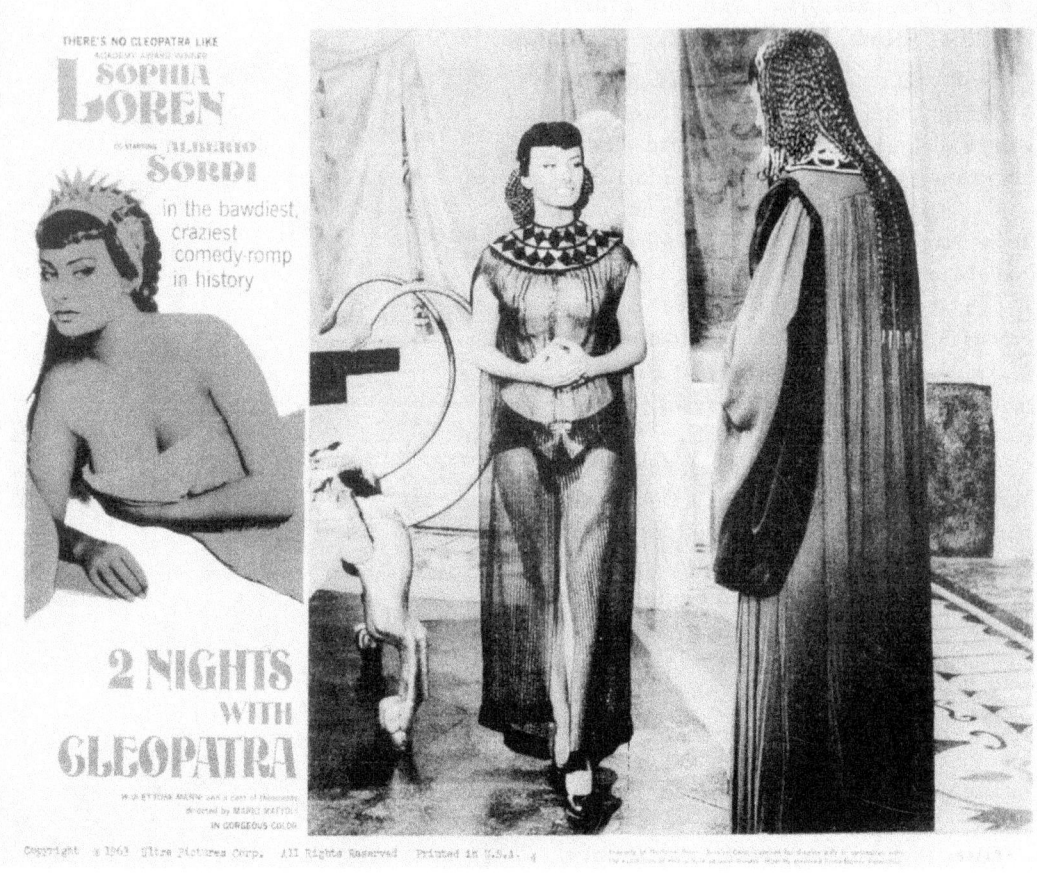

Poster for *Two Nights with Cleopatra*.

Credits: *Director:* Mario Mattoli; *Producer:* Giuseppe Colizzi; *Screenplay:* Ruggero Maccari, Ettore Scola (from their story); *Photography:* Riccardo Pallottini, Karl Struss (Ferraniacolor, aspect ratio 1.37:1); *Film Editor:* Renato Cinquini; *Music:* Armando Trovajoli; *Production Design:* Alberto Boccianti; *Set Decoration:* Riccardo Domenici; *Costume Design:* Gaia Romanini; *Makeup:* Otello Fava; *Hair Stylist:* Goffredo Rochetti; *Production Manager/Production Supervisor:* Totò Mignone; *Production Manager:* Giuseppe Colizzi; *1st Assistant Director:* Roberto Cinquini; *2nd Assistant Director:* Mariano Laurenti; *Production Secretary:* Antonio Negri; *Assistant Production Secretary:* Manolo Bolognini; running time: 78 minutes; released February 4, 1954 (Italy), April 4, 1964 (U.S.).

Cast: Sophia Loren *(Cleopatra/Nisca)*; Alberto Sordi *(Cesarino)*; Paul Muller *(Tortul)*; Nando Bruno *(Soldier)*; Alberto Talegalli *(Enobarbo)*; Gianni Cavalieri *(Innkeeper)*; Ugo D'Alessio *(Cocis)*; Rolf Tasna *(Guard)*; Ughetto Bertucci *(Merchant)*; Ettore Manni *(Marcantonio)*; Andrea Bosic *(Caio Malpurnio)*; Cristina Fantoni *(Dedit)*; Giacomo Furia *(Merchant)*; Enzo Garinei *(Merchant)*; Riccardo Garrone *(Guard)*; Amedeo Girardi *(Prisoner)*; Emilio Petacci *(Prisoner)*; Amerigo Santarelli *(Soldier)*; Mario Siletti *(Prisoner)*; Vando Tress *(Guard)*; *Voice-Dubbing Actors:* Miranda Bonansea (for Sophia Loren as "Nisca"); Lidia Simoneschi (for Sophia Loren as "Cleopatra").

Comments: A beautiful slave girl, an identical twin of Cleopatra, takes the Queen's place and impersonates her. This film was co-produced by Italy's Excelsa Film and Rosa Film. Shot at Ponti-De Laurentiis studios in Rome. This production was originally conceived as a vehicle for Gina

Lollobrigida, who bowed out unexpectedly; Sophia Loren was the hurriedly-cast replacement. The European version contains more nudity of Loren.

The Tyrant of Castile (*Sfida al re di Castiglia*) (Four Star Television, 1963)

Credits: *Director:* Ferdinando Baldi; *Producer:* Virgilio De Blasi; *Screenplay:* Adriano Bolzoni, Andrés Dolera, Piero Pierotti (from a story by Ferdinando Baldi); *Photography:* Francisco Marin (Technicolor, Techniscope, aspect ratio 2.35:1); *Film Editor:* Otello Colangeli; *Music:* Carlo Savina; *Art Direction:* Antonio Visone; *Costume Design:* Gabriella Gabrielli; *Sound:* Mario Del Pezzo, Mario Morigi (Westrex sound system); running time: 100 minutes; released December 24, 1963.

Cast: Mark Damon *(Pietro I, King of Castille)*; Rada Rassimov *Anna Coronel)*; Paolo Gozlino *(Enrico of Trastamara)*; Maria Teresa Orsini *(Maria Coronel)*; Carlos Estrada *(Diego)*; Anna Maria Surdo *(Bianca of Borbone)*; Fernando Cebrián; Andrés Mejuto *(Albuquerque)*; José Luis Pellicena; Goffredo Unger; Ricardo Valle; German Grech; Antonio Moreno; Luis Villar; Adriana Ambesi.

Comments: A take-off on *El Cid* (qv), set in Medieval Spain, and loosely based on historical figures. Co-produced by Italy's Alexandra Produzioni Cinematografiche and Spain's Procusa.

The Tyrant of Lydia Against the Son of Hercules (*Goliath e la schiava ribelle*) (AVCO Embassy Television, 1964)

Credits: *Director:* Mario Caiano; *Producer:* Giorgio Agliani; *Screenplay:* Gian Paolo Callegari, Albert Valentin; *Photography:* Pier Ludovico

Gordon Scott and Ombretta Colli in *The Tyrant of Lydia Against the Son of Hercules.*

Gordon Scott in *The Tyrant of Lydia Against the Son of Hercules*.

Pavoni (Eastmancolor, Euroscope, aspect ratio 2.35:1); *Film Editor:* Nella Nannuzzi; *Music:* Carlo Franci; *Production Designer:* Pier Vittorio Marchi (billed as "Vittorio Marchi"); *Art Director:* Franco D'Andria; *Costume Designer:* Mario Giorsi; *Assistant Director:* Alfonso Brescia; *Sound:* Mario Del Pezzo, running time: 105 minutes (Italy), 86 minutes (U.S.); released September 5, 1963 (Italy), 1964 (U.S.).

Cast: Gordon Scott *(Goliath/Gordian)*; Ombretta Colli *(Princess Cori)*; Gloria Milland *(Zoé)*; Mimmo Palmara *(Artafernes)*; Giuseppe Fortis *(Barbuk)*; Serge Nubret [billed as "Serge Noubret"] *(Milan)*; Paolo Petrini; Nadia Du Montiel; Mirko Ellis *(Politician with Marcius)*; Lea Lander (billed as "Lea Kruger"); Aldo Pina; Amedeo Trilli *(Slave Trader)*; Gabriele Antonini *(Alexander the Great)*; Massimo Serato *(Marcius)*; Nando Angelini *(Soldier)*; Harry Baird *(Slave)*; Calisto Calisti *(Guard at City Gate)*; Luciano Foti *(Soldier)*; Mauro Mannitrizio *(Soldier)*; Emilio Messina *(Macedonian Wrestler)*; Nello Pazzafini *(Ambush Leader)*; Vladimiro Piccia Fuochi *(Soldier)*; Bruno Ukmar *(Libyan Rebel)*; Franco Ukmar *(Macedonian Wrestler)*.

Comments: Goliath aids the kingdom of Lydia in a violent conflict between the forces of Alexander the Great and King Dareios of Persia. Co-produced by Italy's Compagnia Internazionale Realizzazioni Artistiche Cinematografiche (CIRAC), Films Internazionali Artistici (FIA), and France's Les Productions Georges de Beauregard.

Ulysses (Ulisse) (Paramount, 1954)

Credits: *Director:* Mario Camerini; *Producers:* Dino De Laurentiis, Carlo Ponti; *Associate Producer:* William Schorr; *Screenplay:* Franco Brusati, Mario Camerini, Ennio De Concini, Hugh Gray, Ben Hecht, Ivo Perilli, Irwin Shaw (based on the poem *The Odyssey* by Homer); *Photography:* Harold Rosson (Technicolor, aspect ratio 1.66:1); *Film Editor:* Leo Cattozzo; *Music:* Alessandro Cicognini; *Production Design:* Flavio Magherini; *Set Decoration:* Andrea A. Tomassi; *Costume Design:* Carosa, Giulio Coltellacci, Mme. Gres (costumes for Silvana Mangano), Barbara Karinska, Salvini Werther; *Shoes:* Tito Petrocchi; *Makeup:* Goffredo Rochetti, Eugen Schüfftan; *Hair Stylist:* Iole Cecchini; *Production Supervisors:* Fernando Cinquini, Ralph Serpe; *General Production Manager:* Bruno Todini; *Assistant Directors:* Guidarino Guidi, Otto Pellegrini, Serge Vallin; *Art Dept. Manager:* Italo Tomassi; *Sound Engineer:* Mario Morigi (Western Electric sound system); *Sound Recordists:* Bernard Held, Mauro Zambuto; *Sound Mixer:* Mario Amari; *Special Effects:* Eugen Schüfftan; *Camera Operators:* Mario Bava, Mario Parapetti; *Assistant Camera Operator:* Robert Kindred; *Assistant Film Editor:* Tatiana Casini Morigi; *Color Consultant:* Joan Bridge; *Music Director:* Franco Ferrara; *Script Supervisor:* Giovanella Zannoni; *Pre-Production Design:* Georg Wilhelm Pabst; running time: 117 minutes (Italy), 94 minutes (U.S.); released October 6, 1954 (Italy), October 1955 (U.S.); video availability: Lionsgate.

Original Italian poster for *The Tyrant of Lydia Against the Son of Hercules*.

Cast: Kirk Douglas *(Ulysses)*; Silvana Mangano *(Circe/Penelope)*; Anthony Quinn *(Antinoos)*; Rossana Podestà *(Nausicaa)*; Jacques Dumesnil *(Alicinous)*; Daniel Ivernel *(Euriloco)*; Franco Interlenghi *(Telemachus)*; Elena Zareschi *(Cassandra)*; Evi Maltagliati *(Anticlea)*; Ludmilla Dudarova *(Arete)*; Tania Weber *(Eucalicanto)*; Piero Lulli *(Achille)*; Ferrucio Stagni *(Mentor)*; Alessandro Fersen *(Diomede)*; Oscar Andriani *(Cyclops)*; Umberto Silvestri *(Polifemo/Krakos)*; Gualtiero Tumiati *(Laerte)*; Teresa Pellati *(Melanto)*; Mario Feliciani *(Eurimaco)*; Michele Riccardini *(Leodes)*; Andrea Aureli; Andrea Bosic *(Agamemnon)*; Walter Brandi *(Ageleo)*; Lucia Brusco; Daniele Dentice *(Euriade)*; Giovanni Di Benedetto *(Demolteleno)*; Mirella Di Lauri; Jenny Folchi; Piero Ghione *(Anfimedonte)*; Sergio Giovannucci *(Polibos)*; Ettore Jannetti; Victor Ledda; Alberto Lupo; Enzo Maggio; Renato Malavasi *(Medonte)*; Piero Mastrocinque; Carlo Mazzoni; Vera Molnar *(Girl)*; Claudio Morgan; Corrado Nardi; Piero Pastore *(Leocrito)*; Massimo Pietrobon; Aldo Pini *(Polites)*; Roberto Rai; Amerigo Santarelli; Gollarda Sapienza *(Eurimione)*; Gino Scotti; Benito Stefanelli *(Elatos)*; Edoardo Toniolo; Lidia Simoneschi *(Voice Dubbing for Silvana Mangano)*.

Comments: The Greek legend of Ulysses as his wife awaits his return after the Trojan War. A superlative fantasy/adventure, co-produced by Italy's Lux Film, Producciones Ponti-De Laurentiis, France's Zenith Films, and Paramount Pictures. Filmed at Ponti-De Laurentiis Studios in Rome, and on location in Italy and on the coasts and islands of the Mediterranean Sea. Actress Silvana Mangano (Circe/Penelope) was married to producer Dino De Laurentiis. Special Effects technician Eugen Schüfftan had previously worked on Fritz Lang's *Metropolis* (1926).

Ulysses Against the Son of Hercules *(Ulisse contro Ercole)* (Embassy Pictures Television, 1964)

Credits: *Director:* Mario Caiano; *Screenplay:* Mario Caiano, André Tabet (from their story); *Photography:* Alvaro Mancori (Eastmancolor, Totalscope, aspect ratio 2.35:1); *Film Editor:* Renato Cinquini; *Music:* Angelo Francesco Lavagnino; *Set Decoration:* Piero Filippone; *Set Furnishings:* Bruno Cesari; *Costume Design:* Mario Giorsi; *Production Manager:* Luigi Nannerini; *Assistant Director:* Carlo Pompe; *Assistant Director (French Version):* Gérard Ducaux-Rupp; *Special Effects:* Galliano Rico; *Camera Operator:* Sandro Mancori; running time: 105 minutes (Italy), 99 minutes (U.S. theatrical version), 91 minutes (U.S. TV version); released February 3, 1962 (Italy), 1964 (U.S.); video availability: Alpha Video.

Cast: Georges Marchal *(Ulysses)*; Mike Lane *(Hercules)*; Alessandra Panaro *(Elena)*; Dominique Boschero *(Queen of the Bird People)*; Gabriele Tinti *(Mercurio)*; Raffaella Carrà *(Leuconia)*; Eleonora Bianchi *(Prisoner of Lagos)*; Raf Baldassarre *(Prince Adrasto)*; Nando Angelini *(Messenger)*; Tino Bianchi *(King Ircano)*; Gianni Santuccio *(King Lagos)*; Yvette Lebon *(Glunone)*; Oscar Adriani *(Ircano's Advisor)*; Raffaele Pisu *(Assur)*.

Comments: The vengeful gods of Mt. Olympus send Hercules to capture Ulysses, who has incurred their wrath by blinding the Cyclops. Co-produced by Italy's Compagnia Cinematografica Mondiale (CCM) and France's Fidès. Filmed on location in the Canary Islands in Spain. Also known as *Ulysses Against Hercules*.

Ursus in the Land of Fire *(Ursus nella terra di fuoco)* (Embassy Pictures Television, 1963)

Credits: *Director:* Giorgio Simonelli; *Producer:* Giuseppe Fatigati; *Screenplay:* Luciano Martino, Marcello Ciorciolini, Ernesto Gastaldi (from a story by Luciano Martino); *Photography:* Luciano Trasatti (Eastmancolor, Dyaliscope, aspect ratio 2.35:1); *Film Editor:* Franco Fraticelli; *Music:* Carlo Savina; *Art Direction:* Romano Paxwell; *Set Designer:* Giuseppe Ranieri; *Laboratory:* Tecnostampa, Rome, Italy; running time: 90 minutes (Italy), 87 minutes (U.S.); released October 31, 1963 (Italy); video availability: Something Weird Video.

Cast: Ed Fury *(Ursus)*; Luciana Gilli *(Princess Diana)*; Adriano Micantoni *(Hamilkar)*; Claudia Mori *(Mila)*; Nando Tamberlani *(Lotar)*; Giuseppe Addobbati *(Magistrate)*; Pietro Ceccarelli *(Lero)*; Diego Pozetto; Giulio Mauroni;

Nino Fuscagni; Tom Felleghy (*Officer*); Claudia Giannotti; Mireille Granelli; Alba Maiolini (*Villager*).

Comments: Strongman Ursus leads a revolt against Hamikar, a cruel usurper. Co-produced by Italy's Cine-Italia Film and Splendor Film. A sequel to *Ursus (qv)*.

Vengeance of the Vikings (*Erik il Vichingo*) (As Films Producción/ Nike Cinematografica, 1965)

Credits: Director: Mario Caiano; *Executive Producers:* Luigi Mondello, José Maria Ramos; *Screenplay:* Mario Caiano, Arpad DeRiso, Giovanni Scolaro [billed as "Nino Scolaro"] (based on a story by Arpad DeRiso, Giovanni Scolaro, Spanish adaptation by Mariano Ozores); *Photography:* Enzo Barboni (Eastmancolor, Cinepanoramic, aspect ratio 1.85:1); *Film Editor:* Jolanda Benvenuti; *Music:* Carlo Franci; *Production Design:* Luciano Vincenti; *Set Decoration:* Bruno Cesari; *Costume Design:* Maria Luisa Panaro; *Makeup:* Angelo Roncaioli, *Hair Stylist:* Agostina Ferri; *Production Supervisor:* Augusto Dolfi; *Assistant Directors:* Francisco Ariza, Angelo Sangermano; *Assistant Set Decorator:* Luciano Finocchiaro; *Sound Engineer:* Umberto Picistrelli; *Camera Operator:* Antonio Modica; *Assistant Camera Operator:* Mario Cimini; *Assistant Film Editor:* Beatrice Felici; *Script Supervisor:* Liana Ferri; running time: 95 minutes; released September 24, 1965.

Cast: Gordon Mitchell (*Sven/Byarni*); Giuliano Gemma (*Erik*); Eleonora Bianchi [billed as "Ely McWhite"] (*Gudrid*); Elisa Montés (*Wata-wa*); Eduardo Fajardo (*Olaf*); Beni Deus [billed as "Beny Deus"] (*Torstein*); Lucio De Santis (*Erloff*); Roberto Ceccacci (billed as "Roby Ceccacci"); Aldo Pini; Fortunato Arena (*Thormann*); Fedele Gentile (*Viking Chief*); Franco Moruzzi (billed as "Franco Morici"); Aldo Bufi Landi (*Angheropoulos*); Alfio Caltabiano; Erno Crisa (*Eyolf*); Gianni Solaro [billed as "Giovanni Solaro"] (*Danish Ambassador*); Carla Calò [billed as "Carol Brown"] (*Freiodis, Erik's Mother*); Gustavo Salafranca.

Comments: Centuries before Columbus, the adventurous son of a Viking travels to the New World. Co-produced by Italy's Nike Cinematografica, Spain's As Films Producciónes, and Yugoslavia's Triglav Film. Some scenes were shot on location in Spain.

The Vengeance of Ursus (*La vendetta di Ursus*) (Medallion Pictures, 1961)

Credits: Director: Luigi Capuano; *Producer:* Ferdinand Felicioni; *Screenplay:* Marcello Ciorciolini, Luigi Capuano, Roberto Gianviti, Nino Scolaro (from a story by Marcello Ciorciolini); *Photography:* Oberdan Troiani (Eastmancolor, Totalscope, aspect ratio 2.35:1); *Film Editor:* Antonietta Zita; *Production Design:* Alfredo Montori; *Set Decoration:* Camillo Del Signore; *Costume Design:* Antonia Quilici; *Makeup:* Duilio Scarozza; *Hair Stylist:* Adrianna Cassini; *Production Manager:* Ferdinand Felicioni; *Assistant Director:* Gianfranco Baldanello; *Set Construction Architect:* Alfredo Montori; *Sound:* Mario Del Pezzo; *Fencing Master:* Franco Fantasia; *Camera Operator:* Mario Sensi; *Assistant Camera Operator:* Luigi Troiani; *Production Assistants:* Augusto Dolfi, Giulio Pappagallo; *Script Girl:* Nellita Zampieri; *Laboratory:* S.P.E.S., Rome, Italy; running time: 88 minutes (Italy), 85 minutes (U.S.); released December 7, 1961 (Italy); video availability: Alpha Video.

Cast: Samson Burke (*Ursus*); Wandisa Guida (*Sira*); Livio Lorenzon (*King Zagro*); Nadia Sanders (*Sabra*); Nerio Bernardi (*King Alteo*); Gianni Rizzo (*Licurgo*); Franco Fantasia (*Captain of the Guard*); Roberto Chevalier (*Dario, Ursus' Brother*); Gina Rovere (*Lidia*); Ignazio Balsamo (*Andros*); Andrea Costa; Atillo Dottesio; (*Afro, Zagro's Servant*); Fedele Gentile (*Anio's Friend*); Carlo Latimer; Ugo Sasso (*Anio, the Innkeeper*); Amedeo Trilli.

Comments: Ursus leads an uprising to overthrow the evil King Zagro, who lusts after the beautiful Princess Sira. Produced by Italy's Splendor Film. Shot at Incir De Paolis Studios, Rome.

Vulcan, Son of Jupiter (*Vulcano, figlio di Giove*) (Embassy Pictures, 1962)

Credits: Director: Erminio Salvi; *Producer:* Spartaco Antonucci; *Executive Producer:* Decio

188 *Vulcan* SOUND ERA

Top: Gordon Mitchell in *Vulcan, Son of Jupiter*. *Above:* Rod Flash in *Vulcan, Son of Jupiter*.

Salvi; *Screenplay:* Ambrogio Molteni, Gino Stafford, Benito Ilforte, Erminio Salvi (from a story by Erminio Salvi); *Photography:* Mario Parapetti (Eastmancolor, Supercinescope, aspect ratio 2.35:1); *Film Editor:* Otello Colangeli; *Music:* Marcello Giombini; *Production Design:* Angelo De Amicis; *Art Direction:* Ambrogio Molteni; *Costume Design:* Augusta Morelli; *Makeup:* Corrado Blengini; *Hair Stylist:* Evelina Maggi; *Unit Manager:* Franco di Mauro; *Assistant Directors:* Carlo Ferrero, Leo Scuccuglia; *2nd Unit Director:* Spartaco Antonucci; *Set Designer:* Giuseppe Ranieri; *Set Decoration:* Antonio Fratalocchi; *Exterior Sets:* Salvatore Siciliano; *Sound:* Alfredo Neri, Sandro Occhetti; *Special Effects:* Roberto Parapetti; *Fight Choreography:* Luigi Ciavarro, Romano Gaspari; *Assistant Camera Operator:* Giorgio Pasquali; *Special Costumes:* Orlando Giangrande; *2nd Unit Assistant:* Maurizio Pradeaux; *Choreography:* Leopoldo Sovona; *Script Supervisor:* Adriana Bellanti; *Laboratory:* Stacofilm S. p. a., Rome, Italy; running time: 80 minutes (Italy), 76 minutes (U.S.); released March 17, 1962 (Italy); video availability: Alpha Video.

Cast: Bella Cortez (*Aetna, the Sicilian Nymph*); Iloosh Khoshabe [billed as "Rod Flash"] (*Vulcan*); Liliana Zagra (*Sicilian Rebel Girl*); Furio Meniconi (*Jupiter, God of Lightning*); Roger Browne (*Mars, God of War*); Omero Gargano (*Neptune, God of the Sea*); Isarco Ravaioli (*Mercury, Messenger of the Gods*); Yvonne Sire (*Juno, Jupiter's Wife*); Salvatore Furnari (*Geo*); Ugo Sabetta (*Milos, King of the Thracians*); Renzo Stefilongo; Edda Ferronao (*Erida, Goddess of Hate*); Paolo Pieri; Pasquale Fasciano; Giuseppe Trinca; Annie Gorassini (*Venus, Goddess of Beauty*); Gordon Mitchell (*Pluto, God of Darkness*); Romano Gaspari; Amedeo Trilli; Luigi Ciavarro; Leopoldo Savona.

Comments: Jupiter, God of Lightning, decides to punish his daughter Venus for her sexual transgressions. Almost cheerful in its low-budget cheapness, this enjoyable fantasy was produced by Italy's Juno Produzione. Some location filming was done in Iran. This was the first peplum shot in that country.

Bella Cortez and Rod Flash in *Vulcan, Son of Jupiter*.

War Gods of Babylon (*Le sette folgori di Assur*) (American-International Television, 1964)

Credits: Director: Silvio Amadio; *Producer:* Alessandro Tasca; *Executive Producer:* Henry Lombroso; *Screenplay:* Gino De Santis, Diego Fabbri, Sergio Spina (from a story by Sergio Spina); *Photography:* Tino Santoni (Eastmancolor, Totalscope, aspect ratio 2.35:1); *Film Editor:* Nella Nannuzzi; *Music:* Angelo Francesco Lavagnino, Mario Nascimbene, Carlo Savina; *Art Direction:* Franco Lolli; *Costume Design:* Maria Baroni; *Special Makeup Effects:* Joseph Nathanson; *Art Dept. Manager:* Italo Tomassi; *Special Effects:* Antonio Margheriti, Giancarlo Urbisaglia; running time: 88 minutes (Italy); released November 24, 1964 (Italy); video availability: Something Weird Video.

Cast: Howard Duff *(Sardanapolo)*; Jocelyn Lane *(Mirra)*; Luciano Marin *(Sammash)*; Giancarlo Sbraglia *(Arbace)*; Arnoldo Foà *(Zoroastro)*; Stelio Candelli *(Ammurabi)*; José Greci *(Crisia)*; Luigi Borghese; Nico Pepe *(Namtar)*; Calisto Calisti; Omar Zolficar.

Comments: King Sardanapolo and his brother Prince Sammash are rivals for the affection of beautiful Mirra. Produced by Italy's Apo Film and Globe Film International.

War of the Zombies (*Roma contro Roma*) (American-International, 1964)

Credits: Director: Giuseppe Vari; *Executive Producer:* Samuel Z. Arkoff; *Screenplay:* Ferruccio De Martino, Piero Pierotti, Marcello Sartarelli (from a story by Ferruccio De Martino, Massimo De Rita); *Photography:* Gábor Pogány (color, Totalscope, aspect ratio 2.35:1); *Music:* Roberto Nicolosi; *Production Design:* Giorgio Giovannini; *Costume Design:* Tina Grani; *Makeup:* Euclide Santoli; *Hair Stylists:* Adriana Cassini, Marcella Favella; *Production Manager:* Paolo Mercuri; *Assistant Director:* Marcello Crescenzi; *Set Dresser:* Massimo Tavazzi; *Sound Engineer:* Ludovico Scardella; *Microphone Boom Operator:* Piero Leoni; *Special Effects:* Ugo Amadoro; *Pyrotechnics:* Dino Galiano, Paolo Ricci; *Camera Operator:* Mario Capriotti; *Still Photographer:* Aldo Galfano; *Assistant Film Editor:* Lina Caterini; *Production Administrator:* Dante Brini; *Production Assistant:* Pasquale Ferri; *Production Secretary:* Claudia Fedele; *Script Supervisor:* Mariella Vari; *Soundtrack Album Producer:* Luca di Silverio; running time: 98 minutes; released February 13, 1964 (Italy); March 1965 (U.S.).

Cast: John Drew Barrymore *(Aderbad)*; Susy Andersen *(Tulia)*; Ettore Manni *(Gaius)*; Ida Galli *(Rhama)*; Mino Doro *(Lutetius)*; Ivano Staccioli *(Sirion)*; Philippe Hersent *(Azer)*; Andrea Checchi; Livia Contardi; Mathilda Calnan; Rosy Zichel; Antonio Corevi; Giulio Maculani; Luciano Foti *(Armenian Soldier)*; Giuseppe Marrocco *(Armenian Soldier)*.

Comments: An evil magician, Aderbad, attempts to conquer the world with a zombie army of resurrected dead Roman soldiers. American distributor AIP changed the original title, *Rome Against Rome*, to the much more exploitable *War of the Zombies*. Produced by Italy's Galatea Film.

The Warrior and the Slave Girl (La rivolta dei gladiatori) (Columbia, 1958)

Credits: Director: Vittorio Cottafavi; *Producer:* Virgilio De Blasi; *Screenplay:* Gian Paolo Callegari, Ennio De Concini, Francesco De Feo, Gianfranco Parolini, Giovanni Simonelli, Francesco Thellung, Natividad Zaro (from a story by Natividad Zaro); *Photography:* Mario Pacheco (Eastmancolor, Supercinescope, aspect ratio 2.35:1); *Film Editor:* Julio Peña; *Set Decoration:* Vittorio Rossi, Antonio Simont; *Costume Design:* Enzo Bulgarelli; *Assistant Directors:* Augusto Fenollar, Gianfranco Parolini; running time: 88 minutes (Italy); released October 12, 1958 (Italy), March 9, 1960 (U.S.).

Cast: Ettore Manni *(Marcus Numidio)*; Gianna Maria Canale *(Amira)*; Mara Cruz *(Zahar)*; Georges Marchal *(Asciepio)*; Rafael Luis Calvo *(Lucano)*; Fidel Martin *(Osro)*; Vega Vinci; Jesús Tordesillas; Rafael Durán; Nando Tamberlani; Valeria Moniconi; Kerima; Salvatore Furnari; Juan Olaguibel; Eulália del Pino; Santiago Rivero; Conrado San Martin; Francisco Vázquez; Emilio Alonso Ferrer; Rafael Calvo Revilla; Vicente Bañó.

Comments: A Roman, Marcus Numidio, encounters court intrigue and treachery during an uprising in Armenia. Co-produced by Italy's Alexandra Produzioni Cinematografiche, France's Comptoir Français de Productions Cinématographiques (CFPC), and the Spanish companies Athenea Films and Estela Films.

The Warrior Empress (Saffo, Venere di Lesbo) (Columbia, 1960)

Credits: Director: Pietro Francisci; *Producers:* Marcello D'Amico, Gianni Hecht Lucari; *Screenplay:* Ennio De Concini, Pietro Francisci, Luciano Martino (from a story by Pietro Francisci); *Dialogue for English-Dubbed Version:* Patti Manning O'Brien; *Photography:* Carlo Carlini (Eastmancolor, CinemaScope, aspect ratio 2.35:1); *Film Editor:* Nino Baragli; *Music:* Angelo Francesco Lavagnino; *Art Direction:* Giulio Bongini; *Costume Design:* Gaia Romanini; *Production Manager:* Paolo Giovanardi; *Assistant Director:* Pietro Nuccorini; *Art Dept. Manager:*

A pre–*Gilligan's Island* Tina Louise in *The Warrior Empress*.

Italo Tomassi; *Sound:* Oscar De Arcangelis (Westrex sound system); *Camera Operator:* Luigi Filippo Carta; *Orchestra Conductor:* Carlo Savina; running time: 105 minutes (Italy), 89 minutes (U.S.); released August 29, 1960 (Italy), August 9, 1961 (U.S.).

Cast: Kerwin Matthews *(Phaon)*; Tina Louise *(Sappho)*; Riccardo Garrone *(Hyperbius)*; Susy Andersen [billed as "Susy Golgi"] *(Actis)*; Alberto Farnese *(Laricus)*; Enrico Maria Salerno *(Melanchrus)*; Antonio Battistella *(Paione)*; Streisa Brown *(Priestess of Aphrodite)*; Annie Gorassini *(Dyla)*; Aldo Fiorelli *(Scarface)*; Elda Tattoli *(Sappho's Nurse)*; Isa Crescenzi *(Peasant Woman)*; Lilly Montovani *(Cleide)*; Marisa Quattrini *(Temple's Guardian)*; Elena Zareschi *(Sibilla)*; Jacques Castelot; Solveyg D'Assunta *(Elena)*; Mirella Di Centa *(Mina)*; Elena Fontana; Erica Jorger; Litz Kibiska; Erina Locatelli; Elena May; Audrey McDonald; Olga Sievers; Elke Sommer.

Comments: Heroic warrior Phaon discovers a society of women on the island of Lesbos, and falls in love with the beautiful Sappho (Tina Louise of *Gilligan's Island* fame). Co-produced by Italy's Documento Films and France's Orsay Films. Future star Elke Sommer appears in a small role.

The White Warrior *(Agi Murad il diavolo bianco)* (Warner Bros., 1959)

Credits: Director: Riccardo Freda; *Producer:* Mario Zama; *Screenplay:* Gino De Santis, Ákos Tolnay (based on the novel *The White Warrior* by Leo Tolstoy); *Photography:* Mario Bava (Technicolor, Dyaliscope, aspect ratio 2.35:1); *Film Editor:* Riccardo Freda; *Music:* Roberto Nicolosi; *Production Design:* Kosta Krivokapic; *Art Direction:* Aleksandar Milovic; *Set Decoration:* Andrea Fantacci; *Costume Design:* Filippo Sanjust; *Makeup:* Antonio Marini; *Hair Stylist:* Anna Cristofani; *Production Supervisors:* Ermete Paolucci, Dusan Perkocic; *Production Managers:* Thomas Sagone, Milan Zmukic; *2nd Unit Director:* Leopoldo Savona; *Assistant Directors:* Milo Djukanovic, Odoardo Fiory, Mario Bava; *Assistant Art Director:* Milan Todorovic; *Sound Engineer:* Ovidio Del Grande; *Camera Operators:* Sekula Banovic, Kreso Grcevic, Ubaldo Terzano; *2nd Unit Photography:* Frano Vodopivec; *Final Colorist:* Andrea Gargano; *Orchestra Conductor:* Pier Luigi Urbini; *Choreography:* Branko Markovic; *Master of Arms:* Enzo Musumeci Greco; *Laboratory:* Technicolor; *Soundtrack Album Producer:* Luca di Silverio; running time: 91 minutes (Italy); released June 21, 1959 (Italy), February 10, 1961 (U.S.); video availability: Alpha Video.

Cast: Steve Reeves *(Agi/Hadji Murad, the White Warrior)*; Giorgia Moll *(Sultanet, Aslan Bey's Daughter)*; Scilla Gabel *(Princess Maria Vorontsova)*; Renato Baldini *(Ahmed Khan)*; Gérard Herter *(Prince Sergei Vorontzova)*; Milivoje Zivanovic *(Czar Nicholas I)*; Nikola Popovic *(King Shamil)*; Jovan Gec *(Aslan Bey)*; Niksa Stefanini *(Goanzalo)*; Milivoje Popovic-Mavid *(Dr. Eldar)*; Marija Tocinoski (billed as "Marija Tocinowki"); Pasquale Basile; Goffredo Unger (billed as "Goffredo Ungaro"); Antun Nalis *(Melders, Murad's Lieutenant)*; Dragomir Felba; Massimo Righi *(Czar's Orderly)*; June Foray *(English-Language Dubbing Voice)*.

Comments: 19th century Chechen leader Hadji Murad versus the Russian Czar and his invading army in this adaptation of Leo Tolstoy's novel, which the writer based on his own experiences in the Russian Army while in Chechnya. Co-produced by Italy's Majestic Film and Yugoslavia's Lovcen Film.

William Tell *(Guglielmo Tell)* (Fauno Film/I.C.E.T./Atlantis Film, 1949)

Credits: Directors: Giorgio Pastina, Michal Waszynski; *Producer:* Giorgio Venturini; *Screenplay:* Giorgio Pastina, Giuseppe Zucca (based on a play by Friedrich Schiller); *Photography:* Arturo Gallea, Giovanni Ventimiglia (black-and-white, aspect ratio 1.37:1); *Film Editor:* Loris Bellero; *Production Design:* Ernesto Nelli; *Costume Design:* Maria De Matteis; *Production Manager:* Vieri Bigazzi; *Assistant Director:* Giorgio Capitani; *1st Assistant Director:* Carla Ragionieri; *Camera Operator:* Marcello Gatti; running time: 91 minutes; released April 8, 1949.

Cast: Gino Cervi *(William Tell)*; Monique Orban *(Berta)*; Paul Muller *(Gessler)*; Raf Pindl *(Rodolfo di Andas)*; Allegra Sander *(Mathilde)*;

Gabriele Ferzetti *(Corrado Hant)*; Danielle Benson *(Edvige)*; Renato De Carmine *(Bertrando)*; Emilio Baldanello; Enrico Olivieri *(Gualtiero Tell)*; Laura Bigi; Aldo Nicodemi *(Rudens)*; Barbara Deperusse; Giovanni Lovatelli; Alberto Collo.

Comments: The legend of William Tell, produced by Italy's Fauno Film I.C.E.T.

The Witch's Curse *(Maciste all'inferno)* (Medallion Pictures, 1963)

Credits: Director: Riccardo Freda (billed as "Robert Hampton"); *Executive Producer:* Piero Donati; *Producers:* Luigi Carpentieri, Ermanno Donati; *Screenplay:* Oreste Biancoli, Ennio De Concini, Piero Pierotti (from a story by Eddy H. Given; *Photography:* Riccardo Pallotini (Eastmancolor, CinemaScope, aspect ratio 2.35:1); *Film Editor:* Ornella Micheli; *Music:* Carlo Franci; *Production Design:* Luciano Spadoni; *Art Direction:* Andrea Crisanti; *Production Manager:* Lucio Bompani; *Assistant Director:* Giorgio Gentili; *Special Effects:* Serse Urbisaglia; *Fencing Master:* Remo De Angelis; running time: 91 minutes; released April 11, 1962 (Italy), November 1963 (U.S.); video availability: Sinister Cinema.

Cast: Kirk Morris *(Maciste)*; Hélène Chanel *(Fania)*; Vira Silenti *(Young Martha Gant)*; Angelo Zanolli *(Charley Law)*; Andrea Bosic *(Judge Parrish)*; Donatella Mauro; Gina Mascetti *(Barmaid)*; Antonella Della Porta *(Doris)*; John Karlsen *(Burgomeister)*; Antonio Ciani; Pietro Ceccarelli (billed as "Puccio Ceccarelli"); Remo De Angelis *(Prometheus)*; Evaristo Maran *Villager)*; Charles Fawcett *(Doctor)*; John Francis Lane [billed as "Francis Lane"] *(Coachman)*; Veriano Ginesi; Neil Robinson *(Villager)*; Howard Nelson Rubien *(Old Villager)*; Trent Gough *(Dubbed Voices)*.

Comments: Maciste, suddenly appearing in the 17th century, uproots a magical tree and journeys to hell in an effort to find a witch and undo her curse. A wildly-plotted, flamboyant entry, and highly-recommended. Produced by Italy's Panda Film.

The Wonders of Aladdin *(La meraviglie di Aladino)* (Embassy Pictures, 1961)

Credits: Directors: Mario Bava, Henry Levin; *Producers:* Joseph E. Levine, Massimo Patrizi; *Screenplay:* Luther Davis, Franco Prosperi, Silvano Reina, Stefano Strucchi, Duccio Tessari, Marco Vicario (from a story by Stefano Strucchi); *Photography:* Tonino Delli Colli (Eastmancolor, CinemaScope, aspect ratio 2.35:1); *Film Editor:* Gene Ruggiero; *Music:* Angelo Francesco Lavagnino; *Art Direction:* Flavio Mogherini; *Costume Design:* Rosine Delamare, Giorgio Desideri; *2nd Unit Director:* Mario Bava; *Assistant Director:* Alberto Cardone; *2nd Assistant Director:* Franco Prosperi; *Sound:* Vittorio Trentino (Fonolux sound system); *Special Effects:* Mario Bava; *Music Director:* Mario Ammonini; *Choreography:* Dino Cavallo; running time: 100 minutes (Italy), 93 minutes (U.S.); released October 31, 1961 (Italy), December 13, 1961 (U.S.); video availability: New Line Home Video.

Cast: Donald O'Connor *(Aladdin)*; Noëlle Adam *(Djalma)*; Vittorio Di Sica *(Genie)*; Aldo Fabrizi *(Sultan)*; Michèle Mercier *(Princess Zaina)*; Milton Reid *(Omar)*; Terence Hill [billed as "Mario Girotti"] *(Prince Moluk)*; Fausto Tozzi *(Grand Vizier)*; Luigi Tosi; Marco Tulli *(Fakir)*; Raymond Brussières *(Magician)*; Alberto Farnese *(Bandit Chief)*; Franco Ressel *(Grand Vizier's Lieutenant)*; Vittorio Bonos *(Lamp Merchant)*; Adriana Facchetti *(Benhai, Aladdin's Mother)*; Giovanni Galletti *(Midwife)*; Omero Capanna *(Muzda)*; Tom Felleghy *(Doctor)*; Angelo Iacono *(Arab Man)*.

Comments: The fable of Aladdin and the magic lamp. Co-produced by Italy's Lux Film, France's Compagnia Cinématographique de France and Embassy Pictures. Some scenes were shot on Location in Tunisia. Lux Film had originally intended this as a vehicle for Steve Reeves.

Zorikan the Barbarian *(Zorikan lo sterminatore)* (Four Star Television, 1964)

Credits: Director: Roberto Mauri; *Producer:* Aldo Piga; *Screenplay:* Roberto Mauri, Edoardo Mulargia; *Photography:* Ugo Brunelli (color, Pancrorama, aspect ratio 2.35:1); *Film Editor:* Nella Nanuzzi; *Music:* Aldo Piga; *Art Direction:* Giuseppe Ranieri; *Makeup:* Maria Mastrocinque; *Hair Stylist:* Italia Marini; *Costumes:*

Poster for *The Witch's Curse.*

Elide Candidi; *Production Supervisor:* Cesare Scritti; *Production Manager:* Aurelio Serafinelli; *Special Effects:* Augusto Passaura; *Production Assistant:* Bruno Burani; *Camera Operator:* Renato Doria; *Sound:* N. Renda, F. Ancillai; *Script Supervisor:* Wanda Tuzi; *Fencing Master:* Franco Pasquetto; running time: 88 minutes (Italy), 92 minutes (U.S.); released March 30, 1964 (Italy).

Cast: Dan Vadis *(Zorikan)*; Eleonora Bianchi *(Julia)*; Walter Brandi *(Ramperti)*; Philippe Hersent; Vincenzo Musolino; Nello Pazzafini *(Vizir)*; Gino Marturano; Mario Lanfranchi; Luigi Batzella (billed as "Paolo Solvay"); Franco Pasquetto; Anita Todesco; Gino Turini [billed as "John Turner"].

Comments: Heroic Zorikan attempts to recover a Christian relic stolen by the villainous Ramperti. Produced by Italy's Walmar Cinematografica. Some scenes were shot on location at Predjana Castle in Postojna, Slovenia.

Zorro (Zorro) **(Allied Artists, 1976)**

Credits: *Director:* Duccio Tessari; *Executive Producer:* Luciano Martino (presented by Emmanuel L. Wolf); *Screenplay:* Giorgio Arturio (from his story); *English Language Dialogue:* Riccardo Walter; *Photography:* Giulio Albonico (Eastmancolor, aspect ratio 1.85:1); *Film Editor:* Mario Mora; *Music:* Guido De Angelis, Maurizio De Angelis; *Production Design:* Enzo Bulgarelli; *Costume Design:* Luciano Sagoni; *Assistant Costume Designer:* Vera Rita de Reya; *Key Makeup Artist:* Nilo Jacopini; *Makeup:* Michel Deruelle, Alfredo Marazzi; *Wigs:* Grazia Miccinelli; *Production Supervisors:* Vittorio Galiano, Beniamino Sterpetti; *Production Managers:* Maurizio Pastrovich, Averroè Stefani; *Assistant Director:* Marco Risi; *2nd Unit Director:* Mario Forges Davanzati; *Set Designer:* Riccardo Domenici; *Assistant Set Decorator:* Cristiano Tessari; *Sound Editor:* Bruno Zanoli; *Sound Effects:* Renato Marinelli; *Sound Mixer:* Danilo Moroni; *Microphone Boom Operator:* Angelo Amatulli; *Special Effects:* Dino Galiano (billed as "Cataldo Galiano"); *Stunt Coordinator:* Yvan Chiffre; *Stunts:* Alain Grellier; Robert Klein; Marcel Labbaye; Remy Pie; Jean-Pierre Renault; Brandy; Miguel Pedregosa; *Camera Operator:* Sabastiano Celeste; *Still Photographer:* Giorgio Garibaldi Schwarze; *Editorial Supervisor:* Paolo Vochicievich (billed as "Paolo Wochicievich"); *Assistant Film Editors:* Mariella Scalese, Roberto Sterbini; *Color Consultant:* Luciano Vittori; *Orchestra Conductor:* Gianfranco Plenizio; *Composer* (songs *Zorro is Back* and *To You Mi Chica*): S. Duncan Smith; *Master of Arms:* Ivan Chiffre (billed as "Ivan Chiffre"); *Production Secretary:* David Pash; *Script Supervisor:* Vittoria Vigorelli; *Jeweler:* Nino Lembo; running time: 124 minutes (Italy), 120 minutes (U.S.); released March 6, 1975 (Italy), June 1976 (U.S.), video availability: Gemstone Entertainment.

Cast: Alain Delon *(Don Diego/Zorro)*; Ottavia Piccolo *(Contessina Ortensia Pulido)*; Enzo Cerusico *(Joaquin, Don Diego's Servant)*; Moustache *(Sgt. Garcia)*; Giacomo Rossi Stuart *(Fritz von Merkel)*; Giampiero Albertini *(Brother Francisco)*; Marino Masé *(Miguel de la Serna)*; Raika Juri *(Senora de la Serna)*; Adriana Asti *(Aunt Carmen)*; Stanley Baker *(Col. Huerta)*; Yvan Chiffre *(Thug)*; Fabián Conde *(Goat Merchant)*; Tito Garcia *(Chicken Vendor)*; José Riesgo *(Grocer)*.

Comments: Zorro versus the corrupt Colonel Huerta in the Mexican province of Nueva Aragon. Co-produced by Italy's Mondial Televisione Film and France's Les Productions Artistes Associes. Filmed on location in Spain, with studio interiors shot in Italy.

Zorro in the Court of England (Zorro alla corte d'Inghilterra) **(Romana Film, 1970)**

Credits: *Director:* Franco Montemurro; *Producer:* Fortunato Misiano; *Screenplay:* Arpad DeRiso, Franco Monremurro; *Photography:* Augusto Tiezzi (color); *Music:* Angelo Francesco Lavagnino; *Costume Design:* Sibylle Geiger; *Microphone Boom Operator:* Corrado Volpicelli; released September 17, 1970.

Cast: Spiros Focás *(Pedro Suarez/Zorro)*; Dada Gallotti *(Rosanna Gonzales)*; Franco Ressel *(Lord Percy Moore)*; Massimo Carocci *(Pedrito)*; Tullio Altamura *(Manuel Garcia)*; Ignazio Balsamo *(Dice Gambler)*; Bruno Boschetti *(Official with Queen Victoria)*; Barbara Carroll *(Queen Victoria)*; Spartaco Conversi *(Francisco Cortez)*; Angela De Leo *(Luisa)*; Atilo Dottesio *(Cortez

Trial Prosecutor); Franco Fantasia *(Captain Wells)*; Antonio Gradoli *(General Kingston)*; Anna Maria Guglelmotti [billed as "Carol Wells"] *(Patricia Scott)*; Mirella Pamphili *(Cortez's Daughter)*; Daniele Vargas *(Sir Basil Ruthford)*; Liana Del Balzo *(Woman at Party)*.

Comments: A Zorro adventure, produced by Italy's Romana Film.

The Zorro of Monterrey (El Zorro de Monterrey) (Duca Internazionale/ Filmar Compagnia Cinematografica, 1971)

Credits: *Director:* José Luis Merino; *Producer:* Maria Ángel Coma Borrás; *Screenplay:* José Luis Damiani, Lorenzo Gicca Palli (billed as "Enzo Gicca"), María del Carmen, José Luis Merino, Mario Merino, Martinez Román (from a story by José Luis Damiani, Lorenzo Gicca Palli, Maria del Carmen, Martinez Román); *Photography:* Emanuele Di Cola, Antonio Modica (Eastmancolor, 89 minutes); *Film Editor:* Giuseppe Giacobino; *Production Design:* Teddy Villalba (billed as "Tedy Villalba"); *General Production Manager:* Ángel Rosson y Rubio; running time: 89 minutes; released July 29, 1971.

Cast: Carlos Quiney [billed as "Charles Quiney"] *(Antonio Sandoval/Zorro)*; Léa Nanni; Mariano Vidal Molina (billed as "Vidal Molina"); Pasquale Basile; Antonio Jiménez Escribano; Alex Marco; Juan Cortés; Pasquale Simeoli; Santiago Rivero.

Comments: Carlos Quiney stars as Zorro in this adventure, Co-produced by Italy's Duca Internazionale and Filmar Compagnia Cinematografica, with Spain's Hispamer Films.

Zorro, Rider of Vengeance (Zorro il cavaliere della vendetta) (Carthago C.C./Duca Internazionale, 1971)

Credits: *Directors:* Luigi Capuano, José Luis Merino; *Screenplay:* Maria del Carmen, Martinez Román, José Luis Merino (based on their story); *Photography:* Emanurle Di Cola (Kodacolor, Techniscope, aspect ratio 2.35:1); *Film Editor:* José Sntonio Rojo; *Music:* Francesco De Masi; *Costume Design:* Sibylle Geiger; running time: 92 minutes; released April 9, 1971 (Italy).

Cast: Carlos Quiney [billed as "Charles Quiney"] *(Antonio Sandoval/Zorro)*; Malisa Longo; María Mahor; Arturo Dominici; Ignazio Balsamo; Pasquale Basile; José Cárdenas; Anita Farra; Fernando Hilbeck; Enrique Ávila.

Comments: Another Zorro film, with Carlos Quiney in the lead. Co-produced by Italy's Duca Internazionale and Spain's Carthago C.C.

Zorro the Fox (El Zorro) (Magic Films, 1968)

Credits: *Director:* Guido Zurli; *Screenplay:* Guido Leoni, Ambrogio Molteni, Angelo Sangermano, Guido Zurli; *Photography:* Franco Delli Colli; *Film Editor:* Romeo Ciatti; *Music:* Gino Peguri; *Still Photographer:* Ermanno Serto; running time: 89 minutes, released November 17, 1968.

Cast: George Ardisson *(Don Diego di Alcantara/Zorro)*; Giacomo Rossi Stuart [billed as "Jack Stuart"] *(Don Pedro)*; Femi Benussi *(Dona Isabella)*; Ignazio Spalla [billed as "Pedro Sanchez"] *(Sgt. Gomez)*; Paolo Todesco *(John Gardner, Journalist)*; Consalvo Dell'Arti *(Don Gil, Isabella's Father)*; Riccardo Pizzuti; Gianni Pulone; Gustavo D'Arpe *(Alcalde)*; Gippo Leone; Grazia Fei; Aldo Marianecci *(Garcia Rodriguez, a Peasant)*; Spartico Battisti; Juan Valejo (billed as "Juan Vallejo"); Gualtiero Rispoli; Evaristo Maran (billed as "Evaristo Maran"); Artemio Antonini; Lina Franchi; Giancarlo Vignozzi.

Comments: A Zorro adventure, produced by Italy's Magic Films.

Zorro, the Navarra Marquis (Zorro marchese di Navarra) (Romana Film, 1969)

Credits: *Director:* Franco Montemurro (billed as "Jean Monty"); *Producer:* Fortunato Misiano; *Screenplay:* Franco Montemurro (billed as "Francesco Montemurro"), Piero Pierotti; *Photography:* Augusto Tiezzi (color); *Film Editor:* Jolanda Benvenuti; *Music:* Angelo Francesco Lavagnino; *Sound:* Franco Groppioni; *Microphone Boom Operator:* Corrado Volpicelli; running time: 102 minutes; released December 23, 1969 (Italy).

Cast: Nadir Moretti *(Zorro)*; Malisa Longo [billed as "Maria Luisa Longo'] *(Carmen de Mendoza)*; Daniele Vargas *(Col. Brizard)*; Loris

Gizzi *(Don Ignazio Alcalde)*; Renato Montalbano *(Don Ruiz)*; Gisella Arden *(Dolores)*; Dada Gallotti *(Linda)*; Nino Vingelli *(Fra Pistola)*; Ugo Adinolfi *(French Lieutenant)*; Fortunato Arena *(French Sergeant)*; Antonio Gradoli; Rosy De Leo; Gioia De Leo; Gioia Zanetti; Ignazio Balsamo *(Apothecary)*; Eleonora Morana *(Isabella)*; Mimmo Poli *(Taverner)*.

Comments: Nadir Moretti stars as Zorro in this adventure. Produced by Italy's Romana Film.

Zorro the Rebel *(Zorro il ribelle)* (1966)

Credits: *Director:* Piero Pierotti; *Screenplay:* Gianfranco Clerici, Piero Pierotti; *Photography:* Augusto Tiezzi (color); *Music:* Angelo Francesco Lavagnino; running time: 93 minutes (Italy), released September 12, 1966.

Cast: Howard Ross *(Don Ramiro/Zorro)*; Gabriella Andreini; Silvio Bagolini; Ignazio Balsamo; Charles Barromel; Massimo Carocci; Rosy De Leo; Dina De Santis; Arturo Dominici; Giuseppe Lauricella; Valentino Macchi; Eleonora Morana; Nello Pazzafini; Regina Seiffert; Edoardo Toniolo; Gioia Zanetti.

Comments: In old California, Don Ramiro, the secretary of the tyrannical governor he covertly opposes, masquerades as the rebel hero Zorro.

APPENDIX: THE 1980S REVIVAL

A screen adaptation of writer Robert E. Howard's sword-and-sorcery character Conan the Barbarian (essentially Hercules with a sword) was long overdue by the time Universal Pictures released the film *Conan the Barbarian* (starring Arnold Schwarzenegger) in 1982 (the immediate sequel was 1984's *Conan the Destroyer*). Although sword-and-sandal films continued to be produced through the 1970s, their appearance was sporadic. The genre had all but died in the mid–1960, but the box-office success of *Conan the Barbarian* sparked a mini-revival of Italian-produced pepla from 1982 to 1990. These titles are listed here.

The Adventures of Hercules II (Le avventure dell'incredibile Ercole) (Cannon Film Distributors, 1985)

Credits: Director/Screenplay: Luigi Cozzi (billed as "Lewis Coates"); *Producers:* Alfred Pecoriello, Yoram Globus, Menahem Golan; *Executive Producer:* John Thompson; *Photography:* Alberto Spagnoli (color, aspect ratio 1.85:1); *Film Editor:* Sergio Montanari; *Music:* Pino Donaggio; *Production Design:* Massimo Antonello Geleng (billed as "Tony Gelleng"); *Makeup:* Lamberto Marini; *1st Assistant Makeup Artist:* Alvaro Rossi; *Hair Stylist:* Iolanda Conti (billed as "Jolanda Conti"); *1st Assistant Hair Stylist:* Annalisa Coppa; *Production Supervisors:* Fabio Diotallevi, Ricky Sacco; *Production Manager:* Vittorio Galiano; *Assistant Director:* Giancarlo Santi; *2nd Alucio Assistant Director:* Massimo Galiano; *3rd Assistant Director:* Armando Valcauda; *Draftsman:* Lucio Di Domenico; *Set Dresser:* Francesco Cuppini (billed as "Francesco Cupini"); *Props:* Vittorio Zitelli; *Sound Mixers:* Romano Pampaloni, Roberto Petrozzi; *Sound Effects:* Luciano Anzellotti, Massimo Anzellotti; *Post-Synchronization Supervisor:* Gene Luotto; *Microphone Boom Operator:* Angelo Amatulli; *Special Effects:* Giovanni Corridori, Armando Valcauda, Joseph Nathanson (billed as "Josef Natanson"); *Stop-Motion Sequences:* Jean-Manuel Costa; *Cell Animation and Rotoscoping:* Alain Costa, Paolo Di Girolamo, Tiziano Giulianini, Raffale Radice, Marco Ticozzelli; *Miniatures and Models:* Giancarlo Ferrando, Walter Minnelli, Pascal Pinteau, Piergiorgio Pozzi, *Miniatures and Models (Videotape Sequences):* Dario Piana; *Models:* Paolo Zeccara; *Stunt Coordinator:* Rocco Lerro; *Stunts:* Ottaviano Dell'Acqua; *Camera Operator:* Franco Bruni; *1st Assistant Camera Operator:* Guido Tosi; *2nd Assistant Camera Operator:* Daniele Cimini; *Key Grip:* Giancarlo Rocchetti; *Grips:* Mario Occhioni, Arrigo Posta, Pierino Quacquarini, Romolo Siani; *1st Gaffer:* Mario Massaccesi; *Gaffers:* Giancarlo Bachetti, Tommaso Bartolozzi, Domenico Caiuli; *Still Photographer:* Luciano Ronconi; *Wardrobe:* Giovanna Covolo; *Costumes:* Floriana Scalabrelli; *Assistant Film Editors:* Loredana Cruciani, Maria Gianandrea, Roberto Gianandrea, Giorgio Venturoli; *Orchestra Conductor:* Natale Massara; *Transportation Captain:* Pietro Sottile; *Production Assistant:* Olivier Gérard (billed as "Gerard Oliver"); *Script Supervisor:* Fiorella Mariani; *Production*

Secretary: Alessandra Spagnuolo; *Production Accountant:* Renato Pecoriello; *Publicist:* Edilio Kim (billed as "Kim Gatti"); running time: 88 minutes; released May 2, 1985 (Italy); October 4, 1985 (U.S.); video availability: MGM/UA Home Entertainment.

Cast: Lou Ferrigno *(Hercules)*; Milly Carlucci *(Urania)*; Sonia Viviani *(Glaucia)*; William Berger *(King Minos)*; Carla Ferrigno [billed as "Calotta Green"] *(Athena)*; Claudio Cassinelli *(Zeus)*; Ferdinando Poggi [billed as "Nando Poggi"] *(Poseidon)*; Maria Rosaria Omaggio *(Hera)*; Venantino Venantini *(High Priest)*; Laura Lenzi *(Flora)*; Margit Evelyn Newton [billed as "Margi Newton"] *(Aphrodite)*; Cindy Leadbetter *(Ilia)*; Raf Baldassarre *(Atreus)*; Serena Grandi *(Euryale)*; Eva Robins [billed as "Eva Robbins"] *(Dedalos)*; Sandra Venturini *(Teti)*; Andrea Belfiore [billed as "Andrea Nicole"] *(1st Amazon)*; Alessandra Canale *(Delanira)*; Pamela Prati *(Aracne)*; Christina Basili; Paola Marcari.

Comments: This sequel to director Luigi Cozzi's *Hercules* (qv) isn't much better, and in some ways is even worse, particularly in its shameless pandering to the *Star Wars* crowd, although the special effects here are unbelievably trashy, if not inept at times. At one point, a cosmic vision is illustrated with a shoddily rotoscoped sequence lifted from the 1933 *King Kong*! This film uses some recap footage from *Hercules*. Alternate titles are *The New Adventures of Hercules* and *Hercules II*. Produced by Cannon Italia SrL. Filmed at Incir De Paolis Studios in Rome.

Ator, the Fighting Eagle *(Ator l'invincibile)* (Comworld Picture, 1983)

Credits: *Director:* Joe D'Amato (billed as "David Hills"); *Producer:* Alex Susmann; *Executive Producer:* Helen Szabo [billed as "Helen Sarlui"]; *Associate Producer:* Chris Trainor; *Photography:* Joe D'Amato [billed as "Frederick Sionisco"] (color, aspect ratio 1,85:1); *Film Editor:* David Framer; *Music:* Carlo Maria Cordio; *Art Direction:* John Gregory; *Makeup:* Pat Russel, *Production Manager:* Donatella Donati (billed as "Helen Handris"); *Post-Production Supervisor:* Nicholas Wentworth; *Assistant Director:* Sam Stone; *2nd Assistant Director:* Ivanna Masseti; *Sound Engineer:* Wiley Crosby; *Sound Mixer:* Robert W. Harris; *Sound Editor:* May Greenfield (billed as "Max Greenfield"); *Assistant Sound Editor:* Laurie Kellin; *Sound Effects:* John Gayford; *Dolby Stereo Consultant:* Christopher David; *Camera Operator:* Daniele Messaccesi (billed as "Larry Hessel"); *Assistant Camera Operator:* Ed McBride; *Chief Electrician:* Joe Little; *Key Grip:* Henry Noxley; *Stunt Coordinator:* James Hadley; *Wardrobe:* Kim Dascovitz; *Assistant Film Editor:* Shirley Kingston; *Musician (the song "Runn"):* Simona Pirone; *Transportation Captain:* Chuck Mills; *Script Supervisor:* Jean Salzer; running time: 98 minutes (U.S.); released October 7, 1982 (Italy), March 11, 1983 (U.S.); video availability: Scorpion Releasing.

Cast: Miles O'Keeffe *(Ator)*; Sabrina Siani *(Roon)*; Ritza Brown *(Sunya)*; Edmund Purdom *(Griba)*; Dakar [billed as "Dakkar"] *(High Priest of the Spider)*; Laura Gemser *(Indun)*; Alessandra Vazzoler [billed as "Chandra Vazzoler"] *(Woman in Tavern)*; Nello Pazzafini [billed as "Nat Williams"] *(Bardak)*; Jean Lopez *(Nordya)*; Olivia Goods *(Queen)*; Ron Carter; Brooke Hart; Warren Hillman.

Comments: The heroic Ator, son of Torren, avenges the death of villagers slaughtered by the fanatical Spider Cult. Produced by Italy's Filmarage in cooperation with Metaxa Corporation.

Barbarian Master *(Sangraal, la spada di fuoco)* (Cannon Film Distributing, 1983)

Credits: *Director:* Michele Massimo Tarantini (billed as "Michael E. Lemick"); *Producers:* Pino Buricchi, Umberto Innocenzi, Ettore Spagnuolo; *Screenplay:* Piero Regnoli; *Photography:* Pasquale Fanetti (Telecolor, Techniscope, aspect ratio 1.85:1); *Film Editor:* Alessandro Lucidi; *Music:* Franco Campanino; *Costume Design:* Susana Soro; *Makeup:* Marcello Di Paolo; *Hair Stylist:* Lidia Fatigati; *Special Effects:* Giovanni Corridori; *Set Designer:* Francesco Cuppini; running time: 85 minutes (Italy), 83 minutes (U.S.); released November 27, 1982 (Italy), November 4, 1983 (U.S.).

Cast: Pietro Torrisi [billed as "Peter McCoy"] *(Sangraal)*; Yvonne Fraschetti *(Aki)*; Mario Novelli [billed as "Anthony Freeman"]

(Nanuk); Xiomara Rodriguez *(Rani, Goddess of Fire)*; Margaretta Rance *(Sangraal's Wife)*; Hal Yamanouchi [billed as "Al Huang"] *(Li Wo Twan)*; Alex Partexano [billed as "Alessandro Partexano"] *(Galeth)*; Massimo Pittarello *(Rudak)*; Luciano Rossi [billed as "Lou Kamante"] *(Belam)*; Sabrina Siani *(The Golden Goddess)*; Emilio Messina.

Comments: Heroic warrior Sangraal avenges the death of his wife, who has been murdered by Rani, the evil Goddess of Fire. *Barbarian Master* uses footage of the village raid scene from *The Throne of Fire (Il trono di fuoco)* (1983) (qv). The hero's name, "Sangraal," was the original name of The Holy Grail.

The Barbarians *(I barbari)* (Cannon Films, 1987)

Credits: Director: Ruggero Deodato; *Producers:* Yoram Globus, Menahem Golan; *Executive Producer:* John Thompson; *Screenplay:* James R. Silke (from his story; dubbing dialogue by Alberto Piferi); *Photography:* Gianlorenzo Battaglia (Telecolor, aspect ratio 1.85:1); *Film Editor:* Eugenio Alabiso; *Music:* Pino Donaggio; *Production Design:* Giuseppe Mangano; *Set Decoration:* Giancarlo Capuani; *Costume Design:* Francesca Panicalli; *Key Makeup Artist:* Rosario Prestopino; *Makeup:* Franco Casagni, Amedeo Alessi; *Special Effects Makeup:* Francesco Paolocci, Gaetano Paolocci; *Assistant Makeup Artist:* Rosalba Cimino; *Key Hair Stylist:* Vitaliana Patacca; *Hair Stylists:* Gerardo Lepre, Marcello Longhi, Angelo Vannella; *Production Supervisor:* Carlo Carpentieri; *Production Manager:* Luciano Balducci; *General Manager:* Claudio Grassetti; *Assistant Production Design:* Atos Mastrogirolamo; *Construction Coordinator:* Romano Chessari; *Assistant Set Decorator:* Edwin Francis; *Construction Grip:* Amato Gabotti; *Painter:* Giancarlo Sensidoni; *Props:* Pasquale Avvisato; *Sound Engineer:* Massimo Loffredi; *Sound Recordist:* Stanley B. Gill; *Sound Effects:* Tommy Goodwin; *Sound Mixer:* Danilo Moroni; *Special Effects:* Edmondo Natali, Fabio Traversari; *Creature Effects:* Francesco Paolocci, Gaetano Paolocci; *Stunts:* Ottavio Dell'Acqua; *Stunt Coordinator:* Benito Stefanelli; *Camera Operator:* Guido Tosi; *1st Assistant Camera Operator:* Stefano Falivene; *2nd Assistant Camera Operator:* Federico Martucci; *Chief Electrician:* Domenico Caiuli; *Key Grip:* Franco Micheli; *Grips:* Paolo Tiberti, Arnato Gabotti; *Generator Operator:* Giovanni Favella; *Still Photographer:* Sergio Colombari; *Costumes (for barbarian characters):* Michaela Gisotti; *Assistant Costume Designer:* Stefania Del Guerra; *Seamstresses:* Giacoma Manes, Anna Rasetti; *1st Assistant Film Editor:* Nadia Boggian; *2nd Assistant Film Editor:* Silvana Di Legge; *Post-Production Coordinator:* Omneya "Nini" Mazen; *Orchestra Conductor:* Natale Massara; *Musicians:* Cinzia Cavallieri *(synthesizers assistant)*, Maurizio Guarini *(keyboards/synthesizer programmer)*; *Production Administrator:* Alfonso Farano; *Production Accountant:* Silvia Caperna; *Production Secretaries:* Paola Farano, Bruno Macinelli; *Master of Arms:* Benito Stefanelli; *Weapons:* Umberto D'Aniello; *Barbarian Armor:* Michaela Gisotti; *Choreographer:* Giuseppe Pennese; *Location Manager (in U.S.):* Ricky Sacco; *Script Supervisor:* Fabrizia Iacona; running time: 87 minutes; released April 24, 1987 (Italy), March 20, 1987 (U.S.); video availability: Timeless Media Group.

Cast: Peter Paul *(Kutchek)*; David Paul *(Gore)*; Richard Lynch *(Kadar)*; Eva LaRue [billed as "Eva La Rue"] *(Kara)*; Virginia Bryant *(Canary)*; Sheeba Alahani *(China)*; Michael Berryman *(Dirtmaster)*; Franco Pistoni *(Ibar)*; Raffaella Bellazecca *(Young Kutchek)*; Luigi Bellazecca *(Young Gore)*; Wilma Marzilli *(Fat Woman)*, Giovanni Cianfriglia *(Ghedo, the Strongman)*; Angelo Ragusa *(Kadar's Man)*; Nanni Bernini *(Kadar's Man)*; Lucio Rosato *(Kadar's Man)*; George Eastman *(Jacko)*; Franco Daddi [billed as "Franco Dadi"] *(Bluto)*; L. Carroll *(Nose)*; Tiziana Di Gennaro *(Young Kara)*; Marilda Donà *(Kadar's Woman)*; Paolo Merosi *(Kadar's Man)*; Nello Pazzafini *(Jacko's Man)*; Renzo Pavarello *(Bones)*; Paolo Risi *(Pin, the Dwarf)*; Pat Starke *(China's Voice)*; Benito Stefanelli *(Greyshaft)*.

Comments: Twin barbarians exact vengeance on the evil warlord who had captured them as children after wiping out their tribe. Produced by Cannon Films and Cannon Italia SrL. Filmed on location at Campo Imperatore, L'Aquila, Abrusso, Italy, with interiors shot in Rome.

The Blade Master (Ator 2—L'invincibile Orion) (New Line Cinema/Film Ventures International, 1984)

Credits: Director/screenplay: Joe D'Amato (billed as "David Hills"); Producer: John Newman; Executive Producer: Alex Susmann; Associate Producer: Chris Trainor; Photography: Joe D'Amato [billed as "Federico Slonisco"] (color); Film Editor: David Framer; Music: Karl Michael Demer (billed as "Karl Demer," Carlo Rustichelli; Production Design: Massimo Lentini; Art Direction: John Gregory; Makeup: Pat Russel; Production Manager: Donatella Donati (billed as "Helen Handris"); Assistant Director: Sam Stone; 2nd Assistant Director: Julie Morrows; Assistant Art Director: Francis Correl; Sound Recordist: Wiley Crosby; 1st Assistant Sound Recordist: Robert W. Harris; 2nd Assistant Sound Recordist: Suzanne D'Amico; Sound Effects: Lewis E. Ciannelli; Sound Editor: May Greenfield; Assistant Sound Editor: Laurie Kellin; Stunt Coordinator: James Hadley; Stunts: Frank Avila, Fred Peterson, Paul Randors, Marvin Simons, Kevin Strung; Camera Operator: Daniele Massaccesi (billed as "Larry Hessel"); Assistant Camera Operators: Ed McBride, Thomas Burrel; Chief Electrician: Joe Little; Key Grip: Henry Noxley; Wardrobe: Kim Dascovitz; Assistant Film Editor: Shirley Kingston; Apprentice Film Editor: Mark Sofield; Transportation Captain: Chuck Mills; Production Coordinator: Sharon Friendly; Production Assistants: Randy Gleason, Bob Liro (billed as "Bob Libo"), Astrid Miller, Danan Grant Olsey (billed as "Danah Grandsley"); Script Supervisor: Jean Salzer; running time: 92 minutes (U.S.); released December 16, 1982 (Italy), February 15, 1984 (U.S.).

Cast: Miles O'Keeffe *(Ator)*; Lisa Foster *(Mila)*; David Brandon [billed as "David Cain Haughton"] *(Zor)*; Charles Barromel *(Akronas)*; Kiro Wehara [billed as "Chen Wong"] *(Thong)*; Robert Black *(High Priest)*; Donald Hodson *(Village Elder)*; Stephan Soffer *(Ravani)*; Nello Pazzafini [billed as "Ned Steinberg"] *(Wallon)*; Osiride Pevarello [billed as "Hershel Curtis"] *(Sandur)*; Sandra Carle *(Old Woman)*; Nancy Hall *(1st Maiden)*; Linette Ray *(2nd Maiden)*; Robert Karshin *(1st Youth)*; Andy Stradly *(2nd Youth)*; Steve Rivers *(3rd Youth)*; Laura Gemser *(Indun)*; Salvatore Baccaro *(Primitive Man)*; Gregory Snegoff *(Voice for Ator)*; Edward Mannix *(Voice for Sander)*.

Comments: Warrior Ator attempts to save his mentor from the wicked Zor. This sequel to *Ator, the Fighting Eagle* (qv) was quickly-filmed, without a complete script. Some flashback footage from the original film is used. The U.S. television title was *The Cave Dwellers*, and re-used some footage from *Taur the Mighty* (qv). Co-produced by New Line Cinema, Metaxa Corporation, and Royal Film Traders.

Conqueror of the World (I padroni del mondo) (Cinefear, 1983)

Credits: Director:/Screenplay: Alberto Cavallone; Producers: Luciano Ceprani; Nicolò Pomilia; Photography: Maurizio Dell'Orco, Gianfranco Maioletti, Sandro Mancori (color); Film Editor: Alberto Cavallone; Music: Alberto Baldan Bembo; Costume Design: Maria Pia Luzi; Makeup Director: Rosario Prestopino; Makeup Artists: Alberto Biasi, Alfonso Cioffi, Mario Scutti; Hair Stylists: Placida Crapanzano, Nerea Rosmanit; Production Supervisor: Marcello Spingi; Assistant Director: Stefano Pomilia; Set Decorator: Gregorio Cardone; Sound Technician: Raffaele De Luca; Sound Mixer: Walter Polini; Scenic Effects: Roberto Pace; Stunts: Nicola Di Giola; Camera Operators: Giovanni Brescini, Aldo Marchiori; Assistant Camera Operators: Eric Biglietto, David Mancori, Mauro Masciocchi; Production Secretary: Mirella Caballoro; Script Girl: Francesca Montani; running time: 100 minutes; released 1983.

Cast: Sven Kruger *(Bog)*; Saha D'Arc; Viviana Maria Rispoli, Maria Vittoria Garlanda; Aldo Sambrell; Serafino Profumo; Fabio Baciocchi; *Members of the Kon Tribe:* Paolo Bernacchioni; Tristano Iannetta; Adriano Chiaramida; Massimo Pompei; Adriana Giuffrè; Gianfranco Ambroso; Edoardo Terzo; Roberto Trinici; Pierangelo Pozzato (billed as "Pietro Angelo Pozzato"); Nicola Di Gioia; Gina Giuri; Marina Medde; Gabriella Montemagno; *Members of the Akray Tribe:* Antonio Mea; Salvatore Bardaro; Michele Knewels; Renato Moriconi; Maurizio Faraoni; Palmiro Liotta; Sebastiano Tosto;

Luciano Casamonica; Patrizia Salerno; Zaira Zocchedu; Daniela Airoldi.

Comments: Bog, a young Cro-Magnon warrior, struggles for survival in prehistory. Some scenes were filmed on location in the Canary Islands. An alternate European title is *Master of the World.* Produced by Italy's Falco Film.

Conquest (Conquista) (United Film Distribution Company [UFDC], 1984)

Credits: Director: Lucio Fulci; *Producer:* Giovanni Di Clemente; *Screenplay:* Gino Capone, Carlos Vasallo, José Antonio de la Loma (based on a story by Giovanni Di Clemente); *Photography:* Alejandro Ulloa [billed as "Alejandro Alonso Garcia"] (Telecolor, aspect ratio 1.85:1); *Film Editor:* Emilio Rodriguez Oses; *Music:* Claudio Simonetti; *Art Direction:* Massimo Lentini; *Set Decoration:* Mariangela Capuano; *Makeup:* Franco Rufini; *Assistant Makeup Artist:* Mauro Menconi; *Hair Stylist:* Luigi Contini; *Production Manager:* Pietro Innocenzi; *Production Manager (Spain):* José Antonio de la Loma; *Unit Managers:* Domenico Lo Zito, Vincenzo Santangelo; *Assistant Directors:* José Antonio de la Loma, Filiberto Fiaschi, Roberto Tatti; *Props:* Rodolfo Ruzza; *Sound:* Eros Giustini; *Vocal Sound Effects:* Maurizio Guarini; *Sound Effects Editor:* Massimo Anzellotti; *Sound Mixer:* Romano Pampaloni; *Microphone Boom Operator:* Ettore Mancini; *Camera Operators:* Federico Del Zoppo, Claudio Morabito; *Assistant Camera Operator:* Mario Bagnato; *Chief Electrician:* Gaetano Coniglio; *Key Grips:* Roberto Pizzi, Matt Giordano (billed as "Matteo Giordano"); *Still Photographer:* Piero Caputi; *Wardrobe:* Alvaro Grassi; *Supervising Film Editor:* Vincenzo Tomassi; *Assistant Film Editors:* Rita Antonelli, Giancarlo Tiburzi, Patrizia Innocenzi; *Administrator:* Costantino Di Clemente; *Production Secretary:* Francesco Annibali; *Continuity:* Walter Marconi; running time: 88 minutes; released June 2, 1983 (Italy), April 6, 1984 (U.S.); video availability: Blue Underground.

Cast: Jorge Rivero [billed as "George Rivero"] *(Mace);* Andrea Occhipinti *(Ilias);* Conrado San Martin *(Zora);* Violeta Cela *(Sacrificial Victim);* José Gras [billed as "José Gras Palau]; *(Fado);* Giola Scola [billed as "Maria Escola"] *(Girl);* Sabrina Siani [billed as "Sabrina Sellers"] *(Ocron);* Robert Sommer *(Voice for Mace);* Steven Luotto *(Voice for Ilias).*

Comments: A virtuous warrior, armed with a magical bow and arrow, tries to purge a land of all evil and drive away an evil demon. *Conquest,* as one would expect from horror director Lucio Fulci, has plenty of gore and nudity, the latter provided by Sabrina Siani as a naked sorceress.

Gunan, King of the Barbarians (Gunan il guerriero) (Leader Films, 1982)

Credits: Director: Franco Prosperi (billed as "Frank Shannon"); *Producer:* Pino Buricchi; *Screenplay:* Piero Regnoli [billed as "Peter Lombard'] (based on his story); *Photography:* Pasquale Fanetti (billed as "Pasqualino Fanetti"] (Telecolor); *Music:* Roberto Pregadio; *Production Design/Set Decoration:* Francesco Cuppini (billed as "Franco Cuppini"]; *Costume Design:* Silvio Lorenzi; *Stunt Coordinator:* Ottaviano Dell'Acqua; running time: 80 minutes (Italy); released September 9, 1982 (Italy).

Cast: Pietro Torrisi [billed as "Peter McCoy"] *(Zukahn/Gunan);* Malisa Longo [billed as "Melisa Lang"] *(Marga);* Giovanni Cianfriglia [billed as "John Richmond'] *(Nameless);* Emilio Messina [billed as "Emil Messina'] *(Nuriak);* Rita Silva *(Queen of Kuniat);* Fortunato Arena [billed as "Lucky Arias"] *(Mevian);* Franco Galizi (billed as "Frank Gallici"); Philip Bank (billed as "Philips Banks"); Alba Maiolini (billed as "Alba Lines"] *(Midwife);* Sabrina Siani *(Lenni);* Ennio Antonelli; Bruno Di Luia *(Nuriak's Man).*

Comments: Amazon warriors rescue two infant boys from a massacre and raise them to heroic manhood. This low-budget film uses dinosaur footage from *One Million Years B.C.* (1966). Produced by Leader Films.

Hercules (Ercole) (Cannon Film Distributors, 1983)

Credits: Director/Screenplay: Luigi Cozzi (billed as "Lewis Coates"); *Producers:* Yoram Globus, Menahem Golan; *Executive Producer:* John Thompson; *Photography:* Alberto Spagnoli

(Technicolor, aspect ratio 1.85:1); *Film Editors:* James Beshears, Sergio Montanari; *Production Design:* Massimo Antonello Geleng (billed as "M.A. Geleng"); *Set Decoration:* Giacomo Calò Carducci (billed as "Jack Carducci"); *Costume Design:* Adriana Spadaro; *Production Supervisor:* Fabio Diotallevi; *Production Manager:* Vittorio Galiano (billed as "Victor Galiant"); *Production Director:* Ricky Sacco; *Assistant Director:* Giancarlo Santi (billed as "John Santi"); *Sound:* Roberto Petrozzi (billed as "Robert Petroff"); *Sound Mixers:* Robin O'Donoghue, Gerry Humphreys (billed as "Gerry Humphries"); *Post-Synchronization Supervisor:* Louis Elman (billed as "Lou Ellman"); *Dolby Stereo Sound Consultant:* Chris David; *Special Effects:* Armando Valcauda, Germano Natali (billed as "Herman Nathan"), Goffredo Unger (billed as "Jeffrey Unger"); *Models:* Paolo Zeccara; *Camera Operator (Miniature Effects):* Roberto Brega (billed as "Robert Brega"); *Unit Coordinator (Miniature Effects):* Olivier Gérard (billed as "Gerard Oliver"); *Stunt Coordinator:* Enzo Musumeci Greco (billed as "Edward L. Greco"); *Camera Operator:* Franco Bruni; *Assistant Camera Operators:* Sergio Meleranci, Fabrizio Vicari; *Underwater Photography:* Gianlorenzo Battaglia; *Still Photographers:* Mauro Ruspantini, Ram Globus; *Focus Puller:* Marco Sacerdoti; *Assistant Film Editors:* Lizabeth Gelber (billed as "Liz Gelber"), Maria Gianandrea, Roberto Gianandrea; *Keyboard Musician:* Maurizio Guarini; *Orchestra Conductor:* Natale Massara; *Administrator:* Renato Pecoriello; *Production Secretary:* Massimo Galiano; *Script Supervisor:* Egle Guarino (billed as "Leslie Gaul"); *Publicist:* Edilio Kim (billed as "Kim Gatti"); *Master of Arms:* Enzo Musumeci Greco; *English-Language Script Editor:* Frank J. Tsacrios; running time: 98 minutes (U.S.); released August 26, 1983 (U.S.); video availability: MGM/UA Home Entertainment.

Cast: Lou Ferrigno *(Hercules);* Brad Harris *(King Augias);* Sybil Danning *(Ariadne);* Rossana Podestà *(Hera);* Ingrid Anderson *(Cassiopea);* Mirella D'Angelo *(Circe);* William Berger *(King Minos);* Bobby Rhodes *(King Xenodama);* Gianni Garko [billed as "John Garko"] *(Valcheus);* Yehuda Efroni *(Dorcon);* Delia Boccardo *(Athena);* Claudio Cassinelli *(Zeus);* Franco Garofalo [billed as "Frank Garland"] *(The Thief);* Gabriella Giorgelli [billed as "Gabriella George"] *(Mother);* Raf Baldassarre [billed as "Ralph Balassar"] *(Sostratos);* Stelio Candelli [billed as "Steve Candell"] *(Father);* Valentina Montanari [billed as "Valerie Montanari"] *(Chambermaid);* Rocco Lerro [billed as "Roger Larry"] *(The Friend);* Eva Robins [billed as "Eva Robbins"] *(Daedalus);* Giovanni Cianfriglia; Ty Randolph.

Comments: A new version of the Hercules legend, highly touted at the time of its release, but disappointing, largely due to sloppy production design and the unimaginative direction of Luigi Cozzi. Former peplum star Brad Harris, who had starred in *The Fury of Hercules* (qv) appears here as King Augias. Originally, this film was intended to have considerably more sex and violence, but was rewritten on the demands of star Lou Ferrigno, who wanted a more family-oriented movie. Despite shortcomings, *Hercules* was a financial success. Produced by Cannon Italia SrL and Golan-Globus Productions. Filmed at Incir De Paolis Studios and RPA-Elios Studios in Rome.

The Hobgoblin (Ricerca per la potente Spada) (Epic Productions, 1990)

Credits: Director/Screenplay: Joe D'Amato (billed as "David Hills"); *Producer:* Carlo Maria Cordio; *Photography:* Joe D'Amato [billed as "Federico Slonisco"] (color); *Film Editor:* Kathleen Stratton; *Music:* Carlo Maria Cordio; *Art Direction:* Massimo Lentini; *Costume Design:* Laura Gemser; *Makeup/Special Effects:* Maurizio Trani; *Sound:* Keith Young; *Sound Mixer:* Dan Marodan (billed as "Dan Morodan"); *Physical Effects Supervisor:* Michael Deak; *Stunts:* Brian Ricci; *Assistant Camera Operator:* Ken Davis; *Electricians:* Bobby Douglas, Ben Miller; *Grips:* Lee Hughes, Syd Potter; *Still Photographer:* Peter Bates; *Assistant Film Editor:* David Shaw; *Script Supervisor:* Jane Bailey; *Production Accountant:* Walter Kelly; *Casting:* Cleo Lori, Werner Pochath (billed as "Paul Werner"); running time: 94 minutes (U.S.); released August 29, 1990 (U.S.).

Cast: Eric Allan Kramer [billed as "Eric Allen Kramer"] *(Ator);* Margaret Lenzey *(Dejanira);*

Donald O'Brien [billed as "Doan O'Brien"] *(Gunther)*; Dina Morrone *(Sunn)*; Chris Murphy *(Skiold)*; Laura Gemser *(Grimilde)*; Marisa Mell *(Nephele)*; Don Semerano *(Thorn-Grindel Hagen)*.

Comments: A goddess, imprisoned in a mystic ring of fire, is rescued by the heroic Ator. This was the last of the Ator films. The original title, *Quest for the Mighty Sword,* is more appropriate. Produced by Italy's Filmarage.

Iron Warrior (Ator il guerriero di ferro) (Trans World Entertainment, 1987)

Credits: Director: Alfonso Brescia (billed as "Al Bradley"); *Producers:* Maurizio Maggi, Ovidio G. Assonitis; *Associate Producer:* Narcy Calamatta; *Screenplay:* Steven Luotto, Alfonso Brescia [billed as "Al Bradley"] (from their story); *Photography:* Wally Gentleman (color, aspect ratio 1.85:1); *Film Editor:* Roberto Silvi; *Music:* Carlo Maria Cordio (billed as "Charles Scott"); *Production Design:* Franco Vanorio; *Art Direction:* Charles Bikell; *Costume Design:* Valeria Valenza (billed as "Valerie Valenza); *Makeup:* Rossana Parker, Mario Michisanti; *Hair Stylist:* Ferdinando Merolla; *Production Supervisor:* Tullio Lullo; *Unit Production Manager:* Alessandro Altieri; *1st Assistant Director:* Jack Lesina; *2nd Assistant Director:* Andrea Maggi; *Set Dresser:* Carl Lammers; *Props:* Sergio Fabriani; *Supervising Sound Editor:* Joseph Rennie; *Sound Editor:* Irvin Marvin; *Assistant Sound Editor:* Don Knupp; *Sound Mixer:* Giancarlo Laurenzi; *Sound Re-Recording Mixer:* Romano Pampaloni; *Dialogue Looping:* Ken Mitchell; *Post-Synchronization Director:* Leslie La Penna (billed as "Leslie J. La Penna"); *Stunt Coordinator:* Sergio Mioni; *Stunts:* Steve Blay, Vincent Borg, Norman Bottin, Riccardo Mioni, Stefano Maria Mioni (billed as "Stefano Mioni"); Claudio Pacifico; *Camera Operators:* Adolfo Bartoli, Roberto Forges Davanzati (billed as "Roberto Forges"); *Focus Puller:* Andrea Busiri Vici; *Electricians:* Tom Eicher, Sam Fields, Jon Foster; *Gaffer:* Luigi Pasqualini; *Still Photographer:* Mark Pieroni; *Wardrobe Supervisor:* Josephine Mayer; *Assistant Film Editor:* Donatella Taccari; *Negative Cutter:* Robert Queen; *Color Timer:* Mato; *Supervising Music Editor:* Jack Rappaport; *Music Consultant:* Lance Josephson; *Script Supervisor:* John Little; *Continuity:* Mirella Gamacchio; *Master of Arms:* Franco Daddi (billed as "Frank Daddi"); *Production Secretary:* Annette Baird-Smith; *Location Manager:* David Winston; *Supervising Accountant:* Gianna Di Michele; *Assistant Accountant:* Federica Zappalà; *Best Boy:* Elio Bosio; *Casting:* Joanna Lester; running time: 82 minutes; released January 1, 1987 (Italy); January 9, 1987 (U.S.).

Cast: Miles O'Keeffe *(Ator)*; Savina Gersak *(Princess Janna)*; Elisabeth Kaza *(Phaedra)*; Iris Reynado *(Deeva)*; Tim Lane *(King)*; Tiziana Altieri *(Young Phaedra)*; Franco Daddi [billed as "Frank Daddi"] *(Trogar)*; Josie Coppini *(Impostor King)*; Malcolm Borg *(Young Ator)*; Conrad Borg *(Young Trogar)*; Jon Rosser *(Nekron)*; Anna Cachia *(Seductress)*.

Comments: The warrior Ator returns to battle the evil sorceress Phaedra. The third Ator movie, with some scenes shot on location on Gozo island, Malta, with interiors shot at Mediterranean Film Studios in Malta. Produced by Browersgracht Investments and Continental Motion Pictures.

Ironmaster (La guerra del ferro: Ironmaster) (American National Enterprises, 1983)

Credits: Director: Umberto Lenzi; *Producer:* Luciano Martino; *Executive Producer:* Carlo Maietto; *Screenplay:* Alberto Cavallone, Lea Martino, Dardano Sacchetti, Gabriel Rossini, Umberto Lenzi (based on a story by Luciano Martino, Alberto Cavallone); *Photography:* Giancarlo Ferando (Telecolor, aspect ratio 1.85:1); *Film Editor:* Eugenio Alabiso; *Music:* Guido De Angelis; *Art Direction:* Massimo Antonello Geleng (billed as "Antonello Geleng"); *Costume Design:* Rossana Romanini; *Makeup:* Rosario Prestopino; *Assistant Makeup Artist:* Alberto Blasi; *Hair Stylist:* Marcello Longhi; *Production Executive:* Sergio Borelli; *Unit Manager:* Francesco Fantacci; *Assistant Directors:* Riccardo Petrazzi, Alain Sens-Cazenave; *Set Dresser:* Andrea Fantacci; *Props:* Angeluccio Maccarinelli; *Sound Recordist:* Eros Giustini; *Sound Mixer:* Bruno Moreal; *Sound Effects:* Aurelio Pennacchia; *Post-Synchronization:* Frank von Kuegelgen; *Special

Effects: Paolo Ricci; *Miniatures:* Emilio Ruiz del Rio; *Stunt Coordinator:* Nazzareno Cardinali; *Stunts:* Massimo Pittarello; *Camera Operator:* Alessandro Capuccio; *1st Assistant Camera Operator:* Massimo Zeri; *Assistant Camera Operator:* Gianfranco Torinti; *Still Photographer:* Francesco Narducci; *Key Grip:* Matt Giordano (billed as "Giordano Matteo"); *Gaffer:* Armando Moreschini; *Generator Operator:* Egidio Stiffi; *Wardrobe:* Mina Manes; *Assistant Film Editors:* Giuseppe Romano, Silvana Di Legge; *Production Assistants:* Colette Guedon, Alberto Paluzzi, Antonio Saragò; *Master of Arms:* Nazzareno Cardinali; *Script Supervisor:* Olga Pehar Lenzi; *Paymaster:* Anna De Pedys; running time: 98 minutes (U.S.); released March 10, 1983 (Italy).

Cast: Sam Pasco *(Ela)*; Elvire Audray *(Isa)*; George Eastman *(Vood)*; Pamela Prati [billed as "Pamela Field"] *(Lith)*; Jacques Herlin *(Rag)*; Danilo Mattei [billed as "Brian Redford"] *(Tog)*; Benito Stefanelli *(Iksay)*; Areno D'Adderio; Giovanni Cianfriglia *(Vood's Thug)*; Nello Pazzafini; Walter Lucchini *(Mogo Tribe Member)*; Nico La Macchia; William Berger *(Mogo)*; Salvatore Billa; Ottaviano Dell'Acqua; Alessandro Prete; Robert Spafford *(Voice of Tribal Leader)*; Pat Starke *(Voice for Isa)*; Pietro Torrisi *(Mogo's Killer)*; Frank von Kuegelgen *(Voice for Tog)*.

Comments: A prehistoric tribe, struggling for survival, learns how to fashion weapons from iron. Co-produced by Italy's Nuova Dania Cinematografica and Medusa Distribuzione in cooperation with France's Imp. Ex. Ci. And Les Films Jacques Leitienne. Filmed on location at Custer State Park in South Dakota, with interiors shot at RPA-Elios Studios in Rome.

The Seven Magnificent Gladiators (I sette magnifici gladiatori) (Cannon Film Distributors, 1984)

Credits: *Director:* Claudio Fragasso (billed as "Claude Fragass"), Bruno Mattei; *Producer:* Alexander Hacohen; *Executive Producers:* Yoram Globus, Menahem Golem; *Associate Producer:* René Pech (billed as "René Peck"); *Screenplay:* Claudio Fragasso (billed as "Claude Fragass"); *Photography:* Silvano Ippoliti (color, aspect ratio 1.85:1); *Film Editor:* Bruno Mattei (billed as "A. Swyftte"); *Music:* Dov Seltzer; *Art Direction:* Amedeo Mellone (billed as "Armando Melloni"); *Costume Design:* Belle Crandall; *Makeup:* Molly Paige; *Hair Stylist:* Edward Stokes; *Production Supervisor:* David P. Klinger; *Production Manager:* Ned Linke; *1st Assistant Director:* Olivier Gérard; *2nd Assistant Director:* Annie Wise; *Set Dresser:* Bert Dunne; *Props:* Stan Talbot; *Sound Mixers:* Don Lopez, Felix Lamb, Lucien Morris; *Post-Synchronization:* Lewis Lester; *Microphone Boom Operator:* Dede Shub; *Stunt Coordinator:* Hank O'Leary; *Stunts:* Tom Carlisle, Ottaviano Dell'Acqua, Nicola Di Giola, Jeff "Stump" Layman); *Horse Wrangler:* Arnold Schwartz; *Camera Operator:* Ted Carrell; *1st Assistant Camera Operator:* Sam Randolph; *2nd Assistant Camera Operator:* Ed Randolph; *Still Photographer:* Melissa Ling; *Key Grip:* J.D. Owen; *Gaffer:* Alan Horn; *Assistant Film Editor:* Lizabeth Gelber; *Apprentice Film Editor:* Marc Alberti; *Script Supervisor:* Karen de Angelo; running time: 83 minutes (U.S.); released 1983 (Italy), August 1983 (U.S.).

Cast: Lou Ferrigno *(Han)*; Sybil Danning *(Julia)*; Brad Harris *(Scipio)*; Dan Vadis *(Nicerote)*; Carla Ferrigno *(Pandora)*; Barbara Pesante *(Anakora)*; Yehuda Efroni *(Emperor)*; Mandy-Rice Davies *(Lucilla)*; Robert Mura *(Vendrix)*; Emilio Messina [billed as "Ivan Beshears"] *(Goliath)*; Giovanni Cianfriglia [billed as "Jody Wanger"] *(Festo)*; Salvatore Borghese [billed as "Michael Franz"] *(Glafiro)*; Françoise Perrot [billed as "Kristin Kline"] *(Cornelia)*; Antonella Giacomini [billed as "Claudia Bridges"] *(Diana)*; Mary Rader *(Lydia)*; Philip Bard *(Dex)*; Gregg Logan *(Dario)*; Peter Rugge *(Meorio)*; Raul Cabrera [billed as "Gary Levine"] *(Army Captain)*; John Growne II *(Judas)*; Laddy Price *(Leper #1)*; George Wender *(Boy #1)*; Henry Tyre *(Boy #2)*; Eve London *(Girl #1)*; Domenico Cianfriglia *(Roman Soldier)*; Nicola Di Gioia *(Gladiator)*; Mark Urban *(Chief Courtier)*; Carlos Alberto Valles *(Man in Tavern)*.

Comments: In this unofficial remake of Kurosawa's *The Seven Samurai*, a ruthless bandit with supernatural powers is finally defeated by a warrior with a magic sword. Former peplum stars Brad Harris and Dan Vadis are featured here. Produced by Cannon Italia SrL and filmed at De Paolis Studios in Rome.

She (Lei) (Filmhansa, 1985)

Credits: Director: Avi Nesher; *Screenplay:* Avi Nesher (based on the novel by H. Rider Haggard); *Producer:* Renato Dandi; *Executive Producers:* Edward Sarlui, Helen Szabo (billed as "Helen Sarlui"); *Associate Producers:* Michael-John Biber, Sue Cameron; *Photography:* Sandro Mancori (color); *Film Editor:* Nicholas Wentworth; *Music:* Phil Campbell, Justin Hayward, Rick Wakerman; *Production Design:* Massimo Antonello Geleng; *Art Direction:* Ennio Michettoni, Umberto Turco; *Costume Design:* Ivanna Massetti; *Makeup:* Otello Fava, Stefano Fava; *Hair Stylists:* Ennio Cascioli, Giancarlo De Leonardis; *Production Manager:* Annabella Andreoli; *Assistant Production Manager:* Bruno Tribbioli; *Assistant Directors:* Tony Brandt, Paolo Percaus; *Sound Recordist:* Gaetano Testa; *Assistant Sound Recordist:* Giuseppe Testa; *Sound Designer:* Nicholas Wentworth; *Sound Effects:* Elly De Vries; *Dolby Stereo Consultant:* Chris David; *Microphone Boom Operator:* Aldo De Martini; *Special Effects Supervisor:* Ivanna Massetti; *Special Effects:* Armando Grilli; *Stunt Coordinator:* Sergio Mioni; *Stunts:* Ottaviano Dell'Acqua, Stefano Maria Mioni, Angelo Ragusa; *Camera Operator:* Alfredo Senzacqua, *Assistant Camera Operators:* David Mancori, Aldo Marchiori, Giacomo Testa; *Still Photographer:* Guido Simonetti; *Key Grip:* Giovanni Savini; *Gaffer:* Domizio Ercolani; *Electricians:* Stefano Marino, Giuseppe Meloni; *Wardrobe Mistress:* Giovanna Russu; *Assistant Film Editors:* Orfella Cappelli, Lizabeth Gelber, Liliana Serra; *Main Title Design:* Francesco Grasso; *Script Supervisor:* Marion Mertes; *Production Accountant:* Franco Marras; running time: 106 minutes (U.S.); released December 25, 1985 (U.S.).

Cast: Sandahl Bergman *(She)*; David Goss *(Tom)*; Quin Kessler *(Shandra)*; Harrison Muller, Jr. *(Dick)*; Elena Wiedermann *(Hari)*; Gordon Mitchell *(Hector)*; Laurie Sherman *(Taphir)*; Andrew McLeay *(Tark)*; Cyrus Elias *(Kram)*; David Brandon *(Boy)*; Susan Adler *(Girl)*; Gregory Snegoff *(Godan)*; Mary D'Antin *(Eva)*; Mario Pedone *(Rudolph)*; Donald Hodson *(Rabel)*; Maria Cumani Quasimodo *(Moona)*; David Traylor *(Xenon)*; Scott Coffey *(Cult Member)*; Nello Pazzafini *(Tribal Member)*.

Comments: Another in a long line of screen adaptations of H. Ridder Haggard's fantasy-adventure novel, *She*, about a beautiful woman who draws eternal youth from a magical flame, and invites her lover to share her immortality. Previous screen versions appeared in 1908, 1911, 1916 (there were *two* versions in 1916; one was titled *Hidden Valley*), 1917, 1925, 1935 (produced in Hollywood by RKO); 1965, 1968, this version in 1982, and 2001. The most satisfying adaptation remains the 1965 Hammer Films production starring Ursula Andress in the title role. This 1982 film was produced by Continental Motion Pictures, Royal Films B.V., and Trans World Entertainment (TWE).

Sinbad of the Seven Seas (Sinbad dei sette mari) (Cannon Films, 1989)

Credits: Directors: Enzo G. Castellari, Luigi Cozzi; *Producers:* Enzo G. Castellari, Yoram Globus, Menahem Golan; *Screenplay:* Tito Carpi, Enzo G. Castellari (based on a story by Luigi Cozzi [billed as "Lewis Coates"], with additional dialogue by Ian Danby); *Photography:* Blasco Giurato (Telecolor, aspect ratio 1,85:1); *Film Editor:* Gianfranco Amicucci; *Music:* Dov Seltzer; *Production Design:* Walter Patriarca; *Costume Design:* Adriana Spadaro; *Makeup:* Maurizio Trani; *Assistant Makeup Artists:* Alberto Blasi, Laura Borzelli; *Hair Stylist:* Paolo Franceschi; *Assistant Hair Stylist:* Paolo Folcolini; *Production Managers:* David Pash, Giuseppe Pedersoll; *Assistant Directors:* Giuseppe Giglietti, Stefania Girolami Goodwin, Andrea Girolami; *Set Dresser:* Elio Micheli, *Props:* Luciano D'Achille; *Draftsman:* Pasquale Germano; *Head Carpenter:* Armando Vici; *Sound:* Roberto Petrozzi; *Microphone Boom Operator:* Armando Janota; *Special Effects:* Dino Galiano (billed as "Cataldo Galliano"); *Stunt Coordinator:* Riccardo Petrazzi; *Stunts:* Ottaviano Dell'Acqua, Gianluca Petrazzi; *Camera Operator:* Sandro Tamborra; *Assistant Camera Operators:* Giancarlo Granatelli, Carlo Passari; *Key Grip:* Giuseppe Petrignani; *Gaffer:* Nazareno Brescini; *Electrician:* Paolo Leurini; *Wardrobe:* Floriana Scalabrelli; *Assistant Costume Designer:* Carlo

Centolavigna; *1st Assistant Film Editor:* Roberto Amicucci; *2nd Assistant Film Editor:* Mauro Nonnis; *Production Assistant:* Marco Albertini; *Script Supervisor:* Egle Guarino; *Dialogue Coach:* Ray Mottola; *Unit Publicist:* Gene Rizzo; running time: 93 minutes; released April 1, 1989; video availability: MGM Home Entertainment.

Cast: Lou Ferrigno *(Sinbad);* John Steiner *(Jaffar);* Roland Wybenga *(Ali);* Ennio Girolami *(Viking);* Hal Yamanouchi [billed as "Haruhiko Yamanouchi"] *(Samurai);* Yehuda Efroni *(Ahmed);* Alessandra Mertines *(Alina);* Teagan *(Soukra);* Leo Gullotta *(Nadir);* Stefania Girolami *(Kyra);* Donald Hodson *(Calif);* Melonee Rodgers *(Farida);* Cork Hubbert *(Midget);* Romano Puppo *(Captain);* Attilio Lo Pinto *(Zombie King);* Armando Mac Rory *(Town Crier);* Giada Cozzi *(Girl);* Ted Rusoff *(Torture Chamber Keeper);* Massimo Vanni *(Man);* Daria Nicolodi *(Narrator).*

Comments: Legendary seafarer Sinbad must recover five magic stones that will enable him to lift the spell an evil wizard has cast on the city of Basra. This film was originally conceived as a 3-D production in 1983, but that concept was abandoned and the production wad delayed. At one point in this film, optically-modified footage from *Hercules Against the Moon Men* (1964) *(qv)* is used.

Thor the Conqueror (Thor il conquistatore) (Abruzzo Cinematografica, 1983)

Credits: *Director:* Tonino Ricci (billed as "Anthony Richmond"); *Producers:* Roberto Poggi, Marcello Romeo; *Screenplay:* Tito Carpi (based on his story); *Photography:* Giovanni Bergamini (color); *Film Editor:* Vincenzo Tomassi; *Music:* Francesco De Masi; *Makeup:* Pietro Tenoglio; *Hair Stylist:* Maria Fiocca; *Production Manager:* Romualdo Buzzanca; *Assistant Director:* Franco Fogagnolo; *Assistant Production Designer:* Roberto Ricci; *Sound:* Alessandro Sarandrea; *Sound Mixer:* Adriano Taloni; *Special Effects:* Mario Ciccarella; *Master of Arms:* Rinaldo Zamperla; *Assistant Camera Operators:* Aldo Bergamini, Fabrizio Mengoni; *Still Photographer:* Francesco Narducci; *Key Grip:* Nunzio Morales; *Chief Electrician:* Renaldo Tibaldi; *Seamstress:* Anna Lelli; *Assistant Costume Designer:* Gianni Manzi; *Assistant Film Editors:* Massimo Cataldo, Giancarlo Tiburzi; running time: 91 minutes; released February 5, 1983 (Italy); video availability: Substance Video.

Cast: Bruno Minniti [billed as "Conrad Nichols"] *(Thor);* Maria Romano *(Ina);* Malisa Longo [billed as "Malisa Lang"] *(Slave Girl);* Luigi Mezzanotte [billed as "Christopher Holm"] *(Etna);* Raf Baldassarre [billed as "Raf Falcone"] *(Gnut);* Angelo Ragusa *(Thor's Father);* Rosalba Ciofalo *(1st Warrior Virgin);* Elena Wiedermann *(2nd Warrior Virgin);* Artemio Antonini *(Barbarian Chief);* Giovanni Cianfriglia *(Maneater Chief);* Osiride Pevarello *(Thor Tribesman);* Rinaldo Zamperla *(Gnut's Man).*

Comments: Warrior Thor avenges the murder of his parents by the villainous Gnut. Produced by Italy's Abruzzo Cinematografica. The title character is no relation to the Norse God of Thunder.

The Throne of Fire (Il trono di fuoco) (The Cannon Group, 1986)

Credits: *Director:* Franco Prosperi; *Producer:* Ettore Spagnuolo; *Associate Producer:* Umberto Innocenzi; *Screenplay:* Nino Marino (based on a story by Nino Marino and Giuseppe Buricchi); *Photography:* Guglielmo Mancori (Telecolor, Techniscope, aspect ratio 1.85:1); *Film Editor:* Alessandro Lucidi; *Music:* Carlo Rustichelli, Paolo Rustichelli; *Art Direction:* Francesco Cuppini (billed as "Frank Cuppini"); *Costume Design:* Silvio Lorenzi; *Makeup:* Giuseppe Ferranti; *Hair Stylist:* Maria Teresa Carrera; *Production Supervisors:* Giulio Dini, Alessandra Spagnuolo; *Assistant Director:* Mauro Sacripanti; *Special Effects:* Paolo Ricci; *Camera Operators:* Renato Doria, Mario Sbrenna; *Assistant Film Editors:* Mario D'Ambrosio, Maria Gabriella Bonolis; *Continuity:* Rachel Bryceson; *Assistant to the Director:* Remo De Angelis; running time: 89 minutes; released June 17, 1983 (Italy), June 5, 1986 (U.S.).

Cast: Sabrina Siani *(Princess Valkari);* Pietro Torrisi [billed as "Peter McCoy"] *(Siegfried);* Harrison Muller, Jr. [billed as "Harrison Muller"] *(Morak/Belial);* Beni Cardoso [billed as "Benny Carduso"] *(Azira);* Pietro Ceccarelli [billed as "Peter Caine"] *(Tares)*; Dan Collins; Stefano Abbati; Roberto Lattanzio; Isarco Ravaioli; Amedeo Leonardi; Gianlorenzo Bernini.

Comments: The invulnerable Siegfried of teutonic myth vs. the evil Morak. Produced by Italy's Visione Cinematografica. This film reuses the village raid scene from *Barbarian Master* (1983) *(qv)*. The castle scenes were filmed in Bracciano, Rome, and interiors were filmed at De Paolis Studios and Elios Studios in Rome.

Warrior Queen (Pompei) (Lightning Pictures, 1987)

Credits: Director: Chuck Vincent; *Producer:* Harry Alan Towers; *Associate Producers:* Joe D'Amato (billed as "Aristede Massacesi"), Donatella Donati; *Screenplay:* Rick Marx, S.C. Dacy (based on a story by Harry Alan Towers [billed as "Peter Welbeck"]); *Photography:* Gianlorenzo Battaglia (color); *Film Editors:* Joel Bender, Anthony Delcampo, Jim Sanders, Chuck Vincent; *Production Design/Costume Design:* Lucio Parise; *Makeup:* Franco Di Girolamo; *Production Manager:* Egidio Valentini; *Assistant Directors:* Dario Silvagni, Per Sjostedt; *Props:* Valentino Salvati; *Sound:* Larry Revene; *Special Effects:* Franco Di Girolamo; *Stunts/Master of Arms:* Franco Ukmar; *1st Assistant Cameraman:* Daniele Cimini; *Still Photographer:* Claudio Patriarca; *Wardrobe:* Anna Rasetti; *Assistant to the Director:* Andy Christie; *Script Girl:* Luisa Gamba; running time: 79 minutes; released January 1987 (U.S.); video availability: Vestron Video.

Cast: Sybil Danning *(Berenice)*; Donald Pleasence *(Clodius)*; Richard Hill *(Marcus)*; J.J. Jones *(Chloe)*; Tally Chanel *(Vespa)*; Stasia Micula *(Philomena)*; Suzanne Smith *(Veneria)*; David Haughton *(Victo)*; Mario Cruciani *(Roberto)*; Marco Tullio Cau *(Goliath)*.

Comments: In 79 AD, persecuted and sexually exploited slaves attempt to escape during the eruption of Mt. Vesuvius. This film was spiced-up with plenty of nudity and R-rated softcore sex scenes. Produced by Seymour Borde & Associates.

Yor, the Hunter from the Future (Il mondo di Yor) (Columbia Pictures, 1983)

Credits: Director: Antonio Margheriti [billed as "Anthony M. Dawson"] *Producer:* Michele Marsala; *Associate Producers:* Sedat Akdemir, Ugor Terzioglu; *Screenplay:* Robert D. Bailey, Antonio Margheriti [billed as "Anthony M. Dawson"] (based on the graphic novel *Henga, el cazador*, by Ray Collins, Juan Zanotto); *Photography:* Marcello Masciocchi (Eastmancolor, aspect ratio 1.85:1); *Film Editors:* Alberto Moriani, Jorge Sellallonga; *Music:* John Scott; *Art Direction:* Walter Patriarca; *Costume Design:* Enrico Luzzi; *Makeup:* Mario Scutti; *Assistant Makeup Artist:* Giacinto Bretti; *Hair Stylist:* Agnese Panarotto; *Executive in Charge of Production:* Timucin Selgur; *Production Managers:* Michele Germano, Roberto Onorati; *Unit Manager:* Giovanni Loffreda; *Assistant Director:* Ignazio Dolce; *Assistant Art Director:* Yilmaz Zengar; *Set Dresser:* Pasquale Germano; *Set Painter:* Oreste Quercioli; *Props:* Basilio Patrizi; *Sound Editor:* Nick Alexander; *Sound Mixer:* Cinzia Rossi; *Sound Re-Recording Engineer:* Alberto Doni; *Special Effects:* Antonio Margheriti, Edoardo Margheriti; *Models/Miniatures:* Antonella Margheriti; *Stunt Coordinators:* Arnaldo Dell'Acqua, Goffredo Unger; *Stunts:* Massimo Pittarello; *Camera Operator:* Mario Sbrenna; *Assistant Camera Operators:* Luigi Conversi, Mauro Masciocchi; *Steadycam Operator:* Umit Gulsoy; *Still Photographer:* Roberto Nicosia Vinci; *Key Grip:* Orlando Zaccari; *Gaffer:* Tulio Marini; *Seamstresses:* Angela Anzimani, Angela Vittorini; *Wardrobe Assistant:* Umberto Moroni; *Assistant Film Editors:* Muana Hussein, Pina La Rosa, Pietro Tomassi; *Composers (Additional Music):* Guido De Angelis, Maurizio De Angelis; *Music Orchestration:* Neil Richardson; *Music Editor:* Robert Hathaway; *Soundtrack Album Producer:* Benjamin Michael Joffe; *Dialogue Coach:* Paul Costello; *Production Secretaries:* Angelo Corrieri, Marina De Tiberis; *Production Accountant:* Franco Fantini; *Unit Publicist:* Enrico Lucherini; running time: 98 minutes (restored director's cut); released February 10, 1983 (Italy), August 19, 1983 (U.S.); video availability: Sony Pictures Home Entertainment.

Cast: Reb Brown *(Yor)*; Corinne Cléry *(Ka-Laa)*; Luciano Pigozzi [billed as "Alan Collins"] *(Pag)*; Carole André *(Ena)*; John Steiner *(Over-*

lord); Ayshe Gul *(Rea, of the Sand People);* Aytekin Akkaya *(Leader of the Sand People);* Marrina Rocchi *(Tarita);* Sergio Nicolai *(Kay);* Ludovico Della Jojo; Adrian Akdemir; Herent Akdemir; Ali Segur; Zeynep Selgur; Henk Akin; Zenne Poksuz; Nurdan Asar; Nilgun Bubikoglu; Tevfik Sen; Yasemin Celenk; Levent Çakir; Yadigar Ajder; Nick Alexander *(Voice of Blonde Rebel);* Paul Costello *(Blind man);* Larry Dolgin *(Voice of Kai);* Edward Mannix *(Voice of Pag);* Nello Pazzafini *(Tribe Elder);* Gregory Snegoff *(Voice of Yor);* Robert Spafford *(Voice of Tribe Elder);* Susan Spafford *(Voice of Kalaa).*

Comments: In a prehistoric land inhabited by monsters, a young warrior seeks out a desert goddess to learn his origin. Leading man Reb Brown is infamous as the star of the notoriously bad sci-fi stinker *Space Mutiny.* He also played comic book superhero Captain America in two low-budget made-for-TV movies. *Yor, the Hunter from the Future* was originally released at 88 minutes, but a restored director's cut added 10 minutes of previously cut footage. Co-produced by Italy's Diamint Film, RAI Radiotelevisione Italiana, and Kodiak Films.

INDEX

Pages with illustrations are indicated in **bold** type.

Abbati, Stefano 207
Abbrecia, Giuseppe 22
Abbrescia, Giuseppe 22, 153
Abessier, Louis 31
Abruzzo Cinematografica 206
Accursi, Claude 174
Achille Piazzi Produzioni Cinematografica 73
Achilli, Fausto 160
Achilli, Sante 106
Acosta, Armondo Linus 51
Acqua, Antonio 49, 84
A.D. Cinematografica 168
Adam, Ken 158
Adam, Noëlle 192
Addario, Pino 114
Addobbati, Giuseppe 26, 82, 102, 111, 113, 114, 118, 146, 147 165, 172, 174, 186
Addolori, Jolanda 28
Adelphi Compagnia Cinematographica 67, 124, 152, 153
Adelphi Productions 91
Adelphia 153
Adet, Georges 31
Adinolfi, Ugo 196
Adler, Susan 205
Adorf, Mario 109
Adorno, Franco 174
Adrario, Rosina 46
Adriani, Giorgio 158
The Adventures of Robin Hood 178
Adventurer of Tortuga (L'avventriero della Tortuga) 15
The Adventures of Hercules II (Le avventure dell'incredibile Ercole) 197
The Adventures of Mandrin (Le avvventure di Mandrin) 15
The Adventures of Scaramouche (La máscara de Scaramouche) 16
Aeschylus 92
Affronti, Edmondo 29
Ágata Films S.A. 43
Agate, Carlo 91
Agliani, Giorgio 40, 65, 120, 183
Agnoletti, Baccio 135
Agosti, Gus 158, 168

Agostinelli, Claudio 40, 41
Agrebi, Mohammed 175
Agudo, Miguel 40
Ahmed, Hassan 157
Ahmed, Samira 160
Aidei, Sergio 11
Aikens, Vanoye 25, 76, 134, 140
Aimée, Anouk 159
Airaldi, Franco 160
Airoldi, Daniela 201
Ajace Produzioni Cinematografiche 51
Alarcón, José María 51
Alarcón, Juan Benito 111
Alari, Nadine 96
Alarimo, John 54, 132
Albaicín, Rafael 127, 150
Albanese, Giovanni 133
Albani, Enrico 158
Albani, Pietro 131
Albeht, Janez 18
Alberini, Massimo 19
Albertelli, Mario 125
Alberti, Anna Lina 77
Alberti, Annie 77, 166
Alberti, Guido 28, 113
Alberti, Marc 204
Alberti, Mario 174
Albertini, Bitto 32, 36, 44, 65, 69, 102, 126, 129, 134, 135, 147, 152, 160, 165
Albertini, Edda 132
Albertini, Giampiero 194
Albertini, Marco 206
Albonico, Giulio 194
Albressier, Louis 87
Alcardi, Federico 110

Alchimede, Diego 19, 34, 41, 54, 77, 96, 98, 107, 129, 133, 169, 176
Alcón, Manuel 47
Alda, Robert 36, 124, 137
Alderson, John 25
Aldrich, Robert 158, 159
Alessandri, Roberto 26
Alessandrini, Goffredo 47
Alessi, Amedeo 199
Alessi, Francesco 15
Alessi, Ottavio 35, 122
Alexander, Catherine 142
Alexander, Nick 207, 208
Alexandria Produzioni Cinematografiche (Alexandra P. C.) 107, 183, 190
Alexandrief, Anna 25
Alfonsi, Engo 129
Alfonsi, Enzo 139
Alfonsi, Lidia 80, 96, 118, 124, 179
Alfonso, Marí José 26
Alfonzi, Enzo 16, 30, 36, 56, 58, 99, 129, 157, 167, 177, 179
Ali Baba and the Sacred Crown (Le sette fatiche di Alí Babá) 16, **17**
Ali Baba and the Seven Saracens (Simbad contro I sette saraceni) 16
Alianello, Marilù 137
Alias, Bruno 113
Alimonti, Aldo 125
All the King's Men 73
Allasio, Marisa 165
Allegretti, Luigi 34, 60, 87, 88, 95, 98, 106, 143, 147
Allesti, Marussia 13
Allione, Cesare 29, 50, 65, 99, 126
Almirante-Manzini, Italia 7, 12
Alone Against Rome (Solo contro Rome) 17
Alonso, Chelo 20, 21, 69, **69, 70,** 99, 124, 129, 155, **161, 162,** 162, 173
Alonso, Mercedes 116, 154
Alonso, Rafael 127
Aloza, José Luis Jerez 116
Alphaville 150
Alta Vista 29, 36, 37, 69, 82, 112, 114
Altamura, Roberto 167
Altamura, Tullio 20, 34, 77, 81, 82,

210 Index

89, 98, 102, 107, 114, 130, 133, 134, 136, 143, 176, 194
Altariba, Béatrice 58, 153
Altieri, Alessandro 203
Altieri, Nino 9, 46
Altieri, Tiziana 203
Altman, Joan 22
Altoviti, Antonio 21, 22
Altschuler, Modest 14
Álvarez, Ángel 16, 107
Alvaro Mancori Produzioni Cinematografica 161
Amadei, Giovanni 58
Amadio, Silvio 120, 131, 189
Amadoro, Ugo 83, 189
Amanda, Lia 42
Amari, Mario 37, 76, 105, 130, 132, 155, 162, 184
Amato Studios 45
Amatulli, Angelo 194, 197
Amauli, Giulio 130
The Amazons (*Le guerriere dal seno nudo*) 18
Amazons of Rome (*La vergini di Roma*) 18
Ambesi, Adriana 27, 92, 143, 183
Ambrosi, Paola 27
Ambrosiana Cinematografica 76, 91, 140
Ambrosiano, Adelpho 91
Ambrosino, Mario 141
Ambrosio, Arturo 9, 10, 13
Ambroso, Gianfranco 200
Amedei, Anna 32, 127
Ameliese, Brunetta 49
Amendola, Antonio 22, 141
Amendola, Ferruccio 166, 172
Amendola, Mario 26, 29, 49, 129, 165, 166, 167, 172, 181
Amengual, Guillermo 107
Amer, Ahmed 135
American Broadcasting Co. (ABC) 142
American-International Pictures (AIP) 4, 189
Amicucci, Gianfranco 110, 205
Amicucci, Roberto 206
Amidei, Sergio 10, 48
Aminel, Georges 87, 145
Ammarata, Sergio 102
Ammirata, Franco 112
Ammirata, Sergio 65
Ammonini, Mario 179, 192
Amo, Pablo G. del 139
Amords, Francisco 126
Amorotti, R. 154
Anastasi, Luigi 32, 177
Anchóriz, Leo 101, 116, 147
Ancillai, F. 194
Ancillai, Fausto 124, 163, 179
Andersen, Conrad 128
Andersen, Susy 175, 189, 191
Anderson, Annie 31
Anderson, Audrey 84
Anderson, Conrad 40
Anderson, Dale L. 112
Anderson, Ingrid 202
Anderson, Nick 152
André, Carole 28, 207

André, Gaby 72, 73
André, Vittorio 46
Andreini, Gabriella 32, 100, 196
Andreoli, Annabella 205
Andreotti, Giulio 12
Andress, Ursula 110
Andrews, Harry 25
Andrews, Martin 146
Andriani, Oscar 173, 174, 186
Ángel, Antonio Ramirez 167
Angele, Maria Teresa 133
Angeleri, Lia 41, 116
Angeletti, Pio 176
Angeletti, Ruggero 46
Angeli, Pier 124, 158
Angelini, Luciana 19, 49
Angelini, Nando 25, 30, 50, 51, 58, 63, 64, 77, 87, 92, 98, 100, 102, 103, 106, 111, 116, 128, 130, 131, 138, 140, 147, 184, 186
Angeloni, Sergio 55, 164
Angelucci, Angela 167
Angiolillo, Luciana 18, 87, 179
Angiolillo, Tiberio Murgia,Luciana 36
Angiolini, Renato 60
Annacelli, Corrado 106
Anniballi, Francesco 201
Annicelli, Corrado 77, 113, 125, 130, 160
Annuale, Armando 45, 55, 125, 174
Annunziata, Giuseppe 174
Anoria, Franco 63
Ansa Co. 45
Ante, Tony 175
Anthar the Invincible (*Anthar L'Invincible*) see *Devil of the Desert Against the Son of Hercules*
Antinori, Gianni 103, 128
Antinori, Lamberto 124, 141, 167
Antoine, André-Paul 174
Anton, Amerigo 20, 91, 143, 173, 178
Anton, Edoardo 47, 128, 140
Antonelli, Adriano 177
Antonelli, Ennio 167, 201
Antonelli, Franco 65
Antonelli, Maria 103
Antonelli, Rita 201
Antonini, Alfredo 22
Antonini, Artemio 17, 65, 111, 134, 137, 164, 195, 206
Antonini, Gabriele 78, 80, 98, 124, 138, 139, 145, 152, 153, 184, 92–94
Antonioni, Michelangelo 155
Antonucci, Spartaco 187, 188
Anzellotti, Luciano 197
Anzellotti, Massimo 197, 201
Anzimani, Angela 207
Aparicio, Rafaela 24
Aphrodite, Goddess of Love (*Afrodite, dea dell'amore*) 19
Appetito, Enrico 30, 138
APO Film 158, 189
Aquillino, Umberto 50
Aragno, Giacomo 55
Arakelian, Hagop 18
Aranda, Ángel 69, 39, 106
Arandjelovic, Stole 152
Arata, Ubaldo 9, 10, 45, 46

Arbó, Manuel 69, 119, 127, 167
Arbó, Miguel Asins 40
Arbressier, Louis 119
Arcalli, Franco 165
Archetti, Alberto 78, 100, 135, 141
Arco Film 142, 151
Arden, Gisella 102, 111, 133, 196
Arden, Hugo 160
Arden, Mary 138
Ardisson, George 52, 90, 106, 114, 124, 131, 195
Arditi, Mariano 114, 150
Ardizone, Anna 18
Ardizzone, Anna Maria 18
The Arena (*La rivolta della gladiatrici*) 19, 48
Arena, Anna 50, 81, 84, 129, 133
Arena, Ettore 109, 113, 118
Arena, Fortunato 32, 34, 40, 64, 92, 98, 111, 118, 126, 138, 140, 147, 158, 164, 171, 172, 173, 174, 175, 176, 181, 187, 196, 201
Arena, Maurizio 29
Arendt, Elke 59
Arene, Michel 31
Arévalo, José Carlos 84
Arévalo, Juan Antonio 84, 154
Argento, Pietro 48
Arias, Lucky 201
Arias, María Luisa 27
Arié, Bruno 15, 69, 77, 109, 111, 134, 164, 169, 177
Arié, Maria 29
Arion Company 60
Ariston, Michaela 161
Ariza, Francisco 187
Arkoff, Samuel Z. 59, 63, 81, 87, 89, 189
Arlorio, Giorgio 67
Armadei, Giovanni 16
Armendáriz, Pedro 163
Arménise, Victor 10
Armontel, Richard 15
Arnaldi, Arnaldo 12, 20
Arnaud, Fede 49, 158, 162
Arnova, Alba 119
Aroca, María Sánchez 159
Arriaga, Simón 154
Arrie, Bruno 169
Arrieu, René 145
Arta Cinematografica S.P.A. 157
Artale, Carmelo 30
Artale, Lorenzo 150, 174
Arté, Bruno 104, 134
Arteaga, Ángel 26
Artesi, Vittorio 159
Artisti Associati 49
Artix 134
Artuffo, Riccardo 10
Arturio, Giorgio 194
Asar, Nurdan 208
Ascani, Eugenio 20, 111
Ascencio, Francisco R. 16
Aschieri, Pietro 45
Asensio, Francisco Rodríguez 37, 39, 47
Aslan, Grégore 113
Asselin, France 42
Asso, Pierre 96

Associati Produttori Indepenti Film (API) 156
Assonitis, Ovidio G. 203
Asteria Film 177
Asti, Adriana 194
Astolfi, Gianni 17, 55
Atenea Films 120
Athanasiou, Genica 42
Athena, Juan 68
Athena Cinematografica 33, 163
Athenia Films 101
Atlantica Cinematografica Produzione Films 18, 56, 158
Atlas 5
Atlas Against the Cyclops (Maciste nella terra dei ciclopi) 20
Atlas Against the Czar (Maciste alla corte dello zar) 20
Ator, the Fighting Eagle (Ator l'invincibile) 198
Attack of the Giant Leeches 46
Attack of the Moors (I Reali di Francia) 21
Attack of the Normans (I normanni) 21
Attanasio, Ugo 172
Attenea Films 107, 152, 190
Attenni, Giulianna 58, 64, 150, 102
Attili, Giorgio 174
Attila (Atilla il flagello di Dio) 21
Aubrey, Richard 18
Audisio, Carlo 106
Audley, Michael 41, 158
Audray, Elvire 204
Audry, Geneviève 91, 129
Augustus Film 160
Aureli, Andrea 15, 19, 26, 29, 48, 50, 56, 58, 65, 77, 80, 84, 95, 106, 107, 110, 111, 119, 125, 129, 133, 134, 136, 138, 139, 145, 165, 169, 177, 186
Aureli, Giorgio 104
Auriol, Jean-Georges 54
Ausonio, Mario Guaita 14
Autin, Michel 30
Avala Film 23, 78, 113, 115, 152
Avanzi, Lucia 163
The Avenger (Le leggenda di Enea) 22
Avenger of the Seven Seas (Il giustiziere dei mari) 23
The Avenger of Venice (Il ponte d ei sospiri) 23
The Avenger, Zorro (El Zorro justicero) 23
Avesani, Bruno 27, 48
Aveta, Anna Maria 166
Ávila, Enrique 32, 43, 67, 195
Avila, Frank 200
Ávila, Vincente 24
Avis Films 16, 17, 177
Avvisato, Pasquale 199
Axeri, Giovanni 50
Axeworthy, Yvonne 25
Azais, Paul 42
Aznavour, Charles 16
Azzini, Nedo 99

Baca, Robert 175
Baccaro, Salvatore 20, 200
The Bacchantes (le baccanti) 24
Bacci, Gildo 10
Bacciucchi, Erasmo 37, 68
Bacciucchi, Eros 30, 67, 124, 153
Bachetti, Giancarlo 197
Bacic, Vladimir 58, 127, 154
Baciocchi, Fabio 200
Baciucchi, Ditta 19
Badeschi, Franca 67
Badmajew, Maria 41
Bagagli, Renzo 142
Baghino, Gianni 28, 63, 77, 87, 98, 130, 137, 146
Bagnato, Mario 201
Bagni, Luciana 105
Bagnoli, Gualtero 55, 125
Bagolini, Silvio 29, 131, 165, 196
Bailey, Jane 202
Bailey, Robert D. 207
Bailly, Michèle 113
Bain, Agnes L. 13
Baird-Smith, Annette 203
Baird, Harry 171, 175, 184
Baistrocchi, Angelo 150, 166
Bakalyan, Richard 22
Baker, Stanley 158, 194
Bakst, André 178
Balassar, Ralph 202
Balbintlio, Franco 48
Balbo, Ennio 34, 131
Balboa (Il leggendario conquistadore) 24
Balbuena, José 119
Balcázar, Alfonso 163
Balcázar Producciones Cinematograficas 151, 164
Balchin, Nigel 24
Baldanello, Emilio 192
Baldanello, Gianfranco 29, 58, 107, 114, 129, 137, 177, 187
Baldanello, Grazia 58, 91
Baldassarre, Raf 21, 52, 54, 64, 65, 87, 90, 99, 110, 125, 127, 128, 129, 130, 133, 134, 147, 151, 152, 154, 157, 159, 165, 167, 186, 198, 202, 206
Baldenello, Gianfranco 44
Baldi, Ferdinando 44, 50, 115, 160, 166, 168, 169, 183
Baldi, Giorgio 20, 70, 161, 162, 164, 175
Baldi, Joe 40
Baldi, Marcello 54, 64, 70, 102, 113, 122, 150
Baldinello, Gianfranco 169
Baldini, Renato 47, 52, 64, 68, 78, 99, 137, 151, 156, 157, 166, 174, 191
Baldoni, Giorgina 50
Baldoni, Maurizio 44
Balducci, Franco 41, 51, 78, 89, 147, 156
Balducci, Luciano 199
Baldwin, Ferdy 115
Balenci, Noëlle 112
Ballanti, Adriana 65
Ballard, Manuela 130
Ballesteros, Antonio L. 37, 47, 105
Ballistrieri, Gennaro 49, 114
Bals, Gregor 49
Balsamo, Ignazio 34, 60, 63, 77, 81, 84, 87, 102, 114, 129, 130, 133, 141, 146, 176 187, 194, 195, 196
Baltimore, Nadir 82, 143
Baltoni, Fernando 142
Balzo, Liana Del 41, 126, 159, 195
Banciella, Gervasio 116
Band, Albert 22
Band, Charles 22
Bandini, Augusto 8, 9, 10, 12, 13
Bandini, Baccio 168
Baneri, Gianni 84
Banfi, Bixie 131
Bani, Andrea 9
Banks, Philip 201
Bañó, Vicente 107, 119, 167, 190
Banovic, Sekula 191
Banti, Lucia 78
Baquero, Antonio 51
Bar, Jacques 15, 168
Barabbas 24
Baraghini, Giulio 113
Baragli, Nino 155, 190
Baranger, Sandro 28
Barattolo, Giuseppe 10
Barbara, Juan 24
Barbara, Paolo 33, 125, 152, 166
Barbarian Master (Sangraal, la spada di fuoco) 198, 207
The Barbarians (I barbari) 199
The Barbarians (Revak, lo schiavo di Cartagine) 25
Barbaro, Umberto 54
Barberini, Tommaso 49
Barberito, Alberto 122
Barbieri, Romano 80
Barbini, Luigi 92
Barboni, Enzo 50, 105, 156, 187
Barboni, Guido 141
Barboni, Leonida 142
Barboo, Luis 141, 151
Barclay, Peter 152
Barclay, Steve 125
Bard, Philip 204
Bardaro, Salvatore 200
Bardem, Rafael 159
Bardot, André 42
Bardot, Mijanou 129
Barge, Paul 42
Baric, M. 59
Barker, Lex 32, 54, 80, 129, 130, 140, 163, 173
Barnabò, Guglielmo 46, 55
Barnes, Walter 23, 35, 133, 134, 137, 138, 140, 157
Barni, Aldo 114
Baron, Emma 19, 25, 45, 76, 122, 126, 130, 131, 151
Baroni, Maria 92, 95, 158, 189
Barray, Gérard 16, 56, 150, 151
Barri, Barta 40, 43, 65, 67, 101, 150, 151, 159
Barrie, Yvonne 42
Barromel, Charles 196, 200
Barrymore, John Drew 35, 41, 100, 126, 128, 130, 131, 179, 189
Barsacq, Léon 118
Barsanti, Alberto 60
Barsotti, Fulvio 137
Barta, Gian 158

Bartalini, Isa 54
Bartha, John 35, 54, 107, 138, 143, 158
Bartlett, Dennis 22
Bartoli-Avveduti, Maria Antonietta 8
Bartoli, Adolfo 203
Bartolini, Carlo 169
Bartolini, Giancarlo 15, 103
Bartolomei, Franca 112
Bartolomei, Mario 15, 60
Bartoloni, Corrado 80
Bartoloni, Mario 60
Bartolozzi, Tommaso 197
Barton, Jannette 160
Bartrop, Roland 25, 156
Barzman, Ben 51
Basabé, Miguel Ángel Garcia 47
Basaldella, Mirko 27
Basehart, Jackie 28
Basic, Relja 138, 152
Basile, Antonio 30, 110, 138, 157
Basile, Lino 119
Basile, Pasquale 30, 110, 141, 157, 167, 191, 195
Basili, Christina 198
Basili, Mario 175
Bassanelli, Angelo 136
Bassani, Giorgio 15
Bassi, Franco 99
Basta, Ivan 160
Bastianoni, Angelo 18, 157
Bastianoni, Giancarlo 18, 26, 73, 157, 169, 171, 179
Bates, Peter 202
Batisti, Giuseppe 157
Battaglia, Gianlorenzo 199, 202, 207
Battaglia, Rik 15, 21, 31, 41, 52, 77, 107, 119, 120, 131, 141, 149, 158
Battagliotti, August 7
Battelli, Ivo 111, 137
Battiferri, Angelo 125
Battiferri, Giulio 15, 29, 35, 65, 84, 119, 125, 129, 130, 133, 134, 135, 177
Battiferri, Nino 54, 77, 107, 132, 147, 169, 177
Battistella, Antonio 175, 191
Battistelli, Nino 95
Battisti, Spartico 20, 195
Battle of the Amazons (Le Amazoni–Donne d'amore e di guerra) 26
Batzella, Luigi 33, 134, 150, 194
Baud, Antoine 16
Baudo, Serge 118
Baum, Henri 150
Baumann, Anne-Marie 105
Bava, Eugenio 7, 13
Bava, Mario 5, 21, 52, 60, 78, 80, 87, 89, 90, 92, 94, 104, 141, 161, 184, 191, 192
Baxter, Les 52, 69, 70, 73, 77, 112, 143, 145
Bay, Sara (a.k.a. Rosalba Neri) 20
Bayard, Charles 42
Bayarri, Jaime 151
Bazzini, Sergio 154
Bazzocchi, Loris 164
Bazzoni, Camillo 30, 41, 60
Bazzoni, Luigi 128

The Beast of Babylon Against the Son of Hercules (L'eroe di Babilonia) 26
Beauchamp, Edmund 31
Beaumont, Roger 27
Beaver-Champion Productions 41
Beddoes, Ivor 22
Bedi, Kabir 28
Bedini, Leonardo 158
Bedoni, Maurizio 44
Beernardi, Nerio 174
Behind the Mask of Zorro (Il giuramento di Zorro) 26
Belardelli, Augusto 34, 80
Belfiore, Andrea 198
Beli, Marisa 90
Bell, Betsy 36
Bellanti, Adriana 62, 188
Bellazecca, Luigi 199
Bellazecca, Raffaella 199
Bellero, Carlo 23, 77, 110, 114, 133, 134, 143
Bellero, Loris 191
Bellesteros, Antonio L. 159
Belletti, Adolfo 110
Belli, Marisa 23, 92
Bellini, Gianfranco 155
Bellisario, Fabio 22
Beltramme, Franco 139, 177
Beltrone, Annibale 55
Belviso, Antonio 49, 114
Belzo, Liana Del 142
Bembo, Alberto Baldan 200
Bénard, Nicole 42
Benassi, Memo 46
Bencini, Sonia 22, 103
Benda, Georges K. 42, 175
Bender, Joel 207
Benedetti, Ivo 112
Benedetti, Rolando 49
Benetti, Luciano 22, 103, 114, 139, 166
Bengell, Norma 32
Ben-Hur 18
Bennati, Flavio 27
Bennet, Colleen 94
Benoît, Pierre 87, 103
Benson, Danielle 192
Bent, Kirk 161
Bentivegna, Warner 179
Benussi, Femi 195
Benvenuti, Jolanda 29, 34, 63, 77, 80, 84, 87, 89, 102, 104, 129, 130, 133, 143, 145, 147, 165, 167, 171, 187, 195
Berco, Alberto 24
Berenguer, Manuel 51
Berg, Almut 18
Berg, Lorena 55
Bergamini, Aldo 206
Bergamini, Giovanni 110, 122, 151, 163, 179, 206
Bergamini, Sergio 28, 91, 122, 176
Bergamo, Eduardo 175
Bergamonti, Rosella 151
Berganzelli, Sergio 99
Bergen, Birgit 58
Berger, Jean 31
Berger, Monica 163
Berger, William 198, 202, 204

Bergerac, Jacques 59
Bergía, Joaquín 47
Bergman, Sandahl 205
Bergner, Elisabeth 165
Bergonzelli, Sergio 67, 69, 99, 128, 150, 169
Bergryd, Ulla 27
Bériard, René 96
Beringola, Luis 47
Berling, Peter 110
Berlini, Piero 106
Bermejo, Miguel Ángel 126
Bermudez, Dolores 167
Bernacchioni, Paolo 200
Bernal, Francisco 69, 159
Bernalt, José Garcia 47
Bernard-Luc, Jean 56
Bernard, Alex 10
Bernard, Allesandro 7
Bernardi, Nerio 21, 22, 24, 29, 31, 32, 33, 41, 51, 55, 84, 98, 100, 102, 104, 107, 114, 122, 126, 128, 131, 136, 137, 142, 156, 160, 174, 176, 179, 187
Bernardini, Aldo 55
Bernardini, Bianco 176
Bernardini, Giuseppe 70
Bernardini, Luigi 49, 55
Bernardini, Maria 132
Bernardini, Nerio 114
Bernhardt, Curtis 43
Berni, Aldo 166
Berni, Mara 41, 59, 111, 142, 168
Berni, Marcello 29, 83, 112
Bernini, Gianlorenzo 207
Bernini, Nanni 199
Bernini, Vittorio 95
Berri, Robert 56
Berriatúa, Mario 106
Berryman, Michael 199
Berselli, Adriana 40, 43, 49, 131
Berta, Giuseppe 52
Bertheau, Julian 42
Berthier, Jacques 56, 127, 154
Berti, Aldo 102
Berti, Anita 46
Berti, Marina 44, 132, 168
Bertini, Francesca 7
Bertocci, Bruno 113
Bertolazzi, Walter 77, 129, 133, 143
Berton, Léon 42
Bertucci, Ughetto 29, 136, 182
Berutto, Enrico Betti 33, 154
Besesti, Mario 49, 55
Beshears, Ivan 204
Beshears, James 202
Bessi, Carlo 122, 132
Bessis, André 175
Besusso, Vera 34
Bettarini, Cesare 125, 156
Bettex, Sydney 56
Betti, Fiorella 52
Betti, Giuliano 36, 126, 128, 143
Bettini, Silla 126
Bettoia, Franca 21, 47, 50, 107, 135, 147
Bettoni, Robert 22, 56
Bevardi, Franco 43
Bevilacqua, Ettore 104

Bézard, Jacques 178
Bezard, René 31
Biagetti, Giulio 178
Bianchi, Cesare 111
Bianchi, Daniela 166
Bianchi, Eleonora 59, 73, 146, 177, 186, 187, 194
Bianchi, Giovanni 65, 130
Bianchi, Leonardo 158
Bianchi, Mario 112
Bianchi, Nadia 36
Bianchi, Sandro 15, 46, 50
Bianchi, Tino 186
Bianchi, Vittorio 12
Bianchini, Alfredo 104
Bianchini, Cesare 177
Biancini, Ferruccio 10
Bianco, Solly V. 147, 171
Biancoli, Oreste 20, 23, 47, 52, 112, 130, 143, 161, 164, 192
Biasi, Alberto 200
Biava, Claudio 35
Biber, Michael-John 205
The Bible: In the Beginning 27
Bigazzi, Cecilia 24, 99, 128, 131, 147
Bigazzi, Giampaolo 24, 41, 67, 78, 99, 126, 128, 179
Bigazzi, Vieri 191
Bigerna, Luigi 50
Bigi, Laura 192
Biglietto, Eric 200
Bikell, Charles 203
Bilancia, Oreste 13, 14
Bilbao, Fernando 127
Biliotti, Enzo 46, 49
Billa, Salvatore 27, 204
Billery, Raoul 31
Billi, Mimo 164, 176
Billi, Riccardo 173
Billitteri, Salvatore 70, 73, 131, 143
Binarelli, Angelo 50, 176
Binder, Maurice 158
Bindi, Clara 102, 129
Bini, Alfredo 142
Binney, Neil 33
Biraschi, Venanzio 22
Bird, William 164, 179
Birley, Raoul 31
Birri, Fernando 22
Birt, George 25
The Birth of a Nation 8
Biscardi, Maria Luigia 156
Biseo, Vittorio 151
Bistolfi, Erno 115, 116
Bitenc, Demeter 36, 58, 111, 150
Bixio, Franco 110
Bixio, Giorgio 20
The Black Archer (L'arciere nero) 28
The Black Corsair (Il corsaro nero) 28
The Black Devil (Il diavolo nero) 28
The Black Duke (Il duca nero) 29
Black Sunday 60
Black, Robert 200
The Blade Master (Ator 2—L'invincibile Orion) 200
Blain, Estella 130
Blancheur, Jean 31
Blanco, Tomás 101, 107, 119, 139, 151
Blasco, Ricardo 26, 167

Blasetti, Alessandro 54
Blasi, Alberto 203, 205
Blay, Steve 203
Blengini, Corrado 188
Blier, Bernard 30
Bloch, Lars 109
Blondeau, Lucien 42
Blondel, Jean 48
Blondell, Simone 23
Bluhmen, David 125
Blunk, John 27
Blysdeal, Johnny 92
Boby 31
Boccaci, Antonio 139
Boccardo, Delia 165, 202
Boccia, Tanio 20, 30, 31, 40, 91, 136, 143, 173, 178
Boccianti, Alberto 20, 33, 43, 96, 99, 160, 168, 182
Bochart, Pierre 18
Bodina, Liuba 178
Boetan, Ernest 109
Boggian, Nadia 199
Boggiatto, Thea 50
Böhme, Herbert A.E. 32
Boido, Federico 88, 111
Boisset, Yves 37
Bolas, Xan das 16, 40, 139, 154, 159
Bolin, Beli 115
Bolin, Dagmar 118
Bollante, Letitia 102
Bolnand, Bridget 43
Bologna, Enrique 64
Bolognesi, Gemma 135
Bolognini, Manolo 182
Bolongaro, Massimo 20, 143, 163, 179
Bolzoni, Adriano 29, 50, 115, 156, 157, 183
Boman, Mirko 157
Bomba, Leo 47, 140, 174
Bomez, Lucia 111, 118
Bompani, Lucio 30, 77, 119, 192
Bona, Alessandro 13
Bona, Giampiero 164
Bonadonna, Elio 25, 167
Bonagura, Gianni 44
Bonanni, Cinzia 30
Bonansea, Miranda 182
Bonard, Henriette 12, 14
Bonavera, Carla 44
Bondani, Armando 96
Bonelli, Luigi 166
Bonfigli, Gustavo 59
Bongini, Giulio 50, 125, 132, 141, 190
Boni, Luisella 21, 34, 40, 59, 127, 142
Bonifanti, Decoroso 13
Bonifazi, Nadia 59
Bonivento, Giovanni 32, 98
Bonnani, Luciano 114
Bonnard, Giulio 141
Bonnard, Maria 141
Bonnard, Mario 19, 105, 106, 141
Bonnarel, André 31
Bonneau, Gilles 56
Bonnemaison, Louis 18
Bonolis, Maria Gabriella 206
Bonos, Luigi 44, 156
Bonos, Vittorio 44, 192

Bonotti, Guglielmo 29, 31, 44, 48, 54, 125, 177
Bonucci, Alberto 58
Bonzi, Camillo Bruto 12, 14
Bordegas, Roberto 37
Borderie, Bernard 56
Borderie, Raymond 56
Bordi, Mario 125
Borelli, Franco 18
Borelli, Rosario 68, 175
Borelli, Sergio 50, 70, 73, 156, 203
Borg, Conrad 203
Borg, Malcolm 203
Borg, Vincent 203
Borghese, Luigi 189
Borghese, Salvatore 25, 28, 35, 63, 81, 83, 87, 89, 110, 134, 137, 159, 164, 171, 176, 177, 179, 204
Borgiotti, Anita 19, 106
Borgiotti, Maria Grazia 30
Borgnetto, Luigi Romano 9, 11, 12, 13, 14
Borgnine, Ernest 25
Borisavljevic, P. 118
Bornarzi, Renato 169
Borni, Franco 137
Borrás, María Ángel Coma 195, 55
Borromel, Charles 65, 118, 130, 164
Bort, Teresa 47
Bory, Maria 156
Borzage, Frank 103
Borzelli, Gabriella 95
Borzelli, Laura 205
Borzone, Guglielmo G. 49
Bosc, Denise 174
Boscariol, Angelo 27, 124, 167
Boschero, Dominique 68, 186
Boschetti, Bruno 194
Boschi, Eliseo 128
Bosetti, Giulio 67, 124, 153
Bosi, Margherita 84
Bosic, Andrea 23, 30, 44, 51, 131, 147, 149, 167, 171, 182, 186, 192
Bosio, Elio 203
Bossalino, Paola 142
Botta, Leonardo 34, 78
Bottari, Eugenio 89
Bottin, Armando 164
Bottin, Norman 203
Bottin, Pina 77, 129
Bouchet, Barbara 126
Boulais, Roger 18, 31
Bourdon, Jacques 150
Bourvil 31
Bovo, Brunella 110
Boyd, Stephen 27
Bracale, Amalia 141
Bracale, Luigi 163
Bracci, Alfredo 9
Bracci, Enrico 14
Braccialini, Piero 24
Bradley, Al 26, 203
Bradley, Harold 26, 65, 73, 81, 152, 158
Bradley, Rasmo 160
Bradley, Wilbert 92, 133, 134, 144, 149, 178
Brado, Rina 168
Brady, Buff 51

214 Index

Bragadin, Marc-Antonio 142
Bragaglia, Arturo 95, 135, 155, 173
Bragaglia, Carlo Ludovico 18, 19, 58, 77, 95, 119, 135
Bragaglia, Leonardo 119
Braggiotti, Francesca 46
Braido, Rina 25
Brambilla, Franco 46
Bramieri, Gino 91
Bramonti, Antonio 92
Braña, Antonio 159
Braña, Frank 23, 24, 26, 40, 112, 116
Branca, Michele 112
Brancati, Vitaliano 48, 54
Brandi, Walter 33, 150, 176, 186, 194
Brandini, Olga 14
Brandon, David 200, 205
Brandt, Rainer 136
Brandt, Tony 205
Brandy 194
Brankovic, Vlado 50
Brasseur, Claude 104
Brasseur, Pierre 34
Brauner, Artur 164
Braus, Mortimer 77
Brazzi, Rossano 136, 155
Brecia, Alfonso 172
Brega, Roberto 84, 202
Bréhat, Georges 22
Brennus, Enemy of Rome (*Brenno il nemico di Roma*) 29
Breschi, Arrigo 21, 64, 67, 122
Brescia, Alfonso 26, 40, 65, 111, 126, 139, 166, 181, 184, 203
Brescia, Antonio 172
Brescini, Francesco 32, 133, 167
Brescini, Giovanni 200
Brescini, Nazareno 205
Bressan, Carlo 48
Bretti, Giacinto 207
Brice, Pierre 24, 41, 100, 102, 128, 145, **145**
Bridge, Joan 22, 184
Bridges, Claudia 204
Bright, Maurice A. 92
Brignone, Giuseppe 12
Brignone, Guido 8, 9, 10, 11, 155, 165
Brignone, Lilla 165, 176
Brigone, Giuseppe 9
Brigone, Mercedes 13
Brilli, Riccardo 26
Brini, Dante 92, 189
Briones, Félix 47
Brivio, Nadia 128, 129
Brizzi, Anchise 13, 35, 45, 104, 169
Bronston, Samuel 51
Brooks, Julian 164
Brosio, Gino 33, 158
Browers-Gracht Investments 203
Brown, Carol 17, 160, 187
Brown, Don 162
Brown, Harry Joe 159
Brown, Jerry 51
Brown, Laura 36, 58
Brown, Reb 207, 208
Brown, Ritza 198
Brown, Streisa 191
Brown, William Lyon 25

Browne, Roger 113, 131, 138, 152, 153, 171, 176, 188
Brugara, Jose 16
Bruna, Ria 14
Brunacci, Bruno 33
Brunelli, Ugo 192
Brunetti, Sisto 109
Bruni, Bruno 41
Bruni, Franco 197, 202
Bruni, Piera 19, 48
Bruno, Cinzia 84, 92
Bruno, Nando 182
Bruno, Pierrette 31
Brunot, André 42
Brusati, Franco 184
Bruschi, Tullio 26, 29, 165, 167
Brusco, Lucia 186
Brussières, Raymond 192
Bryant, Virginia 199
Bryceson, Rachel 206
Brynner, Yul 168
Bryonne, Lucien 87
Bua, Mario 112
Buazelli, Tino 33
Bubikoglu, Nilgun 208
Buccella, Maria Grazia 56, 126
Bucchi, Cellio 49
Buchanan, Robert 52
Buchholz, Horst 112
Buchs, Luis 106
Bueno, Antonio 51
Buffardi, Gianni 58
Bugette, Louis 31
Bugli, Piero 102
Buhr, Gérard 119
Bulgarelli, Enzo 110, 120, 122, 155, 165, 190, 194
Bullock, Edna 51
Bulwer-Lytton, Edward George 9, 10, 105, 106
Bunker, Larry 112
Buona Vista 178
Bur, Manolo Gómez 32
Burr, Raymond 1
Burani, Bruno 194
Buricchi, Giuseppe 206
Buricchi, Pino 198, 201
Burke, Samson 178, 187
Burmann, Sigfrido 47, 64, 150
Burnett, Don 44, 178
The Burning of Rome (*Il magnifico avventuriero*) 29
Burrel, Thomas 200
Bussières, Raymond 124
Butler, Hugo 158
Buton Film 156
Buzzanca, Gino 36, 91, 104, 124, 140, 141
Buzzanca, Romualdo 206
Byrne, John 132, 133

Ca.Pi. Film S.r.l. 176
C.A.P.R.I. 30
Caballoro, Mirella 200
Cabaud, Pierre 31
Cabiria (*Cabiria*) 1, 7, 13
Cabot, Bruce 69, 70, 134
Cabras, Giulio 119
Cabré, Arturo 39

Cabrera, Raul 204
Caccianti, Laura 138
Cacciottolo, Tonino 37, 90
Cachia, Anna 203
Cadéac, Paul 31
Cadueri, Renato 21, 33, 64, 80, 92, 125
Caesar Against the Pirates (*Giulio Cesare contro I pirati*) 30
Caesar the Conqueror (*Giulio Cesare il conquistadore delle Gallie*) 30
Caffarel, José Maria 40, 126, 151, 159
Caffrey, Colm 25
Cafiero, Vittorio 10
Cagli, Corrado 27
Caiano, Carlo 126, 154, 156
Caiano, Mario 103, 110, 115, 128, 129, 154, 157, 159, 165, 172, 181, 183, 186, 187
Caine, Peter 207
Caioli, Angelo Ron 111
Caisti, Calisto 73
Caiuli, Domenico 197, 199
Caizzi, Renato Terra 17, 152
Cajafa, Gianni 91, 153
Çakir, Levent 208
Cal, José de la 119
Calabrese, Angelo 136
Calabretta, Bruno 46
Calamai, Clara 19
Calamatta, Narcy 203
Calano, Carlo 136
Calatayud, Román 151
Calavetta, Rosetta 159
Calderoni, Rita 18
Calero, Ángel 119
Calhoun, Rory 39, **39**, 112
Cali, Giulio 65, 128, 166
Calisti, Calisto 68, 81, 118, 138, 143, 153, 158, 167, 178, 184, 189
Callegari, Gian Paolo 23, 26, 65, 78, 110, 118, 120, 130, 139, 183, 190
Calles, Alfredo 141
Callindri, Ernesto 177
Calnan, Mathilda 189
Calò, Carla 17, 29, 30, 31, 32, 46, 60, 69, 73, 104, 106, 114, 124, 135, 137, 139, 160, 168, 178, 187
Calò, Sergio 96, 137
Calpini, Aldo 22, 174
Caltabiano, Alfio 25, 39, 73, 118, 152, 153, 158, 172, 187
Calucci, Mario 150
Calvé, Jean-François 134
Calvi, María 150
Calvino, Vittorio 21
Calvo, Eduardo 23
Calvo, José 32, 126, 150
Calvo, Pepe 126
Calvo, Rafael Luis 119, 190
Calzado, Fernando 39
Cam, Cinzia 122
Camarda, Attilio 99
Camardiel, Roberto 39, 116, 119, 159
Cambelloti, Duilio 10, 105
Cambi, Italia 130
Camel, John 167
Cameracanna, Italo 143, 179
Camerini, Mario 10, 184

Cameron, Jeff 35, 73, 89, 98, 111, 140, 152, 158, 164, 179
Cameron, Sue 205
Camille, Valérie 158
Camoiras, Francisco 24, 127
Campa, Miranda 24, 25, 34, 35, 60, 65, 126, 160
Campanino, Franco 198
Campbell, Phil 205
Campi, Alberto 46
Campochiaro, Salvatore 102
Campogalliani, Carlo 14, 23, 32, 69, 119, 161, 166
Campollunghi, Mario 103
Campori, Anna 58
Campori, Grazia 122
Campos, Juan 16, 154
Canale, Alessandra 198
Canale, Gianna Maria 16, 23, 35, 36, 41, 48, 76, 80, 107, 119, 126, 130, 133, 136, 156, 160, 165, 174, 177, 190
Canalejas, José 24, 127
Canales, Ricardo 101
Canales, Susana 139
Cañas, Gonzalo 16
Candell, Steve 202
Candelli, Stelio 28, 49, 127, 179, 189, 202
Candidi, Elide 194
Canelli, Antonio 139
Canet, Francisco 40, 150
Caneva, Riccardo 163
Canfora, Bruno 99
Canghiari, Rossana 113
Canivari, Sergio 28
Caniveri, Marco 28
Cannon Films 199
Cannon Films Italia SrL 199, 202, 204
Cansino, Pilar 24, 87, 139
Cantatore, Nicola 153
Canti, Aldo 118, 137, 164, 171, 179
Canutt, Joe 51
Canutt, Tap 51
Canutt, Yakima 51, 159
Capanna, Omero 192
Capanna, Pietro 15, 22, 50, 64, 107, 140, 149, 174
Capanni, Vittorio 46
Capecchi, Giorgio 155, 174
Caperna, Silvia 199
Capitani, Giorgio 120, 143, 169, 191
Capitani, Roberto 30, 31, 106, 132, 136, 178
Capitol Film 24
Capitole Films 16, 171
Capodaglio, Ruggero 11, 12
Capone, Claudia 171, 175
Capone, Gino 201
Caporale, Aristide 113
Caporali, Roberto 118
Caporilli, Giovanni 55
Capozzi, Alberto 13
Cappelli, Giancarlo 125
Cappelli, Orfella 205
Capponi, Flora 174
Capponi, Oscar 111
Cappuccio, Antonella 158
Capri, Corinne 129, 155, 36–37

Capriotti, Mario 91, 146, 189
Captain Blood (1935) 32, 159
Captain Blood (Le Capitan) 31
Captain Falcon (Capitan Fuoco) 32
Captain from Toledo (L'uomo di Toledo) 32
Captain Phantom (Capitan Fantasma) 32
Capuani, Giancarlo 199
Capuano, Aldo 146
Capuano, Luigi 15, 54, 84, 107, 114, 135, 137, 147, 173, 177, 187, 195
Capuano, Mariangela 201
Capucci, Fabrizio 45, 69
Capuccio, Alessandro 204
Capucine 178
Caputi, Piero 201
Carabella, Ezio 104, 125
Caraco, Paolo 17
Carapelli, Dante Nello 136
Caratenuto, Bruno 17
Carbone, Gilberto 166
Carboni, Rino 128
Carboni, Ugo 91
Carbucci, Sergio 50
Cardarelli, Romano 147
Cárdenas, José 195
Cardinali, F. 59
Cardinali, Nazzareno 204
Cardinelli, F. 142
Cardone, Alberto 44, 122, 124, 138, 142, 192
Cardone, E. 25
Cardone, Gregorio 200
Cardoso, Beni 206
Carducci, Giacomo Calò 202
Carducci, Jack 202
Carduso, Benny 206
Carey, Roland 64, 139, 166
Caribbean Hawk (Lo sparviero dei Caribi) 33
Carini, Cesare Gani 9, 10
Carisi, Mara 91
Carle, Sandra 200
Carletti, Stefano 83
Carli, Laura 41
Carliez, Claude 16, 31, 56, 150
Carlini, Carlo 33, 87, 124, 155, 162, 190
Carlini, Mario 28
Carlisle, Tom 204
Carlo, Rafael Luis 107
Carlucci, Milly 198
Carmellini, Cesare 28
Carmen, María del 195, 55, 84
Carmet, Jean 56
Carminati, Tullio 51, 168
Carmona, Guillermo 24
Carnabucci, Piero 46
Carnavali, Elsa 58
Carnera, Primo 92, **93**
Carnimeo, Giuliano 119
Caro, Cathia 64, 178
Carocci, Massimo 30, 58, 111, 137, 139, 194, 196
Carosa 184
Carosello, Flora 168
Carotenuto, Franca 128
Carotenuto, Mario 33, 46, 91

Carotenuto, Memmo 125
Carpentieri 163
Carpentieri, Carlo 199
Carpentieri, Luigi 20, 30, 32, 112, 143, 146, 161, 162, 164, 192
Carpi, Fabio 70
Carpi, Tito 110, 138, 205, 206
Carrà, Raffaella 20, 31, 60, 122, 130, 154, 186
Carrara, Fulvio 80, 92, 94
Carraro, Tino 41
Carrell, Ted 204
Carrera, Maria Teresa 206
Carrillo, Mary 107
Carroll, Barbara 68, 105, 194
Carroll, L. 199
Carsten, Peter 115
Carta, Luigi Filippo 33, 155, 191
Carter, Carol 130
Carter, Ron 198
Carthage in Flames (Cartagine in fiamme) 33
Carthago C.C. 195
Cartuccia, Vincenzo 28
Caruso, Franco 134
Caruso, Vana 27
Carvajal, Ana 167
Carvajal, Julio 151
Carvalho, Adelino 119
Carver, Jann 19
Carver, Steve 19
Casa, José 42
Casadei, Angelo 140, 163, 169
Casadel, Angelo 163
Casagni, Franco 199
Casagrande, Antonio 29
Casale, Antonio 20, 48, 111
Casale, Tony 173
Casaleggio, Giovanni 9
Casalilla, Juan 107
Casalini, Mario 31, 41, 91, 136
Casamonica, Luciano 201
Casaravilla, Carlos 24, 40, 150, 159
Casas, Antonio 39, 106, 140, 159
Casas, Fernando Izcaino 26
Casas, Jaime Deu 111
Casavola, Franco 135
Cascio, Franco Lo 113
Cascioli, Ennio 205
Casellato, Luigi 137
Caserbib 58
Caserini, Mario 10
Casetti, Tiziana 122, 131
Casile, Geneviève 151
Casini, Mirella 59
Cassel, Jean-Pierre 43
Cassinelli, Claudio 198, 202
Cassini-Rizzoto, Giulia 8
Cassini, Adriana 21, 35, 70, 82, 138, 160, 187, 189
Cassini, Lina 19, 50, 110, 111, 124, 174
Castanyer, José 39
Castedo, Manuel 47, 154
Castellaneta, Donato 165
Castellani, Bruto 8, 10, 14
Castellani, Renato 54
Castellari, Enzo G. 110, 205
Castelli, Ricardo 63
Castelot, Jacques 15, 42, 191

216 Index

Castiñeiras, Manuel 29
Castrighella, Amerigo 113
Castro, Manolita 151
Casu, Domenico 91
Cataldo, Massimo 206
Catalucci, Enrico 132, 179
Catalucci, Ettore 41, 128
Catania, Claudio 29
Catena, Letizia 7
Catena, Victor Andrés 147
Caterini, Lina 36, 52, 102, 189
Catherine of Russia (Caterina di Russia) 34
Catherine, Raymonde 42
Catnoveltaneo, Carlo 13
Cattand, Gabriel 87
Cattaneo, Amelia 13
Cattaneo, Lella 177
Cattania, Luciano 67, 91
Cattozzo, Leo 21, 176, 184
Cau, Marco Tullio 207
Cauano, Luigi 15
Cauchy, Daniel 42
Cavalier in the Devil's Castle (Il cavaliere del castello maledetto) 34
Cavalieri, Gianni 33, 182
Cavalieri, Luciano 106, 131
Cavallieri, Cinzia 199
Cavallo, Dino 192
Cavallo, Nelly 95
Cavallone, Alberto 200, 203
Cavaricci, Nestore 18, 59
Cavo, Angela 34
Cazalilla, Juan 24, 127
C. B. Films S. A. 140
CCC Filmkunst & Co. KG Artur Brauner 165
C.E.A. Studio 107
Cealti, Bruna 118
Cebrián, Fernando 43, 166, 183
Ceccacci, Roberto 73, 83, 168, 187
Ceccacci, Roby 187
Ceccarelli, Pietro 15, 20, 25, 36, 52, 65, 73, 89, 112, 134, 138, 152, 153, 159, 164, 170, 177, 179, 186, 192, 206
Ceccarelli, Puccio 177, 192
Cecchi, Dario 28, 33, 42, 95, 168
Cecchi, Emilio 54
Cecchini, Iole 21, 23, 128, 132, 184
Cecchini, Marcella 32
Cecconi, Aldo 27, 29, 30, 32, 64, 91, 112, 138, 139
Cegani, Elisa 41, 55, 116, 150
Cela, Violeta 201
Celano, Guido 22, 25, 34, 55, 76, 102, 128, 167
Celenk, Yasemin 208
Celeste, Sebastiano 109, 112, 194
Celi, Adolfo 149
Celi, Liliana 84
Cella, Marga 176
Celli, Maria 141
Celsi, Guido Moroni 136
Cély, Célina 26, 65
Censi, Ottorino 29
Centenero, Ramón 166
Centralni Filmski Studios 50, 62, 179
Centro Film 135

The Centurion (Il conquistatore de Corinto) 34
Ceprani, Luciano 200
Cerasoli, Lili 176
Cerchio, Fernando 15, 35, 47, 67, 78, 99, 132, 135
Ceria, Bruno 139
Cerioni, Giorgio 65, 102, 150, 171
Cerulli, Fernando 129
Cerusico, Enzo 36, 51, 92, 155, 194
Cervasato, Tonino 99
Cervi, Gino 44, 47, 49, 55, 125, 132, 136, 140, 155, 191
Cervi, Tonino 50, 67
Cesana, Renzo 77
Cesar, Julio 167
Cesarano, Umberta 58
Cesare, Galo Giulio 31
Cesaretti, Enrico 113
Cesari, Bruno 186, 187
Cespi, Corrado 29
Cester, Peter 20
Cevenini, Alberto 29, 81, 139, 151, 160, 161, 171, 175
CFFF 103
C.F.P.C. 35, 78, 132
C.F.S. Košutnjak 35, 42, 165
Chabert, Roberto 124
Chahine, Yehia 160
Chaliapin, Feodor, Jr. 54, 99, 107, 126, 158–159
Challenge of the Gladiator (Il gladiatore che sfidò l'impero) 35
Chalvet, Jacques 118
Chamarat, Georges 175
Chambois, Jean-Henri 96
Chan, Luong-Ham 145
Chanel, Antony 160
Chanel, Hélène 40, 91, 102, 143, 157, 192
Chanel, Tally 207
Chanteau, Georges 31
Chanteau, Jules 42
Chapalo Films S. A. 139
Chaperon, Micheline 56
Chaplin, Charlie 27
Charge of the Black Lancers (I lancieri neri) 35
Charrat, Jeanine 150
Chart, Olga 177
Checchi, Andrea 35, 52, 137, 189
Checci, Andrea 69
Checci, Dario 176
Chellini, Amelia 13
Chellini, Didaco 13
Chellini, Luigi 7
Chenal, Pierre 126
Chentrens, Federico 173
Chessari, Romano 199
Chevalier, Roberto 187
Chevallier, Christian 177
Chevereau, Robert 56
Chevrier, Jean 18
Chiantoni, Renato 128, 140
Chiappafredo, Enrico 164
Chiappini, Dante 177
Chiaramida, Adriano 200
Chiarenza, Calogero 159
Chiari, Mario 24, 27, 54, 60, 162

Chiari, Maurizio 24
Chiari, Walter 50
Chiesa, Carlo Alberto 48
Chiffre, Ivan 194
Chignone 175
Chimenz, Alberto 40, 131
Chimirri, Sante 155
Chinchilla, José Luis 24
Chinigo, Umberto 103
Chinnici, Giuseppe 130
Chit, Chu Lai 145
Chiusano, Natale 7
Chiusi, Sergio 19, 26
Cholot, Pierre 70
Chooluck, Leon 51
Choquert, Charlotte 31
Chow, Michael 112
Chraibi, Abdou 110
Chretien, Anna Maria 160
Christiani, Aldo 15
Christidès, Robert 118
Christie, Andy 207
Christophe, Françoise 52, 56
Chtarrini, Luciano 37
Ciafré, Michelangelo 139, 40, 58, 60
Cianci, Antonio 145
Cianci, Tonino 112, 145
Cianelli, Eduardo 22
Cianfriglia, Domenico 147, 204
Cianfriglia, Giovanni 51, 76, 80, 92, 109, 124, 129, 131, 136, 137, 149, 157, 171, 179, 199, 201, 202, 204, 206
Ciani, Antonio 192
Ciani, Sergio (a.k.a. Alan Steel) 60, 94, 134
Ciannelli, Eduardo 22
Ciannelli, Lewis E. 200
Cianni, Eloisa 129
Ciarlo, Giovanni 141
Ciarlo, Virgilio 138
Ciatti, Romeo 195
Ciavarro, Luigi 26, 179, 188
Ciccarella, Mario 206
Ciccarone, Luciano 78
Ciccocioppo, Giuseppe 28
Cicero, Nando 94, 124, 141
Cicognini, Alessandro 184
Cifariello, Antonio 141
Cignitti, Enrico 19, 49, 128
Cigoli, Emilio 90, 149, 155, 174
Cimara, Luigi 32
Cimini, Daniele 197, 207
Cimini, Mario 31, 84, 169, 187
Cimino, Rosalba 199
Cindri, J. 59
Cine Produzione Astoria 165
Cine Produzioni Associate (P.A.C.) 40, 164, 171
Cine-Italia Films 120, 187
Cineluxor 21, 91, 173
Cineroma 47
Cinema Television International (CTI) 40
Cinematografica Associati (C.I.A.S.) 59, 69, 106, 127, 131, 142, 154
Cinematografica Filmex S.A. 165
Cinematografica Lombarda 141
Cinematografica Pelimex 26

Index 217

Cineproduzione Emo Bistolfi 116, 118
Cinnecittà Studios 21, 33, 44, 64, 65, 84, 107, 118, 122, 128, 136, 150
Cino del Luca 24
Cinquini, Alberto 49, 129
Cinquini, Fernando 15, 155, 176, 184
Cinquini, Renato 15, 49, 55, 77, 95, 103, 119, 132, 133, 134, 151, 159, 160, 171, 175, 177, 182, 186
Cinquini, Roberto 15, 17, 90, 143, 161, 162, 182
Cintado, Antonio 126
Ciofalo, Rosalba 206
Cioffi, Alfonso 200
Ciorciolini, Marcello 99, 140, 173, 186, 187
Ciriaci, Pietro 136
Circe Productions 43
Cirillo, Emidio 128
Cirino, Franco 33, 49, 158, 168
Cisse, Karamoko 150
Cittadini, Angelo 50
Ciuffi, Sonia 26
Ciuffini, Sabatino 62, 67, 152, 169
Ciulli, G. 29
Civiletti, Massimo 111
Civirani, Cristiano 32, 44, 62
Civirani, Foto 174
Civirani, Osvaldo 54, 55, 84, 103
Civirani, Walter 84, 103
Clair, Jany 40, 83, **83**, 87, 98, 103, 107, 126, 131, 154
Clarasó, Noel 166
Clarin, Hans 127
Clark, James Frank 25
Clark, Ken 46, 81, 82, 160
Claudio, Jean 35, 118
Claudio, Marco 111
Clavel, Robert 42
Clay, Jim 112
Clay, Philippe 124
Clemens, Pilar 26, 104, 150
Clément, Claude 56
Clément, Simone 56
Clementelli, Silvio 33
Clements, Alice 64
Cleopatra 132
Cleopatra's Daughter (*Il sepolcro dei re*) 35
Cleri, Dante 110, 113
Clerici, Gianfranco 156, 196
Cléry, Corinne 207
Clifford, Guido 12
Cline, Roscoe 112
Coach, Donald 115
Coamoiras, Francisco 154
Coangeli, Otello 136
Coates, Lewis 197, 201, 205
Cobelli, Gianna 91
Cobianchi, Franco 40, 111, 129, 141, 172, 173, 175
Cobos, Germán 165
Cocchi, Carlo Alberto 19
Cocco, Piero 49
Cochetti, Ranieri 174
Coffarelli, Maurizio 87
Coffelli, Ciquita 99
Coffey, Scott 205
Cofiño, Adolfo 64

Cogan, Henri 56
Cohen, Gérard 98
Cohen, Maria Pia 36
Cohn, Harry 164
Coignard-Helison, M.J. 112
Colamonici, Raffaele 135, 160
Colangeli, Franz 113
Colangeli, Otello 21, 23, 47, 64, 81, 82, 91, 100, 104, 115, 116, 122, 125, 135, 140, 151, 156, 157, 160, 166, 183, 188, 65
Colanzi, Aldo 39
Colasanti, Veniero 21, 33, 51, 54, 142, 174
Cole, Ignaz 106
Coli, Ombretta 20, 183
Colizzi, Giuseppe 182
Colli, Franco Delli 124, 168, 175, 195
Colli, Mario 124
Colli, Ombretta 65, 156, 173, 184
Colli, Tonino Delli 124, 125, 168, 175, 176, 192
Collin, Alan 102
Collino, Federico 55
Collins, Alan 207
Collins, Dan 207
Collins, Joan 52
Collins, John 103
Collins, Ray 207
Collo, Alberto 12, 13, 192
Collodi, Garzia 90
Collodi, Grazia 73
Colombaioni, Valerio 109
Colombari, Sergio 199
Colombini 141
Colombini, Willi 80, 92
Colossus and the Amazon Queen (*La regina delle amazzoni*) 36
Colossus and the Headhunters (*Maciste contro I cacciatori di teste*) 36, 111
The Colossus of Rhodes (*Il colosso di Rodi*) 37, 106
Colt, Dennis 112
Coltellacci, Giulio 78, 184
Columbia Pictures 25, 164
Columbus Films 99
Coluzzi, Guglielmo 122
Combini, Willi 94
Combret, Arlette 64
Combret, Georges 104
Comerón, Lluís Josep 16
Comin, Jacopo 81, 82, 138, 173
Como, Rosella (a.k.a. Rossella Como) 30, 95, 141
Compagne Industrielle et Commerciale Cinématographique (CICC) 23, 67, 179
Compagnia Cinematografica Champion 43
Compagnia Cinematografica Mondiale (CCM) 16, 159, 186
Compagnia Internazionale Realizzazioni Arisstiche Cinematografiche (CIRAC) 26, 65
Compagnia Italiani Grandi Film 111
Compagnie Cinématographique de France 23, 34, 124, 131, 192
Compagnie Internationale de Productions Cinématographique (CIPRA) 168
Compagnie Internazionale Realizzazioni Artistiche Cinematografica (CIRAC) 184
Comptoir Français du Productions Cinématographiques (CFPC) 36, 40, 42, 107, 126, 127, 129, 190
Comptoir Français du Film Production (CFFP) 59, 73, 87, 98, 99, 100, 131, 149, 153, 154, 169, 177
Conan the Barbarian 197
Conan the Destroyer 197
Conde, Fabián 194
Conforti, Gustavo 46
Congia, Vittorio 116
Coniglio, Gaetano 201
Conino, Isabella 32
Conklin, Gary 153
Connery, Sean 166
The Conqueror of Atlantis (*Il conquistatore di atlantide*) 40
Conqueror of Maracaibo (*Il conquistatore di Maracaibo*) 40, 131
The Conqueror of the Orient (*Il conquistatore dell'Oriente*) 40
Conqueror of the World (*I padroni del mondo*) 200
Conquest (*Conquista*) 201
Conrad, Joseph 142
Conroy, William 50, 160
Consolazione, Tito 49
Consorzio Spartacus 156
Consorzione Scipio L'Africano 46
Constantine and the Cross (*Costanto il grande*) 41
Constantini, Enzo 116
Constantini, Nino 42
Constantini Film 43
Contabiano, Alfo 138
Contact Organization 96, 126
Contalbiano, Alfio 39
Contardi, Livia 21, 40, 52, 119, 189
Contardi, Priscilla 136
Conte, Maria Pia 17, 19, 98, 125
Conti, Edoardo G. 116
Conti, Iolanda 28, 91, 146, 197
Conti, Luciano 112
Conti, Maurizio 64
Conti, Stefano 84
Continental Motion Pictures 203, 205
Continenza, Sandro 49, 65, 77, 87, 89, 95, 113, 119, 120, 136, 140, 143, 151, 168
Contini, Alfio 70, 99, 158, 163
Contini, Luigi 201
Contreras, Federico 24
Conversi, Alberto 17
Conversi, Benedetto 26
Conversi, Cleofe 95
Conversi, Luciano 27
Conversi, Luigi 125, 207
Conversi, Spartaco 80, 92, 102, 155, 156, 177, 194
Coop, Franco 46
Cooperativa Cinematográfica Unión 24
Coos, Lucia 65

218 Index

Copercines Cooperativa Cinematografica 116, 155
Coppa, Annalisa 197
Coppel, Alec 168
Coppini, Josie 203
Coppola, Clara 69
Copro Films 164, 160
Coquelin, Jean-Paul 31
Cora, Claudio 165
Corasello, Flora 113
Corbeau, Roger 42
Corbucci, Bruno 26, 58, 65, 156
Corbucci, Sergio 34, 50, 73, 105, 156
Corda, María 10
Cordaro, Livia 25
Cordella, Myriam 41
Cordero, Emilio 150
Cordio, Carlo Maria 198, 202, 203
Corel, Belinda 24
Corelli, Bruno 125, 129
Corés, Rafael 27
Corevi, Antonio 83, 87, 92, 98, 125, 137, 138, 141, 146, 153, 158, 189
Corey, Brigitte 142
Corey, Isabelle 19, 78, 101, 106
Cori, Graziella 73
Corman, Roger 5, 19, 20, 46
Cormoran Films 16
Corne, Léonce 119
Cornejo, Humberto 16, 159
Cornel, Pina 130
Cornelli, Gino-Lelio 12
Corner, Clarissa 34
Cornes, Paquita 27
Coronet Films 175
Coronet S.R.L. 171
Corrà, Teodoro 77
Correl, Francis 200
Correri, Antonio 118
Corridoni, Franco 65
Corridori, Giovanni 20, 33, 197, 198
Corrieri, Angelo 207
Corrington, John William 19
Corrington, Joyce Hooper 19
Corsi, Jacopo 134
Corso, Angelo 30
Corso, Ettore 46
Cortés, Antonio 16, 39, 119
Cortés, Juan 24, 55, 125, 159, 195
Cortese, Enrico 64, 84
Cortese, Luca 55
Cortese, Nada 19, 77, 130, 133
Cortese, Valentina 25
Cortez, Bella 16, 17, **17,** 62, **62,** 63, 152, 170, 171, 188, **189**
Cortez, Espanita 56
Cortina, Óscar 119
Cortini, Tiziano 163
Cortona, Sergio 104
Corvaisier, Marcel 42
Cosantino, Giorgio 28
Cosmopolis 164, 171
The Cossacks (I cosacchi) 41
Cossu, M. 154
Cossu, Michele 59
Costa, Alain 197
Costa, Andrea 137, 187
Costa, F.M. 10
Costa, Jean-Manuel 197

Costa, Mario 21, 34, 35, 65, 103, 104, 133
Costa, Piero 139
Costantini, Elisabetta 163, 179
Costantini, Giorgio 49, 50, 114, 163, 176
Costantini, Lucia 26
Costello, Paul 207, 208
Coster, Nat 17, 177
Cotroneo, Salvatore 98
Cottafavi, Vittorio 18, 19, 70, 87, 106, 116, 127, 190
Cottance, Pierre 178
The Count of Monte Cristo (Le Comte de Monte-Cristo) 42
Count, Mary 19
Courcel, Nicole 18
Courtland, Jerome 133, 174
Coutan-Laboureur, Jean-Paul 64
Coutet, Henri 31
Couturier, Jacques 42
Covi, Giorgio 46
Covolo, Giovanna 197
Cozzi, Giada 206
Cozzi, Luigi 197, 201, 202, 205
Cozzoli, Michele 34, 77, 129, 130
Crabbe, Buster 80
Crain, Jeanne 100, 130, **132,** 133
Crandall, Belle 204
Crapanzano, Placida 200
Crast, Antonio 163
Craveri, Mario 48, 54
Crawford, Broderick 3, 4, **71,** 72, 73
Cremer, Bruno 113
Crémieux, Henri 43
Cremona, Italo 125
Crescenzi, Gianluigi 27
Crescenzi, Isa 191
Crescenzi, Marcello 21, 189
Cressoy, Pierre 34, 45, 88, 107, 109, 112, 124, 147, 176
Creti, Vasco 10
The Creature from the Black Lagoon 77, 87
The Creature Walks Amng Us 77
Cretinetti and the Boots of Brazil (Cretinetti e gli stivali del Brasile) 8
Crimi, Marisa 30, 60, 99, 161, 164
Crisa, Erno 24, 28, 29, 30, 34, 36, 41, 73, 110, 152, 168, 187
Crisanti, Andrea 192
Crisman, Nino 18, 29
Cristal, Linda 106, 128, 157
Cristal, Perla 23
Cristaldi, Franco 163
Cristallini, Giorgio 70, 87, 106, 143, 163
Cristiani, Aldo 63, 137
Cristiani, Dhia 15, 155, 174
Cristiani, Nino 55
Cristina, Olinto 46
Cristofani, Anna 50, 67, 191
Critérion Films 52, 106
Croccolo, Carlo 58, 91
Crosby, Bob 33
Crosby, Wiley 198, 200
Crovato, Miranda 171
Crovetto, Elio 137, 173
Crowley, Dave 25

Cruciani, Loredana 197
Cruciani, Mario 207
Crudo, Aldo 126
Crugnola, Aurelio 30, 112, 146
Cruickshank, Andrew 51
Cruz, Mara 190
Cuadrado, Luis 143
Cubero, Jaime Pérez 116, 126, 154
Cubi, Alberto 154
Cuby, Joseph 25
Cucchi, Marisa 28
Cuccu, Franco 146
Cueva, Manuel de la 106
Culibrk, Stojan 22, 118
Cummings, Dale 25
Cunillés, José María 113
Cunningham, Beryl 46, 47
Cuocolo, Vittorio 167
Cuppini, Francesco 122, 197, 198, 201, 206
Cuppini, Franco 201, 206
Curia, Domenico 127
Curioni, Federico 45
Curiosi, Frederic 45
Currie, Finlay 164
The Curse of Capistrano (novel) 23
Curti, Giorgio 9
Curtis, Hershel 200
Cyrano and D'Artagnan (Cyrano et d'artagnan) 42
Cyrano de Bergerac 43

Da.Ma. Cinematografica 32
d'Achiardi, Franco 49
D'Achille, Luciano 205
D'Acri, Luigi 34, 63, 133
D'Adda, Francesco 18
D'Adderio, Areno 204
D'Alberti, Della 83
D'Alessio, Ugo 182
D'Aloisio, Gianni 60, 80, 92
D'Amato, Joe 19, 48, 90, 131, 198, 200, 202, 207
D'Ambrosio, Mario 206
D'Amico, Elvira 163
D'Amico, Gianni 28
D'Amico, Lina 49, 77
D'Amico, Marcello 190
D'Amico, Oscar 32, 44, 48, 58, 59, 69, 138, 139, 142, 152, 157, 160, 161, 164, 169, 174, 175
D'Amico, Suso Cecchi 54
D'Amico, Suzanne 200
D'Amiens, M. 59
D'Andra, Franco 143
D'Andrea, Diletta 92
D'Andrea, Emilio 21
D'Andria, Emilio 158
D'Andria, Francesco 65
D'Andria, Franco 34, 103, 118, 172, 181, 184
D'Andria, Luigi 19, 129
D'Andria, Paolo 29
D'Angelo, Alfredo 50
D'Angelo, Carlo 45, 92, 99, 133, 167
D'Angelo, Mirella 202
D'Angelo, Salvo 54
D'Aniello, Umberto 199
D'Annunzio, Gabriele 7

D'Antin, Mary 205
D'Aquino, Rosella 153
D'Arc, Saha 200
D'Arpe, Gustavo 195
D'Assunta, Solveyg 191
d'Ennery, Adolphe 48, 153
d'Eubonne, Jean 18
D'Eugenio, Saverio 19, 21, 50, 59, 106, 129, 139
D'Harcourt, Rita 10
D'Offizi, Sergio 99
D'Oliva, Luigi Pinni 29
D'Orsi, Umberto 30
D'Orziat, Gabrielle 43
Da Roma, Eraldo 37, 42, 73, 105, 126, 140
Dacqmine, Jacques 104, 119
Dacy, S.C. 207
Daddi, Franco 58, 109, 113, 137, 199, 203
Daddi, Wladimir 109, 113
Dafauce, Félix 30
Dagonneau, Maurice 31
Dainelli, Regina 48
Daissé, Amieto 49
Dakar 140, 147, 152, 171, 198
Dakar, Alejandro Barrera 147
Dakst, André 118
Dalcer, Franco 31
Dallamano, Massimo 41, 99, 126, 130, 132
Dallier, Roger 18
Dalumb, Antonio 48
Damiani, Damiano 35, 41, 67, 78, 99
Damiani, Domenico 50
Damiani, José Luis 195
Damiani, Mario 127, 143, 154
Damiani, Riccardo 163, 179
Damiani, Tilde 36
Damicelli, Mario 47
Dammers, Ralph 25
Damon and Pythias (Il tiranno di Siracusa) 43
Damon, Mark 19, 102, 109, 127, 160, 183
Danari, Manta Louisa 48
Danby, Ian 110, 205
Dandi, Renato 205
Dandi, Romano 27
Danelli, Ileana 45
Danesi, Alfredo 15, 18
Danforth, Jim 4, 70
Danieli, Emma 48, 77
Danieli, Lucciana 55
Danning, Sybil 202, 204, 207
Danova, Cesare 176
Dantes, Claude 114
Danton, Ray 135, 147
Darelli, Lilly 23, 29, 138
Darvi, Bella 128
Dary, René 95, 125
Dascovitz, Kim 198, 200
Dauvillie, Simone 130
Dauvillier, Simone 124
Davanzati, Mario Forges 194
Davanzati, Roberto Forges 203
Daves, Dean 179
Davesnes, Edoardo 7
Davesnes, Madame 9

David and Goliath (David e Golia) 44
David, Alfredo 119
David, Chris 202, 205
David, Christopher 198
Daviddi, Leo 163, 179
Davies, Mandy-Rice 204
Davila, Edoardo 134
Dávila, Luis 102, 109
Davis, Ken 202
Davis, Luther 192
Davis, Mac 156
Davis, Ursula 29, 100, 164
Davó, José Marco 23, 154
Dawn, Donald 115
Dawson, Anthony 91, 142, 153, 207
De Agostini, Fabio 30, 138
de Alba, Aurora 131
De Amicis, Angelo 188
De Angelis, Anna 55
De Angelis, Cristina 49, 104
De Angelis, Gualtiero 55, 174
De Angelis, Guido 28, 194, 203, 207
De Angelis, Maurizio 28, 194, 207
De Angelis, Remo 35, 59, 77, 115, 125, 155, 192, 206
De Angelis, Vertunnio 114, 166
de Angelo, Karen 204
de Anguita, Fernando 27
De Antoni, Alfredo 46
De Arcangelis, Oscar 24, 32, 78, 106, 130, 191
De Benedetti, Giacomo 48
de Bengala, Omán 127
de Blain, Luis G. 166
De Blasi, Virgilio 64, 106, 183, 190
De Carlo, Arone 163
De Carmine, Renato 35, 192
De Chiara, Ghigo 127
de Chomón, Segundo 7, 10
De Coligny, Andrey 107
De Concini, Ennio 21, 33, 36, 37, 41, 50, 52, 60, 64, 70, 78, 92, 105, 106, 109, 112, 116, 136, 141, 155, 161, 163, 164, 168, 175, 176, 184, 190, 192
de Córdoba, Luisa 159
de Esquiroz, Gonzalo 151, 154
de Fast, Boris 178
De Felice, Lionello 41, 54, 73, 138, 152, 175
De Feo, Francesco 100, 131, 155, 165, 190
De Filippo, Pasquale 48, 77, 114, 130, 137, 143, 177
De Filippo, Peppino 58
De Florio, Pasquale 99
De Fonseca, Carolyn 25, 44
De Kassel, Julian 169
de Landa, Juan 33, 50
de Lapparent, Hubert 56
De Laurentiis, Dino 21, 24, 25, 27, 73, 135, 176, 184, 186
De Leo, Angela 194
De Leo, Gioia 196
De Leo, Rosy 63, 88, 89, 146, 196
De Leo, Teresa 143
De Leonardis, Giancarlo 205
De Leone, Francesco 77, 131
De Liguoro, Rina 10

de Lirio, Carmen 68
de Loaysa, Antonio Ramírez 47, 159
De Luca, Gianni 109
De Luca, Lorella 35, 141, 150, 155, 168
De Luca, Pupo 109
De Luca, Raffaele 200
de Luna, Álvaro 16, 24, 39, 159, 181
De Marchis, Carlo 27
De Martini, Aldo 205
De Martino, Alberto 46, 65, 100, 115, 116, 120, 140, 151
De Martino, Anna 122
De Martino, Federico 46
De Martino, Ferruccio 52, 60, 80, 92, 189
de Martino, Romolo 32, 62, 70, 110, 116, 140, 151, 175
De Marzi, Marcella 90
De Masi, Francesco 19, 73, 99, 107, 131, 135, 138, 146, 152, 153, 154, 160, 165, 195, 206
de Masure, Louis 18
De Matteis, Maria 24, 27, 46, 49, 160, 161, 162, 164, 191
De Meo, Ennio 146
De Mille, Cecil B. 1, 3, 54
De Nardo, Gustavo 25
de Nesle, Robert 82, 96, 106, 126, 131, 153
De Oliveira, Vera 110
de Orsario, Amando 116
De Pasqualis, Renato 30, 90, 138
De Pedys, Anna 204
De Persio, Mario 167
De Pietro, Elio 28
de Pomés, Félix 166
de Prada, Miguel Fernández 64
de Quevedo, Pedro Rodriguez 154
De Rege, Guido 12
de Reya, Vera Rita 194
De Rita, Massimo 18, 52, 60, 80, 92, 189
de Rivera, Javier 84
De Roberti, Lydia 9, 13
De Robertis, Aldo 158
De Rossi, Alberto 20, 27, 91, 118
De Rossi, Camillo 54
De Rossi, Grazia 51, 166
De Rossi, Lina 34
De Sabata, Eliana 112
De Sanctis, Gemma 12
De Santis, Dina 35, 63, 81, 87, 133, 168, 196
de Santis, Eduardo 134
De Santis, Gino 32, 33, 59, 102, 130, 135, 189, 191
De Santis, Lucio 29, 65, 114, 142, 158, 187
De Santis, Luigi 158
De Santis, Orchidea 176
De Santis, Pasqualino 116
De Santis, Riccardo 33
De Sarro, Raul 132
de Segonzac, Gladys 178
De Simone, Alvaro 11
De Simone, Franco 146
De Simone, Mario 92
de Tana, Sebastián Luca 143

220 Index

De Teffe, Antonio 19, 158, 100
de Tejada, Luis 102
De Tiberis, Marina 207
De Toth, André 67, 122, 124
De Tuddo, Italo 114, 137
De Urrutia, Federico 24
De Vecchi, Jan 114
De Vico, Pietro 65, 114, 135
De Victor, Gabriella 130
De Vries, Elly 205
de Weeks, Harold 159
Deak, Michael 202
Dean, Francesca 36
Dean, Max 112
Dean, Robert 29, 167
Deberg, Chantal 166
Debora Film 115
Deed, André 8
The Defeat of Hannibal (Scipione l'africano) 45
The Defeat of the Barbarians (Re Manfredi) 46
DeGiorgio, Tomasso 9
Degni, Lou see Forest, Mark
Degrave, Jean 56
Dejana, Amedeo 176
Delaître, Marcel 42
Delamare, Gil 64
Delamare, Lise 31
Delamare, Rosine 56, 192
Delattre, Guy 178
Delbo, Jean-Jacques 52
Delcampo, Anthony 207
Deldick, Fraçoise 32
Delic, Stefano 17, 157
Delic, Stipe 17, 138, 157, 165
Delich, Eda 58
Delille, André 31
Dell Publishing 80
Dell'Acqua, Alberto 26, 64
Dell'Acqua, Arnaldo 176, 102, 207
Dell'Acqua, Fernanda 26
Dell'Acqua, Ottaviano 113, 197, 199, 201, 204, 205
Dell'Acqua, Roberto 47, 109, 113 131
Dell'Aguillara, Camillo Mariani 45
Dell'Arti, Consalvo 20, 26, 51, 65, 102, 134, 137, 142, 195
dell'Assinara, Alberto Manca 19
Dell'Orco, Maurizio 200
Dell'Ovo, Giuliano 51, 164, 171, 179
Dellamano, Massimo 46
Delmi, Carlo 134
Delon, Alain 194
Delor, Raymonde 42
Delorme, Guy 31, 56
Delpuech, Roger 118
Demange, Paul 119
Demer, Karl Michael (a.k.a. Karl Demer) 200
Demerik, Elena 102
Demicheli, Tulio 159
Demongeot, Mylène 56, 60, 67
Denic, Miomir 18
Denizot, Vincenzo 12, 13
Dentice, Daniele 186
Deodato, Ruggero 47, 91, 199
Deperusse, Barbara 192
Deréal, Colette 134

Derek, John 130
Derevitsky, Alexandre 70, 126, 174
DeRiso, Angelo 59
DeRiso, Arpad 15, 29, 31, 54, 56, 63, 68, 80, 84, 87, 88, 106, 107, 111, 114, 126, 135, 136, 137, 147, 177, 178, 187, 194
Deruelle, Michel 194
Derval, Jacqueline 50
Desages, Marc 42
DeSantis, Dina 29
Deschamps, Jacques 87
Desecrières, Georges 56
Desert Desperadoes (La peccatrice del deserto) 46
Desert Warrior (Los amantes del desierto) 47
Desideri, Danilo 55, 92
Desideri, Giorgio 29, 32, 60, 64, 65, 67, 69, 104, 110, 137, 150, 165, 192
Desmond, Johnny 33
Desny, Ivan 32
Despotovic, Veljko 112
Dessena, Umberto 33
Dessie, Amleto 54
Dessy, Angelo 36, 49
Detlie, Stanley 51
Detour 78
Dettesio, Attilo 146
Deus, Beni 65, 104, 187
Devi, Antonio 167
Devi, Kamala 110
Devil of the Desert Against the Son of Hercules (Anthar l'invincibile) 47
The Devil-Ship Pirates 152
The Devil's Cavaliers (I cavalieri del diablo) 48
Devon Film 64
Dey, Élida 126
Dhéran, Bernard 32
Di Bari, Dina 140, 156
Di Bari, Vito 26
Di Benedetto, Giovanni 25, 27, 51, 92, 142, 186
Di Biase, Carlo 126
Di Biase, Giuseppe 27
Di Biase, Mario 175
Di Carlo, Toni 64, 150
Di Centa, Mirella 191
Di Clemente, Costantino 201
Di Clemente, Giovanni 201
Di Cola, Emanuele 103, 125, 195
Di Domenico, Lucio 197
Di Filippo, Pasquale 114
Di Fulvio, Mariano 15
Di Gennaro, Tiziana 199
Di Giacomo, Franco 36, 92, 155
Di Gioia, Nicola 50, 52, 84, 131, 200, 204
Di Giovanni, Augusto 50
Di Girolamo, Franco 55, 67, 156, 207
Di Girolamo, Paolo 197
Di Giulio, Pietro 116
Di Lauri, Mirella 186
Di Legge, Silvana 199, 204
Di Lorenzo, Anna 135, 141
Di Luia, Bruno 201
Di Mario, Paolo 118, 167
Di Martire, Marcello 25

Di Masi, Francesco 103
di Mauro, Franco 62, 188
Di Meo, Ennio 146
Di Meo, Maria Pia 52, 155, 159
Di Michele, Gianna 203
Di Mitri, Tony 17, 21, 142, 168
Di Napoli, Nino 158
di Napoli, Raffaele 7
di Nardo, Mario 19
Di Nardo, Maurizio 55
di Nieva, Petra 16
Di Palma, Dario 50, 116
Di Paolo, Antonio 151
Di Paolo, Betto 58
Di Paolo, Mara 159
Di Paolo, Marcello 175, 198
Di Rocco, Rosanna 27
Di Salvo, Alba 34, 87, 91
Di Santo, Oscar 91, 95
Di Savoia, Lionello Pio 28
Di Seta, Gaita 142
Di Sica, Vittorio 192
di Silverio, Luca 26, 52, 87, 90, 92, 115, 163, 179, 189, 191
Di Stefano, Paolo 22
Di Stefano, Vitale 7, 10
di Stolfo, Gianni 55
Di Thiene, Max 29
Di Tocchio, Franco 138
The Diabolical Dr. Z 130
Diamante Co. 28
Diamante, Saverio 48, 104
Diamint Film 208
Diana, Franco 48
Diary of a Roman Virgin (Diario di una vergine Romana) 48
Diaz, Ricardo 47
Dibildos, José Luis 42
Dietz, Jack 77
Dignam, Basil 153
Dilián, Irasima 136
Dimitri, Tony 17
Dimitrijevic, Milutin 99
Dini, Giulio 206
Dino De Laurentiis Cinematografica 31, 41
Dionisi, Anna Maria 49
Dionisio, Anna Maria 83
Dionisio, Silvia 109
Diot, Daniel 42
Diotallevi, Fabio 197, 202
DiPaolo, Dante 20, 113, 130, 145, 164
Divini, Anna 15
Divita, Giuseppe 174
Djakovic, Jurica 178
Djanik, Henry 145
Djukanovic, Milo 191
Dobric, Ivan 59
Dobric, Petar 58, 162
Documento Film 23, 191
Dody, Carla 36
Dogliotti, Guido 14
Dolan, Jim 25
Dolce, Ignazio 39, 55, 59, 68, 87, 103, 106, 127, 154, 162, 168, 175, 207
Dolci, Dario 102, 137
Dolci, Remo 50
Dolen, Jim 56
Dolera, Andrés 183

Dolfi, Augusto 29, 31, 83, 106, 126, 178, 187
Dolfin, Giorgio 131
Dolfini, Giovanni 50
Dolgin, Larry 208
Domage, André 150
Domenici, Arturo 76
Domenici, Beppe 68
Domenici, Riccardo 21, 55, 64, 91, 99, 156, 182, 194
Domiciana 106
Domilia, Nicola 164
Dominici, Arturo 35, 63, 69, 80, 87, 89, 98, 116, 137, 153, 156, 164, 171, 175, 178, 179, 195, 196
Dominici, Franco 77
Dominici, Riccardo 21
Domiziana Internazionale Cinematografica 128
Don Cesare di Bazan (Don Cesare di Bazan) 48, 153
Donà, Marilda 199
Donà, Sergio 122
Donadeo, Alberico 27
Donaggio, Pino 197, 199
Donatella 103
Donati Co. 163
Donati, Donatella 198, 200, 207
Donati, Ermanno 20, 30, 32, 49, 112, 143, 146, 161, 162, 164, 192
Donati, Piero 161, 164, 192
Donato, Luigi 92
Donelli, Alfredo 10
Doni, Alberto 207
Donnini, Giulio 15, 19, 20, 31, 41, 49, 84, 109, 113, 116, 140, 142, 173, 178, 95–96
Dorascenzi, Raniero 113
Dorat, Jean-Pierre 165
Doré, Gustav 11
Dori, Carlo 43
Dori, Liana 150, 174
Dori, Paola Salva 20
Dori, Sandro 30
Doria Film 177
Doria, Bianca 49, 82, 165
Doria, Enzo 52, 78, 127, 165, 168, 176
Doria, Franco 17, 177
Doria, Luciano 95, 125
Doria, Renato 194, 206
Dorigo, Angelo 134
Doro, Mino 15, 19, 50, 77, 87, 90, 106, 107, 116, 135, 142, 147, 189
Dorziat, Gabrielle 43
Dottesio, Attilio 20, 29, 48, 63, 81, 83, 98, 112, 131, 136, 187, 143, 173, 178, 194
Doubrowsky, Kurt 21, 49, 135, 158, 168, 169
Douglas, Bobby 202
Douglas, John 82, 102, 165, 167
Douglas, Kirk 14, 186
Douy, Jacques 42
Dover, Nyta 132, 134
Dovia, Mimi 12
Dower, Julian 164, 179
Drago, Eleonora Rossi 27, 44, 45, 167
Drago, Ely 90
Dragon's Blood (Sigfrido) 49

Dragone, Adolfo 166
The Dream of Zorro (Il sogno di Zorro) 49
Drescoffre, Roger 42
Drudi, Vera 25
Du Montiel, Nadia 184
Dublino, Daniele 109
Dubrava Film 45, 138, 152, 156, 157, 162, 164, 170, 171, 175
Duca Internazionale 27, 125, 195
Duca, Cino Del 153
Ducaux-Rupp, Gérard 186
Duce Compagnia Film 27
Duchesne, Louis 125
Ducos, Jean-Pierre 145
Dudan, Jean 165
Dudarova, Ludmilla 55, 125, 186
Duel of Champions (Orazi e Curiazi) 50
Duel of the Titans (Romolo e Remo) 50
Duff, Howard 189
Dufilho, Jacques 19
Dumanoir, Philippe 48
Dumas, Alexandre 42, 56
Dumas, Noelle 100
Dumesnil, Jacques 186
Dunham, Katherine 27
Dunn, Linwood G. 27
Dunne, Bert 204
Durán, Luis 27
Durán, Rafael 16, 107, 190
Durano, Giustino 68, 133, 134
Durou, Pierre 32
Duse, Carlo 10, 46, 49
Duse, Vittorio 110
Dwyre, Johnny 18
Dwyre, Roger 18

Eastman, George 199, 204
Eastwood, Clint 23
Ebstanian, Luigi 48
Ecelza, Antonio 127
Ecenarro, José Maria 24
Edition et Diffusion Cinématographique (E.D.I.C.) 151
Edwards, Hilton 45
Efrikian, Laura 87
Efroni, Yehuda 202, 204, 206
Egan, Richard 52
Egyptian General Co. for International Film Production (PARC) 160
Ehling, Georges 25
Eichberg-Film 15, 135, 147
Eicher, Tom 203
Ekberg, Anita 122, **123**, 155
El Cid (Il Cid) 51, 67, 166, 183
El-Sabbaa, Mahmoud 40
Elg, Taina 24
Elias, Cyrus 92, 205
Elica Film 49
Elios Studios 84, 156, 207
Elkins, Michael 52
Elledge, Allan 28
Elliot, Leonard G. 146
Ellis, Mirko 35, 48, 65, 77, 81, 107, 127, 137, 139, 168, 171, 181, 184
Elman, Louis 202

Elmes, Guy 130, 164
Elorrieta, José María 24
Elvi 33
Emanuele, Paule 60
Embassy Pictures 192
Emeterio, Jacinto San 30, 43, 167
Emilfork, Daniel 178
Emmanuele, Luigi 18, 105
Emmepi Cinematografica 129
Emperor Maciste (Maciste imperatore) 8
Empire Film Co. 13, 14
Enrici, Carlo 62
Ensascaller, Bob, Jr. 115
Ente Nazionale Industrie Cinematografiche (ENIC) 46
Eory, Irán 16
Eppler, Dieter 115
Época Films S.A. 40
Equini, Arrigo 22, 24, 36, 96, 99, 107, 109, 126, 128, 135, 147, 171
Ercolani, Domizio 205
Ercoli, Luciano 22, 33
Ergles, Matija 59
Ericson, John 158
Erik the Conqueror (Gli invasori) 21, 52
Erikson, Jack 51
Ermelli, Claudio 50
Esbri, Carmen 159
Escoffier, Marcel 118
Escola, Maria 201
Escribano, Antonio Jiménez 167, 195
Espinosa, Luis Pérez 159
Esposito, Giani 51
Esposito, Luigi 37, 58
Esposito, Paola 23
Estela Films 23, 107, 113, 190
Esterhazy, Andrea 77
Esther and the King (Ester e il re) 52
Estrada, Carlos 183
Etcheverry, Michel 119
Euripides 24
Euro International Film (EIA) 58, 147
Europa Cinematografica 35, 179
Eursepi, Enzo 27
Evangelisti, Vittorio 10
Everest, Barbara 51
Excell, Jody 25
Excelsa Film 182
Excelsior Pictures 11
The Executioner of Venice (Il boia di Venezia) 54
Explorer Films '58 36, 42, 78, 98, 99, 126, 135, 154, 169, 177

Fabbri, Diego 24, 41, 51, 54, 189
Fabbri, Roberto 156
Fabbro, Nino Dal 143
Faber, Karin 25
Fabian, Francoise 30, 119
Fabio 20
Fabiola (Fabiola) 8, 54, 140
Fabor, Giorgio 29
Fabre, Dominique 168
Fabre, Fernand 119
Fabriani, Sergio 203
Fabrizi, Aldo 58, 192

Index

Fabrizi, Anna 49
Fabrizi, Franco 50, 127
Fabrizi, Valeria 104
Fabrizio, Alfonso 105
Fabrizio, Arnaldo 73, 118, 143, 152, 153, 171
Fabrizzi, Anna 141, 162
Faccenna, Angelo 125, 156
Facchetti, Adriana 36, 192
Fagioli, Giovanni 174
Fago, Giovanni 20, 67, 95, 164
Faieta, Edoardo 28
Fairbanks, Douglas 23, 175
Fairfax, Audrey 25
Fajardo, Eduardo 187
Falchi, Paolo 36, 112
Falchi, Paola 18
Falciani, Umberto 99
Falco Film 201
Falcon of the Desert (La magnifica sfida) 55
Falcone, Raf 206
Falessi, Enzo 28
The Fall of Rome (Il crollo di Roma) 55
The Fall of Troy (La caduta di Troia) 9
Falletti, Eduardo 104, 139
Fallvene, Stefano 199
Fanano, Gino 174
Fanetti, Maria 28
Fanetti, Pasquale 130, 198, 201
Fanfoni, Vittorio 102, 109
Fanfulla 91, 163, 168, 175
Fantacci, Andrea 191, 203
Fantacci, Francesco 203
Fantasia, Andrea 28, 34, 35, 41, 48, 60, 77, 80, 92, 94, 104, 114, 129, 131, 134, 139, 142, 151, 161, 162, 166
Fantasia, Franco 21, 28, 29, 34, 35, 41, 44, 48, 51, 54, 55, 58, 60, 84, 92, 98, 104, 107, 114, 126, 129, 133, 134, 135, 137, 138, 139, 142, 151, 156, 160, 163, 167, 169, 173, 187, 195
Fantaso 10
Fanti, Elisabetta 88, 172
Fantini, Franco 207
Fantis, Enrica 10
Fantoni, Cesare 21, 31, 33, 34, 69, 94, 96, 119, 124, 137, 141, 155, 178
Fantoni, Cristina 22, 182
Fantoni, Sergio 33, 34, 52, 60, 94, 125
Fanty, Elisabeth 32
Farag, Mahmoud 160
Farano, Alfonso 199
Farano, Paola 199
Faraoni, Mario 137, 143
Faraoni, Maurizio 200
Farber, Bernard 34, 98
Farksen, John 25
Farmer, Mimsy 165
Farnese, Alberto 36, 54, 63, 64, 65, 91, 103, 104, 107, 125, 130, 133, 135, 147, 155, 165, 181, 191, 192
Farnese, Giuliana 54, 135
Farnese, Tatiana 41
Faro Film 42, 67, 78, 99, 126, 128

Faro, Lidia Del 125
Faro, Tigano Lo 30, 31, 58, 64, 118, 136, 161, 163, 181
Farra, Anita 195
Farrell, Guy 150
Fasciano, Pasquale 111, 136, 188
Fassino, Giovanni 40, 41
Fast, Howard 14
Fatigati, Giuseppe 174, 186
Fatigati, Lidia 198
Fattori, Attilo 54
Fattori, Rosanna 30
Fauno Film I.C.E.T. 192
Fava, Otello 18, 60, 92, 118, 172, 181, 182, 205
Fava, Stefano 205
Favella, Adalgisa 30, 62, 175
Favella, Giovanni 199
Favella, Marcella 114, 189
Fawcett, Charles 25, 110, 114, 158, 192
Fawzi, Leila 160
Fea, Pietro 177
Febbi, Vittoria 60
Fedele, Claudia 189
Fedeluca, Nino 78
Federici, Sante 28
Fei, Grazia 195
Feist, Harry 136
Felba, Dragomir 113, 191
Feleciani, Mario 106
Felici, Beatrice 29, 31, 83, 187
Feliciani, Mario (a.k.a. Marco Feliciani) 22, 33, 47, 68, 76, 127, 134, 139, 154, 176, 186
Felicioni, Felice 81, 137, 138
Felicioni, Ferdinand 35, 41, 82, 114, 138, 173, 187
Felicioni, Fernando 114
Felicioni, Guido 65, 98
Felleghy, Tom 20, 28, 128, 137, 159, 168, 169, 187, 192
Felliciani, Mario 58
Fellicioni, Giulio 178
Fellini, Federico 22, 135, 136
Felt, Peter 104
Fenech, Edwige 126
Fénix Cooperativa Cinematografica 126
Fenollar, Augusto 159, 190
Fenollar, Pedro 106
Fenomeno, Jimmy il 87, 118
Fenton-Smith, Basil 27
Feo, Anna Maria 21, 52
Ferando, Giancarlo 203
Ferguson, Roy 152
Fernández, Félix 30, 39, 150
Fernandez, Peter 28
Fernández, Ramón 106
Feroni, Georgio 107
Ferrando, Giancarlo 125, 197
Ferranti, Giuseppe 55, 206
Ferrara, Angelo 50
Ferrara, Franco 15, 22, 24, 25, 33, 44, 64, 67, 77, 103, 120, 122, 132, 137, 160, 163, 164, 168, 174, 184
Ferrari, Gabriele 64
Ferrari, Giuseppe 7
Ferrari, Mario 22, 70, 132

Ferrari, Nicolò 70, 87
Ferrari, Paolo 55
Ferraro, Rolf 177
Ferraù, Alessandro 35, 81, 82, 103, 110, 115, 122, 134, 166
Ferré, Joaquín 166
Ferreiro, José Luis 116
Ferrer, Emilio Alonso 190
Ferrer, José 43
Ferrer, Mel 28, 35
Ferrer, Pilar Gómez 47, 167
Ferrero, Anna Maria 32, 33, 47
Ferrero, Carlo 188
Ferrero, Willy 54
Ferret, Roger 31
Ferri, Agostina 187
Ferri, Liana 30, 84, 118, 138, 181, 187
Ferri, Pasquale 189
Ferri, Riccardo 41
Ferri, Valeria 103
Ferrière, Jacqueline 96
Ferrigno, Antonio 49
Ferrigno, Carla 198, 204
Ferrigno, Lou 198, 202, 204, 206
Ferrio, Gianni 58, 90, 109
Ferronao, Edda 41, 167, 178, 188
Ferrone, Filippo 138
Ferrone, Teresa 119
Ferroni, Giorgio 24, 45, 96, 98, 107, 176, 179
Ferrrara, Franco 27
Ferry, Jean 156
Fersen, Alessandro 174, 186
Ferzetti, Gabriele 27, 55, 77, 192
Feyder, Paul 42
Feyte, Jean 31
Fiasch, Giulio 48
Fiaschi, Filiberto 40, 48, 111, 118, 172, 181, 201
Fidani, Demofilo 23, 54, 114
Fidès 16, 110, 127, 186
Fiedler, Karen 110
Field, Pamela 204
Fields, Sam 203
Fields, Verna 51
Fiermonte, Enzo 22, 24, 44, 67, 77, 78, 99, 107, 118, 128, 130, 139, 149, 156, 158, 160, 164, 165, 171, 179, 181
Fiermonti, Enzo 34
Fierro, Carla 41
Fierro, Jole 125, 126
The Fighting Musketeers (Les Trois Mousquetaires: Premiere Époque—Les Ferrets de la reine) 56
Filippini, Angelo 178
Filippini, Gino 133
Filippini, Reno 179
Filippini, Ugo 40, 55, 111
Filippone, Piero 29, 41, 103, 104, 136, 143, 159, 186
Fillon, Georgette 56
Film Do. Re. Mi. 128
Film Servis 18, 31, 120, 127
Filmar Compagnia Cinematografica 195
Filmarage 198, 203
Filmes 107, 171
Les Films Agiman 151

Les Films Arlane 163
Les Film d'Art 56
Films Benito Perojo 46
Les Films de la Boétie 18
Films Borderie 56, 67, 162
Films Cinematographica 132
Films Columbus 101, 152
Le Films du Centaure 30
Les Films Copernic 164
Le Films Corona 102, 110, 165
Les Films du Cyclope 106
Films International Artistici (FIA) 26, 184
Les Films Jacques Leitienne 118, 173, 204
Les Films Jacques Willemetz 157
Le Films Modernes 56, 119, 178, 179
Films Montana 18
Films Régent 143
Films S.A. 149
Filmsonor 163
Filoni, Fernando 59
Finanziara Cinematografica Italiana (FICIT) 141
Fini, Gianfranco 122
Fini, Giorgio 8
Fino, M. 122
Fino, Savino 49
Finocchi, Augusto 113
Finocchiaro, Luciano 29, 187
Fiocca, Maria 206
Fior, Eugenia Tettoni 10
Fioramonti, Liliana 26
Fiore, Carlo 32, 36, 44, 130, 132, 160, 169
Fiore, Maria 160, 175
Fiorelli, Aldo 80, 94, 191
Fiorelli, Biagio 22, 41, 176
Fiorentini, Enrico 32
Fiorentini, Stenio 26
Fiorenzo, Magia 54
Fioretti, Mario 59
Fiori, Eugenio 91
Fiorini, Guido 15, 33
Fiorino, Paolo 129
Fiory, Odoardo 60, 64, 127, 163, 191
Fire Monsters Against the Son of Hercules (Maciste contro I mostri) 48, 56, **57, 58,** 111
Fire Over Rome (Il incendio di Roma) 58
Fischer, Clare 112
Fischer, Sebastian 49
Fiz, Umberto 32, 45
Fizz, Roberto 25, 50, 175
Fizzarotti, Ettore Maria 49, 55, 67, 141, 166
Flash, Rod 16, 188, **188, 189**
Flash Gordon serials 63
Flaubert, Gustave 110
Fleischer, Richard 24, 25
Fleming, Rhonda 140
Fleming, Thea 171
Florent, Robert 56
Floret, Veronique 18
Florian, Barbara 96, 176
Florido, Antonio 154
Flourens, Pierre 42
Flowers, Dea 104

Flynn, Errol 32, 159, 178
Flynn, Sean 159, 171
Fo, Fulvio 36
Foà, Arnoldo 25, 31, 34, 44, 46, 47, 99, 110, 127, 128, 160, 170, 189
Focás, Spiros 116, 194
Fodor, Ladislas 164
Fogagnolo, Franco 206
Folchi, Jenny 125, 186
Folcolini, Paolo 205
Folgaresi, Elio 167
Fondato, Marcello 124
Fono Roma 42, 56, 178
Fontana, Elena 191
Fontana, Enrico 52, 55
Fontana, Franco 125
Fontenelle, Jean 31
Fonteray, Jacques 112
Fontini, Anacleto 65, 100, 111, 151, 160
Foray, June 191
Forest, Laura 114
Forest, Mark 3, 4, **71,** 72, 73, 81, 82, 84, 104, 107, **108,** 111, 122, **161,** 162, 172, **172, 173**
Forest, Michael 110
Forges, Roberto 203
Forget, René-Christian 31
Foriscot, Emilio 39
Forlenza, Magda 136
Formai, Enrico 136, 137
Forques, Valerie 109
Forrer, Anne-Marie 42
Forsyth, Stephen 32
Fortini, Iolanda 113
Fortini, Romana 64
Fortis, Giuseppe 166, 184
Forum Film 135
Forzano, Giovacchino 13
Foscari, Carla 33, 45, 69, 122, 171, 175
Foschini, Arnaldo 54
Fosco-Giachetti 168
Fossard, Marc 18
Foster, Jon 203
Foster, Lisa 200
Foti, Luciano 184, 189
Fotopoulos, Vasilis 128
Fotre, Vincent 126
Foucard, Franco 31
Foulon, Raoul 56
Foulon, Robert 31
The Four Musketeers (I quattro moschettieri) 58
Fourcade, Christian 31
Fournier, Camille 174
Fowley, Douglas 25
Fox, Jann 20
Fragasso, Claudio 204
Framer, David 198, 200
Franca Film 135
France, Josette 124
France-Cinéma Productions 35, 124
Franceschi, Paolo 205
Franchetti, Rina 25
Franchi, Alfredo 23
Franchi, Fernando 142
Franchi, Franco 30, 91, 110
Franchi, Lina 113, 195

Franchini, Teresa 156
Franci, Carlo 20, 30, 59, 65, 83, 95, 116, 118, 127, 136, 139, 141, 142, 151, 154, 161, 172, 181, 184, 187, 192
Francine, Dolores 140
Francioli, Armando 33, 49, 128, 136
Francioli, Germana 36, 65
Francioli, Luciano 128
Francioni, Renzo 90
Francis, Edwin 199
Francisci, Bruno 19, 119, 137
Francisci, Mario 132
Francisci, Pietro 21, 78, 80, 91, 92, 132, 141, 155, 156, 190
Franco, Franca 68
Franco, Fulvia 28, 92, 94
Francoeur, Richard 60, 174
François, Jacqueline 16
Francomme, Édouard 42
Frank, Fredric M. 51
Franz, Michael 204
Franzi, Celeste 165
Frasca, Fortunato 95
Frasca, Paolo 49
Frascaroli, Valentina 13
Fraschetti, Silvio 15
Fraschetti, Yvonne 198
Fraser, John 51
Frashetti, Silvio 80
Frassinetti, Augusto 15, 36, 60, 67, 175
Fratalocchi, Antonio 114, 169, 177, 188
Frate, Renato Del 120, 122, 163
Fraticelli, Franco 32, 44, 62, 67, 69, 119, 152, 153, 186
Fraticelli, Maria-Luisa 178
Fraticelli, Marisa 54, 120, 158, 177
Fraticelli, Romeo 178
Fraticelli, Sergio 6
Frattaioli, Rodolfo 163, 179
Frattini, Gaio 78, 169
Frau, Maria 67
Frazzi, Franco 39, 103
Freda, Franco 64, 162
Freda, Riccardo 5, 17, 30, 48, 64, 67, 122, 135, 136, 143, 153, 155, 156, 160, 174, 191, 192
Frederica, Aveline 102
Frederick, Hal 135
Freeman, Anthony 152, 198
Freeman, Tony 100
Fregonese, Ferruchio 113
Fregonese, Hugo 112
Frenguelli, Toni 136
Fresco, Jose 84
Fresno, Maruchi 65
Frey, Barbara 127
Freyberger, Manfred 59
Friedman, Georges 118
Friedrichsen, Bente 25
Friendly, Sharon 200
Frieri, Michelangelo 165
Frizzi, Fabio 110
From Russia with Love 166
Fronzetti, Bernardino 63
Fruscella, Nino 64, 163
Fry, Christopher 24, 27

224 Index

Fryd, Joseph 67, 91, 140
Fuchs, Gianni 70
Fuente, Eduardo de la 37, 127
Fuentes, A. Rubio 150
Fugagnolli, Lolly 122
Fulci, Lucio 105, 201
Fulton, John P. 151
Fulton, Rad 103
Fumagalli, Aldo 112
Fumagalli, Franco 30, 112
Fuochi, Vladimiro Piccia 184
Furia, Giacomo 47, 50, 182
Furia, Lilly 32
Furijan, Maks 127, 154, 178
Furlan, Alan 46
Furlan, Rate 99, 166
Furnari, Salvatore 16, 40, 64, 72, 87, 107, 127, 139, 188, 190
Furneaux, Yvonne 35, 107, **108**, 158
Fury of Achilles (L'ira di Achille) 59
The Fury of Hercules (La furia di Ercole) 59, 202
Fury of the Pagans (La furia dei barbari) 60
Fury, Ed 36, 110, 119, **120**, 120, 152, 186
Fury, Wayne 27
Fuscagni, Nino 91, 119, 168, 187
Fusch, Barbara 60, 92, 175
Fusco, Giovanni 22, 35, 41, 99, 128, 135, 147, 179
Fusco, Tarcisio 28
Fusier-Gir, Jeanne 134
Fux, Herbert 165

Gabel, Scilla 104, 133, 138, 153, 158, 160, 191
Gabotti, Amato 199
Gabriel, Eva Maria 156
Gabrielli, Gabriella 183
Gabrini, Misa 92
Gabutti, Raymond 18
Gaffet, Néstor 136
Gaida, Michel 29
Gainsbourg, Serge 59, 140, 142
Gaioni, Cristina 59, 103, 119, 157
Galadini, Eugenio 138
Galas, Orlando 127
Galassi, Angelo 112
Galassia Cinematografica 48
Galatea Film, 21, 26, 36, 52, 54, 60, 80, 94, 106, 113, 155, 171, 189
Galdo, Domenico 9
Galfano, Aldo 92, 122, 189
Galiano, Cataldo 105, 194
Galiano, Dino 47, 55, 65, 105, 175, 178, 189, 194, 205
Galiano, Massimo 197, 202
Galiano, Vittorio 37, 64, 68, 194, 197, 202
Galiant, Victor 202
Galicia, José Luis 126, 154
Galimberti, Gilberto 63, 84, 88, 89, 111, 118, 139
Galitti, Alberto 24
Galizi, Franco 201
Gallagher, Jeanne 21
Gallardo, José 26, 167
Gallardo, Juan Luis 167

Gallardo, Manuel 47, 127
Gallea, Arturo 67, 191
Gallet, Lina 118
Galletti, Giovanni 96, 159, 192
Galletti, Giovannna 27
Galli, Ida 56, 90, 116, 189
Galli, Rossana 132
Galliano, Cataldo 178, 205
Gallici, Frank 201
Gallicia, María Luz 154
Gallina, Mario 46
Gallitti, Alberto 27, 28, 73, 138, 152, 153, 158
Gallo, Emilio 9
Gallo, Nunzio 48
Gallone, Carmine 10, 33, 45, 118
Gallone, Carmine, Jr. 33
Gallone, Soava 7
Gallotti, Dada 20, 59, 88, 168, 194, 196
Gallus Films 145, 162
Galoni, Cristina 58
Galvani, Ciro 46
Galvani, Gilberto 84
Gam, Rita 77
Gamacchio, Mirella 90, 203
Gamal, Samia 47
Gamardiel, Roberto 119
Gamba, Luisa 207
Gambardella, Giuseppe 14
Gambarelli, Cesare 25, 46, 139
Gambino, Domenico 7, 8
Gambino, John 49
Gambino, Joky 49
Gamna, Vincenzo 78
Gance, Abel 42
Gandini, Maria 14
Gandos, Giorgio 134
Garavaglia, Leo 65
Garbini, Amato 15, 33, 73, 95, 122
Garbuglia, Mario 18, 47
Garcia, Alejandro Alonso 201
Garcia, Carmelo 119
Garcia, José Luis 116
Garcia, Juan 106
Garcia, Serafin 154
Garcia, Tito 24, 194, 113
Gardani, Giosue 177
Garden, Floni 160
Garden, Mara 33
Gardenin, Andrej 19, 22, 35, 50, 113, 115, 124, 152, 165, 179
Gardett, Robert 25
Gardner, Ava 27
Gardner, S. 127
Gargaloni, Paolo 118
Gargano, Andrea 62, 154, 163, 191
Gargano, Olimpo 45
Gargano, Omero 16, 62, 88, 152, 188
Gargano, Paolo 25, 73, 122, 163
Garinei, Enzo 182
Garko, Gianni 22, 122, 124, 130, 150, 202
Garko, John 202
Garland, Frank 202
Garlanda, Maria Vittoria 200
Garofalo, Franco 20, 202
Garofalo, Salvatore 27
Garrani, Ivo 19, 34, 43, 60, 65, 80, 87, 124, 126, 141, 142, 157

Garrett, Stephen 122
Garrone, Luigi 160
Garrone, Riccardo 23, 110, 130, 168, 182, 191
Garroni, Guglielmo 156
Garroni, Romolo 31, 100, 111, 136, 167
Gartner, Slava 154
Garvarentz, Georges 47, 112, 151, 171
Garzarelli, Tonino 36, 106, 155
Gaspar, Luis 23
Gaspard-Huit, Pierre 150
Gaspari, Aldo 28
Gaspari, Romano 188
Gasparri, Franco 59, 68, 142
Gasper, Ivan 20
Gasperini, Italo 141
Gasser, Fulvia 58, 127
Gassilli, Raoul 34
Gassman, Vittorio 25, 50
Gastaldi, Ernesto 17, 23, 35, 64, 76, 77, 87, 113, 115, 122, 130, 133, 138, 152, 158, 186
Gastoni, Lisa 58, 118, 133, 174, 176
Gatineau, Michel 87
Gatti, Kim 198, 202
Gatti, Liliana 169
Gatti, Marcello 49, 191
Gaudin, Christian 56
Gaul, Leslie 202
Gautier, Jean-Michel 150
Gava, Andrea 167
Gavin, Maureen 25
Gavo, Rosalia 122
Gavric, Aleksandar 115
Gavrik, Vlastimir 118
Gay, Clementine 13
Gayford, John 198
Gazarelli, Tonino 21
Gazzolo, Laura 55
Gazzolo, Lauro 41, 90, 174
Gazzolo, Nando 41, 140, 147, 155, 167
Gazzoni, Maria Letizia 41, 114
Gec, Jovan 191
Geert, Gisa 22, 80
Geesink, Anton 65
Geiger, Sibylle 194, 195
Gelber, Lizabeth 202, 204, 205
Geleng, Antonello 203
Geleng, Massimo Antonello (a.k.a. M. A. Geleng) 197, 202, 203, 205
Gélin, Daniel 34
Gelleng, Tony 197
Gelpi, Juan 113, 150
Gemma, Giuliano 41, 73, 84, 109, 116, 139, 150, 163, 181, 187
Gemser, Laura 198, 200, 202, 203
Genazzani, Osvaldo 10
Gengarelli, Amerigo 50, 169
Génia, Claude 42
Gennusco, Marinella 30
Genoino, Arnaldo 99
Génovès, André 18
Gentile, Antonio 33
Gentile, Fedele 30, 31, 33, 47, 48, 73, 77, 78, 82, 99, 111, 119, 128, 129, 138, 139, 167, 168, 187
Gentili, Carlo 32, 77, 98, 107, 128, 147, 163

Index 225

Gentili, Ernesto 59, 142
Gentili, Franco 64
Gentili, Giorgio 158, 169, 192
Gentilini, Michele 72
Gentilli, Olga Vittoria 55
Gentilomo, Giacomo 28, 29, 35, 49, 73, 82, 104, 106, 157
Gentleman, Wally 203
George, Gabriella 202
Gerace, Lilliana 19
Gérard, Olivier 197, 202, 204
Gerber, Hela 25
Geri, Adolfo 99
Gerlini, Piero 29, 65
Germani, Gaia 90, 178
Germano, Michele 207
Germano, Pasquale 205, 207
Germano, Romolo 84
Gemelli, Enrico 7, 13
Gérôme, Raymond 178
Gersak, Savina 203
Gervasi, Carlo 163, 179
Gervasi, Eugene 25
Gerzoni, Fausto 136
Gherardi, Giuliana 26, 126
Gherardi, Piero 176
Gherardini, Oreste 14
Ghia, Fernando 119
Ghidini, Giuliana 30, 158, 166
Ghignone, Mario 167
Ghini, Romano 34, 59, 84, 102, 139, 142, 178
Ghione, Emilio 10
Ghione, Piero 22, 24, 78, 99, 103, 126, 128, 186
Giachetti, Bernard Farber Fosco 102
Giachetti, Fosco 41, 46, 59
Giacobini, Franco 52, 90
Giacobino, Giuseppe 125, 195
Giacomini, Antonella 204
Giacomozzi, Ugo 33, 165
Giagnoni, Piero 22, 34, 129, 130
Giambartolomei, Guido 122
Gianandrea, Maria 197, 202
Gianandrea, Roberto 197, 202
Giancotti, Salvatore 80, 87, 143, 145
Giandalla, Roberto 19, 32, 34, 60, 104, 119
Gianese, Gianni 30, 164
Giangrande, Orlando 188
Gianini, A. 59
Gianini, Giulio 152
Giannetti, Alfredo 166
Giannini, Emilio 50, 59, 136, 142
Giannotti, Claudia 187
The Giant from the Dolemites (Il gigante delle Dolomiti) 9
The Giant of Marathon (La battaglia di Maratona) 60, **61**
The Giant of Metropolis (Il gigante di Metropolis) 4, 62, **62, 63**
Giant of the Evil Island (Il mistero dell'isola maledetta) 63
Giants of Rome (I giganti di Roma) 63
The Giants of Thessaly (I giganti della Tessaglia) 64
Gianviti, Roberto 55, 73, 103, 114, 124, 137, 138, 143, 153, 166, 173, 187

Gibson, Carl 51
Gicca, Enzo 92, 195
Gideon and Samson (I grandi condottieri) 64
Giganti, Alfonso 35, 140
Gigi 19
Giglietti, Andreina 141
Giglietti, Giuseppe 205
Gil, Antonio 119
Gil, Jaime Comas 147
Gil, Manuel 119
Gil, Pedro 166
Gil, Salvador 65
Gilbert, Fernand 42
Gill, Stanley B. 199
Gilli, Luciana 40, 135, 153, 166, 186
Gilligan's Island 3, 190, 191
Gilsic, Mira 152
Gimeno, Antonio 23, 24, 40
Ginesi, Veriano 36, 41, 65, 69, 73, 98, 124, 129, 130, 147, 155, 163, 169, 171, 192
Gingarelli, Amerigo 168
Ginnoto, Mirella 36, 77, 122, 124, 155
Gino Mordini Co. 122
Giomareli, Alberto 51
Giombini, Marcello 104, 111, 188
Giomini, Amedeo 127, 142
Giomini, Renato 177
Giomini, Romano 15, 23, 54, 133, 134, 135, 151, 171
Gionannini, Giorgio 167
Gionni, Gustavo 142
Giorda, Marcello 41, 46, 116, 165
Giordana, Andrea 99
Giordani, Aldo 20, 91, 120, 122, 173
Giordani, Eraldo 30
Giordano, Lia 177
Giordano, Mariangela 29, 36, 47, 119, 152
Giordano, Matt 204
Giordano, Matteo 201
Giordano, Roberto Pizzi,Matt 201
Giorgelli, Gabriella 202
Giorgi, Gino 136
Giorgio Agliani Cinematografica 65, 122
Giornelli, Franco 142
Giorsi, Mario 25, 26, 35, 40, 50, 58, 64, 65, 67, 73, 84, 89, 99, 103, 111, 112, 113, 118, 138, 139, 140, 151, 156, 157, 168, 172, 181, 184, 186
Giovagnoli, Lamberto 134, 140
Giovagnoli, Rafaello 14
Giovanardi, Paolo 128, 190
Giovanni, Giorgio 15, 21
Giovanni, Verdi 14
Giovannini, Giorgio 52, 58, 62, 92, 158, 189
Giovannini, Mario 106
Giovannucci, Sergio 186
Giraldi, Franco 50, 156
Girard, Raymonf 42
Girardi, Amedeo 182
Girardon, Michèle 16, 47
Giraud, Hubert 177
Girelli, Margherita 29
Girolami, Andrea 205

Girolami, Ennio 59, 206
Girolami, Fernando Paolo 20
Girolami, Marino 59
Girolami, Romolo 19
Girolami, Stefania 206
Girosi, A. Maria 155
Girosi, Mimmola 34, 36, 50, 156
Girotti, Mario 77, 153, 164, 192
Girotti, Massimo 41, 51, 55, 64, 67, 78, 99, 113, 156
Gisbert, Teresa 119
Gisotti, Michaela 199
Giuffrè, Adriana 200
Giuffrè, Aldo 33, 92
Giuia, Renato 159
Giulian, Giuliano 172
Giuliani, Massimo 102, 158
Giulianini, Tiziano 197
Giunchi, Lea 13
Giuntini, Toscano 59
Giurato, Blasco 205
Giuri, Gina 200
Giusti, Silvano 111, 112, 138, 151
Giustini, Anacieto 36, 77, 84, 88, 130, 141, 155, 169
Giustini, Angelo 124
Giustini, Carlo 19, 25, 51, 116, 125, 130, 156, 164
Giustini, Duilio 19, 40, 91, 103, 120
Giustini, Eros 201, 203
Giustini, Luciano 59
Giustini, Massimo 34, 77, 89, 96, 98, 143
Giustini, Maurizio 30, 67, 91, 133, 146, 153
Giustini, Oscar 109, 113, 169
Given, Eddy H. 192
Givord, Jacqueline 56
Givry, Lucienne 96
Gizzi, Giovanni 14
Gizzi, Loris 41, 48, 63, 77, 87, 125, 130, 133, 136, 146, 165, 168, 174, 195–196
Gladiator Films 26
Gladiator of Rome (Il gladiatore di Roma) 65, **66**
Gladiators 7 (I sette gladiatori) 65
Gleason, Randy 200
Globe Film International 158, 189
Globus-Dubrava Film Studio 156
Globus, Ram 202
Globus, Yoram 197, 199, 201, 204, 205
Glomer Film 36, 130, 131, 155
Glori, Enrico 25, 41, 44, 49, 51, 99, 122, 125, 126, 173
Glori, Mario 176
Glori, Mario Musy 50
Glori, Vasco 135
Glori, Vittorio Musy 50, 155
Gloriani, Tina 49, 59, 96
GMC 58
Goddard, Jean-Luc 150
Goddess of Love (La Venere di Cheronea) 67
Godzilla, King of the Monsters 1, 2, 3
Goddio, Sergio 13
Goetzke, Bernard 10
Gogol, Nicolai 168
Gojira (see Godzilla, King of the Monsters)

Golan-Globus Productions 202
Golan, Menahem 197, 199, 201, 205
Golconich, Vyera 99
Gold for the Caesars (Oro per i Cesari) 67
The Golden Arrow (L'arciere delle mille e una notte) 67
Golec, Manja 59, 142
Golem, Menahem 204
Golgi, Susy 191
Goliath Against the Giants (Goliath contro I giganti) 68, **68**
Goliath and the Barbarians (Il terrore dei barbari) 69, **69, 70,** 145
Goliath and the Dragon (La vendetta di Ercole) 4, 70, **71, 72**
Goliath and the Sins of Babylon (Maciste l'eroe più grande del mondo) 73, **74**
Goliath and the Vampires (Maciste contro il vampiro) 4, 73, **75, 76**
Goliath at the Conquest of Damascus (Golia alla conquista di Bagdad) 76
Goliath, Little 152
Gómez, Ramiro 37, 68, 105, 127, 140
Gonneau, George 69, 143, 145
Gonzáles, Fidel 87
Gónzales, Maria 27
González, Agustin 27
Gonzalez, Marcelo 127
González, Miguel 116
González, Paulino 126
González, Romana 26
Goods, Olivia 198
Goodwin, Stefania Girolami 205
Goodwin, Tommy 199
Gora, Claudio 67, 156, 165, 168
Gorassini, Annie 116, 188, 191
Gordon, Frank 91
Gordon, Mitchell 20
Gore, Laura 55
Gorgano, Paolo 67
Gori, Coriolano 23, 84, 125
Gori, Lallo 23
Gorini, Ariana 136
Gort, Inga 136
Gosálvez, José 119
Goss, David 205
Gotan, Gabriel 160
Gough, Trent 192
Goulian, Ludmilla 178
Goumy, Pierre-Henri 18, 112
Goupil, Pierre 178
Govoni, Armando 52, 60
Gozlino, Paolo 23, 64, 65, 111, 150, 160, 183
Gozzo, Enrico 26
Gracia, Sancho 27
Grad, Geneviève 21, 26, 35, 98, **148, 149,** 149
Grado, Cristina 42
Gradoli, Antonio 16, 23, 30, 88, 96, 114, 137, 195, 196
Gragnani, Piergiorgio 168
Gramigna, Alvaro 19
Gramignani, Valeria 99, 129
Granada, María 150
Granado, Lily 80
Granata, Graziella 33, 122, 129

Granatelli, Giancarlo 24, 103, 147, 205
Grande, Flavia 55
Grande, Nico il 110
Grande, Ovidio Del 54, 122, 191
Grandi Schermi Italiani 96
Grandi, Oreste 8, 9, 10, 12
Grandi, Serena 198
Grandière, Georges de la 150
Grandsley, Danah 200
Granelli, Mireille 91, 187
Granger, Stewart 158, 168
Grani, Tina 52, 92, 189
Grant, Walter 34, 60, 92, 94, 155, 167, 175
Gras, Jean 56
Gras, José 201
Grassetti, Claudio 199
Grassi, Alvaro 201
Grassilli, Raoul 100
Grasso, Francesco 205
Grasso, Giovanni 49
Grau, Jorge 37, 68, 105
Graves, Robert 18
Gray, Dorian 36, 132
Gray, Hugh 184
Gray, Nadia 15, 29
Gray, Roland 29
Graziani, Anna 64
Graziosi, Giorgio 22, 132, 155
Grcevic, Kreso 191
Grech, German 84, 183
Greci, Aldo 28, 33, 58, 167
Greci, José 51, 73, 81, 82, 87, 114, 134, 137, 152, 167, 171, 189
Greco, Edward L. 202
Greco, Enzo Musumeci 28, 33, 34, 41, 42, 50, 51, 60, 70, 80, 92, 95, 110, 120, 124, 125, 129, 132, 134, 141, 160, 165, 176, 191, 202
Greco, Sergio 129
Green, Calotta 198
Greenfield, Max 198
Greenfield, May 198, 200
Gregorin, Jose 138
Gregorin, Joza 138
Gregory, Frank 122
Gregory, John 198, 200
Grellier, Alain 194
Gres, Mme. 184
Grey, Dolly 9
Grey, Elizabeth 10
Grieco, Sergio 28, 30, 99, 110, 125, 126, 128, 129, 138, 157, 167
Grier, Pam 19
Griffith, D. W. 1, 8
Griffin, Jonathan 27
Grignon, Marcel 31
Grilli, Armando 138, 153, 205
Grilli, Mario 28
Grimaldi, Alberto 154
Grimaldi, Eliana 119, 166
Grimaldi, Giovanni 58, 65, 156
Grimaldi, Hugo 87
Grimes, Stephen B. 22, 27
Grisanti, Antonio 10
Grisanti, Remo 67
Grisoni, Angelo 95
Grize, Cyril 31

Grjebina, Irina 178
Gromtseff, Marie 31
Groppioni, Franco 19, 34, 35, 70, 77, 87, 96, 111, 118, 129, 137, 172, 173, 181, 195
Grosso, Remigio Del 96, 98, 99, 103, 107, 128, 135, 169, 176
Grottini, Armando 36, 130, 155
Growne, John, II 204
Grozea, Costel 70, 169
Gruber, Anna 67, 153
Grubmiller, Eva Maria 156
Galimberti, Gilberto 21
Gualabdri, Carlo 10
Gualino, Riccardo 169
Gualtieri, Carlo 37
Guardiola, José 47
Guarini, Alfredo 171, 175
Guarini, Maurizio 199, 201, 202
Guarino, Egle 202, 206
Guarner, José Luis 127
Guarnieri, Armando 81, 87
Guarracino, Umberto 11, 12
Guasco, Luigi 32, 62, 169
Gudin, Michel 87
Guedon, Colette 204
Guélis, Jean 31
Guérini, Camile 96
Guerra, José Antonio de la 151
Guerra, Luigi Antonio 26, 48
Guerra, Mario 116, 165
Guerra, Stefania Del 199
Guerra, Tonino 64, 116, 150
Guerra, Ugo 23, 35, 77, 113, 122, 130, 133
Guerra, Valentina 136
Guerrieri, Romolo 19, 32, 68, 69, 119, 161, 166
Guerzoni, Fausto 128, 130
Guffroy, Jean-Pierre 31
Gugic, Zivojin 118
Guglelmotti, Anna Maria 195
Guglielmi, Marco 22, 126, 153, 164, 173
Gugliemetti, Gastone 30
Guibert, Claire 31, 87, 96
Guida, Ernesto 41, 138
Guida, Wandisa 64, 65, **71,** 72, 73, 80, 104, 131, 134, 137, 140, 146, 187
Guidi, Guidarino 27, 184
Guiducci, Guido 9
Guijarro, Milagros 167
Guillaume, Bruno 70
Guillaume, Ferdinand 43
Guillaume, Matilda 14
Guillén, Joaquin 107
Guillon, Ernest 42
Guillot, Fernando 47
Guisol, Henri 174
Guitián, Manuel 47
Gul, Ayshe 208
Gullotta, Leo 206
Gulsoy, Umit 207
Gunan, King of the Barbarians (Gunan il guerriero) 201
Guns of the Black Witch (Il terrore dei mari) 77
Gustini, Carlo 44

Guthrie, Carl E. 25
Guzmán, Miguel 47, 154
Gwynn, Michael 25

Haas, Ernst 27
Habay, Andrea 9, 12
Hacohen, Alexander 204
Hadley, James 198, 200
Hafenrichter, Oswald 45
Haggard, H. Rider 205
Hahn, Gisela 110
Halain, Jean 31
Hall, Larry 25
Hall, Nancy 200
Hall, Robert 25, 167
Halsey, Brett 23, 30, 153
Hamilton, Sam 152
Hammer Films 90
Hampton, Robert 156, 192
Hanau, John 95
Handris, Helen 198, 200
Hanger, Charles 115
Hani, Pierre 42
Hannibal (Annibale) 77, 177
Hanover Film Co. 13
Hararheet, Haya 103
Haran, Helmut 154
Hargitay, Mickey 95, **95, 96,** 137
Hargous, Lily 56
Haroy, Claude 160
Harris, Brad 3, 59, 68, 84, 127, 142, 154, 202, 204
Harris, John 51
Harris, Richard 27
Harris, Robert W. 198, 200
Harrison, Dan 17, 146
Harrison, Richard 23, 64, 67, **100, 101,** 101, 116, 118, 131, 139, 150, 181
Harry Joe Brown Prods. 159
Harryhausen, Ray 64
Hart, Brooke 198
Hart, John Davis 20, 41, 59, 62, 68, 96, 116
Harvey, Jean-Pierre 160
Hassan, Dori 36
Hatfield, Hurd 51
Hathaway, Robert 207
Haughton, David (a.k.a. David Cain Haughton) 207
Hautecoeur, Louisette 150
Havilland, Liz 152
Hayward, Justin 205
Hayworth, Rita 142, 164
Head of a Tyrant (Giuditta e Oloferne) 9, 78
Hebbel, Friedrich 78
Hecht, Ben 184
Hehn, Albert 165
Heiberg, Brigitte 88
Heinz, Richard 132
Heinze, Peter 27
Held, Bernard 184
Heller, Leone 12, 14
Helm, Alberto 165
Hénaff, René Le 18
Hendy, Gloria 122, 141
Hendy, Janine 118, 122, 124, 141, 171, 175
Henri-Montel, Charles 31

Henry, Guy 43
Henry, Simone 56
Hercules (Ercole) 198, 201
Hercules (Le fatiche di Ercole) **2,** 3, 78, **78, 79,** 94, 161
Hercules Against Rome (Ercole contro Roma) 80
Hercules Against the Barbarians (Maciste nell'inferno di Gengis Khan) 81
Hercules Against the Mongols (Maciste contro i Mongoli) 81, **81**
Hercules Against the Moon Men (Maciste e la regina di Samar) 82, **82, 83,** 206
Hercules Against the Sons of the Sun (Ercole contro I figli del sole) 83
Hercules and the Black Pirates (Sansone contro il corsaro nero) 83, **85**
Hercules and the Captive Women (Ercole alla coquista di Atlantide) 83, **86, 92**
Hercules and the Masked Rider (Golia e il cavaliere mascherato) 87
Hercules and the Treasure of the Incas (Sansone e il tesoro degli Incas) 88
Hercules and the Tyrants of Babylon (Ercole contro I tiranni di Babilonia) 88, **88**
Hercules in the Haunted World (Ercole al centro della Terra) 89, **89,** 90, 92
Hercules in the Valley of Woe (Maciste contro Ercole nella valle dei guri) 90
Hercules of the Desert (La valle dell'eco tonante) 91
Hercules the Avenger (La sfida dei giganti) 92
Hercules the Invincible see *The Son of Hercules Against the Land of Darkness* 47
Hercules Unchained (Ercole e la regina di Lidia) **2,** 3, 80, 92, **93, 94**
Hercules vs. the Hydra (Gli amori di Ercole) 95, **95, 96, 97**
Hercules vs. the Moloch (Ercole contro Moloch) 96
Hercules, Prisoner of Evil (Ursus, il terrore dei kinorghisi) 91
Hercules, Samson and Ulysses (Ercole sfida Sansone) 91
Herlin, Jacques 73, 171, 204
Hermann, Giorgio 83, 128
Hernández, Joaquin Romero 154
Hernández, Rafael 127
Hero of Babylon see *The Beast of Babylon Against the Son of Hercules*
Hero of Rome (Il colosso di Roma) 98
Herod the Great (Erode il grande) 98, **98**
Herrera, José 106
Herrera, Pepe 119
Herrero, Jorge 154
Hersent, Philippe 21, 49, 64, 73, 77, 98, 99, 118, 119, 127, 154, 176, 189, 194
Herter, Gérard 60, 191
Hessel, Larry 198, 200
Heston, Charlton 51
Heston, John 127, 164, 179
Heymann, Claude 55

Heywood, Anne 34
Hidden Valley (She) 205
Higgins, George 31, 68
Hilbeck, Fernando 25, 195
Hill, Gladys 27
Hill, Richard 207
Hill, Terence 34, 77, 153, 164, 192
Hilling, Jacques 56
Hillman, Warren 198
Hills, David 198, 200, 202
Hilton, George 113, 114
Himenes, Julio 26
Hinrich, Hans 55
Hinterman, Carlo 22, 23, 119, 130
Hispamer Films 27, 30, 55, 84, 104, 125, 141, 167, 195
Hitchcock, Claude 25
The *Hobgoblin (Ricerca per la potente Spada)* 202
Hochet, Louis 118
Hodgson, Leslie 27, 158
Hodson, Donald 200, 205, 206
Hoffman, Benno 140
Hoffman, Robert 126
Hold, John 104
Holden, Mike 52
Holder, Ines 37
Holm, Christopher 206
Holmes, Christopher 73
Holzer, Ivy 28, 139, 154, 181
Homer 184
Honoré, Jean-Pierre 83
Honthaner, Ron 33
Hordern, Michael 51
Horn, Alan 204
Horne, Geoffrey 164
Horne, John 25
Horowitz, Margherita 113
Hossein, André 150
Hossein, Robert 113
Howard, Noël 112, 113
Howard, Tom 175
Howes, Rick 25
Hoya, José Antonio 65
Huang, Al 199
Hubbert, Cork 206
Hubner, Sybilla Barbara 26
Hudson, Fred 164, 179
Hudson, Ralph 64
Huerta, Cris 112, 119, 126, 151
Huertas, Ricardo 65
Hughes, Lee 202
Humphreys, Gerry 202
Hundar, Robert 154
Hunebelle, André 31
Hunger, Fredy 157
The Huns (La regina dei tartari) 99
Hunter, Jeffrey 67
Hunter, Tab 68
Hussein, Muana 207
Huston, John 27
Hynes, Fred 27

I.A.C. EI.D.C. 168
Iacobis, Sergio 128
Iacona, Fabrizia 199
Iacono, Angelo 192
Ianiro, Zeus 27
Iannetta, Tristano 200

Index

Iannilli, Fernando 176
Ibáñez, E. 40
Ibáñez, Rafael 30, 84
Ibrahim, Abdel Moneim 68
I.C.D. 92
IFESA 100
IFI Producción S.A. 174
Iglesias, Manuel 111
Iglesias, Miguel 166
Igliozzi, Daniela 81, 178
Igor, Daniele 174
Ilforte, Benito 16, 177, 188
Ilic, Simone 157
Illa, Jorge 16
Illiria Film 119, 122
Imbró, Gaetano 109
Imp. Ex. Ci. 204
Incei Film 113
Incir De Paolis Studio 15, 41, 45, 58, 63, 82, 101, 104, 129, 133, 147, 177, 173, 181, 187, 202, 204, 207
Incontrera, Annabella 76, 126
Incrocci, Agenore 32, 78, 176
Induni, Luis 23, 40, 166
Industrie Cinetelevisive 166
Industrie Cinematografiche Sociali (ICS) 16, 50
Infanti, Angelo 18, 28
Infascelli, Carlo 47, 128, 140
Infiesta, Julio 24, 119, 159
Inglés, Rufino 24, 69, 116, 119, 154
Ingrassia, Ciccio 91
Inkijinoff, Valéry 119, 134, 145, 178
Iniziative Cinematografiche Internazionali (ICI) 113
Innocenti, Camillo 8, 13
Innocenzi, Carlo 20, 21, 30, 35, 44, 59, 68, 69, 95, 137, 139, 142, 143, 152, 161, 167, 178
Innocenzi, Patrizia 201
Innocenzi, Pietro 201
Innocenzi, Umberto 198, 206
Interlenghi, Franco 55, 186
International Germania Film 128
International Motion Picture Enterprises 44
Intolerance 1, 8
Intorre, Libero 174
Invasion 1700 (Col ferro e col fuoco) 99
The Invincible Brothers Maciste (Gli invincibli fratelli Maciste) 100
The Invincible Gladiator (Il gladiatore invincibile) 100, **100**, 101
The Invincible Masked Rider (L'invincibile cavaliere mascherato) 102
Iocono, Angelo 169
Ippoliti, Silvano 17, 91, 158, 204
Iron Warrior (Ator il guerriero di ferro) 203
Ironmaster (La guerra del ferro: Ironmaster) 203
Isabel 154
Isabel, Maria 39
Isasi-Isamendi, Antonio 16
Isleño 119
Isnardon, Monique 168
Isnardon, Robert 168
Isnenghi, Gualtiero 65, 112, 133
Israel, Aviva 27

Israel, Victor 151
Italcaribe 126
Italcine 32
Italaf Kaboul 113
Italgamma 141
Italia Film 171, 175
Italia Produzione 157
Italo Spagnola 126
ITTAC 113
Ivanhoe, the Norman Swordsman (La spada Normanna) 102
Ivanov, Wladimir 112
Ivernel, Daniel 42, 186
Ivkov, Dragoljub 50, 179
Izzarelli, Francesco 40, 59, 127, 142, 154, 171, 175
Izzo, Renato 177

Jaboni, Renato 33, 169
Jachino, Carlo 55, 156, 160
Jachino, Silvana 30, 33, 55, 125, 138
Jacob, the Man Who Fought with God (Giacobbe, l'uomo lottò con Dio) 102
Jacobbi, Ruggero 131
Jacobini, Diomira 13
Jacobs, Irving 165
Jacono, Angelo 169
Jacopini, Nilo 43, 194
Jacovini, Alessandro 50
Jadelica, Nina 99
Jadran Film 41, 58
Jaffe, Sam 43
Jail Bait 3
Jamil, Joudi Mohammed 175
Jamonte, Franco 34, 63, 77, 88, 129, 130, 133, 136, 167
Janey, Alain 31
Janicijevic, Dusan 119, 152, 165
Janin, Joëlle 98
Janisse, Fernand 18
Jannetti, Ettore 19, 176, 186
Janni, Paolo 99, 131
Janota, Armando 205
Janowski, Olga 131
Jaquillard, Henri 56
Jason and the Argonauts 64
Jaspe, José 35, 43, 47, 48, 65, 68, 104, 125, 133, 134, 150, 157, 168
Javert, Nino 55, 135
Javier, Nicholás 47
Jeannine, Sonja 28
Jeffries, Lang 17, 58, 140, 167
Jemma, Jean-Louis 87
Jemma, Ottavio 64, 102, 150
Jhenkins, Jho 20
Joannnon, Léo 18
Joffe, Benjamin Michael 207
John-Mary 32
Johnson, Richard 142
Johnston, Alena 18
Jojo, Ludovico Della 208
Jolly Film 164
Jones, Dickie 22
Jones, Erika 55
Jones, J.J. 207
Jonia Film 41, 81, 82, 114, 137, 139
Jordán, Ángel 116
Jordan, Dick 160
Jordan, Louis 18

Jordan, Mary 152
Jorgen, Erika 124
Jorger, Erica 191
Josephson, Lance 203
Josipovici, Jean 95
Jotta, Elio 146
Jourdan, Louis 19
Journet, Marcel 42
Journey Beneath the Desert (Antinea, l'amante della città sepolta) 102
Jovanovic, Toma 41
Jovic, Ljubica 60
Jovine, Fabrizio 142
Judith and Holophernes (Giuditta e Oloferne) 9
Juillard, Robert 42
Jukas, Ante 59
Junker, Frédéric 31
Juno Produzione 188
Jurado, Katy 25
Juran, Nathan 42
Jurgens, Curt 118, 178
Jurgenson, Albert 112
Juri, Raika 194

Kacic, Mila 154
Kaciceva, Milo 154
Kamante, Lou 199
Kamel, Joe 46, 73, 119, 131, 137
Kamenov, Vasil 165
Kandil, Hussein 104
Kanin, Fay 168
Kanin, Michael 168
Kantof, Albert 164
Kaplan, Nelly 42
Karina, Anna 150
Karinska, Barbara 184
Karis, Vassili 20, 29, 35, 102, 164, 171, 176
Karis, Vic 20
Karlsen, John 131, 192
Karr, Mabel 39
Karshin, Robert 200
Kasapic, Nada 165
Kast, Pierre 134
Kaufmann, Christine 41, 105, 168
Kavouras, Takis 64, 129
Kaza, Elisabeth 203
Kein, Pat 160
Keith, Robert 50
Keller, Hiram 165
Kellin, Laurie 198, 200
Kelly, Walter 202
Kemplen, Ralph 27
Kendall, Tony 29, 114
Kennedy, Arthur 25
Kent, Maria 58
Kent, Stanley 179
Kerim, Son of the Sheik (Il figlio dello sceicco) 103
Kerima 125, 190
Kertes, Arpad 45
Kessler, Alice 52, 159
Kessler, Ellen 52, 159
Kessler, Quin 205
Ketoff, Paolo 92
Khoshabe, Iloosh (a.k.a. Rod Flash) 16, 92, 100, 188
Kibiska, Litz 191

Kieffer, Louis 60, 130
Kiehl, William 25
Kim, Edilio 22, 198, 202
Kindar the Invulnerable (Kindar l'invulnerabile) 103
Kindred, Robert 184
King Kong (1933) 70, 198
King Kong (1976) 49
King of Kings 120
King, Thomas 176
Kingston, Shirley 198, 200
Kirsanoff, Monique 42
Kiss Me Deadly 159
Kitzmiller, John 19, 113, 130, 139, 159, 166, 177
Klaus, Eric 99
Klein, Georges 178
Klein, Pat 160
Klein, Rita 111, 142
Klein, Robert 194
Kleine, George 8, 10, 14
Klimovsky, León 47
Kline, Kristin 204
Klinger, David P. 204
Knef, Hildegard 34
Knewels, Michele 200
Knight Without a Country (Il cavaliere senza terra) 104
Knights of Terror (Il terrore dei mantelli rossi) 104
Knippenberg, Herbert 128
Knives of the Avenger (I coltelli del vendicatore) 104
Knowles, Cyril J. 158
Knupp, Don 203
Kodiak Films 208
Kolosoff, Tersicore 35, 56, 81, 82, 110, 133
Koloss 111
Kores, Raphael 29
Kosanovic, Dejan 118
Koscina, Sylva 43, **78,** 80, 92, **94,** 119, 155, 168
Koster, Nat 177
Košutnjak 100
Kramer, Eric Allan 202
Kramer, Eric Allen 202
Kramer, Stanley 43
Krasker, Robert 51
Kraushaar, Raoul 21
Kresel, Lee 70, 131, 143, 145
Krims, Milton 54, 151
Krivokapic, Kosta 18, 35, 73, 76, 118, 165, 191
Kromberg, Ernest 54, 77, 107, 119, 125, 132, 133, 134, 147, 177
Krstic, Aleksander 99
Krstulovic, Vladimir 138
Kruger, Lea 184
Kruger, Sven 200
Krupa, Gene 33
Krupp, Mara 112
Kubrick, Stanley 14, 138, 156
Kulakowski, Günther 147
Kumar, Ananda 149
Kurland, Norton 51
Kuveiller, Luigi 44, 164

L'Arvor, Yann 143

La Laurette, Huguette 31
La Macchia, Nico 204
La Penna, Leslie J. 203
La Roche, Josette 43
La Rosa, Pina 207
La Rue, Eva 199
La Torre, Giuseppe 56, 165, 174
Labb, Michel Thomas, Benoite 31
Labbaye, Marcel 194
Labussière, Jacques 112
Lacourt, Guy 178
Lacy International Films 147
Ladd, Alan 3, 50
Ladd, Alana 50
Laffargue, Paul 178
Lagerkvist, Pär 24
Lago, Salvatore 178
Lagos, Vicky 106, 163
Lagrange, Valérie 124
Laguna, María Dolores 154
Lalande, Arlette 178
LaMarr, Hedy 54
Lamas, Fernando 138
Lamb, Felix 204
Lambert, Colette 31
Lammers, Carl 203
Lancaster, Alan 164, 179
Lancia, Cesare 77, 178
Lander, Lea 184
Landers, Lilly 150
Landi, Aldo Bufi 15, 34, 102, 106, 113, 125, 135, 143, 146, 153, 166, 176, 178, 187
Landi, Cinzia 103
Landi, Gino 84, 119
Landi, Rossana 146
Landini, Fanny 130
Landolini, Mario 169
Landry, Gérard 21, 24, 28, 29, 46, 104, 125, 129, 130, 134, 166, 168
Lane, Abbe 30
Lane, Francis 58, 192
Lane, Jocelyn 113, 140, 189
Lane, John 142
Lane, John Francis 192
Lane, Mara 127, 154
Lane, Mike 186
Lane, Tim 203
Lanfranchi, Mario 194
Lang, Fritz 186
Lang, Stefy 150
Lang, Stevenson 100
Lange, Claudie 27, 100
Langella, Franco 49
Lante, Diana 46
Lantieri, Franco 163
Lanzano, Umberto 141
Laporte, Leonie 8
Lara, Antonio 47
Lara, Francisco 113
Lara, Nadia 34, 45, 168
Larbi, Benchekroun 110, 158
Lariviere, Colette 130
LaRoche, Maurice 20
Larraya, Aurelio G. 147
Larraya, Federico G. 147
Larreda, Mauel Torres 109
Larry, Roger 202
LaRue, Eva 199

Larvor, Yann 39, 143
Lasala, Luis 37
Laselli, Rinascimento 54
Lassander, Dagmar 28
The Last Days of Pompeii (Gli ultimi giorni di Pompei) [1908] 9
The Last Days of Pompeii (Gli ultimi giorni di Pompei) [1913] 10
The Last Days of Pompeii (Gli ultimi giorni di Pompei) [1960] 48, **105**
The Last Days of Pompeii (1935) 31
The Last of the Vikings (L'ultimo dei Vikinghi) 106
The Last Tzar (Gli ultimi zar) 10
Lastricati, Giorgio 135
Laterza, Giovanni 155
Lathière, Marcel 31
Latimer, Carlo 84, 102, 111, 187
Latimore, Frank 24, 33, 48, 125, 154
LaTour, Joëlle 150
Lattanzi, Tina 34, 49, 122, 132
Lattanzio, Roberto 207
Lattuada, Bianca 168
Laudani, Evelina 129
Laudati, Folco 67
Laurent, Agnès 125
Laurenti, Giuliano 155
Laurenti, Mariano 20, 124, 182
Laurenti, Romolo 135
Laurentino, Mario 158
Laurenzi, Giancarlo 203
Lauri, Mirella D. 22
Lauriault, Andre 43
Lauricella, Giuseppe 196
Laurier, Sara 161
Lautner, Georges 164
Lavagnino, Angelo Francesco 23, 34, 37, 43, 50, 52, 63, 73, 76, 80, 84, 88, 89, 91, 98, 102, 105, 112, 116, 126, 127, 130, 140, 141, 143, 145, 155, 159, 169, 171, 186, 189, 190, 192, 194, 195, 196
Lavi, Daliah 43
Law, John Phillip 165
Lawrence, André 152
Lawrence, Marc 176
Lawrence, Robert 51
Lawrence, Sid 20
Lay, Lore 9
Lay, Ubaldo 33, 129, 176
Laydu, Claude 22
Layman, Jeff "Stump" 204
Lazaga, Pedro 65
Lazzari, Niccolò 33, 43, 118
Lazzari, Piero 25, 122, 152, 158
Lazzaro, Walter 46, 55
Lazzazzera, Assunto 80, 92, 106, 178
L. C. J. Editions and Productions 26, 46, 176
Leader Film 201
Leda Film 142
Lee, Belinda 118
Leadbetter, Cindy 198
Leal, José 16
Leblond, Georges 124
Lebon, Yvette 16, 36, 126, 186
Lecón, Sixto 159
Ledda, Victor 55, 135, 186
Ledoux, Fernand 34

230　Index

LeDuc, Tito 36, 161
Lee, Belinda 41, 67, 116, 127, 164
Lee, Christopher 90, 126
Lee, Margaret **57,** 58, 143
Lee, Paul Mac 161
Lees, Tamara 125, 135, 172, 181
Lefebvre, Robert 118
Lefèvre, Charlotte 31
Lega, Augusto 139
Legions of the Nile (Le legioni di Cleopatra) 106
Leib, Vladimir 154
Lelli, Anna 206
Lemaire, Paul 56
Lembo, Lilli 128
Lembo, Nino 194
Lemick, Michael E. 198
Lemoigne, Denise 56
Lemoine, Michel 98, 131
Lena, Antonio Schiavo 28, 30, 64, 67, 81, 82, 131, 149, 166
Lena, Lia 36
Lenci, Alfredo 8
Lentini, Massimo 200, 201, 202
Lenzey, Margaret 202
Lenzi, Laura 198
Lenzi, Olga Pehar 204
Lenzi, Umberto 34, 77, 102, 118, 133, 145, 147, 157, 171, 178, 203
Leonardi, Amedeo 207
Leondoff, Ileana 9
Leone, Carla 39, 44
Leone Film 73, 122, 152, 153
Leone, Gippo 112, 195
Leone, Ignazio 28, 30, 36, 114, 125, 130, 139, 157, 167
Leone, Sergio 19, 37, 39, 40, 50, 54, 105, 152, 155, 157, 158, 162, 176, 159
Leoni, Guido 195
Leoni, Piero 189
Leonviola, Antonio (*a.k.a.* Leonviola) 20, 122, 170, 171, 175
Lepetit, Pierre 14
Lepre, Gerardo 199
Leri, Piero 46, 87, 178
Leros, Ramón 40
Leroy, Frank 36, 143
Leroy, Michael 18
Leroy, Phillippe 18
Lerro, Rocco 110, 197, 202
Lesaffre, Roland 169
Lesina, Jack 203
Lesoeur 155
Lester, Joanna 203
Lester, Lewis 204
Lester, Richard 59
Leurini, Gino 55, 132
Leurini, Paolo 205
Leutzinger, Eric 27
Levi, Paolo 125
Levin, Henry 192
Levine, Gary 204
Levine, Joseph E. 1, 41, 78, 80, 92, 124, 158, 175, 192
Lévy, Georges 31
Lévy, Raoul 112
Lewis, Jerry 159
Lewis, Reg 58
Leydet, Mirelle 31

Leyva, Mery 159
Liberati, Alberto 104, 158, 162
Liberatore, Ugo 22, 41, 99, 103, 126, 128, 147, 179
Liber Film 54, 78, 107, 135, 147, 151
Libo, Bob 200
Licari, Rod 113
Licari, Rodolfo 113
Licastro, Walter 81, 133
Lieb, Vladimir 127
Lifshitz, Charles 128
Liger, Fernando 116
Ligobbi, Mario 95
Lillo, Nino 104
Lilló, Ricardo G. 27, 150
Lillo, Silvio 130
Limentani, Annalena 119
Limiti, Adriana 166
Limot, Walter 118, 178
Linares, Antonio Navarro 166
Linares, Gonzalo 24
Lindt, Rosemarie 161
Liné, Helga 16, 18, 40, 76, 89, 109, 140, 151, 164, 179
Lines, Alba 201
Ling, Melissa 204
Linke, Ned 204
The Lion of St. Mark (Il leone di San Marco) 107
The Lion of Thebes (Leone di Tebe) 107, **108, 109**
Lionello, Oreste 26, 48, 111
Liotta, Palmiro 200
Lippens, Lucien 118
Lippert Pictures 132
Liro, Bob 200
Lisi, Virna 51
Lissiak 33
Lister, Clement 150
Littera, Giampiero 30
Little, Joe 198, 200
Little, John 203
Livius, Titus 7, 29
Lizalde, José Luis 167
Lizzani, Carlo 50
Llinas, Pierangeli 28
Llopart, Gabriel 126
Lloyd, Richard 92, 100
Lluch, José Luis 24, 127, 167
Lluch, Miguel 55
Loaysa, Antonio Ramírez de 47
Locatelli, Erina 191
Locchi, Pino 155, 174
Loche, Marcel 42
Loddi, Loris 73, 82, 146
Lodi-Fè, Maurizio 158
Lodi, Loris 92
Lodolini, Mario 98
Lofaro, Tigano 22, 106
Loffreda, Giovanni 207
Loffredi, Armando 103
Loffredi, Franco 73
Loffredi, Massimo 199
Loffredo, Gaetano 18
Logan, Gregg 204
Lohman, Augie 27
Lolli, Franco 25, 28, 41, 54, 64, 70, 87, 89, 104, 110, 116, 122, 156, 157, 168, 174, 189

Lolli, Giancarlo 25
Lollobrigida, Gina 136, 182, 183
Lom, Herbert 51
Loma, José Antonio de la 150, 201
Lombard, Peter 201
Lombardi, Angelo 27
Lombardi, Carlo 29, 33, 46, 60, 99, 139, 165
Lombardi, Guglielmo 135, 174
Lombardi, Rodolfo 119, 135, 174
Lombardi, Ugo 46, 136
Lombardo, Goffredo 67, 158
Lombardo, Mara 122, 155
Lombardo, Marilyn 25
Lombardo, Paolo 46
Lombardozzi, Giulio 9, 10, 12
Lombroso, Henry 189
Loncar, Beba 115
London, Eve 204
Long Live Robin Hood (L'arciere di fuoco) 107
Longari, Renata 174
Longhi, Marcello 199, 203
Longmuir, John 18
Longo, Franco 139
Longo, Germano 19, 49, 51, 77, 127, 129, 133, 138, 141, 153, 158, 178
Longo, Guglielmo 46
Longo, Malissa 18, 195, 201, 206
Longo, Maria Luisa 195
Longo, Tiziano 178
Lopert, Tanya 47, 163
López, Antonia 154
López, Charo 113
Lopez, Don 204
Lopez, Jean 198
López, José Timoteo 119–120
López, Manuel Villegas 47
Lopez, Rico 31
López, Simón 16, 47
Lopez, Sylvia 92, **93,** 94, **98,** 99, 163
Loquenzi, Franco 146, 155
Loren, Sophia 22, 50, 51, **181,** 182, **182,** 183
Lorenzi, Silvio 20, 201, 206
Lorenzon, Livio 19, 21, 28, 32, 34, 35, 49, 60, 67, 69, **70, 70,** 73, 77, 80, 89, 101, 113, 114, 118, 126, 130, 133, 137, 139, 140, 141, 143, 151, 160, 163, 173, 174, 187
Loret, Susanne 122
Lori, Cleo 202
Lorys, Diana 139, 154
Loti, Gianni 46, 60, 94, 96, 127, 134
Lotti, Angelo 22, 24, 78, 99, 103, 107, 125, 128, 131, 135, 147, 171
Louise, Marie 19
Louise, Tina 3, 155, **190,** 191
Lousek, Gilda 136
Lovan, Luigina 112
Lovatelli, Giovanni 192
Lovcen Film 50, 179, 191
Love, Lucretia 19, 26, 48, 126
The Loves and Times of Scaramouche (La avventure e gli amori di Scaramouche) 110
The Loves of Salammbo (Salambò) 110
Le Lovre Film 23
Lowens, Curt 25

Lowle, Gianfranco 50, 132
Loy, Barbara 111, 131
Loy, Dina 55
Loy, Mino 63
Loyer, Raymond 145
Lozano, Carmen 159
Lozzi, Edmond 48, 68, 127, 154, 171, 175
Lualdi, Antonella 115, 122, 127, 151, 163
Lubin, Arthur 175
Lucantoni, Alberto 27
Lucari, Gianni Hecht 23, 190
Lucatelli, Marina 36
Lucchini, Maurizio 84
Lucchini, Walter 204
LUCE Studios 64
Luceri, Ignazio 90, 134
Lucherini, Enrico 207
Luciani, Rosa 44, 55, 95
Luciani, Sebastiano A 45
Lucidi, Alessandro 198, 206
Lucidi, Maurizio 32, 70, 87, 92, 113, 124, 127, 163, 169
Lucidi, Renzo 50, 130, 134, 168
Lucignani, Paolo 122
Luda, Gianni 125, 141, 176
Ludovico, Cesare Vico 49
Lugar, Keith 126
Lugosi, Bela 80
Luis Film 126
Luisi, Daniele G. 36, 173
Lukschy, Wolfgang 88
Lulli, Folco 36, 42, 52, 99, 113, 138, 142, 155, 168, 170
Lulli, Piero 21, 23, 26, 30, 32, 33, 35, 40, 46, 51, 59, 64, 65, 73, 84, 89, 99, 106, 111, 138, 139, 140, 168, 181, 186, 76–77
Lullo, Tullio 203
Luna, Antonio 16
Lunda, Elena 9, 10
Luong, Ham-Chau 145
Luongo, Guy 51
Luotto, Gene 140, 151, 197
Luotto, Steven 201, 203
Luparia, Patrizia 26
Lupi, Ignacio 7, 14
Lupi, Roldano 23, 62, 81, 98, 124, 137, 152
Lupo, Alberto 24, 60, 99, 107, 114, 120, 160, 168, 176, 186
Lupo, Michael 37
Lupo, Michele 73, 138, 152, 153, 155
Lupus, Peter (*a.k.a.* Rock Stevens) 35, 63, 76, 89
Luraschi, Luigi 24, 27
Lux Compagnie Cinématographique de France 60, 94, 174, 175
Lux Film 22, 34, 42, 50, 94, 124, 136, 170, 186, 192
Lux Film-Roma 174
Luzi, Enrico 178
Luzi, Lello 30, 138, 167
Luzi, Maria Pia 200
Luzzatto, Guido 33
Luzzi, Enrico 207
Lycan, Georges 67, 178
Lynch, Richard 199

Lyons, Cliff 112, 113
Lyre Film 21, 24, 52, 107
Lyssa 29
Lytess, Natasha 25
Lytton, George Bulwer 10

Macario, Erminio 58
Macasoli, Antonio 29
Maccari, Giuseppe 27
Maccari, Ruggero 49, 182
Maccarinelli, Angeluccio 203
Macchi, Egisto 23
Macchi, Valentino 143, 159, 196
Maccione, Aldo 110
MacDouglas, John 111
Macedo, Enrique 159
Macinelli, Bruno 199
Maciste Against the Sheik (Maciste contro lo scecio) 110
Maciste Against the Sheikh (Maciste contro lo sceicco) 10
Maciste and Prisoner No. 51 (Maciste und der sträfling nr. 51) 14
Maciste and the Chinese Trunk (Maciste und die chinesische truhe) 14
Maciste and the Japanese (Maciste und die Japenerin) 14
Maciste and the Silver King's Daughter (Maciste e la figlia re dell'argento) 14
Maciste Faces Death (Maciste contro la morte) see The Trilogy of Maciste
Maciste in Hell (Maciste all inferno) 10
Maciste in Love (Maciste innamorato) 11
Maciste in the Lion's Cage (Maciste nella gabbia dei leoni) 11
Maciste on Vacation (Maciste in vacanza) 12
Maciste Rescued from the Waters (Maciste salvato dalle acque) 12
Maciste the Athlete (Maciste atleta) 12
Maciste the Clairvoyant (Maciste medium) 12
Maciste the Detective (Maciste poliziotto) 12
Maciste the First (Maciste I) 12
Maciste the Ranger (Maciste bersagliere) 12
Maciste, the Strongest Man in the World see The Molemen vs. The Son of Hercules
Maciste the Tourist (Maciste Turista) 14
Maciste the Warrior (Maciste alpino) 12
Maciste vs. Maciste (Maciste contro Maciste) 13
Maciste vs. the Monsters see The Fire Monster Against the Son of Hercules
Maciste, the Avenger of the Mayans (Maciste il vendicatore dei Maya) 111
Maco, Jerzy 67
Macua, Ángeles 159
Maculani, Giovanna 44
Maculani, Giulio 15, 29, 54, 91, 92, 107, 114, 137, 179, 189

Madal, Jean Claude 64
Madalena, Giorgio Mecchia 168
Maddalena, Renato 91, 140
Maddaleni, Gianni 39, 163, 179
Madison, G. 142
Madison, Guy 15, 54, 135, 147, 157, 167
Madison, Larry 59
Maesso, José Gutiérrez 150
Maestosi, Walter 140
Maestri, Anna 112
Mafai, Giulia 70, 129
Mafera, Vasco 28
Maffei, Livio 20, 112, 143, 161, 164, 175
Maffre, Julien 42
Mafrino, Guido 167
Maggi, Amina Pirani 114, 130, 167
Maggi, Andrea 203
Maggi, Evelina 188
Maggi, G. 165
Maggi, Luigi 9, 12, 13
Maggi, Mario 59, 127, 142, 154
Maggi, Maurizio 203
Maggio, Dante 32, 45, 137, 150
Maggio, Domenico 48
Maggio, Enzo 84, 114, 129, 139, 176, 186
Maggio, Mimmo 56, 58, 111, 167
Maggio, Pupella 27
Maggio, Rosalia 102, 137
Maggio, Tony 176
Maggio, Vincenzo 164
Magherini, Flavio 184
Magic Films 195
Magli, Fiorenzo 76, 107, 177
Magnanti, Elda 27, 181
Magnanti, Renata 118, 172
Magni, Raimondo 64
The Magnificent Adventurer see The Burning of Rome
The Magnificent Gladiator (Il magnifico gladiatore) 111
The Magnificent Robin Hood (Il magnifico Robin Hood) 111
Magrini, Bona 32, 103, 158
Maher, Sherifa 104
Mahin, John Lee 25
Mahin-Rackin 26
Mahor, María 107, 195
Maietto, Carlo 203
Mainardi, Elisa 84
Mainwaring, Daniel 120, 140
Maioletti, Gianfranco 200
Maiolini, Alba 187, 201
Mairesse, Guy 134
Maiuri, Arduino 18
Maján, Juan 107
Majeroni, Achille 34, 46
Majestic Film 191
Majurec, Anna 175
Makowska, Helena 13, 55
Malacrida, Dino 124
Malagoli, Milo 122
Malaguti, Bruna 146
Malandrucco, Angela 37
Malantrucco, Angelo 21, 68, 105
Malasardi, Anna 141
Malasomma, Nunzio 140

232 Index

Malaspina, Michele 15, 50, 126, 129
Malatesta, Mirella 143
Malatesta, Rthe enzo 22
Malavasi, Renato 26, 114, 186
Malcolm, Robert 156
Maldi, Silvana 176
Maleff, Maria 122
Maletesta, Guido 34, 36, 47, 56, 58, 60, 68, 78, 102, 111, 139, 143, 145
Maletesta, Mirella 58
Malevasi, Renato 146
Malier, Carla 58
Mallia, Anna 31
Mallorqui, José 116, 154
Maltagliati, Evi 58, 165, 186
Mambor, Renato 36
Mambretti, Mario 174
Mammi, Fulvia 132
Mamura, M. 143
Mananiello, A. 127
Manara, Luciano 104
Manca, Alberto 19, 21, 95, 110
Mancini, Carla 18, 112, 156
Mancini, Ennio 17
Mancini, Ettore 201
Mancini, M.P. 59
Mancini, Maria Pia 39, 55
Mancini, Mario 49, 58, 92, 141
Mancini, Mauro 55
Mancini, Silvano 19, 62, 103, 169
Mancino, Pasquale 31, 58, 91
Mancori, Alvaro 54, 73, 76, 92, 106, 107, 122, 151, 158, 160, 177, 186
Mancori, David 200, 205
Mancori, Guglielmo 15, 73, 138, 153, 171, 175, 206
Mancori, Sandro 54, 76, 102, 107, 122, 138, 152, 158, 164, 177, 186, 200, 205
Mandini, Galileo 20, 59, 73, 127, 138, 154, 161, 163, 164
Mandini, Guido 179
Manes, Giacoma 199
Manes, Mina 204
Manetti, Alberto 31
Manetti, Lido 10
Manfredi, Manfredo 103
Manganiello, A. 59
Mangano, Giuseppe 199
Mangano, Riccardo 55
Mangano, Rocco Roy 17, 25
Mangano, Roy 17
Mangano, Silvana 25, 184, 186
Mangianello, A. 142, 154
Mangini, Gino 20, 30, 32, 44, 60, 69
Mangini, Luigi 22
Mangione, Giuseppe 47, 102, 110, 119, 122, 155
Maniac 11
Manlandrucco, Angelo 21
Mann, Anthony 51
Mann, Lewis 160
Mannatrizio, Mauro 87, 178
Manni, Alberto 59
Manni, Ettore 18, 21, 22, 36, 64, 67, 87, 91, 106, 111, 129, 135, 140, 169, 176, 182, 189, 190
Mannini, Giorgio 45
Mannini, Ottavio 33

Mannino, Franco 67, 91, 124, 140, 153
Mannino, Vincenzo 140
Mannitrizio, Mauro 184
Mannix, Edward 200, 208
Mannola, Maurizio 102
Mannoni, Roberto 102
Mannuzzi, Nella 181
Mansfield, Jayne 3, 95, **95, 96,** 96
Manson, Héléna 96
Mantovani, Lily 36, 91, 102
Manunza, Masino 60
Manzano, Clemente 159
Manzari, Nicola 165
Manzi, Gianni 206
Manzon, Ginette 56
Marais, Jean 31, 42, 130
Marakova, Jana 18
Maran, Evaristo 192, 195
Marandi, Evi 50, 137
Marangoni, Ada 13
Marangoni, Gina 7
Marangoni, Teresa 8
Marascalchi, Petro 138
Marascalchi, Pietro 21, 98
Maravidi, Mirella 27
Marazzi, Alfredo 194
Marcari, Paola 198
Marceau, Violette 50
Marcellini, Romolo 45
Marcellini, Siro 26, 48, 151
Marcello, Giorgio 46
March, Philippe 56
March, Pier Vittorio 184
Marchal, Georges 39, 106, 151, 155, 174, 186, 190
Marchand, Claude 130, 155
Marchant, Gilbert D. 27
Marchent, Carlos Romero 23, 154
Marchent, Joaquin Luis Romero 154
Marchent, Rafael Romero 23, 154
Marchesi, Marcello 49, 90
Marchesini, Nino 28, 33, 104
Marchetti, Alfredo 167
Marchetti, Giulio 15, 54, 107, 133, 135, 142, 147, 151, 168
Marchetti, Nino 46, 94, 99, 128, 131, 141, 143
Marchi, Maria 25
Marchi, Pier Vittorio 26, 60, 73, 76, 84, 88, 89, 103, 111, 118, 138, 139, 153, 172, 179, 181, 184
Marchiori, Aldo 200, 205
Marciani, Danilo 70, 87, 90
Marco Claudia Cinematografica 112
Marco Polo (L'avventura di un italiano in Cina) 112, 145
Marco the Magnificent (Le fabuleuse aventure de Marco Polo) 112
Marco, Alex 195
Marco, José 40, 67, 101, 151, 154
Marco, Lluis 69
Marconi, Walter 201
Marcos, Arturo 126
Marcus, Alexandre 31, 42
Marcus, Éliane 31
Marelli, Ubaldo 49, 54
Mareschalchi, Alberto 100
Marganiello, Alfredo 163, 179

Margheriti, Antonella 207
Margheriti, Antonio 47, 55, 63, 67, 91, 189, 207
Margheriti, Edoardo 207
Marholm, Alf 104
Mari, Anna 9
Mari, Fiorella 125
Marián, Miguel Pérez 47
Marianecci, Aldo 195
Mariani, Fiorella 197
Mariani, Giuseppe 65
Mariani, Marco 92, 134
Mariani, Vincenzo 30
Marietti, Antonio 49
Marietto 62, 164
Marignano, Renzo 110
Marija, Marin 164
Marin, Christian 165
Marin, Francisco 127, 166, 179, 183
Marin, Giancarlo 67
Marin, Guillermo 106
Marin, Luciano 34, 50, 58, 60, 64, 69, 87, 111, 143, 155, 163, 165, 170, 189
Marin, Luis 167
Marina, José 47
Mariné, Juan 42
Marinelli, Renato 59, 171, 194
Marini, Antonio 49, 59, 73, 83, 138, 142, 191
Marini, Italia 83, 116, 192
Marini, Lamberto 197
Marini, Tulio 207
Marino, Nino 206
Marino, Stefano 205
Marinuzzi, Gino, Jr. 87, 134
Marion, Jean 31
Marion, Mary 119
Mario Voller-Buzzi 12
Maris, Lia 10
Mark of Zorro (E io lo dico a Zzzzorro!) 113
Markov, Margaret 19
Markovic, Branko 191
Marletta, Franco 126
Marlier, Carla 22
Marlowa, Nadia 114
Marlowe, Scott 22
Marmol, G. Cesare 58, 106
Maro, Publius Vergilius 22
Marodan, Dan 202
Marotti, Giuseppe 154
Marquand, Christian 22
Marquette, André 31
Márquez, Luz 150
Marras, Franco 205
Marrazzini, Carlo 134
Marrocco, Giuseppe 113, 189
Marrosu, Amedeo 157
Marrosu, Arnaldo 106, 125, 175
Mars, God of War (Marte, dio della guerra) 113
Marsala, Michele 22, 99, 103, 207
Marsetti, Graziella 177
Marshall, Anthony 168
Martel, Christiane 174
Martella, Giancarlo 138
Martelli, Arnaldo 68, 127, 154, 159
Martelli, Augusto 111, 112
Martelli, Otello 42

Martello, Rodolfo 163
Marti, Eugenio 40
Martignon, Cesare 164
Martin, Carmen 47, 68, 140
Martín, Daniel 166
Martin, Eugenio 32
Martin, Fidel 190
Martin, George 24, 101, 112
Martín, José Manuel 40, 150
Martín, Julián 51
Martin, Leonardo 40
Martin, Lucía 154
Martin, Pepe 65
Martinelli, Alfredo 10, 49
Martinelli, Elsa 31, 113
Martinelli, Sergio 160
Martinenghi, Italo 90
Martinez, Manuel 47
Martini, Antonio 153
Martino, Lea 203
Martino, Luciano 23, 35, 37, 50, 63, 64, 76, 77, 81, 82, 87, 89, 102, 122, 127, 129, 130, 133, 186, 190, 194, 203
Martino, Ray 154
Martino, Sergio 80
Martucci, Federico 199
Martufi, Guido 80
Marturano, Franco 33
Marturano, Gino 88, 102, 134, 137, 149, 194
Marturano, Luigi 68, 133
Marus, Aldo 9
Maruzzi, Franco 109
The Marvelous Maciste (Maciste) 13
Marvin, Irvin 203
Marx, Rick 207
Marx, Samuel 43
Mary, Renaud 18
Marzelli, Giorgio 36, 56, 58, 167
Marzelli, Valerio 58
Marzi, Franca 136, 160
Marzilli, Wilma 199
Marzio, Duilio 136
Marzot, Vera 81, 138
Marzulli, Claudio 90, 134, 173
Mascagno, Renato 87, 88, 98, 143
Mascetti, Gina 34, 59, 175, 192
Mascetti, Rina 92, 129
Masciocchi, Marcello 23, 64, 77, 102, 113, 150, 207
Masciocchi, Mauro 200, 207
Masciocchi, Raffaele 17, 30, 35, 64, 67, 77, 81, 82, 133, 137, 140, 153, 166
Masé, Marino 77, 194
Masetti, Enzo 21, 54, 78, 92, 165
Masini, Giuseppe 64, 103
Masini, Nino 47, 55
Mask of the Musketeers (Zorro e i tre moschettieri) 114
The Masked Conqueror (Zorro alla corte di Spagna) 114
The Masked Man Against the Pirates (L'uomo mascherato contro i pirati) 114
Maslow, Joan 25
Maslow, Walter 25
Mason, Terry 28

Massaccesi, Aristide 19, 32, 48
Massaccesi, Daniele 200
Massaccesi, Mario 197
Massacesi, Aristede 207
Massacre in the Black Forest (Il massacro della foresta nera) 115
Massara, Natale 197, 199, 202
Massari, Aristide 16
Massari, Lea 39
Massay, Arlette 178
Masseroni, Adriana 50
Massetti, Ivanna 198, 205
Massi, Stelvio 20, 49, 50, 119, 143, 156, 161, 164
Massi, Vittorio 103
Massiet, Henri 178
Massimi, Pierre 178
Massimini, Giulio 60
Massini, Pierre 178
Masson, Lucien 42
Masson, Yvette 78, 130
Mastripietri, Augusto 8, 14
Mastrocinque, Maria 192
Mastrocinque, Piero 186
Mastrogirolamo, Atos 199
Mastroianni, Ruggero 156
Masullo, Gennaro 49, 141
Matania, Clelia 133, 141
Maté, Rudolph 25, 152, 153
Mateos, Jaime 27
Mateos, Jesús 37
Mateos, Julián 43
Materassi, Vanni 122, 131
Matesanz, José Luis 151
Mathias, Bob 120, 122
Mathius, Christine 161
Matiradonna, Mario 154, 159
Mato 203
Mattei, Bruno 30, 58, 110, 119, 127, 129, 154, 163, 165, 174, 179, 204
Mattei, Danilo 204
Mattei, Domenico 163, 179
Mattei, Giuseppe 26, 59, 111, 127, 154, 171, 176
Mattei, Pino 154, 171, 176
Matteo, Giordano 204
Mattera, Gino 80, 94
Matthews, Kerwin 191
Mattia, Ettore 80
Mattioli, Luisa 125
Mattioli, Raf 24, 130
Mattioli, Roberto 52
Mattoli, Mario 90, 182
Mattras, Christian 150
Matul, Niko 17, 127, 154
Maturano, Gino 21
Mature, Victor 77, 169, **169,** 170
Maudru, Pierre 104
Maumy, Jean 149
Maunsell, David 25
Maurano, Silvio 45
Mauri, Roberto 100, 102, 149, 150, 176, 192
Maurice, Franck 42
Mauro, Donatella 192
Mauro, Gianni 40
Mauro, Jole 41, 92, 101, 102
Mauroni, Giulio 186
Maury, Jacques 165

Maury, Jean 147
MAX Film 119, 133
Max Productions 134
May, Elena 129, 191
May, Leontine 179
Mayans, Antonio 51, 141, 150
Mayberg, Katharina 49
Mayer, Josephine 203
Mayer, Kirk 160
Mayniel, Juliette 179
Mayo, Alfredo 43, 107, 139
Mayo, Virginia 139
Mayuzumi, Toshirô 27
Mazen, Omneya "Nini" 199
Mazza, Fernando 67
Mazza, Manlio 7
Mazzelli, Anna 173
Mazzi, Gilberto 29, 118, 137
Mazzolotti, Pier Angelo 8
Mazzoni, Carlo 186
Mazzoni, Franca 49, 128
Mazzoni, Mario 91
McBride, Ed 198, 200
McCallum, Gordon K. 51
McCollins, Chris 26
McCoy, Peter 198, 201, 206
McCulley, Johnston 102
McDonald, Audrey 34, 191
McLeay, Andrew 205
McNamara, Richard 36, 40, 54, 59, 62, 68, 80, 84, 96, 103, 107, 116, 131, 147, 164, 169, 172
McReedy, Ed 25
McWhite, Ely 187
Mea, Antonio 200
Mecacci, Pierantonio 59, 127, 142, 154, 156
Mecacci, Piero 20, 127, 143, 161, 163, 164, 179
Medar, Vladimir 58, 115, 119, 165, 168
Medde, Marina 200
Medin, Gastone 49
Medin, Harriet 52, 166
Medina, Patricia 134
Medusa Against the Son of Hercules (Perseo l'invincibile) **115,** 115, 116, **117**
Medusa Distribuzione 204
Megowan, Don 77
Meisel, Kurt 165
Mejovsek, Damir 110
Mejuto, Andrés 16, 23, 166, 183
Melchiorre, Manrico 167
Mele, Luigi 14
Meleranci, Sergio 202
Melidoni, Alfredo 30
Melingò, Renata 51
Melita, Anna 20
Mell, Marisa 203
Mella, Eloy 65, 100, 116, 119, 151
Mellone, Amedeo 20, 31, 77, 83, 91, 132, 133, 134, 136, 141, 151, 173, 177, 178, 204
Melloni, Armando 204
Melnati, Umberto 68
Meloni, Giuseppe 205
Ménard, Roland 96
Menconi, Mauro 201

Méndez, Guillermo 24, 154
Menéndez, Ángel 159, 24, 120
Menéndez, Rafael 39
Mengoli, Marisa 39
Mengoni, Fabrizio 206
Menichelli, Angiolina 91, 116, 167
Menichelli, Pena 7
Menichelli, Rosalba 30, 58
Meniconi, Furio 16, 22, 32, 34, 45, 63, 67, 69, 91, 109, 124, 130, 136, 141, 152, 160, 170, 173, 188
Meniconi, Mario 32, 34, 62, 160, 173
Meniconi, Nello 160, 175
Menzies, William Cameron 132
Mérand, Jean-Philippe 103
Merangel, Charles 42
Mercanti, Pino 29, 106
Mercati, Mario 12
Merchant, W.M. 27
Mercier, Michèle 23, 127, 192
Mercuri, Ardulino 36
Mercuri, Paolo 21, 32, 52, 60, 84, 189
Mercury Films 23, 103
Merino, Antonio 24
Merino, José Luis 125, 141, 195
Merino, Mario 195
Merino, Miguel 154
Merkel, Adriano 19, 21, 65, 103, 120
Merli, Francesco 51
Merli, Silvana 30
Merlo, Maria Luisa 119
Merola, Alfonso 154
Merolla, Ferdinando 203
Merolle, Enzo 36, 129, 130, 155
Merolle, Rino 155
Merolle, Sergio 36, 130, 155
Merosi, Paolo 199
Mertes, Marion 28, 205
Mertines, Alessandra 206
Meschini, Antonio 20
Messaccesi, Daniele 198
Messalina (Messalina Venere imperatrice) 116
Messalina vs. The Son of Hercules (L'ultimo gladiatore) 118
Messeri, Gianmaria 78
Messina, Emilio (*a.k.a.* Don Emil Messina) 20, 63, 73, 89, 111, 118, 163, 164, 169, 171, 172, 179, 184, 199, 201, 204
Messina, Giorgio 55
Messina, Mario 67, 164
Messina, Roberto 20, 55, 107, 134, 159, 164, 171, 172
Mestral, Armand 124, 151
Metaxa Corporation 198, 200
Métehen, Jacques 56
Metheus Film 31, 161
Metropolis 186
Metz, Vittorio 49, 90, 173
Meyer, Godela H. 18
Mezzanotte, Luigi 206
Mezzetti, Danilo 48
MGM 14
Miali, Roberto 45, 102, 122
Miano, Andrea 10, 11
Miano, Andria 129
Micalizzi, Franco 26

Micantoni, Adriano 19, 111, 122, 126, 128, 167, 181, 186
Miccinelli, Grazia 194
Miccinilli, Maria 92
Michael Strogoff (Michel Strogoff) 118
Michaelis, Dario 35, **77**
Michel, Jean-Claude 60
Michelet, Michel 47, 67, 131
Micheli, Elio 54, 96, 98, 107, 114, 133, 135, 137, 205
Micheli, Franco 199
Micheli, Ornella 30, 33, 112, 143, 161, 164, 192
Michell, Keith 153
Michelotti, Diego 30, 43, 89, 107, 163
Michelotti, Serena 47
Michelson, Myriam 113
Michettoni, Ennio 20, 40, 43, 131, 143, 161, 164, 205
Michisanti, Mario 203
Miciella, Raffaella 142
Micula, Stasia 207
The Mighty Crusaders (La Gerusalemme liberata) 119
The Mighty Ursus (Ursus) 119, **120, 121**
Miglardi, Mario 174
Migliarini, Giorgio 119
Migliorini, Lea 129
Mignone, Totò 182
Mijacevic, Slobodan 73, 112
Mikaela 167
Mikailoff, Michele 10
Milano, Lula 99
Milano, Nino 72, 125, 160, 166
Miles, Vera 65
Milic, Stjepan 164
Militon, Albert 118
Milland, Gloria 20, 29, 35, 59, 68, 81, 134, 138, 167, 184
Miller, Astrid 200
Miller, Ben 202
Miller, Bill 152
Miller, Glenn 33
Miller, Mirta 26
Miller, Pat 51
Million, Chery 69, 78, 127
Mills, Chuck 198, 200
Milo, Sandra 99
Milovic, Aleksandar 22, 60, 73, 152, 118, 191
Milton, Inger 51
Mimica, Vatroslav 165
Mincic, Pavle 119
Minervini, Angela 176
Minervini, Gianni 112
Minnelli, Walter 197
Minniti, Bruno 206
Minoprio, Giorgio 110
Minotaur, the Wild Beast of Crete (Teseo contro il minotauro) 120
Minotrio, Carlo 55
Minotti, Felice 7, 8, 9, 10, 11, 12, 13, 14, 166, 176
Minouchkine, Alexandre 163
Minouchkine, Ariane 163
Minuto, Nino 141
Mioni, Fabrizio 80, 94, 141
Mioni, Riccardo 203

Mioni, Sergio 141, 203, 205
Mioni, Stefano Maria 203, 205
Mirabile, Alfredo 124
Miraglia, Emilio 70, 84
Miranda, Isa 46
Miranda, Soledad 119
Mirandi, Armando 70
Mirat, Pierre 56, 178
Miric, Miodrag 112
Mirot, Luc 118
Miserendino, Aurelio 22
Misiano, Fortunato 34, 63, 76, 77, 80, 84, 87, 88, 89, 102, 129, 130, 133, 143, 145, 194, 195
Misiano, Nino 34, 40, 77, 89, 102, 133, 143
Misiano, Pasquale 77, 88, 133, 143, 162
Misraki, Paul 56
Mission Impossible 63
Mistral, Jorge 150, 165
Mitchell, Cameron 21, 29, 31, 52, 104, 106, 115
Mitchell, Gordon 17, 20, 29, 30, 35, 59, 62, **62**, 84, 100, 103, 138, 153, 177, 187, **188**, 188, 205
Mitchell, Ken 203
Mitic, Milan 18, 110, 112, 120, 122
Mitri, Piero 77
Mitri, Tiberio 44, 176
Mitrovic, Drago 138
Mizar, Maria 25
Mochetti, Arnaldo 136
Mocky, Jean-Pierre 42
Modica, Antonio 83, 169, 187, 195
Modica, Giovanni Canfarelli 28
Modio, Jolanda 111
Modugno, Domenico 134
Modugno, Lucia 25
Moffa, Paolo 46, 73, 105, 140, 152
Mogherini, Flavio 21, 67, 78, 92, 175, 176, 192
Moglia, Linda 11
Möhner, Carl 32, 56
Mole Men Against the Son of Hercules (Maciste l'uomo più forte del mondo) 122, 152
Molfesi, Mario 125
Molina, Julio 18, 119
Molina, Mariano Vidal 128, 141, 151, 195
Molinari, Aldo 9
Molinaro, Édouard 42
Moll, Biel 113
Moll, Giorgia 36, 41, 165, 175, 191
Mollier, Jean 99
Molnar, Vera 186
Molteni, Ambrogio 16, 44, 62, 169, 188, 195
Moltini, Cesare 14
Momi, Umberto 136
Momplet, Antonio 100
Monaco, Lea 48, 172
Monaldi, Gisella 50
Monchablon, Jean 178
Mondaini, Sondra 91
Mondello, Luigi 29, 30, 82, 106, 126, 187
Mondial Televisione Film 194
Moneta, Luigi 62

Monfort, Juan 166
The *Mongols* (*I mongoli*) 122, **123**
Monica Film 168
Monicelli, Mario 135
Moniconi, Valeria 190
Monís, Ángel 119, 65, 151
Monlaur, Yvonne 33
Monod, Jacques 113
Monremurro, Franco 194
Montagnani, Nerina 110
Montaigne, Lawrence 44, 124
Montalban, Ricardo 47, 134
Montalbano, Rearmsnato 28
Montalbano, Renato 19, 29, 41, 64, 68, 99, 104, 111, 139, 151, 157, 181, 196
Montalbano, Riccardo 174
Montaldo, Giuliano 50
Montanari, Arrigo 22, 131, 135
Montanari, Sergio 106, 197, 202
Montanari, Valentina 202
Montanari, Valerie 202
Montani, Francesca 200
Montant, Georges 32
Montanti, Alberta 98
Monte, Raffaele Del 24, 65, 77, 78, 99, 107, 114, 119, 128, 135, 137, 143, 164, 169, 173
Montedero, Renata 46
Monteluce Film 18
Montemagno, Gabriella 200
Montemurro, Franco (a.k.a. Francesco Montemurro) 194, 195
Monter, José Luis 167
Montero, Roberto Bianchi 111, 174
Montés, Elisa 143, 187
Montes, José 84
Montesanti, Raul 111, 154, 178
Montesi, Leonilde 138
Montesi, Umberto 135, 160
Montez, María 126
Monti, Carina 141
Monti, Enrico 10
Montori, Alfredo 29, 30, 34, 77, 81, 82, 110, 114, 129, 130, 133, 134, 137, 138, 162, 165, 166, 187
Montovani, Lilly 191
Montoya, Elena 154
Montresor, Beni 47, 49, 128
Montressor, David 25
Montuori, Carlo 49, 135, 173
Montuori, Mario 15, 49, 70, 73, 132, 135, 158
Monty, Jean 195
Moon, Lynne Sue 113
Moore, Clayton 80
Moore, John 51
Moore, Michael 104
Moore, Mike 17, 177
Mora, Mario 194
Morabito, Claudio 84, 112, 126, 136, 201
Morales, Mario 24, 106
Morales, Nunzio 206
Morana, Eleonora 102, 130, 133, 196
Morand, Roger 56
Morandi, Armando 125, 163, 179
Morandini, Albino 26, 111, 118, 163, 172, 181
Morcier, Jean 102

Mordini, Gino 120
Mordini, Giorgio 36
Moreal, Bruno 16, 30, 32, 36, 44, 58, 87, 129, 137, 138, 143, 152, 155, 203
Moreau, Gabriel 8, 14
Morel, Bob 43
Morelli, Augusta 188
Morelli, Manlio 35
Morelli, Maria Teresa 62
Morelli, Rina 55, 136
Morelli, Roberto 127, 142, 154
Morelli, Rolando 59, 119
Moreno, Antonio 27, 183
Moreno, Darío 140
Moreno, Féliz 16
Moreno, José Garcia 18
Moreno, José María 65, 163
Moreno, Julian 24
Moreschini, Armando 204
Moretti, Agostino 33
Moretti, Gaetano 143
Moretti, Nadir 82, 91, 143, 195
Moretti, Roberto 50
Moretti, Sandro 71, 72, 147, 166
Moretti, Ugo 19, 32, 48
Morgan, Claudio 186
Morgan, Michèle 55
Morgan, Terrence 151
Morgan, the Pirate (*Morgan il pirata*) 124
Mori, Bruna 122
Mori, Claudia 30, 158, 186
Mori, Renato 167
Moriani, Alberto 207
Morici, Franco 187
Moriconi, Renato 200
Morigi, Mario 65, 82, 91, 111, 151, 183, 184
Morigi, Tatiana Casini 184
Morin, Pierre 42, 174
Morino Film 124
Morino, Sandrino 49
Morisi, Guido 50
Morley, Robert 164
Morodan, Dan 202
Moroni, Danilo 194, 199
Moroni, Mario 20, 40, 41, 91, 143, 173, 178
Moroni, Primo 159
Moroni, Umberto 207
Morra, Giorgio 27
Morricone, Ennio 24, 27, 142
Morris, Kirk 20, 36, 40, 47, 55, 90, 91, 92, 111, 143, 173, 178, 192
Morris, Lucien 204
Morrone, Dina 203
Morroni, Renata 19
Morrows, Julie 200
Moruzzi, Franco 29, 83, 187
Mosca, Ferrucio 29
Moschin, Gastone 127
Moser, Aldo 28
Moss, Kriss 161
Motion Picture Distributors and Sales Co. 9
Mottet, Jean 42
Mottola, Ray 206
Moulaert, René 56
Mounir Rafla 113

Mountjoy, Eunice 27
Moustache 194
Moya, Alberto 47
Mozzato, Umberto 7, 8, 9
Mulá, Isabel 151
Mulargia, Edoardo 100, 176, 192
Mulé, Francesco 58, 91
Muller, Frederick 130
Muller, Gaston 118
Muller, Harrison, Jr. 205, 206
Muller, Paul 19, 21, 23, 25, 32, 41, 51, 55, 73, 122, 130, 133, 134, 135, 155, 182, 191
Mullet, Pix 118
Mura, Antonio 19, 29
Mura, Robert 204
Murat, Jean 23, 134
Muratori, Luciano 165
Muratori, Primiano 21, 44, 58, 105, 124, 137, 153, 158, 164, 165
Murgia, Antonella 112
Murgia, Tiberio 44
Muro, Venancio 127
Murphy, Chris 203
Murri, Giorgio 174
Musco, Nino 34, 46, 48, 104, 129, 134, 162
Musa Co. 127
Musetta, Gloria 51
Musketeers of the Sea (*Il moschettieri del mare*) 124
Musolino, Vincenzo 33, 178, 194
Musso, Carlo 139
Mussolini, Benito 40, 46, 49
Mussolini, Vittorio 45
Musson, Bernard 32, 42
Mustacchi, Amedeo 7
Mustari, Annamaria 130, 133, 163
Musumeci, Enzo 25
Musy, Gianni 46, 51, 125
Muzio, Virgilio 136
The Mysterious Swordsman (*Lo spadaccino misterioso*) 124

Nachmann, Kurt 133
Nadal, François 31, 56
Nader, George 151
Nadin, Alessandro 114, 126
Nale, Spartaco 25, 73, 80, 112, 116, 167, 170
Nalis, Antun 191
Nannerini, Filippo 151
Nannerini, Luigi 47, 103, 110, 151, 186
Nanni, Léa 195
Nannuzzi, Nella 26, 19, 40, 84, 103, 111, 118, 120, 139, 141, 165, 172, 184, 189, 192
Napoleoni, Maria 91
Nardelli, Franco 139
Nardi, Barbara 131, 167
Nardi, Corrado 186
Nardi, Gianetto 20, 59, 142, 154, 171
Nardi, Maria Grazia 26
Narducci, Francesco 204, 206
Narzisi, Giovanni 52
Naschy, Paul 51, 118
Nascimbene, Mario 15, 24, 33, 35, 41, 46, 49, 122, 164, 168, 189
Nasht, John G. 46

236 Index

Nassiet, Henri 56, 119
Nastasi, Biagio 28
Natale, Roberto 152
Natali, Edmondo 199
Natali, Germano 202
Natalucci, Vitaliano 26, 60, 139, 176
Natan, Emile 118, 177
Nathan, Herman 202
Nathan, Jacob W. 164
Nathanson, Joseph (*a.k.a.* Josef Natanson) 20, 31, 36, 44, 49, 62, 99, 120, 128, 155, 163, 164, 178, 189, 197
Natili, Giovanna 16, 32, 44, 62, 69, 169, 152
Navarrete, Ricardo 47
Navarrini, Renato 28, 29, 46, 81, 87, 113, 129, 134, 165, 172
Navarro, Enrique 27
Nazionale Luce 20
Nazzari, Amedeo 34, 103, 133
Nazzaro, Emilio 130
NBC 26
N. C. Film Co. 64
Nebiolo, Carlo 49
Née, Louis 56
Negri, Antonio 182
Negroni 141
Negroni, Baldassarre 9, 10
Neille, Alma 129
Nell, Krista 102
Nelli, Ernesto 191
Nelson, Burt 23, 25, 137, 140
Nenadovic, Djordje (*a.k.a.* George Nenadovic, Giorgio Nenadovic) 18, 127, 154, 157
Nennati, Flavio 27
Nény, Jean 56
Neptunia Films 141
Neri, Alfredo 114, 188
Neri, Donatella 10
Neri, Rosalba 20, 36, 51, 52, 65, 84, 90, 91, 96, 104, 107, **108**, 135, 176
Nero and the Burning of Rome (Nerone e Messalina) 125
Nero, Franco 27
Nero; or the Burning of Rome (Nero; o la caduta di Roma) 13
Nerval, Nathalie 42
Nesci, Giovanni 174
Nesher, Avi 205
Nessi, Bruno 100
Neveux, Georges 42
Nevola, Edoardo 101
The New Adventures of Zorro (Zorro il dominatore) 125
New Line Cinema 200
New World Pictures 20
Newman, John 200
Newman, Sergio 26, 30, 167
Newton, Margit Evelyn (a.k.a. Margi Newton) 198
Nguyen, Lilian 141
Ngyun, Lillia 23
Niccolini, Flavio 64, 150
Nichols, Conrad 206
Nicholson, James H. 59, 81, 87, 89
Nicodemi, Aldo 192
Nicolai, Alfredo 112
Nicolai, Bruno 141, 142

Nicolai, Elena 49
Nicolai, Sergio 208
Nicole, Andrea 198
Nicolodi, Daria 206
Nicolosi, Roberto 28, 36, 52, 60, 106, 119, 129, 137, 171, 175, 189, 191
Nielsen, Hans 127
Nieto, José 23, 30, 140, 159
Nieto, Toñy 18
Nieva, Alfonso 24
The Night of the Great Attack (La notte del grande assalto) 125
The Night They Killed Rasputin (Les Nuits de Raspoutine) 126
Nightmare Castle 21
Nights and Loves of Don Juan (Le calde notti di Don Giovanni) 126
The Nights of Lucretia Borgia (La notte di Lucrezia Borgia) 126
Nigro, Pasquale 126
Nigro, Pat 126
Nike Cinematografica (CFPC) 84
Nikolic, Miodrag 41, 112, 115
Nin, Carlos 37
Nin, Esther 65
Ninchi, Annibale 35, 41, 46
Ninchi, Ave 91
Ninchi, Carlo 41, 46, 55, 124, 156, 160, 177
Nino, Vittorio 36
Nissoti, Arys 18
Noble, Katina 51
Noce, Luisa Della 102
Noé, Ana Maria 65
Noé, Eduardo 39
Noël, Hubert 87, 96
Nöel, Magali 151
Noël, Philippe 178
Noeppel, Victor 42
Nofri, Pietro 19, 21, 154
Nogara, Edy 111
Noiret, Phillippe 43
Nonibasti, Franco 18
Nonnis, Mauro 206
Nord Film Italiana 33
Northton, Al 152
Nostro, Nick 163, 179
Noubret, Serge 184
Novak, Ivana 112
Novakovic, Lj. 118
Novarese 36
Novarese, Vittorio Nino 15, 32, 49, 78, 99, 132, 135, 155
Novarro, Enrique 116
Novelli, Amleto 8, 13
Novelli, Mario 100, 134, 138, 152, 153, 176, 198
Novelli, Olga Giannini 9
Novelli, Rodolfo 49
Noxley, Henry 198, 200
Nubret, Serge 163, 184
Nucci, Laura 47, 67
Nuccorini, Pietro 80, 92, 155, 177, 190
Nuova Dania Cinematografica 204
Nusciak, Loredana 36, 56, 67, 152
Nussgruber, Rudolf 115
Nutter, Frederica 119
Nuyttens, Paul 56

O'Brian, Melody 25
O'Brien, Doan 203
O'Brien, Donald 203
O'Brien, Patti Manning 190
O'Connell, Pierre 18
O'Connor, Donald 192
O'Cord, Peter 18
O'Dea, Denis 52
O'Donoghue, Robin 202
O'Keeffe, Miles 198, 200, 203
O'Leary, Hank 204
O'Toole, Peter 27
Oakes, Christopher 20
Oath of Zorro see Behind the Mask of Zorro
Occhetti, S. 122
Occhetti, Sandro 111, 160, 188
Occhini, Ilaria 34, 44, 49, 128
Occhioni, Mario 197
Occhipinti, Andrea 201
Ocean Films 149
Oceana Produzioni Internazionali Cinematografiche 102, 110
Ochoa, José María 51
Ocokoljic, Dragan 152
Oddone, Enzo 90
Odoardi, Franco 134
Ojeda, Luis Lucas 26, 167
Ojeda, Narciso 27
Ojetti, Paola 43
Olaguibel, Juan 127–128, 190
Olas, Marcello Bonini 46
The Old Testament (Il vecchio testamento) 127
Olea, Antonio Pérez 127
Olga Chart Co. 177
Oliveiras, Frank 179
Oliver, Gerard 197, 202
Oliver, Juan Luis 151
Oliveras, Frank 151, 164, 166, 179
Olivieri, Cesare 15, 176
Olivieri, Egisto 55
Olivieri, Enrico 29, 49, 155, 192
Olivieri, Mimma 92
Olmstead, Remington 25
Olsen, Rolf 133
Olsey, Danan Grant 200
Omaggio, Maria Rosaria 198
Omegna, Roberto 9
1 Aprile Cinematografica 131
One Million Years B. C. 28, 201
100 Horsemen (I cento cavalieri) 127
Onorati, Maria Luisa 90
Onorati, Roberto 207
Onorato, Glauco 102, 135, 136, 155
Onorato, Maria Virginia 113
Onori, Anna 103
Onori, Roberto 124, 169
Ontañón, Santiago 16, 100
Oppedisano, Stefano 107
Oppo, Ottavio 27, 52, 60
Orban, Monique 191
Orengo, Antonio 128
Orfei, Liana 21, 22, 44, 63, 91, 92, 130, 133, 134, **169**, **170**, 170, 173
Orfei, Moira 20, 26, 46, 58, 64, 95, 103, 119, 122, 133, 137, 139, 143, 145, 173, 181
Oriental Film 137

Origo, Sira 154
Oringer, Barry 43
Orlandini, Antonio 22
Orlandini, Lia 14
Orlandini, Lucio 112
Orlandini, Slia 13
Orlovic, Mica 113
Oro Film 132
O.S.C.A.R. 80
Orsay Films 191
Orsini, Alvaro 31, 84
Orsini, Giorgio 46
Orsini, María Teresa 183, 91
Orsini, Nino 116
Orsini, Orlando 32, 54, 124
Orso, Anna 27, 102
Ortas, Antonio 47
Ortas, Julio 30, 84, 104, 126, 139, 167
Ortenzi, Guido 91
Ortiz, Ángel 24, 69, 106, 128, 159
Ortiz, Maria Teresa 47
Ortolani, Pietro 15, 32, 44, 81, 82, 90, 98, 113, 114, 129, 154, 177
Ortolani, Riz 18, 55
Oses, Emilio Rodriguez 201
Ostenda, Ombretta 52, 91
Osuna, Gloria 29
Otero, José Maria 127
Othello (*a.k.a.* Otello Colangeli) 115
Ouseby, Kay 129
Owen, J.D. 204
Oxon, Paul 156
Ozenne, Jean 56
Ozores, Mariano 47, 187

Pabst, Georg Wilhelm 184
P. A. C. 32, 152
Pace, Anna-Maria 29, 84
Pace, Roberto 200
Pacelli, Cesare 154
Pacelli, Oscar 49, 131
Pacelli, Salvatore Controneo Violetta 143
Pacelli, Violetta 34, 88, 89, 96, 98, 107, 131
Pacheco, Godofredo 126, 139
Pacheco, Mario 106, 190
Pacheco, Rafael 23, 106, 154
Pacifico, Benito 112
Pacifico, Claudio 203
Pacini, Raffaello 60
Padilla, Antonio 128
Padinotti, Aldo 20
Padoa, Clara 46
Padoan, Anna Maria 54, 107, 133
Padovani, Arturo 52, 141
Padovani, Luigi 95
Pagano, Bartolomeo 1, 7, 8, **8,** 9, 10, 11, **11,** 12, 13, 14
Page, Geneviève 51, 118–119
Pageo, Carmen 16, 47
Paget, Debra 3, 36, 142
Paget, Susan 127, 154, 171
Paggioli, Augusto 9
Pagilari, Bruno 116
Pagnani, Gino 113
Pai, Ching Jen 112
Paige, Molly 204
Pailaggi, Roberto 65

Pajer, Ivica 31, 45, 177
Pala, Guido 164
Paladini, Riccardo 91
Palaggi, Franco 50, 73, 135, 156
Palaggi, Roberto 100, 119, 151
Palance, Ivan 167
Palance, Jack 3, 25, 122, 167
Palance, John 25
Palau, José Gras 201
Palazio, Liliana 138
Palella, Oreste 62, 169
Palermi, Enrico 10
Palermini, Piero 31, 35, 50, 56, 126, 131, 133, 135, 160
Pallet, Maryse 42
Palli, Fulvio Gicca 131, 147, 171
Palli, Lorenzo Gicca 92, 195
Pallotini, Riccardo 20, 22, 143, 192
Pallotta, Gabriella 27, 98
Pallotta, Giorgio 65
Pallottini, Riccardo 17, 55, 112, 161, 164, 182
Palmara, Mimmo 20, 22, 39, 73, 80, 81, 87, 94, 104, 105, 141, 147, 149, 155, 157, 159, 171, 174, 176, 179, 181, 184
Palmer, Dick 20, 171
Palmer, Renzo 138
Palmera, Luciano 116
Palmeri, Amleto 10
Palmieri, Alfredo 31
Palmieri, Fulvio 41, 125, 135
Palmieri, Gabriele 90
Palmieri, Remo 140
Palmieri, Wilma 113
Palmiri, Massimo 50
Palolo, Ray 120
Palombi 22, 59, 103, 128
Palombi, Ada 155
Palombi, Franco 24, 32, 90, 99, 128
Palombi, Giovanni 44, 99, 103, 131, 147, 169
Palombi, Nicla 90, 99, 128
Palotta, Gabriella 48
Palou, Teófilo 24
Palumbo, Luciano 25
Paluzzi, Alberto 204
Paluzzi, Luciana 18, 80
Pamec Cinematografica 104
Pampaloni, Romano 197, 201, 203
Pampanini, Silvana 15, 77
Pamphili, Mirella 195
Pamplona, Joaquin 27
Panaro, Alessandra 24, 54, 96, 151, 159, 171, 186
Panaro, Maria Luisa 29, 31, 83, 106, 125, 126, 156, 187
Panaro, Michelangelo 112
Panaro, Milo 141
Panarotto, Agnese 207
Panda Film 20, 112, 145, 163, 192
Panda Società per L'Industria Cinematografica 23, 30, 147, 162
Pandolfi, Elio 30, 163
Panetuzzi, Renato 20, 28, 91, 173
Pani, Corrado 18, 36, 99, 131
Paniagua, Cecilio 140
Panicalli, Francesca 199
Pannaccio, Giulio 30, 138

Panta, Giovanni Del 136
Pantano, Antonio 26
Panzetti, Giovanni 119
Panzini, Alfredo 10
Paola, Dria 10
Paolella, Domenico 23, 35, 46, 76, 77, 81, 82, 89, 110, 130, 134
Paoletti, Alberto 106
Paoletti, Amalia 73, 92, 158
Paoletti, Bice 141
Paoletti, Marco 128, 150
Paoletti, Mario Giuseppe 45
Paoletti, Roberto 26, 102, 112, 142, 163
Paoli, Luciana 28, 111
Paolo, Amerigo 15
Paolocci, Francesco 199
Paolocci, Gaetano 199
Paolucci, Ermete 191
Paolucci, Guido 129
Papa, Leone 13
Papa, Mario Del 158
Papas, Irene 22, 174
Papi, Giuliano 20, 58, 164
Papi, Lorenzo 158
Papp, Emerico 132
Pappagallo, Giulio 81, 82, 114, 187
Parada, Manuel 116, 154
Paradell, Magdalena 51
Paramount Pictures 186
Parapetti, Mario 16, 177, 184, 188
Parapetti, Roberto 188
PARC Film 46
Parédès, Jean 119
Pariante, Roberto 32, 64
Paris Productions (PIP) 96, 126
Paris, Dany 30
Paris, Giovanni 54
Paris, Simone 42
Parise, Lucio 207
Parisi, Franca 30, 33, 127, 134
Parisio, Bruno 48
Park, Reg 3, 87, **86, 89,** 90, 91, 92, 146, **146**
Parker, Judy 102
Parker, Rossana 203
Parks, Michael 27
Parmeggiani, Quinto 165
Parolini, Gianfranco 40, 59, 68, 127, 142, 153, 171, 175, 190
Parra, Julio 139
Parravicini, Renato 166
Parri, Gloria 114, 157
Partexano, Alex (*a.k.a.* Alessandro Partexano) 199
Parvo, Elli 67
Pasco, Sam 204
Pash, David 194, 205
Paso, Alfonso 47
Pasquali, Alberto 10
Pasquali, Ernesto Maria 14
Pasquali, Giorgio 188
Pasqualini, Luigi 203
Pasquetto, Franco 19, 26, 136, 181, 194
Pasquetto, Gianfranco 19
Pasquini, Marco 20, 91, 136, 173
Passalacqua, Giuseppe 154
Passante, Mario 34, 104, 140, 158, 168, 175

238 Index

Passari, Carlo 205
Passaura, Augusto 194
Passeri, Ada 112
Pastina, Giorgio 191
Pastore, Piero 22, 25, 28, 34, 64, 73, 87, 91, 102, 118, 131, 133, 136, 151, 158, 167, 176, 186
Pastorini, Mario 22, 58, 84, 103, 111, 118, 172, 181
Pastorino, Franco 33
Pastrone, Giovanni 1, 7, 9, 12, 13
Pastrovich, Maurizio 194
Pasut, Franca 50
Pat, Angel 160
Patacca, Vitaliana 199
Patellière, Denys de la 112
Pater, Bob 42
Pathé Consortium Cinemá 32, 159
Patorni, Raphael 31
Patriarca, Claudio 207
Patriarca, Walter 20, 34, 76, 84, 87, 88, 89, 91, 102, 136, 138, 143, 145, 153, 173, 178, 205, 207
Patrizi, Basilio 207
Patrizi, Massimo 192
The Patsy 159
Paturel, Dominique 32
Paul, Andreina 114, 137, 138
Paul, David 199
Paul, Peter 199
Pauwels, Paul 56
Pavanelli, Livio 8
Pavarello, Renzo 199
Paven, Elisabetta 90
Pavese, Luigi 50, 136, 165
Pavolini, Corrado 54
Pavoni, Pier Ludovico 24, 26, 35, 40, 65, 78, 99, 111, 118, 125, 128, 131, 139, 140, 172, 181
Pavoni, Vico 131
Paxwell, Romano 186
Payer, Ivo 177
Payne, Laurence 25
Pazzafini, Nello 19, 20, 23, 37, 39, 58, 63, 65, 68, 73, 77, 81, 84, 87, 98, 102, 107, 109, 111, 118, 131, 134, 137, 138, 143, 146, 153, 163, 164, 169, 171, 172, 173, 176, 178, 179, 181, 184, 194, 196, 198, 199, 200, 204, 205, 208
Pazzaglia, Riccardo 129, 134
P E Films (Productores Exibidores Films S.A.) 143
Pearl, Gail 175
Peccerini, Gino 19, 21
Pech, René 204
Pechini, Franco 20, 91, 173
Peck, René 204
Pecoriello, Alfred 197
Pecoriello, Renato 198, 202
Pedersoll, Giuseppe 205
Pedinotti, Aldo 20, 45, 63, 90, 96, 153, 163, 164
Pedone, Mario 131, 205
Pedregosa, Miguel 51, 150, 194
Peguri, Gino 295
Pehar, Olga 163, 179
Pelizzi, Valentino 116, 138, 169
Pellati, Teresa 186

Pellegrini, Amalia 55
Pellegrini, Otto 184
Pellegrino, Fulvio 113
Pellegrino, Mario 141, 156
Pellevant, Antoinette 30, 112
Pellicena, José Luis 166, 183
Pelloni, Raffaella 20
Peluffo, Ana Luisa 165
Peña, Julio 105, 106, 119, 139, 140, 190
Peña, Luis 47
Pengow, Ivan 58
Penkert, Rainer 140
Pennacchia, Aurelio 151, 160, 203
Pennese, Giuseppe 199
Pennoni, Angelo 67, 124, 158
Pensa, Aldo 134
Pepe, Nico 33, 122, 189
Peral, Juan Antonio 24
Percaus, Paolo 205
Percelli, Giovanni 105
Perea, Antonio 128
Perego, Filippo 109, 113
Perelli, Gianni 168
Pérès, Marcel 31
Pérez-Dolz, Francisco 40, 64
Pérez, José Luis 127
Pérez, Manuel 68
Peri, Aldo 46
Peri, Arrigo 22, 24, 54, 107, 125, 169
Pericoli, Ugo 125, 130, 134, 155
Périer, Etienne 168
Perilli, Ivo 24, 130, 184
Perkocic, Dusan 191
Pernana, Charo Tijero 128
Perojo, Benito 47, 159
Perone, Claudio 102, 113
Perotti, Piero 87, 128
Perozzi, Titta 80
Perrella, Alessandro 156
Perri, Arrigo 177
Perrone, Filippo 30, 111, 126, 181
Perrot, Françoise 204
Persello, Nino 23, 29, 146, 150
Persin, Henri 56
Peruzzi, Franco 143
Peruzzi, Giuseppe 30, 64, 174
Peruzzi, Ruggero 70, 128
Pesante, Barbara 204
Pesce, Franco 139, 179
Pesce, Sergio 136, 137, 160
Pescetelli, Ferdinando 99
Pesch, Ulrike 18
Pesquera, José María Alonso 64, 150
Petacci, Emilio 165, 182
Peter Carsten Prods. 115
Peters, Edith 34, 59, 140
Peterson, Fred 200
Petit, Pascale 131
Petitjean, Antoine 150
Petocchi, Anna 18, 167
Petracca, Enzo 31
Petralia, Tito 32
Petrassi, Gofffredo 27
Petrazzi, Gianluca 205
Petrazzi, Riccardo 109, 203, 205
Petri, Aristodemo 166
Petri, Aristodeus 166
Petri, Mario 26, 30, 54, 59, 76, 87, 88,

89, 99, 134, 135, 137, 138, 147, 151, 157
Petricca, Andrea 137, 142, 163
Petricca, Pasquale 26
Petricca, Tulio 19
Petrignani, Giuseppe 205
Petrilli, Vittoriano 135
Petrini, Luigi 166
Petrini, Paolo 26, 184
Petrocchi, Tito 184
Petroff, Robert 202
Petroni, Silvia 113
Petrozzi, Roberto 28, 197, 202, 205
Petrucci, Giovanni 35, 139
Petruca Films 32
Pevarello, Osiride 20, 104, 109, 126, 139, 140, 181, 200, 206
Pevarello, Renzo 102, 109, 113, 140, 181
Pezzo, Mario Del 77, 114, 119, 120, 125, 131, 132, 143, 160, 169, 183, 184, 187
The Pharaoh's Woman (*La donna dei faraoni*) 128
Philippe, Michèle 15, 50
Pia of Ptolemy (*Pia de'Tolomei*) 128
Pia, Ángela 116
Piaget, Paul 154
Piana, Nazzareno 30
Pianelli, Vittorio Rossi 12, 14
Pianforini, Massimo 64
Piazzi, Achille 70, 87, 89
Pica, Antonio 109, 113
Picasso, Lamberto 46, 125
Picciafuochi, Vladimiro 25, 29, 116, 122, 136
Piccillo, Giuseppe 35, 81, 136, 137
Piccioni, Fabio 171, 175
Piccioni, Piero 50, 156
Piccoli, Michel 18
Piccolo, Ottavia 194
Piccolo, Peppino 34, 102, 128
Piccolomini, Nicolò 28
Pichelli, Elissa 104
Picistrelli, Umberto 87, 91, 128, 158, 160, 187
Picó, Tomás 55
Picot, Blanche 31
Pie, Remy 194
Piéral 31
Piergentili, Bruno 17, 146
Pieri, Paolo 102, 134, 188
Pierjac, Albert 178
Pieroni, Mark 203
Pierotti, Piero 23, 28, 52, 63, 80, 84, 87, 88, 112, 129, 131, 141, 183, 189, 192, 195, 196
Pierozzi, Giuseppe 10
Pietrangeli, Antonio 54
Pietrobon, Massimo 43, 102, 159, 186
Pietrostefani, Rometta 65, 176
Piferi, Alberto 199
Piga, Aldo 33, 134, 150, 166, 176, 178, 192
Pigaut, Roger 42, 174
Pignières, René 129
Pigozzi, Luciano 35, 102, 110, 207
Pilares, Manuel 23
Pilcher, Joseph 25

Pili, Enrico 24
Pilotto, Camillo 34, 46, 67, 78, 99, 112, 130
Pina, Aldo 184
Pindl, Raf 191
Pinelli, Tullio 99
Pinelli, Walter 29
Pini, Aldo 22, 26, 29, 31, 41, 52, 80, 92, 94, 124, 125, 130, 138, 153, 167, 186, 187
Pini, Lido 134
Pino, Eulálila del 190
Pino, Maria Luisa 39, 105
Pino, Pasquale Dal 169
Pinori, Giuseppe 109
Pinteau, Pascal 197
Pinto, Attilio Lo 206
Piotrowski, Marciak 51
Piovanni, Pina 15
The Pirate and the Slave Girl (La scimitarra del saraceno) 128
The Pirate of the Black Hawk (Il pirata dello sparviero nero) 129
Pirate of the Half Moon (Il corsaro della mezzaluna) 129
Pirates of the Coast (I pirati della costa) 130
Piretti, Antonio 169
Pirone, Simona 198
Pisacane, Carlo 111, 177
Pisani, Mario 80
Pisano, Berto 48
Pistoni, Franco 199
Pisu, Mario 41, 77, 114
Pisu, Raffaele 186
Pitagora, Paola 25, 116
Pittaluga, Stefano 10, 13
Pittarello, Massimo 199, 204, 207
Pitti, Paola 83, 139, 140
Pividori, Bianca 112
Pizarro, Franco 166, 168
Pizzetti, Ildebrando 7, 45
Pizzi, Pier Luigi 60
Pizzuti, Riccardo 15, 26, 29, 58, 164, 195
Pla, Ángela 119
Place, Lou 22
Placenti, Maurizio 129
Placido, Anna 128
Placido, Fabio 28
Plavsic-Zvonce, Slavoljub 112, 115
Plaza Film 92
Plaza, Julio Ortas 126
Pleasence, Donald 207
Plebani, Alberto 118, 122
Pleboni 141
Plenizio, Gianfranco 28, 113, 194
Plesa, Branko 152
Plesher, Burt 152
Plouvie, Nathalie 18
Po Film 29, 125
Poblete, Ricardo 116, 119
Pochath, Werner 202
Podestà, Rossana 18, 60, 68, 157, 158, 186, 202
Podgorsky, Sacha 25
Pogány, Gábor 67, 91, 156, 189
Poggi, Ferdinando 15, 56, 58, 110, 129, 135, 147, 157, 166, 198

Poggi, Francesco 46
Poggi, Juli 133
Poggi, Nando 157, 198
Poggi, Ottavio 15, 54, 77, 107, 119, 125, 132, 133, 135, 147, 151, 177
Poggi, Roberto 206
Poggioli, Ferdinando Maria 46
Poirier, Henri 32
Poksuz, Zenne 208
Pola, Isa 132
Polacchi, Elio 22, 33, 135, 147, 166
Polacco, Cesare 136
Polack, Luis Sánchez 40
Polaire, Pauline 11, 13
Polani, Anna Maria 77, 83, 88, 89
Polavshenko, Natascia 59
Polentini, Ottorino 109
Polesello, Franca 122, 141
Poletti, Signora 8
Poletto, G.B. 50, 67, 158, 166
Poletto, Piero 17, 65, 102, 113, 119, 120, 131, 140, 151
Poli, Afro 80
Poli, Enrico 125
Poli, Maurice 22, 149
Poli, Mimmo 19, 20, 35, 51, 92, 111, 116, 124, 130, 131, 133, 159, 163, 179, 196
Polidori, Gianni 73, 76, 124, 142
Polini, Otello 46
Polini, Walter 200
Pollentin, Louis 104
Pollentin, Luciano 104
Polletin, Mario 16
Pollini, Joe 56
Pollock, Channing 124, 135
Polombi, Ada 25
Polop, Francisco Lara 113
Polyák, Lilla 175
Pomilia, Aldo 33, 158
Pomilia, Nicolò 124, 200
Pomilia, Stefano 200
Pompe, Carlo 186
Pompei 22, 58, 59, 62, 64, 70, 83, 92, 103, 126, 138, 139, 181
Pompei, Luigi 133
Pompei, Massimo 200
Pons, Paquita 154
Ponte, María Luisa 143
Ponti, Carlo 21, 176, 184
Ponti–De Laurentiis Cinematographica 176, 186
Pontius Pilate (Ponzio Pilato) 130
Popovic-Mavid, Milivoje 119, 152, 191
Popovic, Nikola 191
Popovic, Radomir 118
Porel, Jacqueline 31
Poron, Jean François 168
Porta, Antonella Della 192
Portalupi, Piero 33, 110
Porte, Robert 31
Posani, Dante 91
Possanza, Agostino 114, 139
Possanza, Augusto 100
Post, Robert 22
Posta, Arrigo 197
Postiglione, Giorgio 163, 171, 179
Potok, Rebecca 18

Potokar, Stane 165
Potter, Syd 202
Pottier, Richard 44
Pouget, Armand 8, 10
Pouget, Fernando Negri 10
Poulton, Raymond 24
Pozetto, Diego 89, 186
Pozo, Ángel del 18, 139
Pozzato, Pierangelo (a.k.a. Pietro Angelo Pozzato) 200
Pozzetto, Diego 78, 99, 104
Pozzi, Piergiorgio 197
Pradeaux, Maurizio 188
Prades, Jaime 51
Pradier, Perrette 56
Prati, Pamela 198, 204
Prato, Marcello del 60
Pratt, Marie-Christine 27
Préboist, Jacque 32
Préboist, Paul 32
Pregadio, H. 102
Pregadio, Roberto 102, 201
Pregara, Alessio 37
Preiss, Wolfgang 127
Prendes, Luis 119
Prescino, Carlo 129
Prescino, Giorgio 129
Prestano, Paolo 29, 129
Prestopino, Rosario 199, 200, 203
Prete, Alessandro 204
Prete, Giancarlo 110
Pretetto, Tony 114
Pria, Mario Dalla 67
Price, Laddy 204
Price, Vincent 133, 134
Prieto, Antonio 167
Principe, Albino 46, 134
Principi, Mirra 9, 13
Prinzi, Salvatore 34
Priori, Enrico 49, 112
The Prisoner of the Iron Mask (La vendetta della maschera di ferro) 131
Procaccini, Maretta 150
Procinex 128
Proctor Film S.r.L. 139
Proctor, Sherry 22
Procusa 32, 40, 69, 128, 183
Prodas Co. 139
Prodi Cinematografica 113
Producciones Benito Perojo 16, 159
Producciones Cinematograficas 125
Producciones Ponti–De Laurentiis 22
Le Production Georges des Beaureguard 184
Les Productions Artistes Associés 194
Les Productions Jacques Roitfeld 42
Produzione Gallone 34, 119
Produzione Gianni Fuchs 73
Produzioni Atlas Consorziate (P.A.C.) 40
Produzioni Europee Associati (PEA) 41, 154
Profumo, Serafino 200
Proietti, Mario 113
Promoteo Film S.r..L. 118, 140, 173, 181

240 Index

Prora Industrie Cinematografiche e Dello Spettacolo 67
Prosen, Irena 59, 127, 142, 166
Prosperi, Franco 25, 52, 89, 157, 192, 201, 206
Prosperi, Giorgio 67, 127, 158
Prous, Juan 166
Provenzale, Enzo 128
P. T. Cinematografica 174
Puccini, Aldo 27
Puccini, Luciano 27
Puente, Jesús 24, 27, 43, 106
Puente, Tony 151
Puig, Juan Gelpi 113
Pulone, Gianni 195
Punches, Pirates and Karate (Pugni, pirati e karatè) 131
Punic Wars, the 1
Puppo, Romano 110, 206
Purdom, Edmund 41, 60, **98,** 99, 106, 110, 126, 133, 165, 198
Puri, Luigi 64, 83, 84, 90, 95, 116, 138
Pushkin, Alexander 135

Quacquarini, Pierino 197
Quaranta, Letizia 11, 12, 14
Quaranta, Lidia 7, 8
Quartararo, Gaetano 73, 91, 98, 140, 176
Quasimodo, Maria Cumani 205
Quasimodo, Salvatore 24
Quattrini, Alfio 56, 64, 178
Quattrini, Luigi 41
Quattrini, Marisa 191
Quattrini, Paola 21, 80
A *Queen for Caesar (Una regina per Cesare)* 131
The Queen of Sheba (La regina di saba) 132
Queen of the Nile (Nefertite, regina del Nilo) 132
The Queen of the Pirates (La Venere dei pirati) 133
Queen of the Seas (La avventure di Mary Read) 133
Queen, Robert 203
Quercioli, Oreste 207
Quilici, A. 122
Quilici, Antonia 187
Quiney, Carlos (a.k.a. Charles Quiney) 125, 141, 195
Quinn, Anthony 3, 22, 25, 112, 142, 186
Quiroga, Héctor 128
Quo Vadis? (Quo Vadis?) 13, 14

Rabagliati, Alberto 15
Rabal, Francisco 119
Rabanal, Mariano 128
Rackin, Martin 25
Rader, Mary 204
Radic, Jovan 41, 99, 112, 115, 152, 179
Radicchi, Ruggero 33, 155
Radice, Raffale 197
Radius Productions 64, 104, 176
Raffa, Antonio 177
Raffaelli, Giuliano 83
Raffaldi, Giovanni 67

Rage of the Buccaneers (Gordon il pirata nero) 133
Raggio, Elettra 12
Ragionieri, Carla 191
Ragona, Claudio 30, 91, 95
Ragusa, Angelo 199, 205, 206
Raho, Umberto 35, 50, 133, 153
Rai Radiotelevisione Italiana 208
Rai, Roberto 186
Raineri, Giuseppe 37
Rajapa, Redilly B. 171
Rajic, Nikola 118
Ramacci, Gianfranco 143
Ramazzotti, Gastone 136
Rambaldi, Carlo 49, 58, 64, 70, 116
Ramos, José Maria 187
Ramos, Maria Teresa 119
Rampage of Evil (Capitani di ventura) 134
Ramzy, Ahmed 157
Ranalli, Anna 111, **116,** 116
Ranalli, Carla 40
Rancaño, Jesús 154
Rancati 22, 60, 133
Rancati, E. 22, 64, 70, 92, 103, 120, 126, 128, 181
Rance, Margaretta 199
Ranceri, Peppino 177
Ranchi, Federica 28, 48, 72, 162
Randaccio, Antonio 55, 64, 103, 118, 172, 181
Randall, Mónica 151
Randell, Ron 67
Randi, Lucia 31, 178
Randolph, Ed 204
Randolph, Sam 204
Randolph, Ty 202
Randone, Salvo 142
Randors, Paul 200
Ranieri, Giovanni 58, 107
Ranieri, Giuseppe 16, 32, 34, 36, 40, 49, 59, 62, 100, 114, 127, 137, 142, 154, 171, 178, 186, 188, 192
Ranieri, Katina 33
Ranieri, Raul 26, 99, 103, 131, 147
Rappaport, Jack 203
Rappeneau, Jean-Paul 112
Rapper, Irving 130, 164
Rasetti, Anna 199, 207
Rasia, Bruno 129, 130
Rasputin, the Mad Monk 126
Rassimov, Ivan 27
Rassimov, Rada 183
Ratcliffe, Rosanna 26
Rathbone, Basil 130, 131
Rathnarive, Sardha 147
Ravaioli, Isarco 28, 33, 127, 147, 154, 163, 188, 207
Ravenna, Domenico 113
Ray, Aldo 124
Ray, Linette 200
Ray, Nicholas 120
Raymond, Gary 51
R.C.M. Produzione Cinematografica 37
Re, Gustavo 16, 39
Ré, Stefania 36, 129
Reale, Paolo 137
The Rebel Gladiators (Ursus, il gladiatore ribelle) 134

Recio, Lita 174
Recoder, Antonio 18
The Red Cloak (Il mantello rosso) 134
The Red Falcon (Il falco rosso) 135
The Red Sheik (Lo sceicco rosso) 135
Redford, Brian 204
Redzebasic, Halid 161, 168
Reed, Maxwell 33
Reeve, Christopher 3
Reeves, George 80
Reeves, Steve 3, 4, 22, 51, 60, 69, **69, 78, 79,** 80, 92, **93,** 94, **94,** 105, 124, 147, **148, 149,** 149, 156, **157,** 175, 179, 191, 192
Regina Films 81
Regis, Colette 22
Regis, Dario 24, 99
Regnoli, Daniela 46
Regnoli, Piero 33, 46, 102, 146, 198, 201
Reich, George 168
Reid, Milton 164, 171, 192
Reina, Silvano 157, 192
Reiter, Carlo 10
Relja, Mate 161
Relli, Sina 77, 102, 130, 146
Remarch Film 32, 33
Rémy, Hélène 106
Rémy, Jacques 112
Renaud, Monique 63
Renault, Jean-Pierre 194
Renda, N. 194
Renis, Tony 28
Rennie, Joseph 203
Renoir, Claude 112
Renoux, René 178
Renzi, Nello 91, 95
Ressel, Franco 35, 44, 52, 58, 92, 112, 139, 142, 145, 192, 194
Retix Cinematografica 46
Return of Sandokan (Sandokan contro il leopardo di Sarawak) 135
Return of the Black Eagle (Acquila nera) 135
Revene, Larry 207
Revenge of Black Eagle (La vendetta di Aquila Nera) 136
The Revenge of Ivanhoe (La rivincita de Ivanhoe) 136
The Revenge of Maciste (La rivincita di Maciste) 14
Revenge of the Barbarians (La vendetta dei barbari) 136
Revenge of the Conquered (Drakut il vendicatore) 137
Revenge of the Gladiators (La vendetta dei gladiatori) 137
Revenge of the Gladiators (La vendetta di Spartacus) 138
Revenge of the Mercenaries (Il capitano di ferro) 138
Revenge of the Musketeers (D'Artagnan contro i 3 moschettieri) 138
Revière, Georges 103
Revilla, Rafael Calvo 119, 190
Revolt of the Barbarians (La rivolta dei barbari) 139
Revolt of the Mercenaries (La rivolta dei mercenari) 139

Revolt of the Praetorians (La rivolta dei pretoriani) 139
The Revolt of the Seven (La rivolta dei sette) 140
Revolt of the Slaves (La rivolta degli schiavi) 140
Rey, Fernando 65, 68, 105, 140, 150, 163
Rey, Pedro del 42
Reynado, Iris 203
Reyner, Antimo 46
Rezzera, Mario 134
Rhodes, Bobby 202
Rhodes, Christopher 51
Rhodes, Virginia 18
Rhodios, Apollonios 78
Rhu, Ángela 27, 84
Rialto Film 46, 67, 126, 151, 156
Ribas, Antoni 106
Ribera, Daniel 26, 167
Ribotta, Ettore 142, 159
Ribowska, Malka 56
Ribulsi, Enrico 99, 127
Riccardi, Marina 45
Riccardini, Michele 174, 186
Ricci, Aldo 136
Ricci, Antonio 168
Ricci, Brian 202
Ricci, Luciano 17, 130, 164
Ricci, Orlando 11
Ricci, Paolo 60, 189, 204, 206
Ricci, Renzo 125, 158
Ricci, Richard 56
Ricci, Roberto 206
Ricci, Teodoro 21
Ricci, Tonino 21, 52, 141, 166, 175, 206
Ricci, Vitantonio 65, 178
Riccioni, Abo 13
Richard, Philippe 42
Richards, Tony 106
Richardson, Neil 207
Richelmy, Agostino 15
Richmond, Anthony 206
Richmond, John 201
Rico, Galliano 186
Ridel, Armand 118, 177
Riebauer, Harry 88
Riento, Virgilio 55
Riesgo, José 55, 84, 194
Rietti, Victor 164
Rietty, Robert 22, 27, 51, 164
Rieul, Jean 42
Riffini, Claudio 20
Riganti, Franco 43
Riganti, Giorgio 44
Rigaud, George 16, 39, 151
Rigaut, Roger 174
Rigel, Arturo 16, 47, 159
Riggi, Alberto 46
Righi, Massimo 20, 25, 112, 153, 191
Rigillo, Mariano 28
Rihai, Mansoureh 113
Rinaldi, Antonio 104
Rinaldi, Giuseppe 55, 155
Rinaldi, Lina 139
Rinaudo, Fabio 163
Rio Film 115
Rio, Emilio Ruiz del 18, 65, 105, 116, 204

Rioli, Riccardo 15, 50
Ripamonti, Vittorio 36
Risai, Mansuareh 113
Risi, Marco 194
Risi, Paolo 199
Rispoli, Gualtiero 195
Rispoli, Maria Luisa 36, 163
Rispoli, Viviana Maria 200
Risso, Roberto 59, 65, 114, 138
Riva, Andrea 48, 111
Riva, Miguel de la 116
Rivalta, Giorgio 22
Rivarolo, Leda 132
Rivas, Domingo 47
Rivelles, Rafael 43, 140
Rivelli, Luisa 177
Rivero, Jorge (a.k.a. George Rivero) 201
Rivero, Santiago 24, 126, 167, 190, 195
Rivers, Steve 200
Rivière, George 58
Rizzo, Alfredo 102, 153
Rizzo, Carlo 44, 168
Rizzo, Carmine 48
Rizzo, Gene 206
Rizzo, Gianni 78, 114, 125, 129, 130, 158, 164, 171, 176, 179, 187
Rizzuto, Renato 83
R.K.O. 131
RM Films 112
Roas Produzioni 26, 156
Robbins, Eva 198, 202
Robelli, Aio 48
Robelli, Argy 48
Robelli, Edoardo 48
Robert, Alfredo 49
Robert, Jacques 16
Roberti, Roberto 12
Robertson, Frank 160
Robin Hood and the Pirates (Robin Hood e i pirati) 140
Robin Hood, the Invincible Archer (Robin Hood, l'invincibile arciere) 141
Robin, Jacques 42
Robins, Eva 198, 202
Robinson, Casey 159
Robinson, Joe 25, 52, 169, 171, 175
Robinson, Neil 192
Robledo, Lorenzo 116, 154
Robuschi, Guido 31, 36, 56, 58, 60, 140, 167, 168, 178
Rocca, Daniela 36, 52, 60, 78, 107, 137, 141
Rocca, Emilia Della 137
Rocca, Maria Laura 32, 59, 118
Roccheti, Giancarlo 197
Rocchetti, Gamborino 139
Rocchetti, Manilo 52, 138
Rocchetti, Mara 52, 60
Rocchi, Marrina 208
Rocco, Lyla 134
Rocco, Maria Pia 151
Roche, France 134
Roche, Serge de la 18
Rochetti 48, 58, 62, 64, 92, 126, 181
Rochetti, Goffredo 83, 119, 182, 184
Rochetti, Mara 78, 132, 156

Rodann, Ziva 64
Rodero, José López 51, 64
Rodes Cinematografica 27
Rodgers, Melonee 206
Rodolfi, Eleuterio 10, 13
Rodriguez, Hilda 24
Rodriguez, Inés 27
Rodriguez, Xiomara 199
Rogers, Clyde 136
Rogers, Donald C. 27
Rogoz, Zvonimir 162
Roi, Maria Luisa 31, 34, 41, 106, 166
Roitfeld, Jacques 42
Roitfeld, Wladimir 42
Rojas, Alfonso 104, 167
Rojas, Manuel 24
Rojo, Antonio Molino 67, 101, 116, 150, 151
Rojo, Gustavo 30, 138
Rojo, José Sntonio 195
Rojo, Rubén 165
Roland the Mighty (Orlando e i Paladini di Francia) 141
Rolando, Maria Luisa 19
Rolfe, Guy 25
Rollo, Stefano 163, 179
Roma Film 46
Román, Letícia 130, 35
Román, Martinez 55, 84, 195
Roman, Mirko 157
Roman, Ruth 46
Romana Film 81, 84, 88, 89, 102, 130, 133, 143, 146, 195, 196
Romanelli, Olga 167
Romangoli, Romolo 50
Romani, G. Adami 128
Romani, Giancarlo 130
Romanini, Gaia 36, 92, 122, 139, 155, 182, 190
Romano Film 34, 77
Romanini, Rossana 203
Romano, Carlo 54, 55, 116, 174
Romano, Felice 136
Romano, Giuseppe 204
Romano, Marla 206
Romano, Pasquale 27
Romano, Raffaele 150
Romanos, Lola 8
Rome 1585 (I masnadieri) 141
Romeo, Marcello 206
Romero, Juan Ruiz 150
Romero, Luz 159
Romitelli, Giancarlo 63, 87, 96, 107, 111, 143, 145, 149, 178
Ronald, Paul 99
Roncaioli, Angelo 187
Ronconi, Luciano 197
Rondeau, Suzanne 56
Roni, Adalberto 143
Ronsin, Roger 56
Roquevert, Noël 42
Rory, Armando Mac 206
Rory, Rosanna 32, 140
Rosa Film 182
Rosa, Emilio 49
Rosa, Sergio 19
Rosales, Lina 68
Rosato, Lucio 199
Roscedo, Pasquale 162

Index

Rose, Norman 39, 80
Rosen, Maria Luisa 54, 107, 177
Roses, Luis 120
Rosi, Leopoldo 84, 125, 161, 162
Rosmanit, Nerea 111, 200
Rosmino, Antonio 175
Rosmino, Gian Paolo 19, 59, 60, 68, 80, 138, 141
Rosmino, Gigliola 80, 155
Ross, Frank 104
Ross, Frederic 25
Ross, Herbert 24
Ross, Howard 20, 47, 52, 55, 81, 82, 104, 140, 143, 160, 167, 196
Ross, Red 104, 160
Rosselini, Renzo 156
Rossellini, Franco 156
Rossellini, Renzo 106, 129, 136, 169, 174
Rosser, Jon 203
Rossetti, Franco 41, 50, 70
Rossetti, Livia 40
Rossetti, Mario 64
Rossi-Stuart, Giacomo 22
Rossi, Alvaro 197
Rossi, Andreina 36, 128
Rossi, Cinzia 207
Rossi, Fausto 26, 40, 65, 84, 99, 111, 118, 131, 140, 149, 172, 181
Rossi, Fernando 49
Rossi, Giovanni 67
Rossi, Luciano 142, 199
Rossi, Vittorio 37, 40, 47, 59, 68, 76, 87, 103, 105, 106, 127, 140, 142, 154, 163, 171, 190
Rossin, Sheila 112
Rossini, Gabriel 203
Rossini, Renato 82, 167
Rosson, Harold 184
Rota, Nino 132, 176
Rotundi, Maurizio 91
Rotunno, Giuseppe 22, 27
Roudeix, Pierre 56
Roussel, René 32
Rouzière, Jean-Michel 31
Rovatti, Cesare 50
Rovena, Marcella 128
The Rover (L'avventuriero) 142
Rover Film 20
Rovere, Carla 55
Rovere, Gina 80, 114, 141, 187
Rovere, Luigi 20, 28, 91, 173
Rovere, Patrizia Della 92
Rowland, Roy 150, 151
Roxy, Mirella 54
Roy, Jannette Le 161
Royal Film Traders 200
Royal Films 205
Royer, Michel Le 96
Rozin, Spela 91, 112, 160
Rózsa, Miklós 51, 158
Royal Film 35, 124
RPA Elios Studios 202, 204
Rubener, Asoka 147
Rubener, Sujata 147
Rubien, Howard Nelson 192
Rubini, Giulia 45, 69, 103, 126, 134
Rubinstein, Ricardo 128
Rubio, Ángel Rosson y 84, 125, 195

Rubio, Antonio 67
Rubio, Josefa 16, 47
Rubio, Pepe 27, 68
Rubirosa, Rita 41, 126
Rucavina, Milo 157
Rudel, Roger 145
Rudolph, Oscar 158
Ruffini, Claudio 52, 91, 109, 111
Ruffini, Sandro 10, 55
Ruffo, Leonora 29, 73, 76, 90, 132, 168
Rufini, Franco 201
Rugge, Peter 204
Ruggeri, Ada 162
Ruggieri, Osvaldo 44, 50
Ruggiero, Gene 25, 175, 192
Ruikavine, Milan 138
Ruiz, Capillas 39
Ruiz, Mariano 39
Ruiz, Ventura 120
Rukmini, Subkmanati 141
Ruskaja, Jia 9
Rusoff, Ted 206
Ruspantini, Mauro 202
Ruspoli, Cristina 14
Ruspoli, Esmeralda 153
Russeau, Nadia 26
Russel, Pat 198, 200
Russel, Tony 26, 104, 140, 151, 166
Russo, Alfonso 30, 60
Russo, Vittorio 156
Russu, Giovanna 205
Rustichelli, Carlo 20, 33, 54, 64, 77, 91, 103, 104, 107, 120, 124, 135, 128, 132, 133, 134, 135, 151, 160, 163, 166, 168, 173, 175, 176, 177, 200, 206
Rustichelli, Paolo 206
Ruzza, Rodolfo 201

Sabatelli, Mario 160, 177
Sabatini, Oreste 91
Sabatini, Rafael 159
Sabatini, Stefania 92
Sabatino, Gennaro 46
Sabbatini, Giovanni 20, 64
Sabetta, Ugo 188
Sabu 175
Sacchetti, Dardano 203
Sacco, Ricky 197, 199, 202
Sacerdoti, Marco 202
Sacevic, Tonko 164
Sacripante, Umberto 55, 128, 140
Sacripanti, Luciano 28, 51
Sacripanti, Mauro 50, 206
Sacristán, Gregorio 18
Sadun, Piero 18, 119
Safra, Michael 150
Sagaseta, Enrique F. 47
Sagone, Thomas (a.k.a. Tomasso Sagone) 128, 147, 191
Sagoni, Luciano 110, 194
Said, Fouad 32, 33
Sailer, Tony 88
Sain, Italo 23
Sainati, Bella Starace 55, 125
Sant'Ambrogio, Dino 129
St. George, George 99
Saio, Mario 9, 10, 11
Sakara, Michele 55

Sala, Franz 8, 9, 10, 11, 12
Sala, Margherita 25
Sala, Vittorio 36
Salafranca, Gustavo 187
Saleh, Abdel Khalek 160
Salerno, Enrico Maria 87, 155, 191
Salerno, Patrizia 201
Salerno, Vittorio 141
Salez, Claude 56
Salgado, Rosa G. 30, 84
Salgari, Emilio 7, 15, 28, 33, 135, 147, 162, 176
Salient, Valentin 151
Salimbeni 15
Salimbeni, Giancarlo Bartolini 19, 34, 36, 41, 46, 54, 77, 99, 103, 107, 119, 128, 129, 130, 132, 133, 134, 135, 147, 158, 169, 173, 177
Sallis, Zoe 27
Salou, Louis 55
Saltamerenda, Gino 55
Salvadori, Alfredo 178
Salvadori, Paola 164
Salvadori, Paolo 29, 130
Salvadori, Ruggero 142
Salvati, Domenico 169
Salvati, Rita 91
Salvati, Sergio 95
Salvati, Valentino 207
Salvatore, Alberto 81
Salvatore, Enrico 27, 44, 141, 166, 172
Salvatore, Fausto 8
Salvatori, Alberto 65, 95
Salvatori, Alfredo 178
Salvatori, Goffredo 29
Salvatori, Maurizio 160
Salvatori, Renato 176
Salvatori, Rolando 126
Salvi, Decio 32, 44, 62
Salvi, Erminio 16, 32, 44, 62, 69, 152, 177, 187, 188
Salvi, Luigi 31
Salvietti, Agostino 133
Salzer, Jean 198, 200
Sam, Poing Ping 112
Sambati, Giuliano 64
Sambrell, Aldo 55, 128, 150, 151, 200
Samcro Film SpA. 173
Sammartino, Ennio 118
Samson (Sansone) 142
Samson and Delilah 1, 3
Samson Against the Pirates (Sansone contro i pirati) 143, **144**
Samson and the 7 Miracles of the World (Maciste alla corte del Gran Khan) 112, 143
Samson and the Mighty Challenge (Ercole, Sansone, Maciste e Ursus gli invincibli) 143
Samson and the Slave Queen (Zorro contro Maciste) 145
Samson in King Solomon's Mines (Maciste nelle miniere de re Salomone) 146
San Martín, Conrado 23, 29, 39, 107, 139, 143, 190, 201
San Paolo Films 65, 102
Sánchez, Carmen 106
Sánchez, Flomenica 136

Index 243

Sánchez, José María 106
Sánchez, Pedro Mari 151, 195
Sancho, Fernando 68, 159, 163
Sancro Film 118
Sancrosiap S.p.A. 165
Sander, Allegra 191
Sanders, Jim 207
Sanders, Nadia 64, 187
Sandokan Fights Back (Sandokan alla riscossa) 147
Sandokan the Great (Sandokan la tigre di Mompracem) 147, **148, 149**
Sandokan, Pirate of Malaysia (I pirati della Malesia) 147, 149
Sandri, Anna-Maria 33
Sandri, Gia 92, 100
Sandri, Maria Grazia 33, 60
Sandrine 95, 125
Sanfilippo, Valeria 8
Sangermano, Angelo 29, 31, 83, 111, 187, 195
Sangiorgi, Marilù 41, 139
Sangro, Elena 8, 11, **11,** 12
Sani, Amru 27
Sanipoli, Vittorio 41, 124, 136, 141, 156, 157, 167
Sanjust, Filippo 30, 67, 124, 152, 153, 175, 191
Sanson Films 140
Sanson, Yvonne 125, 136, 141
Sansone, Alfonso 118, 164
Sansoni, Mario 40, 59, 60, 68, 135, 142
Sant'Ambrogio, Dino 28, 114
Santaloce, Silvio 19
Santana, Hugo 168
Santangeli, Otello 84
Santangelo, Guglielmo 41, 130, 134, 164
Santangelo, Vincenzo 201
Santaniello, Angelo 111
Santaniello, Oscar 19, 111
Santarelli, Amerigo 19, 36, 89, 111, 158, 173, 182, 186
Santarsiero, Anna 153
Santi, Franco 33
Santi, Giancarlo 197, 202
Santi, John 202
Santi, Pier Luigi 83, 169
Santini, Alessandro 136
Santini, Gino 114, 146, 156
Santini, Pino 124
Santoli, Alma 21
Santoli, Euclide 21, 52, 92, 112, 158, 189
Santoni, Claudio 29
Santoni, Maurizio 29
Santoni, Tino 19, 58, 128, 163, 179, 189
Santonocito, Carlos 68
Santuccio, Gianni 32, 35, 134, 154, 186
Sapienza, Gollarda 55, 186
The Saracens (Il pirati del diavolo) 149
Sarafian, Richard C. 21
Saragò, Antonio 204
Sarandrea, Alessandro 29, 62, 65, 73, 107, 140, 146, 178, 206

Sarazin, René 56
Sarcey, Martine 145
Sarhan, Shukry 160
Sarlo, Nando 113, 164
Sarlui, Edward 205
Sarlui, Helen 198, 205
Sarno, Antonio 177
Saroli, Elio 88
Sarrazin, Michael 110
Sarrocco, Bernardina 77
Sartarelli, Marcello 91, 189
Sarthre, Gilbert 118
Sarzi-Braga 90
Sassard, Jacqueline 147, 149, 163
Sasso, Ugo 20, 34, 45, 46, 47, 55, 62, 69, 72, 73, 81, 87, 92, 94, 114, 119, 126, 128, 129, 132, 135, 136, 137, 139, 141, 152, 158, 160, 164, 165, 171, 173, 179, 187
Satson, Lucky 115
Saul and David (Saul e David) 150
Saulnier, Jacques 112
Sauro, Sergio 155
Sauvajon, Marc-Gilbert 118, 150, 177
Sauvion, Serge 87
Savage, Archie 84, 158, 163, 175
Savagnone, Giuseppe 44
Savarese, Roberto 42
Savelli, Gianni 103
Savery, Gerald 150
Savina, Carlo 59, 76, 78, 80, 81, 82, 92, 99, 110, 114, 115, 116, 126, 134, 138, 143, 152, 158, 163, 166, 179, 183, 186, 189, 191
Savini, Antonio 28
Savini, Giovanni 205
Savini, Jacobo 138
Savioli, Ageo 37
Savona, Leopoldo 62, 122, 188, 191, 62–63
Savrenti, Mariano 33
Sbardella, Filiberto 174
Sbragia, Giancarlo 56, 72, 116, 189
Sbrenna, Mario 31, 73, 206, 207
Scaccia, Mario 119, 124, 137, 140, 153
Scaglione, Michele 37, 40
Scagnetti, Franca 113
Scala, Delia 50
Scala, Domenico 36
Scala, Gaetano 25, 63, 81, 87, 98, 139, 146
Scala, Gia 178
Scala, Giorgio 99
Scalabrelli, Floriana 197, 205
Scalco, Giorgio 78
Scalese, Mariella 194
Scalia, Sergio 62
Scalo, Giorgio 99
Scandariato, Italia 77, 130
Scandariato, Romano 19
Scandurra, Andrea 34
Scandurra, Franco 68
Scandurra, Sofia 171, 175
Scanzani, Maurizio 84, 163
Scaramouche 16
Scarchilli, Claudio 55, 56, 64, 68, 91, 130
Scardamaglia, Elio 15, 73, 122, 138, 152, 153

Scardamaglia, Francesco 73, 152
Scardella, Ludovico 189
Scarfone, Sina 143, 173
Scaringi, Lilli 127
Scaripanti, Mauro 160
Scarlett, Vorke 118
Scarozza, Duilio 35, 95, 114, 138, 160, 187
Scarpelli, Furio 32, 78, 176
Scarpelli, Marco 21, 33, 116, 141
Scarpelli, Umberto 44, 60, 62
Scarpellini, Giovanni 147
Scatamacchia, Fabio 26
Scatena, Luce 178
Scattini, Luici 22
Scavia, Bartolomeo 26
Scavia, Mimmo 19, 26
Scavran, Luigi 20, 91, 173
Scega, V.S. 59
Scheherazade (Shéhérazade) 150
Schermi Produzione 19, 21
Schermi Riuniti 92
Schettini, Gabriella 173
Schiaffino, Rosanna 120, 141, 142
Schiller, Friedrich 191
Schirru, Fido 7, 13
Schneider, Helmuth 164
Schneider, Sam 99, 106, 161
Schoeller, Ingrid 163
Schöner, Ingeborg 15, 130
Schorr, William 184
Schüfftan, Eugen 184, 186
Schwartz, Arnold 204
Schwarze, Giorgio Garibaldi 147, 149, 194
Sciacqua, Pino 36, 169
Scianizza, Umberto 49
Sciaqua, Pino 102
Scicolone, Sofia 50
Scipioni, Bruno 35, 81, 82, 88, 111, 114, 116, 118, 133, 134, 137, 146, 173
Sciré, Andrea 150
Scisci, Mario 27
Scivicco, Vera 33
Scola, Ettore 182
Scola, Giola 201
Scolaro, Giovanni 178, 187
Scolaro, Nino 29, 31, 80, 114, 136, 178, 187
Scoppi, Andrea 84
Scorcelletti, Rinaldo 126
Scotese, Giuseppe Maria 125, 129, 134
Scotolani, Fausta 19
Scott, Charles 203
Scott, Esther 21
Scott, George C. 27
Scott, Gordon 3, 26, 51, 65, **75,** 76, 96, 98, 103, 107, 114, 131, 145, 176, **183, 184,** 184
Scott, John 207
Scotti, Andrea 21, 26, 32, 40, 48, 84, 88, 89, 95, 99, 122, 138, 143, 146, 168
Scotti, Gino 29, 32, 69, 129, 186
Scotti, Ottavio 36, 47, 64, 67, 122, 130, 155, 156, 163
Scotto, Giovanna 46
Scratuglia, Giovanni Ivan 142, 177
Scratuglia, Ivan 177
Scritti, Cesare 194

244 Index

Scuccuglia, Leo 62, 188
Scuderoni, Pupita Lea 113
Scutti, Mario 200, 207
The Sea Pirate (Surcouf, l'eroe dei sette mari) 150
Seccia, Cesare 37, 68
Séchan, Edmond 177
The Secret Mark of D'Artagnan (Il colpo segreto di d'Artagnan) 151
The Secret Seven (Gli invincibli sette) 151
Segri, Aldo 125, 138
Seguino, Emanuele 48
Segur, Ali 208
Segura, Gregorio García 159, 16
Segurini, Nino 25, 164
Seiffert, Regina 196
Seigner, Louis 41, 42
Seiler, Jacques 56
Sekely, Steve 46
Selgur, Timucin 207
Selgur, Zeynep 208
Seligman, Selig J. 142
Sellalonga, Jorge 207
Sellers, Sabrina 201
Selli, Lulla 22, 103
Selli, Sergio 100
Selmi, Marcello 100, 135
Selmur Productions 142
Seltzer, Dov 204, 205
Selznick, Leon 87
Semerano, Don 203
Sempere, Diego Gómez 64
Sempere, Julio Cesar 51, 167
Sempere, Vicente 51
Sempetery, Wilma 128
Sen, Tevfik 208
Senatore, Paolo 141
Senior Cinematografica 143
Sens-Cazenave, Alain 203
Sensani, Gino 49
Sensi, Mario 21, 54, 62, 114, 138, 151, 154, 178, 187
Sensidoni, Giancarlo 199
Senzacqua, Alfredo 205
Senzacqua, Silvana 55
Seoane, José María 27
Sepúlveda, José 116
Serafin, Enzo 95, 103, 106
Serafinelli, Aurelio 178, 194
Serak, Valentin 59
Serandrei, Mario 20, 33, 36, 41, 52, 54, 60, 67, 78, 89, 92, 139, 156, 158, 164, 166, 174
Serano, Giuliana 111
Serato, Massimo 19, 20, 29, 32, 34, 35, 41, 45, 51, 95, 98, 102, 107, 113, 129, 130, 133, 140, 145, 151, 184
Seratrice, Vincenzo 30, 40, 60, 95, 129, 157
Serena, Gustavo 13, 19
Sernas, Jacques 35, 50, 51, 67, 76, 99, 110, 127, 128, 135, 155, 156
Sernia, Franco 154
Serpe, Ralph 25, 27, 184
Serra, Domenico 11
Serra, Gianna 143
Serra, Liliana 205
Serrador, Pastor 24

Serrano, Rafael Garcia 42, 100
Serravalli, Giancarlo 26
Sertili, Franco 64
Serto, Ermanno 29, 110, 126, 195
Sertoli, Mario 49
Serventi, Luigi 9, 12
Servo, Piero 27
Sestili, Rosetta 114
Séty, Gérard 163
Seven Film 111, 115, 160
Seven from Thebes (Sette a Tebe) 152
The Seven Magnificent Gladiators (I sette magnifici gladiatori) 204
Seven Rebel Gladiators (Sette contro tutti) 152
The Seven Revenges (Le sette sfide) 152
The Seven Samurai 67
Seven Seas to Calais (Il dominatore dei 7 mari) 152
Seven Slaves Against the World (Gli schiavi più forti del mondo) 153
The Seventh Sword (Le sette spade del vendicatore) 49, 153
79 A.D. (Anno 79: La distruzione di Ercolano) 153
Séverac, Jacques 150
Severini, Attilio 17, 52, 54, 88, 107, 111, 141, 157, 160, 177
Severini, Leonardo 145
Severino, Mauro 132
Severova, Sava 127
Sevilla, Carmen 47
Seymandi, Domenico 100
Seymour Brodie & Associates 207
SFA 67
SFF Alfred Rose 81
The Shadow of Zorro (L'ombra di Zorro) 154
Shake, Louis 115
Shannon, Frank 201
Sharif, Omar 113
Sharoff, Pietro 136
Shaw, David 202
Shaw, Irwin 184
She (Lei) 205
She (1911) 205
She (1916) 205
She (1917) 205
She (1925) 205
She (1935) 205
She (1965) 205
She (1968) 205
She (1982) 205
She (2001) 205
Sherman, Laurie 205
Shock, Edith 26
Shub, Dede 204
Siamé, Made 42
Siani, Romolo 197
Siani, Sabrina 198, 199, 201, 206
Sibaldi, Stefano 15, 49, 174
Siciliano, Salvatore 92, 107, 132, 151, 177, 188
Sidewater, Fred 27
Siege of Syracuse (L'assedio di Siracusa) 155
Sienkiewicz, Henryk 13, 14, 99
Sievers, Olga 191

Sign of the Gladiator (Nel segno di Roma) 155
Signore, Camillo Del 29, 35, 81, 82, 114, 126, 129, 138, 175, 187
Signoret, Simone 25
Signoretti, Faustone 110
Signorini, Evaristo 49
Silberman, Serge 150
Silenti, Vira 20, 23, 162, 163, 164, 192
Siletti, Mario 124, 136, 174, 182
Silke, James R. 199
Silva, Franco 35, 77, 132, 122–124
Silva, Giuseppe 55
Silva, María 106, 154
Silva, Rita 201
Silvagni, Dario 207
Silvani, Aldo 34, 44, 55, 159
Silver, Bert 152
Silvero, Daniela 26
Silvestri, Alberto 26, 28
Silvestri, Enzo 21, 124
Silvestri, Gabriele 32, 127
Silvestri, Renato 54, 105
Silvestri, Umberto 55, 132, 156, 158, 174, 186
Silvi, Roberto 203
Sima, Maria 34
Simeoli, Pasquale 195
Simeoni, Simonetta 45, 60, 81, 84, 159
Simi, Carlo 50
Simms, Al 70
Simon, Michel 43, 55
Simoncelli, Leonilde 26
Simonelli, Giorgio 104, 140, 186
Simonelli, Giovanni 40, 59, 68, 127, 142, 150, 153, 171, 190
Simonelli, Idelmo 33
Simoneschi, Carlo 46
Simoneschi, Lidia 15, 39, 44, 55, 155, 174, 182, 186
Simonetti, Claudio 201
Simonetti, Giuliano 32, 40, 41, 60
Simonetti, Guido 205
Simoni 159
Simons, Joan 160
Simons, Marvin 200
Simont, Antonio 65, 106, 119, 190
Simova, Ileana 136
Sims, Al 143
Sims, Sylvia 18
Sinbad and the Caliph of Baghdad (Simbad e il califfo di Bagdad) 156
Sinbad of the Seven Seas (Sinbad dei sette mari) 205
Sinclair, Marie Louise 19
Sindoni, Vittorio 146
Singer, Honoré 25
Sini, Linda 15, 48, 102, 113
Sinibaldi, Claudio 58
Sins of Rome (Spartaco) 156
Sionisco, Frederick 198
Sipioni, Bruno 30
Siracusa, Giovanni 98
Sire, Yvonne 16, 188
Siroli, Edgardo 167
Sisi, Gustavo 19, 91
Sisi, Otello 82
Sissia, Guido 136

Sisti, Mario 58
Sjostedt, Per 207
Skerla, Léna 56
Skiljevic, Ljubo 113
The Slave (Il figlio di Spartacus) 156, **157**
Slave Girls of Sheba (Le verdi bandiere di Allah) 157
The Slave Merchants see *The Devil of the Desert Against the Son of Hercules*
Slave of Rome (La schiava di Roma) 157
Slave Queen of Babylon (lo Semiramide) 158
Slonisco, Federico 200, 202
Sloot, Peter Vander 87, 106
Smacchi, Sergio 20, 109
Small, Edward 80
Smith, Bruno 15
Smith, Constance 104
Smith, S. Duncan 194
Smith, Suzanne 207
Smordoni, Rinaldo 55
Smyrner, Ann 32
Snegoff, Gregory 200, 205, 208
Snidersic, Tanja 58
Sobelli, Olga 21
Société Cinématographique Lyre 60, 64, 155
Société Générale de Cinématographie (S.G.C.) 51, 54, 159
Società Italiana Cines 165
Société Nouvelle de Cinématographi (SNC) 34, 77, 102, 113, 129, 130, 133
Sociéte Nouvelle des Établissements Gaumont (SNEG) 152
Société Nouvelle Pathé Cinéma (S.N.I.P.), 51
La Société des Films Sirius 23, 42, 107, 147
Soderini, Lorenzo 8
Sodom and Gomorrah (Sodoma e Gomora) 158
Soffer, Stephan 200
Sofia, Gioacchino 124
Sofia, Vinicio 15, 55, 102, 165, 178
Sofield, Mark 200
Sofio, Gisella 134
Solano, Domingo 26
Solano, Guido **76**
Solari, Dino 122
Solari, Laura 51
Solaro, Gianni 21, 29, 32, 34, 35, 52, 64, 65, 92, 113, 118, 130, 133, 138, 142, 151, 153, 163, 166, 169, 178, 181, 187
Solaro, Giovanni 187
Solbelli, Olga 95, 125, 160, 174
Soldati, Mario 15, 27, 49, 176
Soldi, Gino 63, 102, 143
Soler, Ángel 27
Soler, Juan Alberto 147, 151, 166
Soler, Tony 104
Soli, Gino 111
Solieri, Fernando 46
Solignac, Guy 31
Soligo, Edda 19, 141

Soliño, Norberto 154
Solis, Pedro 128
Solito, Giacinto 110, 128
Solitro, Gianni 95, 114
Sollima, Sergio 28, 68, 110, 119, 134, 163, 171, 179
Solmesne, Rudolphe 120
Solomon, Jack 51
Solvay, Paolo 150, 194
Sommer, Elke 191
Sommer, Robert 201
The Son of Captain Blood (El hijo del capitán Blood) 159
Son of Cleopatra (Il figlio di Cleopatra) 159
The Son of D'Artagnan (Il figlio d'Artagnan) 160
The Son of Hercules in the Land of Darkness (Ercole l'invincibile) 160
Son of Samson (Maciste nella valle dei Re) 161, **161, 162**
Son of the Red Corsair (Il figlio del corsaro rosso) 162
The Sons of Hercules tv package 47
Sonni, Corrado 73, 92
Sonois, Henri 56
Sonova, Leopoldo 52
Sons of Thunder (Arrivano i titani) 163
Soong, Lucille 113
Sophocles 92
Sorano, Daniel 56
Soraya, Queen of the Desert see *The Devil of the Desert Against the Son of Hercules*
Sordi, Alberto 46, 182
Sormani, C. 120
Sormani, Franco 151
Sormano, Francesco 151
Soro, Susana 198
Sorrente, Sylvia 168
Sorrentino, Alberto 64, 153, 176
Sotirova, Maria 165
Sotlar, Bert 152
Sotti, Andrea 32
Sottile, Pietro 197
Sovona, Leopoldo 188
SpA Cinematografica 87, 90, 113
Spaak, Charles 18
Space Mutiny 208
Spada, Marcello 46
Spadaro, Adriana 160, 202, 205
Spadini, B. 58
Spadini, Grillo 54
Spadoni, Giulio 107, 143
Spadoni, Luciano 192
Spadoni, Pietro 22, 55, 95, 103, 110, 151
Spadorcia, Enrico 140
Spadoro, Umberto 88
Spafford, Robert 29, 81, 204, 208
Spafford, Susan 208
Spaggiari, Erika 163
Spagnoli, Alberto 28, 197, 201
Spagnoli, Manrico 120, 129
Spagnoli, Maurice 21
Spagnuolo, Alessandra 198, 206
Spagnuolo, Ettore 198, 206
Spain, Fay 87

Spalla, Erminio 55, 59, 122, 129, 131, 134, 155, 171
Spalla, Ignazio 195
Spartacus (Spartaco il gladiatore della Tracia) 14
Spartacus (Spartaco) 14
Spartacus (Kubrick) 20, 138, 156
Spartacus and the Ten Gladiators (Gli invincibli dieci gladiatori) 163
Spataro, Rocco 58
Spencer, Bud 24, 77
Sperabene, Giulio 33
Sperli, Alessandro 64, 87
Spettacolo Film 125
Speziali, Renato 113, 168
Spigler, Joseph 118, 178
Spila, Aristide 122
Spila, Otello 65, 130
Spina, Maria Grazia 27, 29, 41, 82, 103, 114, 137, 139, 145, 169, 177
Spina, Sergio 158, 189
Spingi, Marcello 200
Spinola, Matteo 19
Spinolo, Fortunato 14
Spitoni, Stefano 48
Spivack, Murray 27
Splendor Film 134, 137, 187
Sponsali, Valeria 40, 90
Sposito, Carletto 174
Sposito, Carlo 174
Sprovieri, Aldo 22
Sreckovic, M. 118
Srucchi, Stefano 140
S.S.F.A. Studios 174
Staccioli, Ivano 35, 36, 104, 110, 127, 128, 151, 164, 166, 168, 169, 171, 179, 189
Staccioli, Serenilla 175
Stacy, John 25, 131
Stafford, Gino 62, 188
Stagni, Ferrucio 186
Staiola, Enzo 168
Stakovic, Milenko 118
Standard Produzionne 69
Stander, Lionel 113
Stanic, Mila 167
Stankovic, Vladimir 112
Stanojevic, Dragomir 112
Stanojevic, Ljubomir 8
Stany, Jacques 64, 67, 153, 172
Star Wars 198
Starke, Pat 199, 204
Steel, Alan 59, 60, 80, 83, **83**, 84, **85**, 87, 88, 94, 127, 142, 143, 145, **145**, 176
Steel, Anthony 137, 177
Steele, Barbara 21, 138, 138
Stefanato, Angelo 142
Stefanelli, Benito 18, 22, 26, 50, 51, 76, 114, 118, 131, 134, 137, 139, 156, 157, 173, 179, 186, 199, 204
Stefanelli, Marco 26
Stefani, Averroè 147, 194
Stefani, Ubaldo 10
Stefanini, Nico 100
Stefanini, Niksa (a.k.a. Nicola Stefanini) 59, 60, 127, 138, 142, 154, 157, 191
Stefanovic, Lazar 99

Steffanelli, Benito 106
Steffen, Anthony 19, 33, 48, 100, 158
Steffen, Paul 175
Stefilongo, Renzo 188
Stegani, Giorgio 24, 98, 107, 109, 179
Stein, Ronald 77
Steinberg, Ned 200
Steiner, John 206, 207
Steinpichler, Michael 27
Stel, Ermanno 34
Stella Films 110
Stellari, Gian 31, 36, 58, 60, 140, 167, 168, 178
Steni, Antonella 46
Steno 135
Steno, Massimo Patrizi 124
Steno, Vittorio Metz 124
Stephan, Letizia 37
Sterbini, Roberto 194
Sterling, Simon 163
Stern, Mike 142
Sterpetti, Beniamino 194
Steve, Gordon 164, 179
Stevens, Gordon 152
Stevens, Polly 162
Stevens, Rock 35, 63, 76, 89
Stevenson, Bud 152
Stewart, Elaine 152
Stewart, Ivy 127, 154
Stiffi, Egidio 204
Stockwell, Guy 167
Stojkovic, Aleksandar 113
Stokes, Edward 204
Stoloff, Victor 46
Stone, Sam 198, 200
Stoppa, Paolo 34, 42, 49, 55, 136, 160
Stoppa, Tonio 17
Stoppa, Torino 32
Storaro, Vittorio 21
The Story of Joseph and His Brethren (Giuseppe venduto dai fratelli) 164
La Strada 22Stradly, Andy 200
Stragliati, Rolando 174
Stratton, Kathleen 202
Stresa, Nino 21, 22, 23, 35, 69, 103, 133, 137
Strober, Carla 28
Strogoff (Michel Strogoff, corriere dello zar) 164
Stroyberg, Malìs 25
Strucchi, Stefano 164, 192
Strung, Kevin 200
Struss, Karl 22, 182
Stuart, Giacomo Rossi 22, 34, 100, 104, 114, 125, 134, 138, 153, 157, 158, 171, 194, 195
Stuart, Jack 104, 195
Stubing, Solvi 26
Studiya za igralni filmi "Boyana" 165
Sturkie, Dan 25
Suárez, José 34, 157
Suay, Ricardo Muñoz 16, 47
Suleiman the Conqueror (Solimano il conquistatore) 165
Sullivan, Deirdre 25
Sullivan, Susan 139
Sultanovic, Milanka 179
Sun, Sabine 18
Suné, Francois 31

Suné, Michel 31
Surdo, Anna Maria 183
Susmann, Alex 198, 200
Svehlova, Lucie 51
The Sword and the Cross (Le Schiave di Cartagine) 165
Sword of Damascus (Il ladro di Damasco) 165
The Sword of El Cid (La spada del Cid) 166
Sword of Rebellion (Il ribelle di Castelmonte) 166
Sword of the Conqueror (Rosmunda e Alboino) 166
Sword of the Empire (Una spada per l'impero) 167
Sword of Zorro (Le tre spade di Zorro) 167
Sword Without a Country (Spada senza bandiera) 167
Swordsman of Siena (La congiura dei dieci) 168
Swyftte, A. 204
Sylvie 119
Szabo, Helen 198, 205

Tabet, André 47, 103, 110, 126, 186
Tabet, Georges 110
Tabos Film 41
Taccari, Donatella 203
Taccari, Giovanni 49
Taffarel, Giuseppe 69, 152
Tagliabue, Andrea 159
Tagliacozzo, Giulio 58, 60, 91, 92, 110, 166
Tagliacozzo, Guido 80
Tagliaferri, Massimo 60
Tagliani, Renato 36
Tagliavia, Adriano 102
Taglienti, Amilcare 10
Tahi, Moa 102
Tailandier, Jean 31
Takara, Mitsuko 159
Talamo, Gino 29, 106, 133, 135, 178
Talarico, Giuseppe 113
Talavera, José González 159
Talbot, Stan 204
Talegalli, Alberto 182
Talia Films 102, 110
Talione, SetItalo 34
Talli, Ida Carloni 14
Tallone, Italo 98
Taloni, Adriano 48, 155, 163, 206
Tamantini, Franca 132
Tamar, Maria 87
Tamberlani, Carlo 19, 21, 31, 33, 34, 39, 40, 41, 46, 59, 62, 81, 88, 106, 107, 114, 125, 127, 142, 143, 146, 152, 153, 154, 162, 176, 179, 120–122
Tamberlani, Nando 35, 36, 56, 59, 64, 65, 83, 87, 91, 103, 106, 110, 114, 119, 122, 127, 131, 133, 134, 136, 137, 165, 179, 186, 190
Tamborra, Sandro 205
Tamburini, Dolores 140
Tamiroff, Akim 24, 46, 100, 112, 131, 169
Tamiz, Edmond 32
Tana, Raffaele 136

Tancredi, Italo 52
Tanfani, Maurizio 103
Tani 26, 27, 30, 92
Tani, Ditta 138
Tani, Yôko 112, 145, 169
Tanner, Peter 158
Tannuzzini, Franco 84
Tapavica, Mira 165
Tapias, Josefina 166
Tarantini, Michele Massimo 198
Taranto, Nino 58
Taras Bulba, the Cossack (Taras Bulba, il cosacco) 168
Tarchetti, Mario 49
Tarquini, Eschilo 51
Tarruella, Victor M. 166
Tartar Invasion (Ursus e la regazza tartara) 168
The Tartars (I tartari) 169, **169**, **170**
Tasca, Alessandro 70, 158, 169, 189
Tasca, Anna 169
Tasna, Rolf 49, 182
Tasso, Torquato 119
Tate, Lincoln 26
Tate, Sharon 25
Tatti, Roberto 201
Tattoli, Elda 94, 191
Taur, the Mighty (Taur, il re della forza bruta) 170, 175, 200
Taurisano Film 138
Tavani, Eugenia 173
Tavazzi, Alberto 104
Tavazzi, Massimo 52, 60, 67, 92, 141, 147, 166, 175, 189
Tavernier, Bertrand 172
Tavis, Peter 25
Tawfik, Mohammed 40
Taylor, Elizabeth 132
Taylor, Franca Parisi 171
Taylor, Margaret 127
Taylor, Robert 14
Taylor, Rod 36, 153
Tazieff, Haroun 87
Tchang, Giacomo 112, 145
Tchérina, Ludmilla 156
Teagan 206
Tecchi, Jacopo 25, 153, 169
Tedeschi, Carlo 9
Tedeschi, Gianrico 34
Tedeschi, Maria 113
Teixeira, Virgilio 24, 51, 150
Tejeiro, Elena Maria 32
Tele Film GmbH 156
Telexport 16
Tellung, Francesco 155, 160
Témerson, Jean 42
Tempera, Vince 110
Tempestini, Giotto 20
Temple of the White Elephant (Sandok, il Maciste della giungla) 171
The Ten Gladiators (I dieci gladiatori) 171
The Ten Commandments 1, 36
Tenoglio, Pietro 206
Tenorio, Don Juan 126
Tensi, Francesco 159
Teodori, Constantino 177
Ter, Ángel 128
Terascio, Enzo 167

Teresa, Maria 139
Terra, Renato 17, 18, 34, 41, 45, 56, 62, 69, 72, 76, 81, 82, 91, 104, 128, 136, 140, 159, 170
Terra, Stefano 107
The Terror of Rome Against the Son of Hercules (Maciste, gladiatore di sparta) 172
Terror of the Red Mask (Il terrore della maschera rossa) 173
Terror of the Steppes (I predoni della steppa) 173
Terrs, Renato 152
Terry, Susan 125
Terzano, Massimo 8, 9, 10, 12, 60
Terzano, Ubaldo 52, 60, 65, 92, 191
Terzioglu, Ugor 207
Terzo, Edoardo 200
Terzo, Nino 58
Tesei, Giorgio 177
Tessari, Cristiano 194
Tessari, Duccio 23, 33, 36, 50, 70, 73, 87, 89, 105, 112, 116, 140, 143, 163, 192
Tessier, Nicole 64
Testa, Dante 7
Testa, Gaetano 205
Testa, Giacomo 205
Testa, Giuseppe 205
Testa, Riccardo 125
The Testament of Maciste (Il testamento di Maciste) 14
Testi, Fabio 23
Teti, Federico 78
Tevere Film 136
Tharus, Son of Attila (Tharus figlio di Attila) 174
Thébault, Jacques 145, 174
Thellung, Francesco 100, 131, 165, 190
Theodoli, Niccolò 15, 49
Theodora, Slave Empress (Teodora, imperatrice di Bizano) 174
Thévenet, René 30, 125
Thibalt, Henry 18
Thiédot, Jacqueline 112
The Thief of Baghdad (Il ladro di Bagdad) 175
The Thief of Baghdad (1924) 175
The Thief of Baghdad (1940) 175
Thien-Huong 112
Thirard, Armand 56
Thiraud, Armand 112
Thompson, John 197, 199, 201
Thor and the Amazon Women (Le gladiatrici) 175
Thor the Conqueror (Thor il conquistatore) 206
Thornton, Peter 142
Thorpe, Richard 169
Thorys, Peter 126
3 Avengers (Gli invincibili tre) 175
The Three Musketeers (1974) 59
The Three Pirates (I tre corsari) 176
Three Swords for Rome (I tre centurioni) 176
Thring, Frank 51
The Throne of Fire (Il trono di fuoco) 199, 206

Thunder of Battle (Coriolano, eroe senza patria) 176
Tibaldi, Renaldo 206
Tiberi, Piero 77
Tiberius Film 106
Tiberti, Paolo 199
Tiburzi, Giancarlo 201, 206
Tichy, Gérard 51, 67, 151
Ticozzelli, Marco 197
Tieghi, Edmondo 48
Tieri, Arnoldo 116
Tiezzi, Augusto 21, 34, 63, 76, 80, 84, 87, 88, 89, 96, 98, 102, 129, 130, 133, 143, 145, 176, 194, 195, 196
Tiki Film 160
Tiger of the Seven Seas (La tigre dei sette mari) 177
Tiller, Lucy 18
Tinti, Gabriele 18, 45, 52, 69, 103, 153, 158, 186
Tirelli, Singnora 8
Titanus Studios 50, 51, 52, 54, 59, 60, 62, 65, 68, 77, 94, 115, 157, 159, 167, 175
Titi, Franco 106
Titre, Claude 178
Titta, Gualberto 64
Tixador, André 56
Tocci, Bruno 31, 51, 141, 142, 168, 178
Tocci, Franco 103
Tocci, Sergio 16
Tocci, Vincenzo 136
Tocinoski, Marija 54, 191
Tocinowki, Marija 191
Todd, Ann 159
Todesco, Anita 58, 59, 124, 126, 128, 137, 139, 150, 153, 169, 175, 194
Todesco, Paolo 26, 195
Todini, Bruno 27, 176, 184
Todorovic, Milan 99, 115, 122, 152, 179, 191
Todorovic, Radmila 112
Tofano, Sergio 55
Togliani, Alberto 141
Togni, Alex 110
Togni, Darix 55, 156
Toja, Jacques 56
Tolnay, Ákos 191
Tolo, Marilù 36, 111, 118, 150, 172
Tolstoy, Leo 191
Tomadoni, Tullio 25
Tomaselli, Giacomo 28
Tomasi, Italo 90
Tomasini, Giulio 104
Tomassi, Andrea A. 184
Tomassi, Italo 20, 25, 27, 33, 35, 36, 41, 44, 46, 50, 54, 67, 78, 87, 90, 95, 99, 106, 116, 122, 126, 128, 130, 155, 157, 158, 165, 173, 184, 189, 191
Tomassi, Pietro 207
Tomassi, Vincenzo 201, 206
Tomassoni, Gastone 166
Tomatis, Giovanni 12
Tomei, Giulio 35, 88, 111, 137, 167
Tommasi, Paolo 80
Tommasini, Aldo 54, 105
Tonietti, Anne 56

Toniolo, Edoardo 33, 67, 119, 128, 133, 134, 165, 186, 196
Tonnini, Irma 19, 39, 59, 76
Tonnini, Maria 55
Tonti, Aldo 18, 21, 24, 43
Top-Film München 32
Tordesillas, Jesús 154, 190
Tordi, Pietro 29, 47, 49, 64, 65, 92, 99, 104, 124, 132, 135, 141, 152, 160, 164, 166
Tordi, Valerio 98, 107, 176
Torelli, Attilio 41, 102, 146
Torinti, Gianfranco 204
Tornos, Valentin 24
Torodi, Pierre 104
Torre, Giuseppe Della 55
Torremocha, José 27
Tórres, Dolores 159
Torres, José 114, 142, 147, 158, 171
Torres, Lola 106
Torres, Manuel 26, 102
Torres, Tomás 119
Torri, Cesare 119
Torri, Pier Luigi 139
Torrini, Ernesto 46
Torrisi, Pietro 20, 28, 89, 113, 126, 145, 164, 167, 171, 179, 198, 201, 204, 206
Torrs, Manolo 40
Tosato, Attilio 40, 58, 143, 154
Tosatti, Marilyn 25
Tosi, Beppe 55
Tosi, Guido 197, 199
Tosi, Luigi 17, 32, 41, 45, 67, 69, 78, 129, 173, 177, 192
Tosi, Virgilio 128
Toso, Otello 46
Tosto, Sebastiano 200
Tota, Mario 21, 62, 65, 103, 165
Touati, Maurice 31
Tourjansky, Viktor 41, 67, 98, 99, 118, 128, 131, 147, 177
Tourjansky, W. 177
Tourneur, Jacques 60
Towers, Harry Alan 207
Towns, Larby 198
Tozzi, Fausto 18, 41, 51, 104, 125, 134, 150, 168, 192
Trainor, Chris 198, 200
Tramony, Janine 112
Tranché, André 102, 109
Trani, Eligio 54, 107, 132, 158, 177
Trani, Emilio 19, 92
Trani, Maurizio 202, 205
Trans-Ocean Film 106
Trans World Entertainment (TWE) 205
Trasatti, Luciano 22, 23, 40, 48, 103, 139, 146, 155, 157, 165, 186
Traverna, Henri 177
Traversari, Fabio 199
Traversari, Walfrido 165
Traylor, David 205
Treasure of the Petrified Forest (Il tesoro della Foresta Pietrificata) 177
Tréjan, Guy 56
Trent, Peter 136, 160
Trentini, Caterina 40
Trentino, Vittorio 46, 135, 147, 192

248 Index

Tress, Vando 36, 182
Tréville, Roger 60, 130
Trevisaneto, Valentino 160
Tribbioli, Bruno 205
Triesault, Ivan 25
Triglav Film 150, 178
Trilli, Amedeo 16, 17, 33, 34, 55, 60, 63, 65, 69, 81, 88, 102, 104, 111, 114, 122, 129, 137, 139, 146, 165, 177, 184, 187, 188
The *Trilogy of Maciste* (*La trilogia di Maciste*) 14
Trimarchi, Michele 19, 50, 90, 119
Trinacria, Franco 91
Trinca, Giuseppe 188
Trinici, Roberto 200
Trintignant, Jean-Louid 103
Trio Film 135
Trionfi, Claudio 141
Triumph of Maciste see *Triumph of The Son of Hercules*
The *Triumph of Michael Strogoff* (*Le triomphe de Michel Strogoff*) 177
The *Triumph of Robin Hood* (*Il trionfo di Robin Hood*) 178
The *Triumph of the Son of Hercules* (*Il trionfo di Maciste*) 178
Triumph of the Ten Gladiators (*Il trionfo dei dieci gladiatori*) 48, 179
Troiani, Luigi 29, 83, 178, 187
Troiani, Oberdan 29, 62, 83, 114, 178, 187
The *Trojan Horse* (*La guerra di troia*) 177, 179, **180**
Trouche, Liana 166
Trovajoli, Armando 62, 87, 89, 122, 157, 182
Truman, Ralph 51
Tryan, Cecil 10
Tsacrios, Frank J. 202
Tucci, Adriana 114
Tudela, Miguel 47, 159
Tudor, Pamela 177
Tuicovich, Wladimiro (a.k.a. Vladimiro Tuicovich) 25, 91, 92, 136, 167
Tulli, Marco 36, 127, 131, 139, 140, 154, 192
Tului, Fulvio 138, 167
Tumiati, Gualtiero 15, 42, 50, 176, 186
Tunc, Irène 19, 34, 41
Turchetto, Bruno 135
Turco, Giuseppe 37, 40
Turco, Umberto 205
Turi, Renato 155
Turini, Gino 150, 166, 171, 194
Turino, Gianfranco 26
Turlure, Robert 178
Turner, Helene 21
Turner, John 150, 166, 171, 194
Tuset, Francisco 151, 166
Tuzi, Jone 35
Tuzi, Wanda 194
Twentieth Century-Fox 107, 131
Twist, John 52
The *Two Gladiators* (*I due gladiatori*) 181
Two Nights with Cleopatra (*Due notti con Cleopatra*) 181, **181, 182**

Tyberghein, Pierre 178
The *Tyrant of Castile* (*Sfida al re di Castiglia*) 183
The *Tyrant of Lydia Against the Son of Hercules* (*Goliath e la schiava ribelle*) 183, **183, 184, 185**
Tyre, Henry 204
Tyrys Films 141

Ubaldi, Annamaria 150, 158
Ubaldi, Giorgio 29, 40, 67, 101, 106, 116, 127, 151, 163
Úbeda, Diego 154
Udruzenje Filmskih Umetnika Srbije (UFUS) 119
Uhlig, Annelise 49
Ukmar, Bruno 62, 67, 109, 118, 139, 140, 152, 153, 166, 172, 181, 184
Ukmar, Clemente 109, 112
Ukmar, Franco 15, 26, 107, 109, 111, 118, 140, 152, 153, 172, 173, 176, 181, 184, 207
Ukmar, Sergio 145, 152, 169, 173
Ulloa, Alejandro 16, 18, 47, 68, 159, 201
Ulloa, Allejandro 47
Ulmer, Arianne 103
Ulmer, Edgar G. 77, 78, 103
Ulmer, Shirley 77, 103
Ultra Films 140
Ulysse, Jean Paul 56
Ulysses (*Ulisse*) 184
Ulysses Against the Son of Hercules (*Ulisse contro Ercole*) 186
Umilani, Piero 143
Undari, Claudio 33, 73, 112, 141, 154, 172
Uneurop Film 59
Ungaro, Goffredo 191
Unger, Frederico 18
Unger, Goffredo 18, 29, 30, 47, 56, 64, 83, 104, 124, 157, 183, 191, 202, 207
Unger, Jeffrey 202
Unicité 118
Universalia Film 55
1 Aprile Cinematografica 131
Urania Film 80, 94
Urban, Mark 204
Urbinelli, Giorgio 26
Urbini, Luigi 21, 22, 36, 50, 52, 60, 106, 130, 133, 137, 156, 169, 171, 175
Urbini, Pier Luigi 21, 22, 191
Urbisaglia, Giancarlo 158, 189
Urbisaglia, Serse 158, 192
Urias Films 111
Ursus in the Land of Fire (*Ursus nella terra di fuoco*) 186
Ursus, Son of Hercules 47
Urzi, Saro 163
Usuelli, Teo 150, 165

Vaccà, Marino 114, 33
Vaccaro, Ramón 166
Vadis, Dan 3, 134, 160, 164, 171, 179, 194, 204
Vailati, Bruno 60, 67, 92, 175
Valcauda, Armando 197, 202

Valdemarin, Mario 87, 149
Vale, Jerry 112
Valejo, Juan 137, 195
Valente, Antonio 174
Valente, Mario 22
Valente, Renato 135
Valenti, Marisa 94, 141
Valentin, Albert 26, 118, 172, 183
Valentin, Mirko 30, 77, 81, 89, 142
Valentini, Egidio 207
Valentini, Leopoldo 138, 139, 142
Valentinsich, A. 25
Valenza, Mila Vitelli 114
Valenza, Valeria (a.k.a. Valerie Valenza) 203
Valenzuela, Laura 43
Valère, Simone 178
Valeri, Bruno 135
Valeriano, Leo 156
Valérie, Jeanne 110
Valle, Conchita Rodriguez del 167
Valle, Gaetano 77, 110, 143
Valle, Ricardo 78, 84, 127, 165, 183
Valle, Stefano 45, 73
Vallejo, Juan 195
Valles, Carlos Alberto 204
Vallin, Serge 184
Vallon, George 118
Vallone, Raf 15, 51
Valloni, Emma 81
Valmain, Frédéric 42
Valmont, Véra 176
Valori, Bice 91
Van Horn, Buddy 168
Van Hulzen, Joop 176
van Husen, Dan 141
Van Nutter, Rik 136, 174
Van Riel, Mario 28, 50, 51, 166
Van Riel, Raimondo 46
Van Wyck, Francis 25
Vannella, Angelo 199
Vanni, Massimo 110, 206
Vanoni, Ornella 51, 100
Vanorio, Franco 203
Vantellini, Riccardo 159
Vanzi, Luigi 152
Vaquero, Rafael 24, 27, 128
Var, André 42
Varcelloni, Elios 134
Varconi, Victor 10
Vardannes, Emilio 7, 12, 14
Varelli, Alberto 130
Varelli, Alfredo 36, 50, 64, 125, 130, 155, 164
Vargas, Daniele 19, 60, 77, 80, 89, 94, 102, 129, 138, 143, 158, 173, 175, 195
Vargas, Eleonora 65, 69, 100
Vari, Giovanni 29, 114, 129, 130, 137, 141, 167
Vari, Giuseppe 21, 136, 189
Vari, Mariella 189
Variety Film Productions 101
Varone, Domenico 28
Varriale, Gabriele 41, 50
Variano, Emilio 177
Vasallo, Carlos 201
Vasco, Aldo 158
Vaser, Ernesto 9

Vaser, Vittorio 46, 122, 167
Vassalle, Carlo 111, 118, 139, 172, 181
Vasser, Ercole 13
Vasser, Ernesto 13
Vassilli, Marco 164
Vazquez, F. Gomez 107
Vázquez, Francisco 190
Vazzoler, Alessandra 198
Vazzoler, Chandra 198
Vazzoler, Elisa 125
Vecchietti, Alberto 54
Vecchio, Mauro Del 168
Vecci, Amedeo 46
Veevers, Wally 158
Vega, Alfonso de la 24, 127
Vela, Anibal 24
Vela, Antonio 150
Vela, Ivanhoe 69
Velasco, Mahnahén 37, 68
Velinska, Elisabetta 27
Vella, Franca 46
Velter, Jean 107
Venantini, Venantino 198
Vengeance of the Vikings (Erik il Vichingo) 187
The Vengeance of Ursus (La vendetta di Ursus) 187
Ventero, Abraham 107
Ventimiglia, Fernanda 28, 91
Ventimiglia, Giovanni 103, 191
Venturini-Express-Nasht 46
Venturini, Giorgio 22, 41, 128, 131, 191
Venturini, Sandra 198
Venturoli, Giorgio 197
Venturoli, Vittorio 142
Venus Against the Son of Hercules 48
Veo, Anna 128
Veo, Carlo 125, 167
Vera 82
Vera, Guillermo 167
Vercelloni, Elios 62, 134, 169
Verde, Lamberto 50
Verdier, Nadine 47
Vergari, Ezio 125
Vergoz, Fabio 163
Vériat, Claude 178
Vernadet, Maguy 178
Vernay, Robert 42
Verne, Jules 118, 119, 164, 177
Vernon, Anne 151
Vernon, Anthony 20
Vernon, Howard 154
Vernuccio, Gianni 46, 47
Verona, Amelio 36, 155
Versace, Santo 91
Versini, Marie 171
Vesperini, Pierta 52
Vesperini, Pietro 136
Vessel, Edy 153, 167, 175, 179
Vetrani, Tino 64
Vezza, Antonio 143
Vianello, Adriana 35
Vianello, Cesira 134
Vianello, Maria Teresa 64
Vianello, Raimondo 91
Vic Film 78, 99, 128
Vicari, Fabrizio 202
Vicario, Marci 157

Vicario, Marco 17, 18, 55, 157, 192
Vicario, Natalino 55, 91
Vich, Václav 64
Vici, Andrea Busiri 203
Vici, Armando 205
Vicky, Valeria 28
Vico, María 128
Victor Film 29
Vidal, Gil 95, 150
Vidal, Henri 22, 55
Vidali, Giovanni Enrico 14
Vides Cinematografica 84, 163
Vidon, Henri 22
Vietri, Francesco 112
Vighi, Vittorio 116
Vignati, Carlo 125
Vignola, Laura 149
Vignozzi, Giancarlo 195
Vigorelli, Vittoria 64, 194
Vilar, Antonio 150
Vilches, José María 39
Villa, Emilio 27
Villa, Franco 32, 41, 48, 113, 155, 157
Villalba, Tadeo 51, 159
Villalba, Teddy 55, 167, 195
Villar, Luis 183
Villard, André 178
Villasante, José 24, 128
Villé, Paul 42, 87, 174
Villeroy, Daniel 56
Vinà, Giulio 9
Vincent, Chuck 207
Vincent, Roger 42
Vincent, Yves 104, 156
Vincenti, Luciano 154, 187
Vincenti, Silvana 178
Vincenzi, Luciana 153
Vincenzoni, Luciano 18, 50, 139
Vinci, Roberto Nicosia 207
Vinci, Vega 190
Vinciguerra, Gino 163, 179
Vincioni, Guglielmo 77
Vingelli, Nino 63, 88, 130, 196
Violette, Jean 87
Viotti, Ferruccio 100, 111
Viotti, Gino 46
Virgilio, Franco 113
Visconti, Eriprando 164
Visconti, Franco 100
Visconti, Luigi 163, 175
Visentini, Gino 156
Visone, Antonio 24, 35, 64, 98, 103, 110, 135, 169, 183
Vitalani, Italia 10
Vitale, Adriano 22, 120, 128, 133, 134, 135, 138, 153, 169
Vitale, Milly 25, 29, 77, 125
Vitale, Nadia 36
Vitali, Nadia 24, 99, 128, 131, 149
Vitaliani, Evangelina 13
Vitalo, Massimo 128
Vite, Matilde Guerafino 13
Vitelli, Simonetta 23
Vitolazzi, Rocco 76
Vitrotti, Giovanni 9, 13
Vittori, Benilde 29, 161
Vittori, Luciano 65, 194
Vittorini, Angela 207

Vittory, Luciano 65
Vivaldi, Luciana 122
Vivani, Augusto 95
Vivarelli, Piero 34
Viviani, Sonia 198
Vizcaino, Fernando 26
Vizzinibisaccia, Salvatore 139
Vlad, Roman 119, 162
Vochicievich, Paolo 194
Vodopivec, Frano 191
Vogel, Nicholas 18
Voller-Buzzi, Mario 12, 13
Volonté, Gian Maria 87, 103
Volp, Andrea 33
Volpato, Luciano 127, 154
Volpe, Andrea 50, 124
Volpe, Teresa 129
Volper, Albert 56
Volper, Roger 56
Volpi, Franco 51, 131
Volpicelli, Corrado 194, 195
Von Borsody, Hans 40, 115
von Fürstenberg, Ira 126
von Hagen, Ruth 100, 102, 168
von Kuegelgen, Frank 203, 204
von Ledebur, Friedrich 25
von Martens, Lena 152
Voujaklia, G. 34
The Voyage of Maciste (Il viaggio di Maciste) 14
Vrhovec, Janez 34, 41, 113, 154, 165, 178
Vuisic, Pavle 152
Vukotic, Milena 35, 100
Vulcan, Son of Jupiter (Vulcano, figlio di Giove) 187, **188, 189**
Vulpiani, Mario 26

Wachsberger, Nat 150
Wagner, Lisa 104
Wakerman, Rick 205
Wakhévitch, Georges 150
Walerstein, Gregorio 165
Walmar Cinematografica 150, 194
Walowitz, Marvin 27
Walsh, Raoul 52
Walter, Eugene 156
Walter, Ricardo 194
Walther, Léon 42
Wang, George 124, 147
Wanger, Jody 204
Wanguard Film 42
War Gods of Babylon (Le sette folgori di Assur) 189
War of the Zombies (Roma contro Roma) 189
Warren, John 164
The Warrior and the Slave Girl (La rivolta dei gladiatori) 190
The Warrior Empress (Saffo, Venere di Lesbo) 190, **190**
Warrior Queen (Pompei) 207
Wassilli, Mario 92
Waszynski, Michal 51, 191
Watson, Richard 25
Webb, Jerry 52
Weber, André 56
Weber, Tania 186
Wehara, Kiro 200

250 Index

Welbeck, Peter 207
Welch, Raquel 28
Weldon, Alex 51
Welles, Mary 135
Welles, Mel 135
Welles, Orson 3, 27, 44, 45, 113, 169, **170,** 170
Wells, Carol 195
Wells, Veronica 25
Wender, George 204
Wentworth, Nicholas 198, 205
Werner, Paul 202
Werther, Salvini 184
Western Electric 118
Westmoreland, James 103
Weston, Jay 25
Wheeler, René 174
The *White Warrior (Agi Murad il diavolo bianco)* 191
White, Peter 166, 173, 181
Wichard, Michael 18
Wiedermann, Elena 205, 206
Wiener, Jean 42
Wiesenfeld, Suzanne 178
Wilde, Cornel 41
William Tell (Guglielmo Tell) 191
Williams, Fred 138
Williams, Guy 44
Williams, Jack 51
Williams, Nat 198
Willis, Austin 25
Wilmer, Douglas 51
Wilms, Dominique 31
Wilson, Sonia 156
Windish-Graetz, Christa 25, 114
Windsor, Paul 115, 152
Winston, David 203
Wipf, Louis 118
Wise, Annie 204
Wiseman, Nicholas Patrick 8, 9, 54, 140
The Witch's Curse (Maciste all'inferno) 192, **193**
Wochicievich, Paolo 194
Wolf, Emmanuel L. 194
Wolf, R.L. 22
Wolff, Frank 134
Wolkowicz, Emilia 67
Wonder Films 55, 84, 104
The Wonders of Aladdin (La meraviglie di Aladino) 192
Wong, Chen 200
Wood, Ed 3
Wood, Mikaela 167
Wood, Norman 115
Woods, Genie 26
Wooland, Norman 25, 150
Woringer, Bernard 56
Wormser, Richard 158
Worth, Irene 153
Wotruba, Michael 19, 48, 131
Wreim, Huld 160
Wu, Elisabetta 81
Wybenga, Roland 206
Wyler, Richard 25
Wynter, Paul 20, 122

Yago Films 165
Yagunta, Lucia 48
Yamanouchi, Haruhiko (*a.k.a.* Hal Yamanouchi) 199, 206
Yanni, Rosanna 18
Yarza, Rosita 27
Yeh, Ely 145
Yor, the Hunter from the Future (Il mondo di Yor) 207
Yordan, Philip 51
Young, James D. 27
Young, Keith 202
Young, Terence 18, 142
Young, Tiny 112
Yousef, Hassan 160

Zaccari, Orlando 207
Zaccaria, Carla 46
Zador, Eugene 51, 158
Zagni, Giancarlo 142
Zago, Erminia 12, 14
Zagra, Liliana 188
Zagra, Lilliana 16
Zagreb Film 34
Zalewska, Halina 63, 92, 179
Zama, Mario 191
Zambo, Aleksandar Milovic Angelo 122
Zambo, Angelo 91
Zambon, Giorgio 158
Zambuto, Claudia 12
Zambuto, Gero 8
Zambuto, Mauro 184
Zammi, Alfredo 36, 58
Zamperini, Ettore 92
Zamperla, Nazzareno 25, 33, 67, 80, 87, 92, 109, 111, 114, 129, 146, 147, 149, 152, 157, 158, 177
Zamperla, Rinaldo 18, 21, 40, 60, 102, 109, 110, 113, 124, 157, 206
Zamperla, Tony 114
Zampieri, Nellita 82, 114, 122, 138, 187
Zamprioli, Gino 26
Zamurovich, Ceco 68, 106
Zanchin, Nino 77, 95, 163
Zander, Lilli 17
Zanelli, Augusto 174
Zanetti, Athos Danilo 143, 167
Zanetti, Gioia 196
Zani, Pina 164
Zann, Jean 56
Zanni, Aldo 52
Zannoni, Giovanella 184
Zanoli, Bruno 92, 194
Zanoli, Maria 25
Zanolli, Angelo 94, 124, 162, 192
Zanotti, Carlo 20, 175
Zanotto, Juan 207
Zanussi, Lidia 113
Zanussi, Lucia 11
Zanussi, Luciano 113
Zappalà, Federica 203
Zappolini, Walter 22
Zardi, Dominique 56
Zardi, Federico 41, 67, 99, 179

Zareschi, Elena 41, 99, 100, 122, 186, 191
Zarfati, Giancarlo 175
Zarkov, T. 154
Zaro, Natividad 100, 106, 190
Zaro, T. 127
Zarzo, Manuel 102, 109
Zavattini, Cesare 48, 54
Zavitz, Lee 158
Zay, Jean 118
Zebra Films 152
Zeccara, Paolo 197, 202
Zedda, Alberto 65, 150, 165
Zeglio, Clorindo 33
Zeglio, Primo 21, 32, 124, 125, 152, 158, 162, 166
Zengar, Yilmaz 207
Zenith Films 186
Zentillini, Michele 104
Zeri, Massimo 204
Zévago, Michel 23, 31
Zezon, Assia 84
Zicavo, Mario 114
Zichel, Rosy 32, 189
Zignani, Silvano 112
Zingarelli, Italo 65, 100, 106, 119, 151, 165
Zingaro, Corrado 141
Zita, Antonietta 15, 22, 35, 41, 54, 65, 78, 96, 98, 99, 103, 107, 109, 114, 126, 128, 135, 137, 138, 147, 169, 173, 176, 179, 187
Zita, Graziella 98
Zitelli, Vittorio 197
Zito, Domenico Lo 201
Zivanovic, Milivoje 191
Zmukic, Milan 191
Zocchedu, Zaira 201
Zocchi, Nietta 15, 50, 163, 165
Zolficar, Omar 68, 104, 189
Zoppelli, Lia 143
Zoppo, Federico Del 141, 201
Zorcic, Zoran 112, 179
Zorelli, Janine 42
Zorikan the Barbarian (Zorikan lo sterminatore) 192
Zorrilla, José 126
Zorro (Zorro) 194
Zorro in the Court of England (Zorro alla corte d'Inghilterra) 194
The Zorro of Monterrey (El Zorro de Monterrey) 195
Zorro the Fox (El Zorro) 195
Zorro the Rebel (Zorro il ribelle) 196
Zorro, Rider of Vengeance (Zorro il cavaliere della vendetta) 195
Zorro, the Navarra Marquis (Zorro marchese di Navarra) 195
Zschokke, Nuri 175
Zucca, Giuseppe 191
Zuccarelli, Armando 46
Zuccaro, Giorgio 116
Zucchè, Marcello 122
Zuccoli, Fausto 64, 130
Zurbano Films 18
Zurli, Guido 50, 73, 106, 129, 157, 195

www.ingramcontent.com/pod-product-compliance
Lightning Source LLC
Chambersburg PA
CBHW081549300426
44116CB00015B/2815